AN INTRODUCTION TO

ECONOMIC HISTORY

CHRISTINE RIDER

Professor,

Department of Economics and Finance,

St. Johns University

SOUTH-WESTERN College Publishing

An International Thomson Publishing Company

Acquisitions Editor: Kenneth King
Productions Editor: Robin Schuster
Marketing Manager: Denise Carlson
Production House: Ambos Company
Cover Designer: Paul Neff Design
Cover Illustration: The Bettman Archive

HK61AA

Library of Congress Cataloging-in-Publication Data
Rider, Christine
    An introduction to economic history / Christine Rider.
       p.   cm.
    Includes index.
    ISBN 0-538-84710-7
    1. Economic history. 2. Mercantile system. 3. Industrial
revolution. 4. Capitalism. 5. International economic relations.
I. Title.
HC21.R49 1995
330.9--dc20   94-23033
                                        CIP

ISBN:0-538-84710-7

1 2 3 4 5 EB 8 7 6 5 4

Printed in the United States of America

IⓉP   International Thomson Publishing   South-Western is an ITP Company.
                 The ITP trademark is used under license.

To Harry and Eve, with love

Contents

Part III: The Industrial Revolution (18th to early 20th Centuries)

Part IV: The Maturing of Industrial Capitalism (19th and 20th Centuries)

Part V: The Internationalization of Market Capitalism

Preface

The Ideas Behind the Book

Much of the study of economics involves technical and conceptual analysis that quantifies human behavior and creates and tests powerful explanatory theories. We rely on economics, dismal science though some consider it to be, to help us understand a large chunk of our collective and individual reality, but analysis alone is not sufficient to give us a full picture. We also need a sense of economic history to illuminate the concepts and theories.

This book was written to give readers a clear and straightforward understanding of our modern material reality. By looking at the arrangements societies have made to meet their material needs and the ways those arrangements constantly change over time, we can see how history illuminates analysis and how analysis helps us understand historical events. Appreciating the interrelationship of these two aspects of economics helps us form a more complete and thus more powerful picture of the discipline, its concepts and theories, and the economic world.

Special Content Features

- **Focus on both written and and "unwritten" aspects of economic history.** We know a great deal about the famous writers and thinkers and other famous historical figures who have left their mark on economic activity in one way or another. This book gives those important people and their work full due. But to form a comprehensive description of past economic life, the book also looks at the way people lived—their social traditions, farming practices, diets, household arrangements, and so on. Most of our ancestors, after all, were ordinary working people; investigating the conditions of their lives can help us understand the process of economic change.

- **Emphasis on economics in social and political context.** The book views historical experience as a developmental process occasionally interrupted by non-evolutionary shocks or events, both natural and man-made. No economy can be separated from the society in which it is located.

- **Awareness of economics as choice and decision making across time.** This book rejects the notion of historical development always moving toward some better end or ideal of progress. Instead we see that some decisions improve the quality and material success of life for some of humanity, while some choices lead to deterioration for others. We examine how past historical and economic development sometimes affects the present and the future and how, in some instances, choices have created problems along with the means to solve those problems.

- **Focus on patterns of industrialization in different countries.** Industrialization has done more to increase material productivity in the two centuries since the Industrial Revolution than any other behavioral or organizational change. By studying both the common (because most easily transmitted from one country to another) and the culturally and institutionally unique elements in the industrialization process, we identify which elements result in relative success or failure. The results of such investigations can be useful in making policy and in assisting newly industrializing countries in their development efforts.

- **Emphasis on the emergence of markets and market-oriented behavior.** Along with the spread of industrialization, the "market system" came to replace traditional systems and has dominated the organization and coordination of economic activity. Although other methods of organization economic behavior have emerged, as in for example central planning systems, markets and capitalism have proved to be much more resilient. Studying economic behavior and systems over time gives insights into why markets have persisted so well.

Learning and Study Aids

- **Solving Problems in Economic History** sections demonstrate how economic historians investigate important questions, including knowing what questions to ask as well as what resources to use to answer them. In some cases, the use of mathematical or statistical evidence illustrates how these problems were solved.

- **Definitions,** highlighted in italics and set off from the text for emphasis, explain unusual or difficult concepts or terms.

- **Key Concepts,** arranged alphabetically at the end of each chapter, aid review of essential information.

- **Questions for Discussion and Essay Writing** help students synthesize and analyze concepts and events.

- **A Comprehensive Glossary** at the end of the book provides complete definitions or explanations of all historical and economic terms. Since some are historically specific and most are building blocks of economic analysis, access to all these terms can be particularly useful for students without an extensive background in economics.

Acknowledgements

An acknowledgement section is a thank you, and thank yous are always pleasurable to make. My deepest debt, of course, is to the millions of our ancestors whose lives have provided the raw material for history. Their dreams, often shattered, sometimes realized, led to the events that have shaped our lives today. We would not know about them without the recorders, chroniclers, archaeologists, and historians who have distilled a pattern from the immense reservoir of the past. I am grateful to them for their contribution to the study of human society; no present-day historian can hope to embark on an individual work without being indebted to the insights of their predecessors.

Many individuals have provided encouragement, support, and useful comments throughout the gestation period of this book. In particular, I want to thank William Parker, E. Ray Canterbery, and the anonymous reviewers who read and commented on the manuscript at various stages in its development; the students who served as guinea pigs for early versions of the text; and various colleagues who have offered useful advice, including David Colander, Charles Clark, and Ted McGlone. Also deserving thanks are those who assisted with specific aspects of the book including Gregg Buttermore, Erica Gottfried, Christoph von der Decken, Daniel May, Nicholas Smith, Nichole Soto, Marie Tierney (as well as the helpful women in the Word Processing Department at St. John's University), and the staffs of those institutions who helped me locate illustrations; and Mike Tuccinard, who drew the maps. The people at South-Western were helpful throughout the project, and I want to express my thanks to all the editors who have contributed to this book, especially Ken King. Finally, I am especially grateful to Gary Mongiovi, who was always supportive, even when it seemed that no end was in sight. And for all the others, who in so many ways have helped see this work through to the end, I am grateful.

Christine Rider, St. John's University

Part I

Precapitalist Economies

(Third Century B.C. to Fourteenth Century A.D.)

Chapter 1

Introduction

What is Economic History?

ECONOMIC HISTORY, ECONOMIC DEVELOPMENT AND GROWTH are three closely related subdisciplines of economics. The first is concerned with what happened in the past, and with describing how today's developed economies came to be that way. The second, economic development, attempts to understand the present situation of currently developing nations; it has a strong policy orientation. The third area, economic growth theory, is the most analytic, attempting to abstract from reality to develop a theory about how and why economic growth occurs. Both development and growth theory have policy implications.

Inevitably, there are grey, hazy areas of overlap—for example, when does economic history "end" and economic development begin? There is also a considerable overlap with general economic theory, which derives laws or general principles of economic behavior that seem to characterize modern economies. Do these general laws also explain historical events? A simple answer is not possible, and the same event may even be explained in different ways. The problem with economics, as introductory textbooks are careful to point out, is that we cannot run controlled experiments to prove anything. This is even more valid for economic history, where we are unable to go back to doublecheck the events!

This book is an introduction to economic history. It will show how a few countries developed in the past, and will concentrate especially on the emergence and evolution of a market economy and related institutions. This means that we will focus on the history of the emergence of modern economic societies, the framework that modern economic analysis can take for granted. It does not pretend to be comprehensive, covering *all* economic development in *all* countries going back into prehistory, and it also focuses only on capitalist countries, ignoring the development of other ways of organizing and coordinating economic activity.

Relation Between Economic Analysis and Economic History

Let's digress somewhat to look at the relation between introductory economic analysis, which attempts to analyze current reality, and economic history. If you start reading just about any introductory text, one of the first lines you will read will be a definition of economics. It will go something like this: Economics is the study of the allocation of scarce resources among competing ends. There will probably also be a definition of economic behavior: Economic behavior is behavior geared to meeting people's needs. And there will probably also be a definition of an economic system: An economic system is a framework of rules and institutions that influence economic behavior.

Types of Economic System

There may even be a classification of pure types of economic system. These are called "pure types" because they are abstractions; we won't find actual examples of them in real life, but their characteristics can be spotted in real life economies (see Table 1-1). Most texts identify three types:

1. The Traditional Economy. In this type of economic system, people do what they do because things have always been done that way; precedent rules behavior. The motive behind economic behavior is custom; the aim is to maintain the status quo. Inevitably, such systems are not dynamic and do not adapt well to change, because change is a concept that is foreign to experience based on an essentially unchanging reality. Modern exam-

ples of traditional economies include Amazon hunting and gathering family groups, the cattle raising Masai in Kenya or some Eskimo villages in Greenland. There are more, but such societies find it hard to resist the onslaught of 20th century development, and their numbers are dwindling rapidly. However, we can also observe some aspects of a traditional economy within others organized along very different lines. For example, even though the structure of some modern families is changing—there are more working mothers and one-parent families—household organization in Western economies still tends to be patterned along traditional lines, even though the technology of housework itself has changed.

2. The Command Economy. Here, people are told what to do. There is some authority, usually a centralized one, that is obeyed either because it has powers of coercion or because its authority is accepted as legitimate. Le-

Table 1-1
Matrix of Economic Systems

Ownership Form	Operating Mechanism		
	Traditional	**Command**	**Market**
Private	1. Domestic households 2. English agriculture, 15–16th century	1. Germany, 1930s 2. Polish agriculture, 1940s–1980s 3. Military sector	1. U.S. manufacturing 2. New Zealand agriculture
Communal	1. North American Indian, 20th century	1. USSR agriculture, 1930s–1980s 2. U.S. communes, 19th century	1. Hungary, 1940s-1980s 2. Yugoslavia, 1940s–1980s 3. Chinese export manufacturing, late 20th century
Not Indentifiable	1. Amazon tribes 2. European feudalism	1. Pharaonic Egypt	

Note: few economies comprise only one predominant form of ownership of resources and only one dominant operating mechanism; most are mixes. Most common today in capitalist market economies is the persistence of traditional arrangements in household production and a command structure in the armed services within an economy-wide market system.

gitimacy is granted either through some sort of constitution or social contract in which authority comes from the consent of the governed, or it is derived from an instilled belief in some religious or supernatural authority. In any event, justification for authority exists. Modern examples include centrally planned economies and the armed services in all countries; an ancient example is Egypt ruled by the Pharaohs. We could even include modern schools, factories or offices, where authority is accepted as a requirement of social order.

3.   The Market Economy. The organizing element here is not political authority but rather the set of prices emerging from behavior of buyers and sellers operating in many different types of markets. The motive for economic behavior is gain—economic agents respond to and are motivated by monetary incentives. Examples of economies operating largely along market lines include the United States, Western Europe, and Japan.

One word of caution: No economy is exclusively characterized by only one system; all are mixes. However, for convenience, most economies are slotted into a classification depending on which characteristic predominates. This means that the U.S. is classified as a market economy although some of its production takes place under conditions resembling a command economy— the production of military goods is accomplished on command from the Pentagon.

Also, governments buy goods and services in markets, using funds derived from (compulsory) taxes, and some productive activity within the household is not motivated by monetary gain but is done in response to a command mechanism, or by mutual consent.

This classification is based on distinguishing different information/motivation mechanisms influencing economic *behavior*. An alternative classification can be based on property ownership, because whoever (or whatever) owns the eco-

nomic resources needed to meet material needs is in a very strong position to influence what gets done. Again, it is possible to identify three classifications:

1.   Private Ownership of Property. Individuals, families, or legal entities own the material property and labor services used in economic production and trade. Capitalism is an economic system that is characterized by private ownership.

2.   Public or Social Ownership of Property. Society as a whole or the state owns property resources and controls their use. Socialism or communism are economic systems characterized by public ownership.

3.   Unidentifiable Ownership. Only fairly recently has the concept of "ownership" become part of the Western experience, and there are times and places where economic resources have no identifiable owners. (Even today, no-one owns the oceans.) In pre-capitalist societies in general, people would not know how to answer the question "Who *owns* the land?" If pressed, they might say that resources belong to the gods. For example, when the first European settlers arrived in New World, they asked these questions of the native Americans they encountered, who could not understand the concept of *individual* private property. The tribes had hunting grounds or corn fields, but they shifted location as the game or tribe moved on. Similarly, land ownership in the modern sense was nonexistent in feudal Europe in the Middle Ages; land was a gift of God to be used to meet material needs, and its use was circumscribed by a complex set of social regulations.

Although these classifications may be somewhat confusing, it will be useful later on to be able to distinguish between a coordinating mechanism such as a market and the ownership classification. It is misleading and inaccurate to identify capitalism with a market economy: Although capitalist economies are predominantly market economies, it is not an automatic pairing. We are referring to two different, not interchangeable, concepts here. However, the confusion probably arises because the development of the market mechanism as a dominant influence over economic activity occurred at the same time as the emergence of private property rights. Markets where items are bought and sold have always existed to some extent; the important difference in modern market economies is that production, and most economic activity as a whole, is deliberately undertaken for eventual sale in a market; that is, the reason for activity depends on the entire functioning of the market system. Clearly, what then becomes important is to understand how capitalist market societies emerged and evolved.

Why is Economic History Important?

A study of economic history can help us understand economic analysis. This is true even though history is essentially dynamic, an ever-changing process, while most economic analysis tries to explain how stable equilibrium conditions are

---

Equilibrium:
a state of rest in which no change is occurring

---

maintained. In particular, neoclassical theory relies on mathematical model-building set in a network of competitive markets. The technique most commonly used at the introductory level is called marginal analysis. Marginal analysis is grounded on the concept of equilibrium within a framework of constraints that is static and unchanging. It shows the conditions under which a pure, laissez faire market system allocates resources in the most efficient way possible. Given the definitions of economics noted previously, such a system will maximize output (thus meeting more material needs) and wealth. The intellectual roots of this way of thinking lie in Newtonian physics, where,

in the mechanical sense, there is an equal and opposite reaction for every action, so that equilibria positions are stable and in a sense timeless. To the extent that this holds true, then the operation of this laissez faire market system will be self-correcting, provided there are no interfering elements.

To Understand Economic Analysis

Such a static framework is very useful for understanding certain types of economic behavior given certain assumptions about the direction behavior is likely to take, within the model's constraints. Marginalist analysis assumes that each economic agent's behavior is individual, independent of what others are doing, and is motivated by maximization. (That is, workers attempt to maximize income, firms attempt to maximize profits, consumers attempt to maximize satisfaction.) With this framework, it is difficult to analyze economic actions motivated by altruism, emotion, or tradition, and such motivations tend to be regarded as imperfections.

Economic history is very different. It is a study of dynamics, of changes; it observes the changes that have taken place in the framework within which economic activity takes place. By tracing the *structural* changes that have occurred in the past, it becomes possible to understand the emergence of our modern reality. All economic activity takes place in a social setting made up of social institutions, habits, beliefs, and values, and it is as important to understand how these institutions emerged and how the structure of societies change over time as it is to concentrate only on those activities that are somehow measurable.

There is another example of the link between history and analysis. If "good" theories depend on recognizing the nature of the institutions, customs and habits that are usually subsumed under the *ceteris paribus* assumption, then the analysts' awareness of that nature can help build better theories. For example, it is usually assumed that

Ceteris paribus:
all other elements remaining unchanged

the aim of the (capitalist) firm is to maximize profits. If the economist is trying to evaluate the impact of, for example, the privatization of an enterprise in a socialist economy, the analysis will be incomplete unless it takes into account the many different goals that also exist in that society. Even without considering such a change, the differences in economic activity that emerge from any society's past experience can help explain today's differences.

The structure of any society and the values it holds influence behavior—there is no timeless type of purely economic behavior that is universally applicable. For example, the 20th century idea of profit maximization would be totally foreign to a 14th century farmer, while today, Westerners find it difficult to visualize a cooperative society in which an individualist "get ahead" ethic is considered antisocial. Material incentives exist in both these examples, but it is clear that the nature of the incentive and the reaction to it will be different.

So the first reason for studying economic history is to be able to understand the historical context within which current activity takes place. We will be able to understand better how that context emerged and developed and changed. This obviously is an important supplement to the idea that there is a single model of behavior appropriate for all times and places.

Emergence of Economics

In fact, even the emergence of economics as an intellectual discipline is a fairly recent development, dating only from the late 18th century, and the development of the neoclassical model is even more recent. The reason for this emergence is related to real economic changes, especially those associated with the spread of a market society in

which there did not seem to be any clear answer to the question, "What holds society together?"

Economists try to understand and explain reality, which presupposes that there is something that needs to be explained. But until relatively recently, there wasn't that much to understand or explain. That is, for so long as most economic activity was organized along traditional lines, you could *describe* what happened but would not bother to ask *why*. There were few interesting questions to ask about how a traditional economy worked, because the answers were self-evident. People did what they did because their ancestors had done it that way. So barring unexpected shocks like wars, plagues, or famines, there was no reason for economics and therefore no economists. Even those unexpected shocks would not be subject to economic analysis—rather their causes would be ascribed to some extra-human factor, such as the wrath of God.

What changed all this was the spread of market-oriented influences to include more activities and involve more people and groups. As the market economy spread, there were no longer *certain* answers to the questions of who did what and why they did it. In addition, there were other, totally new questions. As the new, money-inspired individualized activities spread, the social cohesiveness that held society together was no longer apparent. It seemed as though society was about to fall apart—and yet it did not. Why not? This was a question that intrigued both economists and political philosophers.[1]

In summary, knowing how and from where our present reality emerged gives us an understanding of that reality we cannot get from the model building approach of economic analysis alone. It also provides a richness to a study of economics that cannot be underestimated.

To Provide Illustrations for Theory

A second related reason for studying economic history lies in the very limitations of the model building approach. Economists have taken pains to develop economics as a science, and as such, it is impossible to conduct controlled or laboratory experiments. We are, after all, dealing with human beings and societies, so cannot subject them to experimental techniques. What economists have done to avoid this problem is to emphasize the role of scientific method, in particular, a method based on setting up propositions in such a way that they can be tested and/or falsified. This is an approach known as positivism which produces a positive science made up of a core of objective, empirically tested propositions. Crucial to this is the idea of falsification: it must be possible to show that a proposition could be wrong, given that it is difficult to prove unambiguously that something is right.

Economic history provides a fertile reservoir of experience to use to test different theories. For example, the relative importance of increasing resource supplies and technological change in expanding output or the impact of resource shortages can also be studied. There are dangers, however, because other explanations beside the one being "tested" may be as valid, logically and empirically. For example, time series studies of the Engels curve relationship summarizing the connection between consumption pattern and income levels show that rising real incomes over time alter the proportions of goods being consumed. To take food as an example, there has been a shift away from cereals to meat and dairy products, a shift that can be explained not only by rising income levels but also by changes in the structure of production.

Another danger comes from the very dynamism of the historical process contrasting with the assumption of a set of stationary parameters for the economic model. That is, using dynamic history to illustrate or test a proposition based on an assumption of stationary conditions (which is necessary to provide validity for mathematical procedures) is suspect. This becomes an even more questionable procedure with longer time periods, because then it becomes that much harder to maintain that conditions are not changing. Be that as it may, so long as an awareness of these problems is understood, economists will continue to use historical illustrations.

To Understand International Relations

A third area where a knowledge of the past distinguishes good from bad practice is international relationships. Although today there does seem to be a trend towards global standardization, the differences between countries remain significant and enable us to appreciate different national experiences. People have met their material needs in a variety of different ways, and it is impossible to say unambiguously that one form of organization is better than another, or that there is a "best" form of economic organization. Taking a purely functional approach, all that one can say is that one form of organization is best if it serves that society's purpose. As the aims of societies change over time, so too will the method of organizing activity. This emphasizes the special qualities of each time and place, and deemphasizes the search for timeless, universal general laws that characterize much economic analysis.

However, knowing how other countries developed is essential for good diplomacy, where an understanding of the other person's point of view is important. This is where historical training comes in; at its very simplest, it gives an understanding of the current situation of other nations that cannot be gained simply by reading newspapers or an entry in a statistical yearbook, as important as these are. Also, and this will become clear as we work through subsequent chapters, international interactions between countries in the past has had an impact on their later development—again, this is not always recognized if we concentrate only on current research.

To Guide Policy

Another relevant reason for studying economic history is the insight it can give into policy making. Again, the introductory chapters of an economic analysis book describe the use of economic models in policy making. Briefly, the procedure goes like this. The economist builds a model designed to isolate and illuminate particular aspects of economic reality. If it is a "good" model (or theory), it will show relationships existing between important elements of reality. Then if anything goes wrong with that reality, we have the insights from model building and can develop policy designed to correct it.

Now applying the same line of reasoning to economic history, the philosopher George Santayana said that if we do not know our past, we are doomed to repeat it—i.e., we have not been able to learn from our mistakes. This is obviously something that we should avoid, particularly those who are responsible for making decisions. It is not easy to identify the specific links between history and policy making, but it is easy to know when they have been ignored, because stupid errors have been made or misinformed judgment has produced poor policy decisions.

In addition, exploring and explaining how material conditions of life emerged in the way that they did has implications for the possibility of future change. This is because any change has a dual effect. New possibilities for development open up, but at the same time other possibilities are closed. Think of cutting down a forest. The cleared land could be used as farmland, or a new city could be built on it. Each of these opens up in turn still other possibilities that may have been unthinkable before. But cutting down the forest is also irreversible; the continuation of that forest as forest is no longer possible. This is a particularly crucial issue in the late 20th century, when many past decisions and events have led to the extinction of many species and threatened shortages of vital resources, even while human population ex-

plodes (see Table 1-2). The implication is clear: We must be much more aware of the reasons for and the consequences of our decisions.

To Be Better Informed

On the more general level, simply being informed about what happened in the past should be part of every informed citizen's education. Often, history seems "messy"—a complex mass of data. It seems uncoordinated, especially when contrasted with the clearcut propositions of economic analysis. But once we know how to approach this complexity (see below) the insights found by linking past cause and effect can be extended to an understanding of modern developments. So we can study economic history simply to satisfy our curiosity about what happened in the past, or as part of a process of learning how to reason logically.

Each reader will accomplish something different with this material, and perhaps will add other reasons to the list. That is how it should be—there is no monopoly on knowledge. The process of learning and discovering does not stop when you've finished the last page.

How? Approaches to Economic History

Having determined that studying the material conditions of life is important, we must now decide how to do it. Any scientific activity is an attempt to understand and explain events and occurrences. So meteorologists attempt to explain and predict weather patterns, while nuclear physicists are concerned with the behavior of tiny particles of matter. The task of social scientists is more difficult. They have to explain the behavior of humans who are not simply existing as part of the "natural" world but who can also change both their environment and their relationships with other people. In other words, humans do not only react to their environment, they can also act and create a change.

Where does the historian fit in? The role of historians is at once both more difficult and also easier. It is easier because *what* they are studying is given, their study will not alter the outcome, and the facts do not change (although clearly the interpretation of those facts can change, and can be influenced by the current point of view of the historian). But it is also more difficult, because the past *is* over, so historians cannot go back to doublecheck the data more thoroughly. They have second chances only with interpretation, not with events. This means that they rely much more than other scientists on other people's observation and description of what were, to them, contemporary events. There is a problem, however: From the point of view of today's historian, these observations are often incomplete or biased or not what is currently considered to be accurate. After all, an observer records only what is thought to be important, and "importance" is a subjective concept that varies from time to time and place to place. If there are many different contemporary observations, it may be easier to fill in the gaps or spot evidence of bias. Unfortunately, the likelihood of ample written evidence becomes less likely the further back in time we go, simply because fewer and fewer people could write then.

One could try to write history simply as a story of what actually happened, a chronicle of events. But this would be difficult to do, confusing to read, and most likely boring. Historians are like other social scientists. When they look at the wealth of data that makes up our past, they have to observe, select, collect, and interpret it. They must have some method of organization to help in determining what is important and what is not as a guide to their work.

What most try to do is look for a pattern that makes the past comprehensible. This may involve searching for timeless, universal laws of behavior, or explaining cause and effect, or trying to prove the existence of a purpose to life, for example.

There are similarities with journalism, when the journalist is instructed to investigate a story by asking the "What, How, Why, and What Then?" questions. If you read a good newspaper story, it will tell you *what* event occurred, *where* it occurred, *who* was involved, *how* it happened, *why* it happened, and perhaps also what the possible implications of the story are. The patterns an economic historian is searching for are contained in the changing material reality of life. This involves focusing on the emergence and development of economic institutions and trying to uncover their implications for economic behavior. Political and social activity are consequently downplayed, and have a role in the story only so far as they influence or are influenced by economic reality.

Universalism vs. Specificity

There are fashions in writing history, and historians from the very first have been influenced by one of two views of historical process. One of these is the universalist approach, which often attempts to write history as a great progression towards a specific end. The other denies the universality of experience, concentrating instead on the specificity of history—each time and each place has its own unique character.

The first Western historians in ancient Greece can be classed with the universalists. While neither Herodotus nor Thucydides uncovered a simple pattern of history, they did believe that there were consistent elements in human nature. For Thucydides, this consistency led him to claim that once it was uncovered, then human behavior could be understood.

A clearer example of a universalist approach geared to uncovering the direction of history is provided by medieval Christian historians, for whom history was simply the working out of the divine plan for the universe. History was a linear progression, beginning with the Creation and it would end with the second coming of the Messiah.

Eighteenth century historians also saw history as a linear progression, but they removed the specifically religious aspects. The goal of the human experience was to attain some kind of secular paradise. Later in the 19th century, two versions of the progression towards this end appeared. One version continued to see history as a linear progression; the other, influenced by Hegel, saw history as moving upwards in a spiralling circle. This implies that "repetitions" could occur, but at a different stage of development, so they would not be absolutely identical.

Some of these approaches were clearly the basis for justifying action. If the goal of human experience was to attain an ideal, then it could be helped on its way—destiny could be shaped. The opposing view, known as historicism, stressed the specificity of each historical event. If all events were unique to each time and place, then nothing could be used to help explain anything else, and no common elements existed.

In the 20th century, the attempt to try to identify a single motive force or end has been discarded, but without implying an acceptance of relativist historicism. There is still an interest in those details that are often left out of the "grand sweep" histories. This is best represented by the French school derived from the work of Fernand Braudel, the school of *Annales*. It focuses on the actual material details of daily living rather than the universal subjects of wars, political changes, or the development of intellectual ideas.

What we will try to do in this book is trace through the themes that are important to economic development, and illustrate them with specific details. We will not take a teleological approach, and in fact, there is no grand conclusion in the last chapter. How can there be when we are still making history?

Mathematical History

In the early 1970s, some economic historians began calling what they did "cliometrics," a more mathematical study of history. (Clio is the Greek muse of history; econo*metrics* involves the use of

Cliometrics:

application of mathematical techniques to the study of history

Table 1-2
Estimates of World Population (Millions)

Year	Africa	N. America	Lat. America	Asia	Europe and Russia	Oceania	World
1650	? 100	1	7–12	257–327	103–105	2	470–545
1750	95–106	1–2	10–16	437–498	144–167	2	695–790
1800	90–107	6–7	19–24	595–630	192–208	2	905–980
1850	95–111	26	33–38	656–801	274–285	2	1090–1260
1900	120–141	81–82	63–74	857–925	423–430	6	1570–1650
1978	450	242	348	2313	785	22	4160

Sources: 1650–1900 data from *Determinants and Consequences of Population Trends*, United Nations, 1953, p. 11; 1978 data from *1980 World Bank Atlas*, World Bank, p. 10.

statistical techniques in the analysis of economic issues.) While it might be thought that this is possible only with recent history—where numbers had been collected and could be used—some early measures of population, harvest, taxes, or trade, for example, also exist.

"New" Economic History

Later on, this became known as "New" Economic History, the systematic use of economic theory and quantitative methods to describe and shed light on the past. There were two approaches. The first is more macroeconomics in orientation, taking such concepts as national income, national product, saving, investment, and consumption, for example, and then applying them to the past. The "new" economic historians have devoted themselves to finding values for these concepts as far back as possible, and then using these quantities and the relationships between them to trace the path of economic growth over time.

The second is more microeconomics in orientation, and is an analysis based on prices and quantities of commodities and services emerging from the operation of various markets. If all markets work in the way specified by an extreme version of neoclassical theory, the result is that rational individuals acting in their own self-interest will produce a socially efficient result. One group of "new" economic historians has also focused on the emergence and development of private property rights. This is because if the owner is responsible for both the costs and the rewards resulting from the use of the resource, this gives an incentive to work and accumulate wealth.

Another device used by New Economic Historians is the counterfactual, intended to measure the impact of one specific element in the growth process. This is done by varying one of the elements of the model, and comparing the new set of predictions with what actually happened. If there is a difference, then it is due to the impact of the counterfactual. For example, take railroads.

We could develop a model of American economic growth using data from the pre-railroad era, then extrapolate to find what the model tells us economic growth would have been if railroads did not exist. These figures are compared to actual growth rates (because railroads *were* built), and we can conclude that any difference between the model's predicted growth rates and actual growth rates must be due to the construction of railroads.

Coherent Narrative

While economic historians have been adding more analytic rigor to their work, other economists have begun to appreciate the qualitative aspects of economic life—those aspects not easily amenable to analytic quantification or generalization. This approaches the methodology of "historians in general" who practice by writing narratives rather than developing formal models, an attempt to describe what happened and link events together in a cause and effect relationship. Such an approach may, but does not have to be, part of a broader world view; it does not need to relate every development to the working out of some general law. It also provides flexibility: the level of explanation can be at the overall level or at the level of detail, whichever is more appropriate for the use to which it will be put. The map analogy is illustrative here. Different types of maps have different uses, so that a street map is ideal for finding a particular address, but useless if one wishes to find the best route to another country.

What this approach implies is that motives must be relevant to the situation and the outcome logically connected. Events do not just happen in a vacuum, and neither are they consciously planned, so if the explanation for the event makes sense, then it is probably right. This type of coherent narrative allows for the complexity of historical events without putting them into the straitjacket of the analytical model. It is also appropriate for an introductory text, and will be used here.

Focus of the Book

Human existence on this planet dates back for millennia, which means that humans have been engaging in economic activity, "trying to make a living," for just as long. Yet this book will be concerned with only a small part of this experience, and will emphasize in particular an even smaller period of time, the last couple of centuries. We will focus on two related issues—the development of economic behavior and the changes in economic systems. Specifically, we will look at the events that led to the emergence and subsequent development of the market mechanism as the dominant control device over economic activity, and to the emergence and subsequent development of capitalism, the economic system prevalent in most of the world today. This is a process of development that is still going on, and by looking at what happened in the past, we may be able to understand and appreciate possible future directions of change.

In an economic history, it is important to do more than simply present a chronological sequence of events illustrated by statistics of various economic magnitudes. So we will be concerned with more than just the growth of output (which measures an economy's ability to produce things), we will also be concerned with the institutional changes providing the setting for economic behavior. We may also overlap with areas usually regarded as social or political history, because it is not easy to isolate the specifically economic aspects of life. There is in fact a two-way process of influence between the economic and socio-political areas of life that will help us understand the interrelationships existing in any society.

Chronological and Geographic Scope

Although we are concentrating on only a short period of time, it is a period that has seen dramatic change. For example, there were fundamental changes in economic organization and technol-

ogy that radically altered both a society's ability to produce things and the way that ordinary people lived and worked. We even seem to be on the threshold of new *places* in which to work, and already space stations have demonstrated the possibility of limited work in places beyond the pull of the Earth's gravity, a potential beyond the comprehension of ancient societies.

To set the stage, to see how ordinary people lived and worked before these changes took place, we will start with the pre-market, pre-capitalist background. Beginning with a very brief survey of the economic aspects of the Roman Empire and its decline, we will devote more time to look at feudalism, medieval Europe's example of a traditional economy. The process of breaking down these traditional ways provided the conditions from which capitalism emerged.

We should be careful, however. The process of economic change took time, and it is impossible to give a date for the emergence of capitalism as such in the same way that we can date a famous battle or a treaty or a monarch's coronation. That is, we know that the prevalent economic system in much of Europe in the 9th century was feudal and that the economic system in the 20th century is capitalist. But like the last straw on the camel's back, there is no one year or even decade that we can identify as the one where capitalism began. All we can say is that in the transition centuries, elements of both were present, but gradually, piece by piece, the structure of the economic system looked less and less feudal and more and more capitalist. To be sure, even today we can still find some feudal remnants, but these are mainly ceremonial and perform no real functions.

The book is limited in geographic as well as chronological coverage, concentrating only on some Western European countries, the United States, and, from the late 19th century on, Japan. The reasoning is as follows. Western European countries shared a more or less common feudal heritage, and its economic aspect, the manorial system, is the system preceding capitalism. As we are concentrating on the transition from feudalism to capitalism, it is inevitable that we look at the countries where this happened first.

In addition, the Western Europeans not only migrated to many other parts of the world, they also exported their new economic organizations and techniques. These took root in some countries, and the United States is the best example of a "new" country with no feudal traditions that adopted early capitalist organizations at the same time that it was being settled. Its development was initially slow, but by the late 19th century, it was clear that the United States had become the largest capitalist market economy. Japan seems like the odd one out, and although it was not one of the countries to be affected by that Western European movement, it must be included because its experience is similar. The pre-capitalist system in Japan was a feudal one, so in that respect, there are many similarities with Western Europe. But there are also differences. Whereas the process of transition in Europe was on a whole slow and evolutionary, in Japan the break with the past was rapid and deliberate. Such planned deliberation may have more implications for currently underdeveloped countries attempting to speed up their transition to modern industrialization. Certainly the experience of other rapidly developing Asian economies in the 20th century, such as resource-poor people-rich Korea or Taiwan, seems to have more in common with Japan than the Anglo-American version.

One final consideration. Although the book is selective by focusing on the development of market capitalism, this should not blind us to the fact that there were other countries in the world with different, equally viable economic systems. Some of these achieved extraordinarily high levels of civilization—at least for some of their inhabitants—at a time when Europe was very far from achieving the dominance that occurred later.

Structure of the Book

In general, the book is organized along chronological lines, although sometimes it is necessary to ignore chronology in favor of the logical development of a theme. The overall theme we are tracing is the development of a capitalist market system. To repeat, this is an economic system in which resources are privately owned, and where the organizing mechanism affording incentives, information, and coordination is provided through the new institution of the market. Markets have always existed; what was new and different about this development was that markets came to dominate economic activity rather than remain a supplement or adjunct to economic life. This had powerful implications for political and social life, as we will see later.

The first part describes the organization of precapitalist economies in the Roman Empire and Western Europe. We go back to the Roman Empire in the 5th century because its collapse after that time influenced the emerging institutions of feudal Europe. There is a lesson to be learned from this, that the development of any society's structure and institutions is not a random process. It responds rather to specific needs and requirements. This is a process that will be repeated. A generalized version of European feudalism appears in Chapter 2, which sketches its early development and its influence on economic life and social ethic. The final chapter in Part I covers the new towns that began to emerge towards the end of the feudal period. These towns, although feudal in some ways, signaled the beginning of the end of feudalism because they were the location of a new commercial activity completely antithetical to the feudal social ethic.

The next five chapters make up Part II: Europe in Transition. We begin to see evidence of the breakdown of traditional forms of economic organization, and their replacment by new forms. The first economic activity to be influenced by the desire to gain was exchange, and a new class of merchants appeared as feudal restraints became weaker.

Many of the changes that we see in these transition centuries will not have a very widespread impact unless they are accepted by society. The acceptability of an economic organization depends on the value system—the set of beliefs that justify and provide a rationale for human behavior. The feudal social ethic provided guidelines for and justified feudal economic behavior, but could not also serve to justify money making or capitalist activity. During this time, an alternative value system more appropriate for the emerging way of life and based on a reaction to the then-established religious orthodoxy appeared (Chapter 5). At first, this had only a minority appeal—but the minority were those most influenced by the new economic ideas, hence the development of a *capitalist* ethic later was no longer confined to just the holders of specific religious beliefs.

The growing influence of the new class of merchants was most clearly revealed in the practice of mercantilism, when the policies of states were geared to providing the favorable environment needed for the merchants' pursuit of gain (Chapter 6). It was during this period too that the search for gain became almost a worldwide activity. The 16th, 17th and 18th centuries are marked by the spread of capitalist ideas from Western Europe, as these nations acquired colonial empires and resources as part of that search for enrichment (Chapter 7).

Something else also began to happen during this transition period. So far, market expansion commercialized the exchange of products, most of which were produced under precapitalist conditions. However, there was an upper limit to the volume of goods that could be produced in this way, which constrained the merchants' further profit making activity. If we jump forward in time to look at the specific characteristics of capitalist production, we will see it marked not only by the deliberate production of goods *for sale* but also by the use of *free labor*. What does "free labor" mean? It does not mean that people work for nothing, but rather that they are legally able to enter into alternative occupations. For example, slave labor is not free because although slaves do not work for money wages, what they are able to do is determined by their owner. Any system in which occupations are based on status at birth or inheritance, like a caste system, is a system of non-free labor, because people are not free to choose their occupation. Thus labor in feudal times, as well as in any traditional system, was not free. Feudal labor, called "serf labor," is not free because it is tied to the land. That is, because serfs were born into the class of serfs, they became farmers, with the right to use land, which meant that they had access to the resources needed to provide for their material needs. Furthermore, this also meant that the output of goods for sale could not expand until the serfs' ties to the land were broken and they became a potential free labor force able to work for others for a wage producing the goods the merchants needed for sale. For so long as people have access to land with which to meet their needs, they have little incentive to face an uncertain life as free wage laborers. So the initial creation of a free labor force, in which the market mechanism spread to encompass people-as-economic-resources, involved a considerable amount of coercion. (Later on, when alternatives became fewer and less appealing, less violence was needed to create this free labor.) The process of producing the first market in free labor began in 16th century England, at which time we also see the creation of a market in which land could be bought and sold (Chapter 8), another example of the spread of markets.

In Part III: The Industrial Revolution, we build on all the preceding changes that were the prerequisites for the expansion of output for sale under capitalist conditions. This part brings us closer to modern industrial reality, and shows the enormous impact of those technological changes—especially those concerned with the use of energy—that ushered in modern manufacturing techniques. We will look at this industrialization experience in Britain, France, Germany, the United States, and Japan.

By this time, market activity dominated economic life, which contrasted to the subsidiary role of markets in precapitalist economies. As a result, several other institutional developments were also occurring. One was the increasing use of money in facilitating the growth of exchange. Money increased in quantity and there were also qualitative changes—the development of paper money and new forms of credit and debt instruments. This accommodating growth of liquidity and other financial developments paralleled the growth on the real side of the economy.

If Part III focuses on each country's experience in turn, Part IV pulls out several features that were common to all and that characterize mature industrial capitalist economies. In Chapter 17, we survey the spread of the factory system, the development of capital markets, and also some opposition to these socio-economic changes. Modern industrialization is characterized by the use of the corporate form of organization. The corporation proved to be highly adaptable to the needs of mature capitalism—in raising funds, spreading risks, organizing the production and distribution of goods and services—and slowly replaced individual ownership of enterprises. This is covered in Chapter 18, while the development of a permanent wage labor force and the institutions associated with it are covered in Chapter 19.

The final section of the book, Part V, looks at the 20th century experience that has been marked by a globalization of economic activity. However, while the post-World War II experience has tended to be cooperative and integrative (Chapters 22 and 23), the earlier part of the 20th century was not—it was marked by crises. In Chapter 20, we look at the increasing international rivalries of imperialism that contributed to the crisis of World War I. In Chapter 21, we see that the need for a cooperative approach to the problems of an increasingly internationalized economy was not recognized, which contributed to the crisis of World War II.

The developments we will trace cannot be unambiguously defined as good for all. For example, our material success seems to herald environmental disaster, there is a growing gap between rich and poor within nations, and economic development does not remove political and ideological hostilities. However, if we understand what happened and what can be done, if we desire to improve the situation, past economic development has provided us with the tools.

A certain amount of overlap has been built into the book. A large book has an advantage if it contains some repetition, because if it becomes necessary to skip over some material, the general theme will not be lost. Obviously, different sections of the book will be more appealing to some readers than others, depending on the use to which the book will be put, but it will still be possible to follow the general theme even while missing out some sections. For example, a short course on the emergence and development of capitalism may wish to skip the chapters in Part III on development in specific countries, and then return to the general theme of development common to many countries in Part IV. Similarly, a course emphasizing either American or European history can eliminate unneeded chapters before returning to the general theme in Part IV. (The Table of Contents is comprehensive enough to enable a more detailed selection, even within chapters.)

NOTES

1. To understand why most economics is taught the way it is today requires studying the history of economic thought, or the development of economic *theorizing*. This is beyond the scope of this book, which is concerned with the development of economic *reality*.

Key Concepts

Capitalism   Equilibrium
Ceteris paribus   Market economy
Cliometrics   Positivism
Command Economy   Traditional economy
Economics; economic system

Questions for Discussion and Essay Writing

1. Does it matter how we study past events?

2. "The past is over and done with, what happened in the past is not going to change. Therefore any approach to the study of economic history is as good as any other." Critically evaluate this statement.

3. Describe the main characteristics differentiating one economic system from another.

4. How would a New Economic Historian set about the study of history?

5. "History is simply a succession of unique events." Discuss.

6. If markets have always existed, why aren't all economies called "market economies"?

7. How are the economic questions of what to produce answered in a traditional, a command, or a market economy?

8. How is economic activity coordinated in a traditional, a command, or a market economy?

9. Why is theorizing useful in economic history?

10. What preconditions are necessary for a capitalist economy to exist?

11. What is the role of a value system?

For Further Reading

Beaud, Michel. *A History of Capitalism, 1500-1980.* New York: Monthly Review Press, 1983.

Braudel, Fernand. *Civilization and Capitalism, 15th -18th century.* (three volumes). New York: Harper & Row (1979), 1981, 1982, 1983.

Cameron, Rondo. *A Concise Economic History of the World: From Paleolithic Times to the Present.* N.Y. and Oxford: Oxford University Press, 1989.

Cipolla, Carlo. *Before the Industrial Revolution: European Society and Economy, 1000-1700,* 2nd ed. New York: W.W. Norton (1976) 1980.

Clough, Shepard B. and Richard T. Rapp. *European Economic History: The Economic Development of Western Civilization,* 3rd. ed. New York: McGraw Hill, 1975.

Dillard, Dudley. *Economic Development of the North Atlantic Community: Historical Introduction to Modern Economies.* Englewood Cliffs, N.J: 1967.

Galenson, David W. *Markets in History: Economic Studies of the Past.* Cambridge: Cambridge University Press, 1989.

Frank, Andre Gunder. *World Accumulation, 1492-1789*. New York: Monthly Review Press, 1978.

Hawke, G.R. *Economics for Historians*. Cambridge: Cambridge University Press, 1980.

Hicks, John R. *A Theory of Economic History*. London: Oxford University Press, 1969.

Heilbroner, Robert. *The Making of Economic Society*, latest ed. Englewood Cliffs, N.J.: Prentice Hall

Hunt, E.K. *Property and Prophets*, 5th ed. New York: Harper & Row, 1986.

McCloskey, Donald. *Econometric History*. London: Macmillan Education, 1987.

North, Douglass C. and Robert P. Thomas. *The Rise of the Western World: A New Economic History*. Cambridge: Cambridge University Press, 1973.

Rosenberg, Nathan and L.E. Birdsell, Jr. *How the West Grew Rich: The Economic Transformation of the Industrial World*. New York: Basic Books, 1986.

Rostow, W.W. *History, Policy and Economic Theory: Essays in Interaction*. Boulder, Colo: Westview Press, 1990.

_____ *The World Economy: History and Prospect*. Austin: Tex: University of Texas Press, 1978.

Note: Most of these texts are general economic history books, and will not be listed again at the end of subsequent chapters. Many journals also have articles of interest to the economic historian and should also be looked at. The following specialize in economic history: *Economic History Review, Explorations in Economic History, Journal of Economic History, Past and Present.*

Chapter 2

Feudalism in Europe

Origins of Feudalism: Decline of the Roman Empire

EVER SINCE THE VERY FIRST AGRICULTURAL REVOLUTION 15,000 years ago, when scattered groups of humans first began to cultivate the soil, farming, whether settled or nomadic, arable or pasture, has always been the basis of economic life. In the centuries before the 19th century, it was the primary occupation of most of the population, as it was essential for sheer survival. But the framework in which farming, or any economic activity, takes place and thus its relative importance, depends on the socio-political framework of the society. It is this framework that has changed in the course of human existence, and which provides a reason for studying history.

Although this book will concentrate on the development of one economic system, capitalism, as it emerged in different places, it is necessary to contrast it with a preceding system. This was feudalism or, more properly, the manorial system that is feudalism's economic counterpart. While any economic history text has difficulty in determining *where* in the past to begin, a useful starting point for this one is with the emergence of feudalism itself, because feudalism seemed so settled and unchanging that it is difficult to conceive of it never having existed. During the time in which it was prevalent, it was also a very practical method of organizing society, determining who

did the work necessary for economic survival, and who got what shares of output.

Feudalism evolved in response to the breakdown of the Roman Empire and was the dominant method of organizing European society from about the 8th century to about the 14th, when it began to disintegrate. In some countries, in less than its purest form, it even remained important until the 19th century; for example, serfdom was not abolished in Russia until 1861. Whether or not change will occur depends on elements specific to different countries, and this will explain the timing of their development.

Roman dominance of Europe began in the 3rd century B.C., started to crumble in the 3rd century A.D., and was effectively obliterated in the 5th century. What was left behind in this vacuum was social disintegration and military weakness, a situation taken advantage of by various warring tribes and peoples. Inevitably, one of the primary needs in such an unsettled situation was to secure personal safety against outside attack. In other words, there was a need for protection. Given this, those individuals capable of providing protection—warriors—became a privileged class because they, and only they, were able to fill this need. As a result, a feudal society became organized into two classes: the upper or ruling class, noble by definition and including those with prized military skills, and the non-noble class. This class included most of the population (be-

18

tween 80 and 90 percent) who were not fighters, but did the work necessary to maintain a military establishment.

This is a different organization of society from that associated with the Romans, whose society was much more settled and who therefore had different political and economic priorities. Roman society, which was originally based on republican principles associated with independent farmers, developed an organized bureaucracy for administration. This can only be done if the society is reasonably certain it will survive, because there is no point in drawing up elaborate rules for the administration of a given society if change is continuous. If change and upheaval are frequent, a basic requirement for social organization is a decision making process flexible enough to meet new demands. This implies locating decision making in individuals, which is why the centuries during and after the breakdown of the Roman Empire saw an organization of society based on personal ties between individuals, not on established rules that may not be appropriate to changing conditions. Once the worst threats to society's survival were past, then these somewhat *ad hoc* decision making mechanisms became formalized as law. And by this time, whether or not the original military need still existed, the social hierarchy became crystallized.

Roman Empire

In contrast to a decentralized feudal society, the Roman Empire was marked by a well developed administrative structure and a highly developed political philosophy. Both societies were based on agriculture, but in Roman times, the few centuries on either side of the birth of Christ, this was at first centered on peasant farming in small agrarian city-states rather than on large estates using unfree labor. Study of the characteristics of the Roman Empire is important because its collapse produced a threat to the survival of European society. Given this situation, adoption of feudal

practice was a very practical response. Thus feudalism, as a political and legal structure, was a response to unsettled conditions, representing an attempt to prevent the complete dissolution of society. In this, it was successful, helped in no small part by the economic arrangements known as the manorial system.

The original Roman city-state was a republic in which all adult male citizens (excluding women and slaves) were equal, bound together by a common allegiance to the state. This could be summed up by the slogan, *civis Romanus sum* (I am a Roman citizen), which expressed both a sense of civilized superiority over non-Romans and a political reality based on common links in an urban society that would rarely be duplicated later.

Expansion

From this small beginning, Roman power and authority expanded. At first, the empire included only the areas around the Mediterranean (literally, "the center of the earth"), but later stretched to include Northern Europe. Initially, the Latin tribes surrounding the Roman state joined it in a Latin league of cities under Roman leadership. Its purpose was defense against rivals, and the league challenged Etruscan dominance in northern Italy and conquered Greek colonies in southern Italy. By 275 B.C., all Italy south of the River Po was Roman, and the peoples conquered gained the rights associated with the Roman system. At this time, the army was made up of peasant-citizens. This is typical when farming is independent peasant farming, because citizens have immediate interest in protecting their lands.

As military expansion continued and new areas were brought under Roman control, commercial opportunities for Roman and Italian merchants increased. However, these merchants' interests began to conflict with those of already-established traders, especially those located in Carthage, a colony established by Phoenicians in what is now

Figure 2-1   Small ships powered by human muscle were the commonest form of water transport in the Roman Empire. Goods were shipped in barrels, like the ones seen here. (Courtesy of Rheinisches Landesmuseum Trier)

Tunisia. (These traders had links with eastern civilizations, and high value items, such as perfumes, enamels, wines, silks and spices were most commonly exchanged.) Commercial conflict climaxed in the Punic Wars, 264-146 B.C., in which Rome defeated Carthage, and in the conquest of Greece.

This phase of Roman expansion had several effects. First, Rome became the strongest power in the Mediterranean area. Second, economic consequences began to undermine the old egalitarian principles on which Roman citizenship was based. The wars, many of which were fought in Italy, had devastated farmland and hurt small farmers, who also faced competition from grain supplies from some of the conquered territories in North Africa. In addition, in Italy itself many wealthy Romans bought large areas of land and began producing grain for city markets, working their estates with slaves from conquered territories. Third, there was an increase in wealth as a result of conquest. But this wealth went to only a few—the mass of the population in Italian city-states only shared in it indirectly. Finally, the expansion of Roman authority required new mechanisms for administration. This was accomplished by establishing Roman provinces in the new areas, with control exercised by the Roman armies.

Internal Disintegration

However, the combination of external problems of administration and internal problems of the polarization of wealth and poverty was too much to be handled by a city-state government. The last century of the Republic was a period of upheaval and civil war, during which the Senate acquired power. The Senate was an aristocratic body, not supportive of the small farmers, a condition leading to further problems.

The Emperor Augustus (31 B.C.-14 A.D.) provided stability. He concentrated power in the hands of the emperor, appointed governors for the provinces, and reduced the authority of the Senate to the governing of Rome, not the whole Empire. The empire Augustus created lasted for the next 300 years, with its peak of power and prosperity occurring in the 2nd century A.D.

Attention was diverted from internal problems with further military successes that expanded the frontiers of the Empire into the Arabian peninsula, transalpine Gaul (modern southern France), the area west of the Rhine and Britain. A disciplined standing army maintained order, but its composition changed. Because military needs were so great, the army was no longer composed only of citizen-soldiers, it also included soldiers from conquered barbarian (i.e., non-Roman and therefore "uncivilized") tribes.

Problems of morale, discipline, and stability developed later. These soldiers no longer felt exactly the same loyalty to the Roman state their predecessors had. Instead, they tended to feel personally loyal to immediate superiors. As the influence of the army grew because of its military success and its importance in governing the provinces, it became more influential in imperial policies. The emperor's survival depended on the army's loyalty to him, but this loyalty was not automatically guaranteed.

However, the army indirectly assisted the expansion of commerce. It built roads for military purposes, but their existence also aided overland commerce and the exploitation of mineral resources from the far flung parts of the empire. Growing wealth permitted the development of an urban civilization in Rome and other cities. It also permitted the empire's "bread and circuses" policy. Circuses were huge, often violent and bloody spectacles featuring fights to the death between captured men, often new Christians, and wild beasts or trained gladiators. To some extent they modified the dissatisfaction felt by the city bourgeoisie and lower classes who were not sharing in the empire's wealth.

But peace and prosperity did not last. Starting in the 3rd century, economic depression, social disintegration, political upheavals, and successive waves of external aggression posed a threat to the Empire that could not be resisted. The external threats were most significant. For so long as the strength and stability of the Empire depended on military success, it could survive, but when military success was no longer forthcoming, it crumbled.

Power Struggles

Internal problems centered around power struggles for the imperial throne and economic problems, including the enormous problem of collecting sufficient revenues to support growing military needs. Depression during the 3rd century was exacerbated by epidemics, and as a result of the fall in population, much land was left uncultivated. More small farmers, no longer able to survive as independent farmers, became *coloni* (tenant farmers), a situation similar to that found in feudalism. The *coloni* obtained use of land in exchange for services rendered to the landowner; they were legally free but economically dependent. Because they were not able to leave the estates, they became in effect a hereditary caste of agricultural laborers. (However, the fact that soldiers were paid in land meant that a small class of free farmers was still in existence.) This encouraged the trend to large scale cultivation, especially in Gaul, Spain, Italy, and parts of north Africa, which were not so oriented to city living as the older parts of Italy.

The movement away from the old republican traditions and towards a more rigid, stratified society was finalized by Diocletian (who ruled 284-305). He increased the power of the emperor and the imperial bureaucracy, and reduced that of the Senate. In the economic sphere, different trades were organized into guilds—associations of producers in the same line of work. This was originally done to make collecting taxes easier, but it also meant that the occupations of merchants and artisans became hereditary, adding an element of inflexibility to the economy.

The taxation problem both encouraged further rigidity and increased internal divisiveness. Land taxes were the most important source of revenue. However, large estate owners could simply defy central authority and refuse to pay, knowing that little could be done to them as the output of their estates was so important to the Empire's survival. General commercial decline further reduced tax collections. Pirates in the Mediterranean threatened shipping, which reduced trading with Persia, Syria, and the other eastern civilizations and effectively resulted in the decline of the Mediterranean as a commercial region. On land, the proliferation of bandits increased the risks of overland trade movements, also leading to a decline in commercial activity.

However, while the western half of the Empire was slowly disintegrating from these internal causes, the eastern half (which would later be known as the Byzantine Empire), centered on the new capital built at Constantinople, was more stable. It was little affected by the barbarian invasions, suffered less from economic depression, and still maintained commercial contacts with Asia. As it became more separate from the west, so it developed more distinct cultural characteristics, although perpetuating the bureaucratic organization associated with Diocletian.

External Aggression

Much more damaging to the survival of the Roman Empire and its centralized authority were waves of invasions by barbarians outside its borders. There were three major waves. The first, in the 5th century, came from the Germanic tribes living to the north. The result was a semi-assimilation of Romans and Germans, the conversion of the barbarians to Christianity (which was first legally tolerated in the Empire early in the 4th century), and an intensification of the trend to the feudalization of European society.

The second wave, in the 7th century, was more disastrous. This time, Moslem invaders from Arabia conquered much of the former Roman Empire and resulted in the Mediterranean becoming a barrier between Christians and Moslems, rather than a center of economic activity, as before. The third wave came in the 9th century, when Nordic tribes from Scandinavia invaded the northern parts of the Empire. These areas had not previously been under serious attack.

Barbarian Invasions

By 395 A.D., it was clear that the days of the Empire were numbered. Although the Germanic tribes (which included Franks, Alamans, Vandals, Saxons, Angles, Lombards, Ostrogoths, and Visigoths) were not allied with each other, they did share one common characteristic. The Roman Empire was characterized by organized bureaucracy, but personal links were more important in these tribal groups: they were not stratified and followed the leadership of a king or war leader.

Why did they become a threat to the Roman Empire? During the 4th century, population pressure forced a movement of thousands of them into the Empire, where they had settled peacefully. However, further peaceful settlement was ruled out as a result of two extra pressures. One was the movement of the Huns, Asiatic nomads, who were moving west and raiding more settled agricultural communities as they did so. By the end of the 4th century, the Huns reached Eastern Europe, defeating the Gothic tribes there. This initiated an attempt by the Visigoths to move inside the Roman Empire. Unfortunately, an inefficient Roman administration bungled these settlement attempts, leading to bad blood between them, so the Visigoths mounted an attack, resulting in further military actions within the Empire's borders.

To counter this and the movement of other Germanic tribes into Spain and North Africa, Roman troops were pulled back from Britain and Gaul. Britain then became open to raids by the Picts from the North, Scots from Ireland, and Saxons, Angles and Jutes from across the North Sea. These invaders successfully pushed the existing Celts and Romanized Britons into Wales and Southwest England, and formed separate Saxon kingdoms in their newly conquered lands. The Franks became established in what is now part of modern France, to move into Gaul in the 6th century; the Burgundians took over the area south of the Rhone; and the Huns controlled the area between the Don and the Danube before moving back to Asia after the mid-5th century.

By the 6th century, the west Roman Empire was in German hands, although Rome came under the control of the Pope. Only Byzantium remained untouched. Germanic traditions mixed with existing Roman institutions. The Roman idea of the state as belonging to and created by all (*res publica*) was replaced by the Germanic idea of government authority as a personal attribute of the king—a product of pastoral existence and individualism. However, with the more settled conditions following conquest came an increased need for some system to preserve order and administer justice. Here, the Germans had no tradition of a permanent administrative organization, so the Roman system of local government was adopted. Economically, little changed under Germanic rule, especially in the provinces where there was less of a heritage of urban and commercial life. Germans too became owners of large estates, and agricultural production continued using economically dependent tenant farmers.

Seventh Century Moslem Invasion

Although it was no longer a *Roman* empire, its central core was still basically a settled, civilized, and Christian world. But a new threat, the second wave of external aggression, appeared in the 7th century, and could not be adapted to as the Germanic invasions had been: the threat from Moslem Arabia, home of a rival civilization.

Islam, established among the nomadic Bedouin tribes of Arabia by Mohammed (570-632) was based on submission to one God, Allah. From early on, it encouraged an aggressive attitude toward non-Moslem peoples because of the desire to subject all people to Allah. Thus inspired, and possibly with the extra incentive of population pressure at home, Arabs on horseback swept across the Mediterranean area. By the mid-7th century, they controlled Spain, North Africa, and Persia—an area including not only unpeopled deserts but also the old Middle Eastern civilizations in Egypt, Syria, Palestine, and Persia. By the 9th century, a later wave of Arabs (called Saracens by then) became established in southern Italy, Sicily, and other islands in the Mediterranean. Resistance was ineffective, although in the 9th and 10th Centuries, some counterattack began. This evolved into the organized Crusades of the 11th and 12th Centuries, which were intended to drive back the Moslem threat.

More completely than before, Moslem control of the Mediterranean eliminated commercial activity and trade, and accelerated the trend to agrarianism. Continual harassment by Saracen pirates localized trade around the coast of Italy, with the surviving links to the East kept in the hands of the Byzantine merchants.

Nordic Incursions

Strangely enough, while the 7th century invasions destroyed the commercial culture of the old Roman Empire, the third wave of external aggression, the Norse invasions from Scandinavia in the 9th century, unexpectedly helped restimulate trade. The Romans knew nothing of Scandinavia, nor did the Germanic tribes who by this time controlled what was then considered the civilized western world. Neither thought the most northern parts of the former Roman Empire worth

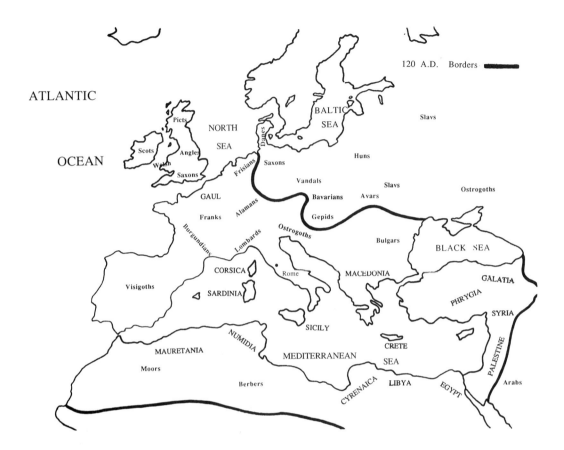

Map 2-1   **External Aggression and the Roman Empire.** Starting in the 5th century B.C., the Roman Empire came under increasing pressure from barbarian tribes located both inside and outside its borders.

bothering about, although these areas were valuable for their mineral wealth. What happened to focus attention here?

By the late 8th century, population pressure resulted in a movement from Scandinavia to potentially more hospitable areas, chiefly England and Northern France. There were limited opportunities for agriculture in the Scandinavian countries, and the invaders first raided, then plundered and terrorized, before conquering and colonizing new areas.

Vikings attacked the east coast of England and successfully conquered the northeast part, while southern England remained in Saxon hands. Norsemen from Norway first attacked Ireland, then began a slow movement across the Atlantic—to Iceland, where a true Norse settlement was established, to Greenland, and perhaps also to America, although no settlement was established there. In the 9th century, Vikings reached the French coast, Spain, and Italy. Settlement was established in northern France, which subsequently became the Duchy of Normandy, bringing the Vikings into contact with the mainstream of what was then civilized Europe. In addition, traders and explorers from Sweden crossed the Baltic and established a new trade route across Russia to the Moslem and Persian worlds.

Feudalism: The Frankish-Carolingian Inheritance

The small-scale, inward-looking nature of feudal society as it developed after the 8th century largely resulted from the overriding need for security, especially security from outside attack. Previously, internal order and security from outside aggression was imposed by the imperial armies and the administration of the Roman Empire. Then, trade and commerce centered around the Mediterranean port cities, which in turn were supported by their agricultural hinterlands. But as external aggression killed off trade, so the reason for the existence of a merchant class disappeared. Consequently, towns shrank, and while some Italian towns persisted as centers of ecclesiastical administration, they no longer had much economic significance.

Especially in the outlying former Roman provinces where towns had never been very important, the change was marked. As trade collapsed, so portable wealth disappeared. Instead, wealth, social, status, and political power came to depend on land—which of course had always been important for material survival. A new organization of society had to be developed to replace the formal structure of the Roman Empire, where society was held together by the acknowledgement of a common citizenship.

Decentralization

This new organization was feudalism, a decentralized system that emerged spontaneously in response to the disturbed social and economic conditions in Europe after the 5th century. A feudal relationship was personal, between man and man. While often looked down on as being a more primitive form of social organization than the centralized bureacracy of Rome, it was a practical form of administration. It stabilized society on a local basis and provided the base from which feudal kingdoms would emerge in and after the 10th century. Feudalism emerged because of the need for security that existed in those unsettled times, and the cost of this security was a surrender of liberty. But this cost was willingly paid—not to have done so implied only a freedom to starve, to be raped, looted, pillaged, and destroyed or enslaved.

While earlier societies also reveal feudal elements, the Franks in Europe during the 8th century under the Carolingian dynasty made it much more organized. Thus those parts of France where the Carolingians were strongest adopted feudalism earlier and to a greater extent than elsewhere. It was only partly applicable in Italy, if at all, where anarchy resulting from power struggles prevented it, and in Germany, where traditions of individualism in many areas persisted. It was not formally introduced in England until the 11th century, where it also lasted the shortest time. While there were many differences depending on time and place, and feudalism itself changed over time, there are common threads applicable to all feudal societies. These common threads, especially those governing social relationships, provided the cohesiveness needed by different societies throughout the Middle Ages, and while beginning to be less important in some areas after the 13th century, persisted for centuries longer in others.

Charlemagne's Empire

It is worth describing the Frankish input because it was so important. The Frankish empire had been consolidated in the 6th century, but was shortlived, and a period of decentralized occurred. Political order was restored in the 8th century, and close links with the Papacy were established.

Charlemagne, who ruled from 768 to 814, extended Frankish rule into Lombardy, Saxony, and other German areas. He relied on dukes and counts to administer these areas, and his agents supervised them to make sure they acted in his interests. This was not like Roman administration, which used clearly defined rules set up in the interests of the central administration.

The empire's economic base lay in large estates owned by wealthy landowners and cultivated by tenant farmers. Some small farms were still independently owned, but this class of freeman shrank as overall conditions were not supportive, as will become clear later.

The Church and Charlemagne were closely linked, and in 800, Charlemagne was crowned Emperor of the Holy Roman Empire. This empire, however, was in no practical sense a restoration of the old Roman Empire. It was a symbolic title describing the Christian semifeudal kingdom then held by Charlemagne, covering most of what is now Germany and parts of France. After Charlemagne's death, the previous tendency of these areas to split away from each other was reasserted, although the idea of a Holy Roman Empire survived into the 19th century.

Two Classes

By the start of the 9th century, feudalism was the most important element in the new social and political order; and it spread as local ruling classes were replaced by Frankish ones. The key relationship was *vassalage*, an honorable status based on military service backed up by possession of land. A vassal was a lord who had reciprocal rights and duties to others in the noble class; each owed duties—military, financial and governmental—to his lord, and expected his own vassals to honor their duties to him. These duties were offset by

Vassal

feudal noble who holds land and has reciprocal rights and duties with other nobles

rights, particularly the right to military support. Vassalage emerged from the practical necessity of fighting the Moslems, who fought on horseback, so that an effective counteroffensive required a well-equipped cavalry rather than the infantry of Roman times. But raising and maintaining horses and horsemen was expensive. Warriors were given grants of land by the king in return for service to him so that they could meet this expense. Thus the numbers of small free landowners shrank because they could not meet the expense of bearing arms, while the prestige and authority of the landowning military class rose because they alone could offer the hope of security and defense against attack. These landlords in turn could grant *benefices*, areas of land called fiefs, held in return for military service. The fief also described an office: as land came with dependent peasants

Fief

area of land held in return for an obligation to provide military services

living on it, holding it involved government jurisdiction over them.

The trend to political decentralization increased with the 9th century invasions. The king alone could no longer provide protection from outside attack, so noble-warriors who could fight were valued because they could provide protection. Thus the surrender of liberty by non-nobles was voluntary and not coerced, because it met a very real, very important need.

The result was a two-class system, with very few people—including shrinking numbers of free farmers and some city dwellers—outside feudal jurisdiction. This two-class division was emphasized by a change from the citizen army of Roman times to the noble cavalry of feudal times. Fighting was a profession open only to a wealthy few. But, especially as it developed in France, only those who fought would be free, and only those who were free were noble. To be a cultivator of the soil, and not a fighter, was to be, by definition, unfree and servile. The servile class, most of the population, had lost their personal freedom and had no political importance at all; they were duty bound to their immediate lord.

Weak Monarch, Strong Lords

Initially, this system worked in the king's favor. Because they received grants of land from the king, and thus were able to bear arms, the new class of nobles owed him their position, reinforced by their oath of loyalty. Within the class of nobles, all vassals were equal (although estates may have been of different sizes) and bound together by mutual obligations. Because of the system of granting fiefs, one man could be both vassal and lord—but all were vassals of the king, who was at the top of the hierarchy.

However, the king's unique position weakened once military expansion ended, at which time his only subjects were the great lords whose landholdings had come directly from him. When there were no more royal estates to be given away, it became more difficult for the king to acquire new subjects (and revenues). This encouraged the decentralizing trend associated with the increasing power of the nobility which came at the expense of the power of the king. However, this trend could not be reversed. Not only were the feudal lords important for internal administration, law and order, they were also needed to fight attacks from outside, which they could do by calling on *their* subvassals for support. This decentralization quickened its pace after the 9th century. Kings retained their titles, but had no effective power to rule an entire country. The king's authority was limited not only by these practical considerations, but also by the development of feudal law and custom. A feudal king was always subject to the law and not above it. The idea that a king was superior to the law did not emerge until centuries later when absolute monarchs who ruled according to Divine Right appeared.

Churchmen were also bound by feudal ties of vassalage, although they did not bear arms (except for the fighting religious orders, such as the Knights Templar). The late 9th and early 10th Centuries were a period of crisis for the Church. During this time, Church discipline broke down; there was interference from the lay nobles or kings who nominated inadequately prepared younger sons who would not inherit a fief to bishoprics, so as to give them wealth from a clerical benefice; and the morality of the clergy, especially the upper clergy, left much to be desired. This ineptness led to much abuse. It also involved gullibility in the collection of holy relics (including not only enough slivers of wood to have made several Crucifixion crosses, but also, reportedly, the skull of John the Baptist when he was 12 years old). The Church tried to prevent decentralization and dominance by local nobles by rebuilding its authority, which became centered around the position of the Pope in Rome, but the anarchy in Italy made the task difficult. Not until later in the 10th and 11th Centuries did cooperation between religious and secular powers emerge in order to encourage a Christian society in which each had a specific role to play.

Feudal Kingdoms

The 10th century was a time of relative peace. The invasions were mostly over, and although some attempts had been made under the Carolingian kings to unify Europe, they were not successful. Instead, feudal kingdoms[1] emerged, based on the principles described above. They were most effective in France, being modified to a greater or lesser extent elsewhere, depending on local conditions. These kingdoms were decentralized: each one was a collection of fiefs, and provided administration, economic security, and justice. No longer did individuals owe loyalty to the state, because there was no state in either the Roman or the modern sense. Instead, loyalty depended on

Solving Problems in Economic History

Was open field farming efficient?

Medieval farming in open fields, where each family held scattered strips on a more or less equal basis, would not be considered efficient to modern eyes. Nineteenth Century historians viewed this system as a form of insurance—co-operative cultivation meant that all shared in bad times as well as good.

Modern economic historians have also investigated open field farming. One particular question remains as a curiosity: if open field farming was inefficient, why did it persist for so long? According to this line of thought, the reason that enclosures occurred in England when they did was to take advantage of the potential for improved farming techniques and thus higher yields on enclosed land. That this must have happened can be assumed from the reality of rising rents on enclosed land: rents rose because the owner of now-private land could appropriate the benefits of the increased yields available. However, this explanation has been questioned, with conflicting results.

Rents did rise on enclosed land, but not necessarily due to increased productivity. The differential between rents on open fields and enclosed land is not very large, according to one study (see Robert C. Allen, *The Efficiency and Distributional Consequences of Eighteenth Century Enclosures*, **Economic Journal**, 92, 1982, pp. 937-953). Unfortunately, there is a methodological problem with comparing a cross-section of open fields with enclosed areas: the market pushes out inefficient farmers on enclosed land, so the surviving open fields must have been "suited to openness," hence the small differential.

Donald N. McCloskey summarizes some of these issues in *The Prudent Peasant: New Findings on Open Fields* (**Journal of Economic History**, 51:2, June 1991, pp.343-355). The problem, as he sees it, is a comparability one. Increased rents on enclosed land probably do demonstrate that open fields were inefficient, but so what? If farmers preferred scattered holdings in open fields even though yields were lower, then scattering must have had other advantages, which is why the open field system persisted for so long. The inefficiency of scattered holdings leading to lower yields results from increased transportation costs moving from one plot to another and from neighborhood effects (livestock and people wandering onto the plot—even though fines were imposed on the trespassers). What were the offsetting advantages?

McCloskey suggests an interesting explanation: farmers were demonstrating risk avoidance, which was prudent behavior in times when the ability to control one's environment was limited. That is, as markets for land and other assets (including grain) developed, risk premiums can be compared. Scattered holdings imply that not all plots will have bad harvests at the same time, making sense of scattering when the risk of holding grain was high. As this risk decreased because the costs of storage fell and as the market for grain became more sophisticated, the advantages of holding scattered plots lessened. Oddly enough, his statistical data contradicts this reasoning. The price risks of holding grain rose between the medieval period and the 17th Century. Given that this period sees the start of enclosure and the ending of the open field system, perhaps this indicates that farmers at this time became less prudent and more willing to assume risk.

the personal bonds between individuals, especially those in the noble class of vassals.

Feudalism was weak in Italy, and surviving cities such as Florence, Genoa, Ravenna, and Venice, remained important. These cities had been centers of resistance to invasion from the Saracens in the 9th century and the Magyars in the 10th century. Cities also developed as ecclesiastical centers. Bishops had always lived in them, and had the rights of fortifying them against outside attack. But to do this required money, and to get the necessary funds (and/or labor and materials required) bishops needed to extend their authority over city dwellers. This inevitably reduced the authority of the counts, who could control only the area outside the cities, especially in Lombardy.

With peace, the revival of agriculture beyond that needed for sheer survival was possible, and especially in the cities of the Lombard Plain, the rebirth of an exchange economy appeared. This became more apparent in the 11th century as Mediterranean trade, and thus Mediterranean port cities, began to revive.

Spain, a frontier state, was recaptured from the Moslems, implying new lands for the creation of new fiefs. But medieval Spain did not become unified, mainly because the French knights who had spearheaded the push against the Moslems were more interested in acquiring fiefs than in leaving a united Spain behind them. Instead, Spain was made up of the kingdoms of Aragon, Navarre, Leon, Castile (and in the 12th century, Portugal).

Feudalism in England

Feudalism was also late in being introduced into England, although a system of protection resembling it was in force ealier. England had been a benighted barbarian backwater to the Romans, and after they left, became a battleground between Angles and Saxons, resulting in the creation of several separate Saxon kingdoms. Starting in 835 and for another century, the Vikings began a concerted effort to conquer the whole country, which almost succeeded. Government was primitive and resistance weak, and the kingdoms in northern and midland England collapsed, to come under Danish rule (the Danelaw).

Danelaw
part of England ruled by Danish conquerors, 9th century

Although it might be expected to result in a dissolution of the society, instead the West Saxon kings mounted a resistance, starting in the late 9th century. (Resistance elsewhere was based on coopting the great nobles into defense duties.) The key element of this resistance, which would be important for later development, was the construction of burhs (fortified places). Originally intended for military purposes, some later became the administrative centers of the shires, areas of local government, and when known as "burgs," became true urban settlements.

Gradually, the Saxons reconquered England, and some feudal elements appeared. For example, during periods of unrest, some of the king's agents allied with local magnates to gain protection that the king seemed unable to provide. But the unique feature was the exercise of power, based on conquest, wielded by the king. Lands reconquered from the Danes were in that sense "liberated," and there was thus no opposition from the inhabitants based on elimination of their own rights. In addition, there was no mechanism for opposition, and the Church supported the monarchy.

As a result, a new administrative organization became established. The monarch was now responsible for enforcing the peace, and the law was no longer the custom of the people only—the king's orders were also law. This system was administered by the king's agents, who became a new, nonhereditary aristocracy based on service to the king rather than on landholding.

However, with the conquest of England in 1066 by the Normans, feudalism proper was introduced. It was made effective as Norman knights were granted English fiefs, which were also given to some of the Saxon nobility as a form of appeasement, although most of the country, including Royal Forests, was kept in royal hands. There was a mixture of both new and old elements. For example, the older Saxon administrative divisions were retained, as was the practice of the writ, the written document that transmitted the king's orders. The lower class, the Saxons, became the feudal tenants of the Norman estate holders, adding a nationalist opposition to Norman rule. Political feudalism was never as complete in England as in France, and many areas were completely outside both political control and the economic organization that went with feudalism. These included some areas of old Norse settlement in the northwest and East Anglia, and those areas that were simply too remote or too difficult to control easily.

The Manorial System

The manorial system, the economic counterpart of the politico-legal structure of feudalism, organized economic life in the Middle Ages. Its core was land. Land was necessary for survival, and an individual's relationship to the land also determined social status and thus wealth. Portable wealth, that associated with an exchange economy best represented by money gained in commercial transactions, was not very important. There was too little trade or commerce, and no exchange economy in the modern sense.

Life reverted to the countryside and was based on the land, with land divided into fiefs (collections of manors). Possession of these land grants—originally given by the king to the great lords who in turn granted parts to lesser nobles—was the basis of the nobility's power. No monarch had the power of national authority associated with later kings. This weakness is

revealed by the frequency of petty wars, of disputes between monarch and nobility, and of disputes over succession to the throne. As an example of the nobles' power and of the monarch's inability to resist, in 1215, King John was forced to concede to the wishes of the powerful English barons and sign the Magna Carta. This guaranteed certain civil and political liberties that provided a basis for the subsequent development of English law. It was significant not only because it called the monarch to account (introducing the idea of limited sovereignty), but also because it removed arbitrariness following arrest of a person by establishing a procedure to be followed.

The Manor

Each manor, which was simply an area of land, had political, economic, and legal/administrative implications. Politically, manors represented the feudal hierarchy in which all land belonged to the king and was granted to others in return for various services. Economically, they governed everyday life through the network of rights and obligations associated with ownership of or access to the land. Legally and administratively, a manor was the area of local administration governed by a noble, reinforced by the "custome of the manor" as expressed in the manor court, which was presided over by the lord as judicial authority. At these courts, village officials (such as the reeve[2] or provost, the villagers' representative) were chosen, arrangements for the forthcoming agricultural year were made, and disputes between villagers-serfs heard. Landowners, whether secular or ecclesiastical, were preeminent, each acting out what they saw as their God-given role of patriarch and defender of the status quo.

Manor
area of land controlled by a feudal noble

No Organized Markets

A manor was basically a self-sufficient economic unit. Given the absence of organized markets, there was little point, need, or desire to produce more than was needed above consumption needs, after making a provision where possible for bad times. From the point of view of the producers, the serfs, why strive to produce more than this? Any surplus would be commandeered by the lord of the manor, but even if this type of exploitation did not exist, a surplus would be difficult to dispose of as there was little organized exchange activity. And in addition, why accumulate wealth for its own sake? The idea was foreign to the feudal way of life.

Any exchange that did exist was on an irregular basis, occurring only when needed. For example, a poor harvest suffered by one manor might force it to seek out another with a surplus. But exchange was not an important part of feudal life, although some took place. For example, some manors had to buy needed salt from others located by the sea or those that contained inland deposits, and certain mining areas, producing, for example, tin, copper, or silver, were specialized. Some examples of local markets where peasants sold small surpluses to townspeople, or even a tiny number of larger ones, especially later in the Middle Ages, were known. But these were hardly a major concession to the concept of making money through exchange, deliberately buying and selling things in order to make a living. Exchange, where it existed, was an adjunct to economic life, not its dominating principle.

Money did exist in the form of coins, but the commercial activity of the time was so limited and so incompatible with the prevailing social and economic ethic that its use was restricted. Only with the later revival of commercial activity was more money used. The largest group of professional merchants were Jews, who had kept up contacts with the East. They traded chiefly for a small, wealthy aristocracy: the Church needed the incense and precious fabrics available in the East for the maintenance of its ritual, while the nobility provided a market for luxuries such as spices and artifacts such as enamels.

The organization of life was based on the land and on one's relation to the land. What follows is a *summary* of the essential details of feudalism: actual conditions varied according to time and place, but all would have some resemblance to this general theme.

Social Classes

Without land and its productive capability, no society is able to exist. But land in medieval times was more than simply a "factor of production." Who you were and what you did were uniquely spelled out by the position you had in relation to the land, and this relationship was further manifested by a complex network of rights and obligations due to and owed by all, which encompassed all but a tiny minority of the European population (estimated at about 42 million at the beginning of the 11th century). This network, reinforced by Church teachings, served to maintain the overriding ethic of "no change." Everyone knew their place in society, and had no desire or opportunity to change it. The ideas of "personal betterment" or social mobility or profit making for personal gain that are familiar in the modern world were irrelevant. This way of life might not be ideal or inspiring to a modern 20th century Westerner, but it was accepted then.

Land and Feudal Tenure

Feudal tenure characterized the "ownership" of land. This means that although one can identify owners (or land holders) of specific areas, landholding came under different rules than is the case today because the institution of private property was unknown. Today, possessing something, having legal title to it, implies that one can do with that possession what one pleases: keep it or sell it.

Feudal tenure

system of land holding under feudalism

In medieval Europe, the idea of *selling* land simply did not exist; ownership might change hands as a result of new political alliances, marriage alliances, or gift, but land was not sold—there was no market for it.

Land was God's gift to mortals, enabling them to live until called to eternal salvation. Therefore it was necessary to preserve the land in good condition, and to pass it on to successive generations so that they too could fulfill their earthly functions. Feudal tenure, thus, incorporates a hereditary right to *use* the land, but not to own it personally.

Lords, Churchmen, and Serfs

There were two social classes in the manorial system. A small percentage of the population, more in Italy, lived in towns and were thus outside or on the fringes of this system. (Town life will be covered in the next chapter.) And some "free" villages existed in remote areas, also outside the system. But everyone else fell into one of these two classes.

The great landowners composed the small upper or ruling class; a minority of nobles and churchmen owned the land. Each owned one or more manors on which the rest of the population lived as tenants. (Later, tenants' rights to use the land became transformed into a hereditary title to it.) Medieval landowners were "lords of the land" rather than modern "landlords."

The Church was dominant economically, politically, and morally. It held many estates and had immense financial resources, which often originated as gifts from the nobles. Ecclesiastics had one extra advantage not possessed by most of the nobility, however—culture. This ability to read, write, and keep records helps explain why effective administration in Europe was so often in the hands of the Church, and why churchmen had

such influence on political affairs—they literally could do what kings and nobles could not. Morally, the Church was the source of, and upholder of, the ethical system justifying the temporal state of affairs.

The serfs formed the second, much larger, class. There were gradations of serfdom—from freeman to body serf—but all, even freemen, had certain duties to perform simply by virtue of living on a manor.

Serf

a person who was "bound to the land" in feudalism

Rights and Obligations

The dominant social relationship was between the lord and the serf, and the network of rights and obligations revolved around one central concept, security. The serfs gained economic and political security. They had a hereditary right to use the land to meet their needs, and the lord could not use his considerable power to remove them from the land, and thus from their access to a livelihood.

The lord provided judicial authority in each manor, covering such matters as land holdings, extent of dues (taxes) and labor services due to the lord in return for services provided the serfs. He also interceded in disputes between serfs, and between lord and serf. In the latter case, although the balance of power determined that the decision would be in the lord's favor, extreme penalties were moderated by the lord's own standing in the hierarchy of nobles: he himself was often accountable to a more powerful noble.

Security

An important aspect of economic security also provided by the nobility was due to the vagaries of the weather. If the harvest failed, the lord was duty bound to provide serfs with what was needed for survival until the next harvest—a very important ingredient in the maintenance of a subsistence life style. After all, this was a time when state-provided services such as unemployment compensation, old age pensions, and welfare payments were many centuries in the future. Security against outside aggression was provided by the lord's castle. Large fortified castles were built all over Europe, many of which still remain today, and these provided the villagers with a place of refuge if needed.

Feudal Services

In return for protection, serfs performed many obligations, of which providing labor services and taxes were the most important. "Week work" describes the work serfs did on the lord's own landholding or for construction projects. This usually took two or three days a week, and as only one family member was required to do it, was not generally too onerous. But "boon work" was a burden. This was work required at specific times such as harvest or planting, precisely when the serfs also had enough of their own work to look after. Serfs were not paid wages for this work; they were under an obligation to perform it for the lords in return for the protection provided by the lord. In other words, money was not exchanged for work, but "protection services" were. In addition, serfs may have been required to provide draft animals for help in plowing the demesne, and they certainly turned over part of the harvest for the upkeep of the noble household. (The proportion of the harvest to be given up depended on the exact status of the serf.)

Serfs were also taxed in various ways, and had other obligations to perform, all of which could be somewhat arbitrary, thus underlying the servile status of bondsmen. Because it was not an exchange economy, most taxes were paid in kind, not in money, but increasingly there was a tendency for them to be replaced by money payments. Examples of feudal taxes include the

tallage, an annual tax imposed for the benefit of the lord; all or part of a landholding went to the lord on death, with a new tenant (most likely the eldest son) paying what was called an entry fine; a fine was paid when a serf's daughter married; and so on. These taxes were arbitrary because they were not based on an ability-to-pay principle, but on the whim of the lord, which could of course change. In addition, serfs were often required to use the lord's mill to grind grain into flour or his brewery to brew beer; requirements reflecting the lord's possession of monopoly power.

Tallage
a feudal tax

Serfs had other obligations imposed on them, too. Their unfree status and the fact that they were tied to the land was reinforced by their inability to leave without the lord's permission. No animal could be sold without the lord's permission, nor could land be sold or assigned without permission. These requirements underscore the importance of continued agricultural production to the survival of feudal society. To have had no restrictions would threaten stability, which was what feudalism was trying to prevent.

Exploitation and Protection

Serfs were thus both exploited and protected. They were exploited in the sense that what they could do was determined by their position at birth and the arbitrariness of the lord of the manor on which they lived. But they were protected in turn. Exploitation was limited by custom—accumulation of wealth through intense exploitation was pointless as well as ethically condemned. Accumulate wealth—for what? Wealth permitted nobles to fulfill their functions, including the function of living a more luxurious life than the serfs to demonstrate that there were differences in position, but any more than this would unbalance

God's design for earthly mortals, and few medieval nobles were willing to tempt God's wrath.

Also, while the serfs were legally in a position of dependency, and in spite of owing many obligations to their lords, they had more economic independence than it seemed. They lived in their own houses; rights to the common land could not be taken away from them; the produce of their strips (after allowance for taxes in kind) and gardens was their own. They could even in some cases purchase their freedom.

While all were servile (with the exception of the few freemen who performed at least some obligations) it is impossible to link economic well-being with precise legal status. For example, some people, known in England as bordars or cottars (cottagers) did not hold any strips in the open fields but rather farmed small plots of land independently, while still having some rights to use the commons. In return, they performed some labor services and paid lower taxes. They may or may not have been better off than the full serfs, who in turn may or may not have been better off materially than the freemen. But while gradations of economic well being did exist, and were not correlated with degree of servile status, they were relatively small and definitely could not compare with the difference existing between lord and serf.

The comprehensiveness and extent of the lord's power varied in different countries, being most powerful in France and least extreme in England. But whatever its extent, it was important in controlling life.

Organization of Production

How people in medieval times actually met their material needs is closely linked to the network of rights and obligations based on the land described above. The land in each country was divided up into large estates, or manors, each consisting of approximately 10,000 acres or 300 families. The size depended on the fertility of the land—larger land areas were needed to compensate if the quality of the soil was inferior. Each manor was under the jurisdiction of one noble or monastery or some other Church institution, and any one noble's holdings could be widely scattered as a result of marriage or shifting political alliances. In fact, this separation of estates could be highly desirable, given the lack of commerce and exchange relationships. For example, a Church estate in a wine growing region was a definite advantage if the rest of the holdings could not support viniculture.

A manor was divided into villages (parishes), each administered by the lord's agent, and having its own church. The center of the manor was the landowner's residence; a fortified castle in the case of lay nobles, or a monastery or abbey. The land area of the manor was subdivided into three basic functional types—again, there could be an intermingling of all three in any given geographical area. These three areas were the demesne, the open fields, and the commons.

Demesne

The demesne covered approximately one-quarter to one-half of the manor, and was exclusively for the lord's own use. Part of it would be cultivated by the serfs, fulfilling their labor services to the lord. Its produce supported the lord's establishment. Although arable (grain) farming predominated, sheep or cattle were also raised—again tended by serfs.

Demesne
part of the manor reserved for the lord's use

Open Field Strip Farming

Each tenant (serf family) had a land-holding large enough to support a family, with the size varying according to the fertility of the land. Tenant holdings were the second division of the manor, and the open field system often prevailed. In this

Figure 2-2   A variety of agriculture tasks are being performed in this miniature from a 15th century French manuscript, De Rustican des Profits Rureaux. (By permission of The British Library)

Strip farming
organization of farming in feudalism

system, which could be cultivated on either a two-field or a three-field system (i.e., at any one time, to protect the fertility of the soil at a time when chemical fertilizers were unknown, one-half or one-third of the area would lie fallow and uncultivated), serfs' holdings were not separated from each other. That is, a field contained a number of strips of land, each owned by a particular serf, but the field as a whole was plowed, weeded, planted, and harvested in common. This system was important to the communal way of life, helping maintain the social ethic of "equality within classes," because it would have been impossible for one peasant to have done something out of line from the rest—even if it was thought desirable for the individual. There was thus neither the opportunity nor the desire for individual betterment. The intermingling of holdings required that all work was done at the same time, and that all serfs received roughly the same rewards from the work.

Strip farming was practical for the times. It shared out land in a way that was seen to be equitable to all, and the common use of jointly-owned equipment and animals economized on these scarce items so each serf did not have to own ploughs and draft animals individually. (This was economically efficient, because labor was the abundant factor of production and capital the scarce one. Thus a labor intensive technique with joint ownership of scarce capital was the best method in that particular situation.)

Common Land

Finally, the third division of the manor was the commons or common land, any uncultivated land including woodlands, marshes, moors, and so on. The commons played an extremely important role in the feudal way of life, not only economically but also ethically.

Economically, all villagers had the right to use it. It affected their standard of living and made arable farming viable. Whatever animals peasants had—working animals and those used to supplement their grain-based diet—grazed here. Serfs could gather timber for fuel and building here and perhaps could also hunt or fish. Socially, the absence of the institution of private property was underscored by the principle of a common right to use the commons. No one owned this land, yet all were free to use it in a way that did not encroach on anyone else.

Commons
uncultivated land

Standard of Living

The net result of this system of production was an adequate, although low, standard of living for the serfs. Each manor was basically self-sufficient in normal times. Just about everyone, except the nobility, worked to produce for their own needs. Food was grown (with the grain being ground in the lord's mill); beer was brewed from grain (probably involving the obligation to use the lord's brewery); and coarse fabric was spun and woven at home. The lord's establishment contained a few more specialized workers, such as a smith, an armorer, and so on. Apart from trade in salt[3] and perhaps an occasional peddler, in normal times each manor was a world in itself.

Although what has been described fits the experience of most of Europe at the time, arable farming along these lines was most suitable on relatively flat land. Marginal or hilly land was usually devoted to pasture, especially sheep raising, and these areas too could be organized along feudal lines, although there were some differences. Because marginal land can support fewer people, and because fewer people are needed to tend sheep anyway, the lord of the manor in such low-population areas was more likely to extract his dues in the form of produce rather than labor services. Where land was more fertile, and the land/labor ratio lower (i.e., where there were relatively more people), the lord was more likely to require labor services because there were more people available and more tasks required in arable farming.

In addition, other manors practiced mixed farming, and some did not use the open field system. In this case, serf holdings could be in compact units. Whatever was done, the absence of an exchange economy and the obligations of lords and servile tenants toward each other are sufficient to demonstrate a feudal mode of production.

Social Ethic

The essentially unchanging way of life in feudal times could only persist because people accepted it. And on the whole, they did—society's values made people believe it to be the "right" way to live. In exactly the same way today, we accept that when adult, we will work for a wage. Absence from the labor force is considered exceptional in today's society because it does not fit in with our ideas of correct behavior expected of an adult.

Church teaching provided much of the justification for this way of life; the manorial system simply reflected a natural, God-given order. So, if man was on earth, marking time before eternal salvation, what was the point of trying to alter God's design? (The promise of immortality also helped acceptance of things as they were.) The purpose of work was not to gain wealth, but to maintain oneself in the position in which one was born.

Feudalism as Organic

Feudal life was seen as an organic, integrated whole, with each part having a particular function to play. Feudal ethics established a hierarchy of values with religion at the apex; and all aspects of life were properly the subject of religion. All classes, all individuals, all activities, thus existed to serve one single idea—the working out of the divine plan of the universe. In this ethical system, there was no division between an individual's inner (spiritual) life and practical activities, such as would emerge after the 16th century. Because each part of society had its role to play, the inequality that existed in feudal society was effectively justified.

That is, because each function was important, it was appropriate that the different classes received different rewards. Hence inequality between classes was rationalized, while the equality that existed within classes assured that each individual received what was necessary to the maintenance of that individual's station. Furthermore, no one went short because this would imply a loss of status, and thus an inability to perform a divinely-ordained function.

Disapproval of Money Making

Poverty was of divine origin, and to try to become wealthy deliberately was to be guilty of the sin of avarice. Wealth was seen as a gift from God, which gave the wealthy a moral obligation to use their wealth to improve the welfare of all. Wealth was thus justified: it enabled the wealthy to fulfill the obligations imposed on them by Divine Providence. But commerce and involvement with money-making activities were despised.

This attitude existed because mere money-making activities were seen as having no functional basis. Everything else provided a service, but the attempt to gain money—through money lending, for example—did not; it did not involve a reciprocal exchange of services between lender and borrower that fulfilled some aspect of the divine scheme of things. Thus labor was necessary and honorable; trade was necessary, although it could become dangerous to salvation if it became more than simply exchange; while financial activities were definitely immoral.

In fact, medieval thinking on economic questions was very practical, and in the later feudal period, when trade and commerce started to expand, the outpouring of writings on the subject represented an attempt to make new developments compatible with traditional morality. To summarize, the two major premises of medieval thought were that economic interests were subordinate to salvation—the main purpose of life; and that economic conduct was simply one aspect of personal conduct on which the rules of morality were binding.

The Church did not condemn wealth—it was seen as necessary because of the role it played in the functional organization of society—but pure economic motives, gain for gain's sake, were suspect. This attitude recognized the strength of economic motives that could dominate men and turn their attention away from salvation, therefore requiring suppression. (Such a view contrasts with the modern idea that man's desire for gain is a constant.) It influenced all the various rules circumscribing those various activities that could be dominated by gain—rules necessary to protect souls.

Just Price

The key to these rules lies in the economic agent's contribution. To seek more wealth than was necessary to fulfill one's functions was to be guilty of the sin of avarice, hence a trader must accept no more "profit" than would compensate for his labor. These rules underscored early medieval Church teachings on the just price and usury, which again make clear the practicality of these rules. A medieval consumer, because of the lack of choice available when the volume of trade and commerce was low, was at the mercy of the seller.

Just price

price intended to keep buyer and seller in their established social positions

---

There was a lack of choice because on the one hand, a few international merchants were responsible for the (limited) supply of imported goods, and on the other, the guilds—organized monopolies—were responsible for the output of domestically produced goods. Thus these monopolies must be prevented from abusing their powers. (How this was achieved will be covered in the next chapter.) So the price should be the just price, a price that guards against extortion of buyers by the seller, and is the price that will enable both seller and buyer to maintain their station in life. This price was not fixed for all time and could change as a result of changing conditions. The important point is that it is not a price based, as are modern prices, on profit making.

Usury

The prohibition of usury was also concerned with maintaining what was felt to be unalterable social reality. At this time, production was mainly for consumption only, and not for expansion of the productive capacity of the economy, so the major

---

Usury

lending money and charging interest

---

types of loan that the Church authorities were most concerned with would be for consumption purposes. For example, a farmer might seek a loan as a result of a bad harvest, or an artisan need funds to replace destroyed tools. In these cases, a money lender who charged interest on loans that occurred because of misfortune was clearly acting immorally. Some exceptions existed, such as large loans made to monarchs or the nobility. What was unlawful was pure interest: interest as a fixed payment determined in advance for a loan of money or goods when there was no risk to the lender. Obviously, as medieval economies grew and the use of money expanded, so the idea of interest became more complex, and many strictly usurious loans did escape the prohibitions, especially those made by the great 14th century Italian banking houses. They escaped because they were considered to be a different order of loans from those connected with the needs of the small craftsman or peasant, where oppression would be the easiest. And even the Church benefited from the divergence between theory and reality, as it too made loans from its huge financial resources.

In fact, it was not easy to administer these laws—there were too many ways of concealing what was in fact usurious. The official penalties ranged from requirements for restitution to excommunication. Church teachings were frequently violated in practice, but it is instructive to investigate what was taught because this shows what principles were valued at this particular time. And here, it is clear that a difference from capitalist ideas is present: in feudalism, wealth was not deliberately used to create more wealth—the *desire* to maximize gain for individual purposes played no part in the feudal ethic.

To summarize, this social ethic was based on the idea that society is a spiritual organism, not an economic machine, and thus economic activity should be controlled by reference to the moral ends for which it supplies the material means. To feudal thinkers, who felt that economic appetites for gain could be overwhelming, it was a sane philosophy. It was therefore rational to institute various rules and regulations to control economic activities to make sure that they served society's purposes, and did not become ends in themselves. Although these rules and regulations were frequently breached, medieval moralists did try to "moralize" and thus justify economic life. They succeeded best with rural life; it was in the newly developing towns and exchange activities that the greatest strains were put on the acceptability of this ethic.

Summary

Feudalism developed as a political organization of society in an attempt to stabilize and protect societies that were disintegrating in the wake of the collapse of the Roman Empire. All features of it, including the organization of economic activity, were thus geared to providing the cohesion necessary to a social organism.

While the early centuries of this period are disparagingly referred to as the Dark Ages, this is unfair considering the social and economic conditions that existed. It is true that the brilliance of Greek and Roman learning and culture did not survive into the Middle Ages, and that political and administrative sophistication—judged by modern eyes—was lacking. But the "benefits" of that former brilliance had anyway only been available to a few privileged citizens. Women, children and, of course, all non-free members of that society, shared in it only indirectly at best. (It is also difficult, because of lack of statistics, especially those concerning the mass of the population, to determine whether or not people were materially better or worse off in different times.)

So although feudal society in many ways was a step backwards to a more primitive form of organization, it was a workable response to prevailing conditions. In most societies, order was restored and maintained, a defense mechanism was established, and a minimum of economic security was available. Feudalism can be seen as a small scale, decentralized system based on land and the rights and obligations associated with land ownership. The serfs, who formed the largest class in society, were tied to the land, but were not owned personally by the lords. Their labor provided them with what they needed for survival, as well as providing enough for the support of the small leisure class of nobles and Churchmen. In return, the lords gave protection and administered justice, albeit weighted in their own favor.

Each manor was basically self-sufficient, and markets and money played only a minimal part in feudal life. Although serfs were obligated to work a certain number of days for the lord, they were not paid wages for doing this—the work was done in return for the services provided them by the lord. Feudal life was based on the idea of community and cooperation as can be seen in the system of agriculture. Although the standard of living was low by modern standards, the economic security of the serf was guaranteed. It was accepted and justified by the prevailing social ethic, which saw society as an organic whole subservient to, and acting out, a Divine order.

Seen in this more positive light, it could also be possible to say that without the period of stability provided under feudalism, later developments would not have taken place. In other, rather flowery, words, perhaps the Dark Ages provided the necessary preconditions for the germination of more modern times.

NOTES

1. At this time, it is difficult to think of Europe as being divided into national entities, as the names France, Germany, or England really refer to geographic divisions, not political ones. But it is convenient to use this terminology because they do relate to concepts familiar to the modern reader. What more accurately describes the political reality of the medieval period is the division into smaller regions—the dukedoms such as Normandy, Burgundy or Flanders are good examples.

2. The modern "sheriff" derives from this word. In England, where the shire was the local administrative unit, the *shire reeve* was the official entrusted with certain administrative duties.

3. Salt was important not only as a nutrient for survival but also as a method of preserving meat. Given the absence of refrigeration, and the relative shortage of winter fodder needed to keep animals alive over the winter, most animals not used for breeding or work purposes were slaughtered in the autumn, and the meat salted down.

Key Concepts

Arable farming	Just price
Benefice	Manor
Burh	Manorial system
Commons; common land	Open field
Danelaw	Provost
Demesne	Serf
Economic Efficiency	Reeve
Fallow	Servile status
Feudal tenure	Strip framing
Feudalism	Tallage
Fief	Usury
Holy Roman Empire	Vassalage

Note: Suggestions for further reading will be found at the end of Chapter 4.

Questions for Discussion and Essay Writing

1. If the structure of a society and the organization of its economy emerge as a response to the needs of the time, what were the *needs of the time* that resulted in the development of feudalism?

2. What were the most important explanations for the fall of the Roman Empire?

3. The Roman Empire was subjected to three important invasions. What were they, and what results did they have?

4. Why is feudalism (and the manorial system) called a decentralized system?

5. Explain the landholding system associated with feudal tenure. In what way or ways does it differ from modern systems of landholding?

6. Feudalism, both as an economic system and as a political system, was held together by a network of rights and obligations between people. Describe this network, and show how it held society together.

7. Describe the medieval social ethic, and how it served to legitimize the organization of economic life.

8. Why were profit making activities looked down on in medieval Europe?

9. Evaluate the manorial system with respect to meeting economic needs.

10. There were two classes in feudalism. What were they? What were the relationships between them?

11. Why is the institution of feudal tenure important to feudalism?

12. How did strip farming serve to maintain the feudal ethic?

13. Why was the institution of common land important to feudalism?

14. Why and how did medieval theologians attempt to control commercial activity?

Chapter 3

Towns in the Feudal Period

THE PREVIOUS CHAPTER sketched out the reasons for the emergence of a feudal system, and described the organization of economic life for the majority of the population who lived in the countryside. To what extent were towns and urban economic activities relevant to this way of life?

Towns and an urban life-style centered around trade, and commercial activities—economic activities we now associate with city life—were not important in feudal Europe. In fact, at the very beginning of the feudal period, towns became less and less important as centers of economic life, and their populations fell as European countries turned increasingly to an inward looking, self-sufficient agricultural life style. The low point was reached in the 10th century. But in the 11th century, signs of a revival of cities became apparent because the causes of the initial decline in activity weakened in their impact on economic activity.

In succeeding centuries, towns became more numerous, larger in size, and there were an increasing number of economic activities specific to towns. Of course, even with this growth, urban population still represented only a very small fraction of total population. Not until the mid-19th century did towns account for a larger population share than the countryside in England (the first country to experience such a shift). The dominance of urban areas is a phenomenon associated with the development of industry, which did not

begin to occur until the 18th century. The initial revival of towns that we are concerned with was associated with the development of trade and commerce—the first economic activities to become influenced by capitalist thinking in Europe.

Investigation of feudal urban life reveals an apparent inconsistency. On the one hand, the structure, organization, and behavior of towns show a distinct feudal pattern in their attempts to maintain the status quo. But on the other, the increase in town economic activity played an important role in undermining feudalism: their activities were, after all, dependent on the existence of markets and exchange relationships that had no part to play in the feudal system. An increase in commercial activities and a change in the organization of towns are both part cause and part effect of the long period of transition from feudalism to capitalism.

Towns in the Early Period (up to 11th Century)

European towns, especially those in the Mediterranean area, flourished under the Roman Empire. Economically, they were based on trade, and in Southern Europe they were centers of political administration because the aristocracy maintained winter residences in towns. We have already seen that barbarian invasions contributed to the breakdown of the Roman Empire, and thus to the introduction of feudalism. However, these invasions were not solely responsible for the dramatic decline in trade between Europe and the East (dealing mainly with goods such as papyrus, spices, oil, fine textiles, wine, and slaves) that occurred after the 7th century.

What happened then, and why was the Mediterranean area practically denuded of trade and traders, emptying the cities dependent on trade? The answer: Islamic invasions swept from the Arabian Peninsula across the Middle East, North Africa and parts of Southern Europe in the 7th and 8th Centuries. Once Persia, Syria, Egypt, North Africa, and Spain became subject to Islamic rule, the old ties to the East that had existed across the Mediterranean were broken with very few exceptions. As trade stagnated, so did the *raison d'être* of the Mediterranean ports. Their markets and sources of goods were gone, and the threats from Saracen pirates made Mediterranean voyages too hazardous for all but the most intrepid merchant-adventurers.

Not only was the climate for commerce discouraging once the Moslems gained control of the Mediterranean, the (less-important) trade centers of Northern Europe around the North and Baltic Seas suffered too as a result of repeated incursions from the Scandinavians up to the 10th century. The result was that port cities lost their economic reason for existence. Thus there was no urban "middle class" involved in trade and commerce; feudal society was a two-class society. The towns that remained were not only numerically insignificant, but also had only a very limited number of functions. One can identify two roles for towns in this early period: as ecclesiastical center and as military fortress. Both were related to the desire for stability in feudal society.

Towns as Ecclesiastical Centers

Although the Roman Empire disappeared, and its pseudo-successor, the Holy Roman Empire, never succeeded in imposing any permanent, cen-

tralized organization and administration within its borders, the Christian Church survived in Europe. Its administrative areas (dioceses) were based on the old Roman boundaries that centered on towns, and the Church's dominance increased throughout the declining years of the early feudal period. Probably because centralized secular authority no longer existed, the Church gained enormous moral and economic influence that was never seriously threatened by the multiplicity of feudal princedoms. The Church administrators lived in the old Roman cities, but the feudal princes had moved back to their country estates, so never had a *physical* presence to provide a counter-influence to this Church power.

Hence those cities in which the bishops lived were the centers of religious administration, populated by the various people necessary for this administration. They included clerics, monks, teachers and students of the Church-run schools, household servants, and those workers, the artisans, necessary to the maintenance of the episcopal household. Market activity in these towns was limited to the local markets where peasants from the surrounding areas sold agricultural produce to the town dwellers.

Somewhat later, the ecclesiastical authorities acquired *de facto* administrative authority over all the town inhabitants, even when *de jure* authority was vested in the temporal prince. This was probably a result of circumstance rather than design simply because the temporal princes were usually absent. To summarize, these towns were restricted in number to the number of Church administrative areas, and were small because of the limited number of functions they performed.

Towns as Military Centers

Other small agglomerations of population occurred as a result of the military need for security that existed in feudal times. Roman cities were always fortified against invaders, and during the insecurities of this early feudal period, such fortifications served as secure refuges for the neighborhood population. But a new military element was added when the local nobles accepted the obligation to defend and protect their lands and population as part of their feudal duties.

This need for defense led the nobles to build strategically located fortresses or castles, called "burgs," in their territories. These fortresses served as military bases; for grain storage against possible famines; and, should the need arise, as safe havens for the peasants in time of war or invasion. The peasants had a reciprocal obligation for the upkeep of the castles: it was one of the feudal services they performed for the lord.

Burgs were generally tiny in population, as the permanent population was composed of military personnel, with very few other civilian personnel living in them. However, in time, these burgs became administrative centers as the nobles' agents acquired more authority over the area. Like the ecclesiastical cities, they often became the locations where the expansion of trade and commerce, and thus the expansion of towns, was located.

Establishing the Preconditions for the Revival of Town Life

Before towns can become permanent establishments, two basic preconditions must be met: there must be a need for towns[1], and there must be a surplus food supply in the countryside. The first means that there must be some economic function or functions requiring the cooperation of many individuals and the ability to tap support services: activities that can be accomplished only when there is a large enough pool of population in a concentrated area. Included here are all the activities associated with exchange, such as transportation, financing, or wholesaling, where contact between people is essential. This is not true of farming, which in contrast requires a relatively large amount of land, so farming communities are typically small and scattered.

The second precondition means that an ability to support an urban population exists; because townspeople typically do not provide all their food needs themselves, there must be a permanent surplus of food and other agricultural necessities of life. The division of town and country, each with its own specific functions, is one of the earliest and most general examples of a division of labor.

In the 11th century, these two preconditions were met. Once towns began to grow again, the stimulus for further growth increased: growth itself made more urban activities possible, which stimulated further expansion of agricultural production.

The reasons for the revival of city growth at this time included the improving environment for trade and exchange activities, and the expansion of agricultural output. The former was helped by a general restoration of peace and an increased feeling of security, as well as by improvements in transportation (see below). The latter was assisted by an extension of usable agricultural land and some improvements in agricultural technology (see below). Both factors helped make the production of an agricultural surplus less an occasional, chance occurrence, and more a permanent possibility. Some other developments also encouraged this urban growth, especially during and after the 13th century. Townspeople increasingly acquired the power to structure urban administration to meet their needs, helping provide a favorable environment for the new money-making activities that had always been despised, if not condemned, by the prevailing Church ethic. Thus, the growth of towns was part effect of and part cause of the breakdown of feudalism in the next few centuries. By providing enduring examples of economic activity centering around markets and exchange, the seeds of the eventual dominance of capitalist relations and forms of economic activity were sown, eventually spreading to encompass all areas of economic life.

It is also possible to distinguish two types of commercially-oriented towns. Both owe their revival or origins to the expansion of trade, but their locations differ. Water-borne trade dominated because of poor road conditions. The first group consisted of maritime ports around the Mediterranean and along the coast of Flanders that owed their growth to the increase in sea-going trade. (But from the 11th century on, overland trade for the first time began to increase, stimulating the development of commercial cities that were in some way connected to the overland trade routes.

Preconditions: Agriculture and Transportation

During the middle feudal period, agricultural output expanded, making possible the development of town communities that lived by trade by providing sufficient food supplies to feed groups of non-farmers. As previously noted, this is a necessary, but not a sufficient, precondition for the development of urban life. Output expanded for two major reasons. First, the area under cultivation increased. This was achieved in several different ways. For example, the lowlying areas on the northwest coast of the Low Countries were dyked and drained, and Flemish experience and expertise in these activities were later borrowed by other countries (as, for example, in the draining of the flat fenland of eastern England). Many wooded areas in Europe were also deforested, and then plowed up and cultivated. And of course, there were always wastelands in every manor—swamps, moors, woodlands—that could be used for the same purpose, a trend that became more important as the permanency of the urban outlets for surplus food supplies encouraged agricultural activity for the market. This development can be seen as a type of "internal colonization" of Europe; the result was a perceptible increase in output.

Second, technical improvements increased the productivity of the land under cultivation. To modern eyes, some of these "improvements" seem rudimentary, but were a big step forward at that time. As previously noted, farm animals were not widely used, partly because of the problem of providing enough winter fodder. This problem became easier to overcome as the feudal period drew to a close, and as agricultural output expanded. As animals were used more often for farm work, and as horses were substituted for oxen, simple equipment such as horse shoes, horse collars and a tandem harness were introduced, making cultivation easier, faster and more productive. Another improvement in the damper climate of Northern Europe, where the soil was heavier, and therefore more difficult to cultivate manually, was the development of a heavier *wheeled* plow with a mold board designed to turn the soil. And finally, the simple switch to a three-field rotation from a two-field rotation system (i.e., leaving only one-third rather than one-half of the land fallow every year to restore its productivity) made it possible, even if nothing else changed, to increase output by one-third. By the 15th century, most of these changes would be in general use, but even earlier, their effect was dramatic.

Transportation also began to improve, although the major improvements came during and after the 13th century. Ships became larger and better constructed; increasing reliance on sails and windpower reduced the need for oarsmen, so freeing up more space for cargo; and navigational improvements such as the compass helped reduce the riskiness of shipping. In the earlier period that we are concerned with here, the changes encouraging a revival of trade are associated mainly with the return of settled, peaceful conditions in the 11th century. From then on, the expansion of trade, transportation improvements, and the growth of towns were linked together.

Development of Maritime Towns

The commercial revival beginning in the 11th century can be explained by many different factors. Trade and urban civilization had declined in previous centuries partly as a result of the Islamic conquest of much of the Mediterranean area—especially those areas important for providing sources of what had previously been in demand by European buyers. But in the 11th century, the Western Church began to face up to the Islamic challenge, and for the next two centuries supported the Crusades, periodic military expeditions sent from Europe to recapture the Holy Land from the Moslems. Even if the Crusades were not militarily successful, they did open up previously closed areas. In addition, they aided the revival of those Italian port cities that were the departure points of the crusading armies through their needs for provisioning and transportation. There was also a rise in population, which not only helps explain the extension of land under cultivation but also helps explain some of the population shifts that occurred. This was a period of the internal colonization of Europe, which in later centuries would be transformed into external colonization of previously unknown lands.

Venice

Venice and the Flemish coast were the centers of this revival. Venice played a unique role, as she had not suffered the same decline as other European cities in the early feudal period. For this reason, Venice deserves special mention. When Venice was first settled, the inhabitants were forced by geography to rely on exchange. Venice's production in these early years consisted of salt, an important element in food preservation, and fish. Her geography—a series of small islands at the head of the Adriatic Sea which leads into the Mediterranean—required use of boats. Venice built on this necessity, and early on developed an exclusively commercial character. Her major trading links were with the Byzantine civilization in the Eastern Mediterranean, and Venice was predominant in supplying Constantinople.

What made Venice unique during the feudal period is that she was never taken by barbarians, hence was never a feudal city, and that she still maintained trading and other links with the East,

Table 3-1

Population Estimates, Major European Countries, 1000–1500 (in millions)

Country	1000	1300	1500
British Isles	2	5	5
France	5	15	16
Germany	3	12	13
Italy	5	10	11
Spain & Portugal			9
Low Counties			2

Note: Total population in Europe as a whole by the 1340s was approximately 80 million; by 1351 about 25 million people had died during the major plague years.

Source: From Carlo M. Cipolla, *Before the Industrial Revolution: European Society and Economy 1000–1700,* 2nd eddition, 1980, W.W. Norton. Table 1-1, p. 4.

thus never declining to the extent of other Mediterranean port cities such as Marseilles. In fact, Venice remained an isolated outpost of Byzantine civilization and never forgot the "secrets" of commerce and trade, which provided the basis for commercial laws and customs subsequently developed in Europe. It is not surprising that Venice was thus regarded as *the* great commercial city of the late feudal period. In the 8th century, Venice was supplying Constantinople with wheat, wine, and salt from Italy, and wood and slaves from Dalmatia (modern Yugoslavia), while importing mainly luxury fabrics (such as damask from Damascus, muslin from Mosul, and gauze from Gaza) and spices.

Another factor unique to Venice was the absence of any feudal ethic that held back commercial development. Gain was important, and Venetians did not care where it came from: During the Crusades era, they were happily—and profitably—supplying both Christian and Moslem armies! Although other Italian cities, especially Genoa and Pisa, later rose to rival Venice, they were always imbued with a Christian missionary spirit, which closed some profitable areas to them.

However, Venice's advantages became greater in the 11th century, which marked the beginnings of her desires to solidify her trading supremacy through political means. In that century, she acquired control over the Adriatic and successfully gained a monopoly over all goods arriving in Venice by requiring them to be shipped in Venetian vessels. At the same time, the Crusaders' attack on Islam had the effect of gradually opening up the Mediterranean, creating once more an environment where trade could flourish. Initially, other Italian port cities such as Genoa and Pisa were important in keeping the sea lanes open, and these cities also expanded their commercial and trading activities. This rise of competitors to Venice ironically added an extra hazard to shipping. Italian cities continually fought one another for supremacy over the Mediterranean during the Medieval period, hence the need for arming merchant ships persisted!

Flanders

During the 12th century, Mediterranean trade became more generalized: Marseilles in southern France experienced a revitalization, as did many cities in Spain, such as Barcelona. The 12th century also saw an expansion of trade in the north of Europe centered around Flanders. Flanders had an advantage Venice did not have: an indigenous cloth industry that could supply cargoes for the return journey. The importance of this industry coupled with the expansion of trade led to the rise of Bruges in particular, and also other Flemish cities such as Ghent, Lille, Ypres, Douai, Arras, and Tournai.

Foreign merchants were very active in Bruges, for example, maintaining warehouses there and using local residents as intermediaries. Cloth made in Flanders was increasingly in demand, and most of it was exported by Hanse and Italian merchants, the former being chiefly responsible for the import of raw wool from England into Flanders. Merchants in some of the Baltic sea towns had formed a league, called the Teutonic Hanse, whose objectives were to gain privileges for their town's merchants in the other towns associated with the League, monopolize northern Europe's export trade, and protect inland trade routes. Such associations were very important in the early stages of trade growth, and cooperation between merchants helped gain stability in this new, relatively untried activity of trading. Later, other towns in the North Sea area joined the League, which had major bases in London, Bruges, and Novgorod; at its peak, 200 towns and districts were included. The products handled by the Hanse were mainly natural products, unlike those in Mediterranean trade. They included wheat from Prussia, furs and honey from Russia, wool from England, and timber and fish. Although profits were large, they were never quite as large as those amassed by Italian merchants, so there was no subsequent development of related, financial activities that later occurred in the great Italian port cities.

Trade in Luxuries

The goods available for trade also multiplied. Increasingly, European products for sale to the East were less often raw materials, and more often manufactured goods. After the 12th century, the most important was wool cloth from Flanders, which was highly prized for its fine quality. Most goods traded—spices are a very good example—were luxuries with a low weight and a high unit value. This is important, because it implied enormous profits to the first merchant traders willing to undertake the risks and hazards of journeys.

Because the cost of transporting goods was extremely high, there were so few merchants that the supply of goods was limited relative to the demand, which in turn was limited to the wealthiest nobles, churchmen, or merchants. In addition, because the experience of market relationships was not generalized, buyers had little idea of what the "right" price should be. The result was a highly monopolistic situation in which high prices existed. There were clear opportunities for making large profits from buying cheap and selling dear. Buyers did not object to this situation, as ability to acquire imported goods implied not only wealth but also power:

"Spices were superb insignia of conspicuous wealth. They were also indicators of ostentatious waste. Given the difficulties of transport, the very presence of imported exotics in a household demonstrated its owner's access to a copious treasury...some condiments were more expensive than others, and yet others were available only to the highest nobility, brought as gifts by ambassadors or bought on noble command by merchantmen. A particular odor or taste in food thus affirmed the political statement: power bought this."[2]

The New Merchants

As a result of these opportunities, it is clear that signs of a capitalist mentality did exist in this new merchant class, indicating an early existence of the idea of capital accumulation and of using these enormous profits to make still more profits. At first, the capitalist spirit dominated only exchange activities. Not until the 18th century did the influence on the production of goods along capitalist lines become widespread.

Where did these new merchant-adventurers come from? It is difficult to identify the origin of this new commercial class. Desire for gain and wealth had always existed, although the Church condemned it as greed or avarice. But the new feature of the desire for gain emerging in the 11th century was its more capitalist character, resting on the idea of rational calculation of capital accumulation. Whatever its origins, a distinct commercial profession did appear, first in Venice and later elsewhere, which did not fit easily into the established social order. As merchants became established in certain locations, their commercial activities attracted migrants from the countryside who could be hired as sailors, dockworkers, servants, and so on. This growth in turn encouraged the development of purely urban services, such as those of bakers, wine sellers, butchers, and masons, for example, as well as those services necessary for continued trade, such as the making of chests and barrels. In other words, all the essentials for growing towns become present.

Development of Inland Cities

Venice helped influence the development of other maritime cities after the 11th century, and merchants borrowed the techniques Venice was developing. But Venice did not influence inland merchants and the subsequent development of inland towns, which were often "new" in the sense that they were not reborn versions of previously important cities.

What the inland cities did have in common with the maritime cities is that they too were focal points for merchants and were located on trade routes. Now, the major characteristic of the earliest development of inland trade was that it was not located in fixed places, and was long distance trade. Merchant-adventurers travelled with their goods in large groups for safety. To them, the advantage of long distance trading was that the

dangers of the journeys would be more than compensated for by the large profits created by the scarcity aspect of the goods in distant lands.

Free Status of Merchants and their Settlements

Because merchant-adventurers moved around, they were always regarded as foreigners and therefore free, unlike the majority of the population who were serfs tied to the land and therefore "belonged" somewhere. They acquired this status

Figure 3-1   Increased building activity was required when towns grew in the late medival period. This scene shows some of the technologically innovative labor-intensive methods used to build tall buildings. From a miniature in a 15th century manuscript, De Rustican des Profits Rureaux. (By permission of The British Library)

as freemen by usage; previously only nobles were free. In order to prove that the merchants were not free would require the existence of a "master," which could not be easily accomplished with people who were continually on the move. This characteristic of freedom was an important element in the development of new towns because the merchants' "freedom" also applied to the institutions they created.

At some point, however, merchants did begin to settle in fixed locations, but little is known about this early stage. Most of the contemporary information from the 11th century was written by clerics who were interested only in the events that affected the Church. But it is possible to derive some common threads, in spite of the great diversity of towns. One common thread is that merchants were attracted to some of the already-existing towns and burgs, for a very understandable reason. These older towns were originally located for strategic, geographic reasons, hence were logical sites for settlement because of the terrain and rivers. The rivers were important for transporting goods, so the major trade routes tended to follow rivers. Some towns became more attractive to these merchants than others. That is, the boost to these early inland commercial towns came not as an expansion of local market activity (which was too local to attract the long distance traders) nor as an extension of the fairs, which were not permanent institutions (see Chapter 4 for more on the medieval fairs).

So some of the early feudal towns developed into late feudal commercial centers, as merchants located their settlements just outside the original town. Given the Church's teachings on commercial activity, merchants would hardly have been welcomed inside the ecclesiastical towns, while there was simply no room in the military burgs. In general, merchant settlements developed around the storehouses or landing places for goods, and these commercial "suburbs" were very important to the later development of cities.

Like the earlier towns, merchants' settlements were surrounded by defense works, which usually distinguished villages (which were not fortified) from towns. As these towns grew more prosperous, the original wooden palisades were replaced by stone ramparts. (The original town or burg was usually encircled by stone ramparts.) A good example of this type of development is the area of London called the "City of London." This was the original trading and commercial medieval city, and it surrounds the Tower of London, the original military fortress built in the 11th century. Because these commercial towns were fortified, they too became *burgs,* and those living inside the walls were called *burghers* or *burgesses* (depending on the language). This term was never applied to the inhabitants of the military burgs, but, in its modern form of bourgeois, is used to describe those involved in urban, capitalist-oriented activities.

Bourgeois
townspeople involved in commercial activities

Towns and Feudalism

The early towns did not have an easy, conflict-free development. In particular, there were problems with land use and population, and consequently, with legal jurisdiction. New towns obviously required land. But not only was the land agricultural (or potentially so) so that the growth of the town reduced the income of the lord who controlled it, it was also associated with the old network of rights and obligations. Because the merchants were "free," they had no intention of performing these obligations. Although this new way of life came into conflict with the feudal ways, the nobles generally found that the money payments made by townspeople for the use of land more than compensated for the loss of agricultural output. However, it was not until much later that the land itself could be bought and sold—feudal ideas still prevailed in this respect.

Another area where feudal ideas posed a barrier was population. While merchants were considered free, the immigrants who came into the early cities were not. They could not hide their origins and could always be claimed by their lords. In the beginning, most of the non-merchant urban population kept the status of serfs; but later, as towns became more powerful and influential, all inhabitants were free by virtue of their residence.[3]

A related problem concerned the internal growth of towns. A merchant who wished to marry could marry only a serf (the nobility kept their distance from acquaintanceship with this society-threatening new class of merchants, hence the only available marriage partners were serfs). But this automatically implied serfdom for the children, as under common law, legal status passed through the mother. Again, this "inheritance" gradually disappeared over time.

City Regulation

By the 12th century, cities were commercial and often also industrial centers, surrounded by fortifications, with their own laws and customs. Even then, however, the process was by no means complete, and different cities developed at different speeds and to different levels. The common thread was that as these commercial cities grew, so the gap between the urban-dwellers—a tiny, but privileged, elite—and the mass of population living in the countryside widened. Political power was still vested in the nobility and the Church, but towns were increasingly able to gain more power for the regulation of their own affairs. Towns, after all, fitted very uneasily into the feudal, two-class scheme.

Because towns were the creation of a new group, inevitably its members built up town institutions and organized its functions to meet their own needs. But because centralized political authority and even the idea of the nation-state were still far in the future, each town developed

its own rules, and the growing strength of towns implied rivalry between them. This can be seen as a preview of future mercantilist policies that adopted extreme protectionism in order to further the *national* interest.

Town Requirements

The developing towns of the 11th, 12th and 13th centuries had several interests. They needed to guarantee a sufficient food supply, to develop an administration and a judicial structure that would best serve their needs, and to create a legal administration to cope with the special problems of the town and its merchants' activities. In general, regulation was the key word. Food supplies and food sales were regulated down to the minutest detail. Deviations were strictly and promptly punished. Urban industry was regulated through the development of craft guilds, patterned after the earlier examples of merchant guilds that regulated, supervised, and encouraged exchange activities. (Guilds also proved to be a powerful means of regulating non-economic matters.) Administrative and legal developments provided an acceptable merging of the interests of the individ-

---

Guild

association of producers or sellers in the same trade or activity

---

ual town dweller and the merchant class as a whole. The result was that the towns guaranteed a low cost of living at the expense of the countryside; guaranteed the quality of products by preventing fraud, abuse, adulteration, and shoddy workmanship; and protected their inhabitants as much as possible from competition from outside. In general, they made most townsfolk into a very privileged minority. They succeeded in these efforts, because without the success and stability of the collective, a single individual would not have succeeded. Given the overwhelming emphasis on tradition, without the development of these commercial towns, it would have been a rare individual who tried to do something different—and could succeed at it!

The Urban Economy

The development of an exclusively urban economy within a legal and social framework that encouraged it, took time, but by the beginning of the 14th century, town economic activity looked very different from the surrounding countryside. But still, although town life was not motivated by feudal traditions, it had many characteristics that would seem to us today to be examples of precapitalist economic activity. In particular, the lack of individual competition is very striking. Every aspect of urban life was regulated. The development of this regulation took time as towns slowly evolved their own comprehensive sets of laws and customs. Work life, production and sale of goods, land use, leisure time—these are many of the activities that came under the control of the municipal authorities and their agents.

Food and Food Sales

The most important need was to guarantee an adequate food supply, and surviving medieval records show that in this area, regulation was at its most detailed. Most towns were small by modern standards. (Although accurate statistics are hard to get, the biggest towns in the 14th century, such as Paris, Venice, and Florence, were no larger than 100,000, and most would have been in the 20,000 to 30,000 range.)

Most food came from the surrounding area, but even with longer-distance imports, the early municipal authorities were concerned to ensure the "common good." This implied controlling monopoly elements and price rises, thus guaranteeing a relatively low cost of living for the towns-people. This was generally accomplished by making all food sales public and eliminating the

role of middleman. It was fairly easy to do this with local food supplies but more difficult when food items were imported from another region or country. In this case, "foreigners," (i.e., anyone not an inhabitant of the town) were either excluded completely from retail trade in order to preserve a role for the town's own merchants, or required to sell their wares at specific places and at specific times.

Standardization

The fact that sales were controlled by time implied an important role for church clocks, which everyone could hear. Also, prices were controlled by measure, which implied in turn the beginnings of systems of standardized weights and measures, an enormous help to the expansion of trade. The standardization of measures was important not only for establishing prices, but also for fixing duties on imports, as import duties were one of the major sources of revenues for monarchs. Most towns had such standards, but there was no guarantee that standards between towns were identical. Standardization is a development that came with the formation of centralized political authority and the development of nation-states, and an ending of the authority of the towns themselves. The lack of inter-city standardization implied that merchants had to keep track of the different measures used in different towns, which can have been no easy task for those merchants active in a large number of towns! The quality of goods, including prohibitions on adulteration and unsanitary conditions, was also firmly controlled. Each producer, whether of a food item or a manufactured good, was required to stamp it with an official seal (the origin of hallmarking) so that if it did not live up to the required standards, the producer could be quickly identified and punished.

What did medieval craft guilds really do? (and who did it?)

Merchant and craft guilds in the medieval period were important for both their economic and their political functions. Craft guilds controlled and regulated the production of those items needed in the urban environment. Merchant guilds dominated trade, both internally and with other countries, especially in the late medieval period (after the middle of the 14th Century). Increasing mercantile wealth gave them much more power over artisans in manufacturing (because they controlled supplies) and was a factor in the change associated with the emergence of more purely capitalist organizations from the 15th Century onward.

Guilds were also closely associated with the administration of towns, and some historians have concentrated more on their role in administering urban societies. But during the late medieval period, various changes took place in England which disturbed the order that towns tried to maintain. Towns also began to lose economic importance as industry, especially the cloth industry, expanded in the countryside.

One way to try to find out what guilds did and how they perceived and tried to organize medieval life is to compare the experience of individuals with documentary evidence. Heather Swanson (*The Illusion of Economic Structure: Craft Guilds in the Late Medieval English Towns,* **Past and Present**, no. 121. Nov. 1988. pp.29-48) does this. She concentrates predominantly on the official records of the city of York and includes an examination of the wills of about 1,200 craftsmen and their female relatives. While her main purpose is to show the role of guilds as instruments of the town authorities,

this investigation also uncovers other relevant findings.

For example, craft guilds were traditionally seen as groups of men pursuing a specific craft; these associations both protected them against competition and provided mutual support and friendship. From this, it would be easy to conclude that women had no productive role. Yet from other evidence we know that women made up half the work force, and were extremely important in some activities, especially in the market for food. Evidence from wills shows that women were active in almost all branches of industry as skilled workers and owners of businesses. They also accounted for a significant proportion of unskilled laborers, a group ignored by the guild system; the guild system, in other words, included only men in skilled manufacturing.

It would also be easy to conclude that the guild system accurately and definitively classified artisans by occupation. However, although administrative records do this, they ignore the reality that manufacturing and service industries depended on the labor of the entire family, and also that most family units were multi-occupational. Secondary occupations include selling food, brewing and providing accommodation. It was difficult to establish craft monopolies because the boundaries between different occupations were not clear cut. For example, knives, an edged tool, were made by smiths, blades-miths, cutlers and armorers; candles were made by chandlers, butchers, skinners and saucemakers - and anyone else with access to animal

(Problem continues on next page.)

(Problem continued from previous page.)

byproducts. Other examples of overlapping interests exist.

So guilds really were organizations with fraternal (mutual support) functions and which provided the methods by which technology and skills could be transmitted. Medieval urban industry, however, was more than just guild industry, because much of the labor force fell outside guild regulations. Later, when towns faced declining economic conditions and change towards a more capitalist system of production

was evident, women were much more at risk, and discrimination against them became overt. Guilds did play an important role in their members' lives, and provided support to them, but over time, these economic functions became subordinated to others. Urban authorities realized the potential of these organizations in regulating the marketplace. Much later, when mercantile dominance was itself threatened, the guild system was used to try to protect the social order, but the underlying forces of change were too strong. So although official records seem to

Enforcement of Regulations

The key to both sales and punishments was promptness and publicity. Special places were set aside for sales of like items, and names such as Bread Street, The Vintry, or Milk Street identify such places in the medieval parts of modern European cities. This also had the effect of controlling competition between individual producers and encouraging sellers' honesty; the importance of social control cannot be overstated. Punishment of violations was also prompt; for example, a baker found guilty of selling an underweight loaf of bread would be carried on a horse-drawn sled through the streets with the offending item strapped around his neck. Or a fishmonger found guilty of selling rotten fish would be pilloried,[4] while the rotten fish was burnt at the base of the pillory! Repeat offenders were denied sales space in that town, effectively eliminating their livelihood, so intense was the rivalry between different towns that it would be impossible to start again.

Sales were not the only activity to be regulated by time. Urban craftsmen's production activities were, too, and in addition, were required to be performed in public view. This meant that these craftsmen worked under a window opening onto the street. (For most produced goods, production and sale occurred at the same place: the producer's workshop, which was part of his home.) There was

another very practical reason for this. In the absence of effective artificial light, requiring production or sales to take place in daylight is another example of the insistence on quality, and also served to keep producers from stepping out of line.

In general, retail stores such as we know them did not exist. Producers of food items, such as bakers (and in most medieval cities, there were four categories of baker, depending on the end-customer and the type of product) worked and sold out of their own homes in the particular area designated for that product. Some types of food were not sold from a fixed location—in London, for example, shellfish were sold by peddlers. And other types of goods could not be sold together—for example, in London, a tavern selling French wines was not permitted to sell sweet or fortified wines (presumably to prevent mixing of poor quality wines).

But the entire spectrum of food laws had the effect of gaining a stability in the towns similar to the stability of the surrounding feudal countryside. The evidence from this period shows the discrepancy between what was desired and what actually happened. The rules and regulations were based on achieving a civic ideal, but their administration recognized the temptations that markets gave rise to. The end result limited competition and individual initiative. This was also a charac-

Figure 3-2   Stocks were a common form of punishment in the medieval period. These stocks were located in the Cambridgeshire village of Meldreth until they were knocked down by a car. Courtesy of Cambridgeshire Libraries' Collection

teristic of the feudal order, although the town and country life were so different.

Urban Industry

The regulation of market activity was also very thorough in medieval towns with respect to manufacturing. Production was literally by hand. Here, however, there were two relevant types of industrial activity, each subject to its own regulations and organizations: local and export industry.

Local Craft Guilds

Local artisans such as bakers, butchers, blacksmiths, and so on produced strictly for the local town market and were subject to a complex web of regulations established by their respective craft guilds. Craft guilds date from the end of the 11th century and were combinations of urban artisans who formed associations on the basis of their particular line of activity. Their models were the merchant guilds that were associations of merchants in different towns who grouped together for their mutual benefit when trade was beginning to expand. (The idea of such collective associations of individuals, in fact, can be traced back to Roman times, if not earlier.) Often, members of merchant guilds shared resources, travelled together (for security) and shared profits on a pro rata basis.

Craft guilds shared many of the same characteristics. Even when formed for charitable reasons, their economic functions soon dominated. In the town environment, they had a dual purpose: to protect both producer and consumer. This obviously met the municipal authorities' needs. In order to protect the consumer, what better way of controlling quality was there than supervising the producer? In this, we see an obvious merging of interests between the town as a whole and individual producers, and we see as well many elements common to the regulation of urban industry and the ethic of the feudal system. In time, many guilds became powerful establishments in their own right, able to participate in municipal administration themselves.

Guilds were privileged bodies. They could reserve the right to practice a craft to members of the guild, eliminating outside competition. The guild operated on a basis of no competition from either outside or inside, in order to make sure that no one grew rich at the expense of the other guild members. To do this, a complex system of rules emerged. These fixed the length of working hours; prices of products (following the "just price" idea that the seller should charge only enough to cover "necessary" costs, which would keep both buyer and seller in their established station in life—there was no element of profiteering here); wages paid to the journeymen; number of apprentices; methods of production and tools to be used.

Although guilds later became restraints on the further expansion of output, they were important in establishing conditions in which production for exchange could be undertaken and become acceptable. Their regulations guaranteed the survival of all producers and guaranteed quality (by specifying techniques and preventing adulteration and inferior workmanship), although at the cost of technological stagnation in later centuries.

Pre-capitalist Production

Guilds are examples of non- or pre-capitalist production for a market. Their regulations prevented excess profits, and thus the idea of individual self-interest being met through expansion, capital accumulation and reinvestment was simply not present. The guild hierarchy started with the apprentice stage. Each guild master trained a certain number of apprentices in the "mysteries" of the craft, which took about seven years. Then the apprentice became a journeyman, who was paid for his work, and after completion of a "masterpiece," which demonstrated proficiency in the craft, the journeyman became a mastercraftsman in his own right. The length of time this took depended on many factors, including the de-

Apprentice
person learning the skills of a craft or trade

Journeyman
guild member who has completed an apprenticeship but is not yet a guild master

mands of the local market. The journeyman also had to prove legitimacy of his birth, possess the freedom of the town, and pay the required entry fee (hence the need to work for wages for a time). As long as population was expanding, there would be no permanent class of wage earners. All journeymen could move out of this stage to the highest level of master. On reaching this level, the mastercraftsman was guaranteed a secure position. This position again is an example of the noncapitalist nature of the guild; masters were proprietors of their own small workshops and owned the raw materials, tools, and output produced.

Later, when guilds became stronger, they not only influenced their members' private lives (such as requiring regular church attendance and proper dress), but also became increasingly involved in municipal and charitable activities. Many founded schools for their members' children—being able to read and write became increasingly a mark of the privileged urban elite.

Export Production

Some towns were centers of export industries as well, such as silk in Lucca, copper in Dinant, and textiles in Flanders and Florence. Workers in these industries are the first examples of capitalist production. They received raw materials from merchants and earned wages for producing the finished output. But this type of work was very small scale and often not permanent. The Flemish cloth industry is a good example, as it declined from about the middle of the 14th century onward. Although these workers were organized along guild lines, they differed from the local town guilds described above by having no direct exchange relations with the final consumers of their products; merchants were the intermediaries.

Also unlike the local guilds, which, by knowing the conditions of the local markets, guaranteed stability by controlling production (through controlling entrance into the guild), these workers were at the mercy of crises such as wars that often affected their economic situation. And as international trade grew, so their numbers grew. For example, at its peak the Flemish textile center of Ghent had over 4,000 weavers alone. Thus the damage that could be done by a loss of markets affected an increasingly large number of people.

This situation led inevitably to a phenomenon more often associated with 19th and 20th century industrialization than with medieval craftsmanship—exploitation and worker protests:

> "Ground down by employers who gave out work to them, the masters were compelled in their turn to grind down the apprentices and journeymen. The preponderance of capital, from which urban economy had

been able to free the small crafts, pressed with all its weight on those producing for wholesale trade...''[5]

These journeymen workers were in a position very close to that of modern workers, and they often reacted in a similar way—the first recorded strike (protesting low wages) was in Douai in 1245! This type of protest was rarely found in the early *local* guilds, simply because those journeymen knew their position as journeymen-wage workers was only temporary. Industrial unrest such as that occurring in 13th century Douai could occur only with a class of permanent wage earners without the option of being anything else. But because the power and influence of the merchants was so great, cities bore down hard on these protests. Too much was at stake, especially as the public interest was seen as being identical to their own.

Summary

The development of urban communities paralleled the expansion of trade and commerce begun in the 11th century, and, while sharing many common characteristics with the surrounding feudal countryside—such as a desire for stability and an absence of competition—these towns were instrumental in hastening the decline of feudalism as a dominant institution. They were based on trade and thus on markets, and the first production for a market took place in them. Craft guilds regulated the production of goods for local use, while in a few towns, chiefly in Flanders and in Italy, examples of capitalist production for export markets took place. Although townspeople were not subject to feudal obligations, the organization of life in most of them was based on feudal ideas of stability and tradition. Even when towns gained recognition as independent legal entities, able to administer themselves and pass and enforce their own laws, it is possible to see marked similarities with the feudal system, although they were among the most powerful forces for change in succeeding centuries.

These early towns made three major contributions to economic history. First, they required a division of labor—a reciprocal exchange of services with the surrounding countryside. Second, they contributed to social change by demonstrating the possibility of a new way of life, one not based on self-sufficient agriculture but on markets, and introducing a new concept, the concept of free labor. Third, they were to show the power of capital. Towns were first established to further the interests of commercial capital, so their organization and administration was geared to encouraging commercial activity. This is important, because commercial activities were the first to be dominated by the capitalist ethic.

NOTES

1. Even if a reason for a town exists, this does not guarantee permanency for the town. For example, many of the boom towns of the 19th century American West had a reason—the discovery and exploitation of gold deposits. But because they never developed any other functions necessary to continued survival, once the gold sources were exhausted, the boom towns became ghost towns. Thus successful communities require linked and self-reinforcing activities to provide continued justification for town life.

2. Madeleine Pelner Cosman, *Fabulous Feasts: Medieval Cookery and Ceremony*, 1976, New York: George Braziller, p. 45.

3. A serf who lived in such a town for one year and a day automatically became free of all feudal ties and obligations. This gave rise to the medieval saying, "City air makes a man free."

4. Stocks and pillories were commonly used to punish offenders and expose them to public humiliation. The pillory locks the offender's head and hands into a wooden frame, while the stocks lock the feet.

5. Henri Pirenne, *Economic and Social History of Medieval Europe*, (1933) 1937 Harvest Edition, New York: Harcourt, Brace & World, p. 188.

Key Concepts

Apprentice
Bourgeois
Burg
Division of labor

Guild
Hanseatic League
Journeyman
Urban regulation

Note: Suggestions for further reading will be found at the end of chapter 4.

Questions for Discussion and Essay Writing

1. Venice became a highly prosperous city by the late feudal period. What similarities or differences exist between Venice and other cities of this period?

2. At the beginning of the feudal period, urban civilization was in decline. Why?

3. What preconditions are necessary for the establishment of towns? (Refer especially to the late feudal period.)

4. "Regulation" characterized economic activity in towns in the late feudal period. How was this regulation accomplished? What results did it have?

5. In what ways would craft guild production be considered "precapitalist"?

6. Why were most traded goods in the late feudal period luxury goods?

7. Why were merchants in the late feudal period considered to be "free"?

Part II

Europe in Transition: The Early Development of Capitalism

(Fourteenth to Eighteenth Centuries)

Chapter 4

The Dissolution of Feudalism (14th to 15th Centuries)

CHAPTER 2 PRESENTED A GENERAL PICTURE of feudal rural economic life as it existed in most of Europe in the early Middle Ages. The main theme underlying feudalism was the desire for security and stability, which in agriculture showed in the organization of production and the network of rights and obligations that existed between lord and serf. Even the development of commercially oriented towns after the 11th century, covered in Chapter 3, included institutions and regulations that aimed for stability. The emphasis on the just price, the continuing prohibition of usury, and the organization of manufacturing production within the guild system make this very clear.

However, the very development of these towns implied the emergence of forces that would irrevocably change that settled, feudal way of life. This is not meant to imply that the emergence of a new class in towns, the urban, commercial class, distinct from the traditional two-class feudal system, was alone responsible for the introduction of capitalism. That would be too simplistic. But its activities helped establish the preconditions for the eventual widespread acceptance of capitalist organization of economic activity.

The most essential change, severing the serfs' bonds to the land, was needed to create a wage labor force (which can be agricultural or indus-trial, employed or unemployed) out of independent producers. The completion of this process, and the result—the dependency of producers on the owners of capital—took time, several centuries in fact, but the 14th and 15th centuries saw the first steps in this process. In addition, economic activity was refocused away from maintenance of the status quo and towards profit making for the purposes of capital accumulation and economic expansion. The value system also changed to make this refocusing acceptable, a change that began in Europe at this time.

Although it is, of course, impossible to put a precise date on the ending of feudalism, the century 1350-1450 saw the manorial system break down. By 1500, feudalism as an economic relationship effectively ended in much of Europe, even if it persisted as a legal, if unenforceable, system. Again, this does not mean an immediate introduction of purely capitalist economic organizations and the wholesale adoption of a supportive value system. What it does mean is that the feudal structure was not strong enough to prevent certain changes from taking place. First in one area, then in another, over the next few centuries European economies looked more and more capitalist in their ethic, organization, and behavior.

Necessary Changes

To recap, three necessary changes had to take place. First, productive methods and organizations had to change in order to generate agricultural and industrial surpluses over and above the needs of the direct producers. This was required to generate a surplus that could be used for economic expansion. An agricultural surplus makes it possible to concentrate people in towns and thus increase industrial production. An industrial surplus permits continued reinvestment in industry, and thus capital accumulation in its modern sense. The important point here is that the surpluses must be used to expand the economic system, rather than for conspicuous consumption or projects not directly contributing to the expansion of the economy.

Second, social relationships had to change so that serfs—the majority of the population—became free of their feudal links to the land and had no other alternatives but to become wage laborers. This process also took several centuries to complete.

Third, the value system had to change away from one that encouraged tradition and stability, and toward one that accepted change (even if it did not welcome or appreciate it). Feudalism was geared to maintaining customary standards of consumption that served to justify its rigid two-class system. To shift to an ethic and economic organization favoring the accumulation of capital for future production was a dramatic shift, but gradually, future generations would come to accept it. We will see the beginnings of such a shift here; a more detailed investigation of the birth of the "capitalist ethic" will be presented in the next chapter.

Spread of Monetary Exchange

The most important cause of the decline of feudalism and the breakdown of the manorial system was the spread of monetary exchange relation-

ships. This began with the revival of trade and commerce centered in towns covered in the last chapter. There were two important implications. First, the new productive methods and purposes (especially the birth of the profit motive and deliberate production for a market) were antithetical to those of feudalism. At the very least, the development of towns and urban activities opened up the possibility of a new way of life, even if few took advantage of it (and only a few did).

Second, these new market-oriented economic relationships were different. They were based on contract, not status; on money, not tradition, so could not be absorbed into the old relationships between lord and serf. This intensified internal conflicts, and again, the feudal system proved too weak to prevent social change from occurring.

So the gradual growth of trade and commerce provides a basic, underlying explanation for the dissolution of feudalism. We will take a second look at these developments to see how they affected rural life, the most important and the most widespread part of feudalism. A related, slowly evolving change also helping undermine feudalism took place in the political sphere. It involved the appearance of the nation-state concept and the rise of the national monarch at the expense of the power of the feudal nobility. This process, however, took centuries—how, then, can we state that in the century between roughly 1350 and 1450, feudalism ended?

The reason lies in a combination of specific developments occurring in this century, which added to the on-going process of change and provided the final catalytic elements for the breakdown of feudalism. These elements were famines, wars, plagues, social uprisings, and the political struggles between old feudal nobility and new monarchs that led to the success of the latter and to the birth of nation-states. Each of these developments is linked to all the others; they were not isolated occurrences that can be seen and evaluated separately. In retrospect, it would have been surprising if Europe *had* emerged from this multiplicity of upheavals unscathed. A modern parallel would be Europe in the last half of the 20th century, which, after having experienced two world wars, depressions and many social and political changes, is very unlike the Europe of the late 19th century.

This chapter will focus on the developments of the fourteenth and fifteenth centuries that effectively killed off *economic* feudalism.

The Growth of a Market Economy

We have already looked at the role of trade and commerce in the development of towns. We will now change emphasis a little and see how the growth and expansion of a market economy undermined the institution of feudalism and altered the way of life of the rural population. The self-sufficiency of the manor was threatened, decreas-

Map 4.1   Medieval Commercial Towns

After the 11th century, many towns located on trade routes became thriving commercial centers

ing the independence of direct agricultural producers. To see how this process worked, we will backtrack to the 11th century, when the growth of trade began.

Local Grain Markets

What had most effect on serfs was not long distance export trade, but the development of local grain markets. Their importance is two-fold. On the one hand an increase in agricultural output, and on the other a ready permanent market for this output in towns, meant that these markets were the first stage of an organized rural-urban exchange directly involving serfs. These markets, in other words, were no longer occasional, sporadic affairs but permanent institutions in centrally located towns in agricultural districts.

As time went on, there was a further development: the rise of middlemen in grain sales. That is, certain merchants bought for inventory purposes, not for immediate use, so as to be able to take advantage of future shortages when they could profitably resell the grain. Very often in these market towns, the first "public" building to be erected after the church was the corn exchange, which became the focal point of these activities.

Such local markets were still only a very small part of total economic activity (because town populations were small), but they were important for two major reasons. First, they introduced serfs to a market economy, although for a time, the old feudal rights and obligations were still the major regulators of serfs' economic activity. Some lords were also affected by this development. Given their increasing needs for money, many encouraged commutation and leased lands to serf-farmers, who then produced for a market. But other lords were subject to a reverse incentive. Often, in cases where population declined, lords had a motive to *increase* their demands for feudal services, which became an important cause of subsequent rural unrest.

Second, because all sales were made using money, serfs began to become familiar with a money economy. Local markets were thus a precondition of commutation, the substitution of money payments for a serf's personal services, which obviously could happen only if serfs had money. A further implication is that feudalism came under greater stress in those areas near market towns than in more remote areas, where there was less opportunity to take advantage of such grain markets.

Medieval Fairs

A second strand in the development of trade affected serfs less directly, but also shows the growing weaknesses of the feudal structure to prevent change: the development of fairs. The fair was a unique medieval market institution. It has no modern equivalent, and in fact declined once merchants' exchange activities became fixed in one location.

Fair

infrequent medieval markets for professional merchants engaged in long distance trade

---

The fairs date from the revival of trade in the 11th century, reached a peak (in number and size) in the 12th and 13th centuries, and then declined at the end of the 13th century, for a variety of reasons. One was the increasing number of merchants establishing fixed operating bases in towns. Another was the establishment of direct shipping routes between Italian ports and those in Flanders and England. Finally, fairs suffered from the upheavals associated with the Hundred Years' War.

Fairs were international markets for professional merchants—they were subsequent to and did not develop from the local markets previously described. Although mainly for wholesale exchange, they inevitably attracted other types of exchange and entertainment activity, so were important events in the lives of those who lived in the surrounding areas. Although fairs took place in other countries—for example, Stourbridge Fair held in Cambridge was an important English medieval fair—the most famous are the Champagne Fairs, so-called because they took place on the Plain of Champagne in France, the location of the major overland trade route between Northern Italy and Flanders.

We have already noted that most of the trading was seagoing trade, centered around the Mediterranean and North Seas. Those few merchant-adventurers who did travel overland did so in large, heavily armed caravans for protection. Increasingly, as trade expanded, one natural line of expansion would be along an overland trade route linking the two major commercial centers. Moving from Venice north to Flanders takes one across the Lombardy Plain in northern Italy, then across northeast France through Champagne. It was at intervals along this and other trade routes that the fairs took place.

Because they were international and large, and therefore required a great deal of preparation, they were infrequent, and each lasted only a few days. In general, the fairs held earliest in the year were the more southerly ones, while the more northerly ones took place later in the year. They attracted merchants from all over Europe. For example, Flemish merchants found buyers for Flemish cloth, and bought imported silks, gold and silver, and spices to take back to Flanders.

The importance of and potential revenues from these fairs attracted the attention of the territorial princes as the old feudal nobility, under increasing pressure for money revenues, realized they could tax the attendees. Consequently, many granted permission to locate a fair in their territory. Often this right was granted to a town—although the importance of a fair preceded the importance of the town where it was held; many of the towns "sponsoring" fairs never became great commercial centers. Thus there is no automatic link be-

tween fair location and the development of an important commercial center.

Another important aspect of fairs giving a special position to new exchange activities was their privileged position. All attendees were under the protection of the territorial prince, therefore not subject to the prevailing laws of the time, which were not very supportive of new commercial developments. Thus, merchants were exempted from reprisal arising out of their activities outside the fair, no lawsuits could take place while a fair was in progress, and even the prohibition of usury was lifted for the duration of the fair.

Mercantile Law

In addition, a body of laws and customs called mercantile law, specific to merchants' activities, gradually evolved. Existing law simply could not or would not handle some of the aspects of these new, developing activities. Common law, based on tradition or usage, could not immediately cope with the implications of events that were new, while canon or church law had a built-in bias against commercial activities in general. Also, existing judicial procedure was too complex and time consuming—requiring, as it so frequently did, proof by ordeal—to be satisfactory to a group of people who were not fixed in one place.

Mercantile law
body of law designed by merchants to regulate trading and exchange

---

This new merchants' law had several aspects. One made contracts binding on all parties, in contrast with canon law which frequently absolved a debtor from repayment, thus not helping the development of commercial practices. The institution of credit became more sophisticated and acceptable to all the parties involved; and each fair was followed by a period for the settlement of debts that also extended to those contracted at a previous fair. This credit and debt network saw the origin of the bill of exchange, one of the earliest forms of credit, which is simply a promise to pay a specified sum of money in a place other than the one where the debt was originally contracted.

The practice of settling debts by compensation and clearing arrangements began in the financial centers of Florence and Siena. The importance to merchants of this body of usage and law was great. So long as trade contracts were few, personal knowledge of other merchants was sufficient to guarantee successful completion. But once trade expanded, it became harder to have this personal knowledge. Hence replacement by agreed-on rules and customs provided the necessary guarantee to activities involving greater numbers and more impersonality.

A faster legal mechanism paralleled it. The old formalistic procedure was inappropriate and the use of witnesses rather than ordeals for proof was introduced instead, as was the idea of using fines for punishments and trial by jury of one's peers. Administration took place in what came to be called the pie-powder courts (from the French, *pied poudreux*, or dusty feet, a reference to the traveling nature of merchants at the time). As merchants became settled in towns, so this body of law developed even further. In towns, the special privileges townspeople gained made it possible to develop a jurisprudence quite separate from that of the surrounding area, which was still subject to existing laws and legal practices.

Trading activities continued to grow and increase in sophistication up to the middle of the 14th century. Then growth halted, but trade was too firmly established to collapse following the catastrophes of the next few decades.

Pie-powder court
medieval law courts enforcing mercantile law

Feudalism's "Last Stand"

This underlying, persistent growth of exchange and market activity and the growth of towns would probably have weakened feudalism eventually. But especially in the years 1350–1450, there were in addition several specific events that hastened this decline, and put too many pressures on the social structure for it to survive intact. In this period, economic expansion ended. Population growth leveled off and fell, economic activity declined, and no new towns were formed or new lands opened up. It was a century of disasters. Any one alone probably could have been overcome, but each was linked or had implications for the others in such a way that a new social and economic order had to emerge. We will analyze these events and see how they fit into this process of transition.

Economic Recession

The decline in economic activity beginning this century of transition had many causes. Much earlier, a famine in the years 1315–17 had a more severe impact than any before, partly because with the growth of towns, many more people were now dependent on the continuation of adequate food supplies. With food supplies hard to get because of poor harvests, towns suffered. For example, in one six-month period in 1316, the town government of Ypres ordered 2,794 burials as a result of the famine—in 1400, its population was estimated at only 11,000. A succession of poor harvests in the 1320s had further devastating effects on peasants and the towns, adding another element to the underlying growth of dissatisfaction with existing conditions.

Improved security in earlier centuries had contributed to the increase in trade and commerce, but was now reversed, depressing further growth. Disturbed political and economic conditions were due to the Hundred Years' War in France, an increase in lawlessness and controversy over the royal succession in England, and renewed fighting between states and cities in Italy.

Any economic decline is always associated with social and political unrest, as the experience of the 1930s shows. A series of peasant uprisings and an increase in dissatisfaction with the existing order were among the results of the unrest in the 14th and 15th centuries. The existing order was attacked because it seemed to be unable to prevent worsening conditions for the bulk of the population.

The Hundred Years War, 1337–1453

This war was called the "Hundred Years War" not because it involved that many years of continuous fighting (the actual fighting was very sporadic), but rather because the issues that led to it took so long to be settled. It was fought between England and France, and commercial motives, especially over who should control the wool trade, helped lead up to it.

Figure 4.1   Wars and political unrest characterized the period of the dissolution of feudalism. This stylized miniature (in an early 15th century manuscript, De Claris Mulieribus) shows a castle being attacked by armed soldiers. (By permission of The British Library)

Before the war started, neither England nor France had achieved real national unity. France, moreover, suffered from problems arising from its high degree of decentralization. French dukes resented both the attempts of successive kings of France to gain authority over *all* of France, and the fact that some French regions were owned by the English king. However, the war strengthened national unity in both countries, ended the power of the old feudal nobility (more so in England than in France), saw the relocation of the wool textile industry—the first to become permanently established along capitalist lines—in England, and overall, accelerated the speed of economic change.

Reasons for Fighting

There were three reasons for the war. First, the traditional territorial excuse for a war lay in the French king's desire to regain possession of English-held areas: Guienne, Gascony, and part of Aquitaine. Second, the commercial reason focused on the important wool textile industry in Flanders and exports of raw wool from England to Flanders. Taxes on traded items were an important source of revenues for governments before income taxes were introduced, so control over this trade gave access to these tax revenues. At issue here was the fact that Flanders was controlled by the duke of Burgundy, and thus a fief of the French crown, but economically had more in common with England—the major source of raw materials for its flourishing textile industry. The Flemish objected to French attempts to gain more authority over Flanders, and many emigrated (with much encouragement from the English king) to England, where some of them settled in a town called Worsted (which thus gave its name to a type of wool cloth). The count of Burgundy retaliated by arresting English merchants in Flanders, which stimulated a counterretaliation by the English king, who put an embargo on all exports of wool to Flanders. This

hurt the Flemish industry, but helped the subsequent development of an English textile industry. A third, minor, reason concerned fishing rights in the Channel, the body of water separating England from France.

Stages of the War

The first period of fighting, stimulated by Edward of England's claim to the French throne in 1337, took place in France. At this time the advantage went to the English. French military weakness was compounded by infighting among the French nobles, the Jacquerie uprising, the Black Death, and pillaging by mercenary armies between battles. (Medieval warfare was characterized by the opposing armies literally living off the land between battles. Thus, even if peasants were not directly involved in fighting, they suffered as a result of looting and pillaging by armies.)

The second stage of the war took place between 1380 and 1420. France was still at a disadvantage, because of its civil war, while previous English unrest had ended with Henry IV's accession to the throne. He was the first English monarch to take a forceful approach to national unity. His son, Henry V, renewed the English claim to the French throne, aided this time by the Burgundians, who now became allied to England. Although Henry achieved military victory, it came at the expense of diverting scarce resources from more constructive activities at home.

The final stage—and the war itself—ended with Charles VII rallying with the Burgundians and driving the English out of all their French possessions, except for the port city of Calais.

Results of the War

France was devastated by the war, which was fought on French soil, and where the activities of the mercenary armies between engagements were not conducive to continued farming. However,

Louis XI (1461–1483) later used his power to break Burgundy's control over large parts of France. He supported the Duke's rebellious subjects, and after the Duke died, Louis simply appropriated large parts of Burgundy's possessions. As a result, he strengthened the power of the nation-state over the old feudal princedoms.

England escaped many of the physical consequences of the war, became unified earlier, and also became more developed along capitalist lines, gaining a textile industry that Flanders lost. The war also meant that many of the feudal nobility were absent from control of their manors for protracted periods of time, which further weakened feudal relationships. The absence of manpower and loss of life resulting from the plagues that swept across Europe during the war period not only created a labor shortage and rising wages for the limited number of wage earners but also helped fire social unrest.

Plagues

The major demographic change in the century after 1350 was that the population of Europe fell after having risen in previous centuries. Much of this decline was due to a succession of plagues, especially the Black Death that alone wiped out one-third of Europe's population, especially in the towns, in the years 1348–1350. Europe's popula-

Black Death
plague that decimated Europe 1348-1350

tion was estimated at about 80 million in the 1340s. The death toll from two years of plague was about 25 million. Later recurrences in the 1360s and 1370s prevented population rebuilding, because younger people of childbearing years had developed no immunity and were at a much greater risk.[1] The population of England suffered even more of a decline than the overall one third experienced in the rest of Europe. It was estimated at about four million at the beginning of

the 14th century, and fell to two and a half million by the middle of the 15th.

These disastrous epidemics led to a labor shortage, encouraged already-building social tensions, and help explain the rise in religious heresies that preceded the Protestant Reformation of the 16th and 17th centuries. Because the plagues spread so swiftly, they discredited confidence in rational theology and encouraged a more mystical world view in which unexplainable, arbitrary catastrophes were both possible and likely. For example, both William of Ockham (d. 1349) and the German Dominican known as Meister Eckhart (d. 1327) had questioned the appropriateness of orthodox rational speculation. The latter in particular, in common with other mystics, appealed instead for a greater emphasis on an "inner experience" of God. Although mysticism represented a reaction both to the Church's scholastic rationalism as well as to worldliness, it appealed strongly to townspeople.

Trade and the Spread of Plagues

Interestingly enough, the timing and spread of the plagues is intimately connected with the development of trade and long distance commerce also marking this period. Isolated populations develop immunities to the endemic diseases in their area, but not to new ones. Although plagues had been endemic in Europe before the 8th century, the cutting of trade ties and the development of spontaneous immunities prevented a recurrence in the early feudal period. But plague remained endemic in some regions where burrowing rodents—the carriers of the disease-carrying fleas—lived, chiefly in Yunan and Burma.

In the 13th century, the spread of trade in Europe was paralleled by the Mongol conquests of much of Asia, which had the effect of transmitting the plague to the steppe areas of northern China, Mongolia, and Russia. From here, it travelled along the caravan trade routes of Asia to reach the Crimea on the Black Sea in 1346. By this time, shipping routes between the Crimea and the Mediterranean and other European ports were well established. Thus the port cities' populations were the first to become infected, and a further spread to inland areas was also possible as people vainly tried to flee from its depredations.

Incidentally, leprosy had previously been a significant—and much feared—disease in Europe, but the plague decimated the leprosy hospitals that had been built outside towns, and it was never again a serious threat. However, this occurred at the cost of rising levels of syphilis (which has the same bacillus as yaws, one of the diseases classed as leprosy in the Middle Ages) and typhus, for reasons closely tied to the economic changes of this period.

To skip a few centuries ahead of the story, plague finally withdrew from northwest Europe only after the middle of the 17th century. By then, various changes in economic behavior and moral attitudes discouraged its spread (but encouraged the rise of other endemic diseases).[2] For example, the expansion of production of wool textiles for a market after the 14th century, made them more widely available for clothing. This lessened skin-to-skin contacts, and thus the possibility of contracting bubonic plague and yaws. More textiles were also now available for bedding, which ironically provided suitable habitats for lice and bedbugs, carriers of typhus (which first appeared in European armies after 1490). In addition, the development of puritanical attitudes brought new ideas about personal decency that presupposed that enough cloth would be available for covering bodies. Hence it is hypothesized that the yaws bacillus altered so that infection could be transmitted not through skin contact but rather through sexual contact as syphilis.

More effects of these experiences with plagues can be noted. First, there was more interest in public health matters—the quarantine of infected people was an example. Second, the strength of city organizations in coping with these disasters shows their permanency and vigor. City governments were active in meeting needs for food, arranging burials, and attempting to maintain public order. Overall, these waves of epidemics had a direct effect in reducing the population of Europe; indirectly, they helped stimulate change from one economic system to another.

Commutation and Alienation of the Demesne

During this time, changes also took place in the rural manors that were both cause and effect of subsequent developments. There were two major changes. The first was commutation, in which money payments replaced the personal services owed by the serfs to their lords. The second was alienation of the demesne, which meant that lords did not farm their land directly by using serfs' labor services, but instead leased parts of it to tenant farmers for money rent.

Commutation

replacement of feudal labor services by money payments

Alienation of the demesne

feudal lords rent demesne land to tenant farmers for money

Incentive to Commute Labor Services

The incentive for lords to commute was clear and again was closely linked to the other changes that were also taking place. The rise of the monarchs and the extension of monarchical authority reduced the nobility's authority as governors of feudal fiefs. In addition, their needs for revenues were increasing. A greater volume of trade and commerce made more of those luxuries associated with a noble life style available and desired. Also, military expenses resulting from their military obligations rose, in spite of the fact that these obligations became transformed from feudal duties to purely monetary obligations. In any event, these pressures intensified during the Hundred Years War. For example, arms became more complex and therefore more costly, while armor also became more costly, especially with the introduction of full plate armor in the 15th century. This also required stronger and healthier horses; a full suit of armor weighs around 40 pounds and is not very maneuverable, hence the need for horses. And as the *practical* reasons for their authority eroded, the nobility increasingly clung to maintaining the outward symbols of their former prestige. For example, they held more complex tournaments, which were expensive.

While population was still expanding, the incentive to commute direct labor services into money payments was strong. When there were excess tenants, it was more advantageous to the lords to collect fixed money rents (called quit-rents) in place of the feudal obligations of at least some of their tenants. Where did the serfs get the money from? As we saw earlier, the development of local grain markets associated with the expansion of towns provides the missing link.

Replacement of feudal services by money payments was more desirable to serfs when population was *declining*, but in this case the lord was less eager. That is, when feudal labor services were imposed on a family, fewer family members meant that the burden on those remaining would increase. In addition, the labor shortage accompanying population decline increased the opportunity cost of being a serf (although we cannot tell whether serfs did in fact make this calculation).

So while population increases had encouraged lords to accept money payments (a trend that was reinforced in cases where they were absent from their estates because of wars), population decline made them more likely to intensify the old feudal demands on serfs. In addition, those who had given up land for the town expansion lost the feudal services associated with it, receiving instead ground rent from the burghers. This also reduced

their willingness to commute the serfs' obligations any further.

Incentive to Alienate the Demesne

On the other hand, while population decrease reduced the incentive for commutation, it increased the lords' willingness to alienate the demesne. The scarcity of tenants made direct farming of the demesne more difficult, so some lords divided up at least part of their land and leased it for money rents to tenant farmers. This process became increasingly common in the 15th century.

Effects

These developments were most frequent in England, France, the Low Countries and parts of Germany; serfdom generally continued unabated in Eastern Europe. The results were many. Materially, peasant farmers were not necessarily better off. The decline in economic activity and the closing of internal frontiers implied fewer alternatives, and an increased burden of feudal services and/or the requirement to make money payments weighed hard when markets were shrinking. In addition, as the nobility ended their demands for feudal services from the serfs, their obligations to provide services in return weakened. That is, the old economic security of the manorial organization eroded as its structure altered. Peasants could no longer depend on the nobility to protect them through times of hardship, and no new method of economic security had emerged as a replacement. This is closely associated with the shift from status to contract. The old feudal relationships based on status were inflexible, but the emerging relationships based on contract could be changed. In this case, the balance of power between the parties involved in a contract was crucial in determining the outcome. The most common contractual relationship came with commutation. The former serfs became copyholders when the commutation fee was recorded on the manor rolls (for record keeping) with a copy being given to the serf-tenant, and a body of *customary* law arose to guarantee them permanent possession of the holdings for which they paid rent. (This produced many economic and social problems for the copyholders in later centuries in England, which will be addressed in Chapter 8.)

Copyholder

former serf whose commutation fee has been recorded on the manor rolls

---

Another contractual relationship emerged from the alienation of the demesne itself. Typically, holdings leased by the lord to tenant-farmers were larger than serf-holdings, thus requiring more labor than could be supplied by one family. This meant that extra laborers had to be hired—a new contractual relationship between tenant-farmer and farm laborer that marked the origin of an agricultural wage labor force joining the small urban wage labor force that already existed in the export industries of some of the larger towns.

In summary, alienation of the demesne and commutation marked the ending of some of feudalism's important relationships. By 1500, feudalism had disappeared in England as an economic relationship, but still survived elsewhere in Europe to a greater or lesser extent. Often, the peasants were not materially better off than before, which, plus other changes, generated a groundswell of discontent.

Social Unrest and Uprisings

All the various catastrophes and developments of the 14th and 15th centuries created a climate where discontent was rife, both among the rural population and in the towns. Discontent manifested itself in both peasant uprisings and some urban protests, when the lower class of urban artisans saw their position deteriorating even further.

The problem arose partly because with the passing of the feudal order itself, those compensations that made it acceptable disappeared. In the countryside, larger segments of the serf population found that freedom from feudal obligations implied lack of a security net that formerly prevented extreme economic hardships from having too disastrous an effect. In the towns, it became apparent that developing capitalism created both extreme wealth and extreme poverty, an ideal condition for urban unrest. But although problems existed, there was yet no organized way that those affected could express their feelings. There were also few instances of a recognition of a common interest between town and country dwellers, so it was difficult for them to get together to try to ameliorate the situation. Hence they were forced into the only avenue open to them: insurrection.

Whether occurring in town or country, these popular uprisings were unsuccessful and did not achieve their aims of improving conditions for peasants and artisans. Even if they were initially successful, rulers quickly reasserted their power in putting them down violently and forcefully; the time was not yet ripe for the voice of the common people to be heard. These uprisings were simply outbursts of anger with no future, especially as the peasants' demands were not clearly expressed. Those affected just wanted protection from the worst abuses they suffered; they did not have a vision of a new society.

Flanders

Of the major uprisings, the first chronologically occurred in western Flanders, 1323–28. Its cause lay in the redoubled efforts of nobles to collect taxes levied on the population to pay fines due to the king of France (Flanders was then part of the French feudal network). This resentment boiled over into riots and then open revolt. The peasants refused to pay not only the taxes but also the tithes levied on them by the Church, and they demanded that the grain stored in monasteries be distributed to the people. There was extreme cruelty by the peasants—matched by the equally extreme cruelty of the forces sent by the King of France to put the revolt down.

Jacquerie

France next experienced a peasant uprising—the Jacquerie in the region known as the Ile de France, in 1357. This occurred at a time when the Hundred Years War was not going well for France, when the peasants were suffering both from the effects of that war and from the intensified demands of the nobility. It was the distress caused by and hatred of the nobles that led to this uprising (hatred that persisted in France up to the time of the French Revolution in the late 18th century).

England

Although the basic situation in England was more favorable to peasants than in France, there was still resentment at the many surviving remnants of feudalism. The Peasants' Revolt of 1381 was a protest against these, and was also a rare example of a common effort between town and country. The unrest began crystallizing after the passage of the Statute of Labourers in 1351. We have already noted that the population decline following the catastrophe of the Black Death led to a labor shortage and rising wages. But the Statute of Labourers was an attempt to return to a pre-plague situation by requiring that wages be restored to their original, lower, levels. Although urban wage earners were few, they obviously resented this—especially as prices were also rising. The final straw came with the imposition of a poll tax in 1381 to raise money for the king to continue waging the Hundred Years War. Resenting the tax and also rural rents, and with no way to make their protest known, mobs in many places destroyed the records detailing the obligations

owed by serfs and former serfs. And a group led by Wat Tyler (an artisan tiler from Kent) led a march to appeal to the king for freedom from the arduous burdens imposed on them. However, as in Flanders and France, the established order had no intention of giving way, and the revolt was put down with much loss of life.

Urban Revolts and Wage Work

Urban revolts occurring in the more export-oriented towns of Flanders, the Rhine, and Italy were a sign, not so much of distress caused by the ending of the old order, as of the inequalities emerging with the new. In Flanders, for example, some of the members of the smaller crafts wanted a greater share of urban government, but they faced the dominance of the great crafts of the textile industry and the power of the international capitalist-merchants. The result was that control of city governments in the major textile centers remained with the wealthiest crafts, although there were continual power struggles between them. The pressures they put on the smaller crafts were passed on by the masters to their journeymen wage workers.

In addition to intercraft rivalry, a new element was added by the end of the 14th century. Wage work was common in the export cloth industry, but at this time, a wage earning proletariat had also begun to appear in the *local* crafts, partly due to the population decline and loss of markets. Previously, there had been few conflicts between journeymen and masters, because expansion implied that one day journeymen too would become masters, hence their status as wage workers was bearable because it was only temporary. But once these opportunities became fewer, journeymen saw their future prospects diminishing, and they became more resentful. So journeymen formed associations for their mutual benefit, increased demands for higher wages, demanded a greater share in the government of their craft guild—in general, signs of an increased antagonism between wage workers and masters that became expressed in constant uprisings. (In Florence, another important textile center, these feelings were accentuated by the autocratic, patrician nature of the owners.) This situation became less tense because the cloth industry in Flanders itself declined after the mid-14th century—there were simply fewer people involved.[3]

In general, unrest in both town and country added to all the other problems being experienced. Although the open uprisings were not successful in a practical sense, they did achieve a symbolic victory: They showed that the peasants were no longer willing to accept automatically everything that the lords did. Peasants had no clear idea of what they wanted the future to look like, except that they did not want the worst abuses and hardships they were experiencing to be part of that future. It took many more generations to achieve effective, organized means of expressing the desires of the lower classes.

Emergence of Nation-States

The weakening of the feudal structure was further evidenced by the rise of national monarchs and the emergence of the idea of the nation-state. As we have already seen, in early medieval times the political structure was organized in a hierarchical pyramid of fiefs, and the king had no real power over all of the dukedoms and principalities that nominally constituted the kingdom. People thought of themselves in regional or local terms, not in national terms.

Alliance Between Monarchs and Merchants

But the various crises we have looked at further emphasized the breakdown of feudalism. Civil war in England effectively killed off many of the nobility who traced their roots and power back to the Norman conquerors of the 11th century. Civil unrest in France, and the need for unity against a

Nation-state

territory whose people share certain common values and who are organized under a single sovereign government

common enemy, England, encouraged the rise of a strong, stabilized, centralized monarchy. In both countries, the demands of organizing and fighting a protracted war, coupled with domestic concerns, stimulated the development of a centralized bureaucracy. Administration required professional councilors with the expertise that feudal barons, serving their monarchs as a feudal obligation, did not necessarily have. Furthermore, there was a common link between the towns and the monarchs; both resented many of the restrictions imposed by the continuing influence of feudalism. Also, the new monarchs were anxious to acquire an effective base, but often did not have the revenue to obtain it. So they turned to the towns and the wealthy merchants, the most important sources of liquid capital available, for loans to finance their schemes. Those financing the rise of the monarchs gained; having their kings indebted to them gave them a voice in the country's administration that could be turned to their financial advantage, and it also gave them the social prestige they lacked so long as social prestige depended on land. Ironically enough, this identity of interests also helped break the power of towns to control the activities of the wealthy merchants, bankers, and shipowners who lived in them or traded with them. Initial town development had helped these people, but the stronger and more independent towns became, the more they rivaled one another. Such a rivalry was not in the interests of the individual merchants, because it restricted their activities. They would gain more from the forging of a *national* viewpoint that was a crucial step forward in creating a larger *national* market—and thus assisting further expansion of capitalist activities.

This was a first step toward the later creation of mercantilism, or national protectionism. In medieval times, the towns had been responsible for regulating their inhabitants' economic activities, but they were effective only within their own boundaries. So the next step was for the monarchs to be able to influence the entire economy; in other words, taking over some of the functions of the towns and seeing themselves as protectors of the common good.

This process went furthest in France and England. Political anarchy still prevailed in Germany, where a centralized government would not appear until the late 19th century. This anarchy held back the development of activity along capitalist lines. (There was, however, a center of growth in southern Germany concerned with the exploitation of the mines of Bohemia and the Tyrol.) Italy also remained politically divided, but the legacy of innovations in financing, banking, and luxury production still implied powerful financial empires for individual Italian families (such as the Medici) until the center of economic activity in Europe shifted from the Mediterranean to the Atlantic coast in the 16th and 17th centuries.

England and the War of the Roses

The process of forging national unity was successful first in England, taking place against a backdrop of political and social unrest and the pressures of a foreign war. One of the first steps came in 1381, when the English king attempted to prohibit imports of foreign cloth (using standard infant industry arguments for a tariff!) and also tried to reserve all trade into and out of the country to English ships. This was impossible to enforce, because there were not enough English ships.

It was civil war—the War of the Roses—that finally broke the power of the old nobility. This war was fought over rival claims to the English throne between the House of Lancaster, whose emblem was a red rose (Kings Henry IV, V, and VI); and the House of York, whose emblem was a white rose (Kings Edward IV and V and Rich-

ard III). This struggle involved considerable bloodshed, but after thirty years, most of the old Norman nobility had been killed off, so when Henry VII (a Lancastrian) defeated Richard III in 1485, the struggle ended. Henry promptly consolidated his victory by marrying a princess of the House of York and renamed his house the House of Tudor.

Economically, Henry VII (1485–1509) was the first systematically protectionist king. He set the stage for the later emergence of the idea of the absolute monarchy by establishing a system of taxes to make the monarch's revenues, and thus power, less dependent on the will of Parliament. His internal security measures were also effective in controlling disorder, and removing most of the opposition to the monarch. By reestablishing internal order, he cleared the way for the economy's subsequent expansion. Thus, for example, those earlier invitations to Flemish weavers now bore fruit in the expansion of the English textile industry; earlier prohibitions on foreigners exporting English wool provided a protected market in England and also contributed to the decline of the great merchants' trading associations, such as the Hanse; and a start was made in encouraging the development of English shipping. These protectionist measures not only hastened the decline of the Flemish wool industry but, more important, encouraged the growth of a merchant marine in the Low Countries, which became *the* great commercial and trading nation in the 16th century. (At this time, Antwerp rose to prominence as both a port and a great financial center, at the expense of Bruges, which declined as a result of its harbor silting up and the loss of the industry that had made it a great medieval city.)

France

French efforts at forging national unity also emerged from the struggles among the French nobility. As we saw above, Louis XI (1461-1483) broke the power of the duke of Burgundy. Both

Figure 4.2   Bruges was one of the most important new towns in the late medieval period, and was at the center of the Flemish wool trade. This photo shows one of the canals that were used for transportation. (Courtesy of the Belgian Tourist Office)

he and later monarchs succeeded in expanding the boundaries of the kingdom of France to something more like its present area. As part of the effort to reduce the power of the nobles, who controlled the king's revenues because they controlled parliament (the Estates General), the king established a direct tax on land to provide permanent revenues to the monarchy. Thus in both France and England, the monarch was able to consolidate a power and a revenue base.

By the end of the 15th century, France and England were nation-states, with a monarch having authority over the whole kingdom. The power of the old feudal nobility had gone, and thus, politically, feudalism was dead. Each country had a more professional, centralized administration, which, given the links with the towns, wealthy merchants, and financiers, was increasingly disposed to favor commercial interests. Because they wanted to wield effective power over the entire country, these monarchs turned against both local vested interests and urban particularism in favor of what they saw to be the "common good". These new style monarchs were later successful in helping to develop the infrastructure of a truly national economy, and their efforts were further extended by the emergence of the idea of absolute monarchy and the practices of national mercantilism. In this light, then, they can be seen as necessary political first steps in establishing the preconditions for the adoption of widespread capitalist practices.

Religious Upheavals

The final element contributing to the weakening of the feudal structure was the growing tendency to secularism and anticlericalism. The Church was an important part of the functioning of feudal society; its teachings encompassed the whole of life and justified everyday existence. As we have already seen, its administration provided one stable link with prefeudal society, and it alone was a centralized, organized force in an age of political decentralization. The authority of the Church over economic life was unquestioned for most of this period.

But in the 14th and 15th centuries, for both internal and external reasons, this authority came under question, and the Church and its teachings became less influential over society. In the 16th and 17th centuries, the Reformation split the Christian Church in Europe into Catholic and Protestant divisions. As a result, a new religious ethic emerged to provide justification for the spread of capitalist ideas. Consequently, capitalist practices could now flourish because the value system was more supportive. Ironically, although the first "protesters" wanted to restore the dominance of religious beliefs over all of life, their emphasis on an *individual's* relationship with God led the way to the subsequent flowering of individualism and to the compartmentalization of life. In turn, this implied that economic activities should be judged on purely economic grounds rather than on the basis of how well they fitted into the divine scheme of things. (Chapter 5 will discuss the development of Protestantism and its contribution to capitalism in more detail.)

Externally, the catastrophes of the 14th and 15th centuries—in particular, the arbitrariness of the plagues—led to a loss of confidence in the idea of a rational world, explainable in terms of a divine order established by a merciful Supreme Being. This loss of confidence manifested itself in mysticism, a renewed belief in witchcraft (and the parallel renewal of witchhunts), and the growth of heresy. The Church was unable to counter these, due in part to its own internal weaknesses and abuses that also contributed to the growth of anti-clericalism. Among these internal weaknesses were the governmental crisis emerging from the dispute over the position of the pope, weakness of the administrative structure of the Church itself, and various abuses and corruption. Some of the most notable examples resulted from the Church's wealth, lax morality among priests, and the increasing substitution of money payments for true spiritual belief (the sale of indulgences and other "pardons" for those who had sinned). This weakness was in fact both intellectual (the Church could not counter the criticisms) and practical (it was unable to cope with the demands placed on it by the various crises of the times).

Weakness was exaggerated by the various plagues that decimated the ranks of the clergy, causing vacancies that were filled too often by poorly trained clerics unable to provide the requisite spiritual guidance or practical expertise. In addition, the administration was unable to handle the problems resulting from the plagues. Instead, it was the towns themselves that demonstrated the organization and ability to deal with these very practical problems.

Summary

The 14th and 15th centuries were times of great change in Europe. Although trade and commerce ceased to expand in the pivotal century 1350-1450, it did not lose its importance, and there was no decline of trade such as that which accompanied the beginnings of the feudal period.

But the feudal period was now coming to an end. On top of the slow erosion of feudalism created by the expansion of commercial activity came a series of disasters, catastrophes and upheavals that the feudal structure could not absorb without being changed. Among these were the population changes caused by the plagues, the upheavals of the Hundred Years War, social unrest among the lower class, and political infight-

ing among the feudal nobility that ended in the emergence of strong, centralized monarchies in England and France. The results of the dissolution of feudalism were that more people were involved in market activity, some exclusively; that the basis for social relationships ceased to be status based on birth and became based on contract; and that for the first time, the unquestioned authority of traditional Church teachings was undermined.

Notes

1. These plagues were transmitted by both person-to-person contact, as with pneumonic plague, where the bacillus is thrown out into the air when an infected person sneezes; and from flea bites, as with the bubonic plague. Before antibiotics, mortality was high: 100 percent mortality rates from the pneumonic plague, and between 30-90 percent for bubonic types.

2. There is a further explanation for the decline in plagues after the 17th century: the shortage of wood and its replacement in housebuilding by brick and tiles. The wood shortage was due to its increased use as charcoal in industry, as well as for shipbuilding and housebuilding. At this time, no attempts were made to reforest logged areas. However, the use of bricks put more distance between plague-carrying vermin and humans.

3. Another result was the decay of the power of the guilds, which also occurred in England. This would have important consequences for the subsequent expansion of production activities along capitalist lines.

Key Concepts

Alienation of the demesne
Artisan
Bill of exchange
Canon Law
Common law
Commutation
Copyholder

Fair
Infant industry tariff
Mercantile law
Peasant
Pie-powder court
Protectionism
Wage labor

Questions for Discussion and Essay Writing

1. Discuss the role played by the new towns of the late medieval period in the dissolution of feudalism.

2. How was the monetization of feudal dues or obligations accomplished in the 14th century?

3. Discuss the importance of location (especially proximity to a growing town) to the breakdown of feudal relationships.

4. Why did merchants need to develop a new body of law (mercantile law) in the late medieval period?

5. Discuss the events contributing to the decline of the Flemish cloth industry in the 14th (and later) century.

6. How did the Hundred Years' War contribute to the dissolution of feudalism?

7. How did the expansion of trade in the 13th and 14th centuries contribute to the spread of disease in Europe? Were there any other effects?

8. "Peasants were often legally free from feudal obligations but this does not always result in economic betterment." Discuss and evaluate.

9. There were many episodes of peasant revolts in the 14th and 15th centuries. What were their aims? Were they successful in achieving these aims?

10. What connection existed between economic changes in the late medieval period and political developments?

11. Explain the pressures contributing to a feudal lord's decision to commute labor services. What pressures existed to cause a reversal of commutation?

12. Why would the development of a strong ruler in a unified state ultimately be opposed to the interests of medieval cities?

For Further Reading

Ashton, T.H. *The Brenner Debate: Agrarian Class Structure and Economic Development in Pre-Industrial Europe,* Cambridge: Cambridge University Press, 1983.

Bailey, Mark. *The Concept of the Margin in the Medieval English Economy,* Economic History Review, XLII:1, 1988, pp. 1-17.

Barraclough, Geoffrey. *The Crucible of Europe: The Ninth and Tenth Centuries in European History.* Berkeley and Los Angeles, Ca: University of California Press, 1976.

Bautier, Robert-Henri. *The Economic Development of Medieval Europe.* N.Y.: Harcourt, Brace, Jovanovich, 1971.

Birrell, Jean. "Common Rights in the Medieval Forest: Disputes and Conflicts in the Thirteenth Century." *Past and Present,* vol. 117 (November 1987): 22-49.

Bloch, Marc. *Feudal Society* (translated from the French), Chicago: University of Chicago Press, 1961.
_____ *Land and Work in Medieval Europe, selected papers,* London: Routledge & Kegan Paul, 1967.

Blomquist, Thomas W. "Some Observations on Early Foreign Exchange Banking Based upon New Evidence from 13th Century Lucca." *Journal of European Economic History, 19:2 (Fall 1990) : 353-375.*

Britnell, R.H. "Feudal Reaction After the Black Death in the Palatinate of Durham." *Past and Present,* vol. 128 (August 1990): 28-47.

_____ "The Proliferation of Markets in England, 1200-1349." *Economic History Review,* XXXIV:2 (1969): 209-221.

Carpenter, D.A. "English Peasants in Politics, 1258-1267." *Past and Present*, vol. 136 (August 1992): 3-42.

Cave, Roy C. and H.R. Coulson, eds. *A Source Book for Medieval Economic History*. N.Y.: Biblio and Tannen, 1965.

Cosgel, Metin M. "Risk Sharing in Medieval Agriculture." *Journal of European Economic History,* 21:1 (Spring 1992): 99-110.

Coulborn, R. *Feudalism in History*. Princeton, N.J.: Princeton University Press, 1956.

Day, John. *The Medieval Market Economy*. Oxford and N.Y.: Basil Blackwell, 1987.

Dixon, Philip Willis. *Barbarian Europe*. Oxford: Elsevier, 1976.

Dyer, Christopher, "The Consumer and the Market in the Later Middle Ages." *Economic History Review*, XLII:3 (1988): 305-327.

Fenoaltea, Stefano. "The Rise and Fall of a Theoretical Model: The Manorial System." *Journal of Economic History*, 1975.

Ganshof, F.L. *Feudalism*. London: Longmans, Green, 1952.

Gregg, Pauline. *Black Death to Industrial Revolution*. N.Y.: Harper & Row, 1974.

Grief, Avner. "Reputation and Coalitions in Medieval Trade: Evidence on the Maghrib Traders." *Journal of Economic History*, XLIX:4, Dec. 1989, pp. 857-882.

Hatcher, John. *Plague, Population and the English Economy, 1348-1530*. London: Macmillan Education, 1977.

Hilton, Rodney et. al. *Bondsmen Made Free: Peasant Movements and the English Rising of 1381* New York: Viking, 1973.

_____ *The Decline of Serfdom in Medieval England*. London: Macmillan, 1970.

_____ "Feudalism in Europe: Problems for Historical Materialists." *New Left Review,* 147 (Sept/Oct. 1984).

Hoffman, R. *Medieval Origins of the Common Fields* in William N. Parker and Eric L. Jones, eds. *European Peasants and Their Markets: Essays in Agrarian History,* Princeton: Princeton University Press, 1975.

Jones, S.R.H. "Devaluation and the Balance of Payments in Eleventh-Century England: An Exercise in Dark Age Economics." *Economic History Review*, XLIV:4 (1991): 594-607.

Lopez, Robert S. *The Commercial Revolution of the Middle Ages, 950-1350*. Cambridge: Cambridge University Press, 1976.

McCloskey, Donald N. "The Prudent Peasant: New Findings on Open Fields." *Journal of Economic History*, LI:2 (June 1991): 343-355.

McNeill, William H. *Plagues and People*. N.Y.: Anchor Doubleday, 1976.

Moore, Barrington. *The Social Origins of Dictatorship and Democracy: Lord and Peasant in the Making of the Modern World*. Boston: Beacon Press, 1966.

North, Douglass and Robert Thomas, "The Rise and Fall of the Manorial System." *Journal of Economic History*. (December 1971).

Origo, Iris. *The Merchant of Prato: Francesco di Marco Datini*. New York: Octagon Books (1963) 1967.

Pirenne, Henri. *Economic and Social History of Medieval Europe*, N.Y.: Harcourt Brace, 1956.

_____ *Medieval Cities: Their Origins and the Revival of Trade*. Princeton, N.J.: Princeton University Press, (1925) 1952.

Polanyi,K. et. al. eds. *Trade and Markets in the Early Empires: Economies in History and Theory*. Glencoe, Ill: Free Press, 1957.

Postan, M.M. *Essays on Medieval Agriculture and General Problems of the Medieval Economy*. Cambridge: Cambridge University Press, 1973.

_____ *The Medieval Economy and Society: An Economic History of Britain 1100-1500*. Berkeley: University of California Press, 1973.

_____ *Medieval Trade and Finance*. Cambridge: Cambridge University Press, 1973.

T and H.J. Habakkuk, eds. *Trade and Industry in the Middle Ages*. Cambridge Economic History of Europe, vol 2. Cambridge: Cambridge University Press, 1952.

Pounds, Norman J.G. *An Economic History of Medieval Europe*. London and N.Y.: Longman, 1974.

Power, Eileen. *Medieval Women*. Cambridge: Cambridge University Press, 1975.

Swanson, Heather. "The Illusion of Economic Structure: Craft Guilds in Late Medieval English Towns." *Past and Present*, vol. 121 (November 1988): 29-48.

Sweezy, Paul *et. al. The Transition from Feudalism to Capitalism*. N.Y.: Science and Society, 1963.

van Caenegem, R.C. with F.L. Ganshof, *Guide to the Sources of Medieval History*. N.Y.: North Holland, 1978.

Verhulst, Adriaan. "The Origin of Towns in the Low Countries and the Pirenne Thesis." *Past and Present*, vol.122 (February 1989): 3-35.

Wallace-Hadrill, John Michael. *The Barbarian West, 400-1000*. London and New York: Hutchinson's University Library, 1952.

Wickham, Chris. "The Other Transition: From the Ancient World to Feudalism." *Past and Present*, vol. 103 (May 1984): 3-36.

Chapter 5

Protestantism and the "New" Classes

THIS CHAPTER SKETCHES OUT THE 16TH AND 17TH CENTURY CHANGES in theological doctrine that altered the value system of European economies. It will show how change affected the conduct of economic activity, and how it encouraged the further spread of capitalist, money-making behavior into previously unaffected areas of the economy.

All throughout the 15th century, those changes in economic conduct and organization that had begun in the new and revitalized towns of Europe continued. However, if these changes were to become dominant and influence an entire *society*, something more was needed. The missing ingredient was the moral justification of money-making activity, necessary if these new activities were to be not only tolerated, but wholeheartedly approved of. By the end of the 17th century, this justification was missing no longer, but had become a fait accompli, especially in the new leading areas of economic growth, Britain and the Netherlands.

Moral sanctions for the new types of economic behavior occurred as a result of a religious upheaval that split the nations of Europe into two Christian camps—those remaining Catholic and those becoming Protestant. From an extreme version of Protestantism, Puritanism, it is even possible to trace the origins of what has been

called "the spirit of capitalism," which gave both an ethos approving economic activity, and rules for personal conduct that were highly encouraging to the rational pursuit of wealth characteristic of capitalist activity.

During the 16th and the 17th centuries, the traditional scheme of Christian virtues was turned upside down. Instead of the monastic life and withdrawal from the world being valued most highly, temporal activity was now seen as most acceptable for a true Christian. Those people already on the forefront of economic change were most supportive of these new religious doctrines, so the effect on the development of capitalism was strong.

To understand the contribution of these religious ideas to the development of an economic system, this chapter has two major sections. The first briefly outlines the historical background of and the events composing the Protestant Reformation; the second explores those aspects of Protestant doctrine that provided the new justification for capitalist activity, assisting the development and spread of capitalism.

Historical Background

Up to the 14th century, the medieval ethic held that all aspects of life were the subject of religion, so that economic interests were subordinate to the main purpose of life, salvation. As such, material wealth itself was not forbidden because it permitted the wealthy to fulfill their part of the Divine plan, but the desire to accumulate wealth for its own sake was forbidden. In this scheme of things, a monastic, spiritual life was the most highly regarded, and Churchmen, monks and nuns were the most assured of salvation. Their separation from purely temporal concerns and their total commitment to purely spiritual affairs permitted them a wholehearted devotion to glorifying and worshipping God, thus preparing for the life hereafter. Economic motives were suspect, because they distracted people from the main purpose of life. So the more important pecuniary motives were to practical activities, the more disreputable the activity was held to be. This led to a grudging acceptance of trading activities, albeit heavily surrounded by restrictions and constraints, but a downright suspicion of finance. Thus the *deliberate* search for wealth, which provides the dynamic for capitalist economies, was missing.

After the 11th century, as we saw, the expansion of trade and commercial activities led to an increasing complexity of economic life. The Church, the major upholder of the medieval ethic, found itself less and less able to handle the ethical problems emerging from this development. There were many attempts to come to terms with them, but doctrinally and administratively, all attempts returned to a reaffirmation of the traditional core of belief: that economic activity must be controlled and/or repressed.

Economic and noneconomic pressures on both Church and European societies intensified in the 14th and 15th centuries. Externally, as we have seen, there was an increase in wealth and trade, a rise of new commercial classes in the towns, a growth of nationalism and a growth of secularism in general. Internally, the Church was split by the crises threatening the position of the pope and the weakness of its own administrative system. This internal weakness showed in its inability to deal with a specifically religious question, the growth and persistence of heresy, as well as the wider questions being raised with the passage of time.

Timing of the Protestant Reformation

By the 16th century, the Church had declined as an institution, and its unquestioned authority over temporal matters weakened. This weakness as well as those secular changes that were pushing up against the inherently conservative limits of feudal thinking help explain the *timing* of the Protestant movement.

Some earlier aspects that also contributed to a distancing of the Church from control over everyday life can be found in previous religious protests. They were denounced by the Church as heresy. For example, the Spiritual Franciscans directly questioned the wealth of the Church and attempted to return ecclesiastics to the practice of strict poverty as exemplified by St. Francis of Assisi. In the 14th century, John Wycliffe (1320-1384) also objected to the vast temporal possessions of the Church and argued that they should be controlled, not by the Church, but by civil governments.

Also important as a forerunner of the strand of individualism that emerged from Puritan doctrine was the Bohemian, John Hus. In 1414, when asked to abjure his "heresy," he chose instead to reaffirm his stand, which was a personal belief based on Scripture, rather than submit to the authority of the Church. The idea of the importance of an *individual* religious experience can also be seen in the growth of mysticism. This was a spiritual reaction against both scholastic rationalism and the external encumbrances that had increasingly come to characterize religious practice at this time.

The opportunities for Church authorities to abuse the Church's role as intermediary between God and humans ironically became greater as material wealth increased. This was possible because of a fundamental doctrine of faith: A divinely established Church was the instrument enabling sinful human beings to attain salvation. All humans were seen as inherently sinful, so faith, participation in the Church's sacraments, and good works would gain a penitent believer salvation. But over time, the Church had developed the practice of issuing indulgences that remitted at least part of the punishment for sins. Originally these were issued only after performance of acts showing true repentance; later on, the acts required were much simpler. Later still, and this was what would stir Luther to action, they could be bought for money, a clear indication that the Church was abusing its special role as intermediary. In fact, the earliest reformers opposed both forms of corruption: The corruption of society made possible by the growth of material wealth and the corruption of the Church.

Martin Luther and John Calvin

Martin Luther (1483–1546) was the first major "protester," because he was incensed by the glaring abuses of the sale of indulgences in Wittenberg (in Germany) in 1517. These were sold for several reasons. First, the current pope, Leo X, wanted money in order to rebuild St. Peter's Basilica in Rome. Second, the secular ruler, Albert of Hohenzollern, also needed money in order to repay a debt he owed to the banking house of Fuggers. (This debt was incurred as the result of another ecclesiastical abuse—Albert had borrowed to finance the purchase of a dispensation permitting him to hold three bishoprics simultaneously.) So there was a natural harmony of interest here: Albert permitted the sale of indulgences in return for a 50-percent share in the revenues. Luther protested this corruption, based

---

Indulgence
remission of temporal punishment for a sin

---

on the premise that the Church as intermediary was unnecessary. His position was that man could be saved only by faith in God's infinite mercy and not by trying to offset sin by accumulating credits for good works in God's account book.

Luther's teachings can be seen not only as antiCatholic, but also as anticapitalist. The former is clear in his attempts to return to the innocence of early Christianity—to simplify and purify religious belief and practice, through a very rigorous, uncluttered simple life and religious ritual. They are anticapitalist in the sense that he opposed the idea that all things—including the salvation of souls—have their price. Hence he distrusted the commercial way of life with its emphasis on gaining wealth, and favored a return to a more medieval view of society where all aspects of life would once more become regulated in accordance with divine law.

Luther's ideas found a ready audience among the peasants of north and central Germany, who, inspired by his teaching, attempted to seize Church property, demand the abolition of serfdom, and require the payment of wages for work. (Luther praised the honorability of labor.) But the 1524 peasants' revolt against powerful vested interests such as the Church, temporal princes, and the landlords was vigorously and bloodily put down with a death toll of 50,000. Luther himself supported the princes. He opposed the sort of drastic social change that the peasants were demanding, and his influence on them weakened as a result.

But between 1520 and 1555, Lutheranism did gain followers, leading to an important development in Church-state relationships, which further showed the weakness of the Catholic Church in retaining hold on all aspects of temporal life. At this time, the two leading European powers, France and Spain, were also engaged in a power struggle for domination over Europe. Charles I of Spain came from the ruling Hapsburg family, which controlled immense holdings in Spain, Italy, America, and Germany. In 1520, when he was also crowned Emperor of the Holy Roman Empire (as Charles V), he found himself facing opposition from the German princes and towns, some of whom were Lutheran, all of whom wanted more rights over government, and all opposed any taxes that would increase Charles' power at their expense. Charles vacillated between attempts to suppress Lutheranism and reconciliation, but in 1529 he ordered that all laws against heretics must be enforced. The Lutheran princes strongly and forcefully protested. Charles was distracted by his many other problems outside Germany and finally agreed to their demands in the Peace of Augsburg, 1555. Its most relevant provisions were that each German ruler was free to decide which religion would be practiced in his state, Catholicism or Lutheranism (no other form of Protestantism was permitted), but that no Lutheran in a German state would be forced to become Catholic. The Peace showed that the Roman Catholic Church and its most prominent supporters were unable to turn back the tide of religious changes, no matter how hard they tried.

Two separate conclusions are relevant: First, the Church's weakness can be seen as the outcome of a political power struggle between temporal rulers and the Church. Second, although the Peace can also be seen as the beginning of "religious freedom," this concept should not be interpreted in a 19th or 20th century way. At that time, it simply meant that the *state* had the freedom to determine which religion its subjects would practice. Put this way, it can be seen quite clearly as a logical outcome of the developing nationalism covered in the previous chapter. It is also connected to the desire (and ability) of secular rulers to gain material wealth, which will be covered in the succeeding chapters. Depending on the outcome of this Church-state struggle, mercantilist policies in the 17th and 18th centuries differed both in their application and in their outcome.

A much more rigorous, cohesive, and powerful Protestantism emerged with the teachings of John Calvin (1509—1564). Calvin was born in France but left for Switzerland after formulating his position. France was a unified, strong power, and still solidly Catholic, so he would have found considerable difficulty in achieving the same influence as did Luther in Germany. (France in fact suffered through a series of religious wars with the Huguenot followers of Calvin between 1560 and 1593, and through either death or forced emigration, successfully repressed Protestantism.) As Calvin is chiefly responsible for the religious ideas that developed into what has been called the capitalist ethic, further consideration will be given in the second half of this chapter.

Anglicanism

A second, doctrinally weaker strand of Protestantism emerged in England, not so much for religious reasons, as with Luther and Calvin, but rather for political expediency. (Later, in the 17th century, the Protestant Anglican Church in Britain would find itself the prevailing orthodoxy. At that time, the British Dissenters or Nonconformists, as the followers of Calvin were called, were dissenting against Anglicanism rather than Catholicism.)

Henry VIII (reigned 1509–1547) was the major actor in this split. He was the son of Henry VII, founder of the Tudor dynasty who had successfully pacified England after the War of the Roses (a civil war fought between rivals for the throne), and had been instrumental in developing the idea of a strong, centralized national government. Henry VIII himself was a religious conservative and had maintained close relationships with Rome. Pope Leo X had in fact conferred the title of "Defender of the Faith" on him—ironically, British monarchs still hold this title. However, marital problems stood in the way of continuing close relations between them, and so between England and Rome.

These arose because his first wife, Catherine of Aragon, although she bore many children, was unable to produce a living son. (Catherine's only offspring to survive to adulthood was a daughter, Mary, who did eventually succeed her father.) Henry wanted to remarry in the hopes of producing a son and heir, and so demanded that the Pope annul his marriage to Catherine to permit this. Naturally, the Pope refused, and in 1531 Henry forced the clergy in England to recognize him and not the Pope as the supreme head of the Church in England. (This was reaffirmed in 1534, after passage of the Act of Supremacy making the monarch the temporal head of the Church in England.) At the same time, Parliament authorized an end to all payments to Rome, and in addition made appointments as bishops the prerogative of the Crown. This was a clear indication of the totality of the split, as it involved a renunciation of both the religious and political authority of the Church in Rome.

Henry, it has been said, was a schismatic but not a heretic, and Anglicanism retains most of the major points of Catholic doctrine with the exception of agreement on the position of the Pope. This was to have importance for the subsequent development of Puritanism in Britain.

Secular Implications

A second important aspect of this split was even more crucial for the practical development of capitalism in Britain and will be further elaborated in a later chapter. As Henry wanted to eliminate all occasions for possible divided loyalties in Britain, he suppressed (abolished) the existing monasteries and confiscated their property. Motivated also by a pressing need for finances, monastery property was given to court favorites for financial considerations or sold. Two important results occurred. First, it created a new class of rich nobles and landed gentry whose wealth was based on land. Unlike the older landed aristocracy, many of them saw land as an income-producing asset to be actively used and not as a God-given gift that had an integral role to play in their way of life. This shows the beginnings of the adoption of capitalist principles as applied to land ownership—a totally new development—and marks the start of a market in land, a reversal of customary social relationships, and a dramatic alteration in the social and economic life in England not matched anywhere else in Europe. For so long as both lord and serf were part of an intact manor, lords had every interest in keeping serfs on the land. But increasingly, a conflict of interest appeared. With the growth of a domestic wool industry added to a debased money, landowners, especially those near the growing textile centers in the south and midlands, had every incentive to find ways to get rid of serfs so that they could convert their lands to profitable sheepraising pastures—a topic that will be taken up in a later chapter.

Moreover, suppression of the monasteries reinforced the trend toward a strong, centralized national government, as well as the religious changes that were by now being accepted by most of the population. The newly wealthy supported the Crown—their benefactor—and were also committed to the new religious situation. They would not have become wealthy unless they had supported Henry.

Continuing Upheaval

However, this change did not occur without opposition, which lasted into the 17th century, depending on which monarch ruled. When Edward VI succeeded his father, the country moved closer to Protestantism. As he was still a child, he was heavily influenced by his Protestant advisors, and during his brief reign, religious freedom increased. But on his death in 1553, he was succeeded by his older half sister Mary, who was determined to restore Catholicism. During her reign, there was heavy repression of Protestant churchmen, and many fled to Germany or Geneva. (Ironically, this had an unexpected consequence. When they returned, they had more extreme Protestant views as a result of their stay in the centers of Protestantism.

The country reversed again when Elizabeth I succeeded her half-sister in 1558 and proceeded to undo all of Mary's work, including the repeal of all laws that had attempted to restore Catholicism. At first, Catholics were repressed, but as an unexpected result of political rivalry between Spain and England, a greater degree of religious tolerance existed later in Elizabeth's reign.

This resulted from the failure of Spanish attacks on England, which culminated in the Great Armada of 1588. This massive Spanish fleet of ships sent to conquer England and claim the English throne was defeated by the English navy (and adverse weather conditions) as it approached the coast of England. Once the Spanish threat was removed, and as most English Catholics had supported their country before their religion, freedom of *private* worship became official law, although other forms of discrimination against non-Anglicans persisted.

At the end of this period of religious upheaval, there was a much greater degree of religious peace and tolerance. Most believed, in common with many of the German states, that it was the right of a ruler to dictate the religious beliefs of the nation's subjects, and given an external threat, it was right to support royal authority to prevent aggression and disorder. The numbers of those holding extreme Protestant views increased, but, while both Catholics and Puritans were prevented from holding certain public offices, the tradition of religious tolerance was slowly being established. However, the Anglican Church itself was by no means a homogenous unit. Within its ranks were those committed to more or less extreme Puritanical views, so that while England was officially a Protestant country, there would continue to be a struggle over precisely *which* aspects of Protestantism to emphasize. This had an impact in the Royalist-Parliamentarian Civil War of the 17th century, although a more important reason

for that war was a more down-to-earth power struggle.

Protestantism and the New Value System

Moneymaking activities were not new, and neither was the desire for material wealth. Many individuals throughout history have provided examples of an intensely acquisitive nature—such as pirates or tax collectors—while many activities such as waging wars have also provided wealth (for the victors). These activities generally showed a disregard of traditional ethical values, especially if an alien group was the one providing the wealth. But, as we have seen, such activities are not characteristic of capitalistic activity as such, which is based on the *rational* pursuit of gain, not merely the acquisition of windfalls. In addition, individuals motivated by what has been called the capitalist ethic could not by themselves establish a new economic order in which this ethic is universally accepted. After all, the development of finance capital occurred first in the cities of northern Italy, and the great fortunes of those banking families show they were successful. But then the center of capitalist activity shifted north and west, and the failure of Italian capitalism to live up to its earlier promise has been explained by the strength of the Counter-Reformation, which successfully reasserted Church-approved limits on the expansion of economic activity. The link between the development of a new value system that encourages intense economic activity and the universal acceptance of that activity that makes possible its further spread owes much to certain principles of Protestant doctrine.

At first, this link seems strange, because up until this time, intense religious belief and intense economic activity were thought to be mutually incompatible, as they had been in feudal times. However, it was precisely the new commercial classes who embraced Protestantism—even at a time when the rigid control Catholicism held over economic life was weakening. But there are aspects of Protestantism that did provide incentives encouraging the rational pursuit of economic gain, giving a *positive* value to worldly activities.

Later, its specifically Protestant nature wore thin, as the very result of worldly success undermined the ascetic way of life. But by that time, the ideas of planning and self control were no longer attributes only of individuals belonging to particular religious sects—they had become characteristic of entire classes and societies. This further implied that while the earlier generations of Puritans *wanted* to work, later ones were forced into the capitalist mold—there was no turning back. By then, the capitalist ethic had lost its original religious sanction and become simply a bourgeois ethic: Religious belief was no longer a barrier to the new type of economic activity.

Predestination

Calvinism and the Calvinist idea of predestination provided this positive justification. Two major effects can easily be identified. First, Calvinism encouraged the development of a capitalist character that was dedicated to hard, unremitting work. (Originally, this dedication was seen as equivalent to a dedication to religious life.) The second major effect was the influence on the correct uses of wealth. Calvinism did not approve of a luxurious life style, so the wealth achieved as a result of the first effect could not be used in a self-indulgent way, but rather should be accumulated and used productively. Together, these gave respectability to material improvement achieved as a result of economic growth.

These ideas represented a reversal of previous religious teaching. They also led to the conception of society as a mechanism, not as an organism as it had been in medieval times. This concept led to

Predestination

doctrine that God has preordained which souls shall be saved

Social ethic

generally accepted set of values giving justification to behavior patterns

the idea of an economy separate from religious criticism and control. It also led indirectly to the idea that the state's justification comes from natural, not divine, laws, and thus that the function of the state is to protect individuals in the pursuit of those natural rights.

The early reformers were attempting to simplify and purify religion and religious practices—in large part, they were as opposed to the corruption they saw in society as to the corruption of the Church. However, Calvin, while also trying to purify the individual and construct a state that would once more become subject to the influence of religion, accepted more of the economic changes that were becoming prevalent. So partly because of this acceptance, and partly because Calvinist theology was much more comprehensive and structured than Luther's, Calvinist principles were much more influential.

Acceptability of Commercial Activity

Calvin started with the assumption that the by now more advanced economic organization was not, *per se*, an aberration, which led on to the idea that trade and commerce were respectable. They were respectable, said Calvin, because it was the merchant's own diligence that created his profits, and diligence is a virtue. This was obviously a very appealing statement to those to whom the traditional scheme of social ethics, which despised money making, was irrelevant. Further, it was not economic motives that were incompatible with spiritual life but their misuse for self-indulgent purposes.

Calvinism

religious doctrines associated with the teachings of John Calvin

The practical applications of this teaching emerge from Calvin's theological premise. The starting point was the idea of predestination: Some people (the elect) are chosen by God for salvation, while others are not. (This contrasts with traditional Catholic teaching, which holds that salvation can be attained through faith, participation in the Church's sacraments, and good works.) Thus there is nothing an individual can do to alter God's decision, and so the purpose of life is not to achieve salvation, because that has been determined in advance, but rather to lead a life that glorifies God. No one can question God's decisions—to do so not only would be presumptuous but would also show a lack of faith.

This turns religion into a much more personal thing; no earthly intermediary between individual and God is really necessary, hence there is no role for the Church. In addition, there is no need for participation in the sacraments as a means of attaining salvation. The outlook for the true believer must thus seem somewhat bleak.

Economic Implications: Work and Wealth

This is where the practical aspects of Calvinism were important, not only for theological reasons, but also for their effect on economic change and individual psychology. Two possible strands of reasoning are relevant here. On the one hand, true believers wanted to believe that they were among the chosen, because any doubt would be seen as succumbing to the temptations of the devil. However, it is also possible to reason that they really could not know with any certainty whether or not they had been chosen; therefore each one, given that nagging uncertainty, must act as if it were so. The end result is the same in either case. Because the chosen, by definition, are diligent, hard work and active involvement in temporal activities not only provided self confidence but were seen as proof that salvation had been granted. The conscientious discharge of this duty to work is a *religious* virtue; it is genuine faith that produces

the work that then becomes the good, or holy, life. This type of work was seen as a calling, and to work in it had positive aspects.

First, hard work enabled a person to avoid temptations such as doubt, and to avoid a waste of time, because time spent not working was time spent not glorifying God. (From this idea derives the popular expression, "the devil makes work for idle hands.") A second positive aspect appeared because if work was the means by which every human was proved to be one of the elect, the results were visible to permit a judgment. This effectively justified profits and wealth, which were the visible end results that could be measured. Furthermore, the more wealth an individual acquired, the more worthy the individual obviously was.

Code of Conduct

The code of conduct the ideal Christian lived by displayed the qualities of thrift, diligence, sobriety, and frugality that were admirably suited to achieve economic success. There are many examples of the plainliving characteristics of this new Christian. For example, plain clothing was the mark of the Puritan: "Quaker grey" was a term used to describe not only a color, but the entire personal appearance of Quakers, one example of a Protestant sect. Also, during the English Civil War of the 17th century, the two armies were the Parliamentarian Roundheads, Puritan followers of Oliver Cromwell, and the Cavaliers, Royalist supporters of the Stuart monarch, Charles I. The Roundheads acquired that name not only because they dressed simply, but also because their hair was short, cropped close to the head. This was an obvious contrast to the lace-adorned fine clothing of Cavalier officers and the long flowing curls that marked Cavalier men's hairstyles of that period.

As the results of economic success could not be wasted in idle, luxurious living, the only option left was to use it to accumulate more wealth. Not only profit making became acceptable: Calvinism would also have an impact later on justifying the work of the growing propertyless classes. That is, if hard, unremitting work was decreed by God as a means of gaining certainty of salvation, then impersonal, mechanical labor for low wages in exploitative conditions, as well as self-directed labor, also gained religious sanction.

Personal Responsibility vs. Social Reconstruction

It is also possible to distinguish two separate strands of Calvinism: the insistence on *personal* responsibility and discipline, and the desire to construct a society containing those institutions that would permit the development of the ideal Christian character. These two strands were not always, or even necessarily, found at the same time or in the same place. Thus, the first tended to predominate in places where Calvinists were in a minority, as in England, and is more directly associated with the new capitalist classes. The second tended to be found in places where Calvinists were a majority, as in the theocracies of colonial New England or Geneva, and where they had the ability to shape social institutions. In these places, it is clear that the laws, rules, and social sanctions were intended to produce the frugal, plain-living Christian. Thus, there was much greater involvement of the social authorities. This involvement included regulating prices and wages, dealing with idleness, attacking personal ostentation, and prohibiting gambling and drunkenness, for example.

From the first strand can be seen the origins of the separation of economics and ethics, and of economic individualism, which would become enshrined by the late 18th century as the economic principle of laissez faire. This was slow to occur. As we have seen, the earliest reformers tried to reassert religious control over material life; however, this led to a problem where the calls for Christian charity conflicted with the potential gains from capitalist activity. This conflict alone

was not enough to produce the separation of ethics from economics. This separation occurred also as a result of inherent aspects of Protestant doctrine, in particular the encouragement given to rational analysis, which implied an ability to learn about and uncover God's truth. But unlike either blind faith or the "inner search" favored by the mystics as a way to salvation, this learning process went in a different direction. A believer could try to uncover divine laws by looking at the results of God's creation, the visible world. That is, if something happened, there must be reason for it. This principle evolved into the idea of *natural* law regulating the world, which gave the go-ahead for the scientific discoveries of later centuries. But most important for our purposes here, removing ethics from economics can happen only when there is an alternative way of explaining society, natural law. For so long as explanations are religious, then all material activity must be ethical, in keeping with religious principles.

Puritanism

The growth of Puritanism in England to include such sects as Quakers in particular and Nonconformists or Dissenters in general had more influence on capitalist development there than the earlier "English Reformation" associated with Henry VIII. This is because it appealed precisely to those industrial and commercial classes who were at the vanguard of economic changes. One reason that they were active in these new capitalist activities is because of continued discrimination against them. That is, because certain positions connected with the exercise of power were closed to them because of their faith, there were greater incentives forcing them into new types of activity

Dissenter (Nonconformist)

Protestant who does not accept the doctrines of the established Church (especially the Anglican Church in England)

where these prohibitions did not apply. However, by the end of the 17th century, these groups were on the whole incorporated into the wealthy, ruling class.

Puritanism in England initially appealed to those who were financially independent, town dwellers and some freeholding farmers in the eastern countries especially. This group of financially independent people formed a larger percentage of the population in the 17th century than later, partly because of the further changes that were to take place in the 18th century. These changes were due to the very success of capitalist activity that would also create a large, propertyless, permanent wage earning class. But their rise to wealth was resented by the older, more conservative aristocracy, who were part of the Anglican establishment and who opposed the new classes for religious as well as economic reasons.

In 17th century England, no public dissent from the State church was possible, but later, pressure from Nonconformists led to a much greater degree of religious tolerance. Influenced by Calvin, economic behavior at this time was subject to personal responsibility. The good Christian must not engage in obvious extortion and must conduct business in a responsible way. However, partly as a result of an inability to crystallize this code of conduct into a society-wide set of rules and institutions, the Puritan's self-sufficiency was increased at the expense of the idea of social solidarity. This represented a contrast both to the feudal ethic and to the idea of the authoritarian state that had emerged with the Tudor monarchy.

The idea of self-sufficiency became widespread in later centuries, when it was no longer confined to Puritans. The stress on individualism in religion led to an individual morality and to the idea of a withdrawal of social responsibility. This will become apparent when later 17th and 18th century developments are discussed. For example, its impact on social policy was to see poverty as a punishment for sin and not as a result of some social or economic cause. This led to the practical conclusion that poverty and its manifestations should be punished and not alleviated by the society. Removing the ethical component also implied that such horrendous activities as the slave trade or such socially divisive actions as enclosures could be judged purely in terms of their profitability.

Summary

Religious upheavals in the 16th century led to the Protestant Reformation, which, especially in its Calvinist offshoots, provided both justification for economic activity geared to profit making and capital accumulation, and rules for personal conduct that all but guaranteed practical success. That is, what had previously been seen as an example of sin and human frailty now became a religious virtue. Those places that combined both capitalist activity and Protestantism—Britain and the Netherlands—took over the leadership of the economic world. However, in time, the qualities needed for success in capitalist activity were no longer confined to just a few select groups but had become part of the way of life of the capitalist classes in all countries.

Key Concepts

Capitalist ethic
Dissenter
Indulgence
Landed gentry

Nonconformist
Predestination
Social ethic

Questions for Discussion or Essay Writing

1. How important is a value system to a society's economic development?

2. How can the timing of the Protestant Reformation be explained?

3. What are the implications for future economic and political development resulting from Protestants being in either a majority or in a minority situation?

4. How did Calvin's visualization of the ideal Christian character contribute to the capital accumulation process?

5. Martin Luther's theology had an anticapitalist element. Explain.

6. How did Henry VIII's suppression of the monasteries in England affect the extension of market relationships to land?

7. In what way does Calvin's teaching legitimize commercial activity?

For Further Reading

Klassen, Peter J. *Europe in the Reformation*. Englewood Cliffs, N.J: Prentice-Hall, 1979.

O'Brien, George A.T. *An Essay on the Economic Effects of the Reformation*, N.Y: A.M. Kelley, (1923) 1970.

Robertson, H.M. *Aspects of the Rise of Economic Individualism: A Criticism of Max Weber and His School*. N.Y: Kelley and Millman (1933) 1959.

Spitz, Lewis W., ed. *The Reformation: Basic Interpretations*, 2nd ed. Lexington, Mass: D.C. Heath, 1972.

Tawney, Richard H. *Religion and the Rise of Capitalism*. Magnolia, Mass: Peter Smith, 1926.

Weber, Max. *The Protestant Ethic and the Spirit of Capitalism*. N.Y: Charles Scribners' Sons, 1958.

White, Lynn, Jr. *Medieval Religion and Technology: Collected Essays*. Berkeley, Cal: University of California Press (Center for Medieval and Renaissance Studies), 1978.

Chapter 6

Mercantilism: Internal Aspects

EUROPE IN THE 16TH CENTURY was characterized by continued commercial expansion, stronger, more centralized national governments, and an increasing acceptance of capitalist principles by a small, but influential, class of people. However, for most people, except in England in some areas, life did not change too much. Farming using centuries-old techniques was still the predominant life style, and contact with the new ways and the new classes through the growth of markets was still only occasional and secondary. The framework for a capitalist market economy was only just being put into place, and capitalist institutions were still at an early stage of development.

In other words, the transition to a capitalist economic system was in the beginning phases. Some vital ingredients were missing. They included a large class of permanent wage earners and production along capitalist lines (just beginning in agriculture in some countries, and mostly non existent outside a few export industries). The most important lack was a general environment—social, political, legal—that was favorable to and supportive of the capital accumulation process.

While it is true that some ingredients can be provided by suitably motivated individuals—for example, an individual capitalist can overcome capital scarcity by borrowing—the scale of the problem must also be taken into account. Private individuals, even acting as a group, cannot alone create that favorable environment, an adequate supply of labor, or even a general capital availability, and all these are needed for continued success. These are the problems that can be tackled only on a national basis.

The implicit recognition of these problems led to policies that have been called mercantilist, which can describe both the policies used to achieve certain goals and also the body of thought justifying them. How these policies were applied and how they contributed to the process of economic transformation will be covered in the next three chapters. The first two will cover mercantilist policies in general terms. However, one result of mercantilism is that the development path of the European countries began to diverge. These countries were more or less similar in the structure of their economies and with respect to the standard of living at the end of the 15th century. But this was no longer true by the end of the 18th century. Partly as a result of the success of mercantilist policies, Britain and the Netherlands in particular began to take on many more aspects of a market economy. The final chapter of this three-chapter sequence will describe the developments that took place in England in the 16th century that also helped account for this divergence. These were the enclosures, part of the process that preceded industrialization along capitalist lines in England. As mercantilist policies themselves help create a favorable environment for capitalist industrialization, the period from the 16th to the 18th centuries can be seen as laying a foundation for subsequent economic development.

Premise: Increase the Wealth of the Nation

The central premise—indeed the central premise of any set of national economic policies—was to increase the wealth of the nation. Mercantilist thinkers attempted to explain what made up this wealth, so that suitable policies could be adopted to help the process along. While mercantilist thought and practice did not constitute a completely homogeneous whole and evolved throughout the 16th, 17th, and 18th centuries, certain common elements are clear. To Spain, *the* dominant European power in the 16th century, and Portugal, gaining wealth through overseas colonization was important. Both played leading roles in the voyages of discovery and Portugal, for a time, successfully monopolized trade to much of the East, replacing Venice. However, while the first phase of mercantilist doctrine is clearly linked to the overseas orientation of these two countries, the final phases owe much more to the domestic production orientation of France and England. These two countries were not major participants in the initial phase of expansion of European influence into either the New World or the Orient, but emerged into dominant positions in the 17th and 18th centuries.

Mercantilists thought that a strong nation—strong militarily as well as economically—was self-sufficient, so that no rival country could cut off vital imported food or military supplies. This was important, as these were not peaceful times for the European nations. It was accepted that the political powers of the state be used to further economic interests to achieve this goal.

Mercantilist Policymaking

Political authorities have always been interested in their economies, and have always tried to encourage "desirable" economic activities. What is thought to be desirable depends on the value system and the balance of power existing at different times and in different places. At this time, national governments' actions were simply an extension of what late medieval towns had been trying to do previously on a local scale. In this sense, mercantilism can be seen as economic state-building.

What determines the aims and actions of the political authorities? The type of state to be built, and therefore the exact nature of mercantilist economic policies, depended on the outcome of political struggle. Although monarchs had gained power at the expense of feudal nobility, a third group, the new commercial class, entered the picture as it attempted to gain political power to strengthen its economic gains. The outcome of this three-way struggle led to three different patterns of mercantilist policy.

In those countries where the monarchs gained total control over the nobility in their push for national unification, and where the commercial class remained weak, mercantilism remained in its earliest, bullionist phase. For example, in Spain and Portugal domestic industry received little encouragement.

A second variation appeared in France where the economic development of the commercial bourgeoisie was supported, but the nobility was weakened and political power remained concentrated in the hands of the Crown. Here, trade and commercial activities were encouraged, but there was no power sharing. This was an unstable outcome, however, leading to a violent denouement in the French Revolution at the end of the 18th century.

Finally, a third variation emerged in England and Holland, where, although monarchs gained power over the feudal nobility, by the 17th century they were increasingly forced to share that power with the new commercial classes. Hence the operation of mercantilist policies in these countries was more oriented to assisting the economic interests of the merchant class.

If the landed nobility retained its hold on power, as in Germany for example, conditions for applying mercantilist policies were unfavorable. The result was only limited development of commercial capitalism in a few areas, with even less encouragement given to development of the economy's productive capacity.

In summary, although mercantilist policies aimed to increase "the nation's wealth," this did not result in a generalized increase in well-being; the monarch and/or the commercial class gained. State power and collective resources were used to implement policies, which presupposed the existence of a unified state able to wield power within its borders, and helps explain the timing of the mercantilist phase of development. And as also noted, there was a close link with military power, seen in the economic aim of self-sufficiency—a country with sufficient domestic production capacity to meet its own needs could not be held to ransom by a foreign rival. This is a more powerful motive than just simply increasing "wealth" in the nation's treasury in order to finance an army. When successful, mercantilist policies were associated with an expansion of national power and prestige.

Figure 6.1   Increasing prosperity made it possible for house interiors to show their owners' wealth. In this painting, *Woman with Child*, by Pieter de Hooch, the floor is tiled, the windows have glass in them and can be opened, and there is a painting on the wall. (By permission of Rijksmuseum-Stichting)

Infrastructure Building

While it became fashionable to criticize mercantilism and mercantilist policies from the time of Adam Smith onwards (Smith, incidentally, was the first to use the term *mercantilist*), it is important to realize the role they played in the development of a capitalist system. As we have already seen, capitalist thinking had changed commercial and trading activities but had barely begun to influence production activities. What held up development in these areas was the lack of many facilities we now take for granted. For example, there were no free, open national markets; there were no uniform monetary systems; transportation was still slow and difficult; and communications were primitive. These and other missing elements, including the lack of a free labor force, could not be remedied by individual investment or individual action.

A more technical way of expressing this situation is to say there was a lack of social overhead capital or infrastructure. These are the basic underpinnings of a developed, modern economy that must be in place before private capital will see an opportunity for profits. Such things as roads, harbors, education, and communications networks, for example, are called "capital" because they require investment—use of productive resources—and last for a long time. They are called "overhead" because they are indirectly productive; these facilities must be in place before private capital can be used productively. And they are called "social" because the funds involved are beyond the reach of any one individual, and provision of them has traditionally been made by public authorities.

Previously, we have seen how the Protestant ethic helped the capital accumulation process by

Infrastructure

Indirectly productive facilities usually provided by governments, such as roads and communications networks

encouraging a simple life style; thrift helped individuals accumulate funds. Chapter 8 will show how the development of the wool processing industry in England, a private undertaking, adapted to capital scarcity by "sharing" capital expenditures between merchant-capitalists and workers. But when the focus of attention is on the broader capital scarcity that was evident in the lack of infrastructure, another remedy was needed, because individual thrift and individual effort were insufficient to meet the much larger need for resources for investment purposes. Once national governments take it on themselves to make good these deficiencies, one way that resources can be diverted into investment uses is to limit consumption, and sometimes this was done by limiting wages. Alternatively, as we will see in Chapter 7, more resources can be gained if one country can exploit and appropriate wealth from another.

Of course, to the degree that mercantilist policies are successful, the constraint of limited resources (especially scarce capital) becomes less pressing. Once infrastructure is in place, private capitalist activity can flourish, and the success of mercantilist policies parallels the redefinition of directly productive capital. In earlier times, productive capital was chiefly in the form of improved land or buildings; when the concept of capital is broadened to include productive equipment, then output can be increased at a faster rate. Again, we see the link with the wealth-as-money concept: The more money capitalists have, the easier it is for them to acquire this productive equipment and thus expand output and wealth. So while later critics were correct in stating that mercantilist policies acted as a brake on private activity because they diverted resources away from "best" uses, they miss the point that without them in the earlier phase, little private activity could have, or would have, taken place. The fastest growing countries were also those where mercantilism was most successful—a comparison of England's later development with that of Spain or Portugal makes this perfectly clear.

Mercantilist Philosophy

At first, the goal was to accumulate bullion, gold and silver, not for its own sake but because it was the *measure* of wealth. Practically speaking, this ties in with the desire for military superiority over rival nations: The country with the largest reserves in its treasury will be able to hire the largest number of soldiers and acquire the needed supplies should this rivalry spill over into actual warfare.

Bullionism

This policy of accumulating precious metals is called bullionism. However, the very narrowest expression of bullionism in practice was shortlived, replaced by policies encouraging production. But the central aim, to accumulate gold and silver, remained, even though the methods changed.

In the earliest period, especially in Portugal and Spain, bullionist philosophy translated into encouraging imports of bullion and forbidding exports of bullion. This seemed relatively easy for them, as they had a head start on acquiring colonies in South and Central America, and were busy looting the wealth of the civilizations there to bring back to Europe. (This will be covered in Chapter 7.)

Favorable Balance of Trade

However, trade and its relationship to acquiring bullion was emphasized next. Now policy shifted toward regulating trade and arranging relationships (especially with a country's colonies) to achieve a favorable balance of trade. This exists when a country exports more goods than it imports, with the difference being made up by an inflow of gold or silver. At the time, there was a general idea that the volume of trade was more or less fixed, which was not too silly an idea, given the relatively low level of production. Thus, if a country imported more goods than it exported, the resulting outflow of bullion to its trading partner as payments were made would leave it poorer and weaker. The main difference between this and pure bullionism is not only the greater emphasis on trade but also the relaxation of the prohibition on bullion export. This was permitted on the understanding that it would subsequently make possible the import of raw materials that could be processed and then re-exported for a greater value than the original bullion export.

Balance of Trade
The total value of all exports compared to the total values of all imports

---

Encourage Domestic Production

This gives a clue to the later development of policy: encourage domestic production within a country itself. The result was the production of more goods for export, which helped achieve a favorable balance of trade and thus a bullion inflow. Here, a favorable balance of trade and a bullion inflow was the side effect rather than the main focus of policy, but the end was the same. That is, while the result would still be an increase in money (wealth), the methods used to achieve that result were more varied and sophisticated.

The progression of thinking parallels the successive building-up of a country's economy toward the original end—the accumulation of gold and silver. Also, as time went on, it was seen that the accumulation of sterile (hoarded) funds was not desirable; what was important was that these funds be used in productive investment, hence the encouragement given to real productive development.

However, we see another change at the end of the 18th century, when the heyday of mercantilist thinking was past, to the more modern idea that the wealth of a country is measured not by its

These Engins (which are the best) to quinch great Fires; are

JOHN KEELING Fecit

Figure 6.2 As Towns grew larger and more crowded, the danger of fire grew more urgent. One early fire engine, the Keelings Fire Engine, using people to pump water, is shown here. (Courtesy of the Masters and Fellows of Magdalene College, Cambridge)

accumulation of gold and silver but by its productive capacity. The very success of mercantilism led to the flowering of industrial capitalism in the 19th century; to the extension of capitalist ways over the entire economy; and, ironically, to the restriction of government intervention in the economy itself—because it was no longer needed.

Mercantilism in Practice

So far, we have looked at the changes that occurred in mercantilist thinking in relation to its given end. Another useful way of looking at mercantilist policies is to classify them into two groups: internal and external. Internal or domestic policies were those applied within a country itself. They had the effect of freeing trade domestically, of creating a larger national market, and of encouraging more production within the country. The relevant words here are *free trade* and *infrastructure*.

External policies were those applied to a country's relationships with other countries, either through trading or with its colonial acquisitions. Here, the aim was to regulate trade so as to achieve a favorable balance of trade and to protect the country's own interests. The relevant words here are *regulation* and *protection*. This chapter concentrates on internal mercantilist policies, the following chapter on the external aspects.

A closer look at the internal policies reveals certain common elements. While application varied according to the country involved, any or all of these elements were present.

Infrastructure

As noted before, development of infrastructure was crucial to subsequent production activity. At this time, some roads were reconstructed and improved to speed up overland transportation and thus reduce the cost of shipping goods, which effectively increased the size of the market. A new development at this time was the construction of canals, especially in the Netherlands. Building such artificial waterways provides an excellent example of improving transportation. Up until this time, overland transportation was slow and costly and shipments had to be small because horses were used. Moving goods by canal was still slow, but significantly cheaper, permitting an increase in shipments of goods that had never been shipped in quantity before. In addition, harbors, harbor facilities, bridges, and other facilities were built. The net effect was not only economic but also political, because improved transportation helped unite a country physically.

Tax Reform

A second element was tax reform. Lower taxes, whether on goods or people, reduces costs and so increases the size of the market. This larger market gives an incentive to expand production by using new capitalist techniques that require a higher volume of sales if they are to be profitable.

A discriminatory tax structure could also affect the structure of production. By lowering taxes on or giving subsidies to goods intended for export while imposing high tariffs on competing imports, it was possible to adjust output in keeping with mercantilist goals. However, in many countries, these tax reforms in practice were often superimposed on an existing tax structure, and the result was a mixture of old and new. That mercantilist policies were less consciously designed to

achieve a grand goal and were more a response to specific needs that happened to move toward that goal can be clearly seen in tax policy. For example, in England taxes were used to protect domestic producers and thus encourage industrial production, but the state also took advantage of the growing wealth of the country to impose many more taxes, which often had a reverse effect. There were taxes on land, on wealth, a poll (head) tax, hearth taxes, a tax on windows, houses, births, burials, marriages, and stamp duties. There were even taxes on bachelors, the idea being to encourage early marriage and thus indirectly a growing labor supply. (Although if this was its purpose, it was oddly structured. In 1695, a bachelor duke paid 40 times what a gentleman paid, who in turn was taxed at a rate six times that of a peasant). There were excise taxes on most food and drink products, especially on imported items, which gave rise to a thriving smuggling industry along the south coast that specialized in smuggling brandy into the country from France.

Excise tax

A tax imposed on a specific item

Loans and Tax Exemption

Industry was subject to direct encouragement using loans and tax exemptions. One aim was to maintain quality while expanding quantity, so production techniques were sometimes specified as well. This resulted in many problems later in the period, when the multiplicity of regulations acted as a barrier to the adoption of new technologies. However, to the extent that costs were lowered and risks reduced, new production was encouraged.

France, for example, used loans, privileges, and tax exemptions to help encourage the commercial production of china, tapestries, silks, and linens. One problem, however, was that the market for such luxury products was limited, and scarcity of labor remained a chronic problem.

In England, attempts were made to stimulate the wool industry by giving it favorable tax treatment and encouraging foreign skilled workers to immigrate. In addition, indirect stimulus was sometimes given; for example, the passage of legislation encouraging people to wear wool.

Monopoly Grants

Any new enterprise is always a risky undertaking. At this time, there were few capitalist organizations with a track record to help make others confident enough to take on such a risk. But if a market could be guaranteed, riskiness is reduced and profitability increased, thus providing an incentive for private capital. This was the reasoning behind state grants of monopoly privileges. Most were granted to trading companies; later in the period, industrial companies could get a monopoly for the production of certain items. Among the more beneficial monopolies granted in England in the late 16th century were those given in the glassmaking, paper making, copper mining, and brass manufacturing industries (the last two were important for military reasons).

Monopoly
Situation where one company dominates a market and captures most of its sales

---

However, like anything else, this privilege could be abused. It was abused frequently, as the monarchs had always-pressing needs for revenues, often met by requiring the entrepreneur to pay for the privilege of a monopoly grant. Then, because of the profitability of the monopoly position, potential holders began to see the money they could gain as more important than the project itself, and monopolies became more and more frivolous and less and less helpful to the industrial structure. Some of these included the monopolies for producing playing cards, for printing the Psalms of David, and for making spangles. The advantages taken by the first Stuart monarchs in the granting of monopolies led to a deepseated mistrust of them. Although the granting of industrial monopolies was abolished in 1639, distrust of them persisted for centuries.

Shipping

An important aspect of policy was to encourage the development of a merchant marine. This was done for several reasons that demonstrate the links between the economic and the political sphere at this time. First, if a country's exports or imports were carried in its own ships, its rivals' carriers were left a smaller share of the carrying trade. Second, this policy expanded opportunities for shipowners and ship provisioners, increased employment for crews and harbor workers, and gave incentives to the shipbuilding industry, all good examples of the economy-building aspects of mercantilism. Third, the military aspect was important, especially at this time of rivalry between countries. If more merchant ships were built, they could be converted to military use if needed; thus the size—and cost—of the fighting navy could be kept down during peacetime.

Policies encouraging shipping had the greatest effect in the Netherlands, which dominated the seaways in the 17th century. Although only a tiny country with a population of about 1.5 million at the beginning of the 17th century, by 1660 it was Europe's chief shipper. At that time, there were about 15,000 Dutch ships, compared to between 3,000 to 4,000 ships flying the English flag and 5,000 to 6,000 French ships.

Dutch ships had always been important in the Baltic trade, but increasingly they gained a large share of Europe's trade with the Near East and an important position in trade with the Americas. While her own colonial holdings in the New World were small, and she was specifically excluded from trading with other countries' colonies, this trade nevertheless flourished. The Dutch found it profitable to supply American colonists (illegally, of course) with goods that they were poorly supplied with from their own mother countries.

Labor force

Another problem was how to ensure an adequate supply of free labor for the expansion of capitalist production. This was not something that could easily be addressed by purely mercantilist policies. Only England "answered" the question by forcefully breaking the peasants' ties with the land (see Chapter 8). France tried to create a free labor force by encouraging the immigration of skilled workers, promoting early marriages, subsidizing large families, and punishing begging and idleness. The point was to increase the numbers of those who could not be supported on small peasant holdings, thus forcing them to turn to wage labor. However, the attempt to create surplus agricultural labor did not have success until the 19th century.

Policies controlling labor costs were also tried, especially in England. For example, there was a wages policy, which established maximum wage rates. While successful in holding down wages, it was deeply flawed, and the attempt to fix wages at the national level died out after 1660. The Statute of Artificers (late 16th century) was another attempt to control the supply of labor. It prevented agricultural workers from entering industry and required the unemployed to take on agricultural work. To solve the problems of unemployment resulting from economic fluctuations, it also required all employers to hire for at least one year, and established a maximum wage. But the law could not adapt to changing conditions, particularly the shrinking of agricultural work accompanying the enclosures. While it remained on the Statute Book for another two and a half centuries, it was progressively whittled down, evaded, and distorted.

Money and the Financial Structure

As production and exchange activities increased, so there was a greater need for the parallel development of money and banking to support and facilitate them. At this time, the use of money became both more widespread—there were more market activities requiring its use—and also more complex. We will see the introduction of different ways of transferring wealth as well as new ways of mobilizing capital in its money form.

Two separate although related components of this issue can be examined. First, the question of the national currency related most directly to the internal unification and state building aspects of mercantilism. Second, increasing sophistication of the financial structure, including banking, accompanied the growth of trading and production. At this time, banking and finance were predominantly in private hands, but their development set the stage for more modern financial structures.

Coinage

An adequate supply of coinage became much more important, as there were simply more transactions taking place that required the use of money. But national rulers also had other reasons to be concerned with the nation's currency.

First, a national currency was one more symbol of national unification. Feudal princes had the right to mint their own currency, which had often been taken over or supplemented by others with mint rights. Then national rulers tried to remove these privileges, and to reserve for themselves the monopoly of issuing money. The widespread practice of minting coins with one side showing the ruler's head was a symbolic way of demonstrating national unity—all persons using coins were constantly reminded of the fact that they were subjects of one ruler.

A single currency improved trading possibilities within the country itself and made it possible to see the entire country as one national market. Previously, if different coins circulated in different parts of the country, the problem of knowing their relative values made trading that much more difficult. By standardizing the currency, the task of the merchant was lightened, and there was no longer the extra burden of evaluating the worth of different coins.

Debasement

Second, national monarchs also had an interest in preserving the worth of the currency, so that a coin of a stated value would continue to have that stated value. It is necessary to keep minting new coins both to keep up with a rising demand for them, and also to replace those that simply wear out. However, when national currencies were first introduced, rulers faced another problem: debasement, connected with the issue of separate coinages. Few issuers could resist the temptation to debase the coinage and thus enrich themselves. Feudal princes were not the only ones to debase coins—anyone who handled them also had an opportunity.

Debasement

A decline of the purchasing power of money

Debasement can occur in two ways. In the first, the issuing authority simply adds a cheaper metal to the coin so that its weight is the same, but its intrinsic value in terms of metal (usually gold or silver) is less. The issuer can then keep the "extra" valuable metal for some other use. This type of debasement is harmful when money is specie—when its value for buying and selling purposes depends on the value of the precious metal contained in it. If coins are debased, suppliers of commodities ultimately lose faith in the worth of the currency and demand more coins in exchange for goods, starting an inflationary process. This sort of debasement makes trade using different currencies much riskier, because coins

---

Specie

Coins; money made out of a material (like metal) which has other uses

---

can no longer be weighed to find out how much metal they have in them, to establish a relative value for them.

The second form of debasement is easier to detect, and can be practiced by ordinary people (although it is unlikely that many do). This involves shaving the edges of the coin very slightly and keeping the shavings until enough is collected to be melted down and used for something else. The debaser gains by collecting these shavings and using the coin, which, so long as the shaving is not too obvious, will be exchangeable at its face value, which is now greater than its intrinsic value because it is a lighter coin.

Rulers on the whole protected their currencies, but were not always able to resist the temptation to debase coins by adding metals of lesser value. For example, Henry VIII of England once started an inflationary process by minting debased coins. However, for most of this period, the English pound rarely deviated from its set value in silver.

Mints did come up with a method of producing coins preventing them being shaved or clipped—a method still used today. The edges of coins are milled (put ridges around) thus making it obvious if someone tried to shave it.

Financial Developments

Even when a currency was established on a national basis, and was not subject to debasement, it was insufficient to meet the needs of an expanding economy. The first supplement to coinage was the bill of exchange (see Chapter 4), originally developed by the international merchants. This was ideally suited to such trading, and also gave rise to intermediate lending with the loan itself standing as collateral. This type of loan was made necessary by the expansion of productive activity itself. As enterprises grew from small ones

Was there a single credit market in England?

In the 20th century, developed countries are characterized by a single, national market for credit. How do we know this? A couple of examples should help. If a company wishes to raise money to expand its productive capacity, it is not limited to its previously-accumulated earnings; it can raise capital by selling new shares to investors all over the country. Or a macroeconomic policy decision by government to raise (or lower) long term interest rates will affect borrowers all over the country.

But this situation has not always been the case. When did a unified market for credit appear? And did changes in financial organization (for example, the introduction of innovative financial instruments) have an effect on the changes in the real economy—the new technologies and new forms of organization associated with the Industrial Revolution in England? Moshe Buchinsky and Ben Polak (in "The Emergence of a National Credit Market in England, 1710-1880." *Journal of Economic History*, 53:1 (March 1993), p: 1-24) attempted to answer this question.

In particular, they wanted to find when, and if, developments in London's financial markets affected the development of the woollen textile industry in West Yorkshire. Briefly, they tried to see whether changes in the price of government debt (more or less equivalent to the interest rate) affected local microeconomic decisions about the formation of new real capital. They compared London long-term interest rates (the in-

dependent variable) with information on property transactions (deed registrations, the dependent variable) in two counties, Middlesex in the south and West Yorkshire. The reason for using deed registrations is that they represent the exchange of real capital, and are related to building, which is one form of capital formation. They ran a regression analysis for various subperiods between 1712 and 1880. They found a statistically significant correlation, which supports the contention that the financial and real markets were no longer regional by the end of the 18th century. This result suggests that England was a nationally integrated economy even before the close of the Industrial Revolution.

Many wars also occurred during this time, so the huge demands for government borrowing could have stimulated the creation of an integrated national market for credit, and could also affect building by, for example, raising input prices and depressing confidence. That is, it is possible that rather than economic changes being endogenous—financial and real side changes influencing each other—they could have been influenced by a third factor, government war finance needs in this case. This is a connection that cannot be proved right or wrong; the value of the Buchinsky-Polak study is that through the imaginative use of imperfect data, it lends support to the proposition that the British economy was substantially integrated by 1800.

serving only local markets, more financing was needed; as they grew, the gap between production and sale lengthened, intensifying the need for a liquid source of working capital.

This development once again raised the question of usury—and in England, the strict law against usury was not repealed until 1495. However, the growth of borrowing and lending, whether or not explicitly legal, restated the original question so that it was no longer, Is interest permissible? but rather, At what level should rates be, and should the state enforce them? By 1713, interest rates were 5 percent in England and lower in Holland—much lower than they had been in previous centuries.

Banking

Banking developments followed trade and other economic practices, so that certain towns became important banking centers because they were centrally located for other reasons. Banking became much more of a separate specialty after the 14th century, and by the 16th, elements of what are now modern banking practices were becoming more common. It is also possible to see the origin of some of these practices at this time.

Central banking and the recognition of the necessity to control private financial activities to retain confidence and keep economic activity on a stable basis emerged in Holland. Antwerp (in modern Belgium) had been the leading financial city in Northern Europe, due largely to its central position in the spice, textile, and metals trades, but this position of dominance was claimed after 1585 by Amsterdam. Amsterdam was a great commercial center. It was a port, and at the beginning of the era of the Dutch commercial supremacy, Amsterdam became a thriving wealthy city of merchants and financial specialists.

Central Banking in Amsterdam

However, at the end of the 16th century, the financial situation was chaotic, to say the least. The toll of the struggle for independence against Spain had led to extensive currency debasement, and there was even more confusion caused by the 14 different mints operating. Because it was a center of international exchange, there were merchants and bankers from many countries working with a variety of different currencies, which gave the money changers a field day in their ability to enrich themselves at their customers' expense.

In this confused situation, the city government of Amsterdam, wanting to retain the city's reputation as a leading financial center, established the Bank of Amsterdam in 1609. This was a public bank with its offices and its vaults in the city hall, presumably to increase the physical safety of deposits. The Bank was given certain responsibilities concerning currency (the "issue" functions of a modern central bank) and deposits (functions today associated more with commercial banks). The Bank initially coped with the currency problem by removing all debased coins from circulation, and by providing the various mints with metal to make standardized coins. It coped with the foreign exchange problem by requiring that all bills of exchange above a certain value (600 florins) be payable only at the Bank. In addition, it changed money at official rates. It eased the transfer of funds by accepting deposits. The depositor was charged a fee and all dealers in large bills of exchange had to make deposits at the Bank. Deposits were credited, not just stored, effectively creating bank money. Withdrawals in coin could be made, but were not very common in practice because bank money, a standardized unit of account, was quickly recognized to be worth more than a possibly debased coin. Thus, accompanying the growth of deposits was the practice of settling debts by transferring funds from one account to another—a purely bookkeeping transaction.

Officially, the Bank was not supposed to make loans—but it did make secret loans to the Dutch East India Company, a monopoly trading company, and to the City of Amsterdam, including the municipal pawnshop. The association with the East India Company, however, lasted only for so long as the Company lasted. When it failed, the Bank collapsed too, and officially ceased to exist after 1819.

Paper Money: Bank Notes

Later in the 17th century the concept of bank paper money emerged more fully. In 1661, the Bank of Stockholm in Sweden went one step further than simply transferring funds from one account to another by issuing its own "promises to pay" that could be used for making payments. These bank notes were printed, another example of the trend to standardizing previously differentiated practices. But what was more important was that they represented the beginning of modern fractional reserve banking: The Bank could extend credit by issuing paper bank notes worth more than was on deposit in metal. That is, the Bank knew that only a few depositors would withdraw actual coins, so it could loan out the rest of the deposits. These loans were not made in coins, but in paper. While each paper bank note could theoretically represent an equivalent amount of coins, this became less true over time. Knowing customers' demands for actual coins, banks could issue a much larger volume of paper, only a fraction of which was backed up by metal.

Bank Note

Paper money issued by a private bank

Paper money reached further levels of sophistication in England. While banking in England during the 13th and 14th centuries had been dominated by the Italian Lombard bankers, increasing xenophobia resulted in their expulsion by Elizabeth I. After this, banking practices were largely adjunct to other types of activity. For example, merchants, scriveners, and goldsmiths all accepted money from others for safekeeping, made loans, and transferred money. Merchants became involved because they constantly dealt in large sums of money. Scriveners (forerunners of today's notaries) were important in commercial affairs and drew up bills of exchange, so attracting "banking" clients because of their legal expertise. Goldsmiths were a natural choice for the safekeeping of money because of their association with precious metals, and they often made loans, too.

Scrivener

A person who prepares documents and draws up contracts

Initially in the 16th century, merchants and scriveners were more important in making loans, transferring money, and dealing with foreign exchange. They often took excess funds over and above what was needed for daily transactions to the Royal Mint for safety. But this was their eventual downfall, as the perennial financial needs of the Stuart kings plus their belief in absolutism led Charles I, in 1640, to refuse to return these deposits until he had been given a loan. This eliminated the role of scriveners as bankers. Customers lacked confidence in them if the monarch could appropriate their deposits. Instead, funds were left with the goldsmiths for safekeeping, and their role as bankers expanded.

Checks

Goldsmiths made both straight loans and discounted bills of exchange, and also initiated something new: the modern check. Depositors could withdraw their funds as cash, but they could also write notes (checks) to the goldsmith-bank authorizing payment to another party—that is, they could transfer deposits to another person. In addition, goldsmiths' receipts for money deposited with them, which represented a goldsmith's "promise to pay the bearer" were another early form of the modern bank note, and were frequently given to depositors who wished to withdraw funds but were willing to forgo withdrawing actual cash. Such bank notes are distinguished from checks because they are not addressed to anyone in particular. They circulated as currency because of confidence in the goldsmiths' ability to live up to their promise and pay cash on demand.

Banking in England

However, the development of banking in England did not follow a steady evolutionary path, and later in the 17th century, the goldsmith banks were to collapse like so many before them. This collapse followed the Restoration of the monarchy, when Charles II was restored to the throne in 1660. He returned with many debts. Some debts were personal; other funds were needed to pay back pay to soldiers. But Parliament had successfully acquired control over taxing and the revenues to be allotted to the sovereign, and was slow to grant funds. So Charles borrowed from the goldsmiths, joining many merchants and landowners as debtors to them. Initially, taxes were raised, and the goldsmiths were repaid, but the Crown repeatedly borrowed from banks, who just as repeatedly raised their charges. The final crisis began in 1667 and came to a head in 1672, when Charles suspended Exchequer payments to the goldsmiths for 12 months. This involved a total of about £11.3 million owed to ten goldsmith banks. The problem was that while goldsmiths had been expecting repayment from the proceeds of future taxes, they had been lending out their depositors' money. Depositors, about 10,000 of them, found that their money had simply vanished, and because of the suspension, were unlikely ever to see it again. Many merchants went bankrupt as a result, and the event destroyed confidence in the goldsmith banks. However, the goldsmith banks had indicated the way that banking would develop. Eventually a national bank, the Bank of England, was created in 1694, following the example of other countries.

Unlike the Bank of Amsterdam, it was a privately owned bank, formed on the joint stock principle (in which many people jointly own the enterprise, the extent of their ownership indicated by their shares of the enterprise's stock that represents the finance capital necessary to establish it), and incorporating both central and commercial bank functions. From the initial stock offering, £11.2 million was lent to the government,

---

Joint Stock Company

A company owned in common by many different individuals

---

which agreed to pay 8 percent annual interest on the loan. A new development was that the loan was made in the form of bank notes bearing the bank's promise to pay; the bank itself kept both capital and the interest payment. The issue of paper money became (and still is) a primary function of the Bank. Acting more like a modern commercial bank, the Bank made loans both by discounting bills of exchange and by making straight loans backed by suitable collateral, and it also bought and sold bullion.

Other Developments

Many other developments occurred at this time, accompanying the growth in the rest of the economy. Insurance as a way of reducing risk in commercial ventures appeared. One of the first was marine insurance, where, for a premium, underwriters agreed to recompense a shipowner or shipper for losses. This obviously became more important as the volume of international shipping expanded.

As land had by this time become commercialized, so mechanisms for financing land purchases also appeared. In France, the *rente* was the device used to finance real estate.[1] The borrower agreed to repay the lender in installments of specific sums of money for a specified number of years, just like an annuity. This idea spread to public financing as well, where the government borrowed money and agreed to make repayments to its creditors over time.

As enterprises, some industrial but chiefly commercial, became larger, the joint stock principle became the favored means of raising initial capital. Accompanying this was the development of stock exchanges, principally in the more important financial centers of Amsterdam, London, and Paris, where shares could be transferred from one owner to another via the services of a new intermediary, the stockbroker. Initially, exchanges were somewhat limited in scope, and reached a significant size only in the 19th century, when enterprises such as railroads, which needed massive amounts of finance capital, emerged. At first these exchanges were mainly concerned with transfers of government debt.

Speculation and "Bubbles"

As with any new developments, there were good and bad aspects. On one hand, these financial developments did help mobilize capital and increase real productive activity. But on the other hand, the 17th and early 18th centuries also generated a mass of speculation or get-rich-quick schemes. Very few had redeeming features; only a few people (the promoters) actually made money in them, while thousands of others, fired by the seeming ease with which fortunes could be made, were taken in by paper promises. Only too eager to find an easy way to wealth, they discovered, too late, that a promise is only a promise. Because many schemes were just so much hot air, as in a bubble which only needs a pinprick to burst, they were called "bubbles."

Bubble

A speculative stock market scheme

While some schemes were started on what seemed like legitimate grounds, their collapse led to disastrous consequences for genuine economic development in many cases. One of the earliest bubbles accompanied the rise of commercial activity in Holland in the 17th century and centered around the tulip bulbs—for which Holland still remains famous. It also illustrates the effects of scientific discoveries—in this case, the principles of crossbreeding to produce hybrids with valued characteristics. (Crossbreeding would subsequently revolutionize farming by making it possible to produce, for example, high yielding dairy cows or heavy beef cattle or grain strains resistant to disease.) Between the years 1633-37, Holland was swept by a tulip mania. Thousands of speculators were eager to pour money into the development of prized bulbs that, if successful, would have anxious growers desperate to buy bulbs, producing high returns for the shareholders. But this bubble collapsed after a failed attempt to produce a tulip with black flowers.

The Mississippi Bubble

A more damaging speculative mania occurred in France several decades later and its collapse slowed down development of more modern financial organizations there. At the end of the 17th century, France had founded a colony near the mouth of the Mississippi River in Louisiana, providing a link in the New World with France's holding in Quebec. In 1717, the Mississippi Land Company, a joint stock company, was founded by John Law, a Scotsman (who had previously set up the Bank of France). This company was founded for two major purposes. First, to take over the debt obligations of the French government, which would be paid off by selling stock in the company, permitting it to finance activities that would be profitable because they were protected by monopoly privileges. Second, the Company proposed to develop this new French Colony. It would have exclusive rights of trading with Louisiana, developing mining rights and importiing slaves. In addition, it gained the monopoly of the beaver trade with Canada. Law's ideas were basically sound: to back paper money issued by the Bank of France with a productive asset rather than with unproductive gold and silver.

Initially, the Company did well, setting off a flurry of interest as potential stockholders fought for the privilege, at ever-rising prices, of buying shares in a company that promised to return fortunes to its owners. Then overextension began as the Company bought the tobacco monopoly in France, took over other trading companies, collected taxes for the government, and minted coins. All this was made possible by raising new capital from the government (which paid for its shares by issuing government securities) and from the Bank of France (which paid by issuing bank notes). Interest income for the government securities would then be used to finance the company's efforts. The Bank would also gain. The notes given to the Company were listed as assets in its investment portfolio, and because so large a part of the Bank's note issue was held by one company, the Mississippi Company, it was felt that this would reduce the danger of a run on the Bank. (Again, remember that these were early days of banking and paper money, when people were used to dealing with actual metals, and the problem of confidence in holding a paper promise to pay was crucial.)

In this situation, the Company had to keep showing rising earnings in order to retain investor confidence, which became more difficult the larger the Company grew. The situation was "saved" by a second wave of speculative interest, and shares in the Company, which were transferable, rapidly rose in price; by the end of 1719, shares that had been issued at 1,000 were changing hands at 10,000. The Company could not resist the prospect of gaining new funds, so more shares were issued, even though the actual productive enterprises were not very successful. At the beginning of 1720, the Mississippi Company merged with the Bank of France, and the prospect of a much stronger entity set off yet another wave of speculative buying bidding up share prices again.

But the mania had run its course. Some large shareholders started selling their holdings, setting off a wave of selling, and prices fell as dramatically as they had risen. By July, the bubble had collapsed, and with it, the Bank of France and the hopes of many speculators. While the project had been successful in repaying some of the government debt incurred in the War of Spanish Succession, the bad effects would have much more serious implication for future French development. Because the Bank was a joint stock company, its failure not only held back the development of French banking (there was no central bank in France until 1800, and this one also suffered from speculative abuses), it also discredited the joint stock principle in general. Even until fairly late in the 19th century, French enterprises tended to remain small, because of the unwillingness to adopt the joint stock form of organization.

The South Sea Bubble

Speculative manias also occurred across the Channel in England, including one of the most famous, the South Sea Bubble. The South Sea Company was incorporated in 1710 as a trading company to hold the monopoly of English trade with Spanish-held areas in South America, and also to try to break the monopoly of slave trading with these areas, at that time held by France. Ironically, the Company achieved a lucky break in 1713, when Spain granted England, not France, the monopoly to sell 4,800 slaves a year in the Spanish colonies, and the privilege of sending one ship a year to these areas for other trading purposes.

This immediately resulted in profits for the company, and speculator interest in acquiring its shares increased. In 1719, the Company agreed to take over part of the government's debts as the price of its monopoly. The government paid 5 percent interest a year on this debt, to be reduced to 4 percent after seven years. Existing government bondholders received stock in the Company in exchange for their holdings of government securities. Company shares were transferrable, which started a wave of buying and sent the stock price soaring. The Company's success continued when it agreed to take over the country's entire public debt (excluding loans to the Bank of England and the East India Company). This was possible because stock prices continued to rise, inducing government creditors to accept company stock instead. The mania had really caught speculators' attention by this time; in six months, shares that had once sold for £100 now changed hands for over £1,000.

Bondholder

A creditor

Success here led to the formation of many other joint stock companies, some simply by greedy promoters who recognized the desire of some people for fast wealth, others based on more legitimate schemes. The most notorious was a project launched "for carrying on an undertaking of great advantage, which shall in due time be revealed"— and inevitably, once the issue had been bought, the promoter absconded without revealing it.

But because so many fraudulent schemes did collapse, confidence in the worth of the South Sea Company shares weakened, and from a high over £1,000, the price had collapsed to £120 by the end of 1720 because of panic selling. This is a classic case of a speculative bubble: The dramatic rise in stock prices was not matched by any increase in trade, the Company's real productive activity, so any lack of confidence for any reason bursts the bubble.

The result of this experience in England led to the passage of the Bubble Act, which required an enabling act of Parliament before a joint stock company could be formed; it remained on the Statute Book until 1825. But unlike the experience in France, the use of the joint stock form of organization remained fairly common in England.

Results of Mercantilist Policy

Although all the western European countries we have considered so far experienced a decline of feudalism, their paths of economic development diverged considerably by the end of this period. As we noted at the beginning of the chapter, these differences depended on the outcome of the political changes that were also occurring. Spain and Portugal experienced the least amount of capitalist development. Although Spain began the period in a dominating position, a power struggle with other European countries resulted in a decline in Spanish influence throughout the 17th century. In the 16th century, Spain ruled many parts of Europe: the Netherlands (1504—1581), Belgium, part of France, Milan, Naples, Sicily, and Portugal after 1580. As a result of Spanish initiative in the voyages of discovery and colonization, Spain's overseas empire spread to North Africa, America, and the West Indies.

Spain itself became unified, but throughout the 17th century was involved in a series of wars that drained the Treasury and led to a loss of most of its non-Spanish European holdings. It lost the Dutch provinces, which began a revolt against Spanish rule in 1566, partly because they felt Spanish rule was hindering Dutch development. An unexpected result of this struggle was the rise of Amsterdam as northern Europe's leading commercial and financial center after the destruction of Antwerp by Spanish soldiers in 1576.

Both France and Spain witnessed the rise of a strong monarchy, but France allowed its new commercial class more economic freedom, hence its development pattern differed. Throughout this period, France's influence increased. France was one of Europe's larger countries (having a population of approximately 18 million in 1600 compared with Spain's approximately 10 million). We have already noted that France had begun a movement towards centralization of power in the mid 15th century, reaching its highest expression under the Sun King, Louis XIV (1643-1715).

Mercantilist policies had mixed success in France, and Louis' suppression of the Protestant Huguenots in the late 17th century removed a vigorous commercial element from French society. While there was more capitalist production activity than before, thanks to various encouragements, the market remained limited. Although the nation's wealth, as measured by the money accruing to the king's treasury, did increase, much of it was wasted. Because a portion of profits made by merchants and new industrialists went to the king, there was less opportunity for reinvestment in other ventures as happened in England. Also, Louis seemed to be more concerned with the prestige of the throne and military glory than with the less glamorous building of the economy. The diversion of resources not only left French prosperity relatively weaker, it also had only a limited payoff militarily, as in the 18th century, France lost much of its colonial empire.

In contrast, the ability of the Dutch and British mercantile classes to gain political power led to a much more successful application of policies. The Netherlands, as we have already seen, became a major sea power, shipper, and financial center. Similarly, this period saw the rise to dominance of England, until then a small, relatively insignificant country (in 1713, just after unification with Scotland, total population was six million). Encouragement given to the development of shipping paid off, and English seapower rivalled Holland's. Agricultural changes (which will be covered in more detail in Chapter 8) achieved the aim of self sufficiency in food production, with some even being exported. More important, these changes led to the emergence of a new landowning class when wealth made in commerce was used to buy land. These new land owners were

not of noble birth and did not live like the aristocracy, but they were instrumental in introducing a capitalist element into agriculture and landholding.

Summary

The 16th and 17th centuries saw the consolidation of early capitalist activity. As we have seen, early capitalist ideas and practices first became influential in commerce and trading, later spreading to agriculture. And as we shall see later, they would revolutionize industrial production, partly because limited output constrained the continued profitable expansion of trading. At the same time, it is important to note several characteristics of this period that would make later developments that much easier.

First, in England and the Netherlands the growing alliance between the commercial classes and the State was mutually reinforcing. The State gained needed revenues from taxing a growing volume of trade, while merchants (and to a lesser extent, early industrialists) gained by having the State provide support for their activities. This support made private profit making not only easier but also more acceptable.

Second, a very important aspect of State support lay in the provision of infrastructure, the underpinnings that must be in place if private activity is to be successful on a large scale. At this time, most attention was given to inland transportation networks, which had political implications by linking all parts of a country together so that it could be seen as a unified whole. (The importance of infrastructure can be seen in today's underdeveloped countries, where state building of transportation networks and education are considered important in improving these countries' development efforts.)

Third, this period marked a growing sophistication (at least among the minority of the population most involved) in the handling of money. States increasingly recognized the advantage of a "sound" unified monetary system, and various financial developments occurred to supplement actual hard cash. Banks—both commercial and central—were more common, even though bank failures were frequent (due to a variety of causes, including simple mismanagement or deliberate embezzlement). Other financial instruments and institutions also developed.

The point of all these developments is that they paralleled and increasingly made possible changes on the real side of the economy. A growing complexity in one area matches a growing complexity elsewhere. However, it must be remembered that in most of Europe, with the exception of parts of England and the Netherlands, life for most of the population, which was still predominantly rural, went on very much as it had for centuries before, with little contact with the emerging market system.

NOTES

1. The connection with financing real estate went back to the Middle Ages, when lords sometimes borrowed money using the only security they had available—their land. If repayment was made from revenues from land, and was used to reduce the principal outstanding, the contract was a "live gage" ("vif gage" in French). If revenues were used only to pay interest and not reduce the principal, it was a "mort gage" because the principal then had to be repaid on the death of the borrower.

Key Concepts

Balance of trade
Bank note
Bondholder
Bubble
Bullionism
Capital accumulation
Central banking
Check
Debasement
Excise tax

Favorable balance of trade
Infrastructure
Joint stock company
Mercantilism
Monopoly
Scrivener
Specie money
Speculative bubble
Stock exchange

Note: Suggestions for further reading will be found at the end of Chapter 7.

Questions for Discussion or Essay Writing

1. How was "wealth" defined in the 17th and 18th centuries?

2. What policies were favored by policy makers influenced by mercantilist thinking?

3. Why was it important for a ruler to gain control over currency issue?

4. In what ways did speculation impede the process of capital accumulation?

5. Why can we begin to talk of "state building" policies in the 16th century, but rarely in earlier periods?

6. What is infrastructure and why is it important?

7. Why did many influential people in this period want to achieve a favorable balance of trade? How did they go about doing it?

8. Why were grants of monopoly thought to encourage expansion of capitalist activity?

9. What did rulers do to solve the problem of currency debasement?

10. What contribution was made with the use of the joint stock form of corporate organization?

Chapter 7

Mercantilism: External Aspects

Voyages of Discovery

DURING THE 16TH, 17TH, AND 18TH CENTURIES, capitalist activity spread around much of the world. This happened as those European countries where capitalist ways of organizing profit-making activities were becoming more common extended their influence to areas previously untouched by the new Western ways of thinking. The expansion of trade and colonization was stimulated by the desire for wealth and helped by State support of the activities of private individuals and companies. Thus, external mercantilist policies complemented those being applied within the country itself.

That such an extension of markets and exploitation of sources of raw materials could be undertaken at all is due in part to the geographic discoveries of the late 15th and early 16th centuries, which opened up "new" areas of potential wealth to Europeans. These discoveries were in turn possible because of the previous resurgence of scientific activity (in areas such as astronomy, for example) and the continuing improvement of shipbuilding and navigation techniques that made long ocean voyages possible. In addition, an interest in science generated a basic curiosity about the natural world that had been suppressed for so long as the medieval ethic remained dominant.

Merchants and traders wanted to expand their areas of influence because selling Eastern products in the West was profitable. At the beginning of this period, Venetian merchants had a stranglehold on such trade, and Venice's wealth was very apparent as it spilled over into non-economic areas. Thus, the thinking went, the rewards would be great if only this monopoly could be broken. The prospect of sharing in these rewards gave an incentive for royal backers to finance the voyages of discovery intended to find new trade routes to the East. These in turn opened up opportunities for the expansion of commercial activity.

Portugal initiated these endeavors, with the first organized efforts made by Prince Henry the Navigator (1394-1460), who also established a school of navigation and colonized the Madeiras and the Azores. Such explorations were revived by King John II, and a voyage of 1487 was the first to reach India by sailing around Africa. Ten years later, Vasco da Gama repeated the voyage around the Cape of Good Hope, and returned from India with spices that sold for 60 times the cost of the voyage—concrete evidence of the profitability of such expeditions. It was so successful that within the next ten years, Portugal had gained effective control of trade with India, replacing Venice.

Discovery of the New World

However, Portugal kept its focus looking East, not West, and refused financial support to Columbus, a Genoan, who instead sailed West with Spanish financing. This gamble paid off, and in

1492 he reached the New World, the Bahamas and the island of Hispaniola (now Haiti and the Dominican Republic), thus opening the way to the European exploitation of the New World. Oddly enough, the pattern of an explorer of one nationality being financed by another country continued. Thus John and Sebastian Cabot, Italians sailing with English financing, reached Canada; in 1501, Amerigo Vespucci, a Florentine sailing for Portugal, discovered the mainland of the continent named after him; and in 1519, Magellan, a Portuguese sailing for Spain, was the first to sail around the southern tip of South America and into the Pacific Ocean, where he reached the Philippines and opened the Western route to India.

Spain's efforts to exploit these discoveries gave it a commanding position in the New World and contributed to Spanish wealth in the 16th century. Spain subsequently controlled much of central and southern America, adding the Philippines in 1564. Portugal's main foray into the New World eventually gave it control of Brazil. France's interests lay mainly in North America, as did Britain's. Both of these two countries were latecomers to the New World, but as it turned out, their holdings had greater value in the centuries to come. And all of the Caribbean islands, important additions to the economies of most of the European nations as well as strategically located, were subject to land grabbing at this time.

Mercantilist Philosophy

Expansion of European influence in the New World and Asia came about in response to the search for wealth. Both trade and colonization in these "new" lands helped this search and were incorporated into the philosophy of mercantilism as it concerned external relations. The mercantilist "systems" that emerged were based on two simple principles—trade and colonies—to assist the growth of wealth (measured by the amount of bullion).

Trade

All trade was to be regulated to achieve a favorable balance of trade. This occurred when the value of exports exceeded the value of imports, causing bullion to flow into a country, which enriched itself at the expense of the deficit country.

Several implications are important here. Remember that the ultimate aim was to increase wealth through the expansion of production and trade, at the expense of one's rivals. However, at this time, there was a widespread view—which continued into the 19th century—that the domestic market was limited, and that the total volume of trade was fixed. The first idea was hardly surprising in the 16th century, when so small a fraction of the population was connected with market activities. But it seems strange as time passed and more of the economy became subject to market influences. The apparent paradox is resolved in two ways. First, domestic policy was oriented to keeping costs down, so policies helping expand the labor supply and keeping wages low did lower costs, but also limited domestic demand. Second, in the pre-Industrial Revolution age, there was a limited amount of what we would call inter-industry sales (sales of machinery or semi-finished items). Equipment used in industrial production, except in a few areas, was simple and often owned, if not made, by its operator. However, in order to continue making profits, market expansion was a vital necessity. So if the domestic market was limited, the only option was to expand sales abroad. Given the idea that total trade was limited, one country's gain in trade came at the expense of another's share.

In addition, both supply and demand conditions were seen as the result of institutional factors, and not, as would be thought after the 19th century, the result of individual, market-oriented calculation. So it seemed perfectly legitimate to merchants and producers to co-opt the powers of the State in order to alter the market to suit their needs. Hence the development of trade regulations. A favorable balance of trade was stressed because it would be caused by an expansion of exports that supplemented sales to the limited domestic market.

Trade regulation was desired because encouraging exports and limiting imports (except, of course, for essential raw material imports) achieved the goal of a favorable balance of trade. It was also desired because in combination with colonial policies, relative prices could be influenced. That is, a wealth inflow is the result of a price times quantity sum, so policies that also generated favorable *terms of trade* were desired, which involved high export prices relative to low import prices. So a favorable balance of trade was the result of increased export quantities *and* favorable prices, and was both cause and result of rising exports and internal prices.

Terms of Trade
The relative prices of imports and exports

To understand this result, two assumptions must be made. First, that domestic costs would not rise; unlikely in this period because labor costs, the largest part of production costs, were controlled. And second, that there was an inelastic foreign demand for exports, meaning that foreign buyers were not very responsive to rising prices. This was also a reasonable assumption to make for two reasons. Many of the important products entering international trade at this time did face an inelastic demand and buyers continued to purchase them, regardless of price. For example, wool from England and spices faced eager buyers in Europe. The second reason lies in the development of mercantilist empires, made up of a more developed European country and its underdeveloped colonies. So long as the parent country monopolized trade with its own colonies (which all of them tried to do), it could also control the prices paid for imports from them (low) and the prices of the exports sold in them (high). What was most important was the ability to import raw

materials at low cost. The limited size of the population of the new colonial areas implied that they were not yet important markets for the output of the developed economies.

The successful application of trade regulation policies generated profits both for traders and later on for producers, even though incomes of the wage earning population at home remained low. Those profits represented an important element in the accumulation of large amounts of capital that later became necessary when capitalist principles were applied to industry on a broader scale than ever before. It might be argued that the large gains generated in trade diverted capital from industrial investment, because most of the profitable trade was in the hands of monopoly companies. But in fact both traders and producers gained initially from the expansion of markets in the 16th and 17th centuries. Only later did the interests of the two groups diverge, partly because an increasing emphasis on the terms of trade at the expense of the volume of trade conflicted with industrialists' need for an ever-expanding market. (The results of this conflict will be taken up later.)

Colonies

The second basic principle of external policies was that a country's colonies should be exploited for the exclusive benefit of the parent country. This idea of the mercantilist empire, made up of the parent and its colonies, saw each playing a specific role for the greater glory of the unit as a whole (but especially for the parent country). Thus, as the colonies were economically underdeveloped, their proper role was to provide raw materials, supplementing the more developed European country which provided produced goods.

Mercantilist Empires

There were two major approaches to the exploitation question. Some empires focused more on trade, while others saw colonies as areas suitable for settlement and for certain types of economic development. For the latter, mining and plantation agriculture predominated, appropriate activities, given the colony's natural resource endowment and its role in the mercantile empire.

Plantation Agriculture

Farming on large estates using large numbers of workers

Portugal's Empire

The Portuguese Empire is a good example of one oriented more to the gains from trade. By exploiting its route to the East via southern Africa, the Portuguese achieved the dominant position of spice traders to Europe. To ensure continuation of these supplies, they established land bases in India, Malacca, and around the Persian Gulf, and in 1557, broke through to the Far East by estab-

lishing a base at Macao in China. However, extensive Portuguese settlements were not undertaken in these areas, which contributed to the eventual decline of Portuguese influence. Without a significant presence, their trading posts were difficult to defend against attacks from other countries' forces. In addition, the Portuguese were not responsible for the further distribution of spices within Europe itself—the Dutch and Italians took over this function. As the 16th century wore on, it became more difficult for Portuguese traders to retain their hold on the Eastern part of the spice trade. After 1580, they lost control of it to the Dutch, who adopted a settlement policy in the Spice Islands (Modern Indonesia) which they took over in 1621. The English also gained some of Portugal's spice trade. In 1622, they captured Ormuz and thus were able to dominate the Persian Gulf. In 1633, as a result of repeated attacks, the Portuguese left Bengal,

Figure 7.1 The expansion of trade relied on wind-powered sailing ships, like these owned by the East India Company, which would be used in the trade between India and Great Britain. (Courtesy of National Maritime Museum, Greenwich)

and the English began to extend control over large parts of India.

One exception to the general trade orientation of Portugal took place in the Portuguese colony of Brazil, initially because there was nothing to trade between Brazil and Europe. After 1532, a policy of settlement was encouraged to exploit Brazil's natural resources, involving some mining ventures, plantation agriculture of tobacco and sugar, and some livestock raising.

Portuguese weakness in defending their possessions was apparent after 1580, when the king of Portugal died, and Philip II of Spain claimed the throne. (Spain ruled Portugal for the next 60 years.) But the need to defend both Portugal and Portuguese colonies imposed a costly burden on Spain, and Spain responded by concentrating attention on the wealthier, bullion-rich lands they had captured in the New World.

Even after 1640, when Portugal regained its independence, the empire was hard to protect, and most of it was lost to the Dutch, French, or English. However, Portugal ousted the Dutch from Brazil in 1660, and as Brazil was Portugal's largest colonial landholding, more attention was devoted to developing its wealth.

This gamble paid off with the discovery of gold; by 1780, Brazil produced more than three-quarters of a billion dollars worth of gold for Portugal. Then came the discovery of large diamond fields, making Brazil the chief diamond producer until the discovery of diamonds in Africa in the 19th century. However, even with this renewed interest in colonies, Portugal still found it difficult to retain hold of its remaining empire; in 1822, Brazil declared its independence from Portugal.

The Portuguese were engaged in one extremely profitable trading venture, the slave trade transporting Africans to work in the plantations

Resource Endowment

The relative supplies of resources available in a country

of the Spanish and Portuguese New World colonies. Portugal initially had a monopoly in this trade (called the Asiento), which, although costing thousands of lives, reaped huge profits for the slave traders. There was intense rivalry between the different countries whose nationals wanted a share in these profits, and the slave trade remained a political and economic plum ripe for the picking. Here again, the Portuguese lost out, as under the terms of the Treaty of Utrecht of 1713, the slave trade to Spanish colonies and Brazil was transferred to British traders.

Spain's Empire

Spain's record in its New World possessions was initially one of sheer exploitation, but eventually turned toward a settlement and cultivation policy. Spanish holdings in the New World were the most extensive and richest of any European country. At its peak, the Spanish Empire reached from Chile to Oregon along the west of the American continent, from Argentina to Florida along the east, and took in Arizona, Central America, and much of South America.

Discovery of massive amounts of gold and silver produced by the Aztec civilization in Mexico prompted the Spanish to claim these lands. After all, simply conquering the Indian population and then shipping hoards of precious metals to Spain was the fastest way to increase national wealth according to the simplest bullionist philosophy. This was made easier by the fact that iron was not among the metals available in Mexico, hence the armaments of the Indians were primitive compared with those of the Conquistadores.

Mexico was taken in 1521, and by 1532, the Spanish had conquered Inca Peru as well. However, when the most easily accessible treasure had been taken, it was realized that wealth from mining in these new lands was potentially much greater than simply looting Indian civilizations. Success required a civilian Spanish presence for administering the colonial areas, so Spain encouraged settlement and the development of a colonial system aimed at increasing Spanish wealth through bullion.

Mining began in Peru in 1545, and in Mexico the following year. At first, gold was the most important commodity produced and exported to Spain, but in the decade of the 1560s Spain imported more silver than gold, a pattern that continued until 1600, after which imports declined.

Gold, Silver, and Bullionism

Access to these enormous quantities of gold and silver turned Spain into the wealthiest and most dominant country in the 16th century. At a time when bullionist ideas were dominant, metals' acquisition counted for more in the calculation of wealth than it would do later. Spain's position as the leading country in the bullion trade was further emphasized in 1576, when an amalgam process using mercury to separate the silver from the surrounding ore was found to increase the yield from mining—and conveniently enough, Spain was the largest producer of mercury.

There was less interest in the cultivation of the new lands, although some Spanish nobles received large grants of land and cultivated some of the new American products for export back to Europe. The result was the introduction of sugar, rice, and coffee in Europe, and also the use of slaves from Africa to work on the plantations. But plantation agriculture was only a small part of colonial activity. Up to 1600, metals continued to account for 90 percent of all exports, and the total Spanish population in the New World was only 150,000.

An elaborate arrangement was also developed to link Spain with its colonies, and to bring the

---

Primary Product

Agricultural products and the output of mines; non-manufactured products

---

wealth into Spain, officially lasting until 1800, although it decreased in practical importance throughout the 17th century. The structure of this arrangement shows how trade was regulated, and the importance the State attached to the control of trade. While mainly intended to ensure that the bullion *did* reach Spain, the arrangements also were designed to protect shipping from attacks from other countries. Two fleets of ships sailed each way across the Atlantic between Spain and the New World each year. All merchandise was carried on these royal ships on behalf of individual merchants. Control was further extended by limiting the ports that were used. All commerce with the New World went through Seville in Spain and a handful of selected American ports for the two centuries between 1503 and 1717. (Trade with the Philippines was added after 1564.) One fifth of all bullion taken went to the Crown. In order to control trade, the House of Trade was set up to register all bullion, impose regulations, and establish penalties to prevent smuggling of goods and bullion out of Spain.

While this seemed all-inclusive, Spain's monopoly on the wealth of the New World was far from complete, and other Europeans became involved. In a few cases, exceptions were made to the requirement that only Spaniards be involved with New World commerce, and some non-Spaniards were legally permitted to sell goods in the Spanish colonies, a provision that became frequently used in the 17th century. There was also a great deal of illegal activity. For example, other European merchants bribed Spanish ones to ship goods for them. There was also outright piracy. (While the organization of trading in two well-armed fleets was intended to increase the security of transatlantic shipping, in practice, the large fleets did present an unmissable, and potentially lucrative, target. Pirates sailing from hideouts in the Caribbean islands specialized in picking out the slower ships for their plunder.)

The other major countries in Europe had a later start in colonization than either Spain or

Portugal, and faced with these two countries' monopolies, had two major options to pursue. One, followed mainly by the Dutch, was to encroach on the monopoly position; this was only partly successful. The other option, followed by France and Britain, was to direct colonization efforts elsewhere. At first, this did not produce the spectacular gains of the Spanish, but the potential for gain was much greater later.

The Dutch Empire

Holland in the 17th century was Europe's major commercial nation. Its colonial policy was closer to Portuguese than to Spanish policy, with a stress on trade rather than settlement; colonies were seen as bases to aid commerce. Even when colonies were acquired, Dutch possession was often temporary. For example, in the Americas, the Dutch settled the colony of New Amsterdam (now New York) and the areas along the Hudson River up to Albany, but were ousted in 1664 by the British. They controlled areas in Guiana, but lost control in 1803; and held some Brazilian ports, which were taken by the Portuguese during the 1650s. The major American colony that remained Dutch was the island of Curacao in the Caribbean.

Dutch East India Company

However, the Dutch held a commanding position in trade, which it dominated and controlled, especially after taking over the Eastern spice trade from the Portuguese. Here, the principle of regulating trade by granting monopoly powers to one company was adopted. The most successful was the Dutch East India Company, created in 1601 by the strategic merger of smaller trading companies. The incentive was Spain's closing the Lisbon spice market to the Dutch, who had been distributing spices within Europe, in retaliation for the Dutch struggle for independence. If it was not possible to get spices from the Portuguese in the

old way, new ways must be found, and a larger company formed by merger would be in a stronger position to do this. Consequently, the Dutch East India Company was given the power to make peace or war, to administer colonies, and to conduct trade. It constantly attacked Portuguese holdings, and had removed the Portuguese from the Eastern spice trade and from many of their Far East holdings by the end of the century.

In the Far East, the Company's most important holdings were in Java and Sumatra (the Spice Islands), where it built fortified ports to protect its trade in places like Batavia (modern Jakarta) and from where it extended its authority inland. The Company also operated forts on the island of Formosa (the name the Portuguese gave to Taiwan) to protect its trade there. And for two centuries, between 1638 and 1854, the Dutch were the only Europeans permitted to trade with Japan. In addition, the Dutch established a supply post at Cape Town to resupply ships on the voyage between Holland and the East, thus establishing a Dutch presence in South Africa for the first time.

The Dutch East India Company was tremendously successful, and became very wealthy. In some years its dividends reached 75 percent, and for two centuries they averaged out at 18 percent annually. This mainly resulted from its successful control of the spice trade, which achieved the aim of keeping spice prices high, further reinforcing the prevailing view of an inelastic demand for traded products.

A less successful example of a monopoly trading company was the Dutch West India Company, founded in 1621 to develop American trade and colonies. As previously noted, the Dutch were not successful in holding on to most of their American colonies, though they did better trading with other countries' colonies, and in naval conflicts with the Spanish (by 1648, they had captured 600 Spanish ships). The problem with piracy as a way of gaining wealth was that while it could bring fast riches, it also invited retaliation, and the Dutch continued to lack manpower for military needs. Holland was the smallest of all the colonizing European nations, hence was at a disadvantage in being able to defend its holdings against attack from its rivals.

This was partly why the Netherlands focused more on its Far East holdings and activities, but even here, its influence declined in the 18th century. One reason was that, after successfully taking over from the Portuguese in the East, the Dutch faced continual attack from the French and English, and, with the exception of the Dutch East Indies, remained in only a few areas in the East after 1713. The second reason for the loss of importance lay in *what* was traded. With the exception of bullion, spices had always been a high value, profitable commodity, and in the 17th century, this gave the Dutch an advantage. But later, trade in textiles, especially the cottons produced by India and Persia, became much more profitable than spices. Here, the French, but more particularly the English, dominated and thus were able to supplant the Dutch in wealth-producing activities.

France's Empire

France's colonial policy was partly a product of its late arrival to the landgrabbing taking place in the New World. Being excluded from the metals-producing areas in South America by the Spanish, and finding it difficult to encroach on the Eastern spice trade, it turned attention to the possibility of finding a northwest route from Europe to the East. (Both France and England were to be haunted by the possibility of the existence of a northwest passage across North America, which led them into repeated conflicts.)

The first pathblazing French explorer was Jacques Cartier, who in 1535 sailed up the St. Lawrence River in Canada. The first successful French settlement in the New World was established in Quebec in 1608, and the French subsequently laid claim to huge areas of the continent as a result of further explorations. An early adventurer was de Champlain, who explored the Great Lakes. Later, Marquette and Jolliet went down the Mississippi River from its source and were succeeded by other explorers who followed the river all the way to the Gulf of Mexico. But efforts to develop French colonies were slow, and there were fewer than 3,000 French inhabitants in French Canada (along the St. Lawrence River and in Acadia) and only a few French-held islands in the West Indies.

Caribbean Sugar and Rum

Louis XIV's chief minister, responsible for economic affairs, was Jean-Baptiste Colbert. Colbert was a dedicated mercantilist and until his death in 1683, attempted to regulate and encourage domestic production to expand French influence overseas. Government action was essential in supporting subsequent French colonial development. As was common in other countries, monopoly companies established by government charter were responsible for colonial expansion. For example, in 1664, the French West India Company was given authority to administer French holdings in the West Indies, Cayenne (Guiana), Canada, and some West African ports. It successfully excluded the Dutch from trade with the French Caribbean islands, which produced sugar, much in demand in Europe both as sugar and distilled into rum. It expanded the French share of the slave trade between Africa and the New World.

One problem did arise with the Caribbean sugar islands. Internal policy aimed at agricultural self-sufficiency, and France wanted to protect its wine producers from foreign competition. Now brandy was produced from French grapes, and rum, produced from sugar, was potential competition so it could not be imported into France. But if islands in the Caribbean were strategically important, the question was, how to retain them within the empire? The way around this dilemma was to use rum as a bartering device in the slave trade and as a tactical device to upset the interests of the other European colonizers.

France in North America

In Canada, the fur trade around Hudson's Bay was encouraged—a good example of mercantilist policy that was appropriate as well as expedient given Canada's wildernesses. However, at times this conflicted with the settlement policy. France wanted to encourage settlement in its new colonies, but was not very successful. The fur trade of North America remained a constant source of antagonism between the French and the English until the middle of the 18th century. Further south, the French established a colony in Louisiana (New Orleans), and overall claimed Canada and the Ohio and Mississippi Valleys in North America. These were huge land claims but were settled by only a small population.

In relations with the East, the French adopted a more trade-related policy, also with mixed success. The French East India Company was never as successful as its Dutch or English rivals, either with its domestic investors or in its overseas activities. Both France and England gained in the East at the expense of the Portuguese, but after 1689, most of the rivalry in this area was between France and England.

India was the scene of the most protracted struggle, especially after the collapse of the Mogul Empire in 1707, when both countries' East India companies tried to expand there. By 1763, the British East India Company was victorious, and the French remained in only a few areas, and then only as traders, not colonists.

Conflict with England

The struggle between France and England had a worldwide aspect, and in the New World, its outcome was the end of French dominance in North America. In the 17th century, fortunes fluctuated. England seized France's possession of Acadia (now the Canadian provinces of Nova Scotia and New Brunswick) in 1613, returned them as a result of a treaty with France signed in 1632, recaptured them again in 1654, restored them in 1667, and finally recaptured them again in 1710. And as a result of the Treaty of Utrecht (1713) France abandoned its claims to Hudson's Bay (and its profitable fur trade).

However, other areas were still left in French hands. Not until the middle of the 18th century were French claims in North America transferred to British hands. Throughout this period, attacks on the borders between French and English areas were frequent.

Constant rivalry led to many outright wars. One, for example, had a particular impact on the outcome of their rivalry in North America. This was the Seven Years' War (also known as the French and Indian War in the Americas), fought in Europe between 1756 and 1763, but involving hostilities in the New World starting earlier than this. French forces had been pushing into the Ohio Valley, and the British countered by building a fort at the junction of the Monongahela and Allegheny rivers (site of modern Pittsburgh). In the war's early stages, the French were successful, as they not only captured this fort but also repulsed British attacks on Fort Niagara and Crown Point on Lake Champlain in New England. Then the British counterattacked successfully. In 1759, Quebec fell into British hands, proving to be the end of French colonial efforts in North America.

By 1750, British territory in North America stretched from Savannah in the South (present day Georgia) to New England and formed a strip of land about 300 miles wide between the Appalachian mountains and the Atlantic coast line. But as a result of the Seven Years' War, French territory was ceded to Britain, which extended its holdings south to Mobile, north into Canada, and west to the Mississippi River (land west of the Mississippi was ceded to Spain). In addition, Spanish Florida was also ceded to Britain.

Britain's Colonies

Britain, like France, was a relative latecomer to colonization efforts in the New World, but ironically finished this phase of European expansion with the largest and wealthiest possessions (even though it lost its 13 North American colonies by 1776). It was one of the first to send settlers, prompted partly by the early recognition that obvious wealth was not available to be exploited as in Mexico or Peru, and also by the desire to expand trading possibilities. In the 13 colonies in North America held by Britain, emigration from the British Isles plus natural increase resulted in a population of two million by 1776, the time of their independence. However, while a settlement policy was encouraged, trade was also encouraged in the interests of expanding production.

New World Settlements

Initial efforts to establish settlements in the New World were not successful until the 17th century. Early colonial development was influenced by

Figure 7.2   The exploitation of cane sugar in the West Indian colonies of European powers gave rise to great wealth for plantation owners. Some built magnificent plantation houses, like this one, St. Nicholas Abbey, in Barbados, probably built about 1650. (Courtesy of Allan Montaine/Barbados Tourism Authority)

several factors. First, conditions in the new country did not permit immediate settlement on European lines. The first few years involved a hard struggle for survival in an unfamiliar environment, emphasizing the need for cooperative action. Although the settlement of North America is often thought of in terms of the rugged, individualist pioneer, this was only rarely true in fact. Much more important, as will be seen later, was the role of the village and town settlements. Towns became the center of American culture and economic life and provided the necessary support to the westward movement of the frontier of settlement.

Second, the first colonial settlements were the products of a capitalist environment. Many were specifically organized by promoters looking to the New World as a source of profitable investment, and as such, were organized along joint stock lines, the principle already being successfully used for commercial enterprises in Britain. So, unlike the French and Spanish colonies that received financial aid for their establishment from their respective governments, British colonizers had to find other, private, sources of funds. What often happened was that a group of investors formed a company and provided the funds necessary to establish a group of settlers (who may or may not have been shareholders themselves) in the New World. Once established, it was intended that profits from the settlers' activities would flow back to Britain to enrich the investors.

Jamestown was the first permanent English colony in North America, the sponsoring company being chartered in 1606 with a monopoly of trade and settlement in Virginia. It failed as a commercial profit-making enterprise, and in 1624 Virginia became a royal colony. However, Jamestown did succeed as a settlement.

What later became the Plymouth settlement in Massachusetts was also financed using the joint stock principle. Unlike the Jamestown settlers, who included some non-shareholding indentured servants, all the Puritans of this colony were shareholders. And also unlike the Jamestown settlement, these pilgrims were not interested in looking for riches, but rather hoped to establish their own community under their own rules and institutions. The Plymouth settlement, which started in 1620, went through severe hardships, and half the original number died. It also was not a financial success, as the original investors got a return of only one quarter of their original investment. The Puritan settlements of New England—by the late 1640s, about 15,000 immigrants had arrived—were important for the later development of New England, and also for the contribution they made to the work ethic that would later be an important aspect of American economic ideology. Other English settlements were Maryland (1634), Carolina (1663), and Pennsylvania (1681).

Other profit-oriented trading posts were established, and many later became attractive to settlers. For example, the Dutch West India Company established a post at Albany in 1624, in New Amsterdam in 1626 (becoming New York in 1664 when it was taken over by the English), and in Delaware, where there was also a Swedish trading company post.

However, the failure of the early settlements as profit generators led to the use of various devices to encourage genuine settlers and also provide financial support until they had become established. For example, a proprietary colony was established in Maryland by Lord Baltimore, with a charter from Charles I, receiving its first settlers in 1634. Profits here were supposed to come from the sale and rental of land. The first settlers were given land in the hope that their success would attract more settlers, so increasing the value of land. To capture this increasing value, land could be sold at higher prices and also quit rents could

---

Indentured Servant

Temporarily unfree labor; one who is contractually bound to work for a master for a specified period of time.

Map 7.1   **Colonial Land Claims in North America**
In the 17th and 18 centuries, the European colonizing powers laid claims to huge areas of North America

be raised. This last was a curious adaptation of a feudal institution to a new country. Land was freehold, but upon its sale, owners were supposed to pay quit rents to the colony's owner, who depended on them both as a source of income and as a source of revenues to finance public services, such as roads. However this, and some other feudal customs written into the Maryland charter, proved incapable of enforcement. Because land was abundant and the different colonies competed for settlers, no potential settler had an incentive to buy land when it was available free elsewhere.

Another early settlement was established by William Penn in the area that is now Pennsylvania. From the first, it was intended to be a farming community. Also, in the original plan for Philadelphia, the area was laid out in accordance with 17th century assumption that a well-planned city was crucial for the development of a civilized culture.

A fairly significant difference between these settlements and those of other mercantilist empires lay in the degree of religious freedom. On the one hand, colonies everywhere were subject to economic control by the parent country through a comprehensive web of rules and regulations. But on the other hand, while both France and Spain required colonists to conform to the official state religion, the emigration of religious dissenters from the British Isles was permitted, resulting in a high degree of religious tolerance in British colonies in the New World. Thus Maryland became a center for Catholics, Pennsylvania attracted Quakers, and the New England colonies were centers of puritanical Congregationalists.

Urban Control Mechanisms

A third influence was that these early colonies were under English jurisdiction, peopled mainly by settlers from England who came with European ideas and institutions. In addition, the 17th century in England saw the English middle class

revolution that resulted in limitations on the monarchy's power, and this influenced the character of the new settlements. For example, the larger villages had a form of self-government similar to that of the English towns and villages they had left. Larger settlements instituted forms of regulation and control they were already familiar with, in keeping with the traditional ideas that the individual's main function was to serve the community, and that regulation of life was the responsibility of the municipal authority. Adequate food supplies had been a primary concern of the new medieval towns in Europe, as in the 17th century settlements of the New World. Regulations covered the same issues: fair prices, quality, adequacy, fair weights and measures, and proper marketing that characterized medieval towns. Towns also attempted to control building, sanitation, apprentices, strangers, security, and all the other issues and problems that face a concentration of population. Their solutions to these problems were largely based on English examples, and there was little incentive to attempt any social experimentation.

Strangely enough, even though it might be thought that a new environment would encourage new ideas, this type of regulation lasted longer than in England. Because many changes were occurring in England beginning in the 17th century, new forms of social institutions were appearing to deal with new relationships and new demands. In the colonies, on the other hand, change was much more gradual, hence urban institutions were much slower to alter. The new settlements did have one advantage over European towns, partly due to demographic factors. Most immigrants were in their economically active years, thus the age distribution was skewed toward a young, active population. This implied that problems of poverty associated with old age were minimal. Only later when the settlements became mature did these towns have to face problems of poverty, old age, and indigence as well as physical decay that were features of European towns.

Outposts of Mercantilism

Finally, colonies were established as part of a mercantilist empire having a particular role to play in that empire. When their initial survival was assured, their role was as providers of raw materials for Britain, and—less important given their limited population—as markets for manufactured goods. This, as already noted, complemented the existing economic conditions.

In this role, towns such as Boston, Philadelphia, New York, Newport, and Charlestown were important because their existence permitted a closer control over economic activity in the rest of the colonies. (A certain irony would be apparent in the 18th century, because as the towns became centers of colonial life, so they also became centers of opposition to mercantilist regulation and imperial rule.) Also in North America, a reversal of development was apparent. Many of the medieval towns in Europe emerged as a result of agricultural development. But in the colonies, and also after Independence with the westward expansion of the 19th century, the towns were settled first, permitting agriculture and other non-urban activities to spread from them. That is, the early towns were seaports and new immigrants had to enter the country through them. In later centuries, towns were the centers for supplies as well as markets. Without them, it would have been difficult to establish scattered farm settlements.

Towns can be seen as control mechanisms, both for colonial authorities and for urban and rural inhabitants alike. They were market centers and centers of religious and political life. Especially for the earliest immigrants, the prevalent idea of the 17th century was that civilized life was urban life, hence the importance of location in or near a town. Most of them had no interest in subsistence agriculture, which was no longer im-

portant in England by that time. And in a mercantilist era, the most important economic activity was commercial. So for a long time, the seaports were commercial centers, linking the colonies with Britain and becoming the main centers of colonial commercial activity.

Economic Activity: Primary Producers

Economic activity in these colonies was conditioned by two major considerations, which, however, overlapped and complemented each other. First, the colonies were part of a mercantilist empire, so there were restrictions on what they could and could not do. They were encouraged to provide those things not available in England (certain raw materials) or those things in which they had an advantage. As it turned out, adapting economic activity to their natural resource endowment was not too arduous. Colonies became primarily providers of agricultural products and raw materials that complemented the greater stress on manufacturing in Britain itself, especially from the 17th century onwards.

Thus agriculture was heavily encouraged. Two patterns of agriculture accompanied by different patterns of land use were important here, and would continue to have importance for the subsequent political development of the United States. The New England colonies were benignly ignored for their economic contribution, mainly because their conditions were much poorer than in the Southern colonies. There was a much greater stress on small individual land holdings, mainly subsistence farming, and consequently only a very limited market participation by farmers. However, in the richer areas to the south, commercial agriculture along capitalist lines predominated, and land was held in large estates, farmed using the plantation system—that is, us-

---

Subsistence Farming
Farming at a level just sufficient to meet a community's needs

ing large numbers of propertyless farm workers. The chief crops in the South were tobacco grown in Virginia, indigo, and rice; while sugar plantations were developed in the West Indies.

Tobacco was by far the most important and profitable product grown in the North American colonies. Its production was prohibited in England, where its consumption was also subject to heavy taxes. Colonial tobacco could be exported only to England, where it was processed and reexported to Europe. Tobacco plantations were among the first to use slave labor, but as tobacco cultivation required relatively little labor compared with the cultivation of sugar, there were only about 300 slaves in Virginia in 1650, compared with 100,000 working the sugar plantations in the British West Indies and 200,000 in Portuguese Brazil.

One problem with tobacco cultivation, which would have implications later in the 18th century, was that although it was very profitable, it rapidly exhausted the soil. Thus, plantation owners required access to new lands and so long as this was available, had no incentive to practice soil conservation techniques. They were violently opposed to any restrictions that would make their movement difficult. This was a characteristic of American agriculture, which remained technologically backward until new land ceased to be so freely available in the 19th century. In England, because land was in short supply, there was an incentive to adopt improved agricultural techniques, but for so long as new land was available in the United States, the same pressures did not exist.

Another commercial crop was rice, grown in the humid swamps of South Carolina, and produced for export to Europe or the West Indies. Indigo, a dye, was encouraged as a complementary crop: It was grown on the high land, and its planting and harvesting demands did not coincide with those of rice. Mercantilist aims can be seen in colonial policies. A special act was passed in 1749 to encourage the production of indigo by paying a bounty, which emphasized the desire for

economic growth. As production of textiles increased in England, so the demand for dyes also rose—and the colonies were the logical suppliers. The chief market for indigo in the 17th century was the wool industry in England, where it was used as a dye; when the cotton textile industry expanded later, indigo replaced rice as a major export. Both of these were very profitable crops: Returns were as high as 50 percent a year. (The increased supply of indigo from the Americas effectively doomed its production in India.) Pennsylvania grew wheat and barley, which were also exported to the West Indies.

This pattern of subsistence agriculture in the northern colonies and commercial export agriculture in the south was matched by a pattern of landholding that complemented it. In New England, smallholdings were farmed on an individual family basis. But in the South, holdings were too large for one family to farm, thus requiring the use of farm laborers for effective exploitation, and encouraging the development of a class of aristocratic planters. Another of the institutions the early colonists brought with them was the idea of class. While the English aristocracy did not emigrate to the New World, gentlemen did, and in the south they became a new landed aristocracy. Even in the northern colonies where there was a merchant rather than a landed aristocracy, it was recognized that inequality would and did exist. So, for example, when town plans were made, different-sized lots acknowledged that the wealthy would build larger houses, and at first, most of the colonies attempted to impose laws that required a person's clothing and behavior to conform to rank.

Extractive Industries

In terms of value and importance to colonial economic development, extractive activities were next in importance. These again depended on existing natural conditions and were encouraged both by various mercantilist regulations and by the emerging merchant class who played an instrumental role in shipping. The existence of forest resources and wilderness areas gave rise to three important industries. First, the fur trade, trapping wild animals for their fur, obviously depended on a wilderness environment. Beaver skins were highly prized for hats, while deerskins were both exported and used for clothing at home. Albany in the north and Charlestown in the south were major fur trading centers. One problem that became more acute was that expanded settlement forced the exploitation of more remote areas, and the fur trade declined in importance in the 19th century.

A second, much-encouraged, industry was shipbuilding. All the seaports developed shipbuilding capabilities, but Boston and other New England ports became dominant, a dominance persisting into the 19th century. Shipbuilding in the colonies was encouraged because of the shortage of suitable wood in England. The availability of timber in North America made the northern colonies, which were not important for commercial agriculture, valued parts of the mercantilist empire. By 1720, Boston alone had 14 shipyards and produced about 200 ships each year.

The third industry that was also encouraged was associated with shipbuilding, naval stores. This is the production of all the items needed to build and maintain ships, most of which were derived from forest products, thus benefitting from the huge forest resources of the continent. These items included tar and pitch for waterproofing, turpentine, masts, hemp for ropes, and flax for sails.[1]

Because of its relative agricultural weakness and its shipbuilding, New England also developed an important fishing industry. However, there was a problem here. Under mercantilist regulations, the British fishing industry was pro-

Naval Stores
Supplies needed for building and maintaining ships, such as pitch, tar and hemp

tected, so American-caught fish could not be sold in Britain. Instead, the fish was exported to southern Europe or the West Indies. Fish was rarely sold fresh; it was usually dried or salted, then packed in barrels. This in turn gave rise to the important subsidiary activity of the cooper, who made the barrels in which these items were shipped.

A special variation of the fishing industry was whaling, and the major whaling towns (Nantucket, New Bedford, Provincetown, and Marblehead) were also located in New England. This industry, unlike fishing itself, was encouraged, because its products were important, so in 1732, a bounty was paid to all whaling ships. The spermaceti was made into candles, whale oil was also used for lighting, and whalebone and ambergris (used in perfumery) were also in demand. In the mid 18th century, as many as 4,000 sailors were directly involved, and many others were indirectly dependent on whaling in processing the catch and preparing the boats for their expeditions. The industry expanded, and in the early 19th century was New England's third most important industry, after textiles and footwear. But overfishing depleted the whale herds, and in 1859, whale oil for lighting faced new competition: mineral oil from Pennsylvania. Then, squeezed between declining demand and declining supply, the whaling fleets shrank dramatically.

One other extractive industry also deserves mention. Before 1750, half of Britain's iron was imported from Europe, but a shortage of suitable timber for smelting ore forced innovations in iron making technology in England. However, when Sweden imposed a 25 percent export tax on iron, it helped stimulate iron production in the Middle Atlantic colonies of New Jersey and Pennsylvania, which had the advantage of plenty of wood for making charcoal. Production was further encouraged with the Iron Act of 1750, which eliminated duties on American pig iron imported into England. However, in keeping with the spirit of mercantilism, further processing of iron beyond the pig iron stage in the colonies was limited to domestic uses, and only pig iron itself was exported. But in fact, iron making in North America was retarded even when these prohibitions were ended, as the availability of cheap wood for charcoal delayed the introduction of the more modern techniques that were introduced in England in the late 18th century. In addition, the slow pace of industrial development limited the market for products made out of iron.

Commerce

An important source of wealth in the colonies was shipping and commerce. Shipbuilding was encouraged by the provisions of the Navigation Acts, and colonial shippers and merchants also benefitted, so the seaports, especially Boston, flourished as commercial centers. Boston became the largest, wealthiest and most populous port. It had a population of 12,000 by 1720, while Philadelphia at that time contained 10,000 inhabitants, and New York was well back in third place. (New York would not become a large important port and city until the 19th century.)

Trading was obviously important, both to export the products of the colonies and to import the needed manufactured items. However, trading patterns varied between the different colonies. Although the growth of trade under the protection of the mercantilist empire initially benefitted merchants, at the same time, it led to resentment of these restrictions—and the weakening of mercantilism itself with the achievement of American independence.

Difficulty of Manufacturing

Manufacturing was not encouraged in the colonies, and in fact, it would have been difficult and costly. The exceptions were small scale, local market undertakings such as printing. As the previous chapters have shown, the transformation of feudal economies into modern industrial capitalist ones

was a long, slow process. While New World colonies did not have a feudal past, they did share other limitations on the introduction of manufacturing techniques that the European countries were only just beginning to overcome. These included a shortage of labor, which would have made the introduction of the then-prevalent labor-intensive techniques prohibitively expensive. In fact, even in situations where paid labor existed, wage rates in America were considerably above those in England, a situation that would persist. (A discussion of how the labor shortage problem was dealt with in colonial times will follow.) A second limitation was the existence of an ideology of free men escaping political or religious repression. This, plus the existence of ample supplies of cheap land meant that it was possible for settlers to acquire land and remain as subsistence farmers, an alternative not available in England, where most landholdings were in the process of being amalgamated into estates for commercial production by a few landowners who effectively expropriated the original small farmers.

The third limitation was the shortage of capital, both private and social. We have seen that financial markets were developing in Europe to make the mobilization of capital easier. But the same development could not occur in a newly settled area where survival was the primary object. In addition, the colonies were wilderness, which made the rapid construction of infrastructure difficult. Capital was universally relatively scarce at this time. The story of how productive capital became less scarce owes much to the development of mercantilist empires. Even without any restrictions, it would have been unusual if large scale capitalist manufacturing enterprise had been attempted.

Forced Labor

The main problem faced by Southern colonists and plantations in the West Indies and South

America was a shortage of labor, which led to the system of forced labor. The use of African slaves for colonial work was initiated by the Portuguese in the 16th century. To begin with, the English were involved mainly with the slave trade, but once the potential profits from plantation agriculture were apparent, slavery became the dominant form of labor.

A less demeaning form of forced labor, indentured servitude, was also used, and about half of the white immigrants into the 13 colonies were indentured. Indenture involved a formal agreement for a limited period of time, usually four to five years, under which the servant agreed to perform the work required in return for passage to the colonies. While this increased the numbers of settlers, it was not enough to provide a large enough labor force for profitable capitalist expansion. Once the period of indenture was over, the servant was free to work for wages. But as wages were high and land was cheap, most soon found themselves in a position to acquire land of their own, so they were no longer part of a potential wage labor force.

Forced labor was not considered suitable for manufacturing enterprises. This is probably due more to the white settlers' prevailing ideas of slaves' racial inferiority rather than any practical barrier to its use. In fact, the use of forced labor is an unusual anomaly in the development of capitalism, which depends on a free labor force.

Trade Regulation

Trade regulation in the entire British empire was extensive. As was the case with the other European colonizers, use of monopoly trading companies was common. One example was the British East India Company, formed in response to the problems individual traders faced from opposition by other countries' traders. Thus, a group of English merchants trading in India formed a joint stock company in 1599, and were granted a charter in the following year for the monopoly of trade between England and India. To begin with, the arrangement was temporary; each trading expedition was organized on a self-contained basis, and the company was reestablished to finance successive endeavors. It became a permanent joint stock company in 1657 and acquired the right of administering its Indian possessions. (In contrast, the American colonies became royal colonies, and were governed from London and not by a commercial company.)

Trade with India presented a problem, because while there was a ready market for Indian products—cotton textiles (calicoes), tea, and spices—England had little to offer in return. The major exports from England were wool textiles, tin (pewter), and lead, but the latter two found only small sales in India, while wool was obviously unsuitable as an export to a hot climate. The only answer was to export bullion. The arguments of the East India Company officials showed the greater advantage that would accrue to England by permitting bullion exports, influencing the alteration of policy away from a narrow bullionist philosophy and toward an emphasis on a favorable balance of trade (see Chapter 6).

Navigation Acts

The policies by which production and trade were regulated were known as the Navigation Acts. A series of these were passed during the 17th century, but two, in 1651 and 1660, consolidated many of the previous ones. The first specified that all goods produced within the empire be brought to England in English ships or the ships of the country of origin, the purpose being to deny this carrying trade to the Dutch. It was successful, and as a result, also increased shipbuilding, especially in New England, to meet the larger demand for ships. The total of merchant shipping increased dramatically to about 420,000 tons in 1751, and was accompanied by complementary dock building and port improvements—a necessity if the desired increase in trade was to be accommodated.

The 1660 Act enumerated (listed) the various products that could be produced and traded. Certain commodities could be produced only in the colonies and exported only to Britain or another colony. This list included sugar, tobacco, indigo, ginger, and dyewoods. While some of these could be produced only in the colonies, the production of items that could also be produced in Britain was prohibited there. Thus, tobacco growers in Virginia gained from the prohibition of tobacco growing in Britain.

In general, commodities requiring extensive processing were produced only in Britain. Thus, iron processing in the North American colonies was prohibited, and a 1721 law prevented the import of calicoes into Britain. This led to the subsequent development of a cotton manufacturing industry in England and the demise of Indian cotton production.

Other measures aimed at increasing trade with other countries. For example, in 1702 a treaty with Portugal arranged favorable deals for trade in wool (from England) and wine (from Portugal). Later, the market for British exports in South America was opened up. The domestic market itself was protected with high customs duties on imports that could compete with domestically produced goods.

Restriction and Enforcement

While there were many policies on the Statute Book, and many more were added especially in the 18th century, not all were or could be enforced. However, increasing restrictiveness irked some North American colonists especially, and

	Table 7-1 Slave Trade, 1451-1700	
Importing Area	**Number (in 000s)**	
	1451–1600	1601–1700
Sao Thome and Atlantic Isles	100	25
Brazil	50	550
Caribbean	—	450
Spanish America	75	300
British North America	1	3
Europe	50	—

Note: In the late 18th century (not shown here) about 100,000 Africans were exported as slaves annually. In 1807, the British slave trade ended, and American slave traders then accounted for the bulk of the slave trade, which reached its peak in the 1830s when about 135,000 Africans were exported annually. A total of about 9.5 million Africans were involved before the end of the trade. In 1820, there were about 1,750,000 slaves in the United States, representing 36% of all slaves in the Western Hemisphere; this figure had grown to 4.5 million in 1860 largely due to a higher rate of natural increase than elsewhere.

Source: derived from P.D. Curtin, *The Atlantic Slave Trade: A Census*, Madison: University of Wisconsin Press, 1969; Robert W. Fogel and Stanley L. Engerman, *Time on the Cross*, Boston: Little, Brown, 1974.

was one element leading to the struggle for independence in the late 18th century. This was more of a political protest against mercantilism, as after independence, the commercial activities of American traders suffered a severe decline because they lost their trading rights within the empire as a whole.

Some restrictions were easily evaded because enforcement was weak, while others were simply unworkable. For example, while most colonial products could be shipped to other parts of the empire, some were required to be shipped only to England. This backfired in the case of rice, which was grown in the Carolinas, and had previously been shipped directly to the West Indies. But when rice was added to the list of goods that had to be shipped first to England, it went bad because of the extra transportation time.

The obvious purpose of these measures was to increase wealth. Those involved in trade and trade-related activities gained from the increasing size of the protected market and access to low-cost raw material imports. (In fact, one motive behind the union of Scotland and England under one crown in 1707 was the desire of Scottish shippers to gain the same privileges as American shippers.) Gains could be made for two reasons. These policies effectively produced favorable terms of trade for British merchants and producers, but those in the colonies, such as sugar and tobacco planters, shipbuilders, and merchants, also gained wealth as a result of access to a protected market. Second, the volume of trade itself grew. In the 18th century, there was more concern with enlarging the size of the trade "pie" rather than with increasing the share of a given trade total. This would eventually lead to conflict between merchants and industrialists.

Between 1622 and 1760, total British trade increased five-fold, with exports increasing at a faster rate than imports. What is also important is a change in the pattern of trade, both by commodity and by area, because this reflects not only the result of mercantilist trade policies but also the economic changes taking place within Britain itself.

Composition and Direction of Trade

A large part of the export trade was accounted for by reexports of colonial products to Europe (a very profitable trade), accounting for about 4 percent of all exports in the mid 17th century. By the beginning of the 18th century, both the absolute amount and the relative share of reexports had risen, to about one third of all exports. For example, 90 percent of all spices, two thirds of calicoes, coffee, tea, and tobacco, and one third of the sugar from the colonies were reexported.

In absolute terms, the greatest growth in exports occurred to non-European countries, rising from almost nothing to one fifth by the mid 18th century. These areas took almost three quarters of manufactured goods exports—a phenomenon accounted for by both the lack of manufacturing production elsewhere and by the barriers erected by the European countries, which were attempting to encourage their own domestic manufacturing. The pattern of imports also reflected this change of dependence away from European trade. By the mid 18th century, half of all imports came from non-European sources.

The type of product being traded also changed, a reflection of the growth and increasing diversification of industrial production that benefitted from protection. Britain's traditional export, woolens, accounted for 80 percent of all exports in the mid 17th century, but declined relatively, although not absolutely, to one third by 1760, as other manufactured items rose to account for a 20 percent share. Products that were produced and exported in increasing quantities in the 18th century included coal and china—both the products of new industries.

The impact of these changes in trade also showed in consumption patterns. Sugar replaced honey as a sweetener, and coffee consumption reached its highest levels in the mid 18th century,

Table 7-2
Geographical Distribution of England's Foreign Trade,
1700–1701 and 1750–1751, percentage of total

	Europe	N. America	West Indies	E. Indies & Africa
Total Imports From:				
1700–1701	66	6	14	14
1750–1751	55	11	19	15
Re-exports to:				
1700–1701	85	5	6	5
1750–1751	79	11	5	5
Domestically Produced Exports to:				
1700–1701	85	6	5	4
1750–1751	77	11	5	7

Source: derived from Phyllis Deane, *The First Industrial Revolution*, Cambridge, Cambridge University Press,

after which it yielded predominance as a nonalcoholic beverage to tea. (Tea imports increased 120 times in the first fifty years of the 18th century.) The consumption of tea, and its rise in popularity, was paralleled by the increasing production of earthenware, which helped make it accessible to a growing proportion of the population. Old spices (like ginger or cinnamon) were more plentiful than before, and new flavors (allspice, chocolate, and vanilla) were now possible because of the opening up of new sources of spices. Totally new products—potatoes, tomatoes, and turkeys— were also introduced from the New World, although they did not have an appreciable impact on eating habits until much later.

Consequences

There were many consequences resulting from mercantilist policies, and some countries gained more than others. In particular, Britain at the end of this period had overcome its initial inferiority

in wealth and industry, even though its domestic population was only one third as large as France's. There were five major consequences, all related to each other: the shift of the center of economic activity to the Atlantic seaboard countries; the growth of trade and the encouragement it gave to the development of new industries; inflation, and the assistance this gave to transferring power to the new capitalist classes; the encouragement given to capital accumulation; and the stimulus given to the development of some of the colonial areas.

Shift to the Atlantic

First, following the voyages of discovery and the start of colonialization in the New World, economic advantage lay with countries on the Atlantic seaboard: Spain, Portugal, France, Holland, and Britain. The centers of European economic activity shifted west, away from the Mediterranean, giving an advantage to locations on the new trade routes and leading to the decline of Venice and other Italian port cities. These five countries were politically unified. In contrast, both Italy and Germany remained politically fragmented until well into the 19th century. The advantage of a strong central authority in the administration of new colonial areas was important and crucial for the successful implementation of protectionist policies.

With this shift in the relative fortunes of countries came an advantage to those port cities, such as Cadiz, Lisbon, Bordeaux, Amsterdam, Antwerp, Bristol, and London, located on the new ocean-trade routes. In particular, London grew into a large, thriving port and commercial city. The bulk of British trade was channeled through it, which attracted both industrial and financial development: the new exchanges, for example, were located here, and London gained from being at the center of a far-flung empire. Similarly Amsterdam also grew in importance as a trading and financial center. However, its earlier development of its financial exchanges and the growth of its financial interests drew attention away from investing in industrial enterprises. It was easier to put money into the commodity exchanges and the monetary returns were greater.

Growth in Trade

In spite of the profits to be made in paper transactions, the second major consequence of mercantilism was the dramatic growth in trade. This stimulated the development of new industries, many specifically designed to process the supplies of raw materials available from colonial possessions. Thus the emphasis on adjusting trade to produce favorable terms of trade implied that potential producers had access to low cost raw material imports such as sugar, tobacco, iron, and timber. The development of such industries, plus the import of other food items like coffee and tea, helped encourage the development of complementary new industries—earthenware manufacture, for example.

Growth on this scale would not have been possible, given the relative scarcity of capital, without an accompanying development in business organization, banking, and finance. Individual capital was insufficient to launch a new, untried enterprise. At this time, we see the initial use of the joint stock principle in business formation, and the development of a more sophisticated organization for launching new enterprises and transferring ownership of shares. The first examples of such exchanges took place at the already existing commodity exchanges, or, in a neat example of simultaneous occurrence, at the newly started coffee houses. But by the late 18th century, exchanges involving only stock transfers became separate organizations.

Inflation

The third major consequence of mercantilist exploration of the New World was an inflation fueled by the increase in imports of precious metals from the Americas. Between 1500 and 1650, prices rose by between 200 and 300 percent. It is impossible to derive a unique cause-effect relationship, as prices had been rising before the start of bullion imports. But it is undoubted that prices continued to rise as bullion supplies increased faster than the stocks of goods plus the rise in commercial transactions. It has been estimated that due to bullion imports from the New World plus production from existing mines in Austria and Germany, stocks of precious metals tripled in this time period. Spain was the major importer of bullion and tried to keep it within the country, but because it had a trade deficit with the rest of Europe, was forced to pay in bullion. This, plus pirates' successful attacks on Spanish ships and other forms of smuggling, helped account for the increase in bullion holdings throughout the rest of Europe.

Prices and wages both rose, but prices rose faster than wages, and this inflationary impact on profits stimulated both merchants and industrialists to expand. The expansionary impact on industrial production was least in Spain and Portugal, where other conditions necessary to start industrial production along capitalist lines were nonexistent.

However, landowners did not gain, especially those who were still receiving rental incomes from land based on feudal customs, who saw their incomes stagnate while prices rose. As a result, in France, for example, many landowners either mortgaged their lands or sold them to the now-wealthy merchants. English landowners were not so affected by this process for two reasons. First, many had modernized the basis of their land rentals as a result of the 16th century enclosures. Second, many had already evicted tenants and were now operating commercial farming enterprises, and thus they gained from the rise in food prices.

With the exception of modernizing landowners, this inflation involved a transfer of economic power from landholders to the newer, commercial classes who were interested in investing in productive enterprises. This shift in economic power was accompanied by a shift in political power, and it is no surprise that mercantilist policies adopted by the state were precisely those that favored commercial activity.

Changes in the Distribution of Economic Power

Fourth, this shift in economic power resulting from inflation gave a boost to the capital-accumulation process by putting wealth into the hands of those who would use it productively. Again, this would not have been possible had not a broad, capitalist framework been in the process of being established. And in Britain, where conditions were most favorable and mercantilist policies most successful, the greatest changes occurred. This shift also encouraged the further development of business organizations: The rise in new activities saw significant use of the joint stock form and parallel financial developments.

Colonial Development

And finally, many of the colonies also gained. In the British North American colonies, for example, the fortunes of plantation owners, shipbuilders, and merchants increased, which would have an impact on the later capitalist development of the independent United States. Colonial ships had the same privileges as British ones, traders received protection on voyages, and access to a large, protected market for colonial products was beneficial. In addition, access to supplies of capital helped development, especially in the construction of infrastructure.

Mercantilism was important in helping to achieve the conditions necessary for sustained growth along capitalist lines because it did permit the transfer of wealth to the classes who would use it for productive investment, rather than for luxury consumption or military purposes. Thus the aims of the mercantilists—to increase the wealth of the nation—would remain desirable, even when mercantilist policies themselves were seen as too restrictive, and thus damaging to continued economic expansion.

Laissez faire ideas later in the 18th century became the favored basis for proposed policies and were especially appealing to the new industrialists. But this was a product of the times. That is, without an industrial base and thus an advantage in industrial techniques plus the developing capitalist framework that state assistance had helped make possible, laissez faire policies would be impractical to implement. The earlier recognition of cooperation—seen in the joint stock company, or in the demands that the state's assistance be used to achieve desired ends—had made it clear that new activities required favorable conditions for their survival. Thus it was ironic that the very success of mercantilism should lead to its overturn.

Notes

1. One center for the production of naval stores, including tar, was located in the Carolinas, which may explain the origin of the "Tarheel" nickname for natives of North Carolina.

Key Concepts

Elastic demand

Inelastic demand

Mercantilist empire

Plantation

Resource endowment

Terms of trade

Indentured servitude

Inflation

Naval stores

Primary product; primary producer

Slavery

Trade regulation

Questions for Discussion or Essay Writing

1. To what extent is it true that "mercantilism opened up the world for capitalism"?

2. Controlling the trade in spices was important to 16th and 17th century merchants and their rulers. What were the results of the struggle for control?

3. Nations attempted to regulate trade under the influence of mercantilist thinking. Why and how did they do this? Were there any differences between regulation in the 16th and in the 18th centuries?

4. To what extent were the British Navigation Acts representative of mercantilist thinking?

5. The creation of mercantilist empires was thought to be important to the wealth-creating process. Why? How?

6. Evaluate trade and colonial policies in the 17th and 18th centuries with respect to their effect on capitalist economic development.

7. Urban settlements in North America represented an important form of control over colonial areas. How did they contribute to material life and to colonial development?

8. Describe some of the scientific and technical discoveries that made long ocean voyages possible in the 15th-17th centuries.

9. What was the relevance of a colony's "resource endowment" to its economic development? Were there other influences on development?

10. What new financial developments occurred at this time? What effect did they have?

For Further Reading

Clark, Alice. *Working Life of Women in the 17th Century,* New York: A.M. Kelley, 1968.

Ekelund, Robert B. and Robert D. Tollison. *Mercantilism as a Rent-Seeking Society: Economic Regulation in Historical Perspective.* College Station, Tex: Texas A & M University Press, 1981.

Elliot, J.H. *The Old World and the New, 1492-1650.* Cambridge: Cambridge University Press, 1970.

Goldthwaite, Richard A. "The Medici Bank and the World of Florentine Capitalism." *Past and Present,* Vol. 114 (February 1987) 3–31.

Heckscher, Eli F. *Mercantilism.* London: George Allen & Unwin, 1955.

Hill, C.P. *Reformation to Industrial Revolution.* The Pelican Economic History of Britain, vol. 2 1530-1780. Harmondsworth: Penguin Books (1967) 1969.

Hopkins, A.G. and P.J. Cain, "The Political Economy of British Expansion Overseas, 1750-1914." *Economic History Review* XXXIII:4 (1979) 463-489.

Lodge, Eleanor C. *Sully, Colbert and Turgot: A Chapter in French Economic History.* Port Washington, N.Y.: Kennikat Press (1931) 1970.

Mettam, Roger, ed. *Government and Society in Louis XIV's France.* London: Macmillan, 1977.

McCusker, John J. and Russell R. Menard. *The Economy of British North America, 1607-1789. 2nd ed.* Chapel Hill: University of North Carolina Press, 1985.

Nef, John U. *Industry and Government in France and England 1540-1640.* Ithaca: Great Seal Books, 1957.

_____ *War and Human Progress.* Cambridge, Mass: Harvard University Press, 1950.

Parry, J.H. *The Establishment of European Hegemony, 1415-1715.* New York: Harper & Row, 1961.

Schama, Simon. *The Embarrassment of Riches: An Interpretation of Dutch Culture in the Golden Age.* New York: Alfred A. Knopf, 1987.

Wallenstein, Immanuel M. *The Modern World System II: Mercantilism and the Consolidation of the European World Economy 1600-1750.* New York: Academic Press, 1980.

Ward, J.R. "The Profitability of Sugar Planting in the British West Indies, 1650-1834" *Economic History Review,* XXXI:20 (1977) 97-213.

Wernham, R.B. *The Counter-Reformation and Price Revolution 1559-1610,* volume 3, The New Cambridge Modern History. Cambridge: Cambridge University Press, 1968.

Williams, Neville. *The Sea Dogs: Privateers, Plunder and Piracy in the Elizabethan Age.* New York: Macmillan, 1975.

Wilson, Charles and Geoffrey Parker, *An Introduction to the Sources of European Economic History 1500-1800.* London: Weidenfeld & Nicolson, 1977.

Chapter 8

Changes in England (15th to 16th Centuries)

Introduction

THE 16TH CENTURY WAS A CRUCIAL TIME in the transition period between feudalism and capitalism, and England was the place in which many developing trends became clear. England had previously been an economic, political, and military backwater, but now emerged from obscurity to play a leading role. Two important preconditions for the establishment of a profit-oriented, private-enterprise economy were met, building on the base put into place since the weakening of feudalism.

These two preconditions were the creation of the institution of private property in land resulting from the enclosure movement, and the related emergence of the first free labor force. At the same time, the capitalist principles that had previously influenced commercial activities now began to influence industry. In the 16th century, we see for the first time a large industry organized along capitalist lines achieving a much greater degree of permanence than those established earlier.

Commercial Capitalism

It is not surprising that commercial activities were the first to be capitalist, nor that production activities should next be influenced by the capital accumulation motive. Merchants are marketers—they distribute and sell already-produced products, and given a demand for what they provide, face the least risk. That is, a merchant's capital is either in money form, immediately after a sale, or in commodity form, immediately after a purchase. When goods turn over quickly, this short time horizon lessens risk and helps explain why merchants were the first to be influenced by capitalist ideas.

And, as we have seen, these activities and the establishment and expansion of a market economy flourished after the 11th century. But the scarcity of goods that could be profitably sold limited the expansion of the market, a limit that began to be noticeable in the 15th century. The obvious next step was to ensure an increasing supply of goods, but how was this to be done? Existing guild regulations limited output, so the merchant-capitalist increasingly became involved in production outside these regulations.

Industrial Capitalism

If the industrial capitalist is defined as one involved in *producing* goods and is the owner of the capital used to produce them (raw materials, machines, and equipment, for example), then three important considerations are relevant. First, production lengthens the time horizon, which increases risk. Unlike the merchant, the industrial capitalist must tie up funds for a long time in setting up production in advance of the goods becoming available for sale. If sales do not materialize, the industrial capitalist suffers a loss. Thus, an already existing market created during the preceding centuries helps explain the timing of this stage of capitalism's development.

Second, because more capital is needed for production than for distribution—increasingly specialized machines and buildings are expensive as well as durable—capitalist production will not take place unless large quantities of output can be produced for an extended period of time. So the scale of production and the time involved increase. Third, once the option of increasing output under existing regulations (meaning guild regulations at this time) is ruled out, workers to operate the machinery and produce the goods must be found. These workers are not available, permanently *and* full time, in a predominantly agricultural community where farmers are independent producers tied to the land.

At first, merchants' involvement was secondary to their primary activity of selling finished goods, but industrial activities became increasingly separated from pure selling. Production was on a large scale, which was possible only if large amounts could be sold consistently, and if all the required inputs were available in the right quantities and at the right time. Production, in other words, had to become permanent and continuous as well as large scale.

This was not possible in 14th century Europe. The necessary conditions were not present in an agricultural society, although as we saw, increasing sales by merchants were compatible with such a society because they were incidental to the main form of economic activity. So the necessary conditions for the establishment of production on capitalist lines had to be created.

One of them, the existence of markets, was being put in place in the 16th century. Now we will see how a permanent free labor force, emerging as a result of the agrarian changes taking place in 16th century England, makes possible the expansion of industrial production. This can occur only in an economy where markets have ceased to be incidental and have become instead the major coordinators of economic activity.

16th Century Enclosures

The decline of feudalism in Europe meant, at least economically if not legally, the end of feudal tenure and the special relationships that existed between lords and serfs. A semifeudal system in which peasants were only partly free then became common over much of Europe. Peasants were still tied to the land, as before, but were free of their previous feudal obligations. In modern economic terminology, the labor resource was still immobile.

Enclosure

The process of creating private ownership of land

In some areas, most notably in the Low Countries, agriculture became much more market oriented. Many urban centers had developed, so there was a ready market for farmers' output, and wealth derived from trade was also available to be used to expand commercial agriculture. But the most far-reaching changes that altered the system of farming, landscape of the country, and rural social relationships occurred in England as a result of what has been called the enclosure movement.

Enclosures began about 1485 during the reign of Henry VII, the first Tudor monarch, and continued to the mid-17th century, when they became less frequent. They began again in 1700 and the last were completed in the middle of the 19th century. While enclosures followed the same pattern and were dominated by the same motives, there are two distinct phases, each with specific characteristics. The first phase, up to the mid-17th century, we can conveniently call the 16th century enclosures, and the second phase the 18th century enclosures. In this chapter, we will look at the first set, and will leave consideration of the 18th century enclosures to a later chapter.

Enclosure has a narrow sense of simply separating one landholding from another by planting a hedge, erecting a fence, or digging a ditch. It indicates ownership and prevents animals from straying onto neighboring land. In this sense, enclosure can occur at any time and in any place.

Conversion to Private Ownership

A broader concept of enclosure was relevant in the 16th century: The conversion of land into privately held land. Now land would no longer be seen as a God-given asset to be used for material needs, but as an income-yielding asset, and land was converted from arable to pasture. Conversion to pasture reduced labor needs and led to depopulation of entire rural communities. It was the origin of the free labor force—a "surplus" population with few economic alternatives except as wage workers for the newly expanding wool industry.

To summarize, feudal land tenure implied community control. No one individual owned the land in any modern sense, and all had customary rights to use it. These rights were matched by certain obligations toward others based on access to the land. The idea of individual ownership, however, superseded the idea of community control, as profit-seeking landlords converted their own holdings into sheep pastures in order to export wool to Flanders. As they did this, they also tried to dispossess peasants from their holdings in order to increase their own pasture land.

The affected area was small, and only about three-quarters of a million acres were enclosed during the first phase. But the number of people involved was significant and the results demonstrated again that feudalism as an economic and social force was dead.

Effects

It is easy to take a narrow economic view and judge enclosures as ultimately beneficial. They did contribute to the rise of an important wool processing industry in England, but the immediate social impact was painful. Many peasants suffered by losing their livelihood, losing their economic independence to become economically dependent. Some have called enclosures a revolution of the rich against the poor. The economically powerful overturned centuries of tradition and custom in their search for gain. The poorer members of society could no longer count on protection: Society was going through a violent social change. Perhaps violence was necessary, because it is difficult to imagine the results emerging from a gradual process of historical evolution.

This social impact, like other economic changes in other times, led to protests and opposition, and prompted a series of measures intended to prevent enclosure. Enclosure in the narrow sense was often an improvement—agricultural yields rose and the value of enclosed land was at least double that of unenclosed land. But the conversion to pasture, the resulting social hardships caused by unemployment, and the perceived (but as it turned out, unjustified) fear that the nation's food supply would diminish, led to countermeasures. While government action did not stop enclosures, it has been argued that it served to slow them down, thus giving society more time to adjust and perhaps preventing a social catastrophe. Interestingly enough, by the 18th century, the emphasis on enclosures as an improvement and the dominance of the idea of individual self-interest were effective in preventing any government opposition. Only in the 16th century did social indignation at what a few landholders were doing result in attempts to ameliorate the situation.

Why Did the Enclosure Movement Happen?

The desire for gain, put into a more rational, capitalist framework, was the underlying motive behind these changes in economic activity. If we now apply this principle to 16th century England, can we discover why this desire affected landholders, and why the result was an expansion of sheep farming?

During the Middle Ages, the most important export from England was raw wool. It went chiefly to the textile centers of Flanders and Florence, and was highly sought after because of its fine quality. The resulting wool fabrics were important commodities for sale in the medieval fairs.

Decline of Wool Exports

The Black Death slowed down the wool trade temporarily by disrupting the wool market. At the beginning of the 14th century, 30,000 sacks of wool (each containing 364 pounds of wool) were exported from England, a total that rose to 40,000 fifty years later. Even while exports were rising, the price of wool rose too; between 1450 and 1635 (when the first enclosure movement was running out of steam) wool prices quadrupled. The reason was that demand for wool from both foreign, and increasingly from domestic buyers, was rising.

However, exports of raw wool declined after the middle of the 15th century, and finished cloth became the leading export from England. This was partly due to the decline of foreign processing centers and partly due to the development of an English wool processing industry. So raw wool exports, which had previously been subject to taxes to provide revenues for the monarch, were now taxed heavily as a protectionist measure. That is, high taxes made exporting raw wool less profitable, so more wool became available to domestic manufacturers, which was encouraged in many other ways, too.

Rising Prices

But whether wool prices were rising because of foreign or domestic demand, there was an incentive to raise more sheep. From the late 15th century on, the move to convert land to pasture for this purpose accelerated. Landholders initially had several options if they wished to take advantage of sheep raising. To keep up the quality of the wool, it was important to prevent contact with possibly diseased animals kept by a peasant farmer, hence the initial move toward enclosure in the narrow sense. But such commercially minded landowners also wanted to expand their scale of operations. So in addition to enclosing demesne land (which was not controversial), some also enclosed waste land (also not controversial if it was genuinely waste, or currently unused land), and some attempted to enclose common land or merge scattered holdings. This last action was definitely controversial, because it often involved dispossessing existing strip farmers.

Change in Landholding Terms

The general rise in prices that occurred in the 16th century gave a second motive. Again, as a result of commutation and the alienation of the demesne, many of the old feudal nobility had exchanged a labor service requirement for money payments. But the level of these payments were geared to standards appropriate to earlier centuries, and the resulting more or less fixed money incomes were insufficient in the 16th century. They were too low, given both the general inflation and the rise in what was now seen as an appropriate life-style for the upper class.

The nobility now had an incentive to end leases granted to tenants farming demesne land or land that had reverted to the lord's control as a result of the decline in population following the Black Death. Alternatively, they could raise rents so high that the tenant was left with no option other than to let the lease lapse. Either way, more land came under the control of a smaller number of large landholders and could then be converted to sheep pasture.

Conversion was also associated with another result of the end of feudalism. England became unified under a strong, centralized monarchy once the Tudors acceded to the throne. The feudal nobility had lost power, so there was less need for each noble to have a loyal peasantry to be used for military purposes; by now, the monarch held military and political power.

In addition, arable farming required more labor than sheep farming, so a landlord who converted land to pasture would not need to employ the former tenant farmers or the farmers whose land he took over. The result was both unemployment and less need for housing as the now unneeded surplus population in affected areas moved elsewhere in search of work. This population shift and the sight of abandoned houses falling into disrepair were among the most visible aspects of the 16th century depopulation of areas most affected by enclosure. In summary, the general weakening of feudal ties and the ideas of personal relationships on which feudalism was based were not strong enough to withstand the onslaught of the new materialist, individualist ethic.

Who Was Involved?

Not all landlords were enclosing landlords—as late as the middle of the 18th century, 60 percent of all cultivated land remained unenclosed, with some of it still being cultivated on the strip system. But enclosing landlords had more in common with the new commercial mentality than with the old feudal ethic. While some enclosures were done by descendants of the old feudal nobility, or, on a smaller scale, by a freeholder who had prospered, most were done by "new" men. They were merchants or clothiers who had bought land or, very rarely, married into an old landholding family.

Original landholders were most likely to enclose and possibly extend demesne land, which was generally not controversial unless it involved a consolidation of strips that encroached on neighboring land. But the easiest way for enclosure to take place on a large scale, and for an entirely new landholding system and a new type of landowner to be introduced, came as a result of the English Reformation.

Enclosure of Church Lands

Henry VIII confiscated all Church lands during the English Reformation. So chronic was the Crown's needs for revenues that this land was sold to men who supported the monarchy and the new religion. The buyers, of course, had to be able to pay, which implied that most of the confiscated land ended up in the hands of rich merchants. Several important implications followed. The new landowners not only were aware of the profit potential of sheep, they were also less likely to be willing to enter into the traditional landlord-tenant farmer relationship. They had no qualms about removing existing tenants and converting land into pasture. Besides, why should they be conscience-stricken when they were only following the example of the Crown, which had appropriated lands from the Church?

Such new owners were the obvious gainers from enclosure, and their wealth and political power grew. Later in the 17th century, many supported the struggle against the absolutism of the Stuart monarchy which succeeded the Tudors. They controlled Parliament, which became increasingly more important in governing the country.

But most of the smaller landholders—descendants of feudal serfs—did suffer. To understand the impact of this change, it is useful to distinguish different categories of landholders. Freeholders accounted for about 20 percent of all landholders. They had permanently secure tenure, possibly achieved as a result of giving some

Figure 8.1   Enclosure of land for sheep pasture was common in England after the 16th century. This scene, of Millers Dale in Derbyshire, shows dry stone walls separating the pasture. (Courtesy of the British Tourist Office)

special service to their feudal lord, that could be passed on to their descendants. They were not affected by enclosure unless they chose to sell their land to an enclosing landlord.

A second group consisted of leaseholders, who made up somewhat less than 20 percent of all landholders. They were small farmers who rented land for a money payment and could farm land as they pleased so long as they paid the rent. This type of tenure was the first example of a contractual relationship to emerge on the land as feudalism declined, and the legal rights involved with the contract were known. Whether or not they suffered depended on whether it was a short or a long lease, and whether the contractual payment was fixed for the term of the lease or was variable.

Those who were most at risk held short leases, because when the lease ended, the landlord had no obligation to renew it. A landlord could indirectly remove leaseholders by offering to renew the lease at an exorbitantly high rent, a practice known as rack renting. What the landlord did ultimately depended on the location of the leased land. If it could be absorbed into his existing holding, then the tenant would be forced out when the lease ended. A second group of leaseholders who were also at risk held leases with provisions for rent increases. These rents could be increased to the point where the tenant farmer could no longer afford to pay.

Rack renting
The practice of charging extremely high rents

Customary Tenants

The least secure farmers, who also accounted for the largest numbers, were the customary tenants. Their problems revolved around the fact that the ending of feudalism did not involve an end of the *legal* obligations of feudalism. While many obli-

---

Customary tenant
One holding land according to traditional practice

---

gations had simply fallen into disuse, strictly speaking a landlord could use these tenants' uncertain legal status to his advantage.

Customary tenants were either copyholders or tenants-at-will. A copyholder had the right to use a particular piece of land, a right that had been recorded in the manor records. That is, some documentation of the right existed, and remained valid for so long as the community was willing to recognize it as a valid claim. However, some landlords used provisions of the copyhold to evict the copyholder. For example, while most could be inherited, an inheritance fee had to be paid when it passed from one tenant to another. If this fee was raised so high that the new tenant was unable to pay, the land reverted to the landlord. But even in cases where the record existed and the inheritance fee was fixed, landlords could always use other means to remove tenants. Copies could be regrettably "lost," and a tenant trying to prove a claim in court had little chance of success when the court itself was made up of large landowners.

Tenants-at-will were the least secure. They had no documentation of their right, and literally could remain on their holdings for only so long as the landlord agreed. Thus they could be the most easily and immediately dispossessed.

Enclosure of Common Land

Even when the landlord did not directly evict tenants, there was an equally effective, indirect way of doing it: To take over the common land, even though they had no legal or moral claim to it. This did not happen often in the 16th century, but if it did, it very effectively removed the viability of arable farming. It also finally signalled an end to an important element of the feudal ethic— the existence of land that was available to all.

Small scale arable farming was viable if the farmers' livestock could graze on common land, or if timber for building or fuel gathered or other supplements to life were available there. But when the commons was enclosed, farmers had no other place to graze cattle or pigs, and arable farming thus became an economically marginal occupation.

Why would enclosing landlords take over the commons? The incentive was that this increased pasture land without the need for conversion from arable land. They could enclose it because the old customs had lost their strength. The major problem was that the villagers' rights to the common land existed only "according to the custom of the manor," and because this right had become legally uncertain, it was only too easy for might to make right. Then the villagers found themselves without rights they always thought they had.

Results

Unemployment

Although only a few tenants were dispossessed outright, the effect on the rural population in many parts of the country was much larger. Many more people were indirectly affected and lost their livelihood or remained on a precariously marginal basis. It is possible to identify four groups involved in this rural depopulation. In the first group were the small farmers who lost their entire holding as a result of enclosure by the landlord. Second were the farmers who kept their land but lost the use of the now enclosed common land, so they were no longer financially viable as farmers. Third were farmers who retained at least some of their land and who had previously supplemented their farm income with some occasional handi-

---

Depopulation
Shift of population out of an area

---

work. Their problem was that neither farming nor their other work was a full-time, year-round option. Their land area was too small or their other work too occasional to provide an adequate source of income; each supplemented the other. The availability of these farmers for other part-time employment depended on the old open field system; once this was destroyed, neither occupation alone was viable. Fourth, villagers with specialized skills, such as the blacksmith, wheelwright, or carpenter, also lost their livelihood. Once their clientele moved away, the market for these service occupations declined, and they were forced to follow.

In summary, enclosures caused rural depopulation and unemployment. Conversion to sheep farming eliminated the small arable farmers, and as sheep farming requires less labor, the dispossessed also became unemployed. Some of this surplus labor was eventually absorbed by the expanding wool industry, but initially the result was the creation of large armies of vagabonds with no means of support.

A few enclosures did increase employment. For example, some marshes near London were drained, enclosed, and used to raise cattle to serve the nearby London market during Henry VIII's reign, and this provided new jobs. But similar examples were rare, and the more common unemployment was a cause for concern.

Development of a Wool Processing Industry

From the point of view of the development of capitalism, as a precondition for later industrialization, and as perceived by landowners and the new textile industry capitalists, enclosures were a resounding success. First, the expansion of sheep raising was a necessary precondition for the establishment and subsequent growth of the wool processing industry in England. It built up the fortunes of sheep farmers and new industrialists. Second, fears that conversion of arable land to pasture would result in food shortages for a grow-

ing population were unfounded and industrial wages did not rise because of rising food prices. Food supplies remained adequate—with corn even being exported throughout the 17th century—mainly because new areas in the northern part of the country were being brought into cultivation, and they offset the arable land being taken out of use because of conversion.

Third, as will become clearer in the last part of this chapter, the enclosures forcefully broke the ties of the peasants to the land, and created a new labor force that had no option but to work for an employer rather than for themselves. This was a necessary precondition for the new industrial activity to be capitalist. Finally, the enclosures increased the wealth and political power of both the large landowners-sheep raisers and the merchant-industrial capitalists. This development altered the political and social complexion of the country by altering the balance of power, and would lead to a struggle between commercial and industrial capitalists for dominance in politics much later.

Protests and Policies

As always, whenever a society is experiencing social change, protests were heard. In the 16th century, there were peasant protests in England, and as was the case with the peasant revolts of earlier centuries, these protesters were not revolutionaries. They were not so much seeking a *new* order as a *restoration* of the old, especially a restoration of old relationships and social justice. And because enclosures were the obvious signs of change, rural protests were often accompanied by destruction of enclosing hedges or filling in of ditches.

One example of the conservative nature of the peasantry shows in the demands of the Ket rebellion in 1549. It began in Norfolk, an eastern county, formerly populated by fiercely independent small farmers which was particularly hard hit by enclosure. Protesters asked that it be made illegal for a manorial lord to purchase land

and then lease it out at high rents; that rents on copyhold land be rolled back; that entry fines (paid when land was passed from father to son) be "reasonable"; that rights to common land be restored; and that no lord of the manor be allowed to use the commons. These were not revolutionary demands, and in fact were completely in accordance with existing legislation. Many of those in power were sympathetic, but in any event, soldiers were dispatched to break up the rebellion, and 3,000 died as a result.

Levellers and Diggers

Other groups later developed more class consciousness and an awareness of the old order's ending. Two groups in particular, the Levellers and the Diggers, originated in the Midland counties, among the most heavily enclosed. They are notable because they survived for so long—they were not simply an ad hoc group of frustrated peasants. (They were given these names because they opposed enclosure in the most direct way possible—levelling fences or hedges and filling in ditches.)

Levellers and Diggers

Groups protesting enclosure

The Diggers, who were basically simple agrarian communists, had developed by the mid 17th century what would now be called a political platform, based on the idea that the common land belonged to the common people. They started living on a commons in the county of Surrey, and were at first left alone. But when they began to cut down some trees, landlords saw this as a direct threat to the institution of private property, and caused the Diggers' crops to be destroyed. Other groups also tried to live on common land but were always opposed and had their crops destroyed.

The Levellers gained more support than the Diggers, probably because they favored peasant land ownership rather than communal owner-

ship. Both groups contained nationalist as well as utopian elements. Levellers thought that slavery in the form of feudal land tenure had been imposed on the originally independent English by the Normans, hence wanted a return to their idea of that pre-Norman idealized society. Enclosures and the accompanying hardships were ways of oppressing independent farmers because they had been made possible by feudalism. Therefore fens and common land should never be enclosed, and any remaining feudal tenure legally abolished because its uncertainties made it possible for landlords to take advantage of peasants.

Levellers also had a political platform that would not have been out of place centuries later but must have seemed damagingly radical at the time. They called for annual or biennial Parliaments at a time when the Crown had most political power; manhood suffrage, which would not be achieved until late in the 19th century; a redistribution of seats in proportion to population; and the abolition of the veto power of the House of Lords.

Movements like these are part of a recurrent theme in human history—the dream of the ideal society or utopia. Whenever the existing material conditions of society are undergoing extreme change producing social and material results that are not regarded as favorable for true human development, there tends to be an upsurge of utopian ideas. The 16th century was no exception; one of the earliest examples of utopian literature was Thomas More's *Utopia*, published in 1516.

What was official government social policy during this time of upheaval? The Tudor monarchs were not much in favor of enclosure, for a variety of reasons. Two related aspects of policy are relevant here: policy concerned with enclosure as such; and the effects of depopulation and the so-called Poor Laws, policies concerned with the unemployed and destitute.

Opposition to Enclosures

The Tudor monarchs wanted to unify the country. Their main aim was to achieve domestic stability at a time when the country was changing from being predominantly agricultural to becoming increasingly commercialized. They did not think that enclosure encouraged stability, for several reasons. First, if the number of independent yeoman farmers was reduced, the security of the country could be threatened, a linkage between economic independence and national security that is repeated often throughout history. Second, enclosures caused depopulation, and depopulation was associated with discontent and rural uprisings, which were destabilizing. Third, both enclosure and depopulation caused increases in unemployment and destitution. Fourth, enclosure and the conversion of arable land to pasture threatened to diminish food supplies.

So they passed several acts, the first in 1489. All were in some way concerned with restoring traditional usage and social justice, the maintenance of an adequate food supply, internal security and defense. By 1597, about 12 had been passed. They tried to prevent conversion, or if that was not possible, ordered a reconversion to arable land, and an attempt to restore abandoned buildings was also made. The content of these acts was based on the work of special commissions appointed to study enclosures and depopulation. They did not prevent or reverse enclosure—at best, they slowed the pace down to a more bearable one, mainly because there were too many conflicting interests both in Parliament and between Parliament and the Crown.

Parliament was dominated by landowning interests, and the interests of the landowners and sheep breeders coincided with those of the newly emerging class of industrial capitalists, but only up to a point. If too much land was enclosed and too many sheep raised, then wool prices would fall, and the landowners would suffer while the capitalists gained. (The counterargument opposing enclosures to protect arable farmers was similarly double-edged: If too much land was kept in cultivation, then production would be too high, so food prices would fall and the arable farmers would suffer.)

Legislation also could do little because enforcement was weak, an inevitable conclusion because enforcement was in the hands of county landowners, precisely those who benefitted from enclosure. However, the work of the special commissions did have value. They publicized the issues, and described the various ways that landlords attempted to bypass legislation. For example, sometimes a single furrow was ploughed down the middle of a pasture so the land could be classified as arable and so not subject to a conversion penalty.

The logical, and only, way to have prevented harmful enclosures would have been to give copyholders full title to their land. But while this would have been popular, it would have alienated the large landlords, and the Tudor monarchs were only too well aware of the limits of their power—they needed the support of the upper class. While the Tudors frequently did not do what they said they would—for reasons of political expediency and financial need—they did want an ordered society. They saw the role of government as one maintaining the cooperation of all groups and individuals, each of which had its own role to play, hence they were careful not to alienate potential support.

Depopulation and the Poor Laws

The very first act attempting to reverse enclosure was passed out of concern with depopulation, which was a concern for two reasons. One was the national security reason, which stated that a country is strong, domestically and internationally, when its inhabitants are free and economically independent. Enclosure removed the economic base of the independent farmer and caused a shift of population from the countryside. Individuals were forced into economic dependency, or worse still, those with no visible means of support were forced into thievery threatening the welfare of others. The second concern centered around this increased number of "idle poor" who roamed the countryside as vagabonds and beggars.

The number of poor and propertyless beggars dramatically increased, and the expansion of the wool textile industry was not progressing fast enough to provide jobs for the newly created labor force. Early Tudor legislation restricted mobility to try to keep the poor rates (taxes imposed to fund relief to the poor) as low as possible, and brutal methods were used on the wandering homeless to try to prevent vagrancy. But neither method solved the problem.

Social Character of Wealth and Poverty

New poor laws introduced by Elizabeth I were remarkable for several reasons. First, the social character of wealth was their underlying premise. It was reemphasized at this time precisely because the emerging problems were caused by the growing individualism that upset the existing order. Second, the poor laws were based on the idea that the cause of unemployment and vagrancy was not an individual character deficiency or personal idleness, but rather due to poor economic conditions that no one individual could control. Hence the relief of the poor was recognized as a social responsibility to be put on a national, secular basis rather than dependent on private charity (or no action at all). To this end, a compulsory poor rate was imposed and local authorities were required to find work for all able-bodied poor. Third, these poor laws were important because it was the last time before the 20th century that the idea of *social* responsibility for unemployment influenced public policy.

The resulting system worked until the Civil War of the 17th century, when it collapsed for two reasons. One was that the central government ceased to exert pressure on the local authorities who were responsible for its administration and financing, so the system simply collapsed. The second reason was the change in attitude about the causes of poverty. Heavily influenced by Puritan thinking, the growing individualism that for a long time had influenced economic affairs now affected social policy. Policy became based on the idea that misfortune and poverty were not the result of some social cause but rather the punishment for sin—poverty was the consequence of individual weakness.

To summarize the social policy of the 16th century is to observe a curious mixture of conservatism and progressiveness. The monarch tried to be enlightened, but attitudes to the poor would be reversed later by the trend toward more popular representation by Parliament, a trend flourishing precisely because of changes taking place in the 16th century. The Tudors' aims were based on a by-now almost outmoded vision of a simple, more harmonious society although their methods were remarkably modern. They tried to use the power of the (new) central government to help victims of social and economic distress. But simultaneously, their successes encouraged the absolutist tendencies of the Stuart monarchs who followed them as well as strengthening the new capitalist class. Both developments ultimately helped weaken the power of the monarch.

Sixteenth Century Industrial Capitalism

The birth of a domestic wool industry producing for both export and domestic consumption paralleled the enclosure movement and helped account for the decline in exports of raw wool. Some small amounts of wool fabric had always been exported, but it was never up to the standards of the main textile centers of Flanders and Florence. However, by the 14th century, both of these areas began to decline. In both, workers resented the fall in their wages and worsening working conditions, while their employers continued to enjoy luxurious life styles, a contrast all too visible in urban areas. So the old textile areas became less competitive with English exports, and English manufacturers took advantage of low labor and raw material costs to underprice their foreign competitors.

A deliberate policy to encourage the growth of a domestic cloth industry in England dates from the late 15th century when its potential benefits were recognized. Encouragement included raising export taxes on raw wool, giving incentives to foreign weavers to immigrate into England, restricting the import of foreign cloth and passing legislation requiring that domestically produced wool should be worn. This one in particular was hard to enforce. The upper classes resented the blurring of class lines implied by this requirement; wearing luxurious imported fabrics were symbols of their wealth they were loathe to give up.

As demand increased, it was important to increase production of a better quality cloth. By this time, the industry could become organized along capitalist lines: finance capital was available (previous trade expansion increased capital accumulation); a labor force existed (thanks to the enclosures); and a market for output and other capitalist market institutions existed. The wool cloth industry went through various stages. Before becoming a market capitalist industry, peasants had been able to make homespun from whatever natural fibers are available for their own use, not for exchange.

Putting Out or Commission System

As the market expanded, better quality cloth was increasingly made by a specialist for sale. Production was typically small scale, controlled by a master, as with guild production for a market. Guild production was characterized by the craft workers owning the raw materials, tools, and finished products; the workers worked at home;

and the market was limited in size. Later, labor became more specialized and capitalists gradually took control of the production process. After the 15th century, this characterized the putting out domestic system of production, an intermediate stage between small scale, precapitalist guild production and large scale, capitalist factory production. The putting out system was used in many other industries at the time. It developed to meet the needs for expanded output for sale, given the constraints of limited capital and labor availability, and reached its most sophisticated form in the wool industry.

Putting out system

Intermediate stage of industrial development; workers own the fixed capital and capitalists own the raw materials and finished products

---

There are many steps involved in the production of wool cloth. The major ones are shearing the wool from the sheep, cleaning, carding, spinning, weaving, fulling, stretching, burling, dyeing, and finishing. Some of these were more appropriate to complete capitalist control than others, while some were appropriate to this intermediate stage. For example, fulling is the process of shrinking the wool fibers, and was one of the first to use a water-powered, mechanical device (wooden hammers) to pound the wool. Building a fulling mill was costly, and typically a manorial lord built one, then required his peasants to pay to use it, a development resisted both by the urban guilds as well as the peasants. However, because fulling required the use of water, most fulling mills were located in the countryside (where the water was) and were thus outside guild control. Also, because of its large capital requirements, it became suitable for control by capitalists. This was particularly true in the northern, hilly areas of England, where the combination of available wool, running water, and fuller's earth (used to remove the grease from wool) gave it an advantage. Florence lacked this combination. Flanders is flat and lacks swiftly running streams; Flanders specialized in the production of worsted, a cloth that is not fulled. (In the 16th century, many Flemish cloth makers emigrated to the eastern part of England which is also flat, and established the production of worsted there.)

Also at this time, guilds increasingly lost control of the various activities connected with finishing cloth (such as dyeing) as capitalist manufacturers gradually extended their control. However, the stages that were most suitable for capitalist takeover were weaving, spinning, and carding.

Increase in Capital Needs

Before any one individual could take over the function of coordinating different stages of production, it was necessary to have greater access to finance capital, as the actual producer is no longer responsible for selling the product to the customer. Financing is necessary for two reasons: The time lag between production and sales lengthened; the scale of operations grew larger; and it had to be possible to hire and pay workers in advance of making sales.

Typically a merchant eager to make more sales initiated the expansion of production, often by contacting a small master (in the north) or weavers (in the east), either one of which avoided guild restrictions. Typically in the putting out system, the merchant-capitalist owned the raw or semifinished materials (which were "farmed out" to the workers) and the finished products, while the workers themselves owned the means of production. Technically this system was not a fully fledged capitalist one as the capitalist owned only the circulating capital, while the workers owned the fixed capital. The producers, who worked on commission for the merchant-capitalist, no longer had contact with the customer. This is a contrast with both guild production, where the producer owned the capital and sold the output, and modern industrial capitalism, where the worker is completely separated from the means of production and contact with the buyer.

Economic Efficiency: Capital Sharing

The resulting system was economically efficient by adapting to prevailing economic conditions—relative capital and labor scarcity—and producing the largest possible output. It marked an increasing control of capital over production, as shown by the separation of the worker from the ownership of raw materials and by the greater use of wage labor. Output expanded because there was a change in the way production was organized rather than a change in technology, although production was on a larger scale than before.

Economic efficiency
Obtaining maximum output from the given resources using existing technology

---

Relative capital scarcity implied that a completely capitalist system could not be introduced immediately. Thus, the best way of achieving as large a volume of output as possible was to spread the available capital out over as large a number of employees as possible. Workers owned their equipment (in the form of spindles or looms, for example) and worked out of their own homes. They were contacted by agents who provided them with raw materials and picked up the finished work. In this way, the merchant-capitalist's resources were devoted solely to acquiring raw materials and paying workers; they need not be siphoned off to pay for buildings or equipment.

The fact that workers "shared" the capital expenses does not mean that there was a voluntary agreement to do so. Most peasants were already familiar with producing homespun, so had the equipment necessary, and it was taken for granted that the workers were responsible for looms. (Later on, looms were rented to workers in an intermediate stage before complete ownership by the industrial capitalist.)

Labor was scarce before the enclosures when the wool industry was just starting its expansion. In a predominantly agricultural society, population is typically scattered, and usually not required to perform agricultural work for a full week, all year round. Farming's seasonal nature implies that the availability of labor for nonagricultural tasks will be erratic. However, the commission system effectively utilized this labor by making use of it during the winter when farm demands were least, or by using the labor of the very small landholder whose farm was too small for a full time farming operation. It was a piecework system where payment depended on the volume of output, so the irregularity of hours worked did not matter.

More and more labor became available as the 16th century progressed, and for many families, especially those left with only a tiny amount of land, the combination of farming and industrial activity was an economic necessity. It also bridged the gap between a rural, agricultural society and an urban, industrial one.

Piecework

Payment for work based on output produced, not hours worked

Increasing Specialization

Some larger enterprises developed at this time. For example, a small master who had previously coordinated the work of a few people may have expanded by hiring outside the immediate circle. Or a merchant middleman or dyer involved at a later stage of production would reach back to earlier stages and bring more workers under his influence and control. With expansion, cloth production became more specialized. For example, wool brokers acted exclusively as middlemen between sheep farmers and clothiers (cloth producers), drapers were the middlemen between clothiers and cloth finishers, and factors were intermediaries between clothiers and drapers. The wool industry became most highly organized in

East Anglia, where many of the Flemish workers located, and the southwest.

However, from the point of view of the new industrial capitalist, the putting out system suffers from some serious defects. Later changes in organization and in technology were attempts to remedy these defects.

Lack of Supervision

The most serious defect occurred because only partial control over the work force was possible, hence the quality of output varied. In large part, the quality of the raw materials determined the quality of the final product, but other problems could arise because workers worked out of their own homes, and inferior work was always a possibility. Sometimes work suffered as workers tried to compensate for declining incomes. Real wages declined throughout the 16th century due to inflation, which resulted in a loss of about one third of wage earners' purchasing power. Also employers tried to hold down money wage rates in order to get workers to work more and harder.

Low wages forced workers to produce more out of economic necessity, but they could also enhance their bargaining power by accepting work from more than one clothier. This meant they would suffer less if work from any one source dried up, and it also protected them to a limited extent against the inevitable irregularity of employment. Other devices were used to try to offset low wage rates. For example, workers were often paid by weight of cloth produced, so dampening the wool made the cloth heavier. But the practice of working for more than one clothier could also mean that work for any one was not delivered on time. As production became more and more specialized, a delay in any one stage held up the others, making it difficult to get everything flowing smoothly. A clothier could avoid this problem by keeping larger inventories on hand, but this tied up too much capital.

Trend to Centralization

Industrial capitalists believed that the basic problem was that the workers were lazy and did not know the value of hard work, a refrain repeated whenever and wherever a first generation of wage workers was introduced to the capitalist work ethic. The belief arose because the employers had more thoroughly internalized the new work ethic than the workers. Workers not only found the transition from self- or nature-paced work difficult, but also found their new status of economic dependent to be demeaning.

Centralization of production

Work performed in a central location (the factory) rather than at the worker's home

---

Employers believed that many of the problems resulted from their lack of control, so the system moved gradually towards centralization of production and the capitalist's full ownership of the means of production. This occurred first at the weaving stage, mainly because looms were more expensive than spindles, and weaving also had to be undertaken for long stretches of time. (Spinning was typically done by women and children and continued to be a domestic operation until the 18th century.) So industrialists' need to exert full control over the work force and work process led them to buy and install looms in a central location where the weavers could be under the constant supervision of a supervisor.

This is the first example of the separation of home from work, and became a characteristic of the factory system, which centralized work. Technical considerations also helped extend capitalist control over other stages. Both fulling and finishing, for example, are areas where large scale production was more efficient, but they also required large amounts of finance capital to establish.

Working Conditions

It is probably true to say that the putting out workers were the first examples of a free labor force that became a permanent feature of the economic landscape. But while they were removed from guild regulations—because production took place in the countryside where the guilds had no power—they were not true, propertyless proletarians either.

What were their working conditions like? What did it feel like to be pushed into a new, nonagricultural status? We will examine specific features of the work life of 16th century employees in an attempt to answer this question.

Property

Most of the workers in the 16th and 17th century textile industries owned not only their own working equipment but also some land. Some of them had previously been full time farmers, but had lost land because of the enclosures, or found that after the commons had been enclosed, they could not survive by farming alone.

But the ability to farm even on a small scale had certain advantages for both employer and employee. The employer could pay lower wages, knowing that the wage was not the sole means of support for the worker. And in an age where unemployment compensation and retirement pensions were unknown, the ability to farm a small holding cushioned the worst impact of lack of work.

Wages

In the 15th century, there were only a few wage workers, but their wages probably rose. However, prices in general rose throughout the 16th century, and real wages fell, not to rise again until the 18th century.

Money wages failed to keep pace with price rises; after 1563, local authorities had the power to set maximum money wage rates, but did not exercise it to prevent the decline in purchasing power. Local authorities, made up of the landed interests and the new capitalists, faced a conflict of interests. As employers, they wanted low wages, but as payers of the poor rates, they wanted high wages and low poor rates. This conflict was made worse by the restrictions on labor mobility imposed by the Elizabethan poor laws: People could not settle in a new community without first demonstrating that they would not require public assistance. This prevented settlement by newly unemployed people from other areas, but also prevented the existing unemployed from moving out of the area, so kept poor rates high.

Working Conditions

To some extent, it is likely that the flexibility of domestic production was more acceptable than the rigorous discipline of the factory would be to later workers. They could, within reason, set their own hours and work at their own pace, although always constrained by economic necessity. In fact, given low wages even for the most skilled workers, while this sort of flexibility was possible in theory, a rather intense degree of self- and family-exploitation was much more likely in practice.

The 1563 Statute of Artificers established working hours for all wage workers. It specified hours from 5 a.m. to 7 p.m. in spring and summer, with 2½ hours allowed for meals, and hours from sunrise to sunset during the rest of the year. The key is the amount of natural light; while the pressure of need forced people to work longer, the lack of adequate artificial light in effect prevented it. Also, while this legislation seems to indicate a rather high degree of regularity in working hours, it was probably more apparent than real, with workers working when they had to.

There was also no guarantee that work would be available on a regular basis, hence the advantage of accepting commissions from more than one employer if at all possible. Even in the 16th century, there were periodic trade upheavals (though not with the regularity of a modern business cycle) when times were hard. For example, 1528, 1586, and 1620-1624 were years when business conditions were depressed, and the absence of either the feudal "economic security net" or modern social security had a tremendous impact on workers experiencing hard times.

Government occasionally intervened for the same reason they were concerned with enclosures, fear of social unrest. Legislation attempted to influence employers to hire employees for a whole year and not lay them off when business conditions worsened. As with the poor laws, the assumption underlying this requirement (which was honored more in the breach) was that the ownership of capital involved a social responsibility. But this was foreign to the capitalists' own view that capital was privately owned to realize private gains.

Other Industries

Other industries began flourishing in England at this time, mostly borrowing better techniques from other countries to remedy deficiencies in existing, backward industries. The exception was coal mining, which became larger and technologically more advanced at an earlier time in England than elsewhere. This was because previous overcutting of forests created a shortage of wood, so industries requiring a heat source had to turn to coal, which was abundant.

Growth industries included the production of military goods (cannon, gun powder, guns) which required large amounts of fixed capital and were established along capitalist lines, thanks to the Crown's assurance of a market and other inducements to establish these vital industries. Consumer goods industries also appeared, to produce items that had previously been made at home—beer, for example—or that had been available only as an imported, luxury item, such as paper, glass[1], and soap.

Summary

The English experience of the 16th century illustrates three important and linked developments. First, the idea of private property spread to land, accomplished via the enclosures. Land was taken out of "social" control and put into private hands, and land sales as a way of transferring property dates from this period. That this occurred is partly due to the fact that feudalism had ended *de facto* but not *de jure*, and the large enclosing landlords took advantage of the resulting legal uncertainties and ambiguities to get their own way. The important motive for enclosure came from rising prices for wool and the increased profitability of sheep raising. So the second development was that large landlords took over large areas of land for conversion into sheep pastures. Unemployment resulted, as although increased demand from the developing textile industry had pushed up wool prices, this industry was not expanding fast enough to absorb the increased numbers of unemployed.

The rise of an important wool industry was the third development. It was a capitalist industry, although modified to meet the specific conditions of the 16th century resource endowment, relative capital, and labor scarcity. The result was the putting out or commission system, which was a partially capitalist, domestic industry.

Notes

1. While English glass was of poorer quality than French or Italian glass, it was cheaper and produced in larger quantities for an expanding market. One interesting aside: when glass containers for drinking came within the reach of a larger number of people and not just the court and nobility, they were made with "bumps" on them. This was not simply an interesting design, but also very practical. At a time when people ate with their fingers and forks were only just beginning to be used, glasses with bumps on them were less likely to slip out of greasy fingers.

Key Concepts

Capital scarcity
Copyholder
Customary tenant
Decentralized production
Depopulation
Domestic industry
Elizabethan poor law
Enclosure
Free labor
Freeholder

Leaseholding
Money wage
Piecework
Putting out system
Rack renting
Real wage
Specialization
Tenant-at-will
Working conditions

Questions for Discussion and Essay Writing

1. What preconditions are necessary if a capitalist economy is to be established?

2. Why did the enclosure movement occur?

3. Why was the enclosure movement controversial?

4. What were the results of the enclosure movement?

5. What were the reasons for the Tudor monarchs' opposition to enclosure?

6. Discuss the Elizabethan poor laws.

7. To what extent is it true that the putting out system was an adaptation to the times?

8. Were the workers in 16th century England well off? What would we need to know before answering this question?

9. Evaluate the economic changes of the 16th century.

For Further Reading

Allen, Robert. *Enclosure and the Yeoman*. Oxford: Oxford University Press, 1992.

Boyer, George R. *An Economic History of the English Poor Law*. Cambridge: Cambridge University Press, 1990

Bradley, Harriet. *The Enclosures in England: An Economic Reconstruction*. New York: AMS Press, (1918), 1968.

Hill, Christopher P. *Reformation to Industrial Revolution*. Harmondsworth: Penguin Books, 1969.

Hudson, P. "The Genesis of Industrial Capital: A Study of the West Riding Wool Industry, c. 1750-1850," in P. Hudson, ed. *Regions and Industries: A Perspective on the Industrial Revolution*, Cambridge: Cambridge University Press, 1989.

Nef, John U. "The Progress of Technology and the Growth of Large Scale Industry in Great Britain 1540-1640" *Economic History Review* (1934), and in *E.M. Carus-Wilson, ed. Essays in Economic History, vol. 1*. London: Edward Arnold, 1954-62.

Ostrom, Elinor. *Governing the Commons: The Evolution of Institutions for Collective Action*. Cambridge: Cambridge University Press, 1990.

_____. "Agricultural and Natural Resource Economics." *Journal of Economic Literature*, 31:1 (March 1993).

Parker, William N. and Eric L. Jones, eds. *European Peasants and Their Markets: Essays in Agrarian Economic History*. Princeton: Princeton University Press, 1975.

Ramsey, G. D. *The English Woolen Industry 1500-1750*. London: Macmillan, 1982.

Roberts, Rebecca S. "Uneven Development and the Tragedy of the Commons: Competing Images for Nature-Society Analysis." *Economic Geography*, 68:3 (July 1992) 248–271.

Turner, Michael. *Enclosures in Britain 1750-1830*. London: Macmillan, 1984.

Wallerstein, I. M. *The Modern World System: Capitalist Agriculture and Origins of the European World-Economy in the 16th Century*. New York: Academic Press, 1974.

Wordie, J.R. "The Chronology of English Enclosure, 1500-1914" *Economic History Review*, XXXVI:4 (1982) 483-455.

Part III

The Industrial Revolution

(Eighteenth to Early Twentieth Centuries)

Chapter 9

Agriculture (18th and 19th Centuries)

AGRICULTURE HAS ALWAYS BEEN IMPORTANT in the economy because the farm sector grows the food for consumers and some of the raw materials needed by industry. Even if the agricultural sector is small and the economy imports at least some of its food needs, these trade ties can have an important influence on the shape and direction of the domestic economy.

Up until the 18th century—or the 20th century for many countries—economies were characterized as pre-industrial because of the dominance of agriculture. During and after the 18th century, farming organization and technology began to change, at first in only a handful of places but becoming more general over time. These organizational and technological changes made up what is known as the Agricultural Revolution. It resulted in larger outputs and lower labor needs that made an industrial revolution possible and provided for its continuation. This chapter will explore the agricultural revolution preceding and paralleling industrialization, and will take us up to the 20th century. To repeat, there are two basic results that are common to such agricultural change:

1. An increase in agricultural productivity and output that makes urbanization effective;

2. A decrease in the number of agricultural workers, both absolutely and as a proportion of the labor force that permits the growth of industrial, nonagricultural output by making possible the expansion of an industrial labor force.

All countries in this history experienced such changes, and changes in agricultural techniques, which were easier to transfer across national boundaries, were basically common to all of them. However, the social change, the reduction in the agricultural labor force and the increase in the industrial labor force, was accomplished in different ways in different countries. This happened because social relationships in general differed, so we would expect the commercialization of agriculture to be undertaken in different ways.

In England, the social transformation of agriculture was continued in a second wave of enclosures, while in Germany, feudal relations were ended in a variety of ways. In both, the small farmer all but disappeared, which was not the case in France, where intensification of the nobles' pressure on peasant farmers climaxed in the French Revolution. As a result, French farming remained small scale. We will discuss agriculture in the United States later, devoting consideration here only to mechanization which affected all countries.[1]

Agriculture in England

Commercialization of agriculture in England dates from the 16th century, and in Chapter 8 we saw how rising agricultural prices, growing towns, and mercantilist policies stimulated enclosure. The result was that capitalist farmers, especially sheep farmers, gained at the expense of consumers, agricultural wage earners, and those "old" nobility who had not maintained their real incomes by shortening the leases they offered to tenants.

Later, improvements such as land reclamation, drainage, and even enclosure required large sums of money. The commercially minded farmer and the new landowners benefitted, and they continued the trend toward an increase in the scale of farming and elimination of small peasant holdings, a trend further encouraged by political developments in the 17th century. The civil wars in England in the 17th century were partly due to increased antagonism between Parliament—composed of landed interests—and the monarchy. Even after the monarchy was restored (1660), Parliament was able to enact legislation that favored its interests because it controlled taxation and thus the monarch's finances.

As we saw earlier, governments had opposed enclosures (although not very effectively), fearing rural depopulation and lack of adequate military manpower. But after the mid 17th century, governments actively encouraged them. Politically weak smallholders still opposed them, but were ignored. Opposition was based on several grounds, none of them new. When the commons were enclosed or other waste land cultivated, there were material losses. The loss of pasture rights, wood for fuel and housing, and opportunities for hunting made the small farmers' existence very precarious. The ideological ground for opposition was based on loss of independence. To the extent that farming was no longer viable, forcing peasants to become fulltime wage laborers demeaned them.

Opposition frequently resulted in scattered peasant protests, but there was never a successful national revolt, mainly because the peasantry was no longer homogenous. There were too many differences of status, outlook, and material conditions distinguishing tenant farmer from marginal copyholder. However, *fears* of peasant revolt probably did slow down the pace of enclosures. But these fears, and any remaining barriers to enclosure, were removed after the mid 17th century. Then, and continuing well into the 19th century, both organizational and technological change associated with the agricultural revolution were allowed full reign.

Formal Abolition of Feudal Tenure

The legal barrier to enclosure was removed in 1646, when feudal tenure was abolished, thus confirming *de jure* what had been *de facto* for generations. While the official ending of feudal political relationships could have had several potential results, the trend toward large-scale commercial agriculture under a system of private property was most significant. Three aspects of the abolition of feudal tenure were relevant to the agricultural revolution. First, landowners no longer depended on the Crown for their lands and positions. This effectively eliminated any remaining feudal relations among members of the ruling class, and the monarch could no longer arbitrarily give estates to favorites or take them away from others. More important, it implied that landowners could act as an independent political force. In this way, the power of Parliament and the recognition of the natural rights of the individual against the absolute power of the monarchy were reaffirmed, effectively reducing royal power.

Second, and obviously associated with the first, landowners gained absolute ownership of their estates. This marked the supremacy of the market relationship, because now landowners themselves were free to transfer property through the market. In addition, they were free from arbitrary death duties, and removing this source of revenue for the Crown further weakened the monarch's power. The principle of primogeniture, or inheritance through the eldest son, was also established. From the point of view of progressive-minded landowners, the way was cleared to full application of capitalist principles in estate management. Freedom from arbitrary taxes meant that financing necessary for improvements would not be siphoned off. The inheritance principle assured that the benefits of land improvement would remain within the family. In effect, long-term planning and capital investment were now possible. However, primogeniture was not an advantage for the lesser gentry. Younger sons could no longer rely on inheriting part of an estate but were instead forced into other occupations (such as the Church or the military). The result was to increase the tendency for land to be concentrated in fewer hands.

Effect on Small Landholders

The third effect was that the abolition of feudal tenure applied only to the upper class and not to smaller landowners. Strangely, copyholders were not granted absolute title to their holdings, and neither were small freeholders, who, unless they could show written evidence of their legal title, were reduced to the same status as copyholders. This could be disastrous, as documents had been lost or destroyed in many cases. The copyhold, as previously noted, was the customary record in the village rolls of a former serf's right to use a particular piece of land. It was not an individual legal title that could be considered a legal prerequisite for an exchange of land in a modern contract economy. However, it assured legitimacy in land-

---

Primogeniture

System of inheritance in which property passes to the eldest son

---

holding so long as there was a social consensus about its validity.

Now that social consensus had disappeared, large numbers of small farmers became dependent on the continuing good will of the large landholder. But the large landowner and capitalist farmers were not interested in the survival or welfare of small-scale peasant farmers, so good will was frequently absent. As a result, they often expanded their enclosures at the expense of peasant farmers using a variety of methods.

These methods intensified financial pressure on small farmers. When combined with the elimination of traditional rights, such as the right to use common land, many of them were forced to sell out. For example, landowners could impose large death duties, and then evict the heirs when they could not pay. Or a landowner would substitute a leasehold for freehold or copyhold, which led to rack renting; charging exorbitantly high rents; at the extreme, the annual rent payable could be equal to the value of the property, which also forced many to sell. And a variety of other fines, taxes, and a simple lack of resources further decreased the viability of small farmers if they lived on the estate of an enclosure-minded landowner.

Removal of Small Peasants

The gradual elimination of small peasants became more intense after 1750, and the trend to large-scale landholdings and commercial farming was further encouraged by some other developments. During the civil wars of the 17th century, the land of many royalist supporters was confiscated and sold, while large fines were imposed on others. There were three important implications. First, many merchants bought this land and were obviously interested in applying profit-making principles to their new estates. In addition, when some former landowners regained their lands after the Restoration, they were forced to become more active in managing their estates in order to recoup their financial losses. Second, many of the smaller gentry were eliminated as a result of fines or land confiscation, further concentrating ownership. And third, these new owners, or "newly motivated" old owners, were not interested in maintaining traditional agrarian relations, which again encouraged more enclosure and elimination of peasant farming. (The difficulties of both peasant farmers and smaller gentry were further increased during the generally depressed agricultural conditions of 1720-1750.) The result was the formation of a class of landowners who were actively interested in their holdings as a commercial proposition.

Resurgence of Enclosure

These legal and political changes *permitted* renewed enclosure. That is, they were a necessary but not a sufficient condition for enclosure and the adoption of new, large-scale farming techniques. Something else was needed to make it advantageous to enclose, and lease out large areas of land to capitalist tenant farmers willing to cultivate for the market. This something else was an increase in demand—first export demand, then the increase in domestic demand associated with 18th century urbanization.

The initial impetus that made commercial farming more profitable came when trade policy was reversed, and is associated with mercantilist encouragement of domestic production. Up to the mid 17th century, the export of grain was prohibited, but was permitted after 1654, and subsequent policies made increased production for export much more lucrative. Thus in 1689, a bounty was paid on all corn exported—a spur to increased production. This was so successful that not until the mid 19th entury did Britain rely on *regular* imports of food, in spite of the increase in population and reduction of the agricultural labor force. While this inevitably increased the price paid by domestic consumers, it also increased farmers' and landlords' profits, encouraging the continuation of enclosure and technological innovation.

In the 18th century, these incentives were continued as urbanization occurred. Incidentally, this policy of stimulating increased agricultural output also indirectly accomplished another policy aim: overcoming the Dutch hold on trade. The Dutch had cornered the carrying trade in spices that were used for preserving meat through the winter. But the increased output of fresh meat, available year-round, meant that a sizable market for spices had disappeared.

Enclosures: Changes in Social Relationships

By this time, little stood in the way of the further consolidation of landholding and the spread of commercial farming. Unlike the 16th century, the new incentive to enclose came from the growing market for food, so now arable farming areas were most affected.

Initially the pace was slow. But after the depressed years 1720-1750, landlords quickened the process of extending private landholding to take advantage of the economies of scale associated with new farming techniques.

Enclosure by Act of Parliament

What was also new was enclosure by Act of Parliament. Until 1801, landlords who wished to enclose specific areas of land petitioned Parliament for permission to do so, but after 1801, general enclosure acts eliminated this requirement. Small farmers whose land was affected had only a limited ability to oppose enclosure. It took knowledge, time, money—and especially courage —to oppose the local large landowner. By 1815, about six million acres (one quarter of all cultivated land) had been enclosed as a result of some 3,300 private enclosure acts, which compares with the half million acres enclosed before 1700.

A large landowner usually initiated the legislative process. When the petition was granted, enclosure commissioners, with the consent of affected villagers, were supposed to oversee the allocation of land and rationalization of landholdings when open fields were involved. They had to make sure that legitimate claimants received a compact holding equal in size to their strips in the open fields. One problem was that strips had been held in different areas. As the point of enclosure was to rationalize by making each holding contiguous, the peasant could end up with a compact farmholding of inferior land. Each farmer involved was also responsible for paying a share of the costs involved. So even though the land area might be equal in size, if it was less productive land, the farmer could suffer a net loss, which often forced a sale to the large landowner. In the 19th century, other areas were also enclosed, including two million acres of common and waste land. By 1850, nearly all agricultural land had been enclosed.

Results of Enclosure

Opinion on the enclosures in general is, and was, divided. On the one hand, it brought uncultivated land into use, permitted the application of new techniques, increased agricultural productivity, and expanded output. But on the other, it led to the concentration of landed wealth and created much class bitterness because of the feeling that the welfare of small farmers had been ignored. It also eliminated that class of small, independent farmers who, in Tudor times, had been considered the backbone of England and important to its strength, militarily and economically.

Looking at these three issues separately, by 1873, a small group of 2,250 people owned half the entire land area of England. One quarter of all land was held in estates of over 3,000 acres (with an average size of over 6,000 acres), and a further 12 percent held in estates of 1,000 to 3,000 acres. This indicates that large landowners increased

their holdings at the expense of both the smaller gentry and small freeholders. Smaller gentry had smaller holdings and were required to pay a land tax, making it difficult for them to finance capital improvements, and they became less competitive. Small freeholders often sold out because they could not compete with farmers who had access to greater resources. They were also more affected by the fall in agricultural prices that, with a few exceptions, characterized the 19th century after the boom years of the Napoleonic Wars. Hence, typically, land was held in large estates and leased out to tenant farmers who worked the land using paid agricultural laborers recruited from the ranks of previous smallholders.

The other two issues are more difficult to quantify. While there was not necessarily any outright coercion forcing small freeholders to sell out, it was harder for them to remain, and this led to a general feeling that enclosure was unjust. Those whose land was included in an enclosure scheme had to pay part of the legal fees, fees for surveyors, and the costs of hedging and ditching lands. Costs were frequently large and burdensome for small farmers, often forcing them to sell. If they did try to hold on, loss of rights to use the commons plus inability to introduce the new techniques (which required capital investment) again made it difficult for them to compete with more efficient large farmers.

Copyholders and an Agricultural Labor Force

It is easier to sum up the position of the copyholders and those who had squatted on what was previously waste land. Anyone without specific legal title to the land simply had no rights and was evicted summarily. Those with records could continue to exist as marginal farmers, but loss of common rights made this a less desirable option, again forcing a settlement with the local landowner. In addition, the combination of the domestic putting out system and a small holding made it possible to survive in earlier centuries. But in the 18th and 19th centuries, as the wool industry became factory-organized, this combination disappeared; factory work depended on a full time labor force. Here, a psychic issue is important, one that is easy to forget. So long as individuals owned land, no matter how little, they had some status and some security. But many observers felt that the rural poor had been degraded as a result of the enclosures. By being forced to become wage workers, they became economic dependents on their employers, and as such were considered inferior.

These enclosures did not result in widespread depopulation, and dispossessed farmers did not immediately become an urban labor force. Most became agricultural wage laborers, but even here, further changes weakened their position.

Traditionally, farm servants were hired annually, lived either as part of the farmer's household or in a tied cottage that went with the job, and received much of their income in kind. But now that workers were in ample supply, living in their own homes, farmers more commonly hired labor for a cash wage as it was needed—by the season, week, or day. So no wage was paid in slack seasons. With the continuing reduction in cottage industry, and with generally falling agricultural wages that did not really begin to rise again until after the 1830s, many were reduced below the subsistence level.

Rural Poverty and Policy

This situation led to enormous financial pressure on agricultural laborers, a breakdown of traditional rural relationships, and another strange reversal of policy in an attempt to deal with the increase in rural poverty. The agricultural areas of southern England were most affected. In northern areas, the growing industrial towns absorbed the dispossessed rural poor, while in Scotland, as yet barely touched by either industrial or agricul-

tural revolution, the old pattern of rural relationships continued.

The problem revolved around low wages and illustrates again the widening differences of attitude between the middle class and the working poor. Low wages were not only thought to be essential for industrial profit making, they were also thought to be morally good for the poor, who were forced to work longer and harder. This was justified as follows: If the rich had money to spend, it was good because it created jobs. If the poor had money to spend, it showed that they earned too much—a signal that wages should be lowered. Anyway, the poor were poor because they did not have the work ethic of the middle class; if they did, they would not be poor.

However, some system of poor relief had always existed, usually on a parish by parish basis, and it is estimated that in 1700, about one fifth of the population received some assistance of this nature. But after 1760, the situation got worse. The living standards of the rural poor fell as a result of enclosure, low agricultural wages, rising prices, and loss of supplementary employment.

Speenhamland System

The policy response became known as the Speenhamland System (or Old Poor Law) after its birth in the village of Speen in Berkshire. It remained in effect until 1834, when the New Poor Law was introduced. In Speen, the Berkshire magistrates determined that where the farmers did not pay a wage high enough to support a family, then the laborer should be paid a supplement, based on the size of family and varying with the price of bread. In effect it established a fixed wage to be paid out of local rates (taxes). This system of outdoor relief was intended to deal with the working poor:

Speenhamland System
Poor relief policy used in rural areas of England

Those unable to work because of age or sickness received indoor relief in parish "poorhouses."

It was quickly adopted in much of the rest of southern England. Although the intention of guaranteeing a living wage was desirable, it demoralized for the recipients, was a further godsend for farmers, and an increasing burden for taxpayers in general.

The problems were many. It removed all incentive for the laborers to work hard, because they could never earn more than the fixed wage, whose proportions between paid wage and supplement varied. Agricultural laborers became demoralized because their living was dependent on parish relief. It benefitted the profit-making ability of the farmers. They could pay low wages, because their wage costs were subsidized by all taxpayers out of whose taxes wage supplements were paid. By permitting labor retention during slack seasons, farmers were also guaranteed that labor would be available during peak harvest times. (They also received export bounties if they exported grain.) It is likely also to have encouraged larger families, because the supplement varied with the size of family. And it definitely increased the burden of local taxes, which rose dramatically as the numbers receiving outdoor relief grew. Probably the only positive statement that can be made is that by guaranteeing at least a subsistence wage, it kept a lid on agrarian unrest. And as agricultural fortunes fluctuated from the boom years of the Napoleonic War period to depressed conditions afterward (when even farmers and landowners came under strain), this was no mean achievement.[2]

To summarize so far, the enclosures of the 18th and 19th centuries effected a drastic transformation of rural life, replacing traditional social relations with those of an impersonal marketplace. But in three major ways, they differed from the earlier wave of enclosures in the 16th century. Then, they were a response to the profitability of raising sheep to provide the raw materials for the growing wool processing industry; in the 18th

century, the impetus came from the increased demand for food, thus arable land as well as pasture was enclosed. Second, in the 18th century, the land area and the numbers of people involved were much larger, which gave rise to social problems on a much larger scale, and led to different mechanisms to deal with them. And last, in the earlier period, official reaction was negative; in the 18th and 19th centuries, government actively supported enclosure as a way of rationalizing and making farming more efficient. It is to this technical aspect of the agricultural revolution that we will now turn our attention.

Technological Changes

Increased productivity and output can accompany changes in organization as well as changes in techniques. Before the mid 18th century, organizational change, mainly increased specialization, was associated with the putting out or domestic system of industry. Later, technological changes involved the application of steam power to industrial uses within the factory. In agriculture, changes in organization due to enclosure and the practice of tenant farming for a market, and changes in technique were the hallmarks of the agricultural revolution. Changes in technique were of two kinds. The first, begun in the 17th century, involved new crops and practices, while the second involved the mechanization of farming. The first phase covers the period up to about 1830, when output grew for three reasons. First, the area under cultivation increased. For example, drainage of the fens in the 17th century, using Dutch techniques, added 10 percent to the area under cultivation. Second, the larger farms that resulted from enclosure were more efficient. Third, the increased practice of crop rotation raised output. By the late 17th century, both England and the Low Countries had incorporated most of the new techniques, with the result that, for example, wheat yields per acre were 40 percent higher than in France, which did not adopt them.

Crop Rotation

The first phase of technical improvement in agriculture started in the 17th century and continued all through the 18th. The practice of leaving land fallow to restore its productivity was now seen by capitalist farmers as a constraint on maximum use of the land. Even much earlier, a simple change from a two-field to a three-field system of cultivation increased the amount of crop-bearing land. Now with crop rotation, this earlier idea was further extended.

The Low Countries, already important for developing new ideas, were among the first to reduce the amount of land left idle by making more sophisticated crop rotations. The small size of the country and growth of commercial towns encouraged intensive farming, to increase agricultural output as much as possible. With the new systems of crop rotation, all land would be cultivated, but the crops grown in succeeding years differed so the soil was not exhausted of particular nutrients used by one particular crop.

A common rotation was grain followed by a nitrogenous legume or clover, which restored nitrogen to the soil and could be used as food for either humans or animals. In turn, the development of livestock raising was encouraged. As fallow land was eliminated, commercial demand for manure grew. (Previously, animals had grazed on the land left fallow, adding their own contribution to soil replenishment.) In Flanders, night soil (human excrement collected from privies), ashes from fireplaces, and city garbage were used, transported to farms from city areas on canals.

Many Dutch techniques, especially in drainage and intensive agriculture, were quickly borrowed by their commercially-minded equivalents in England, and crop rotation became more complex. For example, what became known as the Norfolk four-course system of rotation became common. It was popularized by Charles Townshend (1674-1738), who was also called Turnip Townshend because he emphasized the role of turnips in the rotation. A typical series could be, in successive years, flax (used in the linen industry) followed by turnips (which replenished the soil and also broke up the heavy clay soil found in much of England), followed by oats and clover (used as animal fodder), followed by wheat (for bread). The specific crop grown in any year in any field obviously depended on demand conditions, but the principle of switching each year was widely practiced. The practice of spreading manure on the fields was used, although in England, lime was also used in a process called marling, which decreased the acidity of the soil.[3]

Livestock Production

Commercialization of livestock production was also boosted by the growing demand for dairy products. This development of "new" lines of commercial farming was not totally new; earlier centuries had also seen more commercialized agricultural production. At this time, market gardening and orchards became common near the big towns, while such new crops as potatoes and tobacco, introduced from the New World, also became common. Tobacco had been grown in England in the 1650s, but its cultivation was prohibited a few years later in order to ensure a ready market for colonial tobacco. Potatoes deserve a special mention. While they later became a basic food in both England and Ireland, they were a staple in Ireland. Irish farming did not follow the same trend towards large scale as in England, although farmers were usually leaseholders. They grew grain crops to meet rent payments due to absentee landlords and potatoes to provide much of the family's food needs.

Livestock production involved both an expansion of output and new techniques of stockbreeding utilizing scientific knowledge to produce animals with desired characteristics. Robert Bakewell (1725-95) was one pioneer in breeding. He was a tenant farmer in Leicestershire who selectively bred both cattle and sheep for meat.

His results were very dramatic: The average weight of sheep increased from 28 to 80 pounds, while the average weight of beef cattle increased from 370 to 800 pounds.

Increased Productivity

Improvements in farm equipment and practices also helped improve efficiency and reduce labor needs in agriculture. For example, the increased availability of working horses and the use of horse-drawn ploughs doubled the acreage that one person could plough in a day as compared to the ox-drawn plough. This time saving was increased when lighter ploughs were introduced. By the late 18th century farm implements such as ploughs were made out of iron, which increased their strength and durability.

Jethro Tull (1674-1740) was the innovator whose name is associated with some of these improvements. He invented the seed drill, a simple device that by planting seeds at equal distances from each other avoided the waste associated with the old practice of sowing seeds broadcast by throwing them on the ground. He also speeded up the time needed to weed fields by popularizing the horse-drawn hoe, which cultivated between the neat rows made by seed drills.

The rapid spread of these ideas increased productivity in all types of farms. Information spread partly because the new developments were publicized in newspapers, books, and pamphlets, another sign of a successfully developing economy. For example, Arthur Young (1741-1820) was a notable agricultural propagandist and commentator on rural matters. (Interestingly, while initially in favor of enclosure because of its incentive to introduce more efficient techniques, he later recognized the hardships it produced.)

In recognition of the increased importance of agriculture to the economy, a new government agency was added in 1793, the Board of Agriculture, with Arthur Young as its first secretary. Official approval of the new ideas undoubtedly

help spread them—even George III was enthusiastic, and turned part of the royal estate at Windsor into a model farm utilizing new techniques.[4] All of this information spread rapidly to France, Prussia, and the United States, but how quickly it was adopted largely depended on the extent to which capitalist ideas had affected agriculture. Progress was faster where the trend to large-scale farming was already in progress, and slower where small plot agriculture survived.

Agriculture in France

France did not experience similar organizational and technological changes, and moved more slowly away from basically medieval practices. While cash farming was common and some old feudal practices disappeared (there were no serfs left in France), small-scale peasant farming persisted, and large-scale, completely capitalist farming was rare. This was deplored by the French Physiocrats, who observed the growing wealth of English agriculture during the 18th century, and wished that French farming was as prosperous.

Burdens on Peasants

Much of the reason for this can be explained by the French nobles' lack of interest in the management of their estates. Throughout inflationary periods, these nobles intensified pressure on peasants to try to maintain their own incomes by increasing the burden of feudal obligations that had long since disappeared elsewhere. They applied the letter of the law strictly to collect what was due to them, rewrote the conditions under which peasants lived and worked on their estates, and increased the share of the harvests assigned to them.

Physiocrats
18th century French economic theorists who believed that land was the true source of wealth

---

In addition, there was considerable inequity in landholding. Peasants, who formed 90 percent of the population at the end of the 18th century (a much larger proportion than in England, a sign of the lack of change) had only 30 percent of the land to work for themselves, while the nobles and bourgeoisie each owned 27 percent, and the Church the remaining 15 percent. (The bourgeoisie—representatives of urban commercial interests, such as bankers, merchants, financiers, and shopkeepers—were a numerically smaller class than in England. As a result, they were also considerably less powerful, both economically and politically, even though some, especially financiers, were personally very wealthy.)

This inequity, plus increased pressure on peasants by the nobles, led to the bitterness and resentment that marked France in the years leading to the French Revolution. Political power was still firmly in the hands of the monarchy, which was based on the ideas of absolutism and rule by divine right. Power was not shared with France's parliament, the Estates General (composed of three estates, Church, Nobility, and Bourgeoisie), even though it had been created centuries earlier to approve of tax measures and thus control the monarchy's revenues. Peasants were the largest group in the population and paid the most tax, but had no official voice in political life.

Figure 9.1   This farming scene, although drawn in the 19th century (and appearing in the Illustrated London News, November 7, 1846, p. 300) would be typical of farming practices using horse-drawn farm machines. (Courtesy of The Illustrated London News Picture Library.)

Peasants faced many financial burdens. To the local noble, they paid a money rent or a share of the harvest; a quit rent in place of an obligation to work on the lord's land; a part of the revenues received if a farm was sold; possibly a market fee if goods were sold at the local market; and fees for having grain ground, grapes pressed, or bread baked using the noble's facilities (and usually, peasants were *required* to use these facilities). The peasant paid a tithe to the Church. Then there were taxes whose proceeds went to the Crown, like the *taille*, which varied from year to year as the monarch's needs for revenues changed, and its companions, *capitation* and *vingtiéme*; the salt tax (often with a requirement that a certain amount of salt be bought, to avoid peasants escaping payment of the tax); taxes on beer and wine; and the *corvée*, a duty to work on the upkeep of roads.

Quit rent

Money payment paid in place of feudal obligations

By the 1780s, France's economy was relatively depressed, which hurt many peasants who worked part-time for wages in cottage industry. Prices had also been rising since the 1730s, which led nobles to intensify pressure on the peasants. In addition, the financial situation of Louis XVI had worsened, and in an attempt to find a solution, the Estates General was called into session in 1789. The obvious solution was to impose taxes on the wealthy. The peasants had suffered through two disastrous harvests, and could carry no more tax burdens, but the nobles and clergy refused to consider that option. Also, the Third Estate, the bourgeoisie, like others with commercial interests elsewhere, seized the opportunity to request other reforms to move at least part way to a more representative form of government.

But these demands were followed by the monarch's indecision, and, fueled by rumors of expected resistance by Louis XVI, led to an uprising that started with the storming of the royal prison,

the Bastille. Throughout the summer of 1789 the revolution spread to the countryside, where peasants attacked the nobles' chateaux and burned the manorial rolls in an attempt to eliminate the inequity of 18th century semi-feudalism.

Results of the French Revolution

Some land redistribution did occur at this time. A few of the nobles agreed to surrender their remaining feudal rights in exchange for an indemnity, which would be, on average, equal to about 20 years' revenues from peasants' holdings. (This condition was later eliminated. Had it gone through, it would have meant even greater subjugation of peasants by imposing so large a debt burden for so long.) Later in the French Revolution, lands of the Church and of those nobles who had fled the country were seized. About half of this amount was sold to the peasants, with the rest bought by speculators and some capitalist farmers.

Persistence of Small-Scale Farming

After the Revolution, there was a general reform of the legal system as laws were codified in the Code Napoleon, and peasants eventually gained clear title to their holdings. In addition, the Code eliminated the primogeniture system of inheritance. Both provisions had the effect of encouraging the continuation of small scale agriculture, so that, even as late as 1908, over half of all French farms were smaller than 25 acres. Much earlier, in 1826, small landholders accounted for 89 percent of all landowners, and owned 33 percent of the land in average holdings of about seven acres each. Medium sized landholders accounted for 10 percent of all landowners, and their average holdings were about 57 acres each. Large landowners, who owned 21 percent of the land, had average holdings of about 675 acres. But even when holdings were large, they tended to be rented out in smaller units or farmed on a sharecropping basis, in which case sharecroppers could pay as much as two thirds of the harvest to the landowner. Long-lease tenant farming tended to be in those areas most encouraging to commercial agriculture, such as those nearest urban areas or easily accessible to a transportation route.

The net result was that, although French farmers were as motivated by money incentives as anyone else, they had little desire or ability to introduce new techniques and expand output. Even larger farmers were limited by the slow expansion of the market—population growth remained slow in France, increasing from 27.5 million in 1800 to 36.5 million in 1860 and to 39.7 million in 1913. Between 1800 and 1900, France's total population growth was 50 percent, which compares to much faster growth in both Germany and Great Britain over the same period of time. Germany grew by 200 percent to reach 60 million, and Great Britain by 300 percent to reach 40 million. In addition, and of importance to capitalist farmers producing for a market, the rate of *urban* growth in France lagged significantly behind that of Germany and Britain. By 1913, population in German towns had quadrupled to 40 million, while over three quarters of Britain's population lived in urban areas. But in France, the urban population had only doubled to 18 million by 1913. This limited the commercialization of agriculture and also, because it was combined with the persistence of peasant farming on a small scale, limited the expansion of industrial development by limiting the potential supply of labor.

Slow Modernization

In fact, France's slow agricultural modernization to a certain extent mirrored the slow modernization of industry. It was affected by many of the same influences that retarded industrial development, such as persistence of small units, lack of a good transportation network until later in the 19th century, protection, and limited innovation.

Even in the middle of the 19th century, although France was still self-sufficient in food, traditional methods were still widely used, and agriculture suffered from frequent fluctuations in prosperity. Especially in the first part of the century, periods of rising prices contributed to urban protests as industrial workers faced food scarcity and higher prices. (After this time, the fact that food riots did not occur was largely due to transportation improvements. Because farming was generally undertaken to meet local needs, improving transportation helped break down the tendency to local isolation; the food supply problem was always more one of distribution than of production.)

Traditional production methods limited innovation. For example, in the 18th and 19th centuries, a three-year rotation was common, such as wheat followed by a cereal crop followed by fallow. As in all cases where the practice of fallow was used, it not only limited the use of land, but also meant that little livestock was kept because of the lack of fodder. Thus the amount of manure was restricted, which kept yields low. Although some of the larger, wealthier landowners did begin to adopt English techniques and introduced the planting of fodder crops, it was a slow process. In 1840, only 6 percent of the arable land was planted with such a crop, while 27 percent lay fallow.

For so long as landholdings remained small, this continued to be the case. Even where demand was expanding as a result of urban growth, it was met by bringing more land into cultivation rather than by changing methods. This was especially true in the south where more land was available and where agriculture was more diversified. Most of the technical change occurred in the more heavily populated north. But even where the market and the incentive to innovate existed, it was hard for a peasant farmer to diversify. Farmers were obviously motivated by the need to produce food for their families. But they were also motivated by the perceived need to protect themselves against the possibility of famine, which helped prevent the transfer from a cereal to some other crop.

There were changes. For example, maize and potatoes were often planted on previously fallow land, although it took a long time for the taste of these new items to be accepted. But even diversification did little to raise yields and restore soil fertility. Changes were more common after the mid 19th entury, due largely to the combined effects of increasing demand brought about by urbanization and better distribution due to the completion of the rail network.

Better Transportation in the Late 19th Century

For so long as railroad construction in France remained limited to the major lines linking Paris with other urban centers, agriculture (and regional price differences) were little affected.

After the 1870s more local lines were built and local roads improved, increasing the effective market for local farmers. There were several results. Innovation to improve farming was stimulated and the amount of land left fallow declined. Cereal yields increased by 50 percent in the period 1850-1888. Regional price differences were almost eliminated. Products that had previously been sold only in a local area were now sold in a larger market. For example, the market for ordinary wines increased. (Higher quality wines had always had a national and international market, because even high transportation costs were only a small part of their final price.) However, this was offset by the outbreak of phylloxera, plant lice that attacked the leaves and roots of the vines on which grapes for wine were grown, which devastated French wine production and eliminated smaller producers. Recovery was expensive, as it involved grafting disease-resistant American vine rootstock, and could be borne only by larger producers. Finally, improved transportation also

tended to encourage regional specialization in farming.

Livestock production, both dairying (especially near urban areas) and meat production increased, and the quality of animals improved once they were no longer used as work animals. This development also increased the availability of manure, and in addition, there was a greater use of fertilizer in general. But, as would be expected, change was slowest in the areas where small farms predominated, which also limited the introduction of machinery that required larger capital funds than such farmers had access to. However, improvements were being made, and accessibility to a larger market increased. The net effect on French farming was that by the end of the century, farming was more influenced by the pattern of demand than by the old influence of the need to protect against famine.

Agriculture in Germany

Germany, unlike both France and Britain, had not become a unified nation-state. Previous chapters have shown how the Holy Roman Empire had weakened as a result of religious clashes during the 16th century, which ended in the Thirty Years War (1616-1648). Then the German states split into two camps: those remaining Catholic (chief of which was Austria) and those becoming Protestant (the strongest state here was Prussia). As a result of the devastations of that war, the German states retreated to a condition of semifeudalism. Their economic and political weakness showed later in the relative ease with which Napoleon swept across Germany and formally liquidated the Holy Roman Empire at the beginning of the 19th century.

Fragmentation was echoed in agriculture. There were some large landholdings, following the English pattern, and some small holdings, following the French pattern. The differences depended on how each state reacted to agricultural innovation and the movement away from traditional, feudal landholding patterns. Land re-distribution took place later than in England, and the adoption of new techniques depended largely on whether production was for a market or undertaken by peasants for subsistence.

Prussia and Land Redistribution

In Prussia throughout the 18th century, feudal patterns of landholding persisted untouched. However, the lords were actively involved in managing their estates and in farming for a profit. But Prussia's defeat by Napoleon pointed out the weaknesses of a political and military system based on serfdom. So in return for the peasants' support, the nobles abolished serfdom during the years 1807-1809, and permitted serfs to buy land, although there was by no means a massive redistribution of land to free peasants.

For example, in 1811, those peasants proving their hereditary rights to work the land could get free title to two thirds of it on condition that the remaining third went to the lord. This was made more restrictive later in 1816: Only peasants with two oxen (i.e., the richer ones) gave up one third of the land—all others had to surrender half. (Even as late as 1848, only 240,000 peasants had actually managed to benefit from the freedom promised them in 1811.) And the poorest class of smallholders were not granted title to their garden plots until after 1850. The result was an increase of the size of the lands held by the lords at the expense of the small farmers. However, there was an expansion of capitalist agricultural production using the new technologies in Prussia.

In the rest of Germany, where the lords depended more on the peasants for income and were not actively farming lands themselves, two slightly different patterns emerged. In the states of Hanover, Schleswig-Holstein, Upper Bavaria, and Westphalia, for example, the abolition of feudalism at the end of the 18th century resulted in the creation of large peasant holdings. This occurred because in return for giving up their feudal rights, the lords required compensation from peasants. Peasants differed in economic status, and the poorer ones could not afford the payments required, so sold to the richer peasants who thereby increased the size of their holdings. They were more likely to improve their holdings, although limited by the size of capital investment required.

The second pattern occurred mainly in the west and southwest areas. The abolition of feudalism was accompanied by the peasants gaining complete title to their lands with no compensation given to the lords. Thus here, the French pattern of small scale agricultural holdings persisted.

Landholding in Other Areas

In general, wherever production had traditionally been for a market—as in England, Prussia, southern Italy, and northern Spain—landholdings were large and technological innovations occurred. Large-scale farming also occurred in many of the areas settled by European colonists, such as Australia, where sheepraising on an extensive basis was important and the midwestern United States, where grain production became important in the mid 19th century. Output from these and other "new" areas competed for markets in Europe, and these low-cost producers gained large shares of the old markets. However, because they were empty areas, the availability of cheap land reduced the incentive to adopt soil conservation and other improvement techniques that were necessary in the more densely populated areas of Europe, where land was relatively scarce.

Small-scale farming continued if peasants gained title to their holdings following the abolition of feudalism. It also continued where intensive dairy and poultry farming was important, as in the Low Countries or the eastern United States.

19th Century Mechanization of Agriculture

To a greater or lesser extent, and depending on the pattern of landholding, motivation of the farmer, ability to finance improvements, and extent of the market, the technical changes in farming described were truly international, and were adopted if they could be readily utilized. Changes in this century involved improvements in both knowledge and mechanization.

Better Knowledge

For example, science added to knowledge about what soil really was. This understanding of both soil composition and plant chemistry encouraged the wider use of fertilizers (including guano from Peru) and the development of chemical fertilizers. Science also turned its attention to the development of hybrid plants, especially disease-resistant ones, which was an increasing concern when the urban market served by commercial farming was large.

In the mid 19th century, governments in both Britain and the United States actively encouraged research. They established experimental stations, set up government Departments of Agriculture, and founded special agricultural schools, the first being the Royal Agricultural College in Britain, founded in 1845. In the United States, then still predominantly agricultural, official support came in 1862, when Congress passed the Land Grant Act. Each state got 30,000 free acres for each senator and representative, and could dispose of them as they wished, subject only to the requirement that the education of the masses be furthered. In many states, revenues from the sale of land—to speculators, timber or railroad compa-

nies, or large ranchers, for example—were used to establish what became known as the land grant colleges. These were the "A & M" (for agricultural and mechanical) colleges established in the late 19th century, which became the technical training grounds for those involved in agriculture and industry.

United States Farm Machinery

The United States also took the lead in the 19th century with the development of farm machines. By the late 19th century, when inanimate power was added, they greatly increased productivity per hour. Labor scarcity had always been a problem in this new country; earlier, slaves had been imported to work the southern plantations. An alternative was to investigate the possibility of inventing machinery to replace human labor. There was a strong incentive to do so when potential markets in the industrializing Eastern states as well as in Europe were opened up as a result of the development of a rail network linking the Midwest to the East Coast.

The earliest examples of new types of farm machinery were the McCormick and Hussey reapers, introduced in the 1830s, which replaced the scythe for cutting grain. The twine binder was introduced in 1878 to automatically bundle and tie sheaves of wheat, replacing pitchforks and hand-tied sheaves. The combine combined a reaper and a thresher to remove the grains from the surrounding husks (previously done manually with a flail) and was introduced in the 1880s. It was most suitable for the large fields of the United States and Australia, and contributed to the spread of commercial agriculture in these areas. Machines made extensive agriculture possible with fewer workers, especially when power was added. Other developments, such as the riding plough or winnowing machines reduced the time needed. In wheat production, for example, the number of hours required per acre of wheat production fell from 75 in 1830 to 13 in 1880.

Land grant college

State colleges established with revenues from the sale of land granted to states by the federal government

Figure 9.2   This scene (appearing in the Illustrated London News, August 29, 1946, p. 136) shows the labor intensity of farming at peak times, like harvest time. (Courtesy of The Illustrated London News Picture Library.)

American expertise in agricultural implements was widely recognized when some of the new equipment was shown at the Great Exhibition of 1851 in London, held to glorify the achievements of the Industrial Revolution and the prosperity of Victorian England. (The building itself was a product of many new developments. It was called the Crystal Palace and was made of an iron framework covered with glass, a building style also used to construct the great new railway stations in England.)

Mechanization of field crops was easiest, but the extent to which mechanization improved productivity in any particular branch of agriculture differed. For example, in the United States, a major crop was cotton, but cotton continued to be an extremely labor-intensive branch of farming, and was not mechanized significantly until the 1950s. Similarly, tree crops and market gardening are less amenable to mechanization.

Summary

One mark of an industrializing economy is that the occupational distribution of the labor force changes. The typical pattern is that the percentage of the labor force employed in agriculture falls, while the percentage employed in industry (and service or tertiary occupations) increases. And what is even more important is that while this change is happening, agricultural output does not fall.

It is obvious that the productivity of agricultural workers must rise if this is to happen. Reorganizing work as well as technological changes such as mechanization can raise productivity. Thus, on a very general level, economic development, industrialization, urbanization, and technological change are linked. Rising productivity and output in agriculture reduces labor needs, permits urbanization, and makes possible the development of an industrial labor force. (Whether this occurs depends on what is happening in industry. If industry itself is expanding, then the surplus agricultural workers, willingly or unwillingly, can be absorbed. If not, then they remain as un- or under-employed labor, or can take another option, emigration.)

These changes occurred first in England, then later in France, Germany, and the United States. The framework in which they took place was largely a capitalist one, although as the extent of the spread of capitalist ideas varied, changes could be fast or slow, limited or widespread. Change depended on the extent of the market for agricultural output. Where it was large—where towns were growing fast, as in England or Germany, or where export demand existed, as in the United States—then agriculture became a "modern" capitalist sector of the economy.

Precisely how these changes took place also differed in different countries. In England, the elimination of the small farmer, the last remnant of the feudal past, occurred chiefly through the process of enclosure. This resulted in the forced creation of an industrial labor force, as industry was simultaneously expanding. Small, marginal farmers were also reduced in number in Germany in the 19th century—again, an important incentive was the desire of large landowners to farm land for a profit. The process was slowest in France where small peasant farms remained, and

consequently large scale industrialization was not so widespread. In the United States, the creation of an urban industrial labor force came about in a very different way, and depended heavily on immigration, which occurred in response to the dislocation caused by changes in agrarian relations in Europe. Without an initially large agricultural labor force, the process of increasing productivity in farming involved mechanization. When adopted elsewhere the substitution of machinery for people would continue the process of reducing labor needs in agriculture.

Notes

1. The United States, of course, differs from the European countries in having no feudal past and therefore no feudal ties to break. Landholding patterns ranged from the small, independently owned farms of New England to the large, commercial plantations of the South. The United States was an innovator in mechanization because of its perennial labor scarcity. Mechanization helped open up the rich midwestern farm lands, which had enormous implications for the world economy in the 20th century.

2. Parliament passed the Corn Law in 1815 to cope with financial problems after the collapse of the agricultural boom. It was a protectionist measure designed to keep up the falling price of grain by prohibiting the import of grain into Britain unless the price rose to a predetermined level. While nominally seeming to assure "reasonable" prices for consumers—the effect of a poor domestic harvest would be offset by increased availability of foreign grain—in fact, by limiting availability, it was hoped that prices would remain high, thus protecting the investments of farmers and landowners in improvements. The entire issue of protectionism, as symbolized by the Corn Law, was a controversial one in the early 19th century and will be covered later.

3. Increasing linkages became a feature of economic development at this time, and an interest-

ing one was apparent here. Up to the late 18th century, fertilizers were organic, and synthetic fertilizers were not used until the 19th century. Later in that century, a new technique in the steel industry used a lining of magnesium limestone to permit the use of coal high in phosphorous. The lining absorbed phosphorous and thus produced steel free from impurities. When the lining was completely absorbed, it was broken up to be used as one of the first synthetic phosphate fertilizers.

4. As an interesting aside to the involvement and interest of the upper classes in farming at this time, agricultural innovation also influenced art. Along with portraitists and landscape painters, a new type of painter emerged: the animal painter, such as George Stubbs. In the 18th and 19th centuries, paintings of prize animals, all anatomically correct, permitted their proud owners to display on the walls of their reception rooms the accomplishments of stock breeding they could not display in the flesh.

Key Concepts

Abolition of feudal tenure	Outdoor relief (Old Poor Law)
Agricultural revolution	Physiocrats, Physiocracy
Capitation	Primogeniture
Crop rotation	Speenhamland system
Fodder crop	*Taille*
Intensive agriculture	Tenant farming
Landed gentry	Tied cottage
Mechanization	*Vingtiéme*

Questions for Discussion or Essay Writing

1. What were the major differences between the two major waves of enclosures in England?

2. Discuss the Speenhamland system. In what ways did it differ from or was similar to previous social policies?

3. What were the results of the 18th century enclosures?

4. "Output can be raised with the adoption of organizational change or technological change." Discuss.

5. In what ways were the technological changes associated with 18th and 19th century agriculture related to advances in scientific knowledge?

6. Can any explanations be offered for the differences in agricultural development in different countries?

7. To what extent were economic issues important causes of the French Revolution?

8. Is there a connection between the commercialization of agriculture and the pattern of landholding?

9. What was the impact of agricultural change in the 18th and 19th centuries?

For Further Reading

(and see also readings for Chapters 8 and 10)

Baugh, D.A. "The Cost of Poor Relief in South-East England, 1790-1834." *Economic History Review*, XXVIII:1 (1974): 50-68.

Boyer, George R. *An Economic History of the English Poor Law, 1750-1850.* Cambridge: Cambridge University Press, 1990.

Chorley, G.P.H. "The Agricultural Revolution in Northern Europe, 1750-1880: Nitrogen, Legumes and Crop Productivity." *Economic History Review*, XXX:4 (1976): 429-441.

Grigg, David. *Population Growth and Agrarian Change: An Historical Perspective.* Cambridge: Cambridge University Press, 1980.

Melton, Edgar. "Proto-Industrialization, Serf Agriculture and Agrarian Social Structure: Two Estates in Nineteenth Century Russia." *Past and Present*, v. 115 (May 1987): 69-106.

Mingay, G.E. *Enclosure and the Small Farmer in the Age of the Industrial Revolution.* London: Macmillan, 1982.

Neeson, J.M. "The Opponents of Enclosure in Eighteenth-Century Northamptonshire." *Past and Present*, v. 105 (November 1984): 114-139.

Stone, Lawrence and Jeanne C. Fawtier Stone. *An Open Elite? England 1540-1880.* Oxford: Oxford University Press, 1984.

Chapter 10

The Industrial Revolution: First Phase (1780–1830)

THE PAST FEW CHAPTERS HAVE DESCRIBED SOME OF THE DEVELOPMENTS that prepared the way for the Industrial Revolution. This is the topic of the next several chapters, which will cover the developments beginning in the mid 18th century that totally transformed the economies of the countries we are looking at. Simply put, the Industrial Revolution could be summarized as the widespread application of power-driven machinery in industry. But this single focus on technological change misses the complexity of reality.

What happened? Starting within the context of a capitalist society, the following changes occurred, first in Britain, then elsewhere. Factory production using machines became common, productivity and output in industry and agriculture rose dramatically, manufacturing accounted for a greater share of national output, urbanization accompanied industrialization, and social relationships changed. Previously, as we saw, the family, home, village, or region were more or less self-sufficient. After the Industrial Revolution, most production moved from the domestic unit to the factory, markets existed for just about everything, the scale of operations expanded, economic activity became increasingly internationalized, and products, services, and techniques that were totally unknown before came into existence.

(This last phenomenon became pronounced in the 20th century.)

It was both a social and an economic transformation. It was a movement away from a small-scale economy, influenced by the natural rhythms of climate and seasonal changes and constrained by the limits of human and animal power. It was a movement toward a large-scale economy dominated by impersonal market forces where the ability to tap inanimate power sources seemed to open up unlimited horizons for human ingenuity and achievement.

During the late 18th century and up to the late 19th, only Great Britain was industrialized. When other countries industrialized, trade and financial flows revolved around Britain, a position that persisted until the economic collapse following the First World War.

What we will do now is explore the whys, hows, and whats of the industrialization process. This should help us understand why others industrialized when they did, and why they could compress this experience into a shorter period of time than Britain did. In this chapter, we will concentrate on the first phase of Britain's industrialization from 1780 to 1830, leaving the second phase until the next chapter.

The years 1780-1830 were characterized by the transformation of the cotton textile industry into the leading edge of industrialization. In the second phase, change affected the whole economy. Steam power became widely used in industry, and there was a burst of new technology resulting in both new methods of production and new industries. What also characterized this phase was the growth of the metalworking industries and those industries associated with the use of metal and steam power.

Britain Before the Industrial Revolution

As we have seen, Britain at the beginning of the 16th century was economically backward compared with her European rivals. This was no longer true by the beginning of the 18th century, when although Britain was much less populous than her major rival France (seven million including Scotland, compared with France's twenty million), she seemed much more dynamic. As we also saw, agricultural changes unique to Britain had started a movement of people out of agriculture. In fact, on the eve of the Industrial Revolution, foreign observers were struck by one major result of the enclosures: the absence of a rural peasantry. This contrasted with the persistence of older farming traditions in most of the rest of Europe. They also noted the relatively greater importance of trade in Britain, which grew as a result of two factors. One was the extensive overseas empire Britain had acquired. The second was the growth of manufacturing. This growth of trade[1] stimulated the growth of several cities, including London. London by 1750 had a population of 3/4 million (15 percent of England's population), making it Europe's largest city. Other ports, especially those on the Atlantic trade routes such as Liverpool, Bristol, and Glasgow, were involved in the trade in slaves, sugar, tea, tobacco and, increasingly, cotton.

In manufacturing, wool dominated, but others were also becoming important, including cutlery in Sheffield and small metal goods in Birming-

ham. Most manufacturing, except for brewing and ironmaking, was undertaken along domestic (putting out) lines and was capitalist production for a market. However, little use was made of machines or water power; only in the fulling mills of the wool industry or the grain mills was water power extensively used. Even where "factories," or more properly what we would call workshops, existed, they were relatively small-scale and rare. There was some small-scale mining, such as coal in the north country and midlands and tin in Cornwall.

Involvement of Landowners

One important implication of the decentralization of economic activity is that landowners, by this time a politically important class, were also involved, in contrast with other European landowners. They had an interest in the mines under their land, as royalties went to them and not to the monarch; if manufacturing occurred in villages on their land, they were interested in improving land transportation, so that locally produced products would not be at a disadvantage. (And in the early 18th century, land transportation was neither easy nor fast, so any improvement made a difference.)

While there was not complete harmony or an identity of interests between landed gentry and industrialists, neither was there complete antipathy. With the realization that the ability to make money reflected on the strength of the country, it became easier later in the 18th century to pass laws protecting the home market. This benefitted the new industrialists, even though the much greater strength of merchant interests might have implied trade laws encouraging freer trade.

The phenomenon of landowner support may have been due to greater fluidity in the English social structure. The upper class included both old aristocracy and the new rich who had acquired land in the 16th and 17th centuries. (Land ownership was important because it was seen as conferring social status.) In addition, there was a fairly large number of those who had made money in commerce and trade, the commercial bourgeoisie or what we would now call a middle class. These people too would try to achieve social status by acquiring land, or at least a country house. This meant that wealth was not concentrated in the hands of a small class of aristocratic nobles as in France, but in a larger class of people who were more likely to be economically active in the new way.

Then, whenever the interests of the political decision makers and the economic money makers coincided, the result was likely to be a favorable legislative climate, which remained true until the beginning of the 19th century. By that time, thanks mainly to an increasing number of urban industrialists, there were growing divergences of opinion between landed and urban industrial interests.

Why was Britain First?

In order to answer why Britain was the first country to industrialize, it is necessary to consider the presence or absence of the elements needed for capitalist industrialization, and some special factors (for example, climate and politics).

Population Growth

We will start with the labor factor. Rapid population growth has sometimes been used to explain the timing of Britain's Industrial Revolution, but this is not strictly true. Population growth *per se* will not stimulate the type of revolutionary change that occurred in the 18th century, a reality that also applies to the 20th century, as many developing countries today know.

The population of Great Britain (England, Wales, and Scotland) was seven million in 1707, just after union with Scotland. It reached 10.8 in 1801 (or 16.1 million if Ireland is added), primarily due to a fall in the death rate. This fall has been

explained by the slow improvement in living conditions due to the availability of more and better food on a regular basis, thanks to agricultural changes and improvements in transportation. Other contributing factors included better standards of personal care, as more and cheaper textiles for clothing and more soap became available. The drop was especially noted in the infant mortality rate. In the 1730s, four or five babies out of every ten died before reaching their second birthday, a rate that was halved by the end of the 18th century. Growth was not much affected by a rise in the birthrate, which was very modest, or by immigration or improved public health facilities. The latter, which included better sanitation, waste disposal and water supply, only became important in explaining demographic trends in the mid 19th century.

In general, rapid population growth can affect economic development from both the supply side and the demand side. For capitalist industrialization to take place, three considerations should be noted when looking at the supply of labor. First, even if population growth translates into labor force growth, mechanization could equally well be prevented. Mechanization involves the substitution of capital for labor, and if labor is both cheap and available, there is no incentive to mechanize *unless* other elements are present (for example, a rapidly expanding demand). Also, because mechanization involves large upfront finance capital outlays but no guarantees of a return, the incentive is stifled. Hence population growth *alone* will not cause industrialization. Both Ireland and the Scottish Highlands experienced faster population growth at this time than England, but neither industrialized. The second factor downplaying the role of population growth in stimulating industrialization concerns timing. In England, the rate of population growth rose

---

Mechanization

Use of machinery rather than manual labor

after 1780—*after* industrial change had already begun.

However, the third consideration does distinguish Britain from elsewhere. For capitalist industrialization to occur, the available labor must be free labor. As we have already seen, by the late 16th century there were few effective feudal constraints remaining. In addition, enclosures created a landless peasantry that increased in size as a result of the 18th century wave of enclosures. Even if the existence of a free labor force does not explain the introduction of mechanized techniques in industry, once industrial expansion has begun, industrialists' labor force needs can be met.

Another consideration that was important for the early phase of the Industrial Revolution is that the available labor was already skilled. The early enclosures plus the putting out system of manu-

Free Labor
Workers who are legally free to work for an employer

facture implied that most available workers had skills such as spinning and weaving that were easily adaptable to the expansion of industry, especially before steam power was added. Also the early specialization of industry and the tradition of craftsmanship help explain the origin of many of the earliest technological developments. Most were made by skilled, practical people trying to solve a practical problem they themselves were facing, rather than by scientists working in research laboratories separated from the shop floor.

Thus, to summarize the labor supply aspect, it is impossible to say that a growing population *caused* the industrial revolution. What is more accurate is to conclude that a growing population *assisted* development because the economy was

Figure 10-1 The first machines were typically made out of wood and operated by hand, like this late 18th century carding machine used in the woolen industry (Reproduced by permission of the Syndics of Cambridge University Library)

Solving Problems in Economic History

Was invention narrowly focused or widespread in 18th century England?

The Industrial Revolution in England is often described in terms of technological changes dramatically increasing productivity in a few "leading edge" industries that subsequently affected others in a cumulative and reinforcing manner. However, some researchers believe that innovative activity was more widely dispersed from the start, and it is this dispersion that helps account for the observed industrial changes. How best to examine this issue is the subject of Richard J. Sullivan in "The Revolution of Ideas: Widespread Patenting and Invention During the English Industrial Revolution." (*Journal of Economic History*, L:2, June 1990, pp. 349-362). Because a productivity change depends on the introduction of an innovative process which in turn depends on a creative idea having seen the light of day in an invention, he investigates inventive behavior by examining patents in some English industries between 1711 and 1850.

There are limits to using information on patents as a proxy for innovation because, for example, some inventions are not patentable or were simply not patented. Also, there is a question of which measure of patent activity to use. For example, comparing patents per thousand workers overstates inventiveness in capital intensive industries such as chemicals but understates productivity-enhancing changes in agriculture, which had a large labor force and experienced many organizational changes and non-patentable activity that revolutionized farming. There is the further problem of which industrial classifications to use: Steam engines and production machinery revolutionized industry, but there was no separate "industry" producing them in the 18th century. However, bearing these quali-

fications in mind, patent information can be useful for the following reasons. In a market economy, the expectation of increased rewards to invention arises because of expected profits resulting from expanded production. Expanded production, of course, must be sold if these increased profits are to materialize, so increasing population and other influences affecting the costs of innovation (such as the cost of capital) are also encouraging factors.

Sullivan studied six industries, textiles, metals, field agriculture, ocean shipping, heavy chemicals and railroads, and included patent information on steam engines and production machinery. By far the largest share of patents is accounted for by textiles, in keeping with the traditional view of the central role played by changes in textile technology. But over the entire period, textiles, metals and ocean shipping together account for only 29 percent of all patents issued—so other industries were also inventive. Using a slightly different classification system shows that production machines accounted for 27 percent of total patents issued between 1711 and 1850, although the impact is probably understated because it does not include steam engines or patents for the transmission of power or for nonproduction machines. Recalculating to account for this suggests that mechanical technology was associated with at least 46 percent of patents, and it was widespread mechanization that characterized the Industrial Revolution. Machines in fact were heavily represented in invention in the early part of the period, well before the official "start" of the Industrial Revolution.

(Problem continues on next page)

(Problem continued from previous page)

Patent data also shows bursts of activity in various decades consistent with conventional wisdom regarding the dating of the Industrial Revolution. For example, the three decades 1760 to 1790 showed such bursts—in textiles, metals and ocean shipping (1760s), heavy chemicals (1770s) and in field agriculture (1780s). Railroad technology experienced an acceleration in inventive activity between 1811 and 1820.

This pattern also shows the stimulating feedback effects of inventive activity. For example, it is likely that the expansion of textiles in the 1760s gave an incentive for the development of bleaching chemicals in the 1770s. What is also important about patent data is that it shows invention growing more rapidly in all sectors after 1760, but relatively faster outside a group of technologically progressive sectors, and new classification categories had to be created to account for many of them.

Hence, to summarize, there was a dramatic increase in invention across much of the English economy. However, it is probably true that, as measured by contribution to the growth of total factor productivity, a smaller group of technologically progressive industries accounted for more of the innovation than the inventions. Nevertheless, and whatever classification schemes are used, all the data point to a dramatic acceleration of invention and innovation in the 18th century, largely due to a favorable combination of triggering influences.

already dynamic and changing. This also helps explain why other European countries also experiencing population growth did not industrialize at that time: They lacked the accompanying economic dynamism.

Effective Demand

What role did the increase in population play on the demand side? The important point to remember here is that we are talking about effective demand, demand backed up by purchasing power. This is necessary if increasing demand is to lead to increased production (and thus indirectly stimulate those technological changes associated with the industrial revolution), because in a market economy, only demand that is made effective by money purchases matters to profit-minded producers.

The evidence here is not very strong. Although the cotton textile industry was a consumer goods industry, most of its expanding output was exported during the 19th century. The industries based on metal were mainly investment goods industries so not immediately subject to the stimulus of rising consumer demand.

Did movements of real wages and purchasing power increase demand? Real wages rose in the first phase of expansion, probably in response to the existing relative labor scarcity, which helped encourage some mechanization in the textile industry. But they fell after 1790 and did not start to rise again until after the 1850s. This fall in early 19th century living standards was felt especially by the new urban masses. Their per capita consumption of meat and vegetables fell, and they lived in seriously inadequate housing.

Some classes of the population suffered much more than others. For example, the half million hand-loom weavers in the first years of the 19th century were effectively displaced by power looms. In general, workers in declining industries overtaken by technological change were much worse off—a result of loss of occupation rather than low wages (which affect those who remained

Investment
Acquisition of new productive capital

employed). Agricultural workers were considerably worse off than those in industrial occupations, low paid though most of the latter were. The most dramatic example occurred in agricultural Ireland, where one million of its 8.5 million population starved to death in the great famine of 1846-1847, even though Irish grain was being exported. Only those industries supplying a consumer market—especially household goods—experienced increased domestic sales. The other "leading edge" industries were very little affected.

In fact, widespread poverty in the early years of the 19th century not only limited the expansion of the domestic market but also generated much social discontent, which often reached a boiling point. This discontent was always contained: Britain, unlike most of the other European countries in the 19th century, did not experience domestic revolutions. Increasingly, reform movements attempted to do something. While poverty had always existed, urban poverty, because it was concentrated, was much harder to disguise than rural poverty, hence there was increasing pressure to improve the situation.

Increase in Wealth

Economically, low and falling wage levels were associated with a growing gap between rich and poor. The *share* of national income received by the very wealthy and the middle class increased and was tied in with the investment needs of the industrial revolution. Any country at a fairly low level of income trying to industrialize must somehow finance the increased investment that is needed for this effort. Technically, increasing the rate of capital accumulation requires higher profits and a diversion of income away from consumption. As the very wealthiest were not significant investors in the new industries, this implied that the "new" industrialists, typically small to start with, had every incentive to hold down wages as low as possible. This worked in the initial phase, when new equipment was not

especially costly and could be financed out of relatively small, but growing profits. Not until the 1840s did gross capital formation reach 10 percent of national income. The rise in investment after then was associated with the development of new industries such as the railroads, which were heavy users of capital.

Even economic theory justified this. A major theme of the Classical school of economics was that profits led to capital accumulation; the idea of subsistence level wages was another theme. The advantages of high wages as a spur to higher productivity and increased purchasing power was not realized until later in the 19th century. (When overseas demand for British output stopped growing, attention turned to the possibility of domestic growth compensating for this decline.)

So if increased demand was an ingredient in encouraging technical change, it was not increased consumer demand from the working classes. We shall, however, investigate later the role played by an increased demand from the government and foreign countries (via exports). This increased demand occurred simultaneously with the first phase of industrialization. It provided exactly the stimulus needed in those industrial sectors with significant linkages with others, adding a cumulative effect to this process.

Capital Availability

Turning now to capital as an input, we must separate the concept of capital into two: money and capital goods. This is important, because while a country may be wealthy in the monetary sense—and history provides us with many examples such as Aztec Mexico or 16th century Spain—industrialization is not automatic. That is, money has to be transformed into productive equipment. For this to happen, it is not enough that finance capital be available; it *must* be in the hands of (or accessible to) those who both want to and will take the step of purchasing capital equipment. If this group does not exist, then we would expect a continuation of older patterns of wealth acquisition: through land purchases, trading, or money lending, for example. But as we have seen, a new group did begin to emerge. In addition, the growing importance of the industrial capitalist in England at the expense of the merchant capitalist was mirrored in various changes in the political sphere.

Britain in the 18th century was a relatively wealthy country mainly, but not entirely, due to the growth of trade since the 1660s, assisted by mercantilist policies. Not only had Britain replaced Holland as Europe's most important trader and shipper, but the acquisition of colonies also increased trade in general. Between 1700 and 1800, exports expanded fivefold. For example, acquisition of the sugar islands in the West Indies led to trade in sugar, slaves and food; the East India Company expanded control over India and monopolized trading there; and after 1713, Spanish colonies were opened to British traders. Associated with this trade was the increasing growth and sophistication of financial institutions, which to a limited extent also aided capital movement.

As noted earlier, wealth was not concentrated in the hands of the monarch or a few wealthy nobles. This was the case in France or Spain, for example, where the monarchy had a direct interest in trading companies or monopolies. In England, the monarchy gained when the initial charters of such companies were issued, but actual direct involvement after that was minimal. This meant that trading houses and merchants themselves kept whatever profits they made. Thus the size of the commercial classes was larger than elsewhere.

New Industrialists

However, neither wealthy merchants nor landed gentry were usually directly involved in the industrialization process, although they often provided the financing. What was more characteristic of the new industrialists was that they came from humbler origins (but rarely from the lower ranks of

wage earners). They were often former craftsmen—people who were much more likely to be aware of what was involved in the production process and thus likely to be familiar with the possibilities of technical changes.

But simply having good ideas or even being in control of production was not enough to introduce new technologies. Especially in the 19th century, when innovations and the expansion of the scale of industrial operations became increasingly capital intensive, financing requirements were large. Without a highly sophisticated financial structure—without, for example, a stock market to raise equity capital for new ventures or well-developed investment

---

Innovation

Use of a new technique or introduction of a new product

---

banking—new industrial ventures or expansion required the participation of wealthy individuals, and this was not automatic.

On the one hand, consider the problem of possible payoffs from risk taking. Any new venture, as we have already stressed, is inherently uncertain and thus risky. Those with wealth derived from land or trade, where there is a greater certainty of a fairly certain return, would be less willing to finance a new, relatively unknown venture. But on the other hand, the past had shown that taking risks often did pay off, occasionally very handsomely. Added to this was the fact that the textile industry in the 18th century was not new. Markets did exist and were often monopolized and therefore safe ones. Thus the *idea* of risk taking was more acceptable than in, for example, the 13th century.

Invention and Financing

While it was not easy for the "new" industrialists to acquire financing (it took James Watt, for example, four years after developing the idea of a

Invention

Creation of a new idea

separate condenser for his steam engine to find a partner able to give financial support) it was not impossible. Once the innovations had been put into place, continuing financing was possible from internally generated profits. As the process of industrialization continued, a further characteristic was also obvious—expansion created its own markets. What this means is that mechanization of, for example, consumer goods industries requires new industries to make the machines, which stimulates those industries making or providing inputs as well as expanding demand for what the consumer goods industries are making. Thus emerged the interrelationships that are so important to a modern capitalist economy.

Not only at this time but at any time of capitalist development, both supply and demand conditions must be adequate for continued profitable capital accumulation. Adam Smith, an early Classical economist, realized the importance of the extent of the market—it is no use expanding the ability to produce more if a larger output cannot be sold. However, problems of balance between the two frequently led to recessions. The familiar pattern of business cycles became more familiar once industrial capitalism became more firmly entrenched.

To summarize so far, we have seen that in the most general terms labor and capital availability facilitated industrial change, but it is difficult to state categorically that this availability was the immediate *cause* of the Industrial Revolution. In the same way, the necessary raw materials were either available in England itself, or, like raw cotton, easily available through trade. Before exploring some other explanations of the origin of the Industrial Revolution, it is useful to investigate some other preconditions or advantages.

Extent of the Market

Potential maximum size of the market

Conditions Favoring Change

These other advantages helped provide a general environment in which change could take place and become widespread. Again, they did not *cause* change itself, but their presence made it effective.

First, geography and the development of nationalism can be seen as an advantage. Britain's geographic separation from the mainland of Europe plus the previous centuries' development of national identity implied a certain distance from the political affairs of other European countries. This is not an *absolute* distance, as Britain did fight in the Napoleonic wars, when most of the European countries attempted to prevent France from acquiring domination over Europe. Britain developed a national market relatively early, was united by a common language, and defined by mercantilist-inspired legislation that identified the limits of the national economy as well as the aims of national policy.

Britain was also a Protestant country, and we have previously seen how the Protestant ethic supported the development of capitalist ideas. Again, this is not to say that Protestantism was the *cause* of the introduction of capitalist ideas, and thus of subsequent industrialization. Not all Protestant countries experienced an early industrial revolution, and not all Catholic ones remained unindustrialized. But it was certainly an advantage that this new type of economic activity met with spiritual sanction.

Much has been made of the fact that many of the early pioneers of the Industrial Revolution were not only Protestant but nonconformist— that is, not members of the established Anglican church. This has been explained by the fact that until later in the 19th century, many high level, already-prestigious occupations—in the military, government and trade—were closed to nonAnglicans. Therefore, so the argument goes, those Nonconformists with ambition were channelled into new (industrial) lines of activity. Again, it is important not to derive too rigid a cause-effect linkage between religion and occupation.

A third advantage was undoubtedly the favorable attitude of the government, and the encouragement given by its policies since the mid 17th century. These helped in defining and expanding the national market, in developing a colonial empire, and in encouraging the growth of trade and industry. As we previously saw, almost all governments at this time favored mercantilist policies, but the fact that Britain was first in successfully industrializing again emphasizes the importance of *many* factors contributing to the Industrial Revolution.

Fourth, changes in agricultural organization permitted industrialization and the accompanying urbanization to occur. On the one hand, an expanded agricultural output produced with a smaller work force permitted towns and an urban labor force to exist. And on the other, the elimination of many farmers' livelihood forced the growth of the labor force that could be used in industry. Again, the one does not necessarily lead to the other. Enclosures that took land away from landholding small farmers might only have led to a large class of wage-earning agricultural laborers. Only if industry is already expanding its demand for workers will dispossessed peasants become an urban industrial labor force. In fact, the enclosures, especially in the 18th century, were associated with significant rural underemployment, which caused considerable social unrest.

Peasants did not rush into the cities. This is explained by uncertainty about the future and also by fear of the loss of independence implied by the wage-labor contract. (Thus, in the textile industry as late as 1838, over three-quarters of the work force were women and children, to whom, presumably, fears of loss of independence did not apply, as they did not have the same legal and social status as men.)

Not until the mid 19th century was agriculture significantly mechanized. This means that in the 18th and early 19th centuries, the expansion of agricultural output and reduction of the work force was largely due to changes in organization and the introduction of new, but nonmechanized, techniques. Once mechanization of farming began, the reduction in labor needs continued. Oddly enough, in the later 19th century this coincided with the growth of food imports into Britain. British farming until this time had provided for most domestic food needs and wheat was exported, even though population, especially urban population, was growing. Thus, the increase in productivity was effective well before agriculture experienced an "industrial" revolution.

Productivity
Output produced per unit of input

The Start of the Industrial Revolution

Before discussing the process of industrialization, it is helpful to discuss the relationship between innovation, industrial expansion, and markets. Capitalist production in the wool textile industry was already occurring in England. Industrial expansion would not have occurred unless capitalist producers had some certainty that a larger market existed. That is, if sales expanded at past growth rates, output could grow by simply increasing the scale of existing operations. But expanding by using new methods with higher start-up costs would occur only if higher profits were anticipated.

We have already discounted the domestic market as providing this potential. The domestic consumer market grew slowly and was important only because it was fairly stable. For example, urbanization created a permanent urban market for food; the use of coal for heating homes increased as more houses were built; and the existence of more households increased demand for domestic goods such as cutlery, earthenware, and stoves (made out of iron). Urban growth and the construction of country houses for the wealthy also stimulated the building industry. But the domestic market's growth was certainly not significant enough to lead to the introduction of technologies able to dramatically increase productivity and expand output.

Export Demand

Where did the necessary increased demand come from? To a large extent, from increased exports and from government demand itself. Although exports fluctuated in the 18th century, they expanded extremely rapidly, especially when compared with domestic sales: in the 50 years 1700 and 1750, exports grew by 76 percent while domestic sales grew by only 7 percent, and in the 20 years between 1750 and 1770, they grew by 80 percent while domestic sales increased by only 7 percent.

Part of this increase was due to the exploitation of colonial markets; by 1775, colonial trade accounted for one third of total British trade. Part was a result of the expansion of the reexport market in Europe where British merchants and shippers held a commanding position. Part was simply because of the increasing availability of British industrial products. And part also occurred as a result of the destruction of competition from other countries—the example of India is instructive here. Indian trade was monopolized by the East India Company, which imported many Indian goods, chiefly cotton calicoes, into Britain. In 1700, British wool producers managed to get Indian textile imports banned. While this was intended to boost sales of wool, it had the ironic result of encouraging the production of cotton textiles within England itself. There was some existing cotton production of limited quantities, mainly producing substitutes for linen or for wool and silk hosiery.[2]

The expansion of demand for cotton exports encouraged innovation in this industry, particularly after 1750. Between 1750 and 1770, exports

of cotton increased tenfold, a faster rate of increase than for exports as a whole. A further boost to the cotton industry came in 1813, when the East India Company's monopoly of trade with India ended. This meant that English cottons could now be exported to India. As a result, the Indian textile industry collapsed, as hand production methods could not compete with the cheaper cottons produced using mechanized techniques. Many other products also achieved a dominant position in the export market, especially machinery and iron.

Government Demand

Government through its policies not only aided domestic economic interests but also added demand of its own. During the 18th century, Britain was involved in five wars (losing only one, the War of American Independence, 1775-1783). Wars increased the demand for guns, ammunition, uniforms, ships, and supplies. The increase in demand for guns directly stimulated the iron industry, but in any event, government contracts were large and involved long production runs. This made it worthwhile to introduce new technologies in order to fulfill them.

Britain's situation as an island nation had also been instrumental in the desire to develop sea power. This encouraged the development of shipbuilding and related industries, not only directly but also indirectly, as a strong Navy was important in protecting British mercantile shipping interests. Thus, the Navy's own tonnage increased more than threefold in less than a century, rising from 100,000 tons in 1685 to 325,000 in 1760.

In addition, trade in general increased due to the acquisition of colonies, the opening of other countries' colonies to British traders, the slave trade, and the growth of the carrying trade (by 1730, British shippers finally surpassed the Dutch in Europe's carrying trade). This led to an expansion of the merchant marine. At the end of the 18th century, British ships accounted for a tonnage of 1.8 million, twice that of American ships, while French tonnage amounted to only a quarter of a million tons.

In the 17th and 18th centuries, the slave trade, horrendous though it was, contributed to this stimulus as well as to profit making. In the 16th century, fewer than one million slaves were exported to the New World. But as more New World colonies were developed, and as the potential of using slave labor in the sugar, tobacco, and, increasingly, cotton, plantations was realized, numbers grew to about three million in the 17th century, and seven million in the 18th. The pattern of trade was complex, but generally speaking, victorious African chiefs sold defeated tribes to slave traders who then shipped them to the Americas.[3]

Transportation in the 18th Century

Overseas demand and government demand and policies were, as we have just seen, very important in providing the final catalyst that made the introduction of new technologies to industrial production both possible and profitable. However, one more element is worth considering: the role of transportation improvement in the 18th century before the era of the railroads.

Inland transportation in Britain at the beginning of the 18th century relied on navigable rivers or roads. Roads were bad and unpaved, becoming quagmires when it rained or rutted tracks when it was dry. However, the increase of traffic (mainly freight) in the 18th century led to demands for improvement. This improvement took two major forms, building better roads and constructing canals.

New Turnpike Roads

Although improvements were not particularly startling, the contrast with the previous situation was dramatic, and transportation costs fell sharply because of the shorter journey times. As an example of this reduction in travel time, it took ten days to travel from London to Edinburgh in 1750, but only two in 1830.

Turnpike Road
Toll road on which a user fee is charged

Road upkeep was a parish responsibility, a holdover from feudal tradition when the duty to work on road upkeep was one of the labor requirements imposed on serfs. By this time, road maintenance was poor. To improve this situation, an era of turnpike construction started, resulting in 22,000 miles of turnpikes by 1830 (about one sixth of the entire road system).

Turnpikes were repaired and maintained from tolls levied on users, and their construction had various implications. First, better roads stimulated the coachbuilding industry and led to the development of coaching inns where travelers stayed before the next stage of their journey while teams of horses were changed. Second, a new occupation, that of road engineer, was created. These road engineers incorporated several technical improvements into the turnpikes they constructed. For example, John Metcalfe built roads with curved surfaces to improve drainage (Metcalfe was also remarkable in that he was blind). Thomas Telford, who built bridges, canals and docks as well as roads, stressed the importance of strong foundations. John Macadam's contribution was to construct roads in graduated layers—large pieces at the bottom with a surface of smaller fragments such that when pressed, these fragments became more closely welded together, producing a smooth surface. (Much later, the final addition of a layer of asphalt produced what was called a tarmacadam road, now more familiarly known as tarmac.)

Canals

Canals, the cutting of artificial waterways, were very important to areas not well served by navigable rivers, especially in the Midlands. Producers of household goods, pottery, and small metal wares made there gained from the resulting reduction in shipping costs. Equally important, however, was the reduction in costs of transporting heavy, bulky items such as clay, coal, and ores, which could be as much as 80 percent in some cases. In fact, canals proved to be the cheapest means of transport, which more than offset their slowness. (Goods were loaded onto canal barges and then pulled along the canals by horses walking along banks.) England was behind the rest of Europe in building canals. Her canal era did not begin until 1759 and was relatively shortlived, as the coming of the railroads in the 1840s provided not only a cheap, but more important, a fast way of transporting goods.

The Industrial Revolution in Textiles

In the first phase of the Industrial Revolution, the cotton industry, not the wool industry, was in the forefront of industrial change. This may seem strange, as up to this time, wool was the major manufacturing industry. While new techniques were introduced in wool, two factors combined to slow down further change. First, by the beginning of the 18th century, merchant-capitalists controlled it, and as they had become prosperous using existing techniques, so they were less inclined to take risks on new ones. Second, the fact that cotton is stronger and its fibers longer than wool's made it much more adaptable to mechanized techniques.

Wool manufacture was widespread, although there were significant concentrations in East Anglia, the West Country, and the West Riding of Yorkshire. It was not a factory industry, although some of the work was specialized and done by full- time workers. Most was still done on a part-time basis in the putting out system. In all the textile industries, those areas previously or-

ganized on the domestic system would be most amenable to early factory organization.

Cotton in the beginning of the 18th century was an import-substitution industry. Pure cottons were imported from India, while domestic producers made a cheaper version called fustian. This was a mixture of linen (which was stronger and used as the warp threads) and cotton, and was chiefly used as a cheap substitute for linen, in hosiery or to fill the gap when Indian supplies were inadequate or not forthcoming. Cotton producers were small scale when compared with wool producers. While detailed statistics are hard to come by before the 19th century, some indication of the relative size of the two industries can be gained by comparing what figures are available. Thus, at the end of the 17th century, total wool consumption was about 40 million pounds a year, while imports of raw cotton (all raw cotton had to be imported) averaged about 1.1 million pounds a year.

Transformation in Cotton

What happened to transform cotton manufacturing from an also-ran to a dominating position in the British economy? It became so dominating that when cotton exports declined in the late 19th century, the entire economy began to slow down. Cotton manufacturing became transformed from a small-scale, domestic capitalist industry to a large-scale, factory-centered one; it was transformed both socially and technically. The technical changes increased worker productivity, but output as a whole also expanded as more of all inputs were used.

There were two major incentives for cotton industrialists to adopt new technologies and expand output, one permissive, the second more directly stimulating. The permissive incentive resulted when the import of cotton fabrics into Britain was banned in 1700, and it became possible to expand output without fear of foreign competition.

This alone was an insufficient stimulus. What was also needed was the direct stimulus of an expansion of demand. Demand from overseas did expand—chiefly due to increased exports to Africa and America, which replaced Continental Europe as Britain's largest cotton textile markets, taking half of all textile exports by 1774. Between 1699-1700 and 1772-1774, the export category of "other manufactured exports" (which included cotton but not wool, which was classified separately) grew 419 percent in value. This expansion was paralleled by an increase in imports of raw cotton. In 1700-1709, about 1.1 million pounds of raw cotton were imported; this amount grew to 15.5 million pounds by 1780-1789, and more than doubled again to 43 million pounds by the end of the 18th century. By 1875, half of all exports were cotton goods, and 20 percent of all imports were raw cotton.

By this time, the cotton industry became established in Lancashire due to several locational advantages. First, most of the raw cotton entered Britain through the port of Liverpool, which encouraged location nearby because of the subsequent saving on transportation costs. Second, the area has many swiftly flowing streams, which, once water power became widely used in the industry, was also a major advantage. (Steam power was not widely used until the 19th century, when the existing location advantages of the area gained from proximity to northern coal fields.)

Innovations in Manufacture

While most of the technological innovations in the cotton industry occurred when demand was expanding most rapidly, the first half of the 18th century was not technologically stagnant. One example came in weaving, then done by hand, which limited the width of the woven product to the width of the weaver's arms (most hand-loom weavers were men). This changed after 1733, when Kay developed a flying shuttle to carry the weft, or crosswise threads, across the warp, mak-

ing it possible to produce wider cloth on a single loom. However, by speeding up the weaving process, the ratio of spinners to weavers was upset. Previously, four spinners (usually women) were required to produce enough thread to keep one weaver occupied.

This imbalance led to pressure to introduce new techniques to overcome the spinning bottleneck, although initial efforts were not very successful. But attempts to restore the balance between spinning and weaving continued and encouraged the spread of the factory system. For example, James Hargreaves patented a spinning jenny in 1770. Originally, it spun six threads at once, a tremendous increase over previous methods, and was designed to be used in the domestic part of the cotton industry. Further improvements resulted in 80 separate threads being produced at once. Because the jenny expanded the scale of operations, spinning became relocated out of the home and into spinning mills. By 1778, about 20,000 jennies were in use.

A more important impetus to the development of the factory system came in 1769 with the development of Arkwright's water frame. It used rollers to stretch the threads, producing a stronger yarn, and encouraging the production of all-cotton fabrics. But it was big, and as its name implied, needed water power for energy; thus, spinning mills increasingly replaced cottage spinning, further centralizing the production of yarn.

Steam Power and Factories

Another development in spinning came in 1779, with Crompton's mule (so called because it was a hybrid of the spinning jenny and the water frame), to which water power was added in 1790. The advantage of mule spinning was that it produced a finer (but still strong) yarn, permitting the production of delicate fabrics, such as muslin. The addition of a self-actor in 1825 added an automatic motion to spinning. Steam power was introduced to spinning in the 1780s but was not widely used until after 1815. This cluster of developments resulted in spinning becoming a factory industry and also resulted in another imbalance between spinning and weaving. Because spinning had speeded up, the availability of cheap yarn favored hand loom weavers, who, for a brief period of time, reveled in being highly in demand.[4]

But this was for only a brief period of time. High wages encouraged the entry of new weavers into the industry, putting pressure on wage rates. In addition, European "problems" after the French Revolution (1789) leading to the Napoleonic Wars caused a slump in the fortunes of the cotton industry until after 1815. So the previous shortage of weavers quickly became a surplus, and wages fell dramatically, helping to account for the slow mechanization of weaving. Although a power loom was introduced in 1785, it was not widely used until the 19th century.

Mechanization of Weaving

After the end of the wars, however, weaving mechanized rapidly; 14,000 power looms were in operation by 1820 and 100,000 were being used by 1833. This resulted in massive unemployment of handloom weavers—a classic example of labor-saving machinery resulting in technological unemployment. But the availability of cheap labor permitted a further expansion of the industry.

Thus, the major inventions of the spinning jenny, water frame, mule and power loom, taking place in the existing setting of a capitalist-organized industry, revolutionized cotton and resulted in the first large factories. (By 1841, the cotton industry was the single largest employer of labor in Britain.) However, these changes had relatively few links to other industries, in particular the capital goods industries of coal, iron, and steel. There were some links; for example, the chemical industry saw its birth as a modern part of the economy through its ties to textile production and the desire to overcome bottlenecks that slowed growth of output. One example was the use of chlorine as a bleach. Previous methods of bleaching textiles involved the use of sunlight, which was obviously impractical once output exceeded the limits of cottage production. Another came with the development of sulphuric acid, used to produce the soda needed to manufacture alkalis and soaps for the textile industry. Some other developments with interesting links elsewhere include the introduction of the Jacquard loom in 1801, permitting designs woven into the fabric itself. Its basic mechanical principles were first used in clockmaking and were subsequently, after 200 years, to be further refined in the development of automated office equipment—including the modern computer. Another interesting link came in 1783, when a cylindrical press for printing designs on fabric was first used. Seven years later this was adapted to the printing industry.

Another link involved the internationalization of the industry and the production of raw cotton. The bottleneck here came with the removal of seeds from the raw cotton, a time-consuming task usually done by hand, using slave labor. A rolling mill was sometimes used, but it was effective only when used on long staple cotton. But in 1793, Whitney developed a cotton gin, which doubled the productivity of the rolling mills and could also be used on the short staple cotton grown in the southern United States This had further implications. It secured continuing supplies of raw cotton to Lancashire and also made slavery profitable in the United States cotton growing industry—leading to fortunes for Southern plantation owners and increasing their demand for slaves. (The timing of this increase in demand also coincided with the struggle in Britain over the ending of the slave trade; see note 3.) Cotton grown in the United States replaced that imported from India and the West Indies as the chief source of the British cotton industry. United States output grew from 1.5 million pounds in 1790 to 85 million pounds in 1910; in 1830, three quarters of cotton imports into Britain came from the United States.

Metalworking Industries

Probably nothing else has greater impact on the development of a modern capitalist economy than the iron and steel, machine tool and related industries. These are the industries that refine ores, produce steel and shape it into useful products. They characteristically produce investment goods, capital assets that are required for an industrial economy. Three major considerations are important when evaluating their impact on the Industrial Revolution.

Machine Tool
Equipment used to make machines

First, the new technologies were introduced through the construction of new machines, made first out of iron and later steel. Second, this cluster of industries had much greater linkages—backward, forward, and sideways—than the textile industry, adding a much more dynamic cumulative effect to industrial development after this time. Third, the original location of these industries on the coalfields explains why urbanization in Britain occurred when and where it did.

Expansion of Coal Output

The first changes occurred in the coal industry, leading to the application of steam power and the ability to make good quality steel in large quantities, which made mechanization effective. In the second phase of the Industrial Revolution (to be covered later), machine tool production expanded rapidly, and entire new industries were developed, including one, railways, that had an immense effect on the structure of the economy. This industry was a market for iron and steel and was also important in revolutionizing transportation, making it an input into almost all other industries.

What happened in coal? At the beginning of the 18th century, coal output from scattered surface mines was limited, totalling only 2.5 million tons in 1700. It was mainly used for heating houses. Domestic uses accounted for about two thirds of the industry's output, and coal was used mainly because wood was scarce. Industrial uses of coal were limited to metalworking, brewing, soap manufacture, firing ovens for brickmaking, and sugar refining At that time, coal mining was not very important.

However, demand for coal expanded, first as new household formation increased in the towns, and later in the 18th century as the iron industry expanded (more on this later). Expanding demand led to the exploitation of deeper, underground mines—and thus directly to the development of the steam engine. The linkage between coal and iron production was more complex, but definitely two-way.

Steampowered Pumps

The problem encountered in deep shaft mining was water. Once mine shafts were sunk to levels below the water table, flooding was an ever present danger, a danger that the tin and lead miners had been aware of for generations. Several attempts had been made to devise a mechanism to pump water from mines; one was a not very effective atmospheric engine designed by Savery. However, the idea of creating a vacuum in a cylinder by alternately heating and cooling it, thus forcing a piston inside the cylinder to move up and down was appealing because this motion could be used to pump water out of a mine.

Working on these lines, Newcomen improved on Savery's idea and in 1708 developed a self-acting atmospheric engine. This was a success, and about 140 of them were in use in coal mines by 1781. Its success demonstrated the viability of steam as a power source, although its disadvantages led to continuing attempts to improve it so that it could be used for more than simply pumping water out of a mine. The disadvantage was that it used too much fuel. The cylinder in which the piston moved was alternately heated, then

Table 10-1
Indicators of Industrial Growth: Britain

I Output of Coal* (million tons, selected years)										
1800	1820	1830	1840	1850	1860	1870	1880	1890	1900	1913
11	17	22	34	49	80	110	147	182	225	287

*During the century, technological innovations reduced the amount of energy required per unit of output, so the absolute growth in coal output understates the true amount of industrial expansion.

II Pig Iron Production (000 tons and as percentage of total world output; selected years)									
1740	1788	1804	1820	1840	1860	1880	1900	1910	1920
20	68	250	368	1,396	3,890	7,750	8,960	10,000	8,000
12.5%	24%	41%	36%	50%	53%	43%	23%	15%	13%

III Steel Production (000 tons; selected years)		
1850	1880	1913
49	147	7,500

IV Imports of Raw Cotton for Spinning (million pounds; selected years)			
1701	1781	1799	1802
1	5	43	60

cooled—and the cool cylinder had to be reheated again in order to keep the piston moving. This was no problem on the coal fields where fuel was available, but it obviously limited the application of steam power in, for example, textile mills or other places where access to a primary fuel source was less favorable.

The best known attempt at improvement was made by James Watt, who, as what we would now call a laboratory technician, was working at the University of Glasgow on a Newcomen engine. He developed the idea of using a separate condenser in 1765; the advantage was that a separate condenser was always cool, thus needing less fuel to operate. The efficiency of Watt's engine was four times that of Newcomen's.

But Watt was an inventor and did not have the expertise or financial ability to produce these engines commercially, so he was forced to find a partner. In 1769 Watt formed a partnership with

Figure 10.2 This early steam engine shows the mechanism producing the power in the front and the wheels and belt transmitting power to the machinery in the background. (Reproduced by permission of Syndics of Cambridge University Library)

Matthew Boulton, a manufacturer of hardware in Birmingham, and seven years later, their first engines were sold. These were stationary steam engines, first used to turn the wheels operating bellows in iron manufacturing as well as pump water from mines. More applications became possible after 1781 when Watt patented a rotary motion, so that industrial machines could be powered by attaching them to a moving belt turned by the steam engine.[5]

Impact of Steam Power

Various other patents followed, improving the engine in various ways, and 500 were in use by 1800. Most were used for pumping water, although steam power was quickly adopted for industrial uses, especially in the spinning mills. By 1850, the ratio of steam power to the equivalent energy provided by water was seven to one in the cotton industry and five to one elsewhere. There were also a few early examples of steam producing locomotive rather than stationary power. For example, in 1807 the first steam engine was used to power a boat on the Hudson River in the United States, and in 1814, Stephenson constructed a successful steam locomotive that ran on a fixed track, ushering in the railway age.

The impact of steam power was far reaching. It freed industry from dependence on water power, permitting more flexibility in location, and made the energy contained in coal usable for uses other than heating houses.[6] By making deep shaft mining possible, steam power made larger quantities of coal available and at a low cost. Coal production, which was about three million tons at the beginning of the 18th century, reached ten million tons by 1800, and 65 million tons by 1855.

Both cheaper coal and steam power revolutionized the iron and steel industries—again, with the results of cheapening the production of metals and opening up new uses for them. There is an interesting double link here with the production of steam engines. Previously, industrial machinery was made out of wood, but boilers must be made out of metal to withstand the tremendous pressure building up inside, thus both industries truly relied on each other.

The widespread use of steam power in the textile factories lowered the cost of production of fabrics and led to the start of the mass production of clothes. However, garment manufacturing did not become a factory industry; increased demand was met by "sweating" labor either through homework or in small workshops. As a result, long working hours, limited use of machinery, and low rates of pay were common to the sewing trades.

Later on, steam power revolutionized transport—the railways for land transport and steam-powered ships on water were the major transportation breakthroughs of the 19th century. The entire development of steam power and the transformation of industries where it was used led to an increased demand for people with highly developed technical skills, especially engineers. And as a requirement for the new phase into which the economy was moving—as well as a sign that it had reached a remarkable level of maturity—specialized machine tools and a machine tool industry (making the machines required for industrial production) appeared. So increasingly, production of these items moved out of the hands of the actual machine operator and was taken over by professional machine-making firms.

Iron

By now, it should be apparent that it is difficult to focus entirely and exclusively on developments in only one area. Steam power, the coal industry, the iron industry, and others are all connected. However, we will attempt to isolate the developments occurring within the iron industry for special attention. What happened here shows the combination of technical innovation and profit making that characterized the Industrial Revolution, leading the way to further developments. One of these was the birth of the steel industry, which dominated the second phase of the Industrial Revolution.

Iron had been used in the production of many hardware items for centuries, and steel was also produced, chiefly for armor, guns, and swords. But the quantity of each was limited because production technology was incapable of producing large quantities of good, uniform metal, and in a pre-industrial economy, potential uses of both iron and steel were limited. Not only was iron production limited, it was also geographically scattered. The technology of production required large amounts of energy, as the ore must first be separated from the surrounding rock (by smelting) and then again heated to soften the metal to cast or shape it into useful objects. Up until the 18th century, the necessary heat source came from charcoal made from wood. Because both iron ore and wood are bulky, they are costly to transport, so iron production took place in forests near scattered outcroppings of ores.

Coal at this time was not used to smelt iron, because it did not produce high enough temperatures for this purpose. In addition, much English coal had sulphur in it, making wrought iron (which was shaped into required forms by blacksmiths) too brittle to be worked. High quality iron was imported from Sweden to supplement the small amounts of domestically produced iron.

But during the 18th century, two sets of events occurred to revolutionize the iron industry and increase the ability to produce large quantities of high quality metal. The first, as already noted, was an increase in demand, chiefly a result of increased government demands for military goods, but also because of increased demand from the producers of domestic hardware (stoves, nails, etc.) whose products were needed because of the increase in housebuilding. The second was the increasing shortage of wood. Britain is a relatively small country, and wood use for shipbuilding, housebuilding, and fuel had risen in previous centuries. By this time, the forests were rapidly becoming depleted, especially of wood suitable for making charcoal.

Use of Coke

If coal was to replace wood as an energy source, two problems had to be solved: how to remove impurities from coal and how to make it a more efficient heat source. This was first successfully, if somewhat accidentally, achieved by Abraham Darby, an ironmaker, who reduced coal to coke in 1709. Coke is coal's equivalent of charcoal. It is produced by heating coal in a coke oven to burn off the coal gases. (At first, coal gas was treated as waste, but later it was used as an output in its own right, for both domestic and industrial uses.) The resulting substance burns with a much more stable and intense heat than coal itself, which makes it suitable for iron smelting.

Darby's method was not rapidly adopted, partly because not all coal makes good coke. However, further improvements followed, and by 1750, coke smelted iron was common. Also as this happened, iron production became centralized in the coal field areas, because of proximity to coal.[7]

The first stage of iron production produces pig iron. Next, either cast or wrought iron is made. Cast iron is produced when pig iron is made molten by heating and then poured into moulds to make cannons, stoves, and pots, for example. Wrought iron is made when pig iron is made soft

again, then beaten or hammered into the shapes required.

Removing Impurities

Improvements in these processes linked with developments elsewhere. For example, in the 1780s wrought iron was improved by puddling—stirring the molten metal—which not only burns off the impurities that make it brittle but also reduces the need for hammering (one method of removing impurities as well as shaping iron). In that decade, the steam-powered hammer was first used in iron production. One of the first to use a steam hammer was John Wilkinson, an iron manufacturer who helped make the Boulton-Watt steam engine a commercial success by providing accurately engineered parts for it. Wilkinson was an important government contractor who patented a drill for boring cannons that was easily adapted to producing cylinders for steam engines. Also at this time, the rolling mill was introduced. Here, iron is passed through rollers, which produces sheet iron (opening up new uses for iron, such as plates for ships or boilers) and presses out the carbon.

The net effect of all these improvements reduced the price of iron dramatically and expanded its uses in both old and new areas. Iron output, only 68,000 tons in 1788, rose to 250,000 tons by 1804, 1 million tons by 1835, and 3 million by 1855. Much of this increase was exported. When other countries began to industrialize in the 19th century, their demands for iron and iron products rose, and while their domestic production expanded, it was insufficient to meet all their needs. Even as late as 1865, half of the world's annual production of pig iron was produced in Britain. Among the important new uses of iron was the manufacture of steel, and in association with steam power, the railway. As these are properly associated with the second phase of the industrial revolution, they will be discussed later.

Progress in other Industries

While significant technological and social changes occurred in both textile and iron production, other industries expanded without such a revolution. For example, industries producing metal goods (including many things made out of iron), such as nails, guns, and brass items, were still characterized by a small production unit or even cottage labor. In these and other areas such as the sewing trades, productivity was slow to increase, and some of the worst abuses of exploitation and sweated labor were common as employers attempted to meet demand and raise profits while using old technology. The persistence of many small-scale enterprises meant that, even though workers were wage workers, their identity as a separate "working class" was not strong. This is one reason frequently given to explain the slow growth of trade unions in these industries.

Also, during the 18th century, the demand for earthenware and china increased as population grew, living standards of the middle and upper classes rose, and towns expanded. Pottery manufacture was concentrated in the Potteries (the five towns of Staffordshire), where local clay and the coal used to fire the ovens for baking the finished product were available. The typical pottery had about forty to fifty workers, and although some reorganization of production was possible such as a division of labor to increase productivity, the actual techniques remained largely unchanged and difficult to modernize.

Expansion in this industry and many others was largely dependent on changes elsewhere. Urbanization increased demand for pipes, building supplies, furniture, and china, while rising living standards increased demand for clothing, household textiles, china, and books. In addition, canal building also helped lower costs, and thus expand the potential market, and both the pottery producers and the Midlands hardware producers gained as a result.

Effects of Mechanization

When historians talk about the impact of mechanization and the factory system in the first phase of the Industrial Revolution, they are often talking about the cotton textile industry. Mechanization in wool was slower, although by 1850 the power loom was common here. Expansion of wool production outran available supplies of raw wool in Britain, and by 1850, half of the wool used was imported from Australia. Because older techniques in general persisted longer in other expanding industries, when factory production was introduced, some of the abuses associated with the first factories could be avoided. Hence the focus on the cotton textile industry.

The impact of the first Industrial Revolution can be evaluated from two angles: factory and working conditions themselves, and the stimulus given to urbanization. First, the factories produced a mixture of technological as well as social results; mixed, because few effects can be analyzed in a pure form.

Factories and Centralized Production

Technologically the factory centralized production and was the workplace of large numbers of people; for the first time, it separated home from work. This occurred partly because the new machines were large and needed water or steam power, so the factory in this sense incorporated internal economies of scale. The factory also concentrated workers in one place, aiding employer supervision. This contrasts with the domestic, putting out system, in which each producer controlled the work speed, so that so long as muscle power was the energy source used, the worker controlled the pace at which work was accomplished. This limited the merchant-capitalist's complete control of production and his profit making ability. Control could be exercised only clumsily by varying wage rates paid for completed work. But once workers were grouped in factories, two control mechanisms in addition to wage rates were available. First, now that steam powered the machines, they could run faster—i.e., the pace of the work was no longer set by the worker but by the machine (boss). Second, large numbers of workers were now subject to direct supervision. While this was not too important until later in the 19th century, the typical arrangement was for the "prime" worker to hire assistants and be responsible for their work, a type of sub-contracting. This led the way to the development of the manager as a separate, non-production worker.

A New Work Discipline

The discipline imposed by the factory caused immense problems for the first generation of factory workers, who resented their loss of control and economic independence. They had to be at work at a certain time, leave work at a particular time, work at a machine-set pace. While their previous independence may have been precarious, at least it was under *their* control. They resented becoming subject to the impersonal mechanisms of an all-too-often fluctuating marketplace, over which they had no influence.[8]

Employers always complained that their workers were lazy because they did not accept the new work conditions. In reality, it was not laziness but the difficulty of adjusting to a totally new way of life. (This complaint has been echoed ever since in all countries passing from a peasant economy to an industrial one. Statements made by 18th and 19th century British employers about their employees are remarkably similar to those made in today's newly industrializing economies.) Because workers did not take willingly or spontaneously to a new discipline, a system of low wages, fines for lateness, laws and rules and the structure of work was developed to force them to work. (There was even a wage deduction applied as a penalty for singing while working.)

Partly for this reason, the early cotton factories were largely staffed by women and children, who accounted for 75 percent of the work force in textiles in 1838. Employers believed them to be more efficient, most likely because they were more obedient, and thus a docile, more easily controllable labor force than men. In addition they were low wage workers. Children as young as six years old were employed, and the use of pauper labor—either orphans or children whose parents were destitute—was widespread, again because they were cheap to hire.

The factory depended on the work done by people dependent on their wage income. It was not the labor of the peasant or the craftsman. The link with the employer was impersonal, unlike that between master and servant or apprentice. Some employers practiced a kind of benevolent paternalism, but it was those who did not whose practices would eventually arouse concern that led to factory reform legislation.

Factory Working Conditions

Actual working conditions in the factories were bad and only slowly improved later in the 19th century. The factories themselves were built for maximum use of machines, not for the convenience of workers, so ventilation was bad. (This was a particular concern in the textile factories, where cotton dust in the air caused respiratory problems.) Machines were unguarded, and because wages were low, workers frequently kept them running while they were cleaning them to avoid losing too much income, which was dangerous. Small children were frequently used for this purpose—but at the cost of frequent accidents and dismemberment.

Working hours were typically longer than before. The use of artificial lighting in the factories, beginning in 1805, meant that sunrise to sunset no longer defined working hours. Also employers believed that profits were higher the longer people worked; even for children, work days of 14 hours were common and they were often longer during busy seasons.

There were some attempts to organize unions, to try to exert some control over working conditions and work life, but they met immediate resistance from employers, and Parliament declared all labor organizations illegal and banned them in 1799. A second concern of workers was the lack of social security. In feudal times, hard economic conditions were to some extent softened by the lord's obligations to serfs. In Tudor times, the idea of a person's right to work, to be supported if necessary by social institutions, was prevalent. In the putting out system, absence of paid work, while serious, was mitigated by the rural location, as most workers also had access to a small holding.

This was no longer true in the new towns, and wages could be stopped completely during depressions when employers laid off workers en masse. There were no fringe benefits such as retirement pensions, unemployment compensation, sickness benefits, or health insurance, so workers were periodically exposed to periods of crisis. (The Poor Law existed only to sustain paupers at a bare subsistence level.) That is, the older social traditions upholding the individual as part of an organic, social whole had been replaced by the ethic of individualism, in which the only link between classes was the market wage. If the wage was nonexistent because of market conditions outside the control of the workers—or even the employer—there was no public mechanism to provide support. The response came with the development of Friendly Societies, associations of workers that encouraged saving by members, often provided a modest form of sickness benefit, and most frequently, burial insurance. (Hard though life was, the importance of a decent burial, and therefore of making provision for one, loomed very large in most people's eyes.)

Friendly Society

A mutual aid society established by workers

Urbanization

The second major impact of the factory era was that it changed the total environment in which people lived; it is associated with urbanization. Two points are important here. First, while total population rose, the population living in industrial areas rose even faster. And second, the location of population shifted. For so long as agriculture and the wool industry were dominant, the southern half of the British Isles was relatively heavily populated. But with the development of the cotton textile industry (predominantly in Lancashire) and the coal and the metal working industries, the north gained a relatively larger share of population. In the pre-railway age, this was associated with the advantage of locating near coal fields.

So while in 1750, only London and Edinburgh (capital cities of England and Scotland respectively) had a population of over 50,000, in 1801 eight cities had, and by 1851, half of the entire population lived in an urban area, with over one-third living in a city of 50,000 or larger. Cities and towns, whether fast growing or stagnant, contained 13 percent of the population in 1750, and 25 percent in 1801. This proportion rose to 75 percent by 1901.

More specifically, total population grew by 130 percent between 1751 and 1831 to reach 24.1 million; London grew from 700,000 to 1.9 million—a growth of 170 percent; and the county of Lancashire expanded over five fold from 240,000 to 1,337,000 in 1831. Places such as Manchester, which were formerly sleepy villages, rapidly became large industrial towns. Town growth tied in with the increasing linkages existing between industries experiencing change, and in turn encouraged the location of secondary and service industries. For example, coal mining encouraged location of coal-using industries nearby, which encouraged the development of retailing and printing facilities to service an expanding consumer market.

But because city growth was so rapid, essentially unplanned, and geared toward maximum concentration of people in a given area, living conditions were abysmal. (No more would cities like Bath be deliberately planned to make an architectural and social statement.) Houses for the working masses were small, usually arranged in rows in a back-to-back system (backs of each row being separated by narrow alleyways). Indoor sanitary facilities were not provided, and neither was an indoor water supply. Water, of questionable purity, was available from outdoor pumps. A major problem was the close proximity to the factories. A constant pall of smoke from burning coal hung over the towns when the factories were working. Industrial waste was simply dumped, untreated, into the nearest river, which was also the receptacle for household sewage—and the source of the town's water supply.

Not surprisingly, several epidemics of cholera and typhoid, which are associated with poor sanitation, occurred and there was an increase of respiratory and intestinal diseases. And also not surprisingly, after falling slightly in the 18th century, the death rate rose (especially for babies and children). It did not start to decline again until after 1870, when the rate of population growth also started to decline. Improvements really did not start until after 1848, the year of a particularly lethal cholera epidemic. Then basic public services, such as water supply, drainage and sanitation, became more common, and the industrial towns also began to acquire other public facilities, such as churches, fountains, and parks.

Another effect of this urban growth was that it widened the distance between the classes. In the old village societies, nobility and serfs or landed gentry and farmers lived in the same areas, although there was social distance between them. But the upper classes rarely lived in the industrial towns, and the mark of having achieved middle class status was the ability to move out to the suburbs away from the polluted centers of towns. This movement accelerated later in the 19th century with the development of urban mass transit systems.

Summary

This chapter has covered the first phase of the Industrial Revolution in Great Britain, focusing mainly on the causes of the dramatic increase in productivity and output, principally in the cotton and iron industries. A second focus was on the links existing between different industries and on the impact that industrialization had on life in general.

It is often convenient to concentrate exclusively on the technological changes, which were dramatic. But technological innovation would not have caused such revolutionary changes unless the setting had been right. That is, the problems faced by the inventor are determined by the economic and social environment. While problems can be solved theoretically, what is important for innovation is that the solution does meet a particular need. This comes out most clearly if we make a comparison. Leonardo da Vinci (1452–1519) worked out the principles of the helicopter, but the helicopter did not become a reality until the 20th century, when the need for one as well as the requirements for making one were in existence. On the other hand, the inventors of the 18th and 19th centuries, wherever they lived, were practical people involved in everyday tasks and they were able to see the problem in an actual form, which thus led on to an actual solution. In addition, most successful inventions—those that will be used—are rarely the product of a pure thought process. Rather they are the end product of a whole series of related discoveries that often have their roots in past centuries.

But there is obviously a feedback here too. The general environment in 18th century Britain was a capitalist one, and thus developments that were thought to assist profit making ability would be the ones we see as successful—because they were introduced. But until successful inventions occurred, they would not get financial backing, because money channelled into trade provided higher, much surer returns. Thus, most of the first successful developments occurred as the result of small manufacturers' attempts to improve industrial production, a need that was stimulated by increased export and government demand. The success of these efforts—in particular, the application of steam power to many different areas—not only produced financial success for some inventors but also opened up entire new areas for investment.

Industrial Expansion

Much innovation at this time was labor-saving. That new technology did not cause massive technological unemployment is due to the general industrial expansion. Large supplies of cheap labor (which became cheaper as machines increasingly took over tasks that were once performed by hand) were utilized as output expanded and profit making ability grew. Had labor been scarce, it is unlikely that output would have expanded as fast and as far as it did.

In this first phase, export demand for cottons encouraged the development and growth of the cotton industry. This stimulated the application of power in the major parts of the industry, spinning and weaving, which became concentrated both geographically and also in the factory. Factory production, associated with industrial capitalism in its mature form, thus originated in the cotton industry, both for technological reasons (the size and productivity of equipment) and because it permitted closer control by employers over the work process.

The iron industry also experienced increased demand, and the technological responses made had a tremendous impact not only here but in other industries too. While cotton production was eventually mechanized using steam power, the combination of iron and steam power would lead to more "revolutions" in the 19th century, emphasizing the linkages and cumulative effects of a modern industrial economy.

Social Changes

Finally, the major social changes of this first phase were two-fold. First was the creation of a true industrial proletariat, a wage earning labor force. For these new factory workers, life was hard. They suffered from low wages (real income per capita fell in the early years of the 19th century, not to rise again until after 1870), poor working conditions and poor living conditions.

The second social change was urbanization. For the first time in modern history, towns became home for most of the population. But while these towns were urban, they were certainly not urbane, and observers of the times were horrified by the conditions in them. (Most of these observers were fortunate enough to have a choice not to live in them; no such choice was open to the working masses.) Eventually, these poor conditions did result in attempts to correct some of the worst examples—especially when serious epidemics or the shame of a rising death rate in a country supposedly the world's most prosperous and civilized forced action. (Ironically, massive bombing raids by the Nazi air force during the Second World War achieved what 19th century reformers were unable to achieve: instant slum clearance.)

Notes

1. An indirect measure of the importance of overseas trade is that, in 1700, the largest non-agricultural occupational group was seamen. There were 100,000 seamen at that time.

2. Both the cotton and silk industries were at a further disadvantage when compared with wool, as both depended on imported raw materials. Before 1790, most raw cotton came from the West Indies; after 1790, from the southern United States. In addition, in the pre-industrial period, both cotton and silk products were considered inferior to French silks and Indian cottons.

3. Although slavery is not part of the main theme of this chapter, British involvement in the slave trade ended in 1807. This was the result of considerable opposition to slavery in Britain, beginning in the middle of the 18th century. In 1772, slavery was made illegal in England itself, which was not a particularly significant accomplishment as there were few slaves in England. The battle against the slave trade took longer, because it was a battle against entrenched interests that profited from it. British shippers declared themselves opposed to slavery, but their unwillingness to end the trade in slaves was fuelled by fears that other countries' merchants would gain at their expense. This is precisely what happened. The slave trade was made illegal in England in 1807, and American slave traders took it over instead. The slave trade reached its peak in the 1830s, when about 135,000 Africans were transported yearly.

4. Popular tradition has it that handloom weavers at this time walked around with £5 notes stuck in their hatbands—the equivalent of a modern wealthy magnate lighting cigars with $100 bills.

5. The belt moved most effectively vertically rather than horizontally, which helps account for the style of industrial architecture of the late 18th-19th centuries. Mills and factories built at that time were tall, with many storeys, rather than low and horizontal like 20th century ones. The steam engine would be in the basement, and on the floors above, the machines would be started by attaching them to the belt that moved up from and down to the basement.

6. In areas where coal was not available, such as New England in the United States where the first textile factories in that country were located, water power remained the chief source of industrial energy.

7. Coke was introduced not only in Britain, but later in other countries too, although in areas where ample supplies of wood existed, coke smelting was slow to be adopted. For example, in 1846, 60 percent of French iron was still smelted with charcoal, and not until 1855 did iron produced with coke exceed the quantity produced with charcoal in the United States.

8. Impersonality is indicated by the common practice at that time of referring to workers as "hands." This saw them as adjuncts to machines rather than as whole human beings. It is an example of the increasing social distance between different classes in the society

Key Concepts

Canals
Capital availability
Capital intensity
Centralization of production
Coal
Cotton industry
Extent of the market
Factory system
Financing
Free labor
Friendly Society
Income distribution (functional)
Industrial linkage
Industrialization

Innovation
Invention
Investment
Iron
Machine tool
Mechanization
Metal working
Productivity
Steam power
Technical efficiency
Tolls
Turnpike road
Urbanization
Work discipline

Questions for Discussion or Essay Writing

1. Why did the Industrial Revolution occur when it did?

2. Discuss the preconditions needed for successful industrialization.

3. What explanations have been given to explain why Great Britain industrialized in the 18th century?

4. Does population growth help or hinder mechanization?

5. What were the most important sources of demand growth for British industry during the Industrial Revolution?

6. What is the connection between invention, innovation and financing?

7. How important is adequate transportation to a country's economic development?

8. Why was the cotton industry location of significant technological change in the 18th century?

9. Why was steam-powered mechanization so significant?

10. Industrial development after the late 18th century has been described as being increasingly cumulative and interdependent. Discuss.

11. What developments were necessary to utilize the energy in coal?

12. What was the impact of the centralization of production in factories on the lives of the first generation of factory workers?

13. What aspects of the Industrial Revolution had a social impact?

14. Why did industrialization and urbanization tend to be linked in the 18th and 19th centuries?

For Further Reading

Ashton, T.S. *The Industrial Revolution, 1760-1830*. N.Y.: Oxford University Press, (1948), rev. ed. 1964.

Beard, Charles A. *The Industrial Revolution*. N.Y.: Greenwood Press, (1927) 1969.

Crafts, N.F.R. *British Economic Growth During the Industrial Revolution*, London and New York: Oxford University Press, 1985.

_____ "British Economic Growth 1700-1831: A Review of the Evidence." *Economic History Review XXXVI:2*(May 1983): 177-199.

_____ "Industrial Revolution in England and France: Some Thoughts on the Question, 'Why Was England First?' " *Economic History Review*, XXIX:2 (1976): 429-441.

Deane, Phyllis. *The First Industrial Revolution*. Cambridge: Cambridge University Press (1965), 1979.

Dietz, Fred C. *The Industrial Revolution*. Westport, Conn: Greenwood Press (1927), 1973.

Floud, Roderick and Donald McCloskey, eds. *The Economic History of Britain Since 1700,* Cambridge: Cambridge University Press, 1981.

Hill, C.P. *British Economic and Social History, 1700-1975*, 4th ed. London: Edward Arnold (1957) 1977.

Hammond, J.L. and Barbara Hammond. *The Skilled Labourer 1760-1832*. N.Y: A.M. Kelley, 1967 (1919)

Hobsbawm, E.J. *Industry and Empire*. The Pelican Economic History of Britain, vol. 3, From 1750 to the Present Day. Harmondsworth: Penguin Books (1968) 1979.

Hughes, Jonathan. *Industrialization and Economic History: Theses and Conjectures*. N.Y. McGraw Hill, 1970.

Landes, David. *The Unbound Prometheus*. Cambridge: Cambridge University Press, 1969.

Mantoux, Paul. *The Industrial Revolution in the 18th Century*. N.Y.: Harcourt Brace Jovanovich, 1928.

Mathias, Peter. *The First Industrial Nation: An Economic History of Britain, 1700-1914*. London: Methuen, 1983.

Mokyr, Joel, ed. *The Industrial Revolution*, Totowa, N.J: Rowman & Allanheld, 1985.

Thompson, E.P. *The Making of the English Working Class*. N.Y.: Vintage Books, 1966.

Chapter 11

The Industrial Revolution in England: Second Phase

As we saw in the last chapter, the Industrial Revolution that started in England in the 18th century was based on innovations in the textile industry. The work process was mechanized, work organized in a factory system, and steam power used to power machines. However, there were still large areas of the economy untouched by anything so "revolutionary" as mechanization and steam power: a modern, leading-edge sector coexisted with other traditional industries. Even in the textile industry, some old hand methods persisted.

But after 1830, the Industrial Revolution moved into a second phase marked by continuing innovation in the capital goods industries, and Great Britain emerged as a fully industrialized, mature capitalist economy, in which all but a very few areas were modernized. One extremely important aspect of this phase was the development of the railway. The railway revolutionized transport by providing a fast and cheap method of moving both people and freight, and it contributed to the development of the not-yet-industrializing countries. It was more than simply a method of transport. As both input into and output of other industries, the railway network was the concrete evidence of a more advanced stage of industrialization, and it encouraged the emergence of new industries in its turn. After the coming of the railway, everyone, whether farm worker or factory hand, town or country dweller, was affected by industrialization in one way or another. By demonstrating technical progress in action, it helped underline the unbounding faith in progress characteristic of the Victorian era.

Golden Age of Competitive Capitalism

The mid 19th century from about 1830 to 1870 has always been considered the golden age of industrial competitive capitalism. It was truly a period of British leadership, based on her industrial supremacy, with most of the rest of the world drawn into orbit around her. But it was only a transitory leadership and its passing was in many ways a natural outgrowth of events occurring during this period.

Industrial production continued to expand rapidly chiefly in the heavy industries, but technical changes and changes in business organization also transformed other "old" industries, and marked the appearance of new ones. As always, overseas demand contributed to the stimulus given to industrial production. A new era of trade and commercial policy finally saw an end to mercantilism, and free trade ideas and practices dominated Britain for a long time. Finally, in this period, some of the advantages made possible by industrialization began to filter down to the increased numbers of working people, resulting in a rising standard of living for them.

Change, whether measured by industrial output, extent of trade, growth of towns or other social and economic indicators, marked this period and became accepted as an inevitable part of modern life. The industrial capitalist framework of the society was also by this time accepted as permanent, especially by the working classes who at first lost more than they gained in the transformation of society. Although change was accepted, it was by no means a steady evolutionary process. As always, contradictions were apparent, and they remained, more or less unresolved, to influence development in the 20th century.

Contradiction in Values

Three major contradictions marked this period. They are related, and have noneconomic as well as economic aspects. The first contradiction involves ideas and policy based on prevailing values. During the 17th and 18th centuries, mercantilist ideas influenced relations between the state and the economy. However, at the end of the 18th century laissez faire and free trade ideas gained increasing support, mainly from industrialists and merchants who believed the unfettered working of a free market would best serve their interests and lead to continued economic expansion. But as industry expanded and towns grew, it became clear that there were certain important things an unregulated market could not do. Predominant among these were its inability to deal with the wastes produced by urban and industrial growth, and its failure to provide either protection or an adequate standard of living for the weaker members of society.

Thus, while on the one hand trade and industry became progressively freer, on the other hand the state began to involve itself more with such interventionist measures as legislation regulating work (the factory laws), municipal government, and urban conditions. How can we explain this contradiction? For so long as economic benefits were clear to policy makers, laissez faire predominated, but when intervention was thought to be a more appropriate response to market failure, then intervention was called for. (However, it was heavily opposed, slow and partial.)

Export of Industrialization

The second contradiction occurred as a result of Britain's increased economic strength. It was largely based on the export of capital equipment, technology, skills, and money, which, given the adherence to free trade policies inevitably led to the industrial development of economies that would compete with Britain, thus reducing British exports and slowing down growth. In addition, because these potential competitors —especially Germany and the United States— were larger in terms of land area, resources, and population, they would surpass Britain in industrial production by the end of the century. So while industrial supremacy in the middle of the century resulted from the fact that Britain was the only advanced industrial country, this situation could not last. In the short run, high exports stimulated the British economy, but the long run effect led to a relative decline of Britain's position.

Improving Conditions

Finally, and somewhat ironically, improvement in the social and economic position of the mass of the population was greater after the 1870s, when the rate of economic growth was slower. Up to midcentury conditions improved only slowly, although it is difficult to generalize as different groups and different regions had divergent experiences. But after 1870, during the period called the Great Depression (which is, on the whole, a misnomer, as economic growth did continue in this period, although at a slower rate) indications are that improvement was faster and more generalized. Part of the explanation is due to the changes taking place internationally. A slower rate of growth of exports of both goods and money encouraged greater attention to the possibilities of exploiting the domestic market. This domestic market had not been too important before, because mass purchasing power was low. When real wages rose after 1850, and as municipal government changes led to an expansion of public services, the home market became much more appealing to domestic producers facing increased competition overseas.

With these contradictions forming a general theme, this chapter will first explore the changes in industry, then examine the change in values and its impact on social policy-making, and conclude with a summary of the Great Depression years. We will return to some of these themes in a later chapter, as another important feature of 19th century development is its increasing internationalization.

Golden Age Capitalism

More than anything else, the mid 19th century was the railway age: The railway symbolized everything the Victorian capitalists wanted to be remembered for. The railways could not have been built a hundred years earlier, as they required the existence of an already highly developed economy, permitting the mobilization of huge numbers of skilled and unskilled workers for construction; and the tapping of large amounts of finance capital using a relatively new form of business organization to spread the risks (because rail building required a large capital investment, with an extended pay-back period). Construction also reflected confidence that the monetary rewards would go to the promoters, not the monarchy. In addition, the technical revolution shown by steam-powered locomotion rested on the accumulation of previous knowledge, as well as the existence of freedom for experimentation and the availability of scientifically trained people. Indus-

tries capable of producing the capital goods needed—iron and later steel, engineering, and machine tools—existed, and more important, were capable of responding to the huge demands made by the rail companies. The large scale of railway building, however, implied a new trend at odds with the ideals of competitive capitalism that were being so carefully refined by the 19th century school of Classical economists. There was a dark cloud not apparent to the early railway builders although it characterized economic activity after this time. By requiring large amounts of investment activity at specific times, railways contributed to economic instability: Once the railway was built, demand for new investment fell dramatically and would not rise again until replacement needs appeared.

Railways

Strangely enough, the railways were not built in response to an overwhelming need from industry for improved transportation. In Britain, thanks to the country's small size and earlier improvements in water transportation, easy transportation was both accessible and cheap. Only in a few areas like the coalfields did it make sense to build a fixed track in order to transport coal to the canals or to the coast.

The idea of a fixed track was not new. The very earliest used wooden rails (iron rails were not made until 1767) and horses pulled coal wagons along them. By 1730, such tracks were fairly common in the coal fields. While there were attempts to improve them, they were not yet seen as something that could be either profitable or an entire new area for industrial development. One problem was that the railway was initially seen as just another (although different) type of road, so at this stage, the rails had flanges on them, and carts could travel either on the rails or on the existing roads. This changed later, and by 1790, flanges were on the carts' wheels, not on the rails,

Figure 11.1 This shows an early railroad engine, the Northumbrian, about 1830.
(Reproduced by permission of the Syndics of Cambridge University Library)

so that traffic moving on rails was specific only to the railways.[1]

Another problem was locomotion. Steam power was successfully used in stationary steam engines, and one of the first attempts to use steam for moving power was made in France in 1769, where steam was used to power a vehicle travelling on an ordinary road. This first moving steam engine was very cumbersome and was not developed further. Most of the earliest steam-driven engines were found in mining areas, although a line was built in London in 1801 to move freight. Even as late as 1815, such lines were barely significant either in mileage or in freight carried.

The missing ingredient was an efficient steam locomotive, and not until 1814 was the first really successful one built by George Stephenson. It was based on work done by earlier experimenters and required the availability of precision tools and stronger boiler plates—both necessary for an accurate, and safe, steam engine. Stephenson was an engineer for the Darlington collieries, and the first major private steam line was opened in 1825 under his supervision, although many doubted its ability to survive. In particular, given the high initial costs, its profitability was uncertain, but there were other considerations that eventually converted the doubters.

When the first large-scale public line (between Manchester and Liverpool) was opened in 1830, the railway age truly began. Profitable from the start, the line carried large numbers of passengers as well as freight, and showed the possibility of breaking the canal monopoly, which appealed to railway promoters as a way of making money. The existence of canals proved that there was sufficient freight traffic, but the success of rail lines in attracting passengers, which canals had never done, seemed like icing on the cake. So rail companies promoting new lines met opposition from the canal companies, which they overcame often by simply buying the canal company, and then letting the canal fall into disrepair as a way of guaranteeing traffic.

Capital Mobilization

Simply demonstrating the success of rails was not sufficient to initiate rail construction. Construction demanded huge amounts of capital to acquire land, pay wages to the construction workers, buy rails and equipment, build stations, install signals, and so on, but no revenues would appear until the line was in operation. Such finance capital requirements were out of reach of the resources of even the most highly profitable companies, so it was necessary to widen (and deepen) the finance pool. This was done by using the joint stock form of business organization, pooling the funds of many wealthy investors to finance construction. (That is, many individual investors provided finance capital by buying shares in a corporation and proceeds from the sale

Capital Mobilization

Ability to raise financing for productive investment purposes

Joint Stock Company

A company jointly owned by many shareholders; its shares are transferable

of shares were then used to buy real capital assets.) Such funds were available because the economy was highly developed by this time. Previous decades of capital accumulation had resulted in a large pool of available funds, but by the 1830s, the opportunity for profitable industrial investment seemed to be poor. So by offering the possibility of a return on invested funds higher than that available on government securities, railway promoters successfully attracted the funds they needed. A total of £150 million was invested in 1846–50 alone. (This marks the first time that a significant number of rentiers existed. Rentiers are people who provide funds for investment purposes and receive interest or dividends from them, but who are not directly involved in the organization or the management of the enterprise.)

Rentier

A person who receives income from dividends and interest

However, expansion of stock market activity brought speculation with it. In Britain, there were two major railway mania periods, 1835–1837, and another construction boom in the 1860s (when steel rails replaced iron ones), when there was considerable speculation in railway shares accompanying construction. Each rail line was privately organized, and there was no overall attempt to produce a coherent national network. This led to a great deal of irrationality with duplicating and overlapping lines, and many simply went bankrupt. But the system got built: By 1845, 2,500 miles were in existence, and during the 1840s, 6,000 miles opened, which was almost matched by the 5,000 miles built during the 1860s. By 1870, total mileage was 15,537 miles, and the network was essentially complete. Initially, railway mileage was greater in Britain than elsewhere, but, because other countries were larger, this would not hold for long. Britain had twice the mileage of Germany and four times the mileage of France in 1850, but Germany's mileage was greater in the early 1870s, and France's greater in the 1880s. Outside Europe, the United States quickly surpassed every other country in mileage: 31,000 miles by 1860, which was half the world's total. (However, traffic density on the lines in Britain was always greater than elsewhere.)

Railway building in Britain followed a unique pattern. Before any line could be built, the sponsoring company had to petition for a private act of Parliament to give it the powers to acquire land for the right of way and to construct the line. Petitions were rarely rejected, in spite of considerable opposition from landowners, which often necessitated detours around rather than through a particular area. Opposition was often based on fear of what the steam engine might do to farms. For example, it was alleged that the milk yield of cows would fall, or they would abort their calves after being frightened by this fiery devil. Some towns were avoided entirely because of opposition to the railways. For example, the Cambridge colleges successfully blocked a line into the town itself, so the station was built at what was then the outskirts of the town. In spite of their fears, both landowners and farmers gained from the rail network. They were well compensated for the land acquired by the rail companies, and because of the effect of easier, faster transportation in widening demand for agricultural goods, especially perishable ones, the value of land in general rose.

Canal, coaching, and turnpike companies also objected to rail building and their fear of competition was justified. Few canals remained profitable, although they still had advantages for transporting bulky commodities when speed was not important. The roads especially suffered. Because of the diversion of passenger traffic to the railways, the turnpikes and coaching inns lost their market, and their profits. Not until the 20th century with the coming of the gasoline-powered internal-combustion engine would the railways meet any threat of competition from the roads.

Rail companies were remarkably free of any Parliamentary regulation. One example was the Railway Act of 1844, which required the companies to run one train in each direction once a day, and charge a fare no higher than one penny a mile. (These trains became known as Parliamentary trains.)

Impact of Rail Lines

Railways had both immediate and long term results. The decade of the 1840s was one of serious unemployment and social unrest, and the labor needs of rail construction mitigated the severity of the situation. During the peak construction years 1846–1848, rails accounted for a direct employment of 200,000, and many thousands more in the mining, metallurgy, machine tool, and vehicle building industries, where increased output levels were directly and indirectly due to the railways' demands. Railways provided an outlet for large amounts of accumulated capital, and showed the advantages of the joint stock principle as never before—even before the addition of limited liability for investors in 1855. While money was occasionally lost as a result of

Table 11-1
Changing Shares of the World Trade, 1840, 1900
(as a percentage of total trade)

Year	United Kingdom	United States	France	Germany
1840	32	8	10	—
1900	21	11	8	12

overbuilding or a collapse in the value of shares, railway shares were seen as safer than an alternative use, loans to governments abroad. However, over time, returns on funds invested in railway shares fell to a level only slightly higher than that available on British government debt. When the railways lost their novelty as an outlet for these funds, their place was taken by the shipbuilding and shipping industries.

Limited Liability

A shareholder's risk of loss from a company failure is limited to the initial finance capital provided

---

Longer-term effects were many and varied. The reduction in internal transportation costs stimulated an expansion of both the domestic market for agricultural and industrial goods, and the overseas market. This indirectly helped exporters, especially those selling bulky goods. The export of the railways themselves in the form of finance, engineering skills, rails, and locomotives, was an important factor explaining the increase in exports from Britain before the 1880s. British companies built railways all over the world in Europe, Latin America, the United States, and India. After the 1880s, this source of export growth dropped sharply as most other countries had by this time industrialized sufficiently to tap their own domestic industries to meet needs for future rail building. These networks were important in opening up previously underdeveloped areas such as the midwestern and western United States, the pampas in South America, and the steppes of Russia.

After 1860, building new lines or connections stimulated considerable ingenuity in solving often complex engineering problems, such as construction of lines in mountains, across rivers or under estuaries. Improvements in rolling stock, brakes, and signals as well as amenities for passengers such as heat, restaurant cars, and sleeping cars, also helped reduce the discomfort associated with

early travel by train. At first, companies were unwilling to provide for poorer passengers except when forced to do so, as with the Parliamentary trains, for example. But one railway company (the Midland) took the bold step in 1872 of adding lower fare, third class coaches to all its trains. This was immediately profitable and was soon copied by all the other companies.

Political Unification

Politically, the rail network completed the unification of the country by providing access to previously remote areas. Communications in general were improved. For example, in 1840 the postal system was revamped and rationalized, so that the sender instead of the receiver paid the fees, with the same low rate (the Penny Post) applying wherever a letter was sent. Mail was carried on the trains, which resulted in a national, cheap, and efficient postal system. Socially, the railways broadened the horizons of people, and made them familiar with power-driven machinery as an everyday phenomenon.

There were other effects, too. New railway towns grew as centers of building locomotives or carriages, or where the major marshalling yards were located. Also, resort towns such as Brighton were born, linking in turn with the development of the idea of the holiday, which became a new social habit for almost all sectors of the population. While the middle classes were responsible for the demand for hotels in coastal resorts in which to stay on long holidays—made accessible, of course, by the railways—the lower classes also shared, although to a lesser extent. The introduction of very low fares made a day trip from the major industrial centers to the sea a reality. (One of the earliest organizers of such day trips for factory workers was Thomas Cook, a 19th century parson.) And, although hardly of such major industrial importance, the railways gave a new lease on life to the English public schools, which were boarding schools for the sons of the wealthy.

As the school year was divided into three terms, the logistics of transporting boys and luggage between home and school six times a year were greatly simplified because of the railways.

Other Industries

British industrial supremacy in the middle years of the 19th century rested firmly on a base in the heavy industries, coal, iron and steel, and engineering, and all these were boosted significantly by the rail network. The first phase of the Industrial Revolution was associated with the use of steam power in stationary engines. In the second phase, steam power, as the source of power for the railways, became moveable. In both cases, the basic fuel used was coal, often in the form of coke (as in the smelting of iron ore needed to produce the iron for mechanization).

Because of the pivotal role of coal in this phase of industrialization. the dramatic increase of coal production provides an indirect measure of industrial expansion in the 19th century. From only 11 million tons in 1800, coal output expanded by 1947 percent to reach 225.2 million tons in 1900 and by over 2500 percent to 287.4 million tons in 1913 (see Table 10.1). What is even more remarkable about this increase is that technological advances in the coal using industries *reduced* coal needs per unit of output, so indirectly, it is possible to get an idea of the extraordinary rise of output in these other industries. Although coal was a basic input of the Industrial Revolution, coal mining remained unmechanized until the 20th century, with the exception of the use of the steam engine. So this increase in coal output was accomplished with a large expansion of employment: 200,000 miners were employed in 1850, half a million in 1880, and 1.2 million in 1914, in about 3,000 mines[2].

New Technologies in Iron and Steel

The transformation of the iron and steel industries in the second phase of the Industrial Revolution was necessary to the complete industrialization of the economy. It permitted entirely new developments, especially after the 1890s, because the dramatic reduction in the price of iron and the ability to make large quantities of high quality steel due to new innovative techniques was necessary for widespread mechanization and the use of steam power. Unlike innovations in the textile industry, which were largely but not entirely the work of practical craftspeople, innovations in iron and steel technology involved the conscious application of science to industrial uses. This became more common late in the century as new industries deliberately based on scientific knowledge emerged. The effect of these innovations increased the size of the plant needed for the most efficient, lowest-cost production. Thus, even at a time when the ideology of small-scale, competitive capitalism reached its high point, practical developments in the real world were undermining its validity.

Output in Britain in the iron and steel industries grew as the combined result of two factors, technological advance and a growth in the extent of the market. Market growth occurred both domestically and internationally, and domestically, the demand from the railways was especially important. But international markets for capital goods from Britain expanded even faster, as foreign countries beginning to construct railways and industrialize acquired the necessary imports from the only country then capable of producing them in large enough quantities. In 1840, capital goods exports accounted for 11 percent of the total value of manufactured goods exported, but by 1857–1859, had risen to 22 percent of a larger total, to 27 percent by 1882–1884, and to 39 percent by 1913. This growth in the importance of capital goods' exports came at the expense of Britain's traditional textile exports, which, although rising in absolute terms, had declined to a share of 51 percent of manufactured exports in 1913.

Obviously this expansion in demand could not have been met unless the supply was available. Pig iron output—the basis for cast and wrought iron as well as steel—rose from a mere 190,000 tons in 1800 to 677,000 tons in 1830, 1.4 million tons in 1840, 2.2 million tons in 1850, 3.9 million tons in 1860, 5.9 million tons in 1870, 7.9 million tons in 1890, and peaked at 10 million tons in 1910. For the five decades after the 1820s, Britain accounted for half the world's total production of pig iron, and only in 1890 did output from the United States (then at 9.2 million tons) exceed that from Britain. In 1910, German output also exceeded British output. (Both Germany and the United States are endowed with far larger iron ore deposits than Britain.)

Production of iron was revolutionized in 1828 with the introduction of the hot blast. This innovation expanded the capacity of the blast furnaces in which iron was produced, and throughout most of the century capacity tended to exceed demand. This process also used only half the amount of coal previously required for iron production, and the price of iron fell dramatically. In addition, the introduction of the steam-powered hammer in 1840 made it possible to produce iron in the large bars needed to make railway tracks and steamships.

Easy availability of ample supplies of cheap iron was also a necessity for improvements in steel production. Steel had previously been produced in small batches of uneven quality for specialty uses at high prices. One of the perennial problems in producing high quality steel was the presence of impurities, and in one way or another, the three major technological innovations of 19th century steel production addressed and overcame this problem.

Improving Steel's Quality

The first was the introduction of the Bessemer converter in 1856. The process itself permitted pig iron to be converted directly into steel by injecting hot air into the liquid iron, eliminating the puddling process that had been used to remove impurities. This resulted in large quantities of steel being made at about one seventh the previous price.

Unfortunately, quality was still uneven. This problem was overcome in 1865 with the use of the Siemens-Martin open hearth process, which replaced the closed converter of the Bessemer process with a large shallow pan. The final step was the introduction of the Thomas-Gilchrist process in 1878, which for the first time used phospohoric ore to produce steel. The inside of either a Bessemer converter or an open hearth pan was lined with a basic substance that absorbed the phosphorous, permitting the exploitation of phosphoric iron ore deposits not only in Britain but, more important, in Germany and the United States, where large deposits of such ore are located. (When the lining was completely phosphoric, it was removed, broken up, and used as fertilizer.)

As a result of these developments, output of steel showed a dramatic rise: It increased sixfold between the 1850s and the 1870s, reaching 1.3 million tons in 1880. However, although all these innovations were mainly British in origin, British producers were slower to adopt them than either Germany or the United States By 1890, the United States produced more steel than any other country.

Steel Using Industries

This ability to produce steel in quantity had several effects. Although innovation expanded productivity, employment levels were maintained as growth of output rose even faster. Steel is more durable than iron and replaced iron in the railroads. Steel availability permitted the further development of the engineering and machine tool industries that are necessary for mass production and transformed shipbuilding. These are industries requiring highly skilled labor. The numbers employed in these three areas doubled between 1851 and 1881, and in 1914 accounted for the largest category of employment of male workers. Transportation was also a new growth industry in the 19th century, accounting for 800,000 people in 1881, although these jobs were considered less skilled than those in engineering, machine tools, and shipbuilding.

If steel is to be used to build machines, locomotives, engines, ships, and so on, it must be cut and shaped. This is what machine tools are used for, and the development of the machine tool industry into a sophisticated one is a mark of the maturity of an industrial economy. Early in the 19th century, general machine tools such as planers, grinders, borers, and lathes had been developed in Britain, and were essential for later industrialization. By the 1820s, specialist machine tool producers existed. But the next stage, mass production based on interchangeable parts and precision manufacturing, required that general machine tools be used to produce the specialized ones needed to build accurate parts. United States' firms became important in this area later in the century.

Shipbuilding

Shipbuilding deserves special mention, because the application of steam power to steel ships resulted in a transformation of water transportation as significant as the railways on land. Shipbuilding is not subject to the same limitations as the railroads, which once built will produce only replacement demands. Britain had been a great shipbuilder since the 18th century, but for so long as ships were powered by wind and built of wood, the United States with her enormous forest resources had an advantage. In the first half of the

19th century, American shipbuilding had expanded more rapidly than the British, and in 1860, American tonnage stood at 5.4 million tons compared with Britain's 5.7 million tons.

After then, the development of the steamship saw both shipbuilding and the size of the merchant marine in the United States decline. The percentage of American trade carried in American ships fell from 60 percent in 1860 to 10 percent in 1914. Meanwhile, Britain became the leading shipbuilder and shipper, for two reasons. First, the ability to exploit the new technology was greater in the more industrialized economy. Second, shipping in general was more important to Britain, providing the vital element of demand. As an island trading nation and because of the expansion of trade, plus the fact that Britain was an important shipper for traders in other countries, the size of the merchant marine grew.

Shipping tonnage expanded sevenfold between 1850 and 1900, and tonnage of steamships (which had been minor in 1850) rose from 1.7 million tons in 1873 to 11.3 million tons in 1913. The extent of this rise was dramatic, and more than compensated for the fall in sailing vessels, from 4.1 million tons to 0.8 million tons, over the same period of time. By the end of the century, British tonnage accounted for half the world's total. Various improvements in the application of steam power to shipping, such as the steam turbine, also made steamships fast and efficient, even if dirtier and less graceful than sailing clippers.

One result was a development paralleling a similar one on the railways, the ability to schedule voyages. Now, along with the tramp steamer and the ship that visited the same ports on an irregular basis, the regularly scheduled voyage could be made, which was not possible for as long as sailing ships were dependent on the vagaries of weather, wind, and tides. Regular coastal services were begun in 1816, and in the 1830s transatlantic crossings were regularly scheduled. Not only freight was affected. By the 1870s the passenger liner was a regular feature, both for those at the top end of the income scale and for the millions of emigrants to the United States who crossed the Atlantic in steerage. (Between 1800 and 1840, one million Europeans emigrated to the United States, but between 1840 and 1870 the number shot up to seven million and was even higher by the end of the century.)

Shipbuilding is also important for another reason. Although Britain lost her position as the only industrialized nation by the end of the 19th century, a relative decline shown in comparisons of output totals of both old and new industries, she retained the lead in shipbuilding. This industry was peculiar in that, although it is a product of the Industrial Revolution, and although several important innovations occurred, the new productive techniques and methods of organization characteristic of other modern industries were not used. Shipbuilding was not characterized by a high degree of mechanization and routinized factory production of standardized products. It was an industry where the final product, although built out of "modern" materials using the most modern engineering principles, was essentially a unique product, built one at a time using a variety of highly skilled workers. When shipbuilding became more routinized in the mid-20th century, British shipbuilders increasingly lost ground to those in other countries, especially Japan.

Trade

The 19th century was dominated by Britain. The tiny collection of islands making up the British Isles at midcentury produced about two thirds of the world's coal, half its iron and cotton cloth, five sevenths of its steel, and four tenths of its hardware. At that time, the productive capacity of the economy far outran domestic demands. Dependence on export markets had always been important for manufacturers, and reliance on imports for certain industrial raw materials such as cotton, as well as an increasing volume of foodstuffs, also gave an international bias. To get some idea of the relatively greater importance of trade, in 1870 British merchandise trade amounted to £18 per capita, compared with £6 for France, £5 for Germany, and slightly over £4 for the United States. The only comparable country was Belgium, another industrializing but resource-poor small country.

So trade increased in parallel with the expansion of industry. Until 1873, the growth rate exceeded the growth of national income as a whole. Consequently exports of domestic products, which had accounted for 13 percent of the value of national income at the end of the 18th century, accounted for 22 percent in the early 1870s. And accompanying this growth, a larger share of world trade in general was carried in British ships.

Changing Pattern of Trade

The pattern of trade at the end of the century was very different from that at the start, due to changes occurring within the British economy as it became more completely industrialized. Although reliance on raw material imports remained large, the types of imports and sources changed. At the beginning of the century, cotton was the single largest raw material import, and as cotton manufacturing expanded, so too did these imports: from 31 million pounds in 1790 to 56 million pounds in 1800 and to 280 million pounds in 1830, when three quarters came from the United States. But after the 1850s, and especially after 1870, imports of food such as grain from the United States, wheat and beef from Argentina, and dairy products from New Zealand became more important. By 1914, half of Britain's food was imported, a dramatic change from only a century before. That some foods could be imported, such as meat and dairy products, reflects industrial innovation, in this case, the development of refrigeration as well as faster steamships. New goods entering trade by the end of the century included wool from Australia, nitrate (for fertilizer) and copper from Chile, and guano from Peru. By 1914, seven eighths of all raw materials used were imported, including cotton, wool, oil, tin, nonferrous metals, and iron; Britain was self-sufficient only in coal. These changes reflected not only the inadequacy of Britain's own raw material resources but also the growth of new industries such as oil and chemicals, which required inputs not found in Britain.

Similarly, manufactured textiles were the single largest component of exports before 1850, when they accounted for 60 percent of the value of exports. After then, although their absolute value increased, their relative share declined, while capital goods and coal grew in importance. First iron, then steel and the goods made out of these materials such as railway equipment, machinery, and ships accounted for a greater share of exports.

Changing Markets for Exports

These exports had one thing in common: They represented the export of industrialization, so

Table 11-2
Britain: Export of Industrialization, various indicators

I Export of Capital Goods, As percentage of exports of manufactured goods (selected years)				
1840–1842	1857–1859	1867–1869	1882–1884	1913
11	22	20	27	39

II Export of Coal Millions of tons (selected years)		
1700	1800	1913
2.5	10	73

III Foreign Investment (Export of Finance Capital) £ million (selected years)				
1872	1882	1906	1907	1913
82	82	104	141	225

Note: Before 1840, capital exports were mostly loans to governments; later they represented investment in railroads, public utilities, and other productive assets.

IV Value of Capital Invested Abroad £ million (selected years)				
1840	1850	1870	1873	1913
160	250	700	1,000	4,000

when the importing countries began to industrialize, their imports from Britain fell. Industrial competitors like France, Germany, and the United States did not rely on imports of raw materials or exports of manufactured goods to anything like the same extent as Britain, and they also erected tariff barriers against imports of manufactures from Britain, later becoming actual competitors.

As Europe and the United States became less open markets, new ones had to be found. In the first half of the 19th century, Latin American countries became the largest single market for British cottons, a role taken over by India in the second half. India took up to 60 percent of all cottons between 1875 and 1914. Increasingly trade with developing areas replaced trade with potentially industrializing ones later in the century. Canada, Australia, and South Africa, plus new areas (Malaya and the Middle East) joined the Latin American countries as major markets and sources of raw materials for Britain.

In truth, the period from about 1840 to the early 1870s was probably the only one in which British industrial superiority was basically unchallenged, and all parties to merchandise trade had an interest in keeping it that way. This was true because Britain was either the only outlet for the primary products produced or the only source of the capital equipment needed for industrializa-

Figure 11.2 How textile looms were powered can be seen clearly in this American illustration. The belts that turned the machines can be seen above the looms. (Courtest of the Museum of American Textile History)

tion. Later the situation became one of industrial competitors facing each other, which had an impact on late-19th century imperialism, as developed countries attempted to acquire those colonies rich in the "new" raw materials, such as rubber, oil, and bauxite, needed for the emerging new industries. And it definitely had an impact on the resurgence of protectionism after the 1880s.

Invisibles and Capital Exports

One more change in the pattern of international relations should be noted because it helps explain both the spread of industrialization worldwide and later developments. This was the growth of exports of capital and trade in invisibles. ("Invisibles" include earnings from services such as shipping, insurance, banking, and brokerage as well as interest, dividends and profits from investments made abroad.) Exports of capital had been minor before 1840 when they mainly consisted of loans to governments. But with the building of railways and public utilities, capital exports from Britain increased dramatically, first to Europe then to the United States in the 1850s, and to India and Latin America later. In the 1850s, Europe and the United States together took half of all capital exports, but as this share fell, the share of India and Latin America increased to about 20 percent. Later in the 1880s, developing areas accounted for larger shares.

Without earnings from these sources, Britain's balance of payments would have been in deficit. As it was, there was an adverse balance on merchandise trade throughout most of the century, but this was covered by earnings on invisibles, especially shipping and insurance, before 1875. After then, the trading deficit got larger, and the importance of interest and dividends from abroad as a means of covering it grew.

Great Britain, as would be expected, accounted for a large amount of direct overseas investment. By 1913, this amounted to about £4 billion, which compares with £5.5 billion worth of overseas investment owned by Belgium, France, Germany, the Netherlands, and the United States combined. This is in keeping with a typical pattern of industrial development. A newly industrializing country typically imports capital in both money and equipment forms. As it industrializes, it ceases to be a debtor, and as opportunities for profitable investment at home appear to lessen, so potentially more profitable opportunities abroad seem attractive. By this time, it is sufficiently developed to be able to export capital. This describes Britain in the 19th century, and is a real life development that provides an interesting qualification to both mercantilist and classical schools of economic theorizing: Neither saw the role that exports of money capital would have for either exporting or importing countries.[3]

Effect of Terms of Trade

Analyzing the pattern of British trade provides an interesting practical test of mercantilist ideas. The aim of mercantilism was to generate a favorable balance of trade, accomplished by exporting a higher value than importing and by having favorable terms of trade. At the very simplest, which is what is needed for this discussion, the terms of trade are said to move in a country's favor if a given volume of exports exchanges for a larger volume of imports than before, while they move against a country if a given volume of exports can acquire only a smaller volume of imports than before.

Real life developments, however, showed the weakness of these ideas in explaining industrial development, especially for the world as a whole. Up to 1860, as a result of industrialization, the terms of trade tended to move against Britain. This occurred because the technological innovations associated with industrialization resulted in

Terms of Trade
Relative prices of imports and exports

lower prices for manufactured goods relative to primary commodities. This meant that the underdeveloped countries exporting raw materials to Britain gained purchasing power, enabling them to buy manufactured goods from Britain, further stimulating demand for manufactured exports from Britain. When trade is seen as a circular flow like this, it is possible to recognize the mutual interests that trading partners have.

However, after 1860, the terms of trade began to move in Britain's favor, again a consequence of changes in the pattern of innovation. This time, agricultural and primary product prices were falling relative to industrial ones because the transportation revolution—railroads and steamships—had lowered transportation costs and opened up new areas. Costs fell further in farming as a result of the use of machinery and improved yields following the use of fertilizers. In addition, there was a shift in the composition of exports from Britain, away from relatively cheap textiles and towards relatively expensive capital goods. (There was an additional cyclical factor at work, too. During depressions, prices of primary products tend to fall more than prices of manufactured products, and the spread of industrial capitalism implied that depressions would occur more frequently. The years after 1873 were generally depressed.) This shift implied that Britain could acquire imports on increasingly favorable terms. The resulting lower food prices occurring at a time when food imports were becoming more important helps explain why the standard of living rose in Britain in the late 19th century.

There was a downside to this effect: Relatively lower import prices meant that primary producing countries also had relatively less purchasing power with which to buy British exports. Export demand from industrializing countries was also less than before due to loss of markets and rising protectionism. There were two results. First, there was a tendency for Britain's balance on merchandise trade to become increasingly adverse. Second, there was a tendency for producers

to favor the home market, reversing decades of export-oriented production. Later we will look at other explanations for the relative long-term decline in Britain's international position.

International Financial Network

How this deficit was made good so that the entire balance of payments did balance again reflects 19th century developments. Britain, as the world's largest and most advanced trading nation, was at the center of international financial arrangements. Settlement of overseas payments, brokerage transactions, insurance, and capital flows centered on London, partly because most involved British participation and partly because it was the location of a sophisticated financial community with expertise. In addition, as trading and the settlements network became increasingly multilateral, no one country was ever exactly in balance with each one of its trading partners. This was especially true of the period after 1870. As the newly industrializing countries expanded their imports from the primary producing countries, there was no offset of exports to them or earnings from invisibles. This gap was filled by Britain, which became dominant in shipping goods between countries as well as importing manufactured goods from its new industrial rivals. Thus Britain earned on invisibles, received income from overseas investments, and exported capital sufficient to offset its own excess of imports of goods over exports.

This system worked, at least until its collapse after the First World War, but it was increasingly precarious, especially if compared with the harmony of interests of the midcentury period, or even the stability of the earlier mercantilist empires. That is, although trade between industrial countries is larger in value than that between industrial and primary producing countries, any harmony of interests is more accidental, and in any event cannot be controlled by political means, as in the 18th century, for example. It is potentially unstable and can be affected, as it was in the late 19th century, by artificial barriers such as tariffs, as well as wars, because it is trade between sovereign independent nations.

Changing Values: Free Trade

While these economic changes were taking place, an increasing imbalance was appearing between the economic and the political spheres, with two results. The first was a change in the political structure to reflect more accurately the alterations in economic power that had taken place. The second, closely linked with the first, was a change in values—from mercantilist, protectionist ideas, toward free trade and laissez faire. This was as dramatic as earlier changes away from feudalism and decentralized political power toward central-ized monarchy, or toward reflecting the domi-nance of landed interests and merchants.

Laissez Faire

Principle favoring no government involvement in economic activity

---

The result was a more democratic Parliament more representative of those urban industrial in-terests most critical of mercantilist policies. This came about through an extension of the vote—al-though not until the end of the century would the franchise be extended to propertyless male work-ers, and women had to wait until the 20th century for this privilege of democracy. But more impor-tant, political changes reflected the redistribution of the population that had occurred in the wake of the Industrial Revolution: away from the rural areas of southern England and toward the new industrial towns of the urbanizing north. Change reflected the growing frustration that industrial-ists, and increasingly commercial interests, felt about the perpetuation of mercantilist regulation. Their practical frustration found intellectual sup-port in the new economic theories appearing in the late 18th century. But not until the govern-

ment itself could be persuaded that these regula-tions were not in the country's best interests could the goal of lower tariffs be realized, which is why political restructuring was also necessary.

These two ideas, laissez faire and free trade, are usually taken as synonymous. Both, after all, are based on a belief that the free working of the market, with no government involvement, will maximize a nation's wealth. However, after Par-liament was reformed, and government became more responsive to industrial wishes, a practical divergence appeared. Trade did become freer, but increasingly, the earliest period of pure laissez faire in industry was replaced by concern over social conditions. Thus, commercial policy re-moved restrictions, but domestic policy became more interventionist, although it was a very dif-ferent kind of involvement from that common under mercantilist influences.

Struggle Against Mercantilism

While the struggle between mercantilists and free traders is usually represented by the Corn Law controversy of the early 19th century, in fact both the rise of new ideas and their application began in the 18th. Removing mercantilist restrictions on trade was a slow process, starting in the 1780s, interrupted by the Napoleonic War period, con-tinuing again in the 1820s, and concluding with the repeal of the Corn Laws in 1846. The process was complete by 1860, although to all intents and purposes, free trade dominated commercial pol-icy much earlier. The following period up to the end of the century was not a period of global free trade, but Britain at least remained committed to these ideas, which were rejected only in the very different circumstances of the 1930s. Britain was alone in adopting free trade policies in their purest form. The United States protected its infant in-

---

Corn Laws

Protectionist laws in effect 1815-1846 imposing tariffs on grain imported into Britain

---

Solving Problems in Economic History

Did the working classes' standard of living improve during Britain's industrialization?

One of the most contentious issues that economic historians have grappled with is the impact of industrialization on the standard of living of the working class in Britain. If one takes a relatively late ending point, say the end of the 19th century, it is easy to say fairly unambiguously that living standards did rise. But depending on the measures used, ambiguity creeps in, making it less easy to be so confident.

An excellent survey of the literature on this subject and on the data sources and techniques that can be used to help unravel the problems can be found in "Old Questions, New Data, and Alternative Perspectives: Families' Living Standards in the Industrial Revolution" by Sara Horrell and Jane Humphries (*Journal of Economic History* 52:4, December 1992, pp. 849-880).

The conventional approach (which leads to the optimistic conclusion) is to measure welfare by tracking the real wages of adult males. However, a *family* standard of living depends on more than this. It depends on the wages or contributions of all family members, hours worked, frequency and length of unemployment, and amount of any income subsidies received, for example. After all, in farming districts and before the 20th century, it was uncommon to find a single male breadwinner supporting a non-working spouse and children: such an image is very specific to a relatively short period in the 20th century in developed western industrial economies.

Bearing this in mind, there are several considerations to take into account. If industrialization eliminated women's and children's economic options, tracking the growth of men's earnings would overstate gains. Alternatively, if new options for women and children appeared, then family income growth would be greater than male income growth. Also, were there differences in different regions or among different occupations? For example, it is logical to expect that leading edge industries and occupations would have faster income growth than declining ones. If this is the case, then perhaps inequality within the working classes increased during the 19th century, a feature that would be exaggerated by differential employment patterns. Such differences also make it difficult to generalize.

However, the issue is difficult to examine because of the perennial problem of data inadequacy, discontinuity and noncomparability. The authors here have used a data set of 1350 household budgets giving information on both incomes (for different family members) and expenditures for the period 1787-1865. The data comes from 59 different sources, published and unpublished, and helps to investigate the relative growth of men's earnings and total family income.

The trend in male earnings tends to confirm the view that a rise was experienced; however, this has to be qualified, since recessions prevented steady growth in the incomes of the better-off group, and exacerbated the situation of the worst off, particularly outworkers and agricultural workers.

Total family income changes were more stable in the early part of the period when it tended to offset falls in male incomes, seemingly because of increased participation by other family members. But in the later period, this was not so obvious—that is, declining opportunities for

Problem continues on next page

Problem continued from previous page

other family members increased income in-equality. These changes also tend to show that the growth of income was discontinuous, imply-ing that periods of un- and under-employment had a serious impact on wage-earning families.

In conclusion, the investigation here supports the conventional view that gains in material welfare were made, but qualifies the overall optimism. Both earnings and income growth were interrupted (an effect not picked up by studies concentrating only on wage *rates*, which may have been stable), and evidence of the effect of price changes is unclear. Family income over the entire period grew less than male earnings, and income inequality between families tended to increase, an effect most probably the result of declining work opportunities for women and children.

dustries with tariffs starting in 1816. France had only a brief flirtation with free trade in the second half of the century. By 1880, protectionist policies were restored everywhere except in Britain. But the ideology of free trade and laissez faire persist-ed in people's minds, even though reality (and their own interests) dictated otherwise.

The battle against mercantilism took place on two fronts: practical and ideological. Before 1776, no one doubted the desirability of govern-ment's regulating trade in the country's best in-terests, but on the practical side, the multiplicity of regulations was already weakening mercantil-ism. There were so many regulations that many were being ignored, and the expansion of trade demonstrated that effective enforcement was im-possible. Because many duties were so high, a thriving smuggling industry was encouraged. Opposition to the attempt to enforce old regula-tions in the colonies to raise revenues for colonial defense also involved a high cost—the loss of the American colonies in 1776.

In that same year, Adam Smith published his book, *An Inquiry into the Nature and Causes of the Wealth of Nations*. It was the first comprehensive exposition of the revolutionary idea that govern-ment regulation did not in fact work in the best interests of the nation—i.e., it did not, as mercan-tilists claimed, increase the nation's wealth. Smith wanted to show that free trade resulted in wider markets, thus permitting a greater division of labor which would increase productivity and re-sult in increased output, the true measure of a nation's wealth. He was mainly concerned with the impact of laissez faire on trade, which was hardly surprising, as trade was the most common capitalist economic activity in those early years of the Industrial Revolution. There was also a prac-tical aspect to the demand that the government should let the free working of the market mecha-nism take care of economic activity, already ap-parent in the difficulties of enforcing mercantilist regulations. That is, when the civil service was small and local government corrupt or nonex-istent, nonintervention did make sense.

Laissez Faire and Ricardo's Analysis

Later, the analysis was extended. By positing certain economic laws, it could be shown that free trade and laissez faire would ensure Britain's con-tinued economic superiority. The major econo-mist associated with the 19th century exposition of laissez faire was David Ricardo. The time was immediately after the Napoleonic Wars, when there was no challenge to Britain's leadership, and only landowners were not receptive to free trade ideas.

Ricardo showed that if the goal of self-suffi-ciency in food (made effective by the Corn Laws) was to be achieved, it would require cultivation of less fertile land and need increasing amounts of labor and capital in farming. This increase in costs would cause rising food prices, and as food costs were the most important determinant of real wages, wages would have to rise, raising costs in industry. Although industry was not characterized by diminishing returns as agriculture was, thanks to the effects of technological innovation, it could not expand because resources were being diverted to agriculture. In any event, higher costs in farming squeezed profits. Landowners received higher rents because of the increase in land under cultivation, but were not, by definition, investors in industry. Industrial profits got squeezed, as higher input costs due to higher food prices for workers could not be passed on as higher prices because competitive conditions tended to equalize prices, regardless of productive conditions.

Without industrial profits, capitalists had no incentive to expand. For a small country like Britain, continued prosperity depended on industrial, not agricultural, growth. Thus Ricardo's prescription was clear: Repeal the Corn Laws so that cheaper food could be imported. This would keep down both rents (considered to be unproductive income) and wages, thus increasing profits that could be used for further capital accumulation. In addition, practical considerations also showed that so long as Britain had no industrial competition, the ability to import low-cost raw materials and food from abroad, plus the fact that she was the major source of industrial goods, was not only economically but also politically advantageous.

Removing Restrictions

But it would take a restructuring of Parliament and many more years to remove the last vestiges of mercantilist policies. In the same way that the economic analysis underlying the free trade movement took decades to become a complete, comprehensive statement, so the practical efforts to remove regulations took time. The start came as early as the 1780s. William Pitt the Younger became Prime Minister in 1783, in a very unsettled situation. Trade had been disrupted because of the loss of the American colonies and the

increase in the national debt caused by the cost of fighting the Revolutionary War. Pitt was sympathetic to traders' needs for lower tariffs and less complicated commercial regulations, but his efforts were limited. In 1784 high duties on tea were lowered in an attempt to reduce the enormous amount of smuggling that went on; in 1787 he replaced the complex mechanism used to calculate customs duties with a single rate for each item. What could have been a major step toward freeing trade came with the signing of a commercial treaty with France in 1786, reducing duties on most items traded between the two countries. Unfortunately, any effect this might have had was negated when first the French Revolution took place and then war broke out between Britain and France in 1793.

The Corn Laws

During the war period, free trade ideas were pushed to one side, as the country struggled to retain adequate food supplies and fight against Napoleon's Continental System. A significant mercantilist law, the Corn Law, was passed aiming for self-sufficiency in food. It protected British farmers by keeping foreign grain out of the country with high tariffs (except when a bad harvest occurred, in which case the tariff could be lowered and more grain allowed in to prevent food prices rising too high). This policy kept farming profitable, and, as might be expected, landowners were happy with their increased rents, which resulted from demand for land remaining high. In addition, and in spite of the sliding scale of tariffs, food prices rose dramatically during the war, making this one of agriculture's most prosperous periods.

The free trade movement began in earnest after the war, and a major focus of agitation was the new Corn Law, passed in 1815. This law continued to protect farming, but replaced the sliding scale of the old law with a flat prohibition of any grain imports unless the domestic price reached a certain high level, after which point imports were permitted. (In fact, grain prices fell after 1815 and never reached the threshold level. In 1822, prices were one third the 1817 level, and they never stabilized.) The Corn Law was opposed because now that peace had returned, and given the needs of industry, continued agricultural protection was both unnecessary and harmful, a piece of ammunition based on David Ricardo's analysis. But the landowners who controlled Parliament and thus legislation remained firm—the struggle would not be over until their hold on political power had weakened. Meanwhile, other steps toward free trade that did not affect landed interests were being taken. They recognized the changes that had occurred in Britain's international position during the war, so even without the added boost given by free trade ideology, commercial policy would probably have become less restrictive.

Commercial Policy

Policy regulating commerce and trade

Manufacturers' Desire for Free Trade

By the early 1820s, the effects of the first phase of the Industrial Revolution were becoming clear. Output had increased, and export demand was an important factor in stimulating continued increases in output. As one result of the closing of European markets during the Napoleonic Wars, new markets had been opened up, especially in Latin America. In addition, more territory in India had come under the control of British traders, and Australia, originally used as a penal colony for transported convicts, was no longer seen as only a dumping ground. In particular, its potential for sheep raising was becoming apparent.

Manufacturers wanted free trade for very practical reasons. They did not need protection from foreign imports, because there was no competition from abroad. But they did want access to cheaper sources of raw materials and food, so they favored free trade as a way of preventing retali-

ation from other countries that might close export markets to them. Merchants and shipowners were also in agreement: If fewer restrictions meant an expansion of trade, then their business and profits would expand. While the government depended on customs duties for revenues, the expansion of trade in the 1820s implied that a combination of lower duties and more trade would not result in a loss of revenues. Only landowners remained opposed, but the steps taken in the 1820s did not affect their economic position.

Commercial Policy Changes

Between 1823 and 1827, four major sets of reforms in commercial policy—none requiring Parliamentary approval, which probably would not have been forthcoming—were made. The first set resulted in a general lowering of duties. No duties on imports were higher than 30 percent; previous prohibitions on exports were removed and export bounties were eliminated. This meant that raw wool exports were now permitted, skilled workers were free to emigrate, and, in 1825, that industrial machinery could be exported under license. (These last two reforms were part of the "export of industrialization" that would haunt Britain at the end of the century, but at the time, the impact on machinery producers and the increase of personal freedom was seen as important.)

The second set concerned trade relations with other countries. Under the provisions of the Reciprocity of Duties Act passed in 1823, trade treaties could be negotiated with other countries to lower duties on both countries' exports to each other below the generally prevailing ones. (In effect, this granted mutual Most Favored Nation status.) The act resulted in treaties being made with most other European countries.

Most Favored Nation

Principle of equally favorable treatment of trading partners

The third set dealt with relations with Britain's colonies. For the first time the colonies could trade freely with other countries, but there was still an incentive for them to retain closer ties with Britain. Colonial goods entered Britain paying substantially lower duties than similar imports from other countries (this affected chiefly West Indian rum, Indian silks, Canadian grain, and Australian wool), and colonies in turn charged lower duties on imports from Britain. This was the first step toward the system of Imperial Preference that was later established to create trading ties between countries in the British empire.

Finally, one of the chief mainstays of mercantilist policies, the Navigation Acts, were attacked. They were altered so that, although fishing and the colonial carrying trade were still restricted to British or colonial ships, all the other restrictions on production and shipping were removed. But for all practical purposes, as the Dutch were no longer such a threat as they had been in the 17th century, this provision simply formalized existing practice, and Britain remained the world's chief shipper. (The Navigation Acts were not formally repealed until 1849.)

The alteration of commercial policy thus struck a blow at the unwieldy monolith of mercantilist-inspired policy. Trade flourished, and the lack of regulation did not have an adverse impact on the economy (which continued to grow) as the protectionists had feared. The explanation, again, was that Britain at that time had nothing to lose from free trade. Industrial strength and the increasing complexity of both industry and the financial and commercial institutions necessary to maintain it were well capable of adjusting to new demands.

Protests Against the Corn Laws

But the battle against excessive regulation was not yet over. Although the reforms of the 1820s had made trade easier, the task was not yet complete. In particular, the symbol of everything industri-

alists hated about regulation, the Corn Laws, still remained in effect. The previous changes could be made because landowners were not directly affected, but this was not true with the Corn Laws. Although industry was a larger sector of the economy than agriculture, there were two reasons for focusing on the Corn Laws. First, they kept food prices higher than would otherwise have been the case, which was a concern to industrial capitalists. Second, they were symbolic of the old age that had no place in the new, modern Britain, being kept in place only because of the power of the vested landed interests in Parliament. Thus, repealing the Corn Laws would indicate that the political structure reflected the new distribution of economic power; but they could be repealed only if landowners' control over Parliament were relaxed. Then it would be possible to go further in making laissez faire and free trade policies effective.

Parliamentary Reform

That is why attention turned to the next step, parliamentary reform, accomplished in 1832 with the passage of the Reform Bill. Reform was not easy, as landowners mounted a vigorous opposition to the bill, which was rejected three times by the House of Lords. (Any bill must be accepted by both houses of Parliament before it can be signed by the monarch and pass into law.) Finally, only when threatened with the creation of a sufficient number of new peers who would be in favor of its passage did the Lords relent and accept the bill.

By 20th century standards, the provisions of the Reform Bill were modest but were significant enough to mark the changes that had occurred so that the new Parliament did reflect urban industrial interests. The vote was extended to middle-class males, subject to a property qualification; the working classes could still not vote—the reformers were not yet ready to make that concession. Rotten boroughs, those with a population below

2,000, lost their representatives, and their seats were reallocated to the new towns of the north and Midlands. As the rotten boroughs were towns in the south and west that had lost population as a result of the decline in the wool industry and the rise of industrial towns in the north, the reallocation effectively reduced landowners' political power.[4] The result was a Parliament in which power was shared by industrial interests (represented by the Liberal party, which was born out of the old Whig party) and the landowners (represented by the Conservative party, previously known as the Tory party).

The final stage came in the 1840s, a decade of generally hard times all across Europe punctuated by agricultural depression and serious social unrest. Earlier reform movements in Britain had been thwarted by fears that reform would lead to revolution, and the violence of the French Revolution, even though it had been based on the ideas of liberty, equality, and fraternity, was fresh in the minds of the political elite. But the repressive measures introduced earlier to prevent revolution had not produced a passive, docile working class, and the 1840s, called the Hungry Forties, saw an upsurge of working class protest. This was always contained in Britain, which did not experience a revolution in 1848 as other European countries did. Protests occurred simultaneously with poor harvests, including the failure of the potato crop in Ireland, which intensified pressure to allow grain to enter the country freely. This time the response was favorable, partly because a new series of trade liberalization policies had already been introduced, and finally the time was right for a final onslaught on the Corn Laws.

Free Trade

The new prime minister was Robert Peel, in office 1841–1846, who was the son of an industrialist. Although his previous experience in government was in domestic affairs[5], his intention as prime minister was to free trade from all remaining

duties. Between 1842 and 1846 he managed to accomplish this aim, although he was forced to introduce an income tax to replace lost customs revenues. In 1842, all raw material duties were reduced to a maximum of 5 percent and then completely removed in 1846 except for imports of timber and tallow. Maximum duties on imports of semimanufactured goods were initially reduced to 13 percent then completely removed in 1846. Machinery exports were freely permitted after 1843, and export duties on coal and raw wool were removed. Peel also continued the earlier policy of negotiating trade agreements with other countries.

But his crowning achievement was the repeal of the Corn Laws in 1846, the final ending of the mercantilist era. In the 1850s, trade was completely free; all remaining duties (except for a few used for revenue purposes) were abolished. The major duties, however, affecting Britain's most important imports and exports, had been eliminated much earlier.

Possibly influenced by the surge in trade that marked the 1830s and later decades, other countries also began a movement to modify their protectionist policies. Producers of primary products were strongly in favor of free trade because it would open up markets for them and also permit them to obtain imports of manufactured goods easily, but the new industrialists were not in favor. They wanted to retain protection from competition from British manufacturers in their own markets, so this movement was slow and cautious. The United States began lowering its tariffs after 1833, and the Netherlands reduced tariffs starting in 1845.

The Fall and Rise of Trade Barriers

Success for the free traders internationally was symbolized by the signing of the Cobden-Chevalier Treaty between France and Britain in 1860. Despite opposition from French industrialists, heavily protectionist France agreed to lower duties on imports from Britain, while Britain gained easier access to French wines and silks. The decade of the 1860s was probably the time when trade was least protected, as a protectionist reaction set in after 1873, partly in response to depressed conditions, especially in European agriculture. Farming interests then joined with industrial interests to restore protection to farming, which had suffered as a result of two shocks. The first was the opening up of new farming areas, especially in the United States, Latin America, and Australia, made possible by the railroads and steamships, and producers in these areas were able to undercut European farmers' prices. Second, French wine growers had been devastated by phylloxera which attacked grape vines, while an outbreak of foot rot had devastated sheep flocks. One by one, most of the European countries restored and raised duties in an effort to keep domestic producers profitable; only Britain, the Netherlands, Finland, and Turkey did not.

By 1910, average rates on all imports ranged from 8 percent in France, to 8.4 percent in Germany, 9.6 percent in Italy, 13.4 percent in Spain, and 38.9 percent in Russia, while the average rate on manufactured imports into the United States was 38 percent. Protection was extended by using a variety of other devices in addition to tariffs. These included two-tier rates (the lower rate was applied to countries negotiating a trade treaty), embargoes based on sanitary regulations, and refunds of duties paid by exporters, for example, which all had the effect of limiting trade.

Even Britain, long the bastion of free trade, which had seen the growth rate of its exports decline after the 1870s, was not immune to protectionist pressures. At the turn of the century, there was a movement to restore the tariff to protect domestic industry and also to strengthen ties within the British Empire. However, it was unsuccessful at this time.

To summarize so far, the second phase of the Industrial Revolution was characterized by a high degree of technological innovation, the development and increasing sophistication of the capital goods industries, and a transportation revolution that affected every industry and almost every person in the country. The period between 1840 and 1871 also saw political changes reflecting the change in the balance of economic power, and as a consequence, the popularization and implementation of free trade policies symbolized by the repeal of the Corn Laws in 1846. While other countries also moved toward freer trade, Britain at this time had no effective industrialized competitors, so the impact of her decision was pronounced. After 1870, it was becoming apparent that this unchallenged position would not last, and the final years of the 19th century saw Britain attempt to make an adjustment to a changing world.

Changing Values: Social Reforms

If commercial and trade policy was influenced by laissez faire with the result that trade became less regulated, the same was not true of domestic policy, especially policy concerned with social conditions. Although laissez faire and the individualist ethic were still influential, the recognition gradually arose that there had to be some public involvement, for very practical reasons. So throughout the century laws were enacted and measures taken to improve living and working conditions. These steps were hesitant and ineffective at first, meeting with much opposition, but at least they showed an understanding that national wealth was not just to be counted in output totals. What also mattered was the standard of living of the citizen. It was difficult for policymakers to take these steps. Personal opinions and powerful economic interests were opposed to anything that seemed to interfere with the individual's (read employer's) self-interest. But the changes that had occurred since the mid-18th century made some action imperative.

Population had grown from 10.5 million in 1801, to 18.1 million in 1841, and to 24.1 million in 1867, by which time most of the population was urban or becoming urban. Now the new towns in the industrial areas had no effective system of municipal government—they had grown from tiny villages in most cases—and had been hurriedly built, thus such basic necessities of urban living as decent housing, public amenities, sanitation and pure water supplies were lacking. Industrialization had brought exploitation of workers and had also brought into the open the scandal of child labor, especially of pauper children. Overcrowded urban conditions also produced problems of law and order, and there was no systematic, satisfactory method of handling the new phenomenon of large population aggregations—these were entirely new in the history of western civilization. Health conditions deteriorated, as shown by the rise in the death rate in the first few years of the 19th century. Illiteracy was still pervasive among the lower classes[6], and the problem of poverty remained ever present.

Recognition of Problems

When a problem was recognized, the typical approach was to establish an investigatory commission to look into it, with legislation often occurring after it had reported. But two further developments were needed before effective remedies could be applied. One was the establishment of an efficient civil service responsible for administering and enforcing laws. The second was a satisfactory system of local government, to which could be delegated power and responsibility for dealing with problems on a local level. At the beginning of the 19th century, neither was satisfactory, and thus throughout the century, government involvement was closely linked to improvements in these two sets of institutions.

To a certain extent, these problems were made worse by class attitudes. The middle class was still small, but by the 19th century no longer faced a

generally hostile environment; it had achieved respectability. Middle class attitudes still stressed hard work and individualism but rejected extending laissez faire freedoms to the working classes. Thus employers limited the freedom of workers by adopting employment practices such as contract employment and the truck system (in which workers' pay would be redeemed only for goods at a company store). While strongly opposed to union organization (unions were not legally recognized until 1824), industrialists were frequently participants in their own monopoly organizations formed for price fixing purposes, for example. Because of the development of social and physical distance between this middle class and the working class, the former simply did not know much about the latter—except that they were different. This lack of knowledge about the reality of working class life and the validity of working class ideals and values characterized the 19th century, and contributed to middle class

Truck System
System of paying wages in goods, not money

fears of a revolutionary uprising by those below them on the social scale. Workers themselves, especially at first, were often not willing participants in the new capitalist system. Not only did it offer a limited future to those who remained workers (which was practically all), but also its permanence was not certain.

However, this changed by the 1840s when large numbers were employed in the modern capitalist industries, and when it was clear that a capitalist economy was no passing phenomenon. On the one hand, industrialists had established themselves and thus could afford to make concessions without fear of a working class revolution. On the other hand, living and working conditions were beginning to improve, especially after 1850, thus the permanence of a wage-labor status was no longer to be feared.

This improvement owes much both to reforms undertaken in the century and to industrial changes themselves. At the end of the century, the "average" worker was undoubtedly better off than at the beginning, due partly to rising wage rates but also to shifts in the occupational distribution from low-paying jobs (such as agriculture, a shrinking sector) to high-paying ones, as well as to the greater regularity of employment. (Cyclical unemployment during depressions would remain a serious problem, however, depending on the industry.)

At the end of the century, it was clear that the working class was not a homogenous mass. Although class classifications are ambiguous, perhaps three quarters of the population could be considered lower class, defined as manual workers and their families. Of these, about 15 percent were a labor aristocracy—highly skilled and relatively highly paid workers associated especially with the metalworking and engineering industries. The true middle class made up of independent, self-employed, or professional workers was smaller. However, it was *their* values and attitudes that influenced the characteristic "liberal" ethic of Victorian Britain.

Repressive Measures

This group of merchants, gentry, manufacturers, and traders was in the forefront of the political reform movement of the late 18th century. However, after the French Revolution, it joined its former adversary, the landowning class, in order to impose repressive measures to eliminate the threat of revolution on the English side of the Channel. The result was repeal of the old paternalist legislation regulating wages, apprenticeships, and working conditions, and a ban on the formation of combinations of workers in unions. These measures institutionalized the belief in laissez faire, with industrialists continuing to resent what they saw as interference by government in their decision making, and they also stopped the

outward expression of working class unrest, with very few exceptions.

This unrest focused on the very different nature of employment of the new industrial workers. They had lost status as independent workers; the traditional economy had been shattered, resulting in the emergence of a class of capitalist employers without the traditional authority or obligations that had been common in earlier centuries, which widened the gulf between employer and employee; and both the nature and intensity of exploitation were now different. The issues of concern to workers were not simply monetary issues (important as these were)—they also included resistance to the truck system, dislike of long hours and the rigorous discipline imposed by the factory system, child labor, and repression of union-organizing rights, among others.

Protests by the working classes did not achieve much. For some of the important issues to be resolved required not only a recognition of their importance but also a willingness by those with political power to do something, which took a long time. The first step was the split between industrial and landowning interests that came during the long struggle for free trade. At that time, the increasing confidence of industrialists implied that they no longer needed to depend on the landowners for political influence. Furthermore, with the exception of mutual fear of revolutionary tendencies, their interests were not compatible. Landowners wanted to retain protection and the privileges that went with landownership. Manufacturers and traders wanted free trade and political power, because they perceived their interests to lie in that direction. Thus this struggle for political reform, ending with the triumph of urban industrial interests, was one feature of the 19th century. Another was the gradual introduction of more, and more effective, reforms to remedy the worst abuses of 19th century industrialization and its accompaniments. These reforms took two major forms: legislation covering working conditions and legislation concerned with other social, mainly urban, problems.

Factory Reform Legislation

Factory reforms were the first attempts to correct the failures of a pure laissez faire market mechanism which generated problems that would not be automatically corrected. These were problems that could be remedied only with social action, because individual action would not be able to accomplish much. The first such evil was child labor, and the first factory act was designed to limit the exploitation of children. Legislation was gradually extended to regulate all conditions of employment in factories.

Factory Act
Laws regulating working conditions in factories

The very first act, the Health and Morals Act, was passed in 1802 and was designed to correct the scandal of the use of pauper children in factories. These children were acquired by employers from orphanages and poorhouses as a source of cheap labor. The fact that they were numerous enough to be identified as an issue indicates the poor state of living conditions and high mortality rates. The act limited the children's working hours to 12 a day, with night work to be gradually eliminated. Employers were also to provide housing for these children, provide them with two sets of clothing a year, segregate sleeping quarters by sex, allow no more than two children to a bed, and they were to receive some religious and educational instruction.

While this seemed like a tremendous step forward, it was ineffective, for two reasons. No enforcement provisions were made, and in any case the problem was no longer important. Most factories by this time were in large towns where there was an increasing supply of "free" children (children who lived with their families), so employers could use these children rather than pau-

per children. Free children had a further advantage in being cheaper than pauper children; because they lived at home, the employer was under no obligaton to go to the expense of housing and feeding them. In addition, and unlike pauper children who were hired under contract, free children could be laid off more easily during depressed business conditions.

So child labor was still used, which led to the passage of the 1819 Factory Act, designed to regulate the employment of children in cotton factories. (At this time, the textile industry was the largest manufacturing employer.) This act prevented the employment of children under nine and limited the hours of those between nine and sixteen to 12 hours a day, with no night work.

It met a great deal of opposition. Factory owners wanted the cheap labor provided by children and even protested that productive labor was good for them—that they enjoyed doing it, and it was more like play for them than work! However, although the law was on the books, there were still no enforcement provisions, so it had no practical effect. No attempt was made to deal with the question of child labor in general. Child labor was widespread in agriculture, mining, other textile industries, and domestic industry in general, and it was probably ignored because in these areas it was less visible and therefore less of an immediate concern than in the cotton factories. It is interesting to speculate what the situation might have been if parents had been paid more, thus removing the need for children's earnings to supplement the family's income, and if an effective education system and a commitment to educate future citizens had been in effect. Later developments in Britain and elsewhere showed that child labor was not essential to either economic prosperity or to a healthy democracy.

Ending Child Labor

Factory reform began to be effective only in the 1830s when new laws specifically required enforcement by specially appointed factory inspectors. From this time on, working conditions for adults also became regulated. The first of the new series was the 1833 Factory Act, which prohibited the employment of children under nine in all textile factories, limited the hours of those between nine and 13 to nine hours a day and 48 hours a week (and also required them to attend school each day); and limited the hours of those between the ages of 13 and 18 to 12 a day, 69 a week, with no nightwork for the under-eighteens.

While this was an improvement, it was still very arduous work for those in the textile factories. Progressive encroachment on employers' freedom to maximize output per machine by requiring long hours per worker did lead to the development of intensive techniques of exploitation, such as running machines faster. And how effective was the education provision for children who attended school after work? One interesting development did occur in a related area. A law in 1836 required the official registration of births and deaths, which made it possible to check a person's age precisely, and also prevented families or employers from lying about children's ages.

Another step forward was the 1842 Mines Act, which prohibited the employment of women and children underground where they hauled wagons of coal from the coal face to the lift. It also prohibited the employment of any child under ten, and required that no child under 15 operate machinery. Initially, this was ignored because there were no enforcement provisions, but in 1850, inspectors of mines were appointed. With better enforcement, mining gradually became an all-male occupation.

Limitation of Working Hours

This act was the first to be concerned with the employment of adults. Later, a major step came with the regulation of the employment of women in textile factories, which unexpectedly also affected men. This was the 1844 Factory Act, which limited women's hours to 12 a day, with no night work. Women made up most of the work force, working together with men, so effectively meant that men's hours were also reduced, as the factories could not operate without women. The act also required machinery to be fenced, which reduced the number of industrial accidents and dismemberments that were frequent occurrences.

For a long time, worker movements had campaigned for a ten hour day, and in 1847, the Ten Hours Act was passed, first to apply to the textile industry, and after 1850, to other industries. It was bitterly opposed by employers, who believed that output would fall. (There was even an argument that, as profits were made only in the last hour, by eliminating the last hour, profits would also be eliminated!) This did not happen, as productivity increased, not only because workers were better rested, healthier, and more accepting of their conditions, but also because technical improvements continued to be made.

All these factory acts were consolidated in 1878 and extended to all factory employment. Working conditions in sweatshops and small workshops, as well as domestic service, still remained unregulated, but the acts were significant by showing society's acceptance of responsibility for the working of the labor market. The conditions that produced these laws provide an excellent example of the dilemma facing factory owners. Though they may have been personally sympathetic and willing to improve conditions, an individual making improvements would be at a competitive disadvantage, at least in the short run, when compared with his more unscrupulous competitors. So all factories had to be subject to the same laws in order to improve conditions in any one.

The later laws especially demonstrated employers' readiness to accept public involvement. Earlier laws had not resulted in falling output and profits, and as factories increasingly depended on the absence of labor strife, the advantages of making concessions—better wages, better conditions, shorter hours—were seen in increased output levels. This also shows in laws passed in 1871 and 1875, which gave worker unions privileges they had never had before and indicated an acceptance of unions as a permanent feature of industrial life, not as an evil, revolution-inspiring phenomenon. Greater acceptance of the rights of working people was also acknowledged in the 1867 Reform Bill, which extended the franchise to town workmen. While not all working class men could vote, this marked the first time that workers were recognized as a legitimate part of a democracy, and not revolutionary. Again, by the 1870s, it was clear that industrial capitalism was a permanent fact of life.

Attacking Urban Problems

Improving conditions was also the object of various social reforms aimed at remedying three major problems. The first was that the growth of industrial towns had resulted in large numbers of working class people living in poor conditions, and, as the middle class saw it, this produced a potential for a revolutionary explosion. The second was the danger of epidemics—no longer the plague, but other diseases such as cholera, tuberculosis, typhoid and other fevers, and smallpox, which were mostly dirt-related. The third was the recognition that the unplanned growth and inevitable deterioration of cities not only was ugly and produced shameful living conditions but also adversely affected industrial efficiency—an indirect blow to manufacturers' profits.

While industrial progress had some good effects—cheaper textiles for clothing and increased availability of soap did wonders for individual cleanliness while bricks and iron pipes improved public cleanliness—there were bad effects. These were the overcrowded slums, the problems resulting from unplanned disposal of industrial and human wastes, contaminated water supplies, and so on.

To solve them, faith in laissez faire had to be modified to deal with public problems, and there also had to be a mechanism for action. This came with the reform of municipal government. An 1835 act created elected town councils with the ability to deal with urban problems, and they gradually acquired powers to improve sanitation, public health, water supplies, slum clearance, and education, which would greatly improve living conditions. By the end of the century, a three-tier system of government—central, municipal or rural county, and parish—was in effect.

Epidemics and Public Health

Public health and an improved environment were among the first areas to be tackled, focusing especially on the danger of epidemics. The first major 19th century crisis hit in 1831, when Britain experienced its first cholera epidemic, which had disastrous results, especially in urban slums. For the next forty years, there was an intense interest and activity in questions of hygiene. Because cures for these diseases were unknown at this time, activity centered on prevention, which led to improvements in sanitation and water supplies. Sometimes improvements in one area led to increased problems in another. For example, the laying of drains and sewers frequently polluted rivers from which the water supply was taken. This in turn had to be overcome by tapping water supplies in rural areas far from the towns, which could not have been done without the availability of pipes and engineering technology to solve problems of moving water over long distances.

The most difficult problem to solve was housing which, except for the worst slums, was left until the 20th century for solution. However, urban conditions did improve after the 1870s, although the old 19th century industrial towns never became beautiful, even when attention turned to building imposing municipal buildings or adding parks. For so long as coal was the predominant power source, towns were dirty, smoky, and polluted.

Rising Real Wages

The results of improving conditions were increasingly felt by the lower classes, who finally, after about 1850, began to see some gains in their standard of living. On the personal level, average real wages improved after the 1840s until 1900, mainly due to the shift in the occupational distribution to better paid occupations, and to the greater regularity of employment. In 1900 they were about one third higher than in 1875, and about 85 percent higher than in 1850. However, because such a large part of the population was now totally dependent on wage income, unemployment occurring during depressions was still a major concern, and regional variations also make it difficult to make a general statement. (For example, Lancashire's economy revolved around cotton manufacturing and was particularly hard hit by the cutoff in cotton supplies during the American Civil War in the 1860s.)

Sickness, periods of unemployment, and old age continued to be feared, and would not be adequately addressed in Britain until the 20th century. Until then, a network of friendly societies and other mutual benefit societies provided a partial alternative to the Poor Law. This had been "reformed" in 1834 and was universally hated by the working classes. Under the provisions of the new Poor Law, outdoor relief, as in the Speenhamland system, was abolished and replaced by indoor relief in workhouses, which were deliberately designed to provide conditions that compared unfavorably with those on the outside. Thus, to get relief, families had to live in these places, where the sexes were separated, and adults parted from their children. While poor rates fell from the high levels they had reached under the old Poor Law, the cost in human misery and fear was very high. Although the most inhumane aspects were removed by 1842, the workhouse remained as a symbol of oppression, to be resorted to only by the most destitute and desperate (of whom, unfortunately, there were plenty).

There was still an enormous gulf between the upper and lower classes in terms of income, health, and living conditions. For example, and using early 20th century figures, in 1913–1914, the average adult male earned thirty shillings a week for an average workweek of 54 hours. If employment was continuous all year, this resulted in a yearly income of £77. An adult woman, receiving lower wages, made on average half this amount, or £35. At the bottom of the income scale, two social surveys of large cities made in the 1890s (London and York), where conditions would be much worse, calculated that 40 percent of the working class had a weekly family income of only 18-21 shillings which was defined as a poverty income, and only 15 percent earned above £2 a week. At the upper end of the middle class, however, in 1913–1914, 1.75 million families earned over £700 a year. And the few rich people were really rich: in 1901–1902, 4,000 people left an estate worth over £19 million, and 149 died leaving over £62 million.

However, increasing purchasing power of the lower classes after 1870 did result in more and different food being consumed, and they were catered to by an expansion of retail shops (the hated truck system was finally abolished) for food, clothing, footwear, and increasingly for cheap consumer durables, such as the sewing machine and the bicycle. There was even an expansion of entertainment specifically aimed at the working classes—the music hall. None of these developments would have occurred unless there was discretionary income available in the hands of the working classes. This improvement in conditions showed up in various social statistics. The death rate for males in 1838–1842 had been 23 per 1000; this fell to 15 by 1914, while the rate for females fell from 21 to 13, and the infant mortality rate fell from 150 to 105. Also, as is typical for developed countries, the birthrate fell. But there were still physical differences, related to nutrition and general environment, that separated the upper from the lower classes. In the 1870s, upper class boys aged 11 and 12 were on average five inches taller than those from working class families, and the difference was still three inches for teenagers.[7]

Summary

The period after 1830 saw the introduction of the railway, a revolutionary form of transportation that was the outgrowth of the steam power and metal producing innovations of the Industrial Revolution. The railway had an enormous impact. By providing fast and cheap transportation, it permitted a continued expansion of industry, a widening of the domestic market, and an opening up of new areas overseas. Britain at this time had an unchallenged industrial lead, and the growing confidence in industry underscored the battle to free trade from mercantilist restrictions. Thus, Britain was the 19th century champion of free trade and laissez faire.

But laissez faire *was* challenged on the domestic front, and slowly, amid much opposition, reforms were put into place to correct the faults of an unregulated labor market, and to improve social and living conditions. These reforms plus continuing changes in industrial structure did much to help the working class share in the prosperity they had helped create. As later chapters will show, these changes continued, and became more complex in the late 19th and early 20th centuries.

Notes

1. Interestingly enough, the gauge (width) of the British rail system is a curious holdover from the earlier idea that traffic should be able to switch between railway and road. The distance between the two rails is the *average* of the width of carts used at the beginning of the 19th century. It is also much narrower than gauges of rail systems built later.

2. This had an impact on the development of the union movement in Britain. Miners tended to live in single-industry villages where other sources of employment were limited. The closeness of family and village ties to occupation gave the mining union a very different outlook as compared with unions in other industries.

3. In fact, the 19th century Classical school completely overlooked two of the most significant phenomena of the century—the movement of large amounts of money capital and people across national borders. The Classical theory of international trade is a theory of the movement of *goods*, which are presumed to be a proxy for the movement of economic resources.

4. The most notorious of these rotten boroughs was Old Salem, which had been depopulated so severely that only six people were qualified to vote and elect a representative. As there was no secret ballot, it was an easy matter in such places for the local landowner to bribe the few voters so that they would elect a representative favorable to the landowner's interests.

5. Robert Peel reformed the Penal Code, and also established London's Metropolitan Police Force. Ever since, English policemen have been known as "bobbies" in his honor.

6. In Scotland, however, parish schools had existed since the mid 17th century, so larger numbers of working class children did receive an elementary school education there.

7. That physical differences are a mark of social status had long been known. For example, in children's fairy stories, princes are always tall (and handsome).

Key Concepts

Capital deepening
Capital good

Factory Act
Free trade

Capital mobilization
Capital widening
Commercial policy
Corn Laws
Export of industrialization

Invisible export
Laissez faire
Most Favored Nation
Terms of trade
Truck system

Questions for Discussion or Essay Writing

1. The 19th century in Britain was characterized by contradictions. What were these contradictions and how were they handled and/or resolved?

2. Why was railroad construction so important in the 19th century?

3. Why weren't the railroads built in the 18th century?

4. What was the impact of new technology in the 19th century?

5. How can "industrialization" be "exported"?

6. What was the Corn Law controversy, and why was it important?

7. If laissez faire was so important a principle, why were legislative measures to change social conditions made?

8. Did workers' standard of living improve as a result of industrialization?

9. Discuss the impact of urbanization on society in the 19th century.

For Further Reading

(and refer also to Chapter 10's readings)

Cameron, Rondo. "A New View of European Industrialization." *Economic History Review*, XXXVII:1 (1983): 1-23.

Chambers, J.D. *The Workshop of the World: British Economic History 1820–1880.*

Clapham, John H. *An Economic History of Britain.* (3 volumes). London: Cambridge University Press, 1926–1938.

Evans, Richard J. "Epidemics and Revolutions: Cholera in Nineteenth Century Europe." *Past and Present,* vol.120 (August 1988).

Fieldhouse, David K. *The Colonial Empires.* New York: Delacorte Press, 1967.

Gourvish, T.R. *Railways and the British Economy 1830–1914.* London: MacMillan, 1980.

Habakkuk. H. J. *American and British Technology in the 19th Century.* Cambridge: Cambridge University Press, 1962.

Hammond, J.L. and B. *The Rise of Modern Industry.* New York: Harcourt Brace, 1937.

Horrell, Sara and Jane Humphries. "Old Questions, New Data, and Alternative Perspectives: Families' Living Standards in the Industrial Revolution." *Journal of Economic History*, 52:4 (December 1992): 849-880.

Hudson, Pat and W.R. Lee, eds. *Women's Work and the Family Economy in Historical Perspective*. Manchester: Manchester University Press, 1990.

Humphries, Jane."Enclosures, Common Rights, and Women: The Proletarianization of Families in the Late Eighteenth and Early Nineteenth Centuries." *Journal of Economic History*, L:1 (March 1990): 17-42.

――――――――――― " '...The Most Free From Objection...' The Sexual Division of Labor and Women's Work in Nineteenth Century England." *Journal of Economic History*, XLVII:4 (December 1987): 929-950.

Jenks, Leland H. *The Migration of British Capital to 1875*. New York: Barnes & Noble, 1971.

Levine, David. "Industrialization and the Proletarian Family in England." *Past and Present*, vol. 107, May 1985, pp.168-203.

Lindert, Peter H. and Jeffrey G. Williamson. "English Workers' Living Standards During the Industrial Revolution: A New Look." *Economic History Review*, XXXVI:1 (1982): 1-25.

Mokyr, Joel. Demand and Supply in the Industrial Revolution. *Journal of Economic History* (December 1977): 981–1008.

Nye, John Vincent. "The Myth of Free Trade: Britain and Fortress France: Tariffs and Trade in the Nineteenth Century. " *Journal of Economic History*, 51:1 (March 1991): 23-46.

Platt, D.C. *Finance, Trade and Politics in British Foreign Policy, 1815–1914*.

Polanyi, Karl. *The Great Transformation*. New York: Rinehart, 1944.

Robinson, Eric and Albert E. Musson. *James Watt and the Steam Revolution: A Documentary History*. New York: A.M. Kelley, 1969.

Tann, J. and M.J. Breckin. "The International Diffusion of the Watt Engine, 1775–1820." *Economic History Review*, XXXI:4 (1977): 541-564.

Taylor, Arthur J. *Laissez-faire and State Intervention in Nineteenth Century Britain*. London: Macmillan, 1972.

Taylor, Philip A.M., ed. *The Industrial Revolution in Britian: Triumph or Disaster?* Lexington, Mass: D.C. Heath, (1958) 1969.

Thompson, E.P. "Patrician Society, Plebeian Culture." *Journal of Social History (Summer 1974)*.

Toynbee, Arnold. *Toynbee's Industrial Revolution*. (reprint of 1884 first edition). Newton Abbott: David & Charles (Publishers), 1969.

Williamson, Jeffrey. "Migrant Earnings in Britain's Cities in 1851: Testing Competing Views of Urban Labor Market Absorption." *Journal of European Economic History*, 19:1 (Spring 1990): 163–190.

Chapter 12

Industrialization in France

AS WE MOVE ON TO CONSIDER THE PROGRESS of the Industrial Revolution in other countries, we will see that the pattern was different in each. Obviously, many elements were the same, such as the harnessing of steam power and the building up of heavy industry. But it is the differences that the economic historian finds interesting. How can these be explained?

France's industrialization was slow. In fact, it is difficult to pinpoint a period in which "revolutionary" structural change took place. While Britain's industrialization also took time, this can be explained by the fact that she was the first. Then other countries could avoid making mistakes and industrialize much faster. But France did not. Germany, for example, accomplished more in the forty years following 1870 than France did in the hundred years after the end of the Revolution. This cannot be explained by the role of the State. In both France and Germany, the State played a crucial and active role in economic development in general and in industrial development in particular—a contrast to the dominance of laissez faire in Britain.

France and Germany Compared

France and Germany are frequently compared, because they effectively reversed places in the balance of economic and military power in Europe. At the end of the 18th century, France was Europe's most populous, wealthy, and militarily strong nation. Napoleon's armies had just swept across Europe to inflict crushing defeats on both Austria and Prussia and were defeated only by a combined effort of European (including British) armies. But barely seventy years later France was defeated by Prussia-Germany, and was again subjected to defeat by German forces in 1914 and in 1940. This reversal of roles owes much to the slower growth of economic strength in France. (A word of caution is advisable here. This economic weakness was relative, not absolute, as on the eve of the First World War, France was one of the handful of advanced industrial economies, along with Britain, Germany, and the United States.)

Slow development has been attributed to many causes affecting France either uniquely or more strongly than other countries. Among these influences, to be discussed at length in this chapter, were the nature of the natural resource endowment; the persistence of peasant farming, which delayed the development of a free labor force; the continuing impact of mercantilist policies in the form of tariff barriers; and the slow development of a transportation and communications network, necessary for a coherent, unified domestic market. All these forces had some role to play, and none can be singled out as the *only* explanation.

France and Britain Compared

It is important to evaluate these influences, because at the beginning of the 18th century, France's potential for capitalist industrialization was at least as good as Britain's. Even where she had no observable advantages, there was potential for overcoming difficulties. Capitalist development had a long history in France, with the end of feudalism, political centralization, and mercantilist encouragement to industry and trade all occurring at about the same time as in Britain.

However, this industrial tradition affected only a few areas until well after the mid 19th century. Even in 1896, 45 percent of the economically active population was still in agriculture, and the introduction of large-scale, factory-organized enterprises was very slow. In Britain, the putting out system gave way to factories in the 18th century. In France, because small-scale agriculture remained important, part-time industrial employment was common, and both industry and agriculture tended to be small-scale.

France was more populous than Britain. At the beginning of the 19th century, Britain's population was less than half France's 24 million, which implied a potentially larger home market for France. With large amounts of fertile agricultural land available, France did not depend on food imports. France had adequate supplies of the coal and iron ore needed for 19th century industrialization; less than Germany or Great Britain but more than, for example, Holland, Italy, or Spain. Both countries also had colonial empires, although France lost many of her colonies before the end of the 19th century, while Britain gained more territory (with the important exception of the loss of her American colonies).

On the less positive side, France did not develop a strong shipping industry. Although France has a long coastline, there are few good ports, which are not conveniently located near major industrial regions. This fact, plus the loss of colonial trade, reduced both shipping and the cluster of shipbuilding and servicing industries associated with a merchant marine.

On the other hand, political centralization and the development of an efficient administration was an advantage. Economically, this spilled over into much state support for industry, whether directly as in the establishment of state-built factories, or indirectly through the building of infrastructure, the encouragement of scientific endeavors,[1] or the protection given to domestic manufacturers. France's reputation in engineering and science remained high; for example, Tresaguet's method of road building influenced Macadam in Britain, though ideas were not always applied. Talent, therefore, was not lacking.

Infrastructure

Social overhead capital such as roads, bridges and harbors

So why did large-scale modern industries appear so slowly in France? The basic ingredients, including a commitment to capitalist money making, availability of labor and resources in general, and a generally favorable environment did exist. But somehow, fitting these different pieces together simply took longer. It is often tempting to indulge in national stereotyping to explain what did or did not happen. Thus, a love of beauty, commitment to high artistic standards, and quality workmanship, and an intense individualism are frequently used to explain Frenchmen's reluctance to subject themselves to the indignities of factory life. (These indignities were apparently not important for the French women and children, who, like their English equivalents, formed so large a part of the early factory work force.) But any form of stereotyping is dangerous, especially in this case, as the qualities often ascribed to "the" French could be shown only by a tiny minority of the population—those with wealth sufficient to acquire the finer thing in life. The mass of French workers probably did not experience all the hardships of the English factory worker. There were proportionately fewer of them, and by the time factories were common, most of the worst abuses were no longer present. But there were still vast differences in living standards between the workers and the rich. (Improvements for most of the population up to the mid 19th century have been described as an improvement from misery to subsistence.)

Probably the greatest single drawback to French industrialization was lack of an effective transportation system. While France was politically unified, the country's size and geographic diversity encouraged regional and local differences, which in turn implied that small-scale units were appropriate for economic activity. Even in 1835, it is estimated that of the 173 million tons of merchandise produced or imported in France, 127 million tons were consumed at the place of production or importation, with the rest being consumed within a relatively short distance.

Building the rail network—as in all other countries except Britain—effectively *preceded* the spread of a modern capitalist economy in France. When this was in place, all the other drawbacks, which were linked to transportation in one way or another, gradually became less important in retarding economic growth.

France in the 18th Century

In the 18th century, three features characterized the French economy and continued to do so until the 1840s (refer back to Chapter 9). First, agriculture predominated, occupying most of the labor force either full-time or part-time. The basic concern was to grow enough food, so cereal crops were common and there was practically no permanent pasture. The problem with an economy so dependent on food production was that harvest failures caused periodic crises. This was further accentuated by the lack of good transportation, so failure in one part of the country could not be

offset by movements of food from one region or from abroad.

The second feature was the inadequate transportation network. While France has many rivers, most were unsuitable for regular, waterborne transportation because of fluctuations of water levels, sandbars, and other natural hazards. Roads rarely provided an adequate substitute, so transportation was slow and costly, reinforcing the local orientation in both agriculture and industry. Craft guilds persisted in the towns, although in 1762 a law was passed giving rural artisans the right to make cloth outside guild regulations, stimulating domestic industry. (Guilds were not abolished until 1789.) Only goods of high value, such as silks, fine wines, and some fine woolens, had a national or international market, because their high unit value could more easily absorb high transportation costs. This is the same pattern as medieval trading, where high-value, low-weight items were important.

The third feature was that textile manufacturing predominated and was the most important industrial activity. However, it was mostly oriented to meeting local needs and was based on processing locally available supplies of wool, flax, or silk, using the putting out system of domestic manufacturing. This fitted in well with peasant farming by permitting the use of part-time family labor. However, although demand for textiles increased, as it did for English textile manufacturers, production was expanded by extending traditional methods to more people rather than by following the British route of technical innovation, the use of steam power, and the movement to large-scale factory production.

Most manufacturing was capitalist in the sense that it was organized by a merchant capitalist or mastercraftsman in order to produce for sale in a market and make a profit. Thus, although industry was small scale, and although peasant farming predominated, it was a money economy; peasants had to grow cash crops or work in the putting out system in order to pay the many taxes imposed on them. But there was little incentive to alter production methods in either sector so long as it produced a living. For so long as labor was available at low cost—and peasants frequently accepted lower wages than full-time workers because industrial labor was not their primary occupation—and for so long as foreign competition was minimal, producers felt little pressure to change. Even if the incentive was there, a problem with raising the financing necessary to adopt mechanized techniques existed.

Limited Finance Capital

Because industry was small-scale, finance capital was limited. In fact, industrial expansion in France tended to occur in periods of rising prices and profits, because profits of these small units effectively determined the amount of funds available for expansion. Thus, from 1732 on, rising prices and profits did encourage expansion, but expansion of capacity rarely increased faster than demand. The period 1817-1851, on the other hand, was deflationary, and while mechanization in some areas offset the fall in profits, this period was characterized by a continuation of older methods. Between 1851 and 1873, profits rose faster than prices, and this period is associated with the introduction of new techniques on a larger scale than before.

Outside funds were rarely available before the 19th century, being more attracted to the purchase of government debt or shares in trading companies or tax farming.[2] So, as expansion funds depended on the profits of small enterprises, it is hardly surprising that significant large-scale enterprises were rare. This helps explain why, in the late 18th century but more especially in the 19th, the government took a more active role in encouraging economic development, especially when large-scale enterprises needing large amounts of capital were concerned. Such a role involved not only direct financing, as in the case of the railways, but also improving the mechanisms for mobilizing capital. The problem in France was not so much capital scarcity as capital immobility: Funds were retained within small firms, hoarded to buy land, or used for state loans or luxury consumption, so it was important to increase their availability for industrial uses.

Government Involvement

The government also attempted stimulative measures. For example, where English inventions were known, it tried to encourage their use by granting various privileges to the adopters. Because capital was inadequate and entrepreneurs had limited horizons, private enterprise could not accomplish the task alone, unlike the situation in Britain. State help was most obvious with industries supplying military needs. Thus the iron industry, including foundries and arms factories, and shipbuilding were encouraged, as were industries earning foreign exchange through exports, and Colbert's policy of promoting the cloth, silk, and carpet industries was revived in the period 1740-1780. The government was also active in improving infrastructure, but in the 18th century its impact was limited. Only the coming of the railways would effect a transportation revolution of the size and extent necessary to overcome France's other problems.

In the 18th century, infrastructure improvement focused on roads, bridges, and canals. The best roads were those connecting Paris with the frontiers of the country and the major towns, chiefly in the north and northeast. But "best" is relative, as they were poorly maintained. An attempt to improve them was made in 1738 by extending the *corvée* (the old feudal obligation to perform road work) to thirty days a year for all those who did not live in a town. Although an

---

Tax Farming

System when the right to collect taxes is subcontracted to private individuals who can keep any excess over the contracted-for amount

attempt to overcome a financial constraint, it proved to be both inefficient and obviously unjust. It was inefficient because the unwilling workers required a lot of supervision, and it was unjust because the requirement applied only to peasants, reducing the time they could work in the fields. In 1776 a scheme whereby communities could replace the *corvée* with a tax to provide revenues to pay for the work if they wished was introduced, but this was still unfair, as the privileged classes were exempt from both the tax and the *corvée*— the peasants ended up with the burden in either situation. (The *corvée* was finally replaced by an involuntary tax in 1787, but again the burden fell on peasants.) However, expenditures on road work steadily increased and more were constructed or improved. The result was an improved but still far from ideal situation, even though developing an efficient infrastructure was important.

The final role of the government lay in its commercial policy. In keeping with the spirit of French mercantilism, the aim of policy throughout the 18th century was economic self-sufficiency. French agricultural and industrial producers were protected from foreign competition with a system of high tariffs on imports and in some cases, prohibitions on imports. There was an attempt to liberalize this policy in 1786 with

---

Tariff

Tax on an imported good

---

the signing of a commercial agreement with Britain, but the outbreak of war with Britain in 1793 ended the attempt. However, French commitment to liberalization was weak, and 19th century policy was very much a continuation of 18th century policy, with some exceptions.

France in 1815

Although usually seen in purely political terms, economic causes involving the repression of peasants under the Ancien Régime of absolute monarchy were important in explaining the timing of the French Revolution in 1789 (refer back to Chapter 9). While the Revolution produced a major political transformation in France—from absolute monarchy to republic—it did not have a similar drastic impact on economic development. The structural transformation of the French economy did not become noticeable until the 1840s. The Revolution and the succeeding European wars weakened the French economy and delayed its industrial modernization, partly due to France's isolation from Britain at a crucial stage of technological development. Probably the most significant impact of the Revolution were reforms that had both political and economic consequences.

Effect of the Napoleonic Wars

The economy declined, as would be expected in any area suffering civil strife, and both agricultural and industrial output fell. Only the iron, engineering, and textile industries gained because of increased military demand. In addition, French conquest of much of Europe provided the textile industry with a larger, protected market, free from competition with British textiles. However, although output expanded, it did so using existing techniques. The extent of technological innovation was low but not entirely absent. For example, the process of extracting sugar from sugar beet was further refined at this time to fill the gap left by the British blockade of France which eliminated sugar cane imports. There were also some advances in the chemical industry. The cutoff of Spanish soda supplies led to the development of a process by which soda (a widely used industrial alkali) could be made from sea salt. Because the blockade resulted in a significant loss of trade, those ports and industries associated with trade consequently declined.

Napoleon Bonaparte's acquisition of power and the intensification of war with Britain led to

Figure 12.1 Wine produced in vineyards such as these have been an important export from France. This photo shows the Château du Clos-de-Vougeot (Côte d'Or), which was built in the Renaissance period, and owned by the abbey of Cîteau from the 12th century to the French Revolution. (Courtesy of the French Government Tourist Office)

an application of economic warfare that effectively extended already existing protectionist policies. Napoleon, although motivated by the desire to make France the unquestioned leader of Europe, seriously miscalculated the impact of the Continental System—on both Britain and the rest of Europe. The common perception of Britain as "a nation of shopkeepers" mistook appearances for reality. Napoleon thought that by closing markets to British goods, he could eliminate sales. If European sales disappeared, then Britain would be brought to its knees and forced to submit to French domination. The miscalculation occurred because British goods were widely sold in European markets because of the strength of British industrial *production*, and British reaction to the closing of some markets was to find new ones. As it turned out, the impact on the British economy was less than Napoleon had anticipated, while the impact on the French economy was generally unfavorable. In addition, the system was not complete. There were numerous loopholes; smug-

gling increased—always to be expected when high tariffs existed; and enforcement was frequently slack, partly because the French navy was unable to enforce it.

Continental System

In summary, the Continental System was influenced more by 18th century capitalism in which merchants and the exchange function were dominant than by the emerging reality, the increasing importance of capitalist industrial production. The System did affect Britain, especially by reducing imports and exports. But by this time, the resilience of the economy demonstrated that the economic changes that had transformed the British economy were irreversible. (It is tempting to

Continental System

Economic warfare when France excluded British ships from European ports under French control

speculate about the impact had Napoleon's policy been used one hundred years earlier.)

The specifics of the Continental System, imposed in 1806, were as follows. Importing British goods into France or territories under French control (chiefly the Low Countries, northern Italy, and parts of Germany and Switzerland) was completely banned, and these were areas that had accounted for one third of all exports of British manufactured goods. The policy was enforced by closing the ports of North Germany (which was not directly under French control) as well as France and the Low Countries to British ships.

Britain responded by blockading the entire coast of Europe, preventing, where possible, the entry or exit of all ships to European ports. This had three important implications. First, given the size and superiority of the Royal Navy, the British blockade was more successful than the French action. Second, the continental countries found that their imports from other countries, especially colonial ones, dried up, because Britain was preeminent in overseas trading and two thirds of all reexports passing through British ports normally went to mainland Europe. There were shortages of such important goods as cane sugar (hence the incentive to refine sugar from sugar beets) and raw cotton. Cotton could be imported into France from the Levant, but its supply was irregular, insufficient, and costly. Third, because cotton from the United States was also denied its market in Europe, the new United States retaliated by closing its ports to British ships.

The effect on Britain, however, was not what Napoleon had intended. New markets for manufactured goods opened up, especially in Latin America; the volume of illegal trade increased; and industrial development continued, especially in those industries connected with military supplies. Agricultural output also increased. While inflation picked up steam after 1809 and hardships existed, the British economy was not brought to its knees as Napoleon had hoped.

The effect on Europe was mixed, neither completely devastating nor encouraging. Trade and industries associated with trade felt the worst impact. Port cities declined, especially the North Sea ports, and the Dutch colonial and carrying trade was almost completely lost. Many military and merchant ships were lost through capture or destruction, but there was no revival of shipbuilding, and industries making sailcloth, ropes, barrels, and other items necessary for trading also collapsed. Overseas markets in colonial areas and the Middle East, which had been gained in the 18th century, disappeared. France lost her colony of Santo Domingo (modern Haiti) entirely.

Some industries gained. The Continental System created a huge protected market for French industries in Europe, and France turned her attention away from oceanic trade. But in general, the expansion was only temporary. Expanding industries did not introduce modern methods, and after the war, British goods once again entered the country. Only the cotton industry of Alsace expanded due to the increase in military orders and rising sales to central Europe, while the cotton industry of Ghent, and later Paris, declined. They had relied more on American cotton and were less able than Alsace to acquire alternative supplies. Any industry meeting military needs did well, although as many of them were in Belgium or Germany, they did not remain under French control for long.

While protection resulted in large profits for industrialists, it also retarded innovation, because the incentive to adapt did not exist when there was no possibility of competition with foreign producers. And also because knowledge of what was happening in Britain was nonexistent for a significant number of years, there was even a lack of information about new technology, which contributed to France's delayed structural transformation.

In 1815, after the defeat of Napoleon, France's situation did not particularly encourage change. Roads and bridges had been destroyed and would have to be rebuilt if private industry was to flourish; the loss of a protected market, in addition to the loss of overseas markets during the war, could not be completely recovered; and many of the regions that had been acquired were now potential competitors to France. However, the economy was not totally devastated, and some reforms instituted by the Revolutionary Government and Napoleon cleared the way for continued progress.

End of Feudalism and Other Reforms

First, feudalism was formally ended between 1789 and 1791, and peasants gained title to their lands. This was a permanent gain, although it encouraged small-scale peasant farming that delayed large-scale industrialization along English lines. Second, the administrative system was revamped. The old system of provinces was replaced by a division of the country into eighty-three departments. Originally intended to introduce a more decentralized form of local self-government, their administration was later taken over by prefects acting on behalf of Napoleon's central government in Paris, effectively increasing centralized control. However, economically this system made it easier to introduce and develop an effective transportation and communications network; the initiative for infrastructure development in France had always been in the hands of public, not private, authority. In fact, transportation planning increased under Napoleon. The major links between cities were both built and maintained by the central government, with secondary roads the responsibility of the departments. This division of authority continued throughout the 19th century.

Third, law reform was a major achievement of Napoleon's regime. In the Code Napoleon, five legal codes (civil, civil procedure, commercial, criminal, and penal) replaced all old laws. Its economic impact was to reaffirm commitment to the virtue of private property, so the rights of all property owners were guaranteed. The only ex-

ceptions were for expropriation if it was thought to be in the interests of the State.

While there were no longer any barriers preventing anyone entering any trade or occupation, employers gained more than employees. As in England, workers' associations were prohibited, and collective bargaining and strikes were banned. In addition, but unlike the case in England, all employees had to carry an identity card (*livret*), which contained a summary of the person's work record and previous employers. It was universally resented by employees, but it was very effective in keeping control over workers while enterprises were small-scale. However, even before its abolition, it became less burdensome when large factories replaced personal contact between employer and employee with impersonality, making it easier to ignore or adapt *livret* information.

Livret

identity card carried by French employees

With respect to financial affairs, the fourth development was ambiguous. The Revolution's National Assembly abolished all remaining internal tariffs and tolls, which was good for industry by effectively creating an internal customs union in France. It also tried to ease the tax burden on peasants by extending taxes to all citizens and abolishing excise taxes on goods such as wine, salt, and tobacco. In 1795, only 13 percent of government revenues resulted from tax collections. Lost revenues were made up for by issuing paper money and selling estates confiscated from royalist supporters, but this was only a temporary solution to the problem of government finances.

Under Napoleon, military expenses were covered by requiring payments from conquered territories; for other expenditures, taxes were raised. Local finances were also reorganized (effectively reduced), but this backfired: Public employees such as schoolteachers were paid minimal salaries, and schools remained half empty, while public hospitals were chronically short-staffed.

However, Napoleon did recognize the importance of a good financial system, although France remained less sophisticated in this respect than Britain. Thus in 1800, the Bank of France was established as the Treasury's banker, responsible for paying dividends to holders of government debt. Later in 1803, the bank also got the monopoly of bank note issue in Paris, and in the same year, provincial joint stock banks under government control were permitted. Nine banks were established, operating independently until 1848 when they were absorbed into the Bank of France, creating a nationwide central banking network.

A final reform was also made during the Revolution. France had inherited a medieval system of weights and measures that limited trade, as different areas had their own standards. In an attempt to bring order and thus encourage industrial development and trade, the metric system of weights and measures was adopted in 1795, becoming the only standard in 1840. Coinage also went metric in 1795 when the currency system was reformed—a trend that was eventually followed by every other country in Europe.

None of these reforms directly encouraged economic transformation. But like any other infrastructure development, they helped indirectly by establishing favorable conditions to encourage industrial capitalism.

19th Century Industrial Development

Once France had recovered from years of war and the traumas of political change, what was her situation with respect to economic development in the 19th century? To answer this, it is helpful to describe the economic resources available and then evaluate some of the factors peculiar to France's situation. As a result, it will then be easier

to understand the reasons for France's slower industrialization and assess the contribution that was made. In addition, it is advisable to remember that while France developed slowly, industrialization did occur; at the end of the 19th century, France was one of only a handful of advanced industrial countries.

The first element in 19th century industrialization involved a relative and absolute shift away from agricultural occupations into manufacturing, as increased productivity in agriculture permitted urban expansion and manufacturing. But while France had a large population, albeit growing at a slower rate than her industrial competitors, and thus had an adequate supply of labor in general, the growth of the industrial labor force was slow.

Persistence of Peasant Farming

There are two reasons for this slow growth. On the one hand, as already noted, there was no enclosure movement in France, and instead, peasants' ties to the land were strengthened. In addition, as agriculture was generally prosperous in the first half of the 19th century, agriculture continued to be viable; there were few "push" factors encouraging a basically rural work force to be anything other than farmers. And on the other hand, even as factories spread, the domestic system of manufacturing remained important. By midcentury, only about one quarter of all industrial workers were in large establishments, and most of the rest combined industrial work with farming. Even in 1870, traditional industries, most of which were small-scale, still accounted for 85 percent of France's gross output.

This had several important implications. First, the new industrial labor force included a large number of women and children (up to 20 percent of the factory workers in the most industrialized departments were children), as in every other country in the early stages of industrialization. Second, this labor force was largely unskilled,

Why weren't more irrigation projects initiated in France before the French Revolution?

Economic growth depends on many contributing factors including market considerations, technological development, and institutional change. Even if conditions seem to be right for an economic breakthrough, the absence of supportive institutions can delay it. A good illustration existed in France, where the contribution of the French Revolution to economic development has been discussed extensively by economic historians. Its contribution lies not in the acceleration of technological change, but in improving the institutional climate for entrepreneurial activity.

A case in point concerns the construction of irrigation canals in Provence, the focus of a study by Jean-Laurent Rosenthal ("The Development of Irrigation in Provence, 1700–1860: The French Revolution and Economic Growth", *Journal of Economic History*. L:3, (September 1990) 615-638. Rosenthal presents both quantitative and qualitative evidence to show that although irrigation would have been beneficial, the canals were not built, and suggests that the explanation lies in the division of authority over rights of way. If political jurisdiction is fragmented, then it is likely that this fragmentation also had a delaying effect on other proposed investment projects. After the Revolution, institutional reforms resulted in much more consistency and certainty regarding regional authority, hence the transactions costs associated with investment projects fell. This was certainly true for irrigation projects.

Canals can be built to provide water to towns, for transportation, or for irrigation. The author is concerned solely with irrigation canals in Provence, an arid region where irrigation can have a demonstrable effect in raising yields. He

estimates that total factor productivity per acre would have risen at least 30 to 40 percent as a result of irrigation. This measure takes account of the fact that more labor and capital were applied to irrigated land than to dry land, and also results from the fact that irrigation removes the need for letting land lie fallow. He also calculates that for the region as a whole, if the canals that were planned before 1789 but not built until after had been in place, total regional output would have increased by at least 7 percent, enough to alleviate the recurring problem of food shortage.

In order to estimate the profitability of canals, it is necessary to get information on the prices of inputs and outputs of canal construction, factor shares, and interest rates, which are not readily available. However, with what information is available, Rosenthal estimates that the social return to building a canal (the increase in the price of irrigated land) was positive. All proposed projects were profitable, but they would have been more profitable before 1750, when they were not carried out, than after 1820, when they were. Because the hypothetical profits of the pre-Revolution canals are similar to those realized by projects built after 1820, he discounts the role of technological change. If there had been more technological change, then later projects should have been more profitable.

The proposed canals therefore would have been advantageous; promoters were ready to go ahead, and there is no evidence to suggest that a shortage of financing—from a variety of sources—was the cause for them not being built. As the area of irrigated land expanded by 16
(Problem continues on next page)

(Problem continued from previous page)

percent of what was actually planned to be irrigated, what explains the shortfall?

Rosenthal emphasizes the fragmentation of authority over rights of eminent domain. It is difficult to test this, but investigation of the experience of five 18th century canals shows that the more boundaries they crossed, the more difficult they were to build. If canals were entirely within the estate of the principal landowner, then the benefits could be internalized. But the more areas the canal passed through, the higher the institutional costs—associated with towns and villages demanding payments for permitting rights of way, refusing it entirely thus forcing costly detours, or siphoning off profits by using the water free.

After the Revolution, institutional reform cut these costs by effectively consolidating all powers of eminent domain in the hands of the central government and by eliminating the old organizations and institutions that had previously prevented reform. In addition, there was active state support in the form of engineering advice and administrative oversight. Hence, one can conclude that the French Revolution was a turning point in French economic development because of its impact on institutional change.

which had two feedback effects. One was that for so long as enough unskilled labor was available, there was little incentive to train more highly skilled workers, further encouraging the perpetuation of old methods. The other effect was that where skills were required, for example, in areas where new technologies were being adopted, foreign workers were used, at least in the short run. The first railways were operated using English mechanics and engineers, many of the new developments in metallurgy were introduced using British skills, and even some of the textile establishments required foreign operatives when power spindles or looms were first used. Foreign labor was usually used only for short periods, as once French workers were trained, there was no further need for imported skills.

The third implication was that workers' continuing agricultural connections kept wages down. Both real and nominal wages were either stationary or declining until about 1850, when they began to improve. There was also, as in England, a hierarchy of wages. For example, in the prosperous year of 1836, the average daily wage was two francs for men, one franc for women and .45–.75 franc for children, although skilled workers earned considerably more. (As a point of reference, only those citizens paying more than 200 francs a year in direct taxes could vote at this time, a requirement effectively disenfranchising the mass of French peasants and workers.) However, although wages were low, labor costs per unit of output were higher than in Britain because of low productivity due to the slow introduction of modern methods. French manufacturers found it very hard to compete on price both in France itself and in third markets. Sometimes competition was met by cutting wages and prices, not by introducing new, more productive techniques, or it was simply avoided altogether by retreating behind a tariff barrier. Later in the century, wages and working conditions did improve. As modern factories with a large initial capitalization became more common, so industrial capitalists realized the advantages of a more skilled work force in utilizing this equipment.

And fourth, connected with the issue of both labor costs and population size, domestic demand for the output of modern industry did not expand very significantly. On the one hand, relatively slow population growth provided limits to this expansion and was not compensated for by a growth of export markets. And on the other hand, continued low wages plus a continuing inequity in income distribution retarded the development of a true mass market for French industry, further limiting the incentive to adopt high-speed, mass production techniques. Those areas in which French manufacturing excelled remained those where high quality was important, such as carpets or glassware, and it was Paris that became the center of *haute couture* in the mid 19th century, not London.

Attitudes Toward Labor

The general attitude toward labor throughout most of the 19th century was one of laissez faire, one of the few areas where laissez faire ideas were in force. There was little reaction to the reality of low wages because poverty had always existed. Long working hours persisted, and only in the 1840s were they reduced to an average 12-13 hours. Little was done about child labor or generally poor working conditions, even though discontent among both rural and urban workers was a severe problem contributing to the revolutions France experienced in the 19th century.

French laws designed to prevent the growth of labor unions were more strictly enforced than British ones, and a trade union movement like that developing in Britain consequently did not exist. All the three major classifications of workers—artisans in small workshops, rural outworkers, and factory operatives—found causes for grievances, although the nature of the grievance often differed. For example, the artisans, facing intense competition from factory-produced output, were antimachine, while machine operatives objected to the harsh discipline of the factory. But all were opposed to the generally poor conditions faced by the working classes: poverty, poor housing conditions in some urban areas (although the slow expansion of urban industry implied that conditions were not as universally bad and as widespread as in the new English factory towns), and generally low living conditions. In some in-

dustrial areas, they were so bad that half the army's conscripts failed to meet minimal physical standards.

However, although unions *per se* were illegal, mutual aid friendly societies incorporating functions more commonly associated with unions did emerge. Working class sentiment that was both republican and socialist also appeared, especially during the reign of Louis Philippe (1830-1848). France in fact developed a wide variety of different socialist viewpoints to include the philosophical writings of Saint Simon, the communes suggested by Fourier, Proudhon's anarchism, and Louis Blanc's industrial cooperative societies,

---

Anarchism
Political philosophy advocating the replacement of government by voluntary groups

---

which would all be increasingly influential later.

Most employers, however, in the first half of the 19th century were simply indifferent to the workers' plight, and they were supported by Louis Philippe's increasingly repressive policies. As a result, there was only a limited attempt at social reform: the 1841 Factory Law, which prohibited employment of children under eight and limited the working hours of those under sixteen. But it applied only to establishments with either twenty or more employees or those using steam power, and there were no enforcement provisions, so it had no practical effect at all.

Worsening economic conditions were partly responsible for the revolution of 1848 which overthrew Louis Philippe and led to the establishment of the Second Republic. While the new government—a mixture of middle class liberals, Republicans, and Socialists—did attempt some reforms, nothing much of a permanent nature occurred until Louis Napoleon (Napoleon Bonaparte's nephew) became president. He was interested in social problems, unlike preceding French rulers, and pushed through the Apprentice Law in 1851. This law limited children's working hours and made provisions for education, but like many other laws was not enforced.

This early interest also evaporated. While the French economy generally boomed in the 1850s, workers did not share in this prosperity as wage increases lagged behind price increases. The situation worsened in the 1860s and continuing discontent led to more strikes and riots, which were always firmly put down. This was one ingredient that led to the violence accompanying the rise and fall of the Paris Commune in 1871, after French armies had been defeated in the Franco-Prussian War.

This unsatisfactory condition lasted until the 1880s, when, in order to gain support of the workers, the government adopted a policy of conciliation. Thus, in 1884, *syndicats* (including unions) and other mutual aid associations were legalized. One result was an expansion of the union movement—by 1910, there were over 5,000 unions in France representing 977,000 members—and also a growth of farmers' cooperatives. In 1890, the hated identity card system was finally abolished, although it had become increasingly ineffective as a means of control over workers. More effective factory and mine legislation was passed, and there were also some social welfare provisions, although not on the same scale as those Bismarck introduced in Germany.

Syndicat

French labor union advocating workers' control over production

---

Natural Resources

The second major element in the resource endowment aspect of economic development is land, interpreted broadly here to include all naturally occurring resources. The natural resources most important to 19th century industrialization were coal and iron ore, necessary for mechanizing industry and utilizing steam power. While France had these resources, the adoption of modern methods was delayed by their location, quality, and cost.

For example, coal became widely used in England because of a lack of wood, but at the beginning of the 19th century, France faced no such pressure. Also, water power remained important, partly because of the high cost of coal. This meant that during the century, the use of coal tended to mirror the industrial development of France, rather than being the leading edge. Coal remained a high-cost energy source, due to a combination of factors such as inefficient mining techniques, the high cost of transportation, and high duties on imported coal (over one quarter of the coal used in France throughout the century was imported).

In the first half of the century, coal was mined from scattered deposits in the Central Highlands, where mining was a typically small-scale, higher-cost operation than in Britain. Inadequate transportation made coal even more expensive (coal in Paris was ten times as expensive as coal in Manchester) so there was little incentive to switch to its use. Unlike the situation in England, it was rare to find deposits of coal and iron ore in the same area, so given transportation problems, the development of the iron, steel, and engineering industries was limited. Three other factors are also important. Much French coal is not suitable for conversion into coke, so charcoal continued to be used for smelting iron ore. Ironically, the coming of the rail network gave a new lease on life to small iron producers because reduced transportation costs permitted them to compete. This advantage lasted until the 1860s, by which time the cost and quality advantages of pig iron produced using coke were increasingly apparent—it was at least one third cheaper. After this time, charcoal smelting rapidly disappeared; it accounted for 57 percent of the iron total in 1850 but only 8 percent in 1870 as larger, modernizing establishments produced iron using coke and consequently accounted for an increasing share of iron produced. In 1824, the ten largest establishments produced only 24 percent of the iron, but by 1860, they produced 53 percent, a further illustration of the decline in importance of smaller units using traditional methods.

The second factor is that while western Europe's largest deposits of iron ore were found in Lorraine, this ore is phosphoric. Hence these deposits were untapped until the introduction of the Thomas-Gilchrist process for removing the phosphorous. But Lorraine was annexed by Germany in 1871—just when the new process was becoming adopted—so France lost this important advantage. (German producers, however, were quick to use it.)

The "Wrong" Tariff Structure

Finally, a third artificial factor also contributed to stifling the development of the major 19th century industries: government tariff policy. The situation was somewhat confused early in the century as different groups wanted different policies. Landowners with forests and ironmasters with access to wood supplies wanted high wood prices; ironmasters without access to wood wanted the reverse, but as they had no political power, they contented themselves with supporting tariffs—which everybody wanted. Thus the tariff of 1822 limited imports of iron smelted with coal (i.e., British iron) in order to keep up demand for French iron and so keep wood prices high. There were duties on imported coal, but coal continued to be imported because French output was never sufficient to meet all the demand. The tariff of 1818 limited the import of steam engines, which paid a duty of 30 percent compared with a duty of 15 percent on all other imported machines.

Joint Stock Company

A company whose ownership shares are transferable

The net result was that France never became a major producer of iron and steel. Although in the 1860s France was Europe's second largest producer of iron and steel, Germany's output expanded more rapidly; in 1913, Germany was Europe's largest steel producer with an annual output of 17 million tons, followed by Britain which produced 7.5 million tons and France with five million tons. (In 1914, the United States produced 23.5 million tons and was the world's largest steel producer.)

Problems with Capital Mobilization

The third general element in a capitalist industrialization process is capital. While capital in the production process is specific—capital equipment and buildings—the problems France encountered concerned the mobilization of money capital. That is, given the high cost of establishing new large-scale enterprises using modern technology, finding sufficient financing was a problem. Capital formation proceeded more slowly in France than elsewhere. Capital equipment per employed worker remained at levels below those in Britain or the United States, so relative productivity levels were lower. In addition, because of the late start of industrialization, the problem was intensified because the newest plants using the latest technology were larger, thus needing a larger initial capitalization. This made it impossible for small producers to finance large units out of their own retained earnings.

The problem was not absolute capital scarcity. As already noted, capital was probably adequate, but because some was sent abroad, some held for land purchases, and some used to acquire government bonds, what was available was not accessible to industrial capitalists. The solution lay in a better method of capital mobilization, that is, a larger number of more sophisticated financial institutions.

Also, historical experience had not been favorable to the development of the French capital market. In the past, tax farming and speculative bubbles had siphoned off available funds from productive uses and prevented the development of supportive institutions. The collapse of the Mississippi Bubble (1720) discouraged the establishment of a central bank and joint stock companies and led to a suspicion of banks and paper money in general. Checks were not legally negotiable until 1869, which forced a greater reliance on domestic bills of exchange and bank notes as a means of payment, but required also the existence of a higher level of confidence in paper money which was slow to develop.

In the first half of the 19th century, a major achievement was the creation of a sound system of public credit that encouraged confidence in the government's ability to repay its debts. This was not easy, given the financial problems faced by the country after the war. Private institutions and markets were slower to develop.

Paris Bourse

For example, in 1816 the Bourse (the Paris stock exchange) was created to handle trading in government and private securities. It had sixty brokers, all of them approved by the government. But it remained very small and at first handled very few private securities. The reason was that it took a long time for the joint stock principle to become accepted, and companies organized on these lines were very rare before 1860. (For example, of the over 19,000 new companies founded in the decade 1840-1850, only 1 percent were joint stock companies.) The biggest boost to the acceptance of the joint stock principle came with the introduction of the railroad. On the one hand, railway companies required enormous amounts of finance capital, which stimulated activity in raising it domestically, although much came from overseas investors as well. And on the other hand, government involvement with the planning, construction, and operation of railways

added an element of security that was particularly appealing to the smaller investor.

While there was a small group of influential bankers and financiers in Paris—called the *haute banque*—most of them dealt with large-scale financing. Some specialized in loans to overseas governments or the placement of French government loans, and while they played a significant role in French railway capitalization, they did not tend to become involved in industry. In addition, there was a tendency for those joint stock companies that were established to issue only a few shares of high value, narrowing the pool of available financial resources that could be tapped.

In the rest of the country, the banks, like industrial establishments, tended to have a regional focus and in any event were more oriented toward commercial rather than industrial financing. In general, private banks and financiers were more active in railway finance and short-term loans to heavy industry, not in establishing new enterprises. But to a very large extent, financial institutions were simply reacting to the existing situation, which was not one of large demands for outside capital, and the prevalence of self-financing limited their role.

French Corporate Structure

Two developments helped remedy this. One, most effective in the railway industry, was active government participation that added a degree of security to investing by outsiders. The second was a change in the organization of companies themselves to make it easier to utilize funds: adopting the joint stock form of organization.

While true joint stock companies with transferable shares and limited liability were not very common in Britain in the 1820s, being limited mainly to public utilities, banks, and insurance companies, they did become widely used. In its purest form, such a corporation required authorization from the Crown or enabling legislation from Parliament, a costly and cumbersome process. However, the number of joint stock companies did increase.

It was much more difficult for a French company to adopt this form, as each request for authorization was handled individually. Any company requesting incorporation had to demonstrate its absence of debt, then three levels of investigation were made, with reports from each level being passed to the government official responsible for recommending action. Most requests were denied.

Interestingly enough, as a way around this procedure, many French companies revived the use of the medieval *commenda* form of organization, which in an adapted form neatly solved the problem of limiting investors' liability well before it became legal in Britain. Companies using this form—called *sociétés en commandité*—included sleeping partners who were liable only up to the extent of their initial investment, and they played no part in the active day-to-day management of the business. By the early 1840s, although an attempt had been made to forbid freely negotiable shares in such companies, they were fairly common. There was very little effective difference between *sociétés en commandité* and joint stock companies. Numerically, even though they were still subject to public suspicion, they outnumbered true joint stock companies, which were more common in transportation, insurance, and savings banks.

Société en Commandité
Business partnership with silent partners who have limited liability

---

Investment Banking

By the 1850s use of the corporate form was more frequent because it brought in outside financing. But it was still difficult for new or existing enterprises to acquire the financing they needed. In an attempt to overcome this problem, a significant change in French banking practice took place in

---

Sleeping Partner (Silent Partner)
Part-owner of an enterprise who provided finance but is not involved in day-to-day management

---

the 1850s. New banks were established to provide funds for industrial development—that is, provide long-term loans for new or expanding enterprises rather than only short-term loans for working capital purposes. This was a deliberate attempt to overcome the problem of capital mobilization that was limiting industrial development.

The idea was that these banks would raise capital mainly by selling shares to private investors, with the funds directed to the most promising borrowers. The first one was the Crédit Mobilier, founded in 1852 for the purpose of financing large industrial and public enterprises. It had a tremendous impact initially and was most successful in financing public projects, such as the rebuilding of Paris (a project planned by Louis Napoleon when he became emperor in 1852, which produced the architecturally coherent Paris of today) and public utilities, such as the Paris gas company and the Paris public transport company. But the company became overextended in the 1860s. Its assets were illiquid, and when the companies in which it had invested ran into problems, they reflected back onto Crédit Mobilier. Eventually it was reorganized as a deposit bank in 1867. But the basic idea of providing such long term financing remained influential.

Other industrial development banks included the Crédit Industriel et Commercial (1859) and the Crédit Lyonnaise (1863). Also the Crédit Foncier (1851), while originally established as a land mortgage bank providing low interest loans to landowners and farmers, subsequently entered the urban property market.

In summary, with respect to the basic factors of labor, natural resources, and capital, the French situation was not as favorable to industrial development as the British one, but gradual changes assisted this process. The basic problem was not so much resource scarcity as resource immobility, and in overcoming this problem, the development of an efficient transportation network was a tremendous help. However, at the same time that this more positive development was taking place, there were other issues that tended to have a dampening effect, thus overall, as the historical pattern shows, France industrialized, but at a slower pace.

Rail Network

In the 18th and early 19th centuries, much was done to improve roads and internal waterways, but not enough to produce an efficient transportation network to stimulate industrial development. So while Britain industrialized before the development of its rail network, this was possible only because the country was small and both inland water transportation and coastal shipping were more highly developed. France was larger, and there were gaps in its inland water network as well as problems in using the canals and rivers that did exist.

It soon became obvious that a rail network would stimulate development. It created both a direct demand for the products of the metals and engineering industries (demand from the railways accounted for about 10 percent of their total volume of orders until the end of the century), and also an indirect effect through cost reduction in all other industries. This would effectively expand the internal market and encourage mechanization. But in spite of this, construction was subject to many delays.

The first line was completed in 1827 using horses, not steam, for power. But other early private lines built mainly to transport freight and coal to canals were not very successful as profit making enterprises, and it was not until the 1830s that the importance of a *national* network was recognized. (The main lines were completed by the 1860s and smaller lines added later.)

Even then, the problem of financing remained. But because of the military significance of the network, as well as the old idea that government was responsible for initiating new public works and protecting the public interest, the State became involved in railway construction. Thus the French rail network was a compromise: partly private and partly public, which contrasted with the purely private lines built in Britain and the United States and state ownership in Belgium. While this participation caused delays in construction, there were advantages. There were fewer duplicative lines and failures than in countries relying on unplanned private enterprise, and the partnership was successful in bringing large amounts of previously untouchable funds into productive use.

So in 1833, the Legislature allocated funds to plan a rail network centered on Paris with connections to major ports, the country's borders, and the major industrial regions. The State provided the infrastructure. Central government paid for the land used for tracks and stations, plus one third of the cost of the track, bridges, tunnels, and so on, with local authorities paying for the other two thirds. Private companies were responsible for everything else—rails, stations, signals, rolling stock—and were given concessions for operating the trains. This initial division was subsequently revised, and the State ended up paying much more. It acquired shares in the companies, gave them loans and subsidies, and subsequently extended the length of the operating concessions although retaining some control over fares.

This took time. The first Paris line was not completed until 1837, and even in 1842, only 885 km of lines had been built, compared with 3,600 km in Great Britain and 2,800 km in Germany. But the pace speeded up in the 1840s. The years 1842-1846 were prosperous ones for business in general, and completed rail lines proved to be highly profitable. This led to speculation in rail shares on the Bourse, as investors who had previously not been very interested in acquiring them rushed to buy. By 1847, 1,830 km of rail lines were completed.

Repeated Setbacks

However, there was a crisis that led to major changes in the construction and operation of the French rail network. It started in 1845 in England, where the rail boom collapsed due to massive overbuilding, and inefficient lines went bankrupt. Although French lines were dependent on British technology, labor, and capital (in the period 1840-1843, half the capital invested in French railways came from Britain) France was not at first seriously affected. But the crisis worsened after 1846. In that year most of western Europe experienced a wheat crop failure, and in 1847 France bought grain from abroad. Also in 1847, business conditions were depressed, and the rise in unemployment added fuel to the increasing hostility to Louis Philippe's government. This resulted in the 1848 Revolution and the establishment of the Second Republic. Consequently, much British capital was withdrawn from France. Speculation in rail shares collapsed, and the rail companies got into difficulties, especially where the lines were incomplete and thus not generating operating revenues.

After the 1848 Revolution, matters improved. The rail companies received compensation for property damage suffered during the revolution, and the control of the lines was reorganized. Between 1852 and 1857, the thirty companies that had previously controlled half the total trackage were amalgamated into six large companies. Expansion continued, and by 1857 the railroads were responsible for hauling more freight than the waterways.

There was another business depression in 1857, which temporarily set back rail expansion, and the companies were once again rescued by the State. This time, in order to prevent further speculation and to try to retain the participation of smaller investors, the State effectively guaranteed

interest paid to shareholders and also provided construction funds for new lines to be built in rural areas. In response to the 1878 rail crisis, the government bought the lines of some of the smaller rail companies that had failed, and built some new ones, which were subsequently turned over to private hands. The basic problem emerging in the latter part of the 19th century was the inherent conflict between private profitability and the national interest. While the rail network had demonstrated its social benefits, smaller rural lines were not appealing to private companies because traffic was too light. A similar conflict had appeared in the canal network, which was resolved with the nationalization of the major canals by 1909. Gradually the same thing happened in the railroad industry, and by 1936, all French lines had been nationalized.

The importance of the rail network to France's industrial development was great. Industry's local orientation due to high transport costs (as much as half the final price, depending on the item) was a perennial problem. It has been estimated that manufacturing costs in France were high because of the inadequate system of transportation existing before the rail network was in place. Even protection, which imposed high tariffs on imported goods and materials, was not such a significant deterrent to expansion. Thus the creation of a truly unified internal market made possible by reduced transportation costs and easier accessibility had a very positive effect on those enterprises able to take advantage of the new opportunities. In fact, the pace of industrialization increased during 1851-1870, the period when the major lines were making their impact felt. It has been estimated that the constraints on industrial competition imposed by high tariffs in France late in the century were more than offset by the increase in internal competition made possible by the railways.

Protection

If railroads stimulated French economic development, it is difficult to say the same for commercial policy, which, except for a brief period, continued to protect industry from foreign competition. While it could be argued that a high tariff policy made sense in the years immediately following 1815, when an effort to speed up industrialization was starting, it was less justifiable later. Some industries needed no protection at all, and the impact of other countries retaliating against French goods hurt. Thus, French foreign trade was probably much more affected than would have been the case if tariffs had been lower or nonexistent. In some cases, the introduction of the most up-to-date technologies was delayed,

especially steam power, which adversely affected French competitiveness.

While all countries had a tariff policy, the historical experience with purely free trade is limited. Britain liberalized her trade policy only when it was profitable to do so—when her industrial strength was significantly greater than that of any other country. Then the elimination of tariffs did not expose her industries to the threat of competition from other countries because competition did not exist. The issue is more complex in France's case. If protection was justifiable, the important point was to make sure that the right tariffs were imposed, but this did not happen in France. So one could argue the point that it was not so much that having tariffs was wrong as that the tariff structure was poorly designed.

Figure 12.2 The Eiffel Tower in Paris represented many structural and technological advances when it was built (1889). At the time, it was the tallest edifice in the world at 984 feet. (Courtesy of the French Government Tourist Office)

Early Protectionism

In general, there are three distinct periods in the operation of French tariff policy. The first period up to 1860 was protectionist, followed by a brief period of liberalization until 1881, when protectionist policies were restored. However, it is impossible to relate the speed of economic growth with the existence of tariffs or free trade directly. The first period generally coincided with slow, steady growth, with the exception of some minor crises and the major depression of 1847-1851. While growth was faster during the second period, it was faster in the 1850s before tariffs were reduced and slower in the 1860s after liberalization. Again, the economy was stagnating before tariffs were raised in the 1880s, but experienced very rapid growth after 1892, when an extremely high tariff was imposed. The problem with attempting a general conclusion about the relation between growth and free trade is that in reality, *ceteris* are not *paribus*: It is difficult to isolate just one effect and explore its consequences.

One very important difference between French and British policy existed in the 19th century. In Britain, opinion was divided over the advantages of free trade, with landowners and farmers favoring continued protection while industrialists favored free trade. But in France, no important industry or interest group was in favor of free trade. Thus the fear of these groups about the increasing economic strength of British industry was compatible with the traditional prejudices and political hostility that marked relations between these two countries for much of their history.

At first, in 1816, coal was subject to a 30 percent import duty, while iron paid a 50 percent duty. The reason was to protect the wood suppliers and landowners by keeping demand for charcoal high, but the result made coal-using manufacturing high-cost, delaying the use of coke. Manufacturing was high-cost anyway, given the inadequate transportation network;

coking coal was twice as expensive in France as in Britain or Germany, and as French mines could not meet existing domestic demand, coal continued to be imported.

However, concern over the iron industry increased when larger imports of British iron began entering the country. In an attempt to protect both coal mines and iron producers, the tariff on iron smelted with coal (i.e., British iron) was raised to 120 percent in 1822, and in 1826, various types of steel (cast steel, sheet steel, wire) had tariffs of 100 percent imposed. Imports were not reduced by any significant amount, as French output remained low. But, combined with the 15 percent duty on machines (raised to 25 percent in 1841), the effect was to raise manufacturing costs, delaying improvements in metalworking, and limiting the use of steam power.

Tariffs had a greater protective effect on the production of pig iron. In 1830, only 9 percent of pig iron was produced with coke, although half of the iron products were produced using coal. While steam power was introduced only slowly, mainly because of the expensive fuel needed, a complicating factor was the continuing use of water power. Even in 1845, water provided three times the amount of power that steam did.

Steam power was introduced much faster in the larger establishments, becoming more common in metalworking, because reliance on unpredictable water supplies was too costly. By the 1860s steam generated 70 percent of the power they used, while the proportion was only 40 percent for French industry as a whole. Steam power to provide the blast of hot gases was essential once the Bessemer process of making steel was introduced in French steelmaking in 1858.

The combination of duties on machinery imports and the prohibition on the export of machinery from Britain (lifted in 1843) implied a much slower acquisition of the latest advances in technological knowledge. However, it did encourage a variety of illegal means to acquire machinery or machinery designs and forced a development of French ingenuity. The first steam engines used in France were British, but increasingly they were French-made. Steam engines used to power river boats underwent continual modification to meet specific French needs, and in the iron industry there were continual small-scale innovations to overcome high fuel costs. But in general, the transformation of these industries to large-scale, steam-powered enterprises remained gradual.

Similarly in the important textile industries, protective tariff policy encouraged the persistence of small-scale, inefficient units. In many cases, it was poorly designed, with results that went beyond merely guaranteeing high profits to protected manufacturers. For example, French silks enjoyed a worldwide reputation and market and three quarters of the industry's output was exported. But some exports were not made because the French market remained closed to imports of wools and cottons, and foreign buyers retaliated by limiting their imports of silks from France. Tariffs in the cotton industry also had a stunting effect on the modernization of this industry. Imports of cloth were completely prohibited, which should have encouraged French production for a protected market, and imports of cotton yarn were prohibited until 1834 (when the prohibition was replaced by a duty), with many dyes either prohibited or taxed heavily. Only raw cotton paid low duties of about 3-4 percent plus navigation dues. This situation favored only the cotton spinners, whose inputs paid the least duties, but was obviously not beneficial to the weavers, who had to buy inferior but more expensive yarn than their foreign competitors. The result was that cotton cloth was very expensive in France.

In general, the effect of protection in the textile industries delayed mechanization by continuing to make the domestic system viable even though high cost. But the problem was that so long as important political groups did not suffer from it, there was no incentive to change.

Mid Century Trade Liberalization

Such an incentive, however, began to emerge once the framework of the rail network was in place. Although trade liberalization represented a reversal of traditional practice and was bitterly opposed, it began as a practical necessity. Thus, as the output of the iron and steel industry was insufficient to meet the increased demand from the railways, import duties on iron and steel were reduced in 1853. However, while a small change could be made, further reductions met too much opposition in the legislature.

There was an alternative, a method used by Louis Napoleon, who had the power to sign commercial treaties without legislative approval. The result was the Cobden-Chevalier Treaty between France and Britain in 1860 and similar treaties with other European countries later. Its main provisions were that France repealed import duties on raw materials, replaced outright prohibitions with duties (with a uniform maximum rate of 30 percent falling to 25 percent in 1864), and gradually reduced duties on food and drink items. Britain abolished duties on silk and lowered those on wine and brandy (which had a serious effect on the smuggling industry). In general it covered the most important items traded between the two countries.

The problem with evaluating its impact is that while trade in Western Europe did expand, other unfavorable events occurring at the same time had a depressing effect on trade. These included the Crimean War (1854-1856), the widespread cholera epidemic of the early 1850s, the commercial crisis of 1857, war with Italy in 1859, the American Civil War in the 1860s, and recessions in the same decade. This makes it difficult to determine how much change in the economy can be attributed to any one cause.

There was a switch to more modern processes in iron and steel making, with coke smelting accounting for 92 percent of all output by 1870, and the Bessemer converter in steelmaking and the Siemens-Martin process beginning to be used. But still, metal producing enterprises complained that trade liberalization was hurting them. What was most likely was that, depending on the area, small iron works could no longer compete against the larger, modern establishments, whether they were located in France or elsewhere, and this, combined with a decline in iron ore reserves and a timber shortage, led to their disappearance.

In textiles, the silk industry stagnated, but this was partly due to the epidemic that killed silkworms in France, as well as to the rise of new competition in England. New supplies from the Far East replaced domestic raw silk, but as the French shipping industry was weak relative to the British, raw silk was transported on British ships. But before reaching France, imports went for transshipment through London, where new producers established a silk industry. It was more mechanized than the largely domestic industry in France and produced lower-priced silks, so silk exports from France declined. (Silk further declined in the 20th century as a result of competition from Japanese silk producers and the development of synthetic substitutes.)

The cotton industry, the largest on the European continent, suffered as a result of wars. The first crisis came during the American Civil War (1861-1865), which cut off nine tenths of the supply of raw cotton. In Normandy, which was completely dependent on American cotton, there was massive unemployment and a consequent decline of its cotton industry. Alsace had access to supplies of Egyptian cotton (where cotton was first grown in 1820) and survived by running mills and factories at a low capacity utilization rate. The second crisis came as a result of Germany's annexation of the province of Alsace, where the most important part of the French cotton industry was located, after the Franco-Prussian War. As a consequence, the cotton industry stagnated and was unable to meet the competition from other textiles and from other countries.

So while in general much industry modernized after 1860, and although trade and industrial output expanded, several important groups were anti-free trade, although many of the problems they suffered from owed little to trade liberalization. But another major crushing blow—which added strength to the protectionists' arguments—came with France's defeat in the Franco-Prussian War. While there was a rapid, noninflationary recovery from the war, and an economic boom in the years 1870-1873, there was a brief return to protectionist policies starting in 1872. The most serious conflict between free traders and protectionists occurred as the previous trade agreements were about to expire.

Late Century Tariffs

In the 1880s, the Protectionists regained influence, and they had many examples of depressed conditions to support their arguments for a return to an effective tariff policy. In particular, agriculture was depressed and prices fell, due to the disaster in wine growing regions, devastation from the silkworm disease, and increased competition from wheat growing areas such as the United States, the Ukraine, Hungary, and Australia. Initially, the reaction was small. In 1881 a ban on the import of American pork was imposed, followed in 1884 by an increased surtax on foreign sugar, the reimposition of duties on cereal imports (oats, barley, rye) in 1885, and the successive raising of duties on wheat after 1885. This resulted in an increase in food prices and consequently wages, but met no resistance from industrialists who were themselves facing higher tariffs on French exports to Germany, Austria, Italy, and Russia. Increased protection to French farmers was one more explanation of the slow shift of labor from farming to industry.

In any event, manufacturing costs were higher as a result of various influences. These included the lack of coal and iron ore resources and the uncompetitiveness and small size of the French merchant marine, which hurt exports. In 1913, only 1.8 million tons of its 2.2 million tons of shipping were powered by steam, while the British merchant marine accounted for 18.7 million tons; even Germany's fleet was larger at 5 million tons. Although steam-powered vessels had revolutionized British shipping, French sailing boats were still being built and subsidized. Other causes of higher French manufacturing costs were the lack of major, concentrated industrial regions, which, even after the transportation system was improved, still implied high transportation costs and a lack of linkages between French industries. There was also a fear that improved social legislation would raise costs. (The effect that this might have on increasing productivity by producing a more contented work force was conveniently forgotten.) Thus, there was a growing groundswell of support among French industrialists—large modern ones as well as smaller ones—for the reimposition of tariffs on imports to make it possible for them to compete in France itself on a more equal basis with foreign producers.

This resulted in a third high tariff period for France, which became generalized in 1892 when a new two-tier tariff was drafted. One tier was a high tariff on all products imported from countries with whom France had no trade treaty. The other imposed a minimum tariff on those items coming from countries that had negotiated a trade agreement.

The new tariff imposed a 25 percent duty on all farm products that had been exempt from duties in the 1880s, and all manufactured and semi-manufactured imports were now subject to high duties (only textile raw materials were exempt). In addition, bounties and subsidies were paid to encourage the expansion of shipping and the shipbuilding industry, the production of flax (for the linen industry), and the entire silk industry. Most of these tariffs were increased in the period up to 1914. The results were almost predictable. France relied much less on imported goods as domestic production expanded, but consumer prices rose. Also, other countries retaliated by imposing higher tariffs on French goods. This particularly hurt the silk industry, which always relied on exports. (Only Britain did not discriminate against French silks, and in fact consumed more than French users.) However, the silk industry also suffered from other developments, such as the introduction of the sewing machine, which reduced demand for the highest quality silks (which continued to be sewn by hand). There was also foreign competition in the form of cheaper silks and silk blends, and, increasingly, synthetic fibers. However, on the other hand, the introduction of electric power enabled some small

Table 12-1
Indicators of Industrial Growth: France

I Coal Production (million tons; selected years)							
1852	1860	1870	1880	1890	1900	1905	1913
5	8	13	19	26	33	35	40

II Imports of Raw Cotton for Spinning (million pounds; selected years)	
1830	1846
70.4	143

workshops to compete more effectively against larger enterprises.

But in many ways the new tariff structure could not compensate French producers entirely for their relative lack of competitiveness, especially when other factors prevented complete self-sufficiency. For example, continued expansion of industry and the gradual conversion to steam power provided an incentive to increase coal production. By 1913, coal output had increased to 40 million tons (up from only 5 million tons in 1852), but this was only a fraction of Britain's 287 million tons or Germany's combined coal and lignite output of 277 million tons. Even this met only two thirds of domestic demand—some 22 million tons were imported. And much domestic production still came from small mines that could continue in operation because of their protected status. However, by the end of the century the use of steam power and, in some cases, the new electric power, was widespread, especially in the larger enterprises that controlled most of the production in heavy industry. Elsewhere the small firm was still the typical production unit.

Direct encouragement of shipping and shipbuilding at this time was also not very effective. One major problem limiting the expansion of shipping was the relative lack of bulky output for export, which reduced the demand for French-built cargo vessels. Shipbuilding thus faced not only low demand but also high costs. All imported materials used were taxed, and ports were also a considerable distance from domestic sources of supply, increasing transportation costs.

The new tariff structure did little to help emerging new growth industries such as chemicals and electrical manufacturing. While French producers had an early lead in chemical production, this lead was lost to Germany after 1871, and a variety of reasons have been offered in explanation. One was that an important branch of chemical manufacturing depended on coal as a basic input, where Germany had an advantage. In addition, the education system did not adapt

sufficiently to produce the middle-level technicians and chemists needed. The most important branches of chemical manufacturing in France were medicine and perfumes, in keeping with traditional French superiority in high-value production, but unfortunately lines with only a limited market. France's electrical industry was only about one third the size of Germany's.

Summary

Although France did industrialize, the structure of industry differed from that in either Germany or Great Britain, her two European rivals. By the end of the century, both these economies had gone further in introducing large-scale enterprises than France, where small-scale manufacturing still predominated. And also by that time, France was no longer the strongest, wealthiest nation in Europe, having been overtaken first by Britain and then by Germany.

Inadequate Transportation

A mixture of reasons account for France's slow development, some of which reinforce the effect of others. Probably the single most important explanation was the inadequacy of the inland transportation network, which made it both difficult and expensive to move raw materials and goods, reinforcing the tendency to small-scale, locally oriented establishments. Being small in scale, these enterprises were less likely to adopt what could be seen as risky new production methods. Once the rail network was in place, French industry developed rapidly, more modern techniques were introduced, and, especially in heavy industry, large-scale units became more common.

Natural Resource Problems

Linked with this was the comparative disadvantage of France in natural resources. Coal deposits were far from the iron ore deposits, which limited the development of the metals industries as well as the use of steam power. Both of these were further limited by the abundance of wood, with high transportation costs making any manufacturing process using coal or iron high cost. Other domestic resource-using industries suffered in midcentury as an epidemic killed off silkworms and phylloxera denuded vines—both silk and wine production were examples of production where France was a leader.

Labor

A third factor was France's slow population growth. This limited the expansion of a large domestic market and was not compensated for by an expansion of export markets. Also, and in spite of several revolutions, the persistence of considerable inequality in income distribution did not encourage the development of mass production industries geared to a mass market—effective purchasing power simply did not warrant it.

On the labor supply side, again France experienced only a gradual shift toward the development of a large factory work force. Partly because the French Revolution had strengthened the peasants' ties to the land, and partly because of the continuation of small industrial establishments, the effective supply of labor to large units was reduced.

Capital Mobilization

A fourth factor was inadequate capital mobilization. Financial institutions such as banks and stock markets were weak, and although improvements occurred, the ability of large enterprises to tap outside funds was limited, which had further implications. Caution rather than risk taking was dominant, partly because France had suffered from speculative panics and financial collapses in the past, so there was a tendency not to trust outsiders with funds. Because these collapses had been associated with joint stock companies, the joint stock form of organization was viewed with

deep suspicion. Also, the prevailing tendency for firms to be family-owned and reliant on their own profits for expansion reinforced the tendency to cautious decision making and further limited the possibilities for growth.

This was even further reinforced by political instability and wars. Including the late 18th century, France experienced four revolutions and two major wars before the end of the 19th century, and two major varieties of government, monarchy and republic. While most of these governments tended to be repressive and probusiness, the changes, or fears of changes, further limited the development of confidence that had been important to 18th century Britain, which had its revolutionary period behind it before industrializing. Lack of confidence limited long-term new investment. New enterprises whose payback periods were extensive would not be started if there was fear of property damage or expropriation, which further reinforced the tendency to keep funds within the firm, hoard them, or send them out of the country.

Protectionism

Finally, throughout most of the 19th century France remained protectionist, but without the encouraging effects its supporters hoped for. On the negative side, protection probably delayed the introduction of new technologies, made manufacturing costly, and encouraged the persistence of small enterprises. On the positive side, observers credit French producers with their achievements in areas where high-quality, individual work is important. Areas such as the silk industry at its peak, perfumes, the Paris fashion industry, and wine are good examples. And inventiveness was not lacking. In textiles, the Jacquard loom, first introduced in 1804 and perfected by 1850, was widely adapted for use in other industries and other countries, while French pioneering efforts in auto manufacturing were very successful. Also, the development of sugar beet refining, chlorine bleach, and improvements in ironmaking were important. For example, the Martin brothers developed an open hearth process that extended the Siemens process by heating gases before they entered the furnace where steel was made, and the Siemens-Martin process gradually replaced the puddling of iron. French engineers were widely regarded. As an example of the combination of engineering skill with a rare example of entrepreneurship and political acumen, the cutting of the Suez Canal (1859-1869) through Egypt to link the Mediterranean and the Red Sea, and provide a shorter route from Europe to the East was remarkable. (The Panama Canal was also a French idea and design, but the organization of the Panama Canal Company left much to be desired, and this canal was eventually built with United States resources.)

But the cost of the commitment to artistic achievement may have limited the economy's flexibility and ability to adapt to change. France suffered through numerous crises in the 19th century, economic as well as political, although it would be foolhardy to say that these were caused only by French problems. As will be shown in a later chapter, modern industrialization in the 19th century involved a much greater degree of international linkages, and one country could not for long isolate itself from the rest of the world behind a tariff barrier.

Notes

1. For example, engineering training was early encouraged in the College of Highways and Bridges (established 1747) and in the College of Mines (established 1793).

2. Tax farming is the procedure in which certain individuals agree to collect taxes for the government, i.e., tax collection is not done by a specialized government agency. Any sum in excess of the contracted-for amount is retained by the tax farmer.

Key Concepts

Capital mobilization
Continental System
Infrastructure
Investment bank
Nationalization
Peasant farming
Protection

Sleeping partner
Société en commandité
Syndicat
Tariff
Tax farming
Trade union

Questions for Discussion and Essay Writing

1. Does a protectionist policy encourage economic growth as compared with a less restrictive policy? Evaluate carefully.

2. Discuss France's economic situation at the turn of the 18th century. To what extent did its various elements encourage or discourage economic development?

3. Why did France industrialize slowly?

4. Compare and contrast French and British approaches to industrialization.

5. Using France as an example, is it possible to say that political uncertainty does not encourage innovative economic activity?

6. What was the role of the government in French industrialization?

7. Do wars retard or stimulate economic development? Why?

8. What was the role of agriculture in the French Industrial Revolution?

9. Discuss the various labor issues involved in 19th century French industrialization.

10. Discuss the issues surrounding the adoption of steam power in 19th century France.

11. Capital mobilization has been offered as a problem area in 19th century French development. Why?

12. What was the impact of the railroad on French economic development?

For Further Reading

Ardagh, J. *The New French Revolution*. N.Y.: Harper & Row, 1968.

Baum, W.C. *The French Economy and the State*. Princeton: Princeton University Press, 1958.

Cameron, Rondo. *France and the Economic Development of Europe, 1800–1914*. Princeton: Princeton University Press, 1961.

Caron, François. *An Economic History of Modern France*. N.Y.: Columbia University Press, 1979.

Clapham, J.H. *The Economic Development of France and Germany, 1815–1914,*

4th ed. Cambridge: Cambridge University Press, 1936.

Clark, Samuel. "Nobility, Bourgeoisie and the Industrial Revolution in Belgium." *Past and Present,* vol. 105 (November 1984): 140–175.

Dickinson, H.W. *A Short History of the Steam Engine*. Cambridge: Cambridge University Press, 1939.

Dunham, Arthur L. *The Industrial Revolution in France, 1815–1848*. N.Y.: Exposition Press, 1955.

Fremdling, Rainer. "The Puddler: A Craftsman's Skill and the Spread of a New Technology in Belgium, France and Germany." *Journal of Economic History*, 20:3 (Winter 1991): 529–567.

Grantham, George. "Agricultural Supply During the Industrial Revolution: French Evidence and European Implications ." *Journal of Economic History*, XLIX:1 (March 1989) : 43–72.

Henderson, W.O. *The Industrial Revolution in Europe*, 1815–1914. Chicago: Quadrangle Books, 1961.

Heywood, C. "The Role of the Peasantry in French Industrialization, 1815–1880." *Economic History Review*, XXXIV:3 (1980): 359–376.

Kindleberger, C.P. *Economic Growth in France and Britain, 1851–1950*. Cambridge, Mass: Harvard University Press, 1964.

Maurice, Marc, François Sellier and Jean-Jacques Silvestre. *The Social Foundations of Industrial Power: A Comparison of France and Germany*. Cambridge, Mass: MIT Press, 1986.

Milward, Alan S. and S.B. Saul. *The Economic Development of Continental Europe, 1780–1870*. Totowa, N.J: Rowman and Littlefield, 1973.

O'Brien, Patrick K. and C. Keyder. *Economic Growth in Britain and France, 1780–1914*. London: George Allen & Unwin, 1978.

Price, Roger. *The Economic Modernization of France, 1730–1880*. N.Y.: Halstead Press-John Wiley, 1975.

Rosenthal, Jean-Laurent. "The Development of Irrigation in Provence, 1700–1860: The French Revolution and Economic Growth." *Journal of Economic History*, 50:3 (Sept. 1990): 615–638.

Stearns, Peter N. *Paths to Authority: The Middle Class and the Industrial Labor Force in France, 1820–1848,* Urbana: University of Illinois Press, 1978.

Sussman, Nathan. "Missing Bullion or Missing Documents: A Revision and Reappraisal of French Mining Statistics, 1385–1415." *Journal of European Economic History*, 19:1 (Spring 1990): 147–162.

Trebilcock, Clive. *Industrialization of the Continental Powers 1780–1914*. London: Longman Publishing, 1981.

Velde, François R. and David R. Weir. "The Financial Market and Government Debt Policy in France, 1746–1793." *Journal of Economic History,* 52:1 (March 1992): 1–39.

White, Eugene Nelson. "Was there a Solution to the Ancien Régime's Financial Dilemma?" *Journal of Economic History*, XLIX:3 (September, 1989): 545–560.

Chapter 13

Industrialization in Germany

OF ALL THE COUNTRIES COVERED IN THIS TEXT, GERMANY'S TRANSFORMATION in the 19th century was the most rapid and the most spectacular. Between 1800 and 1900, Germany transformed itself from a collection of backward, militarily weak, semi-feudal states into an industrialized, unified country that not only pioneered in the development of totally new industries, but was also, a few years later the aggressor nation in the First World War.

Unlike both Britain and France, the story of Germany's economic transformation cannot be separated from the story of its political unification. The motivating force was largely due to one man, Bismarck, and one country, Prussia. And again in contrast to both France and Britain, economic development did not occur in parallel with a movement toward political liberalism and representative government. If both Britain and France were emergent capitalist economies in 1700 before their industrial revolutions, the same cannot be said of Germany in 1800; it was semi-feudal economically, and politically autocratic and decentralized. The price Germany paid for political unity and economic strength was a high degree of political repression. But ironically, although opposed to liberal reform movements, the conservative Bismarck successfully introduced the most far-reaching social welfare legislation—well before any other country in the world.

Germany at the Beginning of the 19th Century

In the 15th and 16th centuries, southern Germany was the location of a highly developed commercial and financial capitalist culture, but after then, for a variety of reasons, development retrogressed. One reason for this was that the center of economic activity shifted to the countries bordering the Atlantic following the opening up of the New World. As a result, the importance of the Rhine as an inland trade route lessened, and led to the decline of the Hanse ports of the Baltic. None of the German states shared in the general overseas expansion of the 16th and 17th centuries, which, as we have previously seen, was so important in generating profits to be used in the capital accumulation process. The German mercantile fleet, second only to the Dutch until the early 17th century because of the importance of the Hanseatic League, then shrank, while both the British and Dutch fleets grew. (Although Germany is a large country, it has only a short coastline on the North and Baltic Seas, and consequently has fewer ports.) Also, many political factors that were important in explaining why both France and Britain were started on the path of commercial and industrial capitalist development were absent in Germany.

While the German states were nominally united under the Holy Roman Empire, the central authority of the Empire was effectively limited. The Empire included about one thousand separate territories, ranging from independent city-states to large states; three hundred of them were entitled to issue their own currency. The ties holding these states together grew weaker, and political rivalries caused further erosion throughout the 16th and 17th centuries. Population also fell during this time to a low of about ten million in 1650, although rising to approximately seventeen million a century later. Austria was the dominant state in the Holy Roman Empire, and tried to extend its control over several non-German states in the 16th century through a series of power plays. These included the conquest of Hungary and other parts of central Europe and the strategic and marriage alliances linking the Hapsburg monarchies of Austria and Spain. But this activity distracted attention from more purely Germanic issues, and the Thirty Years War (1618-1648), which divided Germany along religious and political lines, proved to be the final blow to the hope of uniting Germany under one ruler. After then, the Holy Roman Empire was more a name than a real entity.

Most of the German states were small, but Prussia in the 18th century, especially under the leadership of Frederick II (known as Frederick the Great, ruling 1740-1786), extended its borders and increasingly challenged Austria for domination over the rest of Germany. (Frederick's role in helping lay the basis for subsequent German industrialization was also unusual among German leaders at this time.) This challenge continued to be mounted throughout the 19th century, but resulted in the smaller states fearing a political takeover by one of them, which further discouraged both voluntary efforts to create closer political ties and economic development. With the exception of some isolated examples, such as the production of fine wools in Saxony, serf-peasant farming under semi-feudal conditions was the predominant economic activity.

Germany's weakness was finally demonstrated when Napoleon defeated Austria and Prussia in his sweep across Europe, occupied large areas of Germany, and formally dissolved the Holy Roman Empire. At the conclusion of the Napoleonic Wars in 1815, Germany consisted of thirty-nine different states, loosely linked together in what was called the Germanic Federation, which was an association imposed on Germany by the Great Powers (including Great Britain and Russia). The Federation, however, had extremely limited powers. Each state operated independently, and was responsible for its own commercial policies (including tariffs), its own currency and its own communications. This fragmentation was a disadvantage for modern industrialization, as the small size of most of these states provided only limited markets, thus restricting opportunities for the capital investment needed for an industrial revolution.

Napoleonic War Shock

Defeat in the Napoleonic Wars was, naturally, a shock, especially for Prussia which was considered to be efficiently governed (it was an autocratic monarchy) and militarily strong. That its military strength was not as great as thought has been explained by the lack of relevance of the army commanders' thinking to 19th century conditions. They believed that the economically and politically oppressed peasants would willingly defend their country, but the peasants had little incentive to do so, and it is hardly surprising that the Prussian armies went down to defeat.

Recognition of this and similar problems began to be made even before the end of French domination, and it initiated a pattern of change that characterized Prussia. Pressure for change came from the *top* of the social and political hierarchy, not the bottom. The first change came when the structure of the army was reformed; now all male citizens were liable for military service, and officers were chosen for their ability, rather than on the basis of their aristocratic birth as before. Domestic reforms in Prussia included the emancipation of the serfs as an attempt to co-opt them into more willing and effective military service. In addition, and of great importance for later industrial development, the role of education in helping produce a strong state was recognized; the first step was the founding of the University of Berlin. (Saxony was the most progressive of all other German states at this time, and established vocational schools for teaching technical and practical skills.)

Lack of a Middle Class

While such changes did subsequently aid development, one aspect marking both Britain and France in their precapitalist days was missing in Prussia and most of the other states—a middle class of urban commercial interests that was supportive of capitalist development. To some extent, this derives from the "top down" philosophy of the landowning aristocracy and their unwillingness to share political power, which led to continued repressive policies throughout the 19th century. It also prevented the development of a more representative form of government and sufficient private enterprise to initiate significant capitalist industrial development. In turn, this implied that the State would take on a much greater role in encouraging such development.

In Prussia, this was most obvious at the beginning of the century, when the State attempted to break the powers of the towns (whose inhabitants were exempt from military duty) by removing all legal barriers between town and country. The towns were dominated by craft guilds, which were unable to oppose this policy initiated by the governing landowning aristocracy, and some apparently hoped that it would prevent the emergence of new non-guild competition in the towns, which they feared more than they feared the dominance of landowning interests. In any event, guilds were weakened. Strangely, such cooperation between oddly paired interest groups such as urban guilds and landowning aristocracy delayed the emergence of middle class liberalism.

Problems to Overcome

At the end of the Napoleonic Wars, the Germanic states had both long-term and short-term problems to overcome. The long-term problems included a generally inefficient farm sector (although some larger farms were exporting grain), made worse by the fact that soil fertility was uneven. The small industrial sector was still predominantly organized along craft guild and artisan lines, and there was little incentive to organize large-scale industrial enterprises because the domestic market was too small. There were large deposits of coal and iron ore in the Ruhr, Saar, and Saxony, but they were on the country's borders, and required the existence of a rail network for effective exploitation. As elsewhere, transportation in the pre-rail age was poor and inefficient. The Rhine was a major water route, but it was expensive to use because of the frequency of toll barriers along its length. The labor force was large, but it would not be a free one until a combination of emancipation, erosion of peasant farming, and a growth of capitalist industry existed. Overall, there was a general lack of all those other elements contributing to that "generally favorable environment" necessary for an industrial revolution.

The biggest problem was political fragmentation. Of particular economic importance, the fact that each state controlled its own borders and imposed its own commercial policy was significant. The number of internal tariff barriers and amounts of tariffs paid resulted in high shipping costs, further narrowing the domestic market. As one example, a 300-mile journey on the Elbe to Hamburg involved thirty different tolls and took one month to complete. Market fragmentation was one of the first problems to be tackled.

Economically, the short-term problems resulted from the disruption caused by the Napoleonic Wars; only the iron and arms industries gained from the war. The states were heavily indebted. Overseas trade had declined even further; only the port of Hamburg did not because it picked up shipping relocated from Dutch ports after France occupied the Dutch Republic in 1795. (Hamburg at that time handled a sizeable proportion of the coffee and sugar exported by French colonies to Europe.)

Industry and trade found it difficult to recover. After the war, many countries had raised their tariffs against imports, which lowered Germany's traditional exports of cereals and timber. Although they had imposed their own tariffs, the German states experienced a flood of imports of English manufactured goods once warfare was over, and this produced three major results. First, having such goods available reduced the incentive to manufacture them domestically, especially given that domestic producers were at a technological and cost disadvantage. Second, existing domestic producers continued to use traditional production methods, so they were not price-competitive with imports, and many producers went bankrupt. (The few factories that had been established were mostly in the mining and metallurgical industries.) Finally, the general economic weakness of the economy and the specific problems of the end-of-war depression, made worse by a failure of the harvest in 1817, provided cause for concern.

Prussia and the Zollverein

Prussia initiated the drive for the modernization and unification of Germany, later becoming its most highly industrialized state. But at the same time that this drive was being made, the ongoing struggle between Prussia and Austria for domination over Germany helped shape the unified state that emerged in 1871; Austria was not part of it.

Zollverein
German customs union formed in 1834

When the Germanic Federation was established in 1815, it was intended that both Austria and Prussia would be responsible for "managing" Germany. At that time, Austria had the greatest influence. Austria's chief minister then was Prince Lothar von Metternich, whose ambition in life seemed to be to crush liberalism, constitutionalism, and parliamentarism. Political reality being what it was at the time, he faced no opposition, and in Austria, the press, the universities, freedom of expression, and other attributes of modernizing states were suppressed by various repressive policies. However, in the 1830s, the effectiveness of such policies began to weaken. The end finally came with the revolution of 1848, which led to the downfall of Metternich and the disappearance of the old, autocratic Austria. Although Prussia was hardly the most liberal of states, it did survive the 1848 revolution intact, and the economic changes that were beginning to produce a modern state were accepted as the trade-off for a certain degree of political reactionism.

This transformation had begun soon after 1815 and later expanded to include the movement for the unification of Germany. At first, the Prussian government and business cooperated to revive trade and industry. Infrastructure projects, direct involvement in industry, and changes in commercial policy were started in the 1815-1845 period, and included road construction and improvements and the encouragement of education, especially technical education—the Berlin Technical Institute was founded and the Association for the Promotion of Industrial Knowledge was established. Direct involvement in industry resulted in several publicly owned enterprises such as textile factories, flour mills, iron works, and chemical plants. Some of these were located in territory Prussia had gained in 1815, which included not only coalfields but also parts of some of the main commercial routes along the Rhine and other river valleys.

Commercial Policy Simplification

Prussia's greatest achievement in uniting Germany came with commercial policy. The first step taken in 1818 was the introduction of a single moderate tariff to replace all existing town and provincial tariffs within Prussia. This tariff was structured to exempt some raw materials from duty, impose low duties on manufactured items such as cotton and pig iron that would be raised as industrialization proceeded, and impose higher tariffs on all other imports, especially colonial products such as coffee and sugar. The immediate effect was to stimulate new industry within Prussia by protecting new producers from foreign competition.

In 1819, Prussia suggested that all the German states adopt a single tariff, but nothing came of it although the idea remained. By 1828, some independent enclaves within Prussian borders were absorbed into the Prussian tariff system, and in later years, Bavaria and Wurttemberg established their own customs union.

Customs Union

a group of nations with free trade between themselves and a common tariff on trade with outsiders

---

By this time, Prussia had gained an important strategic advantage in constructing the tariff, because it was designed to benefit those within the union and hurt those outside. So, although the new tariff was much lower than those it replaced, industry and trade expanded because artificial barriers to trade had been lowered and simplified. While some states had been nervous about joining because they worried about losing customs revenues—an important source of revenues of governments at that time—in fact they found that their revenues, allocated in proportion to popula-

---

Artificial Barrier

A man-made impediment to the free movement of goods and resources

---

tion size, were considerably higher than before because of the expansion of trade.

Austria's Metternich opposed the Prussian tariff system, seeing it as a direct threat to Austrian leadership in Germany, but his counterproposals and resistance went nowhere. Many other German states wanted to avoid taking sides in the Austria-Prussia struggle by remaining neutral, but the economic advantages of being linked with a modernizing Prussia proved too strong. By 1834, this customs union, officially called the Zollverein, covered a population of 23.5 million, and only Austria, Hanover, Mecklenburg, and Oldenburg remained outside.

Attraction of the Zollverein

The general principles of the Zollverein were simple. All states adopted the Prussian tariff system, and were responsible for collecting customs duties at their own frontiers. Revenues were distributed in proportion to each state's population. Prussia alone negotiated commercial treaties with foreign governments on behalf of all members, the idea being that better terms could be gained by bargaining from the position of strength produced by a united market of nearly all Germany.

Eliminating artificial barriers to trade within Germany itself produced many benefits. Economically, lower shipping costs within the country stimulated manufacturing by increasing the effective size of the market. Competition between different areas of the country increased, and a localized, inward-looking attitude was gradually eliminated. The united approach to negotiating with other countries resulted in many concessions being made in overseas trade, and the increase in trade led to almost doubled revenues from customs duties in the nine years after the Zollverein's official birth—a definite gain to the participants' treasuries.

Ad Valorem Duty

A duty or tariff calculated as a percentage of the item's price

A problem arose in the 1830s: Because duties were specific, levied by weight or quantity, and were not *ad valorem*, falling prices after 1818 meant that the real burden of duties rose as a proportion of the price. There was some controversy over the solution. On one side were the free traders who wanted to lower duties to restore their original impact. This solution was opposed by the protectionists who saw the encouragement given by protection to domestic industry, and who therefore wanted higher duties. A compromise solution raised duties on pig iron and textiles only.

Building a Rail Network

The Zollverein had two important accomplishments. It successfully removed artificial barriers to the economic unification of Germany and formed the base for its eventual political unification. However, it could do nothing to overcome an important natural barrier to the complete achievement of economic unity, the large size of the country. Lack of an efficient transportation network held back exploitation of Germany's rich resources and limited the expansion of industry.

Starting in the 1830s, this barrier was overcome with the development of a rail network that had a greater impact in encouraging economic expansion than in any other west European country. Germany in the first half of the 19th century lagged far behind Great Britain and France in industrializing, so falling transportation costs and improved transportation would have a much greater impact. The first major line was opened in 1839 between Dresden and Leipzig, and Germany's network was built faster than in any other

Continental European country except Belgium, which is a much smaller country. By 1850, a total of 3,660 miles had been built, including three north-south and three east-west through routes, compared with only 1,872 miles in France. The system's two major hubs were Berlin and Cologne.

However, there was one problem: The states could not agree on a uniform rail policy, so each built its own railroads, missing an opportunity for a unified *national* network. There was also a different pattern of financing in each state. Some lines were built privately by joint stock companies; some were built by cooperating public and private groups; and in 1847, the first state-owned railroad was built through the Saar, location of an important coalfield that later became a major industrial area. However, after 1871, the lines began to be nationalized by state governments, which helped unite them into a national network; in 1919, the entire system was transferred to national government ownership.

The impact of the rail network was predictable. Easier, faster, and cheaper transportation enabled Germany's natural resources to be fully exploited. Coal production and use had been minor before 1840—only about one million tons in 1820—but expanded rapidly to reach six million tons by 1850, partly due to the growing rail network's expanding demand for coal. The railways also stimulated the iron industry, both directly for its own uses and indirectly by encouraging the expansion of iron-using industries. At this time, the major industrializing regions were the Saar and Upper Silesia; the Ruhr coalfield began to be exploited only in the 1840s, and charcoal smelting was still common before then.

Specific Duty

A tax or duty of a certain absolute amount imposed on a good

Steam Power

Steam power was first introduced in the 1830s and became more common after 1840 as factories in the metal-using and textile industries began to replace small workshops. By 1850, one third of the nonagricultural work force was employed in factories. Steam power was also used in the mining industry, where German firms used the latest, most efficient technology because of their late start. Steam also increasingly powered steamships on inland rivers, although facing much protest from the Rhine boatmen who found it difficult to compete with the faster steamships.

This early phase of industrialization, stimulated by the Zollverein and the railroads, involved a two-way flow of people, goods, and capital into and out of the country. As might be expected, and to compensate for the low level of technology in Germany, imported technology, machines and skills were utilized for the initial development of textile mills, machinery workshops, steamships, and railroads. Although a considerable amount of emigration took place, mainly to the United States, population rose from about 25 million in 1815 to 35.5 million in 1850, making Germany the second largest country in Europe (after Russia).

As would also be expected, the spread of factories produced many of the same results as in Britain. Child labor was common, and health and living standards were poor, which caused concern because of the military's need for strong, healthy recruits. This concern led in 1839 to Prussia's first factory law, which prohibited the employment of children under nine years of age, and limited the working hours of those under sixteen. The spread of factories also adversely affected craftsworkers and workers in domestic industries. For example, Silesian weavers and linen workers suffered, and their protests in 1844 were widely publicized. (Linen was used for peasants' clothing and had always been an important industry.)

The entire decade of the 1840s, when the old peasant and artisan traditions increasingly faced competition from capitalist industry, was a decade of serious social unrest, as it was throughout Europe. Many textile workers died of hunger in the 1840s; there were strikes and riots in towns where both domestic industry workers and factory operatives protested their poor conditions; and peasants in the countryside suffered from a series of bad harvests and erosion of traditional farming. In many places they had lost their traditional rights to pasture, and so were in the same position as English farmers after enclosure. In Prussia, even decades after the official emancipation of the serfs, effective freedom was slow to appear. This social distress is one explanation for emigration; in the first half of the century, peak emigration periods usually coincided with depressed conditions, but this pattern changed in the second half.

1848 Revolution

These real grievances combined with ideologies to generate the 1848 Revolution in Germany. The revolutionary movement incorporated both nationalism and liberalism; its theme was that national unity could be achieved by representative governments and constitutions. It had surprisingly broad support, uniting intellectuals and workers who wanted expanded voting rights and improvement of economic conditions with peasants who wanted an elimination of feudal obligations. So for a variety of both political and economic reasons, there was opposition to the repressive policies of Metternich and the other rulers. There were demands for constitutional reform in many German states, to include parliaments, jury trials, freedom of the press, and freedom of speech. Urban riots occurred throughout 1847 and 1848.

The final spark was lit in France where a revolution took place in February 1848. Popular uprisings in Germany followed, and later that year, every (frightened) ruler had either agreed to a more liberal constitution or appointed a liberal ministry. There was even a German National Parliament, made up of bourgeois representatives from all the states but with few landowners and no labor or peasant representatives, which met to propose a constitution for the economic unification of the country. It had no effective power, but was permitted to continue in existence, remaining as a symbol of unity.

However, this revolution was short-lived. By late 1848, reactionary regimes were restored as Austria crushed uprisings of non-Germanic groups within her borders, stopping the reform movement. Then Prussia abolished its National Assembly and also assisted other groups in putting down their revolutions, which caused concern in Austria where there was worry that Austria's influence in Germany would be eroded while Prussia's rose.

Thus, in 1849, while some economic freedom—especially the ending of peasant servitude—had been achieved, it was achieved at the cost of stamping out emerging liberalism and more modern political constitutions. In addition, as elsewhere, unions were banned and workers could not hold political meetings. The restoration of repressive regimes was so successful that there was no effective political opposition to them until the 20th century, and even where constitutions had been liberalized, most rulers still favored and practiced absolutism. What did survive was the idea of nationalism, an idea championed especially by conservative Prussia.

Germany after 1850

The Zollverein survived both this political upheaval and the continuing antagonism between Austria and Prussia, which even led to war between them from which Prussia emerged victorious. Austria remained outside the Zollverein, although trying to regain influence over the other states by proposing a single customs union for all

of Germany and Austria in 1849. Some states favored it, but Prussia opposed it and the Zollverein states renewed their existing agreement, effectively killing the Austrian plan. Only later in 1853 did Austria and the Zollverein agree to institute trade preferences.

The Zollverein economies continued to grow, especially in the period up to 1857, while Austria did not. The period 1850-1870 is usually described as the time when Germany was preparing for her Industrial Revolution. During this period, the economy finally began to change from one predominantly dependent on agriculture and domestic industry to one where manufacturing was important, although 64 percent of the population was still rural in 1871. In particular, this changing economy showed sufficient strength to survive the 1857 commercial crisis, the American Civil War (which cut off supplies of raw cotton), and Prussia's various wars.

Much of this progress can be attributed to the impact of the Zollverein, which provided a large, free market protected from outside competition, and the rail network. Although fragmented—there were over 60 independent railway administrations and 1,400 different rates for freight in 1871—it still provided a much easier, faster, and cheaper method of transportation than had ever existed before.

Progressive Developments

Three other elements also helped encourage and sustain industrial development. First, various restrictions on economic activity were relaxed. Peasants were no longer subject to remnants of feudal servitude, although in many cases they were being eased off their land. Guilds were no longer able to count on legal protection, and they faced increased competition from factory production. Factories were easier to establish once owners no longer had to get a license to do so. And in the 1860s, there was a fairly sympathetic audience for free trade ideas, although they would never be as influential as in Britain and were not put into practice.

Second, some changes in the financial sector facilitated the increased amount of economic transactions. Most states established a central bank authorized to issue the bank notes that were important in providing new means to complete transactions. New joint stock credit banks, similar to the ones in France, were helpful because they assisted the establishment of new enterprises by marketing corporate shares, often even holding these shares themselves, and made direct loans to new businesses; they effectively acted as investment banks. This was a significant step because Germany's late start meant that there was no preceding period of capitalist development as in France or Britain, so there were few sources of accumulated profits that could be tapped for new enterprises. Hence, late starters needed to find finance capital from sources other than existing enterprises' profits. This is why investment banks played a larger role in economic development than in Britain, where there was less need for them.

Third, and closely linked to the second point, the joint stock form of corporate organization began to be used more widely. At first, corporations were formed to find financing for the new rail companies, which needed large amounts of capital, appearing later in other industries. By 1860, there were over three hundred such companies in existence.

Textiles

As was typical of early industrialization, textiles were the single most important industry until 1870. This industry employed about three quarters of a million people, and was the single largest user of labor, with the exception of farming. Production of cotton textiles was the largest, and because it was a new industry in Germany, was from the start organized almost entirely along large-scale factory lines. The tendency for large

units to predominate was further encouraged as a result of the American Civil War, which cut off raw cotton imports. Although alternative supplies were available from India, they cost more, and only larger, more modern producers were able to make effective use of them; the smaller producers were unable to compete and went out of business. By 1870, the cotton industry in Germany was about one-sixth the size of Britain's cotton industry.

Older, established textile industries did not expand. Wool did not adopt new techniques, and domestic production of woolens remained important for so long as raw wool from domestic German sources was available. When the industry became dependent on imported supplies of wool after 1850, the domestic manufacturing system declined as factory production became more common. Linen had once been a very important industry; at the end of the 18th century, one quarter of Prussia's exports were linens. But production of linen for peasant clothing declined throughout the 19th century, unable to compete with cheaper, factory-produced substitutes such as wool and cotton. The linen industry remained unmechanized, and even markets for fine linens were lost to competition from Belgium and Ireland, whose industries did mechanize and subsequently produced at lower costs.

Coal

The rapid changes occurring in the period before 1870 show most clearly in the coal and metal industries, those characteristic of 19th century industrialization. Exploitation of the major coalfields was encouraged after 1851, and because of their late start, mining companies used the latest technology, were large scale operations, and in general operated very efficiently. Coal output was 17 million tons in 1860, rising to 38 million tons in 1871, twice as much as France; at this time, Germany was second only to Britain in coal production in Europe. Coal consumption, however, exceeded that in Britain where one third of output was exported. In the 1870s, Germany's coal imports declined, for a variety of reasons. Domestic output increased, and costs were lower, thanks to the completed rail network, the building of the Saar Coal Canal, and a general reduction in freight charges, making it possible to utilize more domestic coal.

The demand for coal increased once steam power began to be more widely used and as a result of the expansion of the iron industry. Germany is less richly endowed in iron ore than in coal, and iron ore deposits are scattered, requiring the efficient transportation provided by the railroads before they can be effectively exploited. So even while demand was expanding, output was small at midcentury—only one half of France's output and one-sixth the size of Britain's. But it expanded rapidly after then, partly due to the exploitation of new deposits (chiefly in the Rhineland and Westphalia) and partly due to the more efficient working of old deposits: Between 1850 and 1870, iron ore output expanded fivefold, reaching 4.3 million tons.

There was also a feedback effect. Production of pig iron also expanded dramatically at this time—

1.2 million tons of pig iron were produced by 1870, more than France's output—and this increased demand for Ruhr coal, which was especially suitable for conversion to coke. Throughout this period, as was common in other countries, too, there was a change in the location of iron production and a change in technology. Increasingly, iron production using modern methods was concentrated in large establishments on the coalfields, rather than using charcoal as fuel at the iron deposits themselves.

The Unification of Germany

What would have happened to German industrialization if the country had not been unified in 1871 is, of course, an unanswerable question. It is likely that industrialization would not have been as fast or as thorough, because although movement toward economic unity had already been taken with the Zollverein, the advantages associated with being a nation state are much greater than those associated with cooperation between different sovereign states. And as political events in Germany are so closely related to economic events, we should cover political developments.

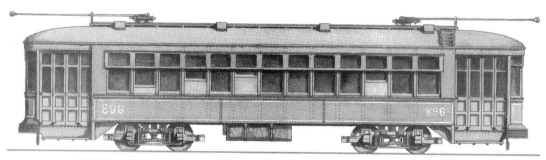

Figure 13.1 Electric street cars, like this one from New Orleans, revolutionized urban mass transit at the end of the century with their ability to move large numbers of people quickly and efficiently.

Bismarck

After the 1848 Revolution, conservative Prussia dominated the push for German unification, especially after Otto von Bismarck became chief minister in 1862. Bismarck was a conservative Prussian landowner with strong antiliberal views. However, he recognized that political strength depended on industrialization, and he favored unification because he thought that Prussia would be able to dominate a united Germany. Oddly enough, he also introduced the first social insurance legislation, not so much for humanitarian reasons but because it reasserted the old principle of *social* responsibility for individual economic distress that had been absent since the end of the medieval period.

Bismarck became chief minister of Prussia at the request of William I, who was facing increased pressure from liberal members of Prussia's National Assembly. Bismarck successfully resisted demands for liberalization and continued to strengthen Prussia's position against Austria. Two issues are important.

Austria's Loss of Influence

First, the Zollverein states wished to get the same concessions when trading with France that France had granted to Britain with the 1860 Cobden-Chevalier Treaty. (Germany already had trade concessions from Britain.) France granted them in 1862, to become effective in 1866. When Austria found out that France had a more favored position when trading with the Zollverein countries than she did, she began to negotiate for a new treaty. Unfortunately, Austria was not negotiating from a position of strength, because her economy had not developed to the same extent as the Zollverein countries and Austria's involvement in the Crimean War and in war with Italy in 1859 had encouraged a surge of protectionist attitudes—a strong implication that Austria had lost the economic leadership of Germany.

Second, Austria also lost political and military influence in Germany. The first signs of this resulted from the Schleswig-Holstein affair: Denmark and Germany both claimed "ownership" of these provinces, and Austria was involved in a disputed claim to the Danish throne. While Denmark claimed authority over the two provinces, ethnically they were German, and were even nominally part of the Germanic Confederation. The dispute led to war in which Austria and Prussia (for once acting together) defeated Denmark, but continuing disputes between Austria and Prussia over these two areas broke out into the open in 1859. This time Austria lost.

As a result of the victory, Prussia annexed several north German states and dissolved the 1815 North German *Con*federation, replacing it with the North German Federation. This was a smaller union of states north of the River Main

Table 13-1
Indicators of Industrial Growth: Germany

I Pig Iron Production (000 tons; and as % total world production)											
1740	1800	1820	1840	1860	1870	1880*	1890	1900	1910	1913	1920**
18	39	89	167	522	1,240	2,429	4,035	7,429	12,905	19,300	6,299
11%	8%	9%	6%	7%	10%	13%	15%	19%	20%	—	10%

* includes Lorraine
** excludes Lorraine, Saar, Upper Silesia

and was not so much a league of existing states as an entirely new type of federation. The Zollverein now consisted of this Federation, Baden, Bavaria, and Wurttemberg, a grouping that would be the foundation of a united Germany. Bismarck then rewrote the Zollverein's constitution, replacing its Congress with a Customs Council and a Parliament, in which majority vote (essentially Prussia's) would determine administrative decisions. He was not able at this time to extend Zollverein links to include political ones. The South German states remained hesitant. While they clearly saw economic benefits in continued membership in a customs union, they were not ready for closer political ties.

Preparation for the Franco-Prussian War

How closer ties were eventually achieved is a story of diplomacy and duplicity on Bismarck's part, involving preparations for war with France. France in the 1860s had proposed a deal with Prussia, in which France would not object to Prussia's recent annexations if Prussia remained neutral while France annexed Belgium and part of Bavaria. Bismarck publicized his objections, thus gaining support in Germany for his protection of German rights against French aggression. France then retreated in humiliation. But the tension between them continued and came to a head in 1870 over a question of disputed succession to the Spanish throne. Bismarck this time made public a false version of what happened, and war broke out in 1870.

Prussia was victorious in the Franco-Prussian war. There was an element of revenge present when the peace treaty and the agreement establishing a united Germany was signed at Versailles in 1871 (the King of Prussia was made German Emperor). This united Germany excluded Austria, but included the North German Federation and the South German states. They had been drawn to Prussia by a common nationality, the economic advantages of the Zollverein, and Prus-

sian support for them against France. It probably also helped that Prussia had recaptured military glory from France, their former conqueror. These factors successfully overcame centuries of political fragmentation and feelings of suspicion frequently held by the smaller German states about the large powers' designs on them.

The constitution of the new Empire was Bismarck's masterpiece. It was an adaptation of the North German Federation Constitution, with the Emperor at its head, and a two-chamber legislature, the Bundesrat, which represented the rights of the states, and the Reichstag. The Reichstag was elected by universal secret suffrage, and although it seemed to be a triumph of democratic liberalism, it had only very limited powers, less than the Bundesrat, thus could also be seen as a triumph of conservative reaction. The central authority took over most of the economic functions of the states, which, however, still retained control over direct taxes, transportation, and technical education.

Germany After 1871

By the turn of the century, Germany completed her industrial revolution and became one of the most industrialized nations of the world. Much of the growth in the earlier period—stimulated by the Zollverein and the rail network, which was completed in the 1870s—provided a solid base for future development. But there were some factors specific to the early 1870s that were also advantageous.

First, one result of the Franco-Prussian War was Germany's annexation of Alsace and Lorraine. This immediately doubled the size of the German cotton industry, and Lorraine contained western Europe's largest iron ore deposits plus some important ironworks and engineering establishments. Second, the incorporation of Schleswig and Holstein into the Empire added ports on the North Sea. Later on, between 1887 and 1895, the Kiel Canal was built across the peninsula to join the North and Baltic Seas. Third, this war was followed by a short boom that affected many industries. Besides giving up two provinces, France also paid Prussia an indemnity, some of which was used for military purposes, and the building of barracks and forts led to an expansion of the building industry. The iron industry also gained, partly due to demand from the railroad companies, and partly to the establishment of new iron, steel, and engineering works. (In the years 1871-1873, nine hundred new companies were established.)

The boom ended in 1873, and the following years saw the eventual nationalization of the remaining private railways (in 1919, all railroads were turned over the State), a return to protectionism, and the beginnings of state-provided welfare services. Here, Bismarck was ahead of his time in recognizing the social consequences of the Industrial Revolution and in providing such services, although his motives were political rather than humanitarian.

Protectionism

Commercial policy protecting a nation's domestic industries from foreign competition

---

Role of Cartels

There were some other factors that also aided German industrialization at this time. One was almost unique to Germany—the use of cartels as a device for helping manufacturers. The other two, acquisition of a colonial empire and a resurgence of protectionism, were shared by all the other industrial nations at this time. (Only Britain remained true to the ideals of free trade, which had never been particularly strong in Germany anyway.)

A cartel is a group of independent producers that agree to cooperate rather than compete with each other. It can involve agreement on any or all of the following: market shares allocated to each participant, the level of prices charged, how much

---

Cartel

An association of producers agreeing to cooperate rather than compete with each other

---

production should be produced and by whom, and profit sharing. Cooperation tends to become common when the size of the firms increases, especially in a stationary or only slowly growing market. It occurs because, if all firms want to increase sales in order to tap economies of scale and achieve lower production costs, the market becomes saturated, and a price war could lower everyone's profits. Thus there is an incentive for some firms to agree not to compete in this way and to allocate market shares and fix prices so as to keep all member firms profitable; it adds an element of stability in an uncertain world. (And if noncartel firms can be squeezed out, so much the better.)

While the earliest German cartel, the Neckar Salt Union, dates back to 1828, most were established in the depressed conditions of the 1870s. Some were established to share the costs of developing new lines of activity, especially in the highly capital-intensive chemical and electrical manufacturing industries. Most were in heavy industries, coal, iron, and steel especially. Cartel activity was assisted by developments in the financial sector, where banks were also showing a tendency to increase in size, often by merging. Large banks also saw an identity of interests in encouraging industrial mergers and cooperation agreements, especially in the new electrical manufacturing industry. (This trend will be covered in more detail in a later chapter.)

Protectionism

The return to protective policies was stimulated by the depression of the 1870s, and was also a response to the increased protection of industry in other European countries at this time. Depressed conditions led to many bankruptcies in companies facing competition from foreign imports, in spite of the growth of cooperative agreements. Losing enterprises like this did not help the development of a strong economy, and many domestic industrial and agricultural producers agitated for new and/or higher tariffs. Farmers and landowners had previously been in favor of liberal trade policies, but in the 1870s, facing competition from new grain exports from the United States, German farmers lost their former markets in France and Britain and now wanted at least to be able to hold onto domestic markets with tariff protection. German exports were further limited because France was beginning to reverse her brief period of liberal trade policies, and both Russia and Austria had extremely high tariffs.

There was another, political reason for new tariffs. The new German empire received revenues from customs and excise duties and also from annual contributions made by the various state governments. Bismarck felt that this made the Reich too dependent on the whim of these governments, which threatened his ideal of a strong united Germany. So he favored an increase in tariff rates to raise the independent revenues of the central government, and in 1879 a list of new duties was introduced. Most were still low, with no duties imposed on imports of raw cotton, wool, scientific instruments, or ships, but they were subsequently revised and increased in 1885 and 1887. The continuing expansion of the economy stimulated an increase in trade, achieving the goal of increasing the Reich's revenues. Tariff policy also had the effect of providing a more stable environment for domestic manufacturers, although agriculture continued to decline. Tariffs do not seem to have had an adverse impact on prices, which remained stable until 1900, although the expansion of industrial capacity also had an influence.

Colonies

Finally, Germany began to acquire a colonial empire, a new development. Germany had no existing colonies, and although there was opposition to a colonial policy before 1871, opinion changed after unification. Colonies, it was thought, would provide new markets for increasingly prosperous industries that needed continuing expansion of demand for sustained profitability. The acquisition of new sources of supply under German control was another influencing factor, and it was believed that having colonies would make it easier for German traders to compete with British ones, who gained not only from their protected position in British colonies but also from protection given by the British navy.

After 1884, Germany began to acquire a colonial empire through negotiation, mainly in those areas of Africa and the Pacific where German traders already had commercial interests. By 1914, German holdings amounted to over one million square miles containing a population of fourteen million people.

But while this policy was motivated by commercial interests, acquisition of colonies did not produce the desired results, either in expanding markets or in providing new materials sources; even in 1913, colonial trade accounted for only 0.05 percent of total German trade. It also proved to be extremely expensive for the Reich government. Bismarck had hoped that because of the potential profits, chartered companies operating in colonies would take over the burden of administration, but the companies did not wish to do this. In fact, they gained considerably by getting land, rights to build or sink mines, and outright cash grants from the government for operating in these areas. The government was left with the responsibility for governing the colonies, which was costly, and furthermore picked up the costs of meeting the colonial companies' demands.

An additional factor can also be noted at this point. After Germany was unified, government policy was very encouraging to industrial development and it tried to create conditions favorable to further capitalist advance. As industrialization proceeded, it brought new problems with it. These problems included poor working conditions, pollution and congestion in towns, an urban housing shortage, poverty, and severe health problems. The introduction of social insurance policies in Germany was intended to try to manage some of these to help maintain a favorable environment for business; at the same time, Bismarck was hoping to reduce the appeal of a socialist alternative.

Social Welfare Legislation

Throughout most of the 19th century, little was done in any country to remedy social problems. There were some private social organizations, including charitable foundations and worker mutual aid societies, but their impact was limited. Some employers were benevolent, but again, their impact was limited. To a very large extent, the combination of traditional ideas plus laissez faire attitudes plus an increasing class polarization explained the inaction. The traditional view was that poverty had always existed, although it became much more visible now because it was concentrated in the towns. The class division meant that those with the wealth and power and ability to do something had no incentive, because they did not suffer from any of the problems.

While it may seem that Bismarck was an unlikely champion of pro-worker legislation, his political savoir faire should not be underestimated. As previously mentioned, he was no friend of liberalism. He wanted a strong Germany and recognized that strength depended on industrialization—which at this time was capitalist industrialization—but capitalist industrialization also produced problems. He wanted to address these problems in order to consolidate the hold on

Social Welfare Policy

Social policies aimed at improving the population's well-being, in areas such as health, education, pensions

power of the reactionary forces at the head of the German government. Having successfully squashed middle class liberalism, he recognized that doing nothing about labor problems raised the possibility of an even more potent threat to the existence of a united Germany based on capitalist industrialization: socialism. Even in the 1870s, socialist ideas, which had gained a large following among workers, were beginning to move out of the realm of theory and into practice. In 1877, socialists polled half a million votes in the elections for the Reichstag and held 12 seats.

This resulted in intensified pressure against socialists. Employers were instructed not to hire anyone thought to be a socialist; there was considerable harassment of socialist meetings; and in 1878, the Socialist Party was banned and fifty newspapers suppressed. However, the stick approach did not work: Socialism continued to appeal to workers. So Bismarck decided to adopt the carrot approach, hoping that if the provision of state welfare services improved conditions, workers would accept the inevitability of the capitalist system and be less inclined to support a socialist alternative.

"Carrot and Stick" Approach

Pleasant promises designed to encourage some behavior patterns combined with threats intended to deter other types of behavior

Thus, in 1883, the first part of the program was adopted. This was a Health Insurance Law, making insurance for factory workers, miners, and lower-paid white collar workers compulsory. It was later extended to farmers, but those already covered by state or municipal schemes were exempted. By 1889, 5.5 million workers were insured for benefits that included free medical attention and benefits to be paid in case of sickness. Contributions were paid jointly by employer and employee, and the actual administration was carried out by friendly societies. In 1884, coverage was extended with the Accident Insurance

Law, which paid grants or widow's benefits in the event of an industrial accident that prevented a worker from earning a wage. By 1889, 13 million workers were insured against this sort of catastrophe. The final part, which made the system almost completely comprehensive, came in 1889 when an old age and disability pension scheme was added, funded by contributions from employers, employees, and a subsidy from the government. This scheme provided a retirement pension to workers once they reached the age of seventy, or a pension if they were no longer able to work because of disability before then. In 1899 widows and surviving children of insured workers who died before reaching this age also became eligible for pensions.

Health, accident, and retirement pensions provided an element of security to a work force dependent on wage income by providing an alternative source of income if the wage was no longer forthcoming because of illness or old age. In earlier times, this security had been provided through the network of rights and obligations that were part of the feudal tradition, or through an explicitly societal responsibility for the misfortune of its individual members, who were at the mercy of events they could not control. But in every country since the 14th century, this network was eroded, and with the coming of laissez faire and the individualist ethic, society as a whole no longer accepted the responsibility. For so long as economies were not heavily monetized, market economies, and if subsistence was available through a family's own efforts, survival might be hard but was possible. But the creation of a permanent wage earning class solely dependent on a money income for survival, especially one concentrated in cities, produced problems beyond the control of any one individual. Depressed business conditions leading to unemployment were outside the worker's control. Industrialists' concern for profits above all led to factory conditions that invited accidents, while generally poor working and living conditions in the industrial towns

were not conducive to the maintenance of good health.

The recognition of state responsibility to provide remedies for the inevitable occurrences of modern industrial life was a significant achievement, and one that would be copied later by other industrial countries. In Germany, employers criticized these policies, but criticism was offset by the feeling of security gained by employees and the contribution they made to an improved standard of living. As an example, the death rate declined from twenty-seven per thousand in the 1870s to sixteen per thousand in 1910.

However, Bismarck's hope that a social insurance scheme would prevent workers from being attracted to socialism was not realized. The socialist vote in the Reichstag steadily increased. After 1890, the law banning the Party's existence effectively lapsed, and by 1910 the Socialists were the largest party in the Reichstag, holding 110 seats, thus for the first time being capable of providing an opposition element in Germany. In addition, many unions and friendly societies were controlled by the Socialist party.

Expansion

In the early 1880s, Germany truly became an industrialized country: In 1882, for the first time, the same numbers of people were employed in industry and commerce as in agriculture. Industrialization speeded up after that, and by 1907, twice as many people were employed in industry as in agriculture. This paralleled increases in the urban population; by 1910, there were 23 cities in Germany with over 200,000 people in them. All this occurred as population grew from 35.5 million in 1850 to 48 million in 1888 and to 66 million in 1913, making Germany the second largest country in Europe after Russia. Emigration also dropped significantly by this time, a probable indication that conditions were improving within Germany itself.

Economic growth took place with much state support. The transportation system, including both railways and waterways, increasingly came under public ownership, and further improvements were made. The railways and new canals, such as the Dortmund-Ems Canal, which linked the Ruhr industrial area to Emden, the Berlin-Stettin Canal, and the Rhine-Herne Canal, plus the construction of new harbor facilities made it possible to move bulky goods quickly and cheaply. This was important, as Germany's industrial strength lay in heavy industry, which outranked textiles as the dominating element in the economy after 1870. This late-century spurt of canal building was almost unique to Germany, for few other important canals were built in other countries once the rail network was in place.

Heavy Industry
Core industries in an industrialized nation, such as power generation and metalworking

---

Industrial Development

By 1913 Germany was second only to Britain as a coal producer in Europe, producing 190 million tons of coal and an additional 87 million tons of lignite to Britain's 287 million tons. Most, 112 million tons, came from the Ruhr, where large companies increasingly dominated— one third of the Ruhr's output came from only six companies. The same sort of expansion also occurred in the iron and steel industry, one dominated by a small number of vertically integrated producers. They controlled production from the mining of coal and iron ore through the production of iron and steel all the way through to machine making and engineering establishments.

The introduction of the basic process in steel making in 1878 spurred the exploitation of Lorraine's ore deposits. Steel production was lower cost than Britain's, as German producers' late start meant they adopted the latest technology. By 1913, Germany produced 13.1 million tons of

steel—more than Britain—and was second only to the United States in steel production. Most of the incentive to expand in iron and steel was due to increasing internal demand from industry, the railways, and construction, but export demand was also important for machinery production, and Germany became a leading supplier of industrial machinery.

A related industry that also expanded rapidly at this time was shipbuilding. In the mid 1880s, Britain was the world's largest shipbuilder, and Germany had only a small capacity for shipbuilding. In addition, only half her 1.2 million tons of merchant shipping was powered by steam, although steam was becoming the prevalent power source in shipping. But by 1913, the situation had changed, and an increasing volume of trade encouraged an expansion of the merchant marine to 4.4 million tons. At this time, Germany was second only to Britain as a trading nation. Shipbuilding boomed, and large shipyards were established at Hamburg (which also became more important as a port once steamships were common), Bremen, and Stettin. These yards even successfully competed with British yards for export orders.

Development of heavy industry was a characteristic of all industrializing countries in the 19th century. This is because it involved steampower and machinery that stimulated the coal, iron, steel, and related industries.

Importance of Scientific Applications

Where Germany made a special contribution was in the application of science to industrial uses. The result was the development of two 20th century industries, chemicals and electrical manufacturing. Although Germany did not invent all of the ideas that were subsequently used by industry, German firms were very active in putting many of them to use.

Among the explanations for this success, two are almost unique to Germany. The first was state assistance to industrial development, especially in new areas, to encourage activities enhancing Germany's strength. This assistance came in various forms. One was the recognition of the legitimacy of public involvement; in contrast, laissez faire influence in Britain, for example, implied that research that might lead to practical application of laboratory experiments would not receive public financing as a matter of course. A second one was the absence of an anti-monopoly policy, which permitted firms wishing to exploit new areas to combine, and pool the funds and knowledge necessary for these new, expensive, and risky undertakings. A third was that public authorities frequently provided a market for some of the resulting output—explosives were used by the army, while the gas produced by the coking process was used in municipal street lighting systems, for example. A fourth factor was the education system, which through technical high schools, for example, was increasingly oriented toward producing the technical skills needed by a changing industrial structure. This orientation toward science had been started early in Prussia, when education was removed from church control to become the responsibility of the State.

The second explanation was the existence of close ties between academic research laboratories and industry. This was unlike the situation in Britain, for example, where although the universities were improving, they were more likely to advance in basic research. But in Germany, close links between universities and industry implied a closer focus on applied science. For example, von Liebig was a German chemistry professor whose work on the chemical composition of plants led to the development of the inorganic fertilizer industry.

The New Chemical Industry

A third factor, but one not unique to Germany, was the existence of the raw materials necessary for these new industries. In chemicals, the most important resource at this time was coal, which Germany had in abundance. Coal is a surprisingly versatile mineral. When heated to produce coke, five major groups of byproducts emerge, each used to produce a wide variety of further products, ranging from asphalt, aspirin, and baking soda through cosmetics, dyes, explosives, fertilizers, hosiery, insecticides, linoleum, mothballs, paints, photographic developers, and plastics, to synthetic rubber and waterproofing materials.

Coke is the largest byproduct (76 percent) and can be burned as fuel and used to smelt metal (its first major use) and to produce graphite, carborundum, baking soda, and washing soda. Gas produced in the coking process accounts for 17 percent of coal's byproducts. It can be used for lighting or as a fuel; the sulphur is used to produce sulfuric acid which is then used in the agricultural chemical industry to produce fertilizers, fungicides, and insecticides. Cyanogen gas has further uses: in producing dyes, pigments, resins, and artificial silk; in photography; and in gold and silver plating. Tar accounts for 5 percent of the coal byproducts and is used to produce dyes, plastics, phonograph records, radio parts, preservatives, insulating materials, storage batteries, and perfumes, among others. Light oil accounts for 1.5 percent, and one of its byproducts is toluol, used to produce the TNT (trinitrotoluene) explosive. It is also used to produce solvents, dyes, plastics, and insecticides. Finally, some residual chemicals include nitric acid and ammonium nitrate (fertilizers, dyes, and explosives), ammonia (paper manufacturing, pharmaceuticals, and disinfectants), ammonium phosphate (fertilizers), ammonium persulphate (photography and oxidizing agents), and ammonium sulphate (fertilizers and explosives).

Naturally, the chemical industry did not emerge full fledged with all these branches in operation at one time. The first use of coal as a chemical raw material occurred in 1856 in England, when the manufacture of a synthetic dye from coal tar was established. Previously, all dyes

Synthetics
Artificial equivalents of natural things

used were organic, produced, for example, from plants such as indigo (blues) or madder (reds). But with the rapid expansion of the textile industry, a major user of dyes, it was difficult for organic sources to expand sufficiently fast to keep up with demand. Thus the impetus given to finding alternatives. In the 1870s, leadership in the production of synthetic dyes shifted to Germany, and by 1913 Germany produced 88 percent of the world's total, with 80 percent of this output being exported. (As one consequence, indigo farming in India declined.)

Germany also led in the development of a modern inorganic chemical industry producing pharmaceuticals, photographic chemicals, explosives, plastics, synthetic fibers, and fertilizers. The consequences of some of these developments would not be apparent for many years. For example, the development of synthetic fibers (the first produced from coal was nylon) later posed a serious challenge to the traditional textile industries. The production of pharmaceuticals, including aspirin and the antibiotic sulfa drugs, revolutionized the practice of medicine. Availability of inorganic fertilizers led to dramatic increases in agricultural productivity. The entire phenomenon of photography would revolutionize ordinary people's leisure time as well as lead to the development of the movie industry and the transformation of the advertising industry, both of which were still only in their early stages. Development in chemicals was dominated by large firms associated with one of the two major combinations, the Bayer group and Höchst group. (In 1916, these two groups combined forces to produce the unit called I.G. Farben.)

Electricity

Progress made in science and technology was also important in the development of the electrical industry, which began in Germany in the 1880s. The principles of electricity had been known for some time, and its first practical application came with the development of the telegraph. The United States and the United Kingdom took the lead in the manufacture of telegraphic equipment in the 1850s and 1860s; then in 1866 Werner von Siemens invented the electric dynamo. This permitted mechanical motion to be produced from electric power, and led to experimentation with electric traction. Electricity's potential as a new energy source for both lighting and power was quickly recognized, and companies set up to develop it got financial support from banks. The result was electric street lighting and electric powered trams or trolleys, a new form of urban mass transport replacing the old horse-drawn omnibus. Provision of these services was increasingly taken over by municipal authorities from private companies in the late 1880s, in recognition of their importance to the cities' economic health.

Private manufacturing of electrical equipment expanded and included telephone and telegraph communications equipment, electric furnaces for steel making, electro-chemical processes, and appliances using electric motors. Germany became the world's leading manufacturer and exporter of electrical equipment. This industry too was dominated by cartels, formed in reaction to the depressed conditions following the boom in electrical manufacturing in the 1890s. The two cartels formed in this period were AEG, which focused on electric lighting uses, and Siemens-Halske, which manufactured dynamos and equipment for electric railways.

Vertical Integration
A merger of enterprises at different stages of production

Summary

Bismarck's rule ended in 1890, by which time it was clear that his dream of a united Germany as an industrial power was being realized. Germany's special contribution came with the development of science-based industries that were to become characteristic leading edge industries in the 20th century.

German development was unique in the 19th century in that political changes and economic changes occurred almost simultaneously. The drive for German unification is inseparable from the progress made in industrialization. While many countries in the 20th century are faced with the same problem—the need to develop a modern state *and* a modern economy—Germany's experience is not a blueprint, because conditions today are so completely different. Part of the explanation of Germany's rapid transformation to its position at the end of the century can be found in the encouragement given to private industry by the State. Without this, even with the advantages of unification and a larger market, it is doubtful whether the new industries Germany pioneered could have been established, given their enormous finance capital and skill requirements.

What was true of 19th century industrialization was that it produced "old" or already-known products in a new location, the factory. But, as was demonstrated with the development of the chemical and electrical industries and would be even more apparent later, 20th century industrial expansion depended on producing "new," previously unknown, products. In an atmosphere of laissez faire, producing what was never known before is difficult and risky. It is easier with active encouragement of research, help with the development and extension of markets, and a safe environment for producers. New research then makes it more likely that new products will be discovered, even if the search was originally for something else—the serendipity effect of subsidized research. The problem for private industry is how to develop a market to make production profitable. In other words, the focus of production changes; before then finding markets was not one of the industrialists' basic concerns because whatever they produced could be sold, barring depression. The question of how such markets are developed and maintained, a 20th century issue, will be taken up in a later chapter.

Key Concepts

Ad valorem duty
Artificial barrier
Cartel
Customs union
Electricity
Heavy industry
Political fragmentation

Protectionism
Social welfare
Specific duty
Synthetics
Vertical integration
Zollverein

Questions for Discussion or Essay Writing

1. Compare and contrast the approach to industrialization taken by Germany, France, and Great Britain. Is it possible to say that one approach is better than another?

2. Describe the disincentives to capitalist industrialization that existed in Germany at the beginning of the 19th century. What were the major problems that had to be overcome before Germany could industrialize?

3. To what extent is an urban "middle class" necessary to economic development?

4. To what extent is an active state necessary to economic development?

5. Describe the developments that helped the exploitation of German coal resources.

6. Do wars help or hinder economic development? Discuss with reference to Germany.

7. To what extent does national unification have advantages for a country's economic development?

8. What was the impact of the introduction of social welfare policies in Germany?

9. Are there advantages for a latecomer to industrialization?

10. Discuss the emergence of the chemical industry in Germany.

11. "New" industries began to appear in the late 19th century. What was new about them? What was their impact?

12. Discuss the emergence of electrical manufacturing in Germany.

For Further Reading

Barkin, Kenneth D. *The Controversy over German Industrialization 1890–1902*, Chicago: University of Chicago Press, 1970.

Brown, John. C. "Market Organization, Protection and Vertical Integration: German Cotton Textiles Before 1914." *Journal of Economic History*, 52:2 (June 1992,): 339–352.

Clapham, John H. *The Economic Development of France and Germany, 1815–1914*, 4th ed. Cambridge: Cambridge University Press, 1936.

Evans, Richard J. and W.R.Lee, eds. *The German Peasantry: Conflict and Community in Rural Society*. London: Macmillan, 1985.

Forbes, I.L.D. "German Informal Imperialism in South America Before 1914." *Economic History Review*, XXXI:3 (1977): 384–398.

Hagen, William W. "How Mighty the Junkers? Peasant Rents and Seigneurial Profits in Sixteenth-Century Brandenburg." *Past and Present*, vol.108 Aug. 1985 80–116.

Henderson, W.O. *The Industrial Revolution in Europe, 1815–1914*. Chicago: Quadrangle Books, 1961.

_____ *The Rise of German Industrial Power 1834–1914*. Berkeley: University of California Press, 1975.

Lee, W.R. "Economic Development and the State in Nineteenth Century Germany." *Economic History Review*, XLI:3 (1987): 346–367.

Maschte, Erich. *Outline of the History of German Cartels from 1873–1914*, in F. Crouzet, W.H. Chaloner and W.M. Stern, eds. *Essays in European Economic History, 1789–1914*. New York: St. Martin's Press, 1970.

Moeller, Robert G. *Peasants and Lords in Modern Germany: Recent Studies in Agricultural History*. Boston: Allen & Unwin, 1986.

Overy, R.J. *The Nazi Economic Recovery, 1932–38*. London: Macmillan.

Stolpe, Gustav. *The German Economy 1870 to the Present*, new ed. London: Weidenfeld & Nicholson (1940) 1967.

Tilly, Richard. *Financial Institutions and Industrialization in the Rhineland, 1815-1870*. Madison: University of Wisconsin Press, 1966.

_____ "Mergers, External Growth and Finance in the Development of Large-Scale Enterprise in Germany, 1880-1913." *Journal of Economic History* (September 1982).

Chapter 14

Capitalism in the United States: The First Phase (Up to 1860)

IN CHAPTER 7, WE WERE FIRST INTRODUCED to the economic development of the New World, seen as part of the development of mercantilist empires. In this chapter, we will focus on the experience of the former British colonies of North America that were the original United States. The country grew after independence when the former French and Spanish colonial areas as well as the relatively unpeopled western territories were added, preparing the basis for the emergence of a powerful economy. While much of the focus of this text has been on the role of industrialization in the wealth-creation process, the experience of the United States also provides another important lesson—that an agricultural country is not doomed to poverty. While the United States does have a world-class industrial sector, its agricultural sector is world class as well.

Capitalist industrialization in the United States did not begin in earnest until after the end of the Civil War (1865), but its earlier experience helps make clear what is needed for industrialization. The American Industrial Revolution was compressed into a very short period of time, the happy result of an extremely favorable resource endowment plus the advantages connected with making a late start. By 1900, while it was clear that the United States was becoming the world's indus-

trial leader, there were some special factors accounting for its different pattern of development.

The most significant is that the United States was never a feudal country. When the first European immigrants, influenced by the emerging capitalist environment they had left, began to structure a new economy, they did not have to overcome remnants of the past. Another related difference is that to the European immigrants, it was a new, wilderness country, which had both stimulating and delaying effects. On the one hand, the absence of traditions meant that it was easier to adopt new ideas. But on the other, the absence of towns, roads, communications, and all the other necessities for a civilized life and a flourishing economy meant that it would be harder and take longer to achieve the same levels of economic development as the European countries.

A third unique and somewhat unusual difference was that the United States relied on slave labor in its development. This is unique because, as we have already noted, capitalism is associated with the existence of a free labor force. The use of slaves in the United States was a response to some special features of its development. How slaves were used in profit-oriented production and the struggle for their emancipation resulted in distinct differences between the American and the European economies.

In addition, while capitalist institutions were accepted and established, there was nothing automatic or preordained to indicate that development would be *industrial* development. Not until the middle of the 19th century did industry and industrialists show signs of becoming dominant, with business (manufacturing) interests taking over leadership roles. Throughout the earlier period of the country's existence, there was a very strong antipathy to industry and urbanization, an antipathy partly rooted in the ideology of colonial America. The early immigrants were influenced by the demands for political freedom present in the England they had left behind. More important, the availability of ample land made it possible for people to own and farm their own land, which fitted in well with the desire for economic independence no longer possible in England. Also, later on the conditions existing in industrializing, urbanizing Britain were seen as threatening to a strong political democracy, and for a long time, industrial activity was seen as degrading. Only when land became scarcer —when the frontier of western settlement was closed—was industrialization favored.

In this chapter, the first topic to be covered will be the role of economic resources in economic development put into an American context. This will provide a background for a discussion of economic activity in colonial America, the impact of political independence, the importance of the railways, and initial industrialization in the first half of the 19th century. Focus will initially be on the thirteen English colonies (what are now the states of New Hampshire, Massachusetts, Rhode Island, Connecticut, New York, New Jersey, Pennsylvania, Delaware, Maryland, Virginia, the Carolinas, and Georgia), because these were more important in the explanation of the capitalist development of the United States than the French or Spanish colonies that subsequently became part of the United States.

Resource Endowment

Any economic activity in any country is ultimately dependent on its resource endowment: its relative supplies of land, labor, and capital; their nature and quality; and, for a capitalist economy, the nature and extent of its market. How resources will be used depends on the level of technological development. In the first two centuries of American development, two major features of its resource endowment stood out. First, the abundance of land and natural resources on or in the land, and second, the relative scarcity of labor.

Resource Endowment

The relative supplies of land, labor, and capital in a country

---

The land area of North America is immense (just how immense the first settlers did not know). The land was fertile, filled with rich virgin forests and deposits of potentially valuable mineral resources, and there was a range of climatic conditions. But it was primitive wilderness. There was no social overhead capital, no roads, bridges, harbors, or canals, making it impossible to introduce European techniques immediately. These techniques flourished in Europe only when all the supporting conditions were present, which would not be the case in the United States until the 19th century.

Capital, in both money and real form, was also scarce. Money capital had to be imported, and imports of capital equipment remained crucial until well into the 19th century. However, not until late into the century did the capital shortage cease to be a constraint on economic activity.

Labor Shortage and Development

Labor scarcity also gave development a peculiar character. The immigrant population was tiny in the first years. It was estimated at 52,000 in 1650, but expanded rapidly. A century later, it had reached 1.2 million; at the time of the first census in 1790, it was 3.9 million, and it increased dramatically after that to reach 76 million by 1900, by which time, thanks to massive waves of immigration, labor scarcity was no longer an issue.

Applying economic reasoning to this situation, we would expect those activities requiring much land and little labor or capital to be important, delaying labor-using manufacturing until much later. Agriculture was necessary for sheer survival in the first centuries, but other primary activities involving the gathering or production of raw materials continued to be important. We would not expect any large-scale manufacturing. Labor scarcity, other things being equal, tends to imply a high wage rate; manufacturing could expand in England because large amounts of labor kept wage rates low. In addition, as previously noted, the supporting infrastructure simply was not present, so much private productive activity would have been impossible or extremely high-cost.

Also, other things were not equal. Until about the 1830s, most of the immigrants to the English colonies had no intention of becoming employees. The availability of land and the ideology of free men seeking a new start implied that most wanted to be independent farmers and not permanent wage laborers. This easy access to land also delayed the full-scale introduction of industry organized along capitalist lines later on.

Were there any options available to deal with this situation? Perhaps the indigenous Indians could have been used as a labor force, as the Spanish had done in their New World colonies in South America. This was not even considered in the thirteen colonies. Native Americans were seen as an obstacle, but not a serious one initially, as a large land area implied that there was room for everyone. However, this view changed in the 19th century, when farmers, ranchers, and mining companies saw Indian claims to the West as blocks to settlement. Starting after the Civil War, an implicit policy of eliminating Indians and

pushing the survivors onto smaller and smaller reservations began. The Indians for their part, with a noncapitalist culture, could not understand either the whites' desire to own land privately or their destruction of those resources such as buffaloes and forests that had sustained Indians for so long.

Since there was no free labor force to do the work the capital owners needed done, they used forced labor. Throughout the 17th and in part of the 18th century, indentured servitude was a common way of providing labor. This meant that a potential immigrant would agree to work for an employer for four to five years, after which time there would be no further link between them. In return—and this was its appeal to the poorer servant—the employer paid for passage across the Atlantic. While the use of indentures made it possible for owners to use capital productively, the problem was that at the end of the contracted-for term, the servant was a free person and no longer willing to work for an employer. (About half of all white immigrants to the colonies came over in this way.)

Indentured Servant

A person who is contractually bound to work for a master for a specified period of time

---

The lack of a permanent work force was a particular problem for the commercial exploitation of agriculture and led to the second form of forced labor, slavery, which accounted for all the black immigrants to the United States. Slave labor made the plantations pay but involved its own special costs in turn. It made economic activity inflexible because the slaves were part of the plantation's capital assets and could not be fired when demand for plantation products was low. As we will see later, in theory slaves could be sold, but if all slave owners tried to sell at the same time, the resulting fall in prices did not make it a satisfactory solution.

Looking at resource endowments alone implied an emphasis on primary activities such as agriculture and the extractive industries, with manufactured goods being imported. During colonial times, an institutional factor reinforced this tendency: the thirteen colonies were part of the British mercantilist empire, and as such, had a special role to play. This role was as a provider of raw materials to Britain, and certain activities were not permitted in the colonies. Although these mercantilist restrictions were eliminated once political independence was attained, the underlying economic conditions did not change. There was no spurt of industrialization after Independence, as there was still no incentive to industrialize. Manufactured imports were easily available, investors saw higher returns in trade or land acquisition, the technological problems limiting manufacturing still existed—and on top of all this, the Jeffersonian idea that manufacturing was inherently degrading was influential. Not until infrastructure was put into place, capital became more widely available, the labor shortage overcome through immigration, and a mass market developed did the United States industrialize on a large scale. This did not happen until the 1860s.

Economic Issues and Independence

Although the struggle for independence for the thirteen colonies is usually presented in political terms, there were also economic causes revolving around resentment of mercantilist restrictions imposed by Britain. Most of the population, in particular small independent farmers and urban artisans, was not really affected by these economic issues but still supported the independence movement, which included demands for greater political freedom and greater representation in legislatures. However, two groups, merchants and shippers in the North and plantation owners in the South grew increasingly resentful of mer-

cantilist restrictions. Although these two groups were in the minority, their wealth and economic importance gave them a much greater influence than numbers alone indicated.

Trading Patterns and Problems

First, why was trade an issue? This is an important question, especially given that the protected status of the colonies formed the basis for the development of a wealthy, aristocratic merchant elite in Boston and the other seaports in the 17th century. Trade was most affected by the colonies' status within the British mercantilist empire, linking Britain and the colonies in ways that were political and cultural as well as economic. But the very success of a protected economic status led to a desire to expand further, and thus to a resentment of continued colonial status that blocked such further expansion.

This was felt more in the northern colonies where trade was more important. The pattern of commerce in the South during colonial times was a fairly simple, two-way trade with Britain. Exports were agricultural and primary products: tobacco from Maryland and Virginia, rice, indigo, and naval stores from the Carolinas. With the revenues received from the sale of exports, the southern colonies bought manufactured goods such as textiles, furniture, glassware, and hardware from Britain, and they also imported slaves from Africa. Trade with Britain was approximately balanced.

The northern pattern was more complex, mainly due to the fact that not all of what the colonies produced was complementary to Britain's production, thus third markets had to be found. This was necessary in order to acquire revenues to buy the desired manufactured items in Britain for importation into the colonies. There was a direct link only with furs, ships, and naval stores. Thus, Pennsylvania and New York both produced wheat and flour, and the New England colonies had an advantage in fishing, but these items were not needed in Britain, which was self-sufficient in grains and fish. Several trade patterns illustrate the adjustment to the situation.

For example, grain and fish could be sold in southern Europe, wine and fruit bought with the proceeds, and then shipped to Britain for sale. The resulting revenues would be used to acquire manufactured goods. This was noncontroversial. Another pattern, however, did lead to problems as it involved trade with the West Indies, the most valuable of Britain's western hemisphere colonial possessions because they produced sugar. Food (flour and fish) and lumber could be sold to the West Indies, which did not produce enough food to feed all the slaves required to work the commercial sugar plantations. Then a cargo of sugar or molasses could be shipped to Britain and exchanged for manufactured goods. Variations on this pattern also occurred. For example, molasses could be taken to New England, distilled into rum, and then used in the African slave trade to acquire more slaves for shipment to the West Indies or the southern colonies. (Newport's merchants in particular became important in this slave trade.)

However, this pattern involved not only increasing conflicts with Britain, as will become clear later, but also conflicts within the colonies themselves. (The colonies were not subject to a unified government, and there was no coordination of commercial relations between them.) This conflict also involved the growth of Boston as the leading commercial city. New England, unlike the other areas, had few internal resources that could be used in trade. Hence Boston merchants early on became exclusively concerned with the importation and distribution of foreign manufactures, as well as the export of goods from the other colonies, and Boston dominated the coastal trade between the different colonies. However, because so much of the import trade was concentrated there, money drained from the other colonies to Boston merchants. More technically, Boston had a surplus on its balance of trade with the other

colonies, which they resented. Hard currency was always scarce, and later became another cause of resentment leading up to Independence.

Currency Problems

Currency was a problem, as most of the available money was used to offset the adverse trade balance with Britain. So from fairly early times, coins were supplemented with paper money (bills of credit), giving rise to two problems, with one continuing to be a major issue until the early 20th century. This was the question of control: Specifically, how much paper should be allowed to circulate? On the one hand, merchants and urban interests favored a very tight control over money issue but came into conflict with farmers and landowners in country districts. These groups favored a much more liberal expansion, mainly because, as they held large amounts of debt, it was to their advantage if currency depreciation (inflation) occurred. Then their debts could be repaid with a smaller real burden as money then would be cheaper. (In the colonies, South Carolina's paper money depreciated considerably, and in 1730, bills of credit exchanged in a seven to one ratio with sterling.)

The second issue concerned the legitimacy of paper money and brought the colonists into head-on conflict with the British government. For a long time, a policy of benign neglect characterized the administration of the colonies. But by the middle of the 18th century, many old regulations began to be tightened up and new ones imposed to try to return the colonists more firmly to the mercantilist fold. Thus, in 1764 the Currency Act was passed, prohibiting the issue of paper money in the colonies. If enforced (which it was not), colonial economic activity would have been severely restricted by limiting the available medium of exchange.

Limits of Mercantilism

By the 18th century, colonial merchants were coming up against the limits of mercantilism in their search for profitable opportunities, especially in two areas. One possibility came with a limited westward expansion, fueled by the expansion of the fur trade and by the realization that continuing population growth and settlement would increase land values. If this happened, more agricultural and extractive goods would be available for export or for sale in the growing urban markets of the eastern seaboard, and there would also be a demand for imports into these same areas. Colonial merchants wanted to retain control over this expansion. Boston merchants were still dominant but faced an increasing amount of competition from rivals in Philadelphia and the other seaports after 1730.

It was the second aspect, the search for new opportunities beyond those permitted by the Navigation Acts that led to most conflict with Britain, resulting in northern merchants' eventual leadership of the movement for independence. This concerned trade with the West Indies. The colonies were important suppliers of food to these islands, were heavily involved with the slave trade to them (there were then more slaves in the West Indies than on the North American mainland), and also shipped sugar and molasses from the islands. Ironically, it was the Navigation Acts themselves that gave a role to colonial merchants and shippers.

Sugar and Rum

All the colonizing European countries claimed sugar islands in the Caribbean, but until the passage of the Navigation Acts, the Dutch had a commanding position in the carrying trade between non-Dutch islands and Europe. The Navigation Acts successfully eliminated the Dutch by requiring that all trade between Britain and British colonies or between British colonies be carried in British or colonial ships. Because colonial ships were in demand and colonial merchants on an expansion path, they quickly became involved in this trade.

The problem arose when these merchants began trading with non-British sugar islands, which was more profitable for them due to an inconsistency in French policy. This inconsistency arose because policy in France aimed to strengthen the agricultural sector, including the production of wine and brandy. French Caribbean islands were important for strategic as well as commercial reason, as indeed they were for the other European colonists. The problem for France was that sugar was used to produce rum, and importing rum into France competed with the interests of French brandy producers. So while sugar production was important—rum was used as a bargaining item both in the slave trade and in the fur trade with American Indians—the market for French-island sugar was not restricted to French buyers only. In particular, and unlike sugar from British plantations, it was not subject to an export tax. Thus, although colonial merchants were supposed to buy sugar only from British islands, they frequently bought it more cheaply from French plantations.

Naturally, this was not in the interests of the British West Indies sugar planters, who saw their market weaken. They were a powerful interest group in Britain, and in 1733 succeeded in getting the Sugar Act passed, prohibiting the importation of any foreign sugar, molasses, or rum into Britain or the colonies. But it was not, and could not be, enforced, given the difficulty of policing both the Caribbean area and the entire New England coast.

In fact, the sugar growers suffered, but nothing was done until the end of the Seven Years War with France in 1763.[1] During this and earlier wars, New England merchants had been profitably supplying both sides. So when hostilities ended, they were accused of trading with the enemy. This action initiated the end of the period of benign neglect of the colonies, and the start of a more rigorous attempt to enforce mercantilist policies in the colonies.

To this end, a new Sugar Act was passed in 1764. It lowered the import duty on sugar and molasses imported into the colonies in an attempt to make sugar from British islands more competitive with French-island sugar to reduce the incentive to smuggle. In addition, and this was what most incensed the merchants, enforcement activities were stepped up. Colonial merchants thus disliked continued colonial status because efforts to tighten mercantilist policies conflicted with their plans for expansion. Expansion was important to them, because it promised profits.

Restrictions on Land

The second strand of irritation against continued colonial status affected landowners and land speculators in particular, and again the end of war with France brought it out into the open. For so long as Canada and the Ohio Valley had been in French hands, British authority had encouraged settlement there to encroach on French claims and upset the fur trade. Landowners approved of this. The recognition that an expanding population would increase land values had already led to some land speculation in what are now the states of West Virginia and Ohio. In addition, farmers and plantation owners wanted to move west to new fertile areas, and this was especially important for tobacco growers.

However, between 1763 and 1774 colonists were effectively prevented from doing so. In 1763 all the land west of the Appalachians came under the control of British authorities, and colonial governors were not permitted to continue their former practice of making land grants to colonists. In addition, settlers already in the area were required to return, the reason being that no protection could be given them against Indian hostilities if they stayed. Then the Quebec Act of 1774 annexed land north of the Ohio River to Quebec, effectively channelling the northern fur trade through Montreal and out of the hands of American merchants.

Given the small numbers of people involved, these provisions would probably have been accepted, even if unwillingly. But there was a further, obvious injustice: While colonial landowners were excluded from western lands, land grants were still being made to British landowners and merchants. This was shortsighted, as it alienated southern landowners who had always been the most loyal to British rule.

Catalysts for Rebellion

On top of these two underlying strands of resentment against trade and land policies were other events that brought the colonies to the boiling point. During the Seven Years War, the colonies had enjoyed an economic boom; providers of provisions and merchants especially gained. But with the end of the war, this extra demand disappeared and depression set in, lasting until the end of the decade. This depression was felt most severely in the seaports.

There were also some repressive measures, imposed as part of the effort to tighten mercantilist policies and justified in Britain as part of the effort to make the colonists pay more for their own defense. Although the economic impact was small—it has been estimated that the average tax paid by colonists was 5 percent, which compared favorably with an average of 30 percent in England—what was most important was the perception of injustice felt by colonists. That is, some of these measures were internal taxes, and previous procedure had always been that internal taxes could be imposed only by colonists on themselves and not by Parliament in London.

The most notorious of these was the Stamp Act, passed in 1765. This followed the Sugar Act of 1764, which, while it lowered import duties on foreign sugar, had also increased duties on indigo, coffee, wine, and textiles, therefore raising the price of many items imported into the colonies.

The Stamp Act required stamps (of varying prices) to be put on documents such as licenses, contracts, wills, newspapers, and pamphlets. This again was shortsighted as it affected lawyers and publishers who had the most influence on public opinion. Resistance to it was great, leading to an effective boycott of imported British goods. As it affected economic interests in Britain itself, the Stamp Act was repealed in the following year.

Again, repeal might have satisfied colonial aspirations but for the effect of other repressive measures. One, passed in 1765, required that colonists must provide the necessary lodging for army units in their districts. A second, the 1767 Townshend Act, imposed tariffs on items such as tea, glass, and paper. They were low duties, but because the goods were used by a broader cross section of the population than wine and silk, they had the result of raising the cost of living. Another act reorganized the colonial customs service in an attempt to crack down on smuggling.

By this time, resistance had broadened to include small farmers, tradespeople, and urban artisans, whose motives for supporting the movement for more freedom in the colonies were varied. Farmers, for example, wanted representation in colonial legislatures equal to that of larger property owners. (At that time, only large property owners could vote.) Resistance successfully resulted in many of these acts being repealed by 1770, although the duty on tea was retained.

In 1770 the depression was effectively over and trade expanded again. But once more, another shortsighted action renewed opposition to British rule. This time it was the Tea Act, passed in 1773, which gave the East India Company the monopoly of selling tea in the colonies. While this actually resulted in the price of tea becoming lower than ever before, it aroused the opposition of colonial merchants, who were denied further participation in the tea trade. What was more, they feared that a complete loss of their trade in other items could follow if other such monopolies were granted. Hence, merchants once again were in the forefront of opposition to British rule.

War with Britain

This led to a period of war with Britain (1775-1782) and the attainment of American independence, uniting the thirteen colonies into one nation. However, in spite of resentment against British rule, the colonists were not completely united, either in breaking with Britain or in what they wanted the newly independent country to be, and some of the issues that emerged were not handled entirely successfully. They would also have considerable economic impact.

Conservative defenders of colonialism emphasized the economic advantages of continued colonial status, which included the advantages of trading in a large protected market, the protection to shipping given by the Royal Navy, and protection against Indians. But they were also aware that, as the American colonists had always had more freedom, more prosperity and more rights than colonists elsewhere, it was important to defend these privileges against encroachment. This led to a problem, because while they wanted more political rights, if independence was needed to achieve them, it was not only treason against an established government, but could also be seen as a precedent for future revolutionaries—who could encroach on their rights. This dilemma was not satisfactorily solved. Some Loyalists (at least 35,000, probably more) eventually left to reestablish roots in Canada, others went to the new areas west of the Appalachians, while others simply accepted the changing situation.

Political Implications

While support for independence came from all parts of the population, it was led mainly by men of property such as planters and merchants. Some radical democrat leaders wanted independence and the elimination of British rule. But another inconsistency appeared, first in the Declaration of Independence (1776) and later in the Articles of Confederation. Thus, the Declaration of Independence was a social revolutionary document stressing the rights of all. However, if taxation could be imposed only on those who had political representation, then poorer colonists must be given rights they had never had before, which was inconsistent with the preferences of large property owners.

It was partly out of fear that established privilege and property could be overthrown that the Articles of Confederation, outlining the shape of the new nation, was weak. This document limited the powers of the central government, leaving the new states sovereign and in a very strong position. The new federal government could not regulate commerce between the states in the new confederation; it could not negotiate with foreign nations; it could not establish a uniform monetary system; and it had no powers to impose taxes. In other words, this new government had none of the powers that the European governments had slowly come to recognize were required for a strong nation. Unless it was revised, the new country would be weak because it effectively encouraged decentralization of political and economic power.

However, this weakness presented as many problems as the British rule it replaced, and unity became increasingly important for the states, in spite of the lack of common interests. Unity required a strong, representative central government, so during the years when the Federal Constitution was being drafted, the minority who believed that a weak central government threatened the safety of their property were successful in getting their point of view across. The resulting government would be able not only to ensure the safety of property rights against the threat of social disorder, it could also ensure the strength of the nation against the threat of outside aggression. This view was opposed by those who saw a strong central government as authoritarian, with

political power concentrated in the hands of a small minority and not the people as a whole.

The constitution, as a product of the 18th century and thus influenced by 18th century reality and ideas, did make property the central institution of the new country. The new federal government gained control over commerce between the states, could levy taxes, control trade with other countries, and would be able to develop a uniform national currency. In short, it provided a new mercantilist-inspired government in place of the old one it had rejected. However, two more points are relevant here. First, the issue of states' rights and central government power continued to be controversial. Second, the *application* of the new federal government's powers to achieve a strong, prosperous economy did not meet unanimous approval, creating various problems throughout the 19th century.

Independence

Achieving political independence had little impact on economic development because it did not alter the basic economic conditions. Land was, if anything, even more ample as new additions to territory were made and the Appalachian barrier surmounted, and labor remained scarce. After the political adjustments, the United States still remained, in effect, an economic colony of Great Britain. Most trade was still with Britain, with the United States specializing in exporting primary products and importing manufactures.

The major change was in what was exported, which had nothing to do with independence. Tobacco had been the most important export, but after 1790 cotton began to rival and then surpass tobacco as the major export. This occurred for two reasons. First, the revolution in cotton manufacturing expanded Britain's demand for raw cotton, but while cotton could be grown in the southern states, it suffered from a disadvantage. That is, the cotton grown in the United States was short-staple cotton, and unlike the long-staple cotton grown in the West Indies and India, removing seeds from it was time consuming (taking one person one day to remove seeds from one pound of raw cotton) and therefore expensive. But second, the invention of a cotton gin in 1790 speeded up the process of seed removal by using a machine that successfully removed seeds from short-staple cotton. Now the southern states did have an incentive to expand cotton growing for the British market. (This development had further implications in expanding the use of slaves, which will be discussed later.)

Barriers to Manufacturing

There was still little incentive to industrialize. Not only was the resource endowment pattern still unfavorable to manufacturing, but there were other limiting factors. First, imports of manufactures were easily available on favorable terms. Second, for so long as higher returns were obtainable in trade or in land, capital owners were unwilling to risk something new and untried. This began to change in the 19th century, but the opening up of the empty lands west of the Appalachians, made possible with the coming of the railways, implied that land speculation continued to attract capital away from industrial uses until well into the 19th century. Third, there were technical problems. Britain's ban on the export of skilled workers and machinery (until the 1820s) implied that underhand methods had to be used to acquire the new manufacturing technology. Finally, the idea persisted that manufacturing was inherently degrading, although a few prominent people favored it. One supporter was Alexander Hamilton, who issued his *Report on Manufactures* in 1791, proposing the introduction of manufacturing in the interests of producing a strong, prosperous, and diversified economy. To this end, he favored specifically mercantilist proposals: the imposition of tariffs to protect new industrialists from foreign competitors, subsidies and bounties to help manufacturing get started, and prohibi-

tions on some raw material exports as a way to redirect resources into manufacturing. Some of these proposals subsequently became official policy in the 19th century.

Some immediate effects of independence had implications for later development. Land owned by Loyalists was confiscated and redistributed, with some bought by promoters for speculative purposes. More important, western lands were now open, and the process of distributing this land had a significant effect on subsequent development. There was a controversy over how to proceed—it was, after all, a situation with no precedent. (This will be taken up later.)

Declines in Trade

The effects on trade were most significant. With independence, the international position of the United States altered: It was no longer a privileged colony in a large, protected, mercantilist empire, but just another trading nation. So all the previous bounties and encouragements to export certain items were gone, tobacco lost its exclusive position in the large British market, traders no longer had access to the important West Indian market, and shipping in general lost the protection previously received from the British Navy. Because some markets were either closed or available on less favorable terms than before, new markets had to be found. The most important of these markets was the Orient, and American furs were sold in China, while tea and silks were the most important items imported in turn.

While trade in general declined for these reasons immediately after independence, a much more damaging blow came during the Napoleonic Wars. Initially, American merchants gained from these wars by being able to enter trade areas abandoned by European merchants, but the indirect effects of Napoleon's Continental System led to actions that ended this initial prosperity. Under the Continental System, European ports were closed to British ships and products. In retali-

Continental System

During the Napoleonic Wars, British ships were excluded from European ports, and any ships sailing to British ports could be seized

ation, Britain blockaded Europe's coast in order to prevent any ships from entering or leaving. This directly affected American shippers attempting to trade with Europe, and in retaliation, the United States government imposed the Embargo Act in 1807, prohibiting American ships from leaving for foreign, in particular British, ports. The impact was dramatic. From a level of $108 million in 1807, exports fell to only $22 million in 1808.

Trading improved after the War of 1812, with the resumption of normal relations with Britain, but shipping experienced fluctuating fortunes. Although American shipbuilding had an important cost advantage—at the end of the 18th century, wooden sailing ships could be built for slightly over half the cost of British ones—this advantage did not spill over into shipping. The percentage of foreign trade carried in American ships reached a peak in the 1820s. In 1826, 93 percent of all United States foreign trade was transported in American ships, but the proportion declined steadily thereafter and was less than 10 percent in 1913.

There are two major explanations. First, dependence on international trade effectively declined after the 1830s, when domestic manufacturing began to become more significant. This, plus the internal expansion that took place in the 19th century and the development of production capabilities and a mass market on an unprecedented scale, implied that the major focus of capitalist activity would turn to exploitation of domestic resources, away from the international economy. Only coastal shipping expanded as domestic manufacturing for domestic uses grew. By 1860 the tonnage of shipping used in coastal trade was larger than that in international trade.

The second reason lies in the changing technology of ocean transportation itself. So long as wooden sailing ships were used, and periodic fluctuations caused by wars and depressions were ignored, the American merchant fleet grew. In 1815 it was half the size of Britain's, and in 1850 it had almost equalled Britain's tonnage. But with the coming of steam-powered steel ships, American shipbuilders were at a disadvantage; the lack of a modern industrialized economy and supporting industries meant they could not compete. The fleet declined, and in 1907, actual tonnage was less than it had been a century earlier, even though the volume of world trade had expanded dramatically over this period.

Early Textile Industries

Although there was a general antipathy toward manufacturing and industrialization, declining fortunes in trade affecting New England merchants resulted in the first factories being established early in the 19th century. However, these early attempts were curious: They were not totally capitalist, as not all the characteristics of capitalist production were present, and not until after mid century would genuine capitalist industrialization occur. Early textile manufacturing in New England is an interesting example of a capitalist adaptation to predominantly noncapitalist conditions.

In the 18th century, there was some manufacturing and, as is typical of a prefactory age, it was small-scale, domestic manufacturing along the lines of the putting out system in England, serving small, local markets. Textile production was concentrated in New England (Massachusetts, Rhode Island, Connecticut, and New Hampshire) where the absence of large scale commercial agriculture implied that it was possible for part-time industry to complement subsistence agriculture.

In order to move toward a factory-oriented production system, several preconditions had to be met. Technology had to be imported; capital to finance the buildings, equipment, and materials was needed; a source of power was necessary; and free labor in the amount required had to be available. These preconditions could be acquired, but the existence of a free labor force was the major obstacle, and it was the adaptation to this problem that meant the early textile industry in New England was not a pure capitalist one.

Meeting the Preconditions

Taking the necessary preconditions first, technology acquisition was difficult, and designs for the new equipment had to be smuggled out of Britain. Thus, in 1791 the first Arkwright spinning mill was set up in Pawtucket, Rhode Island, based on designs brought there by Samuel Slater. Slater employed children, paying them in truck, and the yarn produced was then woven by families working out of their own homes. These early mills (there were only five in operation before 1808) were powered by water, so the early mill towns in New England were located along rivers.

The necessary capital began to become available during the Napoleonic Wars as a result of both the decline of trade and the rise of competition from New York, which led to a shift of capital from commerce to industry. New England merchants had always been the most profit-oriented of any group in the United States, and the elimination of their source of profits, due to war with Britain and the Embargo Act, opened up a new use for their accumulated capital. Most textiles were imported until 1807; thus the ending of trade with Britain implied the existence of unsatisfied domestic demand that could be met through domestic manufacturing of textiles.

New York as Cotton Trading Center

In addition, there was increased competition from New York merchants. New York at the beginning of the 19th century was just starting a process of growth in which the city first overtook

Boston as the country's chief port and later became an important manufacturing city. It was a major entry point for British imports, and via the Hudson River and its coastal trade attracted buyers from the mainland. One advantage it had over Boston, whose merchants still used traditional practices, was the use of the consignment method of selling. This eliminated two sets of middlemen—the British exporter and the American importer—so prices were lower than in either Boston or Philadelphia, diverting trade from Boston to New York.

Another development leading to New York's growth was related, and would have further implications for political and economic events later in the century. While shipments coming west from Europe were assured, initially New York shippers lacked something to send east to Europe. This led to the beginning of northern dominance and control over the southern states and their most important product, cotton, which met the New York shippers' requirements for a return cargo.

That a market for cotton existed in England was certain, and as coastal shipping expanded, New York became involved with the export of southern cotton, beginning, in effect, a new triangular trade pattern between New York, the South, and Europe. This advantage was further strengthened by New York's expansion of banking, which extended credit to southern planters. New York bankers and merchants gained at the expense of the South, which did not meet the challenge by expanding financial and trade institutions itself. By 1830, only sixty cents of each dollar paid for cotton was retained by growers; the rest was absorbed in interest payments, commissions, freight charges, and insurance paid to Northerners.

So New England merchants faced threats to their continued profits from two sides. The problem was to convince merchants, who were used to the ready liquidity of short-term trading, to undertake long-term investments in fixed capital in which returns did not appear immediately. This is a common problem of the transition from commercial to industrial capitalism and was overcome by pooling resources from several merchants, thus to some extent limiting the risk of any one.

The major problem, given that a market for textiles existed and that the supply capability could be put into place, was the labor force. In 1800, barely 10 percent of the total labor force were employees. New England was a predominantly agrarian society, and even though agriculture was not very profitable, the dislike of factories and manufacturing had forced the use of an outwork system to accomplish what little manufacturing there was.

The Waltham-Lowell System

However, there was a solution, found by Francis Cabot Lowell, who set up what became known as the Waltham-Lowell system in 1816. Lowell, a Boston merchant hurt by the war, established a unique factory, combining (unlike English factories) spinning and weaving in the same plant. New England farmers were poor, and while they would not degrade themselves to work for an employer, they would let their daughters work in order to accumulate funds for their marriage or for land acquisition. Thus the first factory labor force in the United States was largely composed of these women. It was not a true capitalist labor force of propertyless, permanent wage earners. As later developments showed, these women *did* have alternatives to factory work, and by the 1840s, were replaced by a work force that was a permanent one because no alternatives were open to it. New England was also very Puritanical, and while the Puritan virtue of hard work was a plus,

the strict concern over morality led to the unique aspects of the Waltham-Lowell system. Farmers let their daughters work only if housing was also provided and nonwork hours strictly supervised in order to safeguard their virtue. To this end, Lowell built dormitories, run by chaperones, for the female work force. The women were subject to a curfew of 10 p.m., and they also had to attend church on Sunday. As a further recruitment device, educational pursuits were also encouraged. (The fact that this early work force had a higher status than the average industrial work force is indicated by the fact that wages were higher than those paid to female schoolteachers, and teachers were also recruited to work in the mills.)

These efforts succeeded. The town grew from 2,500 in 1825 to 21,000 in 1840, and in 1834, 3,800 of the factory's 5,000 employees were farm girls. However, conditions soon deteriorated. Wages were between $2 and $4 a week, for a 72 hour week, with $1.25 deducted for room and board; those who expected to accumulate funds rapidly for a nest egg were soon disappointed.

Neither living nor working conditions were desirable. Those who complained and protested against pay cuts and work speedups were fired and blacklisted, which meant that they could not get a job anywhere else. The expansion of the work force outran the pace of building, and overcrowding was common. In the early 1840s, the women attempted to press for a 10-hour day but were unsuccessful and most of those active in this movement were fired. This effectively ended the Waltham-Lowell system, which had tried an unusual method to ensure an adequate work force because the conditions at the time of its introduction were not yet ready for full scale industrialization.

Waltham-Lowell System

System of early textile manufacturing in New England which provided dormitories for its female workers

---

Blacklist

A list of people who are being discriminated against; often used by employers to deny employment

In the 1840s, the farmers' daughters were replaced by Irish immigrants, who were more docile and willing to accept low wages because they did not have an alternative. *This* labor force was the first permanent one in the United States. Increasing immigration throughout the rest of the 19th century was instrumental in overcoming the labor shortage that held back capitalist industrialization by creating a permanent industrial proletariat.

While many of the new textile mills established at the beginning of the century failed following the resumption of British imports after 1812, textile production was the leading manufacturing sector until the 1860s. At that time, it was one sixth the size of Britain's, with three quarters of all production located in New England. American textile production concentrated at the coarser end of the market (fine fabrics continued to be imported), and this was appropriate for the situation. Coarser fabrics like denim found a ready market among the farmers who formed the majority of the population, and in addition were

Figure 14.1 Textile production in the United States was turning into a factory industry in New England, where this spinning frame was used by the Merrimack Manufacuring Company. (Courtesy of the National Museum of American History, Smithsonian Institute.)

encouraged by the American textile producers' emphasis on quantity. This in turn was helped by the invention in 1831 of the ring spindle, which permitted continuous spinning, and one operative could attend more of them than the mule. The cost, however, came in the lower quality of the yarn. Water power continued to be the chief source of power, and even as late as 1860 was more important in all American manufacturing than steam power.

Other Industries

After 1820, conditions for all types of manufacturing improved. Population almost doubled between 1820 and 1840 to reach seventeen million, partly because of increased immigration, although most of the increase was due to natural causes. The American birthrate was higher than in Europe, and the average number of children per family was six or seven, while four or five was more common in Europe. This increase expanded both the potential market and the labor supply.

Government policy also helped by imposing a moderately protective tariff in 1816, which put duties on cotton, woollen, and iron imports. Tariffs were raised in the 1820s but reduced in 1833. However, domestic manufacturers still found it hard to compete not only with better quality, lower-priced imports, but also with domestic or sweated industries that were especially important in the footwear and textile industries. Also, opportunities available in land speculation, agriculture, commerce, and transportation reduced the flow of funds to industry. Because of this, and unlike their equivalents in Britain, American manufacturers were always protectionist, favoring tariffs and not free trade—even when they did not need protecting.

In the first half of the 19th century, other industries besides textiles faced the basic problems

---

Sweated Labor

Work done for low wages in poor conditions

Protection

Tariffs imposed on imports protect domestic producers from foreign competition

---

of resource availability that limited their expansion. In 1815, only about 15,000 people were employed in manufacturing of all kinds. One major drawback was transportation. Lowell had shown it was possible to overcome the labor shortage (although his was only a temporary solution), and the accessibility of the industrial river towns of New England to coastal shipping meant that raw cotton could be easily shipped from the southern states and finished textiles transported to the major urban markets of the East. New England was the most important manufacturing region, accounting for half of all manufactured output in the United States even as late as 1860. Other areas did not have New England's accessibility, which helps explain their slow development. This relative isolation meant that it was cheaper to import iron from Britain than to transport it ten miles inland; hence iron production remained small scale, technologically backward, and limited to small market areas.

Iron Production

Pig iron production was important in colonial times because there were large supplies of wood for charcoal, and charcoal smelting in scattered locations characterized American iron production. But ironically, what was an advantage in the 18th century became a disadvantage in the 19th, when new technologies using coke transformed British iron production. Only in the Civil War period, stimulated by the increase in demand for iron for military purposes and by demand from the railways, did coke smelting outweigh charcoal smelting in the United States, a century later than in Britain. Even in 1850, 60 percent of all iron used was imported. However, by the 1880s, the situation had changed so dramatically that by then United States production was larger than Britain's.

There were changes before 1860 that resulted in the concentration of iron production and also show the process of adaptation to specifically American conditions. For example, to produce wrought iron from pig iron required alternately heating and hammering pig iron, but this took a large amount of labor, and labor scarcity limited its adoption. The introduction of the puddling process and rolling mills to remove impurities required less labor and also meant that coal could be used as the heat source. Because the coalfields were more concentrated than iron ore deposits (in Pennsylvania, New Jersey, and Maryland), this stage of iron processing tended to be located in towns such as Philadelphia, Pittsburgh, Scranton and Baltimore, which were near the coal deposits. Initial pig iron production was slower to concentrate in a few locations in the same way.

Food Processing

Three other industries are also significant at this early stage of development. Two were food processing industries based on the existence of rich agricultural resources. The way they developed also shows the importance of transportation in providing access to both raw material supplies and final markets. For example, flour milling was an early example of a semimanufacturing process, and in colonial times, New York and Baltimore were two major centers of flour milling. Both were accessible by river to what were then the most important grain growing areas, and by sea to the major markets in the West Indies. As other areas, the Ohio Valley and the Midwest, opened up, towns such as Rochester also became important flour milling centers. Rochester was accessible to the agricultural area to the south of the Great Lakes and was linked to New York via the Erie Canal and the Hudson.

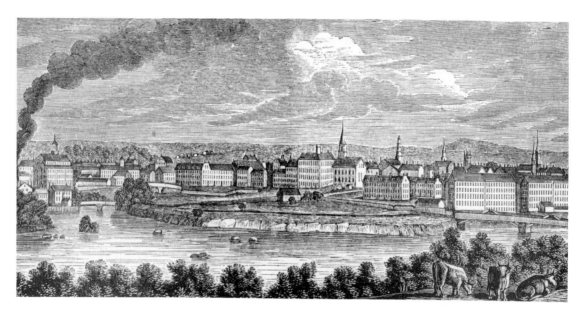

Figure 14.2 The Massachusetts town of Lowell grew into an inportant textile manufacturing center, and is seen here in an engraving made at a time when the town's surroundings were still rural. Note the height of the buildings (Courtesy of the Museum of American Textile History)

A second agricultural processing industry, meat packing, also saw its beginning at this time, although it did not become a large industry until the opening of the West to cattle ranching. However, in the 1820s, a new development with immense implications for later industrialization occurred. Cincinnati, linked to the southern port of New Orleans via the Ohio and Mississippi Rivers, was the leading center of meat processing, especially of pork products, whose major market was the slave south. In 1826, for the first time in the United States, the principle of the assembly line was adopted. This is a method of organizing work in which, unlike traditional methods, the worker has a fixed location while the materials/product move past on a moving belt. (It was first used during the Napoleonic Wars in a British Navy biscuit factory.) Oddly enough, as it was applied, it was first a disassembly line: Live animals entered the plant, were slaughtered, and as the carcasses moved past, each worker had a specific task—removing the hide or entrails, cutting the pieces, and so on. By the 1850s, however, Chicago became the leading meat packing center, chiefly due to its advantages as a railway center and Great Lakes transshipment port.

Guns and Armaments

The third industry also introduced a new technique for producing items for a mass market and was one in which the United States took a commanding position. The industry was small arms production, and the technique used standardized interchangeable parts. It was first adopted during the war years at the beginning of the century, when there was an increased demand for munitions, and although it took time and capital to tool up the plant for production, once these preliminary steps had been taken, production of finished items was very rapid.

Traditionally, craftsmen were responsible for making each unique gun from start to finish. Eli Whitney and Simeon North redesigned the process so that the parts were made first, each to a standard pattern, and were then fitted together to assemble the final gun. The necessary finance for producing the tools and machines needed to stamp out the components came from a government contract to produce muskets. In 1813, North adapted the process to pistols, and it was later used by Samuel Colt for the production of revolvers.

New Technology

These innovations and others appearing later in the century were a response to two issues. First, the need to come to grips with the labor scarcity problem; second, the desire to reduce labor costs by using unskilled and therefore lower-paid labor. Mechanizing meat packing and small arms production helped speed up the output produced with a given number of people, which solved the first problem. But as the country industrialized and the extent of its market widened, although the quantity of labor was no longer a problem, the quality was.

That is, immigration, which had been running at about 100,000 a year in the early 1820s, speeded up rapidly to 500,000 a year in the late 1850s, and to close to a million a year at the end of the century. At first, these immigrants included large proportions of Irish and Germans, most of whom had no industrial experience. In addition, most immigrants did not speak English, so there was an added communication problem.

The ability to utilize these potential workers in the most profitable way depended on being able to simplify industrial tasks so they could be done by unskilled labor. This is especially clear in meat packing; each worker had only one specific task to perform, which would be repeated thousands of times each day. While more skills were needed to design and manufacture the equipment making each separate part, only a small number of people were needed to do it, thus overall skill requirements were less. That it also involved a higher degree of capital intensity implied early on that production would tend to become concentrated in the hands of a relatively small number of capitalist industrialists able to acquire the necessary financing to start up production.

Transportation

In the first half of the 19th century, industrialization was slow, although its potential was great. As the country grew in land area (Louisiana was added in 1803, Florida in 1819, Texas in 1845, with the western areas later moving to statehood status) the potential wealth of its natural resources became recognized. But the problem of adequate transportation remained. Without it, these rich resources had no economic value at all, because there was no easy connection between supply and markets and thus no way of using them. This problem would not be successfully overcome until the coming of the railways.

Water Routes

Before then, natural features dictated both the location and the pattern of economic activity. The Appalachian range had effectively limited economic activity in colonial times to the area between it and the Atlantic coast, and for a long time coastal shipping was the most effective link between seaports. Internal roads were poor or nonexistent. The area to the west was relatively underpopulated. Where settlement existed, it was either self-sufficient or, if commercial, located within easy access of the Ohio and Mississippi Rivers, thus becoming oriented to the South, especially to New Orleans. Water routes, both sea and river, were crucial, and early towns were located either on the coast (Boston, New York, Charlestown, for example) or at strategic points on the rivers (Cincinnati and Pittsburgh for example).

The importance of water routes helps explain why steam-powered river boats were so impor-

tant in the United States The first effective one was used on the Hudson River in 1807, but they became much more widely used on the Mississippi River, increasing the orientation of the Ohio Valley to the South, not the East. But even here, the first engines were imported, because producing such technologically advanced equipment required a more highly developed heavy industry than was currently in place.

As is true of all other large countries, the improvement of transportation and communications, especially the building of the railways, was crucial to economic expansion. Such a network made it possible to tap new resources effectively by linking them with potential markets, making them economically useful. In the United States, improved transportation lowered shipping costs, contributed to the emphasis on internal development, and helped the export of traditional products. Because access from new grain-growing areas in the West was improved, these areas could be cultivated commercially for the first time to produce food for the industrializing East as well as for Europe. The improvements in transportation taking place in the first half of the 19th century are closely linked to the spread of settlement and the westward expansion of economic activity, and to the land policy adopted by the federal government.

Turnpike Roads

These improvements determined where and when new settlement would take place, which in turn made commercialized development possible. At the end of the 18th century, the first improvements came in the construction of roads in the older, settled eastern areas. These were turnpike roads on which user fees were levied, but most were poorly planned and by the mid 1830s half were simply abandoned. One road, however, the National Road, was significant because it was the first to overcome the Appalachian barrier between east and west. Its construction was financed with federal funds, and it ran from Baltimore on the Atlantic coast across the Appalachians to the Ohio Valley, reaching Columbus, Ohio in 1833, and Vandalia, Illinois in the 1850s. However, it was too expensive to use for freight shipments.

Canals

There was also some canal building, starting later than in Europe. Canals, with one important exception, were less significant, especially because they were soon made redundant by the railways. Canals were less important to the development of the United States than elsewhere for two reasons. First, canal construction was more expensive and thus rates charged were higher, simply because the distances were too great, and the population and centers of economic activity too scattered, so there was never a sufficient density of traffic to make canals profitable. In 1816, only 100 miles of mostly short canals had been built.

The second problem applied mainly to the canals built further north, where winters were cold. If the canals froze during the coldest winter months they were unusable, reducing their ability to compete with the railroads, which could be used all year round. In spite of this, canal companies continued to attract funds, chiefly from the state governments but also from British and East coast establishment financiers, until the 1830s when funds began to be diverted to the railways. Between 1820 and 1838, 18 states authorized credits of $60 million for canal construction, and in the decade of the 1830s, 3,326 miles of canals were dug, only slightly less than the 3,328 miles of railway track laid.

Erie Canal

The one exception was the Erie Canal, started in 1817 and completed in 1825. While relatively short, 363 miles between Albany and Buffalo in New York, its significance was greater than its mileage indicates. This is because it provided a final link in a water route connecting the Great Lakes with the port of New York and thus the rest of the world. For the first time, it was now possible to transport goods between east and west at low rates. Before it was built, transporting grain from western New York to New York City cost three times as much as the cost of growing wheat, six times the value of corn and ten times the cost of oats—an obvious disincentive to cultivate commercial grain crops. But after construction, freight rates fell by 90 percent, and ranged between 1/2 cent and three cents per ton mile, comparing extremely favorably with rates on the National Road, which ranged from twenty-five to fifty cents.

Economic effects of the canal were many. It stimulated the commercialization of western agriculture, first in western New York, then in the area surrounding the Great Lakes, by providing easy access to eastern urban markets and to markets in Europe. It stimulated industry in the east, especially in New England, by providing access to western markets for manufactured goods and by dealing a death blow to commercial agriculture there. It further encouraged the growth of New York, not only as a port and commercial city, but also as a manufacturing city. Other cities also owed their birth and subsequent development to the Canal, including the Great Lakes ports of Duluth, Detroit, and Buffalo, as well as Chicago, which gained further with the coming of the railway.

Importance of Rail Building

But all this development paled into insignificance when compared to the railroad revolution, which effectively completed the political unification of the country as well as making it a single economic entity. The rail network, coupled with huge amounts of immigration later in the century, made the United States the largest mass market in the world.

The pattern of rail building first coincided with the already-settled area of the Eastern seaboard but was later important in making new settlement possible in the West, opening up new areas to economic activity. Most attention in the westward movement has focused on the individualist pioneer in a new environment, but the expansion of activity that did occur would not have been possible without town development and adequate communications—first using rivers, later using railroads. Some early towns in the West began as forts or trading posts but developed into commercial centers for the surrounding agricultural areas. Others simply began as speculative enterprises, when a town was planned on paper. Whether a town would grow and produce returns for town promoters, which many did not, depended on the agricultural and commercial development of the surrounding area that in turn depended on connections with the East.

Towns in the West made settlement possible because of their banking functions as well as their communications role. New settlers were heavily in debt; their land was mortgaged, and they needed credit for the tools, animals, food, and other necessities of life before new farms were in operation. This credit availability in turn was dependent on Eastern banks, and the pattern of control over westward settlement by eastern finance houses led to frequent crises and political confrontations. Without the Easterners' desire for more trade with the West, which encouraged the building of new rail lines to provide access to supplies and markets, the area west of the Appalachians would have remained relatively underdeveloped.

Government Support for Rail Network

This makes it possible to understand why rail building received government support at both state and federal levels, as well as private financing. Governments were involved because the settlement of the country made the dream of a strong

and prosperous United States more of a reality. Private investors hoped not only for lucrative returns from the railways themselves but for gains from the rise in land values that accompanied railway building and the development of new towns. They also hoped for profits to be gained from the expansion of agricultural, commercial, and eventually, industrial activity.

Without this public support and finance, and without equipment from Britain and other European countries, the rail network could not have been constructed as fast and as extensively as it was. Technology had to be imported, and until 1860, most of the rails and equipment were imported. Financing for projects as extensive as the American lines was also crucial. The joint stock principle was utilized, and with various other methods (including loans from governments and the ability to issue bank notes to cover financing), more than enough was raised to build lines. There was no attempt to avoid duplication of lines in most cases. The private promoters built lines where they wanted, which resulted in overbuilding and eventually in bankruptcies, amalgamation of lines, falling share prices, and a lower return on investment than investors originally anticipated. Up to 1839, British investors put about $170 million into railway companies in the United States, but after the financial panic of 1837 and the world depression of the 1840s, United States companies were no longer so attractive to foreign funds.

Land Grants

Much more important as a source of gain was the assistance provided by governments in the form of land grants. They provided land either free or on very favorable terms to railway companies who in turn sold the land and financed construction with the profits. The principle behind land grants was simple. Construction of the railroads increased the value of land by improving access, so the companies should be able to recoup some of

Land Grant

Grants of land made by governments to railroad companies as an inducement to build rail lines

that increased value as a reward for their enterprise. In addition, government subsidies helped attract other funds, thus speeding up construction and consequently economic development in general.

Federal land grants were large, and between 1850 and 1871, when the program ended, railway companies gained possession of about 129 million acres, covering alternate sections of land on either side of the line. Such grants amounted to one quarter of Minnesota and Washington, one fifth of Wisconsin, Iowa, Kansas, North Dakota, and Montana, one seventh of Nebraska, one eighth of California and one ninth of Louisiana. The rail companies preferred to sell much of this land to farmers rather than land speculators, because the necessary freight traffic would build up faster. As one example, the Union Pacific transcontinental railway did extremely well from its land—it netted $136 million on land sales, out of which it paid construction costs of only $70 million. In addition, federal loans of over $64 million were made, most going to the transcontinental lines of the Union Pacific and the Central Pacific.

Some states also made land grants of about 51 million acres to the rail companies and provided subsidies of $95 million after the Civil War until 1890. Up to 1860, at which time total investment in the railroads accounted for about 25 percent of the total capital of the United States, government aid, including land grants valued at the federal government's low selling price, amounted to $1.2 billion, and in the period 1865-1890, amounted to $1.5 billion. Foreign investment, especially in the prewar period, amounted to about one quarter of the railways' needs, while public investment accounted for another 15 percent.

Early Lines

Inevitably, in a situation where so much money was available, there were abuses and many promoters were corrupt. There was overbuilding, and many lines were not profitable; in 1872, of 364 listed railways, only 104 paid dividends, and only 35 paid dividends of 10 percent or more. Also, many lines were built so quickly and so badly that they had to be rebuilt after fifteen years. But the network did get built. The first line, the Baltimore and Ohio Railroad, was started in 1828, but the real start came in the 1830s, and only after 1850 did railways become more important for internal transportation than the existing rivers, canals, and roads. During the 1830s, over 3,000 miles of track were laid, but this construction boom collapsed in 1836 when a financial panic led to the withdrawal of many foreign funds. A further 6,000 miles were built in the following decade, mainly in the eastern states.

There was a major boom in the 1850s, ended by another panic in 1857, which added 21,000 miles and connected the Great Lakes area and the Midwest to the East. By 1860, lines had reached Milwaukee, St. Louis, Memphis, New Orleans, and Chicago. Chicago especially owed its rapid growth to its position as a Great Lakes port and transshipment point between lake shipping and rail lines (by 1853, four lines had reached Chicago). Chicago is the northernmost point through which a complete, landbased transcontinental line can pass, and this location as a railway terminus led to its growth as an agricultural processing and industrial city. The railroads attracted stockyards, meat packing plants, and grain elevators, giving a boost to commercial agriculture in the surrounding area. Industry included farm machinery plants and iron and steel mills. Later, supporting banking and financial services were established. At the beginning of the 19th century, Chicago was only a trading post. But its population of 40,000 in 1852 increased 50 percent in one year, thanks to the stimulus of the railroads,

---

Solving Problems in Economic History

Were the railroads necessary for the economic growth of the United States?

Conventional historical interpretations hold that the construction of a rail network in the United States was important to the industrialization of the country. Many reasons have been offered, including the impact that lower transportation costs plus speedier transportation had on creating and enlarging a national market for many industries as well as providing a direct stimulus to the iron, steel, construction, and instrument industries themselves. Improved communications and transportation, it was held, led to increased productivity and thus increased output by expanding the possibilities for the further division of labor. As far as the railroads' role in assisting the country's settlement goes, historians have noticed that the spread of western settlement accelerated after railroads were in place; reliance only on water or wagon transportation implied a much slower rate of new settlement.

Robert Fogel (in *Railroads and American Economic Growth: Essays in Econometric History,* Baltimore: The John's Hopkins Press, 1964) summarizes one of the first statistical tests of this interpretation, and concludes by casting doubt on it. In order to test whether railroads were indispensible for economic growth, Fogel maintains that it is necessary to show that substitutes for railroads could not, or would not, have had the same effect. How can this be done? One device is to estimate the difference in the actual cost of shipping goods by rail and the alternative cost of shipping using alternative methods; only if the costs of rail transportation are considerably lower can the necessity interpretation be maintained. However, there is a problem, because if a differential exists, it will be peculiar to the pattern of settlement induced by the railroads; if the rails did not exist, then different cities would have been important shipping points. Fogel also estimates the direct and indirect effects on the iron and other industries generated by the railroads to see whether they are larger than would otherwise be expected.

His conclusion is that while the railroad did grow rapidly, and did become important in inland transportation, it did not make an *overwhelming* contribution to the economy's production potential. That potential, and actual growth, was more the outcome of many different factors and applications of innovative knowledge—which were in existence before the railroads came about. In sum, observed growth was induced by several innovations in manufacturing industries combined with transportation innovations that lowered costs and expanded markets. Given this background of innovation, if railroads were not built, other forms of cheap transportation would have been, and American economic growth would have been just as rapid. While historians see merit in the multiple-causation hypothesis, few would accept Fogel's claim that growth would have been as rapid in the absence of railroads.

---

and by 1860 had reached 109,000, when 15 lines connected to Chicago.

The boom in railway construction and speculation in railway company shares contributed to the financial panic of 1857. Construction was based on expectations of large amounts of traffic, so when it did not materialize rail profits fell, bursting the speculative bubble, and rail shares fell dramatically.

In the 1860s, the rail network was further expanded by the completion of the first transcontinental rail line between east and west coasts in 1869. The Union Pacific-Central Pacific line was authorized in 1862. It may seem odd that such an undertaking would be started during a period of civil strife that would be expected to slow down the pace of economic activity. That this did not happen has been explained by the pressure exerted by President Lincoln, who believed it would help unite the nation. Thus the North's success in winning the Civil War could be interpreted as a political accomplishment of this goal, with completion of the transcontinental line as a means to make unity more effective. After 1865, and before 1900, almost half the new mileage built was in areas west of the Mississippi, with mileage in the east mainly filling in the gaps left earlier. By 1906, there were 228,000 miles of rail lines in operation, more than in any other country.

Contribution of Rails

The major accomplishment of railroad construction, especially before the structural transformation of the economy that came after the Civil War, was that it permitted the exploitation of the vast natural wealth of the country. By making possible the spread of settlements, the railways helped the absorption of millions of immigrants in agriculture and especially in industry. It was possible to develop the previously empty areas of the west where natural resources were now economically valuable because they were accessible by rail to the major markets. However, the very success of the rails marked the decline of the rivers as major transportation routes; by 1873, the Mississippi in particular had lost most of its traffic. Because the establishment of a rail network is so closely linked with American land policy that governed the extension of the frontier of economic activity to the West, attention will now turn to it.

Land Policy

After independence, one of the most important decisions that had to be faced by the new government was what to do with all the unexploited lands west of the Appalachians. There was never any disagreement that these lands, then nominally owned by the federal government, would eventually pass into private hands. Within the next hundred years, practically all did, which was a remarkable phenomenon of American history. But there was a disagreement over how it should be accomplished, which in turn determined both the pace and the pattern of economic development.

Agrarian Democracy

On the one hand, the idea of agrarian democracy was expressed most forcefully by Thomas Jefferson. The principle of freedom had become effective with independence and must be guaranteed by providing easy access to the land for all individuals. It was the most extreme statement of the anti-industrialization, anti-urbanization ethic, reflecting the belief that the United States could be strong as a new democracy only if it was peopled by independent farmers who were not dependent on industrial employers for their livelihood, and who could thus make their own political decisions uninfluenced by pressure from employers.

On the other hand, there were those who favored disposing of land in large blocks to industrial and mining interests (and later to rail companies), to speed up economic growth. That is, permitting capitalist interests to acquire land would accelerate the pace of settlement and exploitation of natural resources on which economic progress and strength depended.

Agrarian Democracy
The principle that effective democracy depended on the existence of strong independent farmers

While the idea of equal access seemed to be uppermost, in practice policy shifted between the two extremes. The net result was that while much agricultural land did go to small farmers (about fifty million acres, although some was bought first by land speculators), business interests gained more. About half a billion acres of mineral-rich and timber lands ended up in the hands of large companies, which included cattle ranchers, mining companies, timber companies and railway companies.

Government Revenues from Land Sales

There was a further political complication that was not resolved until much later in the 19th century. That is, the new federal government initially relied for revenue on customs duties and handouts from the states. But in order to strengthen the central government, it was thought desirable to reduce dependence on the states by reserving revenues from land sales for the federal government itself. This meant that land should be sold, not given away, and not until the Homestead Act of 1862 did land become free to settlers. However, there were two implications of making sales. The first was that settlers became heavily in debt to banks, which had further implications for the financial panics that erupted throughout the 19th century, as well as for the development of periodic agrarian unrest and political agitation. The second was that it slowed the settlement of the country by limiting it to those people with greater access to resources.[2]

Changing Land Sales Strategy

The first stage of land sales in 1785 attempted both to raise revenues and to encourage settlement by selling large parcels of land, 640 acres, with a minimum price of $1 per acre. Few aspiring farmers had this sort of money, so most of the land was bought by land companies and speculators who then resold the land in smaller lots. But

this was enriching the latter and not helping settlers, and abuse also occurred because holders of federal war bonds could pay for land with the bonds accepted at face value. As speculators had acquired many of these bonds at a fraction of their face value (because many of those who originally bought them did not expect the debt to be made good), they thus gained a large windfall by redeeming bonds for land.

Policy then changed in 1796 in order to remove speculation by raising the price to $2 per acre and giving a year's grace before payment was due. This did not succeed either. It did close out speculators, but it also closed out settlers: One year was not enough time to go to the farm area, build shelter, and undertake all the necessary clearing and preparation in order to produce a harvest that could be sold to repay a debt of $1,280 plus whatever was needed to equip the farm and support a family in one year.

This led to another shift to try to encourage new farmers. In 1800, the minimum size was reduced to 320 acres (and further reduced to 160 acres in 1804), and more liberal credit terms were introduced. This did not solve either problem: There was still a great deal of speculation, and the credit terms were not liberal enough for settlers, so many farmers were foreclosed. Even in 1820, when the price was reduced to $1.25 an acre, the problem of making enough of a commercial success of a totally new farm in a short period of time in order to pay back loans was too great.

A partial solution came with the Preemption Law of 1841, which permitted squatters to settle on land and make the initial steps toward developing a farm into a going concern. Then when the land was offered for sale, the squatters had the first option to buy it—by which time, it was hoped, they had accumulated funds with which to do so. However, this still took a long time to accomplish, and even then, most were heavily mortgaged with little hope of being able to repay.

Conditions for commercial farming did not improve in most of these western areas until the railroads improved accessibility, which was not until the 1850s and until the 1870s for the most western regions. Until then, and depending on the location, farmers either were self-sufficient and not predominantly part of the market system, or they were producing for a market but were heavily in debt. This was, and would continue to be, a problem. Without credit (available only at high rates), farmers were unable to grow grain, but with the high rates, grain growing was not very profitable.

The final stage of land policy followed the passage of the Homestead Law in 1862, which explicitly endorsed Jefferson's ideal of agrarian democracy for the first time. It eliminated the speculative element but also any revenues the federal government received from land sales. This law gave any citizen title to 160 acres of land free after a claim had been filed and the land occupied for five years. This was the aspect that removed speculation—no speculator could wait that long.

By this time, with the expansion of railroads (by 1872, some 70,000 miles had been constructed) and the sale of railroad lands, more settlement and the expansion of commercial farming was possible. But population was scattered and agriculture overextended, and a series of crises would continue to plague agriculture, even while the secular trend in agricultural output was upward.

Summary

By the middle of the 19th century, the United States was ready to complete its transformation into a developed, industrial capitalist nation. However, the Civil War, which broke out in the 1860s, delayed this last step. From its beginning as new British settlements in the 17th century, American economic development shared common elements with European development but also had many unique features. In the 17th century, as well as in the 18th, the most highly developed form of capitalist economic activity was commerce. Thus, the merchants in the Eastern seaboard towns became the economic elite of the new country. But because this was a new country for European settlement, and because the original thirteen colonies were part of a mercantilist empire, differences appeared. Much early activity was designed to ensure permanence for new settlements, which had to be built from scratch. (In one way, this was an advantage, as they would not have to deal with the same urban problems to the same extent as the older towns in Europe.) Because they were colonies, they were seen as providers of primary commodities such as furs, timber, and tobacco, and not of manufactured commodities. This fitted in well with the resource pattern of abundant land, scarce labor, and scarce capital, especially social overhead capital.

Even after political independence, economic dependence remained a reality: Given the relative availability of resources, capitalist activity remained oriented to trade and land speculation because returns were higher than in manufacturing. Early textile manufacturing in New England adopted a device for attracting labor that in essence was precapitalist rather than capitalist. Similarly, on southern plantations another noncapitalist device was used to overcome the labor scarcity problem: the institution of slavery.

Two features mark the first half of the 19th century. Both contributed to establishing the preconditions for the successful exploitation of natural resources, the coming of extensive industrialization, and the establishment of a potential mass market that would be important to development after the Civil War.

The first was the construction of a transportation network, in which railroads were most important. By providing access to the ports of the east coast, and subsequently to the world as a whole, they permitted the opening up of rich agricultural lands in the country's interior and made commercial farming possible. At the same time, they also encouraged industrialization in the east by opening up markets for manufactured goods in the newly settled areas. The second feature was related to the first. This was the shift of population to the west as new lands were sold to settlers and to industrial interests. This would not have been possible without the construction of transportation routes that not only got people to where they could settle but also made it possible for them to live there by connecting them to urban areas and by making their economic activity, whether agricultural, extractive, or industrial, part of a wider national market. Railways, in other words, ended local specialization and self-sufficiency.

By the 1860s, conditions were right for the country to become fully industrialized. The labor scarcity problem was being overcome through immigration as well as the introduction of labor-saving machinery. The infrastructure necessary for this was also being put into place. And by this time, even ideas and values were beginning to accept, and later wholeheartedly approve, industrial activity and industrialists.

Notes

1. After the Seven Year War, France relinquished claims to North America. Thus Canada then became part of the British empire, and the Ohio Valley was also added to territories under British control.

2. Another implication of this policy resulted in the pattern of western political geography. Land was initially sold in parcels of 640 acres, which is one square mile. Townships were laid out to cover six miles square, which is equivalent to 36 sections of one square mile each. Thus the original intention was for each township to consist of 36 farm families.

Key Concepts

Agricultural processing
Agrarian Democracy
Anti-industrial bias
Forced labor
Immigrant
Infrastructure
Labor shortage

Land grants
Mechanization
Protection
Rail network
Resource endowment
Slavery
Waltham-Lowell System

Questions for Discussion or Essay Writing

1. Discuss the importance of a country's resource endowment to its economic development. How does the United States illustrate this constraint?

2. Evaluate the impact of the War for Independence, the Napoleonic Wars and the War of 1812 on United States economic development.

3. Discuss the implications of the various trade patterns used by American merchants in the 18th Century.

4. To what extent did economic issues contribute to the demand for independence?

5. Why didn't the United States industrialize at the very beginning of the 19th century?

6. How did New England textile manufacturers overcome the problem of finding labor when textile manufacturing was first established?

7. To what extent did innovative activity in the first part of the 19th century compensate for perceived problems of economic development?

8. Evaluate "transportation" as a precondition for or input into the industrialization process.

9. To what extent is it true to say that the existence of transportation networks determines the location of economic activity?

10. Discuss railroad building in the United States. To what extent did it differ from the experience in other countries?

For Further Reading

Abbott, Edith. "A History of the Industrial Employment of Women in the United States." *Journal of Political Economy* (14 October 1906): 461-501, and 17, (January 1909).

Billington, Ray.A. *The Genesis of the Frontier Thesis*. San Marino: Huntington Library, 1971.

Bridenbaugh, Carl. *Cities in the Wilderness: Urban Life in America, 1625-1742*. N.Y.: Capricorn Books, 1964 (1938).

Bruchey, Stuart W. *The Roots of American Economic Growth, 1607-1861: An Essay in Social Causation*. N.Y: Harper & Row, 1965.

Cohn, Raymond C. "The Occupations of English Immigrants to the United States, 1836-1853." *Journal of Economic History*, 52:2 (June 1992),: 377-388.

Conrad, Alfred And John Meyer. "The Economics of Slavery in the Ante-Bellum South." *Journal of Political Economy* (April 1958): 95-122.

Dublin, Thomas. *Women at Work: The Transformation of Work and Community in Lowell, Mass. 1820-1860*. N.Y.: Columbia University Press, 1979.

Field, Elizabeth B. "The Relative Efficiency of Slavery Revisited: A Translog Production Function Approach.." *American Economic Review 78* (June 1988).

Glaab, Charles N. and A. Theodore Brown. *A History of Urban America*. New York: Macmillan 1967.

Goldin, Claudia. "The Economic Status of Women in the Early Republic." *Journal of Interdisciplinary History* (Winter 1986): 375-404.

Gutman, Herbert G. *Work, Culture and Society in Industrializing America*. N.Y.: Knopf, 1976.

Habakkuk, H. J. *American and British Technology in the Nineteenth Century: The Search for Labour-Saving Inventions*. Cambridge: Cambridge University Press, 1962.

Heilbroner, Robert L. and Aaron Singer. *The Economic Transformation of America: 1600 to the Present*. 2nd edition. N.Y.: Harcourt Brace Jovanovich, 1984.

Hindle, Brooke. *Emulation and Invention*. N.Y.: N.Y. University Press, 1981.

Lindstrom, Diane. "American Economic Growth Before 1840." *Journal of Economic History* (1979): 289-301.

Montgomery, David. "The Working Class of the Pre-Industrial American City, 1780-1830." *Labor History*, 9 : 3-23.

North, Douglass C. *The Economic Growth of the United States, 1790-1860*. Englewood Cliffs, N.J.: Prentice-Hall, 1961.

Schmidt, Louis B. "Internal Commerce and the Development of the National Economy Before 1860." *Journal of Political Economy* (December 1939): 798-822.

Sokoloff, Kenneth L. "Inventive Activity in Early Industrial America: Evidence from Patent Records, 1790-1846." *Journal of Economic History*, XLVIII:4 (Dec. 1988), 813-850.

Stover, John F. *American Railroads*. Chicago: University of Chicago Press, 1961.

Taylor, George Rogers. *The Transportation Revolution, 1815-1860*. White Plains: M.E. Sharpe, 1977.

Wade, Richard C. *The Urban Frontier: Pioneer Life in Early Towns*. Chicago, University of Chicago Press, 1959.

Walton, Gary M. and Ross M. Robertson. *History of the American Economy*, 5th ed. New York: Harcourt, Brace, Jovanovich, 1983.

Ware, Caroline F. *The Early New England Cotton Manufacture: A Study in Industrial Beginnings*. N.Y.: Russell & Russell, 1966. (1931).

Chapter 15

Capitalism in the United States: Second Phase (After 1860)

AS WE SAW IN THE LAST CHAPTER, THE UNITED STATES experienced rapid economic growth in the half century before the Civil War. By 1860, the total value of manufacturing was $2 billion (an increase from only $200 million as recently as 1810), the labor force had grown to 11 million, and the country was second only to Britain in manufacturing. But it is the period *after* the Civil War that marks its emergence as fully industrialized, as measured by the distribution of the labor force or comparative value of output from agriculture and industry.

In 1860, 60 percent of the labor force was still engaged in agriculture, but this percentage declined as manufacturing grew; by 1910, only 30 percent of the labor force was in farming. Similarly, it was not until the 1880s that the value of manufacturing output first equaled the value of agricultural output. A third measure of industrialization is the percentage of the population living in urban areas. This measure is used because 19th century industrialization was associated with urbanization, thus the statistic is a general, although indirect, measure of industrialization. While the rate of urban growth was faster than the rate of growth of rural population, not until later in the 20th century did urban population exceed rural. In 1900, only one third of the population of seventy-six million lived in urban areas, less than the equivalent percentage in Germany or Britain, indicating the much greater importance of agriculture in the United States economy.

The Civil War is more than just a convenient period dividing a developing from a developed country. It was also a political struggle with a result that was as significant for the future pattern of growth and the balance of economic power as the struggle against mercantilism had been in Britain earlier. It was a struggle between an older aristocracy based on land attempting to hold onto political leadership and the new economic industrial elite that now attempted to influence the direction of policy making. However, two very important distinctions between this and the earlier battle for power in Britain should be noted. In Britain, the older landed interests wanted to retain protection while industrial interests favored free trade. This was reversed in the United States, where industrialists favored protectionist policies and southern plantation owners wanted free trade. The second distinction is that the struggle in Britain was peaceful, but in the United States, it led to a bitter and bloody period of war between the States. One possible explanation is that in Britain, industrialists were found all over the country, but in the United States, because industrialist-protectionists were concentrated in the North while plantation owners-free traders were

315

in the South, so regional differences could be exploited.

Civil War Crisis

Conflict between the states essentially became a conflict between the northern industrializing states and the southern slave-owning states, with the new western areas often acting as pawns. These western areas were appeased by the generous land grants of the Homestead Act and the promise of improved transportation following authorization of the transcontinental rail lines. Southern states attempted to secede from the new Union in 1861, less than a hundred years after its formation. While they had many reasons, they all seemed to revolve around the institution of slavery. The South's economy—and indirectly the wealth of the whole country—depended on slave labor. The single largest export from the United States throughout most of the 19th century was raw cotton, and northern merchants' involvement in selling it and importing those goods that sales revenues from cotton made possible depended on cotton production continuing.

But cotton was produced using slave labor, and the South, for this and ideological reasons, refused to consider freeing slaves. In the North, where there were very few slaves, opinion favored abolition (which, of course, led disgruntled Southerners to argue that it was easy to give up something one had never become used to).

Economic Importance of Slavery

As cotton production grew, so the number of slaves grew. In 1810, there were 1.3 million slaves, accounting for 19 percent of the total population, although most were in the South. By 1860, there were 4.5 million slaves, at this time accounting for only 13 percent of the population, largely because of the tremendous increase in overall population due to immigration and natural increase. While Southerners in general as a matter of principle favored the continuation of slavery, in fact less than 5 percent of the white population of 8 million in the South owned slaves in 1860. However, this minority's view was influential: They opposed abolition because slaves were valuable property to them as well as a mark of social status.

Although slavery was probably beginning to disintegrate as a result of internal causes, by midcentury a combination of developments led to a worsening crisis that affected the entire Southern economy. While slaves were mainly used as domestics and on the cotton plantations, after 1820 the institution itself came under strain as the presumption of the moral and intellectual inferiority of the blacks was questioned. This occurred especially in the Southern cities, undermining the insistence on keeping slaves ignorant and uneducated (most Southern states had laws preventing slaves from learning to read) precisely by providing opportunities for education and skill acquisition.

In many cities slaves *had* learned skills, becoming more valuable to their owners because they could be hired out profitably to employers as clerks, chefs, draymen, and steamboat workers, for example. Savannah even had all-slave units in its firefighting force, including a top-rated engine unit. Because there were greater opportunities for contacts, many slaves had learned to read and write, which gave them the ability to question the validity of their status. In the 1820s and 1830s, there were some scattered slave protests, but they were crushed, and the result was an intensification of various mechanisms to perpetuate slavery.

By 1860 the numbers of slaves left in the cities had declined from an average of 20 percent of city population in the 1820s; most were now in the countryside. But this led to another dilemma. Selling urban slaves to plantations removed a disruptive element from the cities but added one to the plantations, where there were larger numbers congregated in one place.

While these internal contradictions were slowly gnawing away at slavery from the inside, there were external problems that involved the entire Southern economy. By 1860, although cotton was still important for the country, the growth of manufacturing and the expansion of Western agriculture implied that it was proportionally less important than it had been, which weakened the economic basis for the Southern landowners' claim to political power.

Inflexibility of Slavery

The basic cause was slavery. As previously noted, capitalism depends on profit making by producing output for sale in a market, using a free labor force with the aim of accumulating capital. While Southern plantation owners were certainly not averse to making profits, they were not pure capitalists either. The difference lies in the labor aspect. Both industrial capitalists and plantation owners had a large, initial fixed investment—the former in plant and equipment, the latter in land. While the industrialist saw labor as a variable cost (free labor can be hired or fired as conditions indicate), this was not true of the planter. The planter also had a large fixed investment in slaves, which occurred when the slaves were bought. This meant that a much larger amount of capital was tied up for longer periods of time, which added an element of inflexibility to an economy based on the use of slave labor and also made slavery very hard to eliminate, as slaves were property and therefore valuable. Even if an individual slave owner could sell slaves and thus reduce his fixed investment, it was not a viable alternative if all slave owners tried to sell slaves at the same time, especially in a slave-dependent monoculture like the South.

Monoculture
Situation where only one crop is cultivated

This inflexibility hurt plantation owners and their profit-making ability throughout most of the first half of the 19th century. Profits were squeezed from both the cost and revenue sides. On the cost side, the ending of the slave trade (1808) combined with an increasing demand for cotton from European and New England textile mills meant that the supply of slaves did not increase as fast as the demand for them: natural increase was insufficient, and the price of slaves rose. In 1800 a field hand could be bought for between $300 and $450, but in 1860 the price had risen to about $2,000. This affected smaller slave owners the most, because they could rely less on the natural increase of their slave holdings. In addition, cotton exhausted the soil rapidly. The South was a monoculture where modern ideas of crop rotation, soil improvement, and conservation were not applied; instead, cotton planters relied on the ability to acquire new lands when old areas were no longer productive. Hence over time, the center of cotton cultivation shifted west from the original areas in South Carolina and Georgia to new areas in Alabama, Mississippi, Louisiana, Arkansas, and Texas. However, new land purchases required large initial outlays, with little immediate return.

Both factors implied that the costs of producing cotton rose but they were not offset by increases in productivity due to technological innovation. Profits were squeezed from the revenue side as well; from 1810 to 1860, the trend of prices for raw cotton was down. But because the system was inflexible, the expected capitalist response of a movement to an area of production where returns were higher was missing because too much capital was tied up in land. So the financial position of the planters weakened.

Southern Dependence on the North

This was further intensified by the planters' dependence on the North for credit and trade. Some cotton was shipped directly from Southern ports,

Solving Problems in Economic History

Was slavery economically efficient?

One of the earliest, and most controversial examples of cliometric analysis came in the study of American slavery by Robert Fogel and Stanley Engerman (*Time on the Cross*, 2 volumes, Little, Brown, 1974). Slavery has been particularly suitable for quantitative analysis because there is a wealth of data available on all aspects of slavery, such as sales figures and prices, cost of upkeep, location, and so on.

This study aroused considerable controversy because it reversed what the authors referred to as common misconceptions about slavery. Among their findings: slave owners encouraged family stability—-few children were sold, and most slaves stayed on one plantation all their lives; that the rate of expropriation was lower than is usually thought, with the typical slave receiving up to 90 percent of income produced; and that the material conditions of the typical slave's life compared quite well with that of a free industrial worker. Possibly some of the controversy arose because of the moral abhorrence of slavery, but the authors took pains to emphasize the absence of moral implications: They undertook a strictly quantitative analysis.

Some of their other findings perhaps have fewer emotional overtones. For example, when

Southern plantation agriculture was compared to Northern family farming, they found no evidence of inefficiency. The best explanation offered is one borrowed from industrial trends, the advantages of economies of scale. That is, because plantations were large, the organization of slaves into gangs permitted a high degree of specialization that was efficient. In addition, evidence supported the image of the typical field hand as hardworking and efficient; some slaves, both on plantations and in the towns, developed highly valuable specialized skills. In general, the purchase of a slave, the authors found, was highly profitable, generating rates of return that compared favorably with investment in manufacturing, which would hardly have been possible if slave labor was inefficient.

Although both the methods as well as the conclusions of this study have come under fire (see, for example, Elizabeth B. Field, "The Relative Efficiency of Slavery Revisited." *American Economic Review*, June, 1988) it remains important as one of the pathbreaking examples of the use of quantitative analysis of historical problems.

but the imports demanded by the South from Europe were always shipped to a Northern port, and then, via coastal shipping, sent South. The nature of credit dependency was a particular irritant, and there were many ways that Northern financiers and banking houses had taken advantage of the South for years. For example, loans were frequently secured by future crops or land or slaves. In the case of loans secured by crops, planters received bills of exchange or drafts that

matured when the cotton was finally sold. As planters usually needed funds immediately, they were discounted earlier at substantially less than face value. In any event, loans carried high interest rates, and commission charges asked by cotton factors (selling agents) were also high.

This dependency was fragile and frequently disrupted by commercial crises. For example, in 1857 the New York money market was in crisis. Railroad stock prices were falling, and banks were demanding repayment of loans advanced to stock purchasers. In addition, New York banks acted as reserve banks for others in the country, which were withdrawing their funds from New York banks to meet demands for cash from their own depositors following overspeculation in land. This led to more pressure on banks and many collapsed. What followed next was a withdrawal of foreign funds and a fall in the international exchange value of the dollar. The end result was that cotton planters suffered as the dollar price of cotton fell, even though they had nothing to do with the fall.

No attempts were made to diversify the economy to lessen the dependence on cotton and thus on slavery, or even to lessen the dependence on Northern financial institutions. The South remained predominantly rural, and while some towns, such as New Orleans, Savannah, and Mobile grew, they grew more slowly than elsewhere. Industrial activity was consequently limited, apart from some tobacco processing. While a slave labor force *could* be used in industry (slaves were used in Richmond tobacco factories and ironworks) the system was not really adaptable to such uses because the prevailing Southern ethic ruled against it. Also the South did not share in the population increases resulting from immigration. Immigrants were either factory workers, and the South had too few factories; or independent farmers who were attracted to the West.

Effects of the Civil War

The outcome of the Civil War was largely determined by economic strength, as modern wars tend to be. At first, conditions were depressed: Ocean shipping fell 60 percent between 1860 and 1864, new railway construction ended, the cotton textile industry (both in New England and Europe) was severely disrupted, and New York's banking industry declined because of the withdrawal of Southern activity (Southern debts were uncollectible).

But while war in general limits economic expansion, some industries gained, both directly from military demands and indirectly. So, for example, while uniforms and munitions for the armies were at first imported, after 1863 Northern industry under the stimulus of large government orders began producing them domestically in the quantities required. This helped the expansion of wool textiles and the footwear industry, which in addition became a factory industry as the sewing machine was adapted for use on leather. The iron industry, which had been technologically backward for so long, received the final impetus to modernize as war demands stimulated the use of coke instead of charcoal in iron production.

An indirect stimulus was given to the farm machinery industry and to agricultural mechanization, because so much of the work force was conscripted for fighting. From the military point of view, the North's superior railway network was vital in moving men and materials, whereas the South's rail lines were usually short and lacked interconnections. So although the South had an impressive military tradition (including the best generals), its fighting men lacked the support necessary to wage a successful offensive.

Reconstruction: Post Civil War South

After defeat in the Civil War, the Southern States went through a difficult period. Plantations, towns, villages, and railways had been destroyed during the war, the result of the Northern "scorched earth" policy intended to weaken southern resistance. This had to be made good, but the Reconstruction government imposed on the South did little to help Southerners in general. It did benefit Northerners however, and this, plus antiblack feeling led to white resistance (including the formation of openly racist organizations such as the Ku Klux Klan) and a deliberate policy of racial segregation that marked the South until the mid 20th century.

One immediate result of the war was the abolition of slavery, but in the beginning the impact on economic activity was negative, and the longer-range impact resulted in the persistence of a system of semidependence of blacks on white landlords. Freed slaves did not gain any rights to land. Instead, the practice of sharecropping was used, in which former planters owned the land but advanced the tools and seeds to the sharecroppers who worked it. In exchange, the landlord received from one half to two thirds of the crop. While this system did keep land in production, it also perpetuated black dependence (in 1900, three quarters of all black farmers were sharecroppers) and white dependence on Northern merchants and financiers. Property values had fallen, so many former plantation owners sold out to new commercial owners, including war profiteers. Those who remained still required financing, but the advances they received from merchants were based on the continued cultivation of cotton, which limited agricultural diversification.

By 1869, cotton prices were firming and harvests were large. Ironically, this further discouraged diversification, although in the 1870s some manufacturing was begun, primarily agricultural processing such as sugar refining or production of cottonseed oil and oil cake, or lumbering. After the 1880s low labor costs in the South plus a lack of union organizing activity saw textile production shifted there, away from New England. But the South remained the country's poorest region and was marked by poor race relations. Significant industrialization did not occur until well into the 20th century.

Sharecropper

Tenant farmer who pays "rent" to the landlord with a share of the harvest

---

Western Expansion

Colonial America was important as a producer of agricultural and primary products, and this tradition continued in the new areas opening up in the West. Westward expansion picked up after the Civil War, encouraged by completion of the transcontinental railway and construction of a nationwide rail network. Opening up the area to commercial farming and mining involved overcoming two major obstacles as well as requiring improved transportation. First was the elimination of the immense buffalo herds of the Plains, which the cattle ranchers believed "wasted" the grass on which cattle could feed. This extermination, completed by the mid 1880s, was itself the waste of a unique natural resource. Second, there were the Indians, although by the 1870s they no longer presented a hostile threat to the expansion of capitalist activity.

Up to 1851, the area from the Missouri to the Rocky Mountains was recognized as sovereign Indian territory, but discoveries of gold and other metals plus pressure from Western ranchers and settlers reversed that. The 1860s was a period of intense hostilities and the army was used to "pacify" the Indians, who were being removed from areas thought to be rich in minerals. By the late 1860s, Western Indians had been pushed into two major reservations—well away from the rail lines—and in 1871, Congress rejected Indian claims of sovereignty and took over jurisdiction of Indian affairs.

The first westward expansion after independence was into the grain-growing lands of the Midwest, in Ohio and Illinois. With expansion later into the Plains states, cattle raising became profitable once the Indians were suppressed. However, in these new areas, settlers who wanted to cultivate land came into conflict with ranchers over fencing and water rights. As settlers were supported by the government, ranchers' cattle drives north from Texas to rail termini, from where they were shipped to meat packing plants, became rare by the 1880s. (Although this period was a brief one, the legend of the independent, rugged cowboy has persisted as a part of American culture. Perhaps the reason is that it perpetuates the old Jeffersonian idea of independence, albeit in a new form, as a contrast to the crass materialism of the eastern industrial cities.)

Rail construction also helped timber companies move operations west, and they, like railroad and mining companies, also gained huge areas of new land for exploitation. Much of the boom experienced by the timber companies can be traced to continuing population growth, which increased demand for housing and thus for lumber.[1]

In mining, there was a pattern of large capitalist mining companies, particularly in industrially useful minerals such as copper and iron, coexisting with individual prospectors. The hopes of striking it rich by finding gold or silver lured many individuals west, first to California gold in 1849, then to silver in Nevada in 1858-1859, and then to Montana after the Civil War. However, because machinery was often required, mining companies gained from the discovery of precious metals made by individuals who then were unable to afford the capital investments needed to exploit subsurface lodes. In any event, it was rarely the individual prospector who gained a fortune: The best way of making money out of these finds was to provide support services, such as food, liquor, or transportation.

But the expansion of grain farming in the Midwest and West affected more people and had a more significant, if less colorful, impact on political life and policy. The explanation lies in the problems faced by Western farmers, problems that were both natural and manmade.

Farmers' Problems

In 1860, the western border of grain growing reached into eastern Iowa and southeastern Minnesota, then spread to Kansas and Nebraska by 1870 as the rail network expanded. By 1880, the population of these four new states had risen to 2.5 million from practically nothing in 1860. The natural problems faced by grain farmers—the right amounts of rainfall and sunlight at the right times—were intensified by artificial problems such as credit availability and crop marketing. Although large markets for farmers' output existed, fluctuations in export demand plus fluctuations in supply caused by natural factors resulted in frequently alternating periods of prosperity and hard times throughout the rest of the 19th century. In addition, the expansion of farming resulted in a tendency toward overproduction, such that when prices in general were falling, farm prices tended to fall faster. This could be offset by continued movement further west, which kept up land values, but even here, there was much speculation in land that often had an impact on the financial institutions in these new areas, which in turn affected credit terms and availability for farmers.

Immediately after the end of the Civil War, farming was prosperous, but this prosperity collapsed in 1868 because of overproduction and a general lag of world demand behind supply. The outbreak of the Franco-Prussian War saw prices rise again, only to fall in 1871 when European production resumed. These problems were made worse by the injustice farmers perceived in their dealings with the railways and middlemen such as grain elevator and storage companies. Farmers believed that the better-organized companies took advantage of the unorganized individual farmers. For example, while the railways provided access to markets for farmers, the *terms* on which this access was provided discriminated against farmers and in favor of large shippers in general. Where water transportation was not an alternative, farmers had no option but to use the railways.

Farmers also protested against the rates charged by middlemen. Again, grain elevator companies usually had a monopoly in particular areas and were able to exploit this monopoly power because farmers did not deal directly with their final consumers. Farmers also protested against national tariff policy, which effectively raised prices of manufactured goods to farmers but did not at the same time provide them with any compensatory treatment. They were also heavily in debt to banks because of mortgages on their land or loans to buy equipment, which in turn often involved paying high commissions to agencies selling farm machinery. Because of their high debt load, farmers suffered during deflationary periods when the real value of debt increased, irrespective of how productive farmers were, how hard they worked or how much output they produced.

Political Reactions of Farmers

In general, farmers' grievances were based on the perception that although they formed a valuable part of the American economy and American democracy, they were exploited by powerful, well organized special interests against which they had little redress. This growing protest finally led to political action. In 1867, groups of farmers in Illinois attacked rail lines and in the same year forced passage of the Warehouse Act, which required state inspection of warehouses and elevators and imposed penalties on companies refusing to deliver grain to the warehouse it was consigned to. In 1871, the Illinois legislature passed a law banning rate discrimination in rail rates and imposed maximum charges.

This was followed by similar action in other state legislatures. However, rail rates did not fall significantly until the late 1870s, because it required more than legislation at the state level to accomplish. In any event, the tendency to increasing monopolistic practices implied that any improvement in profits from lower transportation rates would be captured by intermediaries. Grain farmers were affected the most. Of all farmers, they had the least market power, so that wheat

farmers received only 17 percent of the final price paid by consumers, while dairy and cattle farmers received 50 percent.

The Grange

Political action was a second way to approach farming problems. The major organization was the Grange, founded in 1867. By 1874, its membership (including women, which was unusual for any organization at that time) had grown to 1.5 million, but it was only moderately successful. In general, the Grange tried to educate farmers and improve their financial situation. It pressed for legislation for the regulation of transportation and storage costs in order to end discrimination against farmers and promoted cooperative efforts, both in buying and selling. While some local granges owned cooperative grain elevators, they met a great deal of opposition from rail companies that preferred to deal with farmers individually and not as a group, and most of them eventually closed down. Cooperative efforts in buying to reduce the prices farmers paid were more successful. In fact, this also stimulated the growth of the mail order industry, which eliminated agencies and permitted farm families to buy direct at lower retail prices in rural areas. (The first mail order company, Montgomery Ward, was established in 1872.)

Ultimately the Grange tried to do too much with too little and failed to meet the wishes of all farmers, especially when prosperity returned. As a result, rival organizations emerged, many with a specifically political orientation. For example, in 1874, independent agrarian parties formed in nine prairie states, California, and Oregon. In addition, many more states began to regulate rail charges, which helped eliminate a major source of farmer discontent. However, in one very important respect, these organizations were successful. They showed the potential dangers of monopolies, which were later recognized on the federal level with antitrust legislation, and specifically brought agrarian issues into politics.

The Greenback Issue

One very important issue on which farmers had pronounced opinions was currency, and farm support for the "greenback" issue led to a controversy between easy money and hard money advocates. The issue dates from the Civil War. Before then, the banking and currency system was chaotic, with no direct federal regulation of banking, and with paper money consisting of bank notes circulated by state-chartered banks. Among the

---

Greenback

United States paper money printed with green ink on the back

---

reforms intended by the 1863-1864 National Banking Act was establishment of nationally chartered banks. Their note issues would replace the state banks' bank notes and would be supplemented by greenbacks, legal tender notes issued by the government itself. Greenbacks were pure paper, not convertible into gold or silver. They were issued to help pay for Civil War debts and had contributed to inflation during the 1860s.

However, prices were declining after the war, and attempts were made to contract the money supply by withdrawing greenbacks from circulation and returning to specie payment. This movement was supported by bankers, merchants, and other commercial interests, but opposed by farmers and manufacturers. They wanted cheap money, as inflation made it easier to finance expansion and pay off old debt. To make their point, cheap money advocates formed the Independent National (Greenback) Party in 1876, with a platform specifically favoring continuation

---

National Bank

A United States bank chartered by the Federal Government

---

of a paper money standard. While never achieving national power (the Republican and Democratic parties were not particularly anti-inflation themselves, and all three parties shared considerable overlapping interests), this party did keep concern over banking and currency questions at the forefront of national politics.

Continuing Problems

In the 1870s some farmers attempted to improve their position by diversifying, but this only brought more problems. First, wheat farmers found much wheat land unsuitable for other uses, and second, diversification implied taking on additional debt, keeping farmers under the control of financial interests. As a last resort, and this applied especially to those in Wisconsin, Indiana, and Illinois, farmers simply gave up under competitive pressures and moved further west to start all over again. The land they left behind was frequently taken over by farmers with more capital resources who did diversify, especially into dairy farming.

The underlying problems were not resolved. After a return to prosperity, a drought affected the Plains states in 1886-1887, and many farms were foreclosed. A recovery later was followed by the financial panic of 1893, which led to more years of depressed conditions. In 1894, wheat prices were the lowest they had ever been. However, after 1896, the depression ended, climatic conditions improved, and continuing population growth improved market conditions for farmers. Export markets, especially for the traditional products of wheat, pork, cotton, and tobacco, remained important, which indirectly reduced the incentive to diversify. But the domestic market's continuing growth implied less dependence on overseas demand whose fluctuations contributed so much to the shifting fortunes of farmers, and this helped improve the farmers' position.

In the 20th century, the era of laissez faire in farming began to come to an end as federal government efforts to even out price fluctuations and adopt other interventionist measures started. This was limited at first. Government agents first provided information to farmers in 1914, and in 1916 the Farm Loan Act gave favorable mortgage terms to farmers. However, the rise of exports stimulated by World War I resulted in renewed debt as farmers expanded their activities, and the same problems of fluctuating incomes returned again once Europe's farmers resumed production and the export market declined.

The 1920s were generally depressed years for farmers, with many contributing factors. Weather conditions were poor. Second, a declining export market was made worse by the protectionist tariffs of 1922 and 1930, which limited European exports to the United States and thus European ability to buy American agricultural commodities (see Chapter 21). Then a slower rate of growth in the domestic market due to the restriction on immigration led to overproduction, a fall in farm prices, and reduced land values in wheat growing areas. Many farmers were foreclosed as they were unable to repay their debts. In addition, the introduction of the gasoline-powered tractor made it harder for small farmers to compete with larger farmers who adopted it. There was also a trend to conversion from independent farmer to tenant farmer status, especially in southwestern states. All these conditions encouraged the actively interventionist measures designed to stabilize farm incomes and restore farm purchasing power associated with national policies of the 1930s.

Industrialization: Mass Production

Although agriculture remained an important part of the economy, the major change taking place in the period from the end of the Civil War to the

Figure 15.1 Huge numbers of immigrants poured into the United States in the late 19th century, providing an important source of labor for expanding industry. These immigrants are leaving Ellis Island, the most important center for processing immigrants between 1892 and 1943. (Courtesy of the Museum of the City of New York)

end of the century was the spread of industry, with a big industrial boom occurring between 1865 and 1873. Unlike farming, the secular trend in industry was toward increased concentration. Progress was not steady, as there were currency problems, three financial panics, and two long depressions before 1900. But by then the United States had become the world leader in manufacturing. (In 1893, New England alone produced more manufacturing goods per capita than any other country.) Some individual businessmen and enterprises proved much more capable than farmers of protecting themselves against market fluctuations. However, they were charged with not acting in the national interest, and a process of legislating against certain undesirable business practices intended to restore competitive conditions in business began, although it was not very effective in practice. By the end of the century, manufacturing was characterized by a large number of small enterprises, and a smaller number of very large enterprises concentrated in core industries: capital goods, oil, chemicals, and food processing.

Concentration

The extent to which an industry is dominated by a small number of firms

---

Meeting the Preconditions

The transformation of the economy to being predominantly industrial by the 1880s was extremely rapid; once the Civil War was over, all the necessary ingredients were in place. The United States, a large country, possessed all the major natural resources needed for 19th century industrial expansion: coal, iron ore, timber, cotton, as well as those needed for the newly emerging industries based on oil. The labor shortage that had plagued industrial activity for so long was overcome as millions of immigrants poured into the country and as more mechanized and labor-saving technologies were developed. The extent

of both industrial expansion and mechanization is indicated by the use of energy. In 1865, 16 million horsepower of energy was used, rising to 1.6 billion by 1929. Population growth provided a much larger internal mass market than was available to any European country. Hence the need to rely on export demand, always difficult for a newly industrializing country, was reduced and there was also a much greater incentive to extend the technologies of standardized mass production, in which the United States became a world leader.

Also by this time, capital was easily available, either as foreign funds borrowed through the London money market or increasingly from domestic sources, especially industrial profits. (Other sources of funds were more attracted to the higher rates available in land or stock market speculation, which tended to slow the pace of industrial development.) Social overhead capital was in place. Government had early on built roads and canals and subsidized the rail lines, so the necessary transportation and communications networks needed for mass movement of people, goods, and information were present. Government also helped the acquisition of skills and technical knowledge by providing public education facilities, which represented a larger investment in education than occurred anywhere else. And finally, tariff policy was generally protectionist, so that domestic producers could exploit the huge domestic market without fear of foreign competition.

The growth in output was extraordinary. Annual average total output was $9.1 billion immediately after the Civil War, rose to $35.4 billion in the last years of the century, and was $59.7 billion in the 1912-1916 period (in 1929 dollars). Between 1869 and 1899, agriculture and manufacturing essentially reversed places in their relative share of value added to output. In 1869, agriculture contributed 53 percent and industry accounted for 33 percent of value added, but in the latter year, agriculture's share fell to 33 percent while industry's rose to 53 percent. Between 1860 and 1900, population increased from 26.9 million to 75.9 million, expanding both the number of consumers and the supply of labor. In 1860, of a labor force of about 10 million, 60 percent were in agriculture with only 18 percent in manufacturing and other nonagricultural jobs, but by the end of the century, agriculture accounted for 30 percent of the labor force with 20 percent in manufacturing alone. (In 1910, of a labor force of 37 million, 2 million were children under 15, while women accounted for 7.4 million.)

Although the growth of the domestic market in the second half of the 19th century was the major factor stimulating industrial growth, foreign trade also grew, and it too reveals industrial change. Between 1870 and 1900, exports tripled to $1.5 billion, and the percentage of manufactured goods exported rose from 15 percent to 32 percent, a sign of industrial maturity. Changes in the composition of output also mirrored the developments occurring in British and German industrial development. But in many important respects—the role of immigration, business ethics and tariff policy—American development was very different.

Cotton textile production was the leading industry before the Civil War, but because industrial expansion was faster in other areas, was only the sixth largest by 1914. In terms of value of total output, food processing remained the most important until 1914, but because output also includes the value of inputs, a more commonly used measure to indicate industrial change is value added, which excludes the cost of the original raw materials. If this measure is used, then the heavy industries were more important. During and after the Civil War, the iron industry finally adopted more modern European technology, which contributed to the doubling of pig iron output each decade, so that by the late 1880s iron output was greater than Britain's. In 1890, the United States produced 9.2 million tons, while Britain produced 7.9 million tons.

Steel

The major development however, occurred in the steel industry. Although the Bessemer process for converting pig iron into steel was introduced in England in 1856, it was not used in the United States until 1864. By 1875, there were about 12 converters in existence, steel production was slightly less than 400,000 tons as compared with less than 100,000 tons in 1871, and the industry began to expand rapidly. By 1880, 1.2 million tons were being produced; by 1900, 10 million tons; and in 1915, 32 million tons, at which time the United States was clearly the world's leading steel producer.

Steel production is important in a modern industrial economy because it has so many linkages with other sectors of the economy. This means that, for example, improvements in production technology that lower costs and prices can be passed on to stimulate steel users, giving them an incentive to expand, which in turn increases the demands the steel industry makes for iron ore and coal. Whereas previously it took a day or more to convert three to five tons of iron to steel, the Bessemer converter now took only ten to twenty minutes. The capacity of the converters also increased. Early ones held five tons, but by 1900 capacity had risen to twenty tons. In the early 1870s, steel sold for about $100 a ton; later in 1873, the price had dropped to $50, and by the late 1890s to $12. Steel use expanded because of the enormous demands made by the construction of railroads (which in turn lowered other industries' transportation costs), the expansion of the farm machinery industry due to the expansion of agriculture and mechanization of farming, the growth of the machine tool industry because of the expansion of industry in general, and mechanization in particular, and even construction.

Steel became a basic building material. It was used in the construction of suspension bridges, such as the Brooklyn Bridge in New York City, started in 1879, and it also permitted the construction of modern, high-rise buildings using a load-bearing framework of metal rather than heavy masonry, which increased the amount of available interior space. As early as the 1840s, cast iron had been used in the construction of warehouses, but the height of buildings for residential or office uses had been limited by human lung and muscle power. After the 1880s two more related developments made the construction of tall buildings possible. The first was the improvement of the elevator; the second was the development of electricity as an alternative power source. Once a safe, reliable electric-powered elevator was practical, then the era of high rises began. (The first

modern apartment house was built in New York in the 1870s.)

Many other linkages also existed. For example, increasing farm mechanization increased demand for steel for farm equipment, and the use of steel in refrigerated cars on the railroads and in steamships made agricultural output more marketable over longer distances. In addition, steel was increasingly used in new areas—in the production of consumer durables and in a new industry, automobile production. Only in shipbuilding did improvements in steel have little effect in the United States, and American-built shipping tonnage was lower at the end of the century than it had been at the beginning.

Steel production is also a good example of the trend toward increasing scale of operations coupled with increasing concentration. In 1870, 808

Table 15-1
Indicators of Industrial Growth: United States

I Coal Production (million tons; selected years)				
1860	1870	1880	1890	1900
15.1	42.5	64.8	143.1	245

II Steel Output (000 tons; selected years)	
1870	1890
100	10,200

III Pig Iron Production (000 tons and as % of total world production)										
1740	1800	1820	1840	1860	1870	1880	1890	1900	1910	1920
1	40	110	290	821	1,665	3,835	9,203	13,789	27,304	36,926
—	9%	11%	10%	11%	14%	21%	34%	35%	42%	59%

companies in the iron and steel industry employed 78,000 workers, produced an output of 3.2 million tons and had a total invested capital of $121 million. By 1900, only 669 firms employed 272,000 workers, produced 29.5 million tons and had invested capital of $590 million. The giant here was the United States Steel Corporation, a holding company organized in 1901. This company alone accounted for half of all pig iron capacity, all of the country's output of barbed wire (important as fencing for western farmers), and 60 percent of the structural steel and wire markets.

Oil

A similar trend to increasing scale and concentration accompanying increased output occurred in a new industry pioneered in the United States, the oil industry. Previously, whale oil, candles, and gas had been used for lighting, but mineral oil soon replaced the first two. The first oil well was sunk in Pennsylvania in 1859. At that time output was small, and its uses were limited to lighting and lubrication. Growth, however, was fast as new uses emerged. By 1865 oil was the sixth most important export from the United States, and its domestic market had also expanded dramatically. One early problem with oil was the difficulty of storing and transporting it. Two major solutions emerged. The first was to use pipelines (the first was built in 1865) to transport oil to storage tanks near refineries and markets, a totally new form of transportation. The second was to build special tank cars to hold oil and then ship it by rail.

Oil cannot be used as is but must be refined (essentially distilled) into different grades of oil products for different purposes. The early refineries were concentrated in Cleveland, which had an advantageous location near the Great Lakes and on rail lines, and was thus accessible to both the production sources and the markets for oil. (Transportation needs and costs are an important aspect of the development of the oil industry, and

more attention will be paid later to the monopoly trends apparent in the 19th century.)

The story of the concentration of the oil industry is inseparable from that of the Standard Oil Company and its founder, John D. Rockefeller. He was a commission dealer in Cleveland, and with funds from profitable business deals made during the Civil War he established a refinery in Cleveland. By 1870, through a process of acquiring other refiners, the Standard Oil Company of Ohio accounted for one seventh of Cleveland's production, which at that time totalled five million barrels a year.

The next stage was to dominate the entire industry. Using secret deals with the rail companies, Standard Oil received preferential rates that helped keep its costs low. With the strength gained in refining, Standard Oil then moved to control production and retailing, becoming a vertically integrated company. By 1875, the Company controlled 90 percent of the country's refinery capacity and was acquiring a dominating position in production and marketing, so that by 1904 it controlled about 85 percent of the domestic market and 90 percent of all exports of oil from the United States. Output expanded rapidly. Total output of 51 million barrels in 1899 increased to 379 million barrels in 1919.

Its position was challenged, and the legal ones will be covered more fully later. On the supply side, Standard Oil had achieved dominance by its control over oil in Pennsylvania and Ohio. The Company's advantage in the industry gained by its control of transportation and pipelines, which were mainly in the East, lessened with the opening up of new fields in Texas, California, and the southwest. But in spite of this, the Standard Oil Companies always remained dominant in the oil industry.

While it did not develop better technology itself, Standard Oil did take advantage of new improvements which, combined with its sometimes shady operating tactics, gave it a commanding position in the oil industry. However, these technological advances increased the size of plant needed for efficient operation, which became an effective barrier against the entry of new competitors; the initial finance capital requirements were simply too great. As with all other industries that showed a similar trend to large scale and concentration in only a few hands, the competing issues of efficiency and marketplace competition led to considerable agitation late in the 19th century and in the 20th.

Motor Vehicles

Another new industry that also showed the same trends in the 20th century was the auto industry. Its emergence depended on a combination of several factors: improvements in steel and machine tool technology, advances in the technology of the gasoline-powered internal combustion engine, availability of glass and rubber—in general, the advances being made in chemical and electrical knowledge. And in turn, the auto industry would stimulate construction: Cars need good, paved roads to travel on, and this plus the building of service stations selling gasoline—an important new market for the oil industry—provided added demand for the construction industry all through the 20th century.

Although the first automobiles were pioneered and produced in France and Germany, unique opportunities in the United States eventually made it the world's leading auto producer until it was displaced by Japan in the 1980s. These opportunities occurred because of the much longer distances and the larger potential market in the United States They could be made effective because of the cooperation of governments at all levels in building roads for the cars and trucks to travel on. By 1910, there were sixty separate companies in the United States producing cars, but the trend toward merger and a reduction in numbers had already begun when in 1908-1909, William Durant organized General Motors out of a merger of several companies.

Table 15-2
Immigration into the United States

Decade	Immigrants (000s)
1830s	538.4
1840s	1,427.3
1859s	2,814.6
1860s	2,081.3
1970s	2,742.1
1880s	5,248.6
1890s	3,721.3
1900s	8,202.4
1910s	8,513.7

But the most significant step for the industry came in 1909, when Henry Ford applied the principle of mass production on an assembly line basis to the Model T. This was a far cry from his first car, which was built in a small workshop using parts from bicycles and horsedrawn carriages. Mass production enabled lower skilled workers to be used, in contrast to the early craftsman-built cars, and for the first time lowered the price to turn it into a potentially mass market product. By 1913, Ford's sales of 168,000 cars a year were one third of the nation's entire output, and a year later Ford had almost one half of the industry's sales.

Not only cars but also gasoline-powered tractors and trucks were being produced. Trucks later represented a real threat to the railway's monopoly of freight transportation. By 1917, total output of all gasoline-powered vehicles was almost two million a year, most of it accounted for by a small handful of large firms.

Immigration

The Industrial Revolution was revolutionary in Britain not only because it had such a dramatic

Figure 15.2 Woman workers were an important part of the American industrial work force. Shown here is an illustration of a march by striking shoemakers in Lynn, Massachusetts (from Leslie's Illustrated, March 17, 1860). (Courtesy of the Tamiment Institute Library)

impact on people, their social relationships and way of life, but also because it revolutionized the technology of producing material things, the basis of economic life. The technological revolution permitted an expansion of output, all other things being constant, because it increased the productivity of the individual worker. If it had not done so, capitalist industrialists would never have introduced mechanization because it would not have resulted in increased revenues and therefore profits. Thus in Europe, application of these new techniques accounted for much of the output increases that were achieved.

In the United States, adoption of new techniques alone would have had much the same impact as in Europe. But the extent of the expansion of output owed much to that unique feature of United States development, immigration, which meant that all other things were not equal. The labor supply expanding at the same time that productivity improvements were taking place accounts for the dramatic growth of output in the United States in the second half of the 19th century.

Immigration was not important in the European countries, although after the 1840s there was considerable immigration into England from Ireland. Rather *emigration* was a safety valve for these countries in the face of the transformation in social life and the initially declining opportunities for work following the introduction of the first factories. The experience of the United States in the 19th century was very different. On the individual level, the new immigrants were affected by the breakdown of the old society in Europe, but in the United States, there was no old society in the process of transformation. In this sense, while the process of emigration was an upheaval, requiring breaking the ties of community and learning new skills (most came from a rural background), a new way of life, and a new language, it was an upheaval of a very different type when compared to the process of change occurring in Europe.

On the national level, without the enormous increase in labor supply and the potential increase of the market made possible by immigration, the continual development of mass production methods would not have occurred. This trend toward the mechanization, standardization, and deskilling of the work process was further aided by other features of immigrants, especially later in the 19th century. They were usually industrially inexperienced, because in most cases the push factor resulting in emigration from Europe had been the breakdown of peasant agriculture in the face of competition from more efficient commercial farming in the United States, and the coming of factories, which eliminated domestic industries. Industrialists had an incentive to keep labor costs low by adopting those techniques requiring repetition of simple skills that could be done by low-wage, unskilled immigrant labor. So important was this that agents were sent to Europe after the 1860s to recruit new workers, and the effect on the entire labor force was to hold down wages.[2] In addition, after 1880 an increasing proportion of immigrants spoke no English, which further encouraged the development of industrial techniques that did not require literacy in English.

After 1860 and before the closing of immigration in 1915 due to the First World War, some thirty million immigrants entered the United States, most becoming part of the new urban work force in industry. The pattern of immigration as well as the numbers also shows significant changes that had an influence on the reception of the newcomers. Throughout the century, the absolute numbers of immigrants increased and accounted for a larger and larger proportion of the total population increase. (The birthrate had always been high, partly because of the bias in the age distribution of the population toward younger age groups.) Naturally, immigration, especially from the British Isles, had always been an important factor, but the changes that occurred in the 19th century added other implications.

As a point of reference, immigration before the Civil War was just beginning to show the increases that characterized the last half of the century. In the 1830s, immigrants numbered over 500,000 and accounted for 13 percent of total population increase. One third came from Ireland and one quarter from Germany. (German immigration had been insignificant before 1830.) In the 1840s, there were over 1.4 million immigrants, nearly half from Ireland (this was the decade of the Irish potato famine), and they accounted for a quarter of the population increase in that decade.

Immigration in the 1850s was 2.8 million, one third of the total population increase, mostly from Ireland and Germany. After 1854 there were also a few Chinese immigrants, hired to build the rail lines in the West, although some also became miners or fishermen. Unfortunately, their presence as a completely different cultural group later led to many racial problems in the West.

Population inflows were temporarily slowed by the Civil War, but still a total of over 2 million new immigrants, mostly from Ireland and Germany, arrived in the 1860s, and a further 2.7 million came in the 1870s. During the 1880s, the number of immigrants almost doubled to 5.2 million, or 41 percent of the population increase of that decade. What was noticeable for the first time was the shift in the area of origin; 10 percent, mostly Jews, were from central and eastern Europe and 6 percent came from Italy and southern Europe.

Depression during the 1890s contributed to a reduction in numbers, but still 3.7 million people crossed the Atlantic, half from eastern and central Europe (Poland, Russia, Austria, Hungary) and Italy. Between 1900 and 1909, immigration more than doubled to 8.2 million, most from the new areas of eastern, central, and southern Europe, and this was half the total population increase. This pace more than kept up in the decade 1910-1920, with a concentration of immigration before 1915. Then the First World War

cut immigration off, and it was further restricted by the 1917 Immigration Act. By that time, 8.5 million people entered the country, 61 percent of the total population increase, and again largely from the "new" areas of Europe.

Impact of Immigration

The impact of this massive flow of immigrants was immense, not only on the economy, as noted above, but also on social and political life. Immigration was encouraged in the early years after independence. After all, a new country needed peopling, and as most immigrants then were white Protestants from the British Isles, many with the skills needed for emerging industries, there was little conflict between old and new. There was only a little opposition from the growing towns of the Eastern seaboard, which for the first time were beginning to see urban problems such as poverty on a larger, although still limited, scale than before. (This marked the start of the tendency to blame foreigners for problems.)

However, the overall harmony was disturbed in the 1830s. Then, the appearance of a large number of Catholic, mainly Irish, immigrants aroused opposition. Not only religious differences, but also the fact that many were poor, unskilled, and, given the limited expansion of industry at that time, unemployed, led to the crystallization of opposition into a nativist movement advocating immigration restriction to prevent the entry of more Catholics. To a certain extent, this reflected the still agrarian nature of the country. Other non-British, non-English speaking peoples had arrived from Scandinavia and Germany, but because they tended to be "pulled" by opportunities to become farmers, rather than "pushed" by poverty, their impact was scattered. However, Irish immigrants tended to remain in the coastal towns, especially Boston and New York, and thus were much more visible.

Opposition resurfaced in the 1840s, and this time developed into a political party, the Know-

Nothing Party, which added an anti-Chinese element to the existing anti-Catholic theme. While unsuccessful in achieving legislation to curb immigration, it did lead to some anti-immigrant legislation in some states, aimed especially at easily identifiable racial groups such as the Chinese. For example, in California, there was much hostility to the 50,000 Chinese there, mainly because they worked for lower pay, and licensing requirements were imposed only on *foreign* miners and fishermen. (Between 1850 and 1870, half the state's income came from such anti-Chinese impositions.) The Know-Nothing Party became weaker after 1855, and first the Civil War and then the postwar boom turned attention away from the immigration issue.

But increases in immigration in the 1870s, plus the depression after 1873, led to renewed anti-immigrant attitudes. In particular, and this would be a charge levied against newcomers in the 20th century too, the depression was blamed on foreigners taking jobs away from white Americans. As in the 20th century, this did not stand up to scrutiny: Most of the newcomers worked in menial jobs that native Americans did not want. However, pressure against the Chinese was successful. In 1882 Congress passed the Chinese Exclusion Act, which cut off further immigration from China, led to the deportation of those not entitled to reside in the United States, and prevented those remaining from applying for citizenship. (This anti-Asian sentiment was extended to the Japanese in 1907.)

Social and religious bias against Jews and Catholics was also a recurring feature, especially if later generations attempted to break the white Anglo-Saxon-Protestant hold on positions of power and authority. Most of the first generations of immigrants worked in factories or urban sweatshops, and it was almost impossible for them to do anything else. However, municipal politics, which was not very appealing to those with economic power, was one alternative route to power. Many city political organizations then became dominated by Irish Catholics, and the "boss" system was widely used. This was a version of an old patronage system adapted to the special needs of immigrants who were not otherwise politically represented, and who, as uneducated non-English speakers, found it difficult to adjust from a simple village environment to the complexities of 19th century urban life.

The immigrants in general, exploited by employers and others as they were, and often resented by an "older" population, made many contributions. These included building the economic strength of the United States, its greater heterogeneity, and its cultural variety. However, pressures for standardization and assimilation remained strong.

To a large extent, anti-immigrant (read "alien") feeling influenced the 1917 Immigration Act, which codified existing immigration law. Its intent was to limit immigration as much as possible to those western and northern European peoples believed to be most adaptable to existing "American" culture. It did this with a quota system restricting the numbers of immigrants from each country. There was some easing of restrictions in the 1952 Act and its 1965 Amendments, but the basic principle of restricting the entry of those with few skills remained. The quota system protected the domestic labor force by permitting immigration only when immigrants had skills needed by employers that were not available in sufficient quantities domestically. However, immigration has continued to be a reality of American life, and even in the 20th century, with substantial numbers of immigrants from new Asian and Latin American areas, anti-immigrant attitudes still echo those of the 19th century.

Business Ethics

Accompanying the spread of industrialization was acceptance and widespread admiration of the businessman. This was new in American culture, as previously a strong anti-urban, anti-industrial strand existed, and economic and political power, to a very large extent, rested on land. But after the Civil War, as economic growth became almost synonymous with industrial growth, the most admired people were industrialists and businessmen. This cult of admiration of businessmen and their practices was not shared by European countries.

Social Darwinism

To some extent, this partly reflected the recognition of the importance of manufacturing in the nation's continued prosperity, but it also reflected the emergence of a new philosophy, Social Darwinism. It effectively justified the behavior of the new elite, even though abuse and corruption was involved in many cases. This abuse and corruption was not limited to the private sector. Government officials at all levels were also involved in behavior that was definitely not ethical, and even the courts could be bought.

Social Darwinism

Philosophy adapting Darwin's theory of biological evolution to explain social and economic progress

---

The new values were based on recasting Charles Darwin's ideas of evolution in a sociological context. Darwin had shown that species evolve through the hereditary transmission of those traits that best adapted them to the surrounding environment. As reinterpreted by the philosopher Herbert Spencer, an idea of progress toward the emergence of a more "perfect" being was added. As further applied to economic life, the wealthy were obviously the most perfect yet attained: They had gained wealth because they were the economically best adapted. This gave businessmen a respectability and justified exploitation, because whatever they did was required for the working out of inherent social evolution. It also simultaneously explained and excused the tendency toward monopolization practices, large-

scale enterprises, and inequality of wealth. On one aspect, however, Social Darwinists were conveniently silent. This was the issue of *inherited* wealth, in which the beneficiaries were wealthy simply because of their birth and not because of anything they had done.

In order for a philosophy such as this to have been accepted to the extent that it was, there had to be both agents willing to participate in the expansion of the economy and opportunities for them to do so. The timing can be explained by the Civil War, which provided the possibility of gaining wealth that could later be used in industry. The war opened up opportunities because it involved enormous expenditures, and contractors supplying equipment and collectors of federal revenues enriched themselves as a result. In addition, the war broke with the continuity of the past. On the one hand, the fact that some groups lost wealth, power, and prestige opened up the social hierarchy to others, but without at the same time providing any social constraint on what could or could not be done. And on the other hand, the expansion of economic activity to the West provided new areas for potential profit making, and again there was no accompanying growth in social or civic responsibility. Possibly the fact that the country had such a short past, unlike the European countries, accounted for the lack of social constraints on business ethics.

Margin Loan

A loan used as a partial downpayment to purchase stocks

Robber Barons

While most of the country's businessmen were solid, respectable people, the few really flamboyant ones, whose behavior and ostentation caught the public's attention, were those who left their mark on this period. Because of their practices, they were called "robber barons," and they thrived at a time when there was no established

Robber Baron

Name given to some United States industrialists who used exploitative or ruthless means to gain wealth

code of business ethics, very few legal or statutory limitations on what they could do, and immense public gullibility, which enabled the most notorious to take advantage of people's desire to make money the easy way. While there was inefficiency and waste involved, the robber barons simply responded to the situation and the time in which they lived. (Inevitably, over time, as the worst abuses in both business and government were uncovered, loopholes were closed.)

The explanation of this phenomenon has been based on the combination of the relative newness of the country plus the realization of its enormous wealth, which was only just beginning to be tapped. There was a willingness to try to share in this wealth, but often without a corresponding recognition of exactly what was involved or of the responsibility that went with wealth.

For example, as new companies were formed or old ones expanded, share speculation and other practices equalled if they did not surpass the old European bubbles in the promoters' audacity. There was much stock watering, in which proceeds of the "excess" shares sold went to only a few people and not to productive uses within the company. One of the most notorious of these schemes involved the battle between Jay Gould and Cornelius Vanderbilt for control of the Erie Railway. In the 1860s, Vanderbilt attempted to wrest control of the Erie away from Gould and his associates Daniel Drew and Jim Fisk. Gould then issued $8 million in watered stock to reduce Vanderbilt's control, so Vanderbilt got a judge to stop the issue. However, Gould retaliated by bribing another judge to permit it, and capped it

Stock Watering

An excessive number of new company shares are sold, with the revenues going to the promoters

off by bribing the New York State legislature to legalize the stock issue. At this point, Vanderbilt withdrew and turned his attention to the New York Central Railway, where he issued shares worth $23 million, with most of the proceeds enriching him and his associates.

Stock Manipulation

Gould was later involved in another scheme in 1868 that led to a collapse of the New York money market which ruined many. For this scheme, he issued more watered stock in order to push the price down so that he and his associates could then buy back shares at the lower price, pocketing the difference between the revenues received from the new issue and the repurchase expense. But to do this without raising the share price again (which would defeat the purpose) required producing a money panic. This was done by taking advantage of the role played by national banks in New York as central bankers (there was no official central bank in the United States until 1913).

These banks were required to hold 25 percent of their liabilities (customers' deposits) in reserve as nonearning assets, and if this proportion was not maintained, they had to call in loans (the other major asset held), many of which were margin loans made to stock exchange dealers and stock holders, in the ratio of $3 for every $1 in cash lost through withdrawal. These banks also had to report their financial position in early October when their books had to be in order.

What the Gould group did was to deposit $14 million in national banks and then withdraw it, in cash, in early October. This forced the banks to call in loans to keep their books balanced, and in order to repay, many stockholders sold their shareholdings. This increased amount of selling pushed down share prices—including the price of Erie stock—which permitted the Gould group to purchase it at bargain basement prices.

Gould used other tactics for forcing stock prices to move up or down, thus helping him manipulate the stock market in order to make money. He bought the New York *World* newspaper in 1879 and had a controlling interest in Western Union (the telegraph company) after 1881. With this potential influence on public opinion, he used these two media vehicles to question the profitability of companies he was interested in. When this manipulation successfully lowered stock prices, he bought shares. Then the process was reversed, and glowing reports on the same companies appeared. This stimulated interest in their shares and stock prices rose, at which point Gould could sell out at a profit.

This was sheer paper manipulation, doing little to help the real growth of underlying productive capacity. Gould was not the only manipulator; there were many schemes based on the desire to make money. The desire to increase profits was also a motive behind the trend to combinations of companies: If competition could be eliminated, the remaining company would have more market power and therefore could raise prices and thus profits. But not all such schemes succeeded—many companies did collapse during depressions.

Another scandal involved the Union Pacific transcontinental rail line. In this one, the controlling shareholders of the Union Pacific formed the Credit Mobilier in 1867. This new company was given the contract for constructing the line under terms that effectively left the owners with the revenues gained from selling UP's stocks and bonds. That is, the cost of construction would be exactly equal to the UP's resources, while government subsidies to the line would be siphoned off to the Credit Mobilier's owners. In order to avoid Congressional interference with this scheme, many representatives and senators were sold Credit Mobilier shares at extremely favorable prices. Although there was a subsequent investigation in 1872, few of those involved admitted any wrongdoing.

Some questionable practices hurt those least able to afford it. For example, in 1872 three New York savings banks failed, and as there was no system of deposit insurance, this meant that depositors lost their savings. Between 1870 and 1878, twenty-eight life insurance companies failed in New York, with similar consequences.

At the same time that industry was expanding, business was getting bigger, and a few "captains of industry" were achieving fame and fortune, a new type of businessman emerged: the corporate manager. This development was an inevitable outgrowth of the trend in business organization. As the scale of operations grew, no single individual, no matter how talented and capable, could possibly control it. Thus there was a need for an organization to manage the different aspects of a business.

This was also a period of maturity for industry. If the flamboyance of the robber baron had been an ingredient in achieving widespread industrialization through new company formation, its continuation required different skills for survival. These were the skills of the corporate executive, who presumably was better able to steer an enterprise in an environment where business had become established. The executive was rarely a majority shareholder or owner of a company, but increasingly, corporate management was the route to positions of power and prestige as it became more difficult for an individual to become established in an environment where large size was prevalent.

Tariff Policy

In the period after the Civil War, the expansion of the domestic market was a major factor stimulating industrialization, while foreign trade was much less important, especially when compared with the role of foreign trade in Britain's industrialization. Up to 1914, foreign trade accounted for only about 10 percent of United States Gross National Product, a much lower percentage than in the European countries, where it could account for up to half. However, United States foreign trade did increase its share of a rising world total to about 10 percent by the 1880s. While agricultural exports, especially cotton and foodstuffs, continued to be important, industrial exports were increasing their share.

Although government policy in this period was nominally laissez faire, with the exception of land grants and subsidies to the rail companies, tariff policy was not. Neither major party was unilaterally pro-free trade: It has been said that the Democrats favored high tariffs, while the Republicans favored very high tariffs. As the Republican party dominated government for most of the period to the end of the century, commercial policy was marked by a high degree of protection of American industrialists against foreign competition, reflecting the party's business orientation.

Congress was simply following a long established pattern of protectionism, although more widely than before. The very first tariff, in 1789, was the outgrowth of a political controversy. On one side was Secretary of the Treasury Alexander Hamilton, who as one of the few pro-industrial interests, wanted access to British capital. On the other side were those who wanted discriminatory tariffs on British goods as punishment for the recent hostilities. The tariff ended up reflecting Hamilton's views, and was only mildly protectionist, with no discrimination against or favors granted to specific countries. There were duties on imports (which were raised in 1792), but the main thrust was to encourage American shipping by imposing only a moderate duty on cargoes brought in American ships, but a very heavy one on cargoes carried in foreign ships.

Then trade was disrupted by the Napoleonic Wars, and relations with Britain and France deteriorated due to British seizure of about 900 American ships sailing for France and the capture of about 750 ships by French privateers. This was followed by the War of 1812 with Britain, which was not resolved until 1815. At the end of the war, the resumption of trade resulted in a dramatic increase in the volume of imports, which

jumped from $13 million in 1814 to $147 million in 1815, most coming from Britain. Trade resumption also produced many bankruptcies of new American manufacturers due to renewed competition, encouraging the introduction of the first truly protective tariff in 1816. Because infant industries in cotton and wool textile production were to be saved from competition, this Act imposed 25 percent duties on competing imports, especially of the lower-quality imports, and 20 percent duties on iron and some other imports. The trend in tariff rates was upward until 1828. In 1824 woollen textiles, iron, glass, and lead received protection, while in 1828 duties were raised on raw wool, naval stores, molasses, and iron; the duty on imported wools was the highest at 45 percent.

Infant Industry
A newly established industry

However, opinion was divided over tariffs. Manufacturers liked them, even when, as in the case of cotton textiles, they were long past the infant industry stage and faced little competition for the products they produced. Merchants and cotton planters objected because of the possibility that trade would decline. They feared the effect of the tariff on the prices of the manufactured goods they bought (whether imported or domestic) and also feared retaliation by the countries to whom they sold cotton.

Increased sectional conflict led to the beginning of a period of more moderate tariffs starting in 1832, which removed duties entirely from some items (but not iron) and reduced others to a maximum of 20 percent over the next ten years. This was due less to the example being set in Britain and more to political realities at home. In particular, there was a need to reassert federal authority over the protesting south by making some concessions to southern planters. However, it is likely that the protection given to iron producers reinforced technological backwardness in the American iron industry. This domestic reality, reinforced by the free trade movement in Britain, surfaced again in the 1840s, when Southern Democrats favored still lower tariffs, but were temporarily thwarted in 1842, only to succeed in 1846. In that year, tariff reductions represented a triumph for agrarian interests. Tariff policy was still moderately protectionist but, especially when reinforced by further reductions in 1857, marked a brief commitment to free trade that would remain until reversed during the Civil War.

Tariffs, Politics and Protectionism

The problem with tariff policy in the United States was that it became a political issue because tariffs were both protectionist measures and revenue raisers. They were important in providing revenues for the federal government between 1790 and 1860, when new sources of revenues were used. (The income tax as a source of federal revenues in peacetime was not introduced on a permanent basis until 1913.) A duty that provided sufficient revenues for the government often conflicted with protectionist interest: The former would still permit imports, the latter would prefer them to be eliminated. Oddly enough, the federal government actually had a budget surplus in the 1850s and again from 1875 to 1879, which reduced the effectiveness of an appeal for tariff increases to provide it with revenues.

During the Civil War, new and higher tariffs were introduced and subsequently raised in following years, making a commitment to protection even as the economy continued to grow and strengthen. In 1862 and 1864, tariffs on many manufactured goods were raised, with manufacturers' approval. They approved because many taxes imposed in the special circumstances of the Civil War had raised their costs and they wanted tariffs on competing imports in order to reduce the competitive advantage of foreign-made goods. However, some of the other new duties

had a wider impact. Duties were imposed on both tea and coffee and raised on sugar, which increased the cost of living for just about every household.

After the Civil War, and in spite of the declining need for higher tariffs to raise revenues, protectionist sentiment hardened, although some minor concessions were made to the now not very influential free traders. From the 1880s on, tariffs were increasingly protectionist, and given the size of the internal market that was free from foreign competition, industrialists especially gained from this policy. The 1883 Tariff Act increased the number of duty-free goods (which included only those goods that were not produced in the United States anyway) but raised rates on all the others. This had a particularly protective impact on textiles, iron, and steel products. This trend was continued with the 1890 McKinley Tariff, which raised rates on wool, textiles, cutlery, and tin plate, leaving most of the other duties at their existing high levels. A sop was thrown to agricultural interests: Sugar now entered the country duty-free, which helped American sugar growers owning plantations in Cuba.[3] To offset the impact of the entry of this cheaper sugar, and as a form of appeasement, sugar growers in Louisiana were paid a production bounty of two cents a pound.

A slight reduction in some tariffs and removal of duties on wood, wool, and copper were features of the 1894 Tariff Act, but policy in general was still heavily protectionist and the average tariff was now about 40 percent. Even after further reductions in 1913 and removal of steel, coal, and footwear duties, protectionism remained; by then, the average rate of duty was 29 percent.

Throughout most of the 19th century and into the 1920s the United States followed a heavily protectionist path. The pattern of tariff revisions reflected the pressure of special interests. Industrialists were the most influential special interest group after the Civil War, and as they favored protection, tariffs were raised in this period. Even when protection from foreign competition was not needed, and the tariff only raised profits for the affected producers, special interest groups still succeeded in getting their way. This was particularly noticeable after the First World War. Although the United States was the world's leading steel producer by this time, had gained a strong position in the new chemicals industry, and was one of the lowest-cost agricultural producers, all these industries were protected with new high tariffs in 1922.

Economic Fluctuations

The United States economy grew absolutely after the Civil War and became more industrialized, but growth was not steady, being marked by a pattern of prosperity followed by depression. Fluctuations in economic activity are not a modern phenomenon, and depressed conditions have often occurred, usually because of a poor harvest or disruption of trade due to war. But with the spread of industrial capitalism, such fluctuations changed in character and an element of regularity was added. With the internationalization of industrial activity through trade, business cycle fluctuations spread from country to country. While one country can to a certain degree isolate itself from others with a completely prohibitive tariff policy, for example, this rarely occurred after the mid 19th century. A country can even try to modify these fluctuations, but the international linkages existing between economies implies that all will be affected to a greater or lesser extent.

Why Business Cycles Occur

At its simplest, a business cycle occurs because what is produced is rarely exactly equal to what is bought. An imbalance between production (and productive capacity) and sales will then start off a process of adjustment in either direction in an attempt to restore an approximate balance. No fluctuation occurs if producers produce exactly what will be bought. The economy *could* grow steadily over time if the expansion of productive capacity involved in an industrialization process

or an expansion of agriculture occurs at the same speed as the growth of markets.

This is a chance occurrence, especially given that 19th century industrialization was largely unplanned; each potential producer's decisions being made without considering the two-way linkage existing between the producer and the rest of the economy. Small imbalances are frequent and are constantly in the process of being worked out, either through price adjustments, expansion of plant capacity, or bankruptcy and collapse, for example. In the presence of competition, even many of these small upsets affecting individual producers will rarely have a major effect on the economy as a whole.

But where there are more than a few problem areas the result is significant on the national level, and then the entire economy can be thrown into a depression. How long it takes for recovery depends on the nature of the causes. In a modern capitalist industrial economy, the chances for fluctuation and the element of regularity in business cycles are much stronger. Thus, the search for profits to be used for capital accumulation and expansion of operations requires that new investment must constantly take place, at an expanding rate, because it is the return on invested funds that is counted as profit. But the larger the total of investment, the harder it becomes to achieve even a stable rate of return, let alone an increasing one. This occurs because markets and sales must expand sufficiently fast to absorb the increased output, which is unlikely.

While the United States on the whole saw a much greater expansion of markets throughout the 19th century—an increasing population bought more of everything, including the new products that were becoming a feature of modern life—it was not immune to fluctuations. Railroad overbuilding coupled with huge amounts of speculation led to periodic crises. Balance was then restored by the literal wiping out of paper gains, but this does not encourage new productive activity. The problem of finding sufficient new profitable opportunities for expansion was influential in stimulating the imperialist period of the late 19th century, the extension of investment and production activities to other countries, which will be taken up later.

While business cycles in modern economic analysis are usually looked at in terms of real factors, such as declines/rises in output and profit, extent of unemployment, number of bankruptcies or net new company formations, monetary factors also reinforce any fluctuation. This was particularly true in the United States in the 19th century, which suffered from a relatively chaotic banking system. When paired with the appeal of speculation in land as well as securities, this implied that a collapse in the financial area could have real economic consequences.

The Great Depression of the 1870s

One such panic occurred in 1873 and, combined with various international factors, led to a full-scale business depression. The Great Depression of the 1870s was the first of the modern age to be shared by the industrial countries. There were two major reasons why it was international, and they go part way to explaining its length and severity. One was that since 1850, every then-industrial country had been involved in some military action. The United States fought its own Civil War, France had invaded Mexico and had also fought Prussia, which in turn had previously fought Austria, and Britain had attacked Abyssinia.

Wars have several effects on economic activity in an *industrial* country. New military demand exists, so businesses producing to meet this demand flourish. There is also pressure on prices, as productive capacity strains to meet demand for both civilian and military goods, and this encourages inflation. But when the war is over, military demand disappears, and those companies unable to adjust to only civilian needs may also disappear. There is, consequently, downward pressure on prices, unemployment rises as companies collapse

and the army is demobilized, and incomes in general fall.

The second reason concerns transportation. There had been excessive construction of railways in Central Europe and Russia, excessive in the sense that traffic did not materialize as quickly and as voluminously as expected, and therefore operating revenues were low. It affected foreign investors who saw little or no return of their money. The impact of the construction itself had helped exporting companies, mainly in Britain and Germany whose steel products were used, and this added another inflationary element. The same reasoning applies to the construction of the Suez Canal.

Thus the early 1870s were generally inflationary years. This was definitely true in the United States, where there had also been domestic railway overbuilding, plus a large amount of speculation in railway company shares. Inflation is encouraging to businesses, especially new ones taking on heavy debt loads in order to start production. (With the increase in the size of plant needed, the debt load becomes larger.) Easy access to credit had made it possible to borrow for this purpose. So while 431,000 business firms of all sizes existed in 1870, the number had grown by more than one third to reach 610,000 in the following year.

This inflation was a credit inflation. Between 1868 and 1873, deposits in national banks rose by $43 million, but bank loans rose by $283 million, in large part due to demand by railway companies (30,000 miles were built between 1867 and 1873) and other new companies for financing, plus demand for loans for stock purchases that were fuelled by speculation. In addition, in the same period, fires in Portland, Boston, and Chicago had stimulated a demand for credit for rebuilding purposes.

No problem exists if the expansion in productive capacity is well-founded, but this is not always the case. Leaving aside the issue of speculation (which never has productive results), many of the new rail lines did not generate sufficient immediate revenues to start paying off debt. In 1872, 260 railway companies out of a total of 364 were not profitable enough to pay dividends to shareholders, and in 1873, 89 simply defaulted and did not repay bondholders the funds that had been loaned. One major problem that affected the railways in particular and many other large companies was the existence of very large initial fixed costs. These paid for the plant and equipment that had to be in place before production could begin, thus borrowing to finance it well in advance of the receipt of operating revenues could backfire if estimates of the size of the market later proved to be overestimates.

That credit had been extended so far and so fast owes much to the lack of effective regulation over banking and the absence of a central bank to provide liquidity when necessary. The New York national banks, which had been acting as reserve banks for out-of-state banks—in effect, performing the function of a central bank—proved not to have the resources to continue once the crises hit and other banks began to withdraw funds they held in New York.

There were additional factors. The expansion of agriculture further west had left much eastern agriculture noncompetitive, and land values were falling in these stagnating areas. While American enterprise continued to be attractive to foreign investors, foreign debt was growing large, reaching $1.5 billion by the end of the 1860s and involving interest payments of $80 million. To this was added an adverse trade balance, which resulted in an outflow of gold.

With the background of overenthusiasm in new companies, overextension of credit, and overebullience in the stock market, the beginning of 1873 saw further adverse events. New York had experienced scandals in its insurance and

Fixed Costs

Costs of production that do not change as output changes (e.g. rent, interest on borrowed funds)

banking industries, while the Credit Mobilier scandal was also unfolding. The money market could not cope with demands made on it—indebtedness was far out of proportion to the available cash held by the banks.

The crash came in September as securities firms failed, initiating an attempt by shareholders to sell their stocks before the price fell; their very actions resulted in falling stock prices. This then led to a collapse of confidence, and the collapse of financial houses and companies snowballed when they were unable to get the cash needed to repay debts owed to creditors. The banks did not have sufficient cash in reserve to meet all demands. In 1873, over 5,000 companies failed, compared with only 2,900 in 1871 and 4,000 in 1872. This number included 89 defaulting rail companies. Had there been an immediate expansion of liquidity, it is likely that this would have remained a financial panic, but it became a full-scale depression instead.

Initially, work stopped in railway construction, throwing half a million people out of work. This then filtered through to those iron and steel and engineering companies associated with rail transportation, and unemployment rose. Prices and wages fell, and the number of business failures continued to rise, reaching a peak of well over 10,000 in 1878. Recovery did not start in any meaningful way until 1896. Germany also suffered a panic in 1873, and the combined effect of these crashes on international trade and payments spread depressed conditions first to France and Belgium, and then to Britain.

Similarly in 1893, another panic followed a decade of more railway building accompanied by more speculation, several bankruptcies of large companies, and an outflow of gold. This had started in 1890 when a financial crisis in Britain led to the demand for repayment of American loans, and was continued in 1893 when a poor harvest and drop in agricultural exports led to the United States running an adverse trade balance. Over 600 banks failed this time, and by the end of 1894 about 195 railway companies had failed, with the number of commercial failures in 1893 alone being 15,000. Heavy industry as before was most affected, but the farm sector also suffered, and unemployment was widespread.

One important reaction to these periods of depression was the stimulus it gave to various forms of business combination. At a time when prices were falling, sales were down and competition for survival increasingly took the form of cutthroat price competition, such combinations were seen as providing a better chance of survival. By eliminating price warfare, profits could be protected, and it was felt that the market power of a monopolizing combination could achieve more control to ensure a more stable environment.

Summary

By 1900, the United States was fully industrialized. After the schism of the Civil War, the basic heavy industries of iron and steel were built up, and there were many new emerging growth industries: autos, chemicals, electrical manufacturing. Much growth was due to the progress made in the first half century, which saw the necessary infrastructure, especially railways, being put into place.

Improved transportation was vital not only to improve the business climate for new manufacturing but also to open up the West to agricultural and extractive activities. While land speculation remained ever present, diverting funds from use in industry, it did not prevent the growth of an important agricultural economy. In fact, of all the countries that were industrialized by 1900, the United States was unique in the size of its farm sector and the importance, though relatively declining, of its share in exports. This importance also gave a particular flavor to political life, as farmers frequently felt their interests were not being attended to.

The ability to borrow technology and capital from abroad also helped rapid industrialization.

But one very special feature, large numbers of immigrants, solved the old problem of labor scarcity. The depth and extent of United States industrial growth also owes much to the increased mechanization that, by simplifying industrial tasks, permitted the use of industrially unskilled immigrants without a prolonged period of training.

As in Germany, a protective tariff structure throughout most of the century helped manufacturers, although it was bitterly opposed by landowners, most farmers, merchants, and bankers. This was the reverse of the British experience, where manufacturers were solidly behind free trade. In the United States, ideas of laissez faire remained more influential on the domestic, not the international, front, and not until fairly late in the 19th century would there be any attempt to limit the freedom of business.

This relates to the unique position of power and authority businessmen had achieved for themselves after the Civil War. Even when they made wrong decisions, which affected millions adversely, these were seen as only errors and did not result in a questioning of their right to lead the country. But the flamboyance of the late 19th century robber barons would be followed by the more sober conservatism of the corporate manager. That a corporate bureaucracy was beginning to emerge is a symbol both of industrial maturity and of the increasingly large scale of business enterprises, which could no longer be controlled by one individual.

Many of the developments seen at this time in the United States also occurred in other countries. This shows both the maturing of capitalism and its increasing internationalization.

Notes

1. There is another example of American adaptation to labor scarcity in housing construction. This is the use of the balloon frame construction in residential housing, which replaced the old

brick-by-brick method because it utilized lower-skilled labor and speeded up construction. It also required the use of nails, thus it was another development that could not have happened before the industrial revolution.

2. In the 1860s, male workers received on average $2 a day for an average of 10 hours work. Women workers always got less and in some places were the most exploited of all groups. For example, in the 1870s in New York, 15,000 women received $5.50 a week for working 13½-hour days. The average male wage at that time was considered barely sufficient to support a family, especially in industrial cities where living costs were high.

3. Cuba was the scene of clashes between Spain and the United States leading to the Spanish-American War. At the end of this war, Cuba ceased to be a colony of Spain and instead became a protectorate of the United States in 1901.

Key Concepts

Business cycle
Discounting
Fixed costs (of production)
Greenback
Industrial concentration
Infant industry tariff
Legal tender
Mass production

Monoculture
Monopolization
National bank
Paper money
Robber Baron
Sharecropping
Social Darwinism
Variable costs (of production)

Questions for Discussion and Essay Writing

1. How is it possible to determine if one country is industrialized and another is not?

2. To what extent were economic motives important causes of the Civil War?

3. What economic problems did the institution of slavery create for the southern economy?

4. To what extent do wars help or hinder economic development?

5. Discuss the problems faced by farmers in the western states after the Civil War. How did they deal with them?

6. To what extent did the United States have an advantage in introducing mass production techniques that was not shared by the other countries we have investigated?

7. Modern industry is characterized by interdependencies. How does this affect development?

8. Why was there a trend to concentration in industry in the late 19th century?

9. "Industrialization in the United States would not have been possible without an input from foreigners." Discuss.

10. Discuss the impact of immigration into the United States

11. Can you explain the appeal of Social Darwinism?

12. Evaluate the impact of tariff policy on U. S. development in the 19th Century.

For Further Reading

Brown, Dee. *Bury My Heart at Wounded Knee: An Indian History of the American West*. New York: Harper & Row, 1971.

Broude, Henry. *The Role of the State in American Economic Development, 1820-1890,* in Hugh Aitken, ed. *The State and Economic Growth*, New York: Social Science Research Council, 1959: 4-22.

Bruchey, Stuart. *Enterprise: The Dynamic Economy of a Free People*. Cambridge, Mass: Harvard University Press, 1990.

Clark, Victor S. *History of Manufactures in the United States*. N.Y.: McGraw Hill, 1929.

Cochran, Thomas C. and William Miller. *The Age of Enterprise: A Social History of Industrial America*. rev. ed. New York: Harper & Row, 1961 (1942).

Conrad, Alfred and John Meyer. "The Economics of Slavery in the Ante-Bellum South." *Journal of Political Economy* (April 1958): 95-122.

DuBois, W.E.B. *Black Reconstruction in America, 1860-1880*. Millwood, N.Y: Kraus-Thomson Organization, 1976.

Engerman, Stanley L. "Some Economic and Demographic Comparisons of Slavery in the United States and the British West Indies." *Economic History Review*, XXIX:2 (1975): 258-275.

Fogel, Robert W. *Without Consent or Contract: The Rise and Fall of American Slavery*. New York: Norton, 1989.

_____ and Stanley L. Engerman. *Time on the Cross: The Economics of American Negro Slavery*. Boston: Little, Brown, 1974.

Folbre, Nancy and Barnet Wagman. "Counting Housework: New Estimates of Real Product in the United States, 1800-1860." *Journal of Economic History*, 53:2 (June 1993): 275-288.

Gates, Paul. *The Farmer's Age: Agriculture 1815-1860*. New York: Holt, Rinehart & Winston, 1960.

Genovese, Eugene. *The Political Economy of Slavery*. New York: Pantheon, 1965.

Hill, Peter Jensen. *The Economic Impact of Immigration into the United States*. N.Y.: Arno Press, 1975.

Hounshell, David. *From the American System to Mass Production: The Development of Manufacturing Technology in the United States*, Baltimore: Johns Hopkins Press, 1984.

Josephson, Matthew. *The Robber Barons: The Great American Capitalists, 1861-1901*. N.Y.: Harcourt Brace and World, 1962.

Limerick, Patricia Nelson. *The Legacy of Conquest: The Unbroken Past of the American West*. N.Y.: Norton, 1987.

Mayr, Otto and Robert C. Post. *Yankee Enterprise: The Rise of the American System of Manufactures,* Washington, D.C.: Smithsonian Institution Press, 1982.

Nevins, Alan. *The Emergence of Modern America, 1865-1978*. N.Y.: Quadrangle Books, 1971 (1927, 1955).

Ransom, Roger L. and Richard Sutch. *One Kind of Freedom: The Economic Consequences of Emancipation*. Cambridge: Cambridge University Press, 1977.

Rosenberg, Nathan ed. *The American System of Manufactures*. Edinburgh: Edinburgh University Press, 1965.

Thomson, Ross. "Technological Change as New Product Development." *Social Concepts* (1986).

Turner, Frederick J. *The Frontier in American History*. Huntington, N.Y: R.E. Krieger, 1975 (1920).

Wright, Gavin. *Old South, New South: Revolutions in the Southern Economy Since the Civil War*. New York: Basic Books, 1986.

And see also references at the end of Chapter 14.

Chapter 16

Economic Development of Japan After 1868

Introduction

JAPAN'S DEVELOPMENT HAS OFTEN BEEN RE-GARDED as the economic success story of the 20th century. Today, this resource-poor small country, which only just over a century ago began to emerge from a feudal-like past, is one of the world's industrial powerhouses. In absolute size, Japan's economy is the third largest after the United States and the former Soviet Union. With a commanding position in international trade, especially in cars, electronics, and shipbuilding, Japan became the first Asian nation to break into what had previously been an exclusive American-European club of mature industrial nations.

As a late starter, Japan could borrow from the experience of other countries and compress its development into a short period of time. Although there are many differences in Japan's development compared with the experience of other countries, there are also similarities. It is impossible to focus on any one ingredient and identify it as the sole cause of Japan's economic miracle. What we can say is that any economic development experience is the outcome of many contributing factors, both economic and noneconomic, many of which have their origins in the past.

Some of the differences that distinguish Japan are the result of a unique combination of influ-ences. One is that Japan is resource-deficient, especially for an industrialization process based on coal, iron ore, and oil. Another was its fear of becoming colonized or at least dependent on a Western country. Together, these two encour-aged a process of industrialization that was paired with external aggression and the acquisition of colonies (or areas of influence) to compensate for the lack of resources and increase self-sufficiency. That this path was taken rather than another is largely due to the control of government at sig-nificant times by a group of military leaders who encouraged industrialization in order to achieve military goals. Their ability to wield power in this way can perhaps be explained by Japan's rapid change from a predominantly feudal society to a centralized, modernizing one, a change largely the result of top-down government initiative. There was no period when an urban middle class had influence, as there had been in Britain, and there was no significant opposition to the greater role played by government. Although the indus-trialization process involved severe hardships for various segments of the population at different times, their protests did not reverse it. In fact, many of the dramatic economic changes were not accompanied by upheavals in the social structure, which remained relatively undisrupted by economic change, and even today traditional elements still coexist with modern ones.

Possibly the experience most similar to Japan's was Germany's. Both industrialized late, both were politically authoritarian, both emphasized military goals, both were military aggressors in the 20th century and were devastated as a result (although Japan was not a belligerent in the First World War), and both became economically powerful in the postwar period. However, Germany's industrialization was paralleled by political unification that was not necessary in Japan, and Germany did not acquire or attempt to gain such a significantly large colonial empire as did Japan at a similar stage of development. As we explore Japan's development, many other parallels and differences will become apparent.

Many of the pre-industrial elements of the socio-economic structure look remarkably feudal. Many of the policies adopted by the government in the late 19th century have characteristics reminiscent of mercantilism in the search for self-sufficiency. The ethic of frugality looks Calvinistic (although it resulted from different influences). In spite of these similarities, it is important to remember that the general environment was Asian, Pacific, and Japanese—not Euro-American and influenced by the Judeo-Christian ethic.

Pre-Industrialization: The Tokugawa Era

Japan is made up of a group of islands separated from the Asian region of the former Soviet Union and the Korean peninsula by the Sea of Japan. Its land area is slightly less than the size of California, but much is mountainous, and with 65 percent of the land area forested, good fertile farmland is at a premium. For a long time, Japan lay within the sphere of influence of China, and many Chinese elements were borrowed and adapted to the Japanese environment, including the language, culture, and religion. In the 16th century, when European explorers, traders, and missionaries were active in spreading out into Asia and the New World, Japan attracted the attention of the Portuguese and the Dutch. However, these advances were not welcome, and their ideas and values were seen as threatening to Japanese integrity. So in the 1630s, the country became effectively closed to Europeans.

Feudal-Like System

Isolationism was the achievement of the Tokugawa shoguns, who dominated Japan after 1603, and who played a role similar to that of the most powerful lords in feudal Europe. There was an emperor at Kyoto, but his functions were largely ceremonial, and the real power rested with the shoguns. The structure of Japanese society looked very feudal. There were about two hundred territorial lords (*daimyo*) who owed nominal allegiance to the emperor and who controlled their fiefdoms. The dominant military family was the Tokugawa, who ruled Tokyo (then called Edo) and owned about one quarter of the agricultural land.

Daimyo
powerful nobles who effectively ruled Japan; similar to Europe's feudal nobles

---

Below them were about two million samurai, the warrior class who had the status of feudal retainers. Peasants made up approximately 80 percent of the population, and as in Europe, the taxes they paid supported the *daimyo* and the Tokugawa; about 40 percent of the peasants' output was appropriated in this way.

Tokugawa rule did produce peace and unity (unlike the early medieval period in Europe), and there was some growth of cities and the development of handicrafts and trade during the 17th and 18th centuries. Urban artisans lived in these towns, and their primary function was to provide luxury goods such as silks, porcelain, and enamels for the nobles. Some tradesmen-merchants (*chōnin*) also lived there and were intermediaries in internal trade. This internal trade was dominated by the movement of rice from peasants in the countryside to the cities as payment for feudal dues. Both artisans and merchants were an inferior class at the bottom of the social ranking, even though merchants were beginning to increase their wealth and power.

Chonin

Japanese merchants

What really distinguishes Japan from medieval Europe is the persistence of this traditional economy and lifestyle. As shown in earlier chapters, feudalism gradually broke down as the result of various pressures. Among the most influential of these were the growth of trade, markets and commercial activity, and the slow emergence of the nation-state. Political change and the development of nationalism did not exist in Japan, as the strength of the Tokugawas imposed a unity on Japan. If there was any tendency for change to occur as a result of evolving economic forces, it was tightly controlled by a deliberate policy choice. The Tokugawas attempted to retain hold on power by preventing any change from occurring and by isolating Japan from undesirable foreign influences.

To this end, foreign contacts were severely restricted after 1640 and could be made only through the few remaining Chinese and Dutch merchants located in Nagasaki. Although Japan had a long maritime tradition, no ships capable of long ocean voyages were constructed, and the movement of Japanese merchants was effectively limited to internal travel only. This isolationist policy had the effect of keeping Japan ignorant of the changes that were transforming many of the European economies during this time.

Economic Effects of Isolation

However, although the economy was a low-income one, it was by no means a purely subsistence economy. It did produce a surplus, but because it was not a capitalist economy, the surplus was appropriated by and used mainly for the luxury consumption of the nobles. The growth in the wealth of the merchants—whom the shoguns found increasingly difficult to control in the 19th century—is another indication of the potential wealth of the economy.

Many agricultural improvements were made, chiefly connected with irrigating the rice fields (rice was Japan's staple crop). Also, some industry was developing in rural areas following a pattern very similar to the commission or putting out system in which part time industrial work was combined with farming. This was especially important in the silk industry. Silkworms fed on the mulberry trees in the forests, and the silk was reeled off the cocoons by the farmers. As had happened in Britain, this type of industrial experience helped provide a small pool of skills for later industrialization. But unlike Britain, Japan did not show significant innovative and research activity in the period before its Industrial Revolution; again, this was to characterize subsequent development as well.

There were also some infrastructure developments that would have a helpful impact later. Markets were in existence, as was a credit system. There was a good road system (although few wheeled vehicles existed) and a high level of literacy—nearly one half of all male children received some formal education. If measured by social statistics, the economy also provided an above-subsistence standard of living. Life expectancy was fairly high and the birthrate was low, more like that of an economically developed nation than a low-income one. On the eve of the Meiji restoration in the second half of the 19th century, population was about 34 million.

Growing Pressures for Change

Tokugawa attempts to impose a rigid "no-change" pattern on Japan came under increasing pressure after 1750. While they would reach a crisis point in the 1850s when foreign influences forcibly broke open Japan's isolationism, several internal developments began to present challenges that were not adequately dealt with, partly because the Tokugawa shogunate was becoming more corrupt and ineffectual. Failure to manage these developments when they first occurred helped contribute to the upheavals associated with post-1868 modernization.

Isolationism

deliberate policy of limiting or eliminating contacts with other countries

Although total agricultural output remained adequate, imbalances and increasing pressures occurred as a result of population growth and rising demands from the ruling class. Agricultural improvements were inadequate to meet these increasing demands, and productivity remained low. Burdens on the peasants increased as taxes were raised, but tax revenues were still not enough to meet the needs of the rulers, mainly due to inefficiency in handling public finance.

These problems were one ingredient in increasing conflicts between social groups. Peasants suffered the most because they were the most easily exploited. They were also affected by fluctuations in the price of rice caused by natural variations in crop size and by artificial reasons, chief of which was currency debasement resulting from the rulers issuing too much currency as a way around their own financial difficulties. Peasants were easily manipulated by merchants who took advantage of them. The samurai were also becoming increasingly restless and intensified their power struggle with the *daimyo*. But they found this struggle difficult to finance, because as a rentier class, they had no natural source of revenue, so they became increasingly indebted to the merchants. (The material standard of living of the samurai was closer to that of the peasants than of the *daimyo*.) In turn, the slow rise of the merchant

class as merchants grew wealthier helped undermine all the old traditional institutions.

A series of famines and natural disasters—including earthquakes which strike Japan from time to time—further intensified the plight of the peasants and contributed to declining support for the Tokugawa shoguns. One noneconomic factor also helps explain this weakened support and the solution that emerged in the 1860s. Toward the end of the Tokugawa era there was a rediscovery of national traditions as well as a revival of interest in Shintoism, an indigenous religion that gives a special role to the Japanese emperor. In the face of increasing foreign activity in the area—Russia had expansionist interests to Japan's north, Britain was expanding in China, and the United States was also interested in expanding in Asia—it is hardly surprising that there were demands for Japan to mount an effective resistance against those foreign interests.

Commander Perry's 'Black Ships'

Japan's isolationist phase was forcefully changed after 1853–1854, when United States Navy ships under Commander Perry sailed into Tokyo's harbor and threatened to bombard the city unless Japan opened up diplomatic and commercial relations with the United States. Faced with this threat, and recognizing the country's military weakness, the shogunate capitulated and signed treaties first with the United States and with other Western countries later. As had happened with China, these treaties reflected the unequal balance of power. Japan was forced to grant rights of extraterritoriality to foreign traders and could not levy tariffs of more than 5 percent on imports. However, although trade was opened up, Japan did not have much to export except tea and silk, and its small cotton industry was almost destroyed by competition from foreign imports. The immediate result of this opening up of trade was an outflow of specie.

Extraterritoriality

principle in international diplomacy; the host country grants another the right to treat its occupation of a site in the host country as if its own laws, not those of the host country, applied

The situation was humiliating. Once again, the links between a modern industrial economy and military strength had been demonstrated, and Japan's rulers realized that they were incapable of defending their country against advanced Western military might. Socially, there was upheaval, and several antiforeign riots occurred. This crystallized into a movement to restore the Emperor to a position of significant power, with many overtones of nationalism. The ideas of bourgeois democracy or liberalism that were influencing many European movements in the 19th century were not an issue in Japan at this time. After a series of clashes, the western *daimyo* defeated the shogunate. In 1868 the Tokugawa shogun abdicated and Emperor Mutsuhito ascended the throne, to reign until 1912.

Meiji Restoration

The policies adopted under the new Emperor reveal themes that have characterized much Japanese development since then. They were also mercantilist in spirit, combining as they did state building and economy building to achieve self-sufficiency. In Japan's case, the goal of self-sufficiency also involved territorial expansion outside its borders, apparent first in the 1890s and later developing with alarming consequences in the 1930s. To begin with, it was quickly recognized that if Japan were to become a modern power, it had to industrialize in order to build up the military strength necessary for defense. This would require domestic reforms—initially just enough was done to satisfy the foreigners.

What happened in the early years involved the infrastructure development that was necessary for subsequent industrialization and some structural changes that gave Japan a more Western appearance as well as providing a suitable framework for industrialization. The aim of appeasing foreigners plus the ability to borrow from them and adapt to the Japanese context was very clear with some of these changes. The old feudal system was abolished in 1871, and the samurai and lords were pensioned off. The administration of the country was taken over by a centralized bureaucracy modelled on the French system. Modernization of the legal system borrowed ideas from the British, French, and German legal systems. The military establishment was revamped: The Imperial Army was redesigned along Prussian lines, and the Imperial Navy designed after the British. The education system used France as its model for schools and the United States university system was the model for Japan's higher education. A new banking system based on the United States national banking system was introduced, in which banks' holdings of government bonds provided the collateral for their issue of bank notes. Many of these new banks were established by the old aristocracy, whose start-up capital came from the government bonds they received when their feudal rights were commuted. (Later on there were problems with this system, as it contributed to inflation, and in 1881 the banking system was remodelled along European lines, with a central bank, the Bank of Japan, monopolizing the note issue.)

The Meiji government next faced the problem of industrialization by adopting two strategies. The first was to build infrastructure, initially a rail system. As Japan had no heavy industry at this time, this necessitated using foreign capital, real and money, as well as foreign skills and technology. Foreigners were utilized in other areas as well in these initial stages, but always on a temporary basis and under carefully controlled conditions—the inheritance of wishing to preserve Japan from undesirable foreign influences lingered. In the 1880s, private Japanese companies took over the rail lines, but they remained heavily subsidized by the government via a mixture of concessions and guaranteed rates of return. The outcome was not completely satisfactory, so the major rail lines were nationalized and taken into government ownership in 1906.

Meiji Industrialization

A large role for the government also appeared necessary in the second strategy: helping stimulate industrialization. The major problem resulted from the sudden structural change from a feudal economy, because no group of people with the finances, skills, experience, and motivation to undertake a broad-based industrialization effort existed. The merchants had experience with profit making, and some of the former samurai also became industrial administrators, but all the ingredients for a capitalist industrialization effort were simply not present.

As a result, the government built and operated shipyards, armaments factories, metal-producing foundries, machine shops, and model factories for the production of textiles, glass, chemicals, cement, and sugar. Many of these (with the exception of armaments) were sold to private owners in the 1880s once they had become established, although many still received subsidies. Shipyards in particular were heavily encouraged, since the government was concerned to build up a ship-building capability as well as a shipping presence. So both builders and the merchant marine were subsidized, which helped Japan achieve a dominant position in shipbuilding. As the 18th century mercantilists were aware, this area of the economy also had significance for military purposes, an insight not lost on the government.

Subsidy
financial support given to encourage certain types of activity

---

Financing

All these activities required financing, and this also required attention. How were the needed imports of equipment, technology, and skills to be acquired? The burden fell on the agricultural sector, and it was a heavy burden: increase agricultural exports to earn foreign exchange. Tea was the major export, but exports declined by the end of the century. Two traditional textile industries using domestic raw materials were cotton and silk, but the cotton industry could not meet foreign competition, so the burden fell largely on the silk industry, which could compete internationally. Silk yarn in particular provided between one fifth and one third of export revenues in the late 19th century. Exports of raw silk rose from two million pounds in 1868 to ten million pounds in 1893 and to thirty million pounds by 1914. Some silk fabric was also exported, accounting for 10 percent of export revenues. As late as 1930, silk exports were the chief source of foreign exchange.

These agricultural exports were insufficient to provide all the needed revenues. Because Japan did not wish to become dependent on foreigners (after all, the whole point of the industrialization exercise was to achieve economic self-sufficiency), initially there was very little foreign borrowing. This was unusual—most economies at an equivalent state of development are chronically capital short and rely on capital imports. Japan took out only two foreign loans in the early period, one to finance the first railway in 1870 and the second to finance the pension commutation of the lords and samurai. In any event, isolation has two sides. Not only had Japan been isolated from the outside world, but the outside world knew little of Japan; hence, even after 1868 lending to Japan did not appeal to foreign lenders. Little was known of it, except that it was not well supplied with exploitable primary commodities, and there were also questions about its political stability.

This reinforced the burden on the agricultural sector. In 1873, the tax system was revamped.

The peasants still paid the bulk of the taxes, but a new land tax was introduced. It was assessed on the potential productivity of the land itself, rather than on the harvest produced, and was intended to encourage the full cultivation of land so that it would be put to its best use. In the 1870s this tax provided up to 90 percent of the government's revenues, a proportion that was still as high as 60 percent in the 1890s, but fell as development proceeded and new taxes (excise and business taxes in particular) were introduced.

In spite of this, the government resorted to deficit financing in the 1870s and 1880s, which produced currency problems because government borrowing became the basis for new bank note issues. Excessive issue of new bank notes helped fuel a moderate inflation that, with the new taxes, diverted resources away from peasant farmers to the government and private capitalists. There were occasional peasant protests against the burdens of industrialization, but they were always contained.

Creating a Favorable Environment

The Japanese government was not only directly involved in the industrialization effort, it also attempted indirect stimuli. It tried to encourage an import substitution policy, but had only limited success because of the tariff restrictions imposed under the unequal treaty provisions, restrictions that were not lifted until 1898. However, the cotton industry made a comeback, possibly because it did not require imports of Western technology. Using a predominantly female labor force, cotton output rose and in the 1890s enough was produced to meet domestic needs. By 1900, output had risen further and

---

Import Substitution

policy encouraging industrialization by promoting domestic manufacturing of previously imported goods, often to reduce a foreign exchange drain

---

some was exported. Exports were mostly cotton yarn, but some cloth was exported to China and Korea. Heavy industries took longer to develop, but tariff protection was added after 1898, and by 1914 Japan was meeting most of its iron, steel, and machinery needs. Protection against foreign competition had a greater effect in the period after World War I.

Other elements of the environment-creating process included supportive fiscal and monetary policies and exchange rate policies, although results were not too encouraging at first. As part of its desire to become ranked as a world power, Japan adopted the gold standard in 1897. Exports were still predominantly primary products and were growing rapidly, accounting for 14 percent of total expenditures by 1904. But because they faced competitive pricing conditions on the world market, and with the extra burden of various military engagements, Japan faced a balance of payments outflow and reversed its previous reliance on self-finance. Between 1897 and 1914, the balance of payments was in deficit and Japan experienced an inflow of foreign capital. (In fact, in the period 1868-1940 Japan had a surplus on its current account in only 27 years; only in the 1970s did surpluses begin to appear.) In 1914 over 60 percent of Japan's public debt was owed to foreign governments. While this capital inflow was typical for a developing industrializing economy, and although it did not represent debt owed to private individuals, it was seen as a violation of the aims of self-sufficiency.

Farming and Labor

Japan's population was about 34 million in 1870 and it grew fairly slowly until 1925, which was unusual for a country at that stage of economic development. The labor for the early industrialization effort came predominantly from agriculture—until 1920, the availability of surplus labor held down real wage increases in industry and encouraged labor-using technologies in industry.

Solving Problems in Economic History

Were Japanese workers lazy?

The social revolution involved in the transition from farm to factory work during initial industrialization had a dramatic impact on the first few generations of factory workers. An influential argument describes the difficulties encountered by the first English factory workers in dealing with a new sense of time, clock-time, which differed from the natural rhythms of work in an agricultural environment. The struggle between employers and employees over the imposition of this new time discipline was lengthy, and seemingly repeated wherever industrial development was begun. Workers often objected to their inability to control their own pace of work. Employers said that workers were simply lazy.

Factories in Japan in the late 19th and early 20th centuries also saw conflicts between management and workers. But it does not seem likely that workers resisted the new time discipline (as elsewhere) so much as they resented other aspects of industrial life. Thomas C. Smith (in "Peasant Time and Factory Time in Japan." *Past and Present*, v. lll, May 1986, pp.165-197) suggests that the reason is an already well-established appreciation of time by Japanese peasant farmers. Their time sense was not clock-time, but a sense of time as precious and therefore to be used as productively as possible. In addition, peasant culture emphasized the social value placed on the group control of and use of time. Once factory managers learned to appreciate the importance of the social control of time, many of their earlier problems with workers disappeared.

Where did the peasants' attitude to the productive use of time come from? Smith uses a variety of sources, including peasant diaries, farming manuals, and pamphlets and various other tracts mainly from the late Tokugawa

period and early 20th century, to show an extraordinary emphasis on the virtues of minutely accounting for time. Work for long periods of time was an economic necessity, a moral virtue, and an intergenerational family obligation. Interestingly enough, one work diary of a farmer who was also a low-ranking samurai and a village official, shows only 18 rest days out of a 354-day lunar year. (Not considered by Smith as one explanation of this minutely detailed use of time is the nature of Japanese agriculture itself. There is little land suitable for cultivation, so it is farmed intensively with different overlapping crops whose peak labor needs cannot coincide with each other if maximum harvests are to be obtained.) Farms remained small, and any family unable to manage its farm adequately lost its land and therefore brought dishonor on the family. The family was the relevant unit for administrative and legal control, and educational and moral pressure on individuals promoted correct behavior as a social obligation.

This emphasis on the social context of work created problems after the Meiji restoration because the idea of an individual contract between equal parties voluntarily entered into was a totally foreign one. The status of a factory worker was dishonorable because the idea of working for oneself without respect to social obligation was unwelcome. Such an attitude persisted into the early 20th century.

Many of the problems of the early factories were overcome by the gradual introduction of an organizational hierarchy (similar to the village's social control mechanism) and corporate practices compatible with other traditions. However, working hours remained exceptionally long, like those on the farm, even though

(Problem continues on next page)

(Problem continued from previous page

hours in other industrial countries were shortened. Long hours were not objected to by Japanese workers, most likely because there was considerable acceptance of lateness, absenteeism, and general laxness at work. Smith concludes that the later acceptance of factory time occurred because the older traditional time sense became incorporated into the workplace. Hence workers worked—and continued to work—long hours (not necessarily produc-

tively) because time became enmeshed in the social structure, even though at first there were problems with the moral implications of the employer-employee relationship.

So the perceived laziness of the early Japanese factory worker was more likely due to the problems encountered in the new environment. It may also have been a practical response to the requirement to work very long hours—to take time off or ask for shorter hours for one's individual benefit would not be socially acceptable.

However, unlike what happened in Britain, the absolute growth of agricultural output and a relative shift away from agriculture was accomplished with small family farms continuing to predominate. Even as late as 1940, about five and a half million family farms remained. At the turn of the century, most were freehold, but there was an increase in tenant farming in the early years of the 20th century as falling farm prices made it difficult for many small farmers to meet their tax bills. Farms were small—even in 1940, less than 1.5 percent of all farms were larger than twelve acres. Most of them, 57 percent, were between one and five acres, although one third were smaller than one and a fifth acres. Although technological improvements were being made, farming was not capital-intensive, and significant mechanization began to be effective only after the 1960s. The small size of farms and the initially large numbers of farmers provided the labor needed for industry.

More important, it helps explain an aspect of the Japanese economy that is distinctively different from the European experience. Structural change did take place—the shift first from agriculture to manufacturing and then to capital intensive large-scale industry makes that clear. But it took place without the destruction of a small-scale and traditional sector, and with agriculture remaining a fairly important employment source. The paradox is explained by the fact that because farms were small family farms, they were compat-

ible with holding part-time or second jobs elsewhere, either in a primary industry (such as fishing) or in a small enterprise in the traditional manufacturing sector. This has become less important since 1960 because of the continuing demand for labor, but it does illustrate a pattern of Japanese development characteristic of much of the 20th century. It also helps explain the pattern of labor relations that is also associated with Japanese development (see below).

Results of Prewar Industrialization

By 1914, Japan had essentially completed the first stage of its industrialization. Its overall growth rate in the preceding forty years matched that of the European economies and was even faster in manufacturing. The change can be seen very dramatically in the usual measures of industrialization. The share of agriculture in Net National Product fell from over 30 percent in the 1880s to 21 percent by the mid-1930s. Manufacturing's share rose from 18 percent to 36 percent over the same period.[1] The composition of the labor force showed a shift out of primary activities (agriculture, fishing, and mining) and into manufactur-

---

Industrial Policy
deliberate government action to stimulate industrial development

Figure 16.1 Modern Japan still contains some traditional elements, as this scene of a Japanese woman wearing traditional dress in the middle of a modern street shows. (Courtesy of the Japan National Tourist Oraganization)

ing. In 1880, out of a total labor force of close to 20 million, 81 percent worked in the primary sector and only 6.4 percent worked in manufacturing and construction. The equivalent percentages in 1900, when the labor force had risen to 25.3 million, were 69 percent and 13 percent, and in 1920, were 55 percent and 19 percent. Also in 1920, a further 15 percent were employed in commerce and transportation, an employment category that typically grows as the economy becomes more industrialized and diversified. The composition of exports mirrors this shift. Exports were dominated by primary products in the 1870s, but by the 1930s they had fallen to 7 percent, while manufactured exports had risen to 93 percent. Early exports of manufactured goods were mostly textiles or foodstuffs (bean paste, soy sauce, or sake), but in the 1930s, and associated with the industrial maturity achieved in that decade, heavy industrial exports became dominant (discussed later).

Military Successes

As Germany had demonstrated the effectiveness of its industrialization by overpowering France in the 1870 Franco-Prussian War, so too did Japan show that it was capable of success in modern warfare. In 1894–1895, Japan defeated China and annexed the island of Taiwan, which it renamed Formosa. Japan also gained indemnity payments from China that were used to finance imports needed for the continuing industrialization effort and for a further military buildup.

In 1902, Japan and Great Britain signed an Alliance treaty, which indicated to Japan the achievement of equal treatment with the great powers—no longer would the country be looked on as a potential colony because of its exploitability. Achieving the rank of significant power was further emphasized in 1904–1905, when Japan went to war with Russia and won. Russia had occupied Manchuria (the location of potentially valuable natural resources) partly to attempt to secure claims to China, and was threatening Ko-

rea, which Japan felt was within its sphere of influence. As a result of this military success, Japan replaced Russia in Manchuria, acquired more territory including Port Arthur and part of the island of Sakhalin, and gained Russia's acknowledgement of its interest in Korea, which Japan subsequently annexed in 1910. In 1915, Japan also gained a concession from China to mine iron ore in the northern provinces, which, added to the already acquired rights to coal in Fushun, went part way toward meeting Japan's needs for these basic resources.

World War I and the Impetus to Growth

Japan was not actively involved in fighting in the First World War, and in fact gained economically, first by not having to divert resources for a military effort and second by experiencing increases in demand, especially for textiles and shipping. As a reward for allying with the winning side, Japan gained a presence at the Versailles Peace Conference, and was given the former German concessions in Shantung (China).

Table 16-1
Japan: Industrial Structure
(% shares, annual averages)

	Primary (agriculture, fishing, mining)	Secondary (manufacturing, construction)	Services
1880s	32	18	50
1900s	41	21	36
1910s	35	28	35
1920s	26	37	44
1930s	21	36	43

Source: Estimates by Yuzo Yamada, quoted in W.W. Lockwood, *The Economic Development of Japan*, Oxford: Oxford University Press, 1955, p, 135.

In spite of this recognition as a world power, the incentive to militarism and territorial expansion was reinforced during the War. While Japan felt that it could fight a short war and rely on financing and supplies from neutral countries, it did not think it possible in a long war where economic strength counted. The reason for such a conclusion was based on Germany's experience during the war. Germany was a larger country, with resources, manpower, and a mature economy, and it had still been defeated.

United States As Japanese Ideal

Although it may seem strange because they are so different, Japan looked on the United States with admiration. Japan wanted to be self-sufficient and to develop a strong industrial base, which was what the United States had done. Of course, the difference was that the United States had access to all the necessary resources within its borders. Japan did not, which was why the pressure for territorial acquisition grew. Government policy—always playing a more dominant role in Japan—was increasingly influenced by how national defense, militarist needs, and imperialism related to industrialization and economic strength.

The basic natural resources needed for industrialization at this time were coal and iron ore, hence the appeal of Manchuria. Since 1911, Japan had in fact been increasing its role there, taking advantage of China's weakness, which left it unable to control Manchuria. By 1920, it was also clear that oil was another basic resource Japan needed to acquire, once oil-fired engines began to replace coal to power warships. The need to find controllable oil resources added extra pressure to expansionist aims.

Although the protectionist tide was rising in Europe and the United States, the persistence of liberal free trade ideology as expressed by the new League of Nations made it difficult for Westerners to understand Japan's push for self-sufficiency and territorial expansion. If trade made economies interdependent, it was a powerful tool for peace, so why would a resource-poor country not wish to participate in the world economy as a trading partner? Japan was criticized in the West and by China—at this time undergoing domestic upheavals that progressively weakened it—for its expansionary role in Manchuria, but this had little effect on Japan.

Domestic Reform

In the 1920s the militarist aspect became somewhat muted as attention was focused on domestic reform and economy building. A major role in modern industrialization was played by *zaibatsu*, business combines or groups of enterprises. They played a role similar to that of monopoly or vertically integrated companies by reducing risk. In trade they were especially important, as they helped reduce the risks associated with fluctuations in demand, provided information and transportation services, helped to improve experience and skills, and economized on scarce capital. Large enterprises and groupings coexisted with small ones through a system of subcontracting (which is still common). There are advantages for both large "parent" firms and small contractors. The contractor can eliminate the effects of fluctuations in demand by contracting out work only when demand rises, while keeping work in-house when new orders are scarce, hence retaining a core of skilled, loyal workers who are guaranteed lifetime employment at the expense of the subcontractor's employees. It keeps labor costs low and economizes on hiring/firing and training costs. The subcontractor gains by having a guaranteed market for its semi-finished output and is usually also provided with financing, materials, and technical or managerial assistance as well, hence sur-

Zaibatsu

Combinations of enterprises acting together to further their mutual interests

vival is easier than it would be in a purely cut-throat competitive market. This is a system based on mutual trust and loyalty—characteristics valued in the Japanese cultural tradition.

Adaptability: Electricity and Oil

Two examples of Japanese adaptability also appeared at this time, and one further helps explain the persistence of small units in the traditional sector. Both relate to energy. First, because Japan was a late starter, it was easier for its new enterprises to adopt the latest technology—in this case, the use of electricity as energy. This implied that steam power would not be quite so dominant in Japanese industry, and in fact, even as early as 1917, energy from electricity exceeded that obtained from steam power. A second implication of electrical power is that it is easily adaptable to small units. Given the availability of labor in the 1920s ("pushed" out of agriculture and also from large scale enterprises adopting labor saving technology), wages were low. Low wages plus the availability of small electric motors helped the survival of small enterprises, especially those involved in labor-intensive export activities such as silk and metal toys.

The second example concerns oil, although here the result was not so impressive. Search for a controllable source of oil led Japan to Manchuria and Sakhalin, but oil from these sources was insufficient to meet all Japan's needs. Relying on imported oil was not thought to be the answer, because imports could always be cut. Various attempts to develop synthetic oil had been made previously. Germany, for example, had experimented with oil derived from coal. Japan attempted to produce synthetic petroleum from Manchurian oil shale, but this was not very successful, and synthetic oil accounted for only a tiny percentage of Japan's oil needs.

1930s Expansion

In the 1930s, the militarist aspect of policy began to resurface, reflecting the desire for military strength based on the self-sufficiency of the Japanese Empire, which would be expanded in this decade. To a large extent, militarism was fueled by increasing domestic economic and social problems that resulted from the generalized economic problems of the 1930s. The response increased the pressure for overseas expansion and also borrowed from the experiments with central planning that were beginning in the Soviet Union. This was compatible with the approval for government involvement in the economy and was seen by some military leaders as a suitable method for increasing control over the economy as a way of meeting their priorities. The military elite knew that Japan, in spite of its rapid industrial progress, was too weak to fight an extended war and hence would need economic restructuring and a prolonged period of peace in which to make this effective.

Domestic Problems

Steady growth was interrupted in the 1930s, and Japan did not experience the peace necessary for continuing growth. Domestic problems resulted both from the impact of the Great Depression and from the effects of rapid industrialization. The rural areas were affected most severely, the areas already bearing most of the costs of industrialization, and social distress increased. There was also increased hostility to capitalism, which was seen as the cause of the problems. Against this background, there was competition for control of policy-making between those wishing to increase Japan's military strength and the political moderates.

In 1930, Japan readopted the gold standard just at the time the Depression hit East Asia. The result was that markets dried up even while Japan was continuing to import, so the trade imbalance led to an outflow of specie to make good the adverse balance of trade. By the end of 1931, 60 percent of Japan's entire international reserves had evaporated. Because currency issue was tied to the level of reserves, the result was deflation, which affected the prices of agricultural commodities the most, causing hardship in agricultural communities. Once Britain left the gold standard, the possibility of increasing exports to the West decreased, encouraging both a focus on Asian markets (which became more important to Japanese trade) and the militarists' pressure for more isolation. Initially, the response was a tightening of requirements for obtaining foreign exchange, and in 1933 monopoly control over foreign exchange was put into the hands of the Bank of Japan.

Internally, a program of reorganizing industry to encourage the creation of larger, more efficient units began. The idea was that if efficiency increased, exports would become more competitive internationally. The problem was that world trade levels remained low throughout the 1930s, and although Japan's exports were growing until 1938, Japan still needed to export more to earn foreign exchange for imports. Western markets were not receptive. This is one of the reasons that expansion into Asian areas to create the so-called co-prosperity sphere was encouraged. Not only would these areas provide the needed raw materials, but they would also provide new markets. This was a motive remarkably similar to the old mercantilist empire idea.

Centralized Control and Reallocation

Increasingly at this time, more control over the economy was seen as the solution to many problems, and the close links between the powerful *zaibatsu*, the military oligarchy, and the government bureaucracy were important in influencing the direction of the economy. Ironically, although the militarists favored control in order to strengthen industry so as to improve military

strength, it required a prolonged period of peace to be effective. But this was not to be. Japan's adventurism in the mid 1930s led to aggression that prevented the achievement of industrial strength.

Some of the programs adopted to deal with domestic problems had an effect on the defense buildup as well as illustrating Japan's adaptability. For example, northeast Japan was least industrialized and suffered most in the early 1930s because of its dependence on agriculture. Programs were established there to produce alcohol from potatoes (using a technology developed in France and Germany) which would be mixed with gasoline to economize on scarce oil supplies. (A similar program was adopted in Formosa, producing alcohol from sugar cane.) Plants to produce magnesium from seawater were also introduced.

Another problem faced by the military was the poor physical condition of many of the recruits. To deal with this, Japan introduced a program following the European example to pay medical expenses for those needing treatment, and treatment itself could be obtained in hospitals that were subsequently brought into public ownership. Both had a direct impact on military goals, while the second was in keeping with a general trend toward the introduction of social welfare programs.

A third program attempted to deal with domestic problems at the same time that it met military needs—the provision of electrical power. One justification was to provide electricity for rural areas along the lines of the Tennessee Valley Authority in the United States. Of more interest to the military was the provision of cheap electricity for those industries involved in the military effort—steel, shipbuilding, machine making, and chemicals, for example. The idea was to nationalize power generation and distribution so as to meet the aims of a social relief program and military preparedness. The stumbling block was the companies themselves, who were uninterested in moving into rural areas unless properly compensated, which did not happen until 1938.

By the mid 1930s, some new directions were also opening up for the Japanese economy that would have significant implications in the postwar period. At this time, automobiles were assembled in Japan from parts imported from Ford and General Motors plants in the United States In 1936, two Japanese producers, Nissan and Toyota, were licensed to produce cars, receiving significant government assistance for doing so. Government provided half their capital requirements as well as tax and trade concessions. By 1939, United States producers were no longer involved in Japanese car production. During the Second World War, auto production capability was important, but it was not until after the war that independent Japanese auto production expanded significantly.

At the same time that these initiatives were being worked on, Japan was developing an agency capable of taking over central planning functions. Initially called the Investigative Bureau, it had a primary task of strengthening control over industry and achieving Japan's self-sufficiency in the production of militarily vital outputs such as ships, steel, aircraft, and fuel. In 1937, the Bureau was renamed the Cabinet Planning Office and was authorized to prepare a national policy guide. This was exactly what the militarists were hoping for, as it gave them powerful controls over the shape and direction of the economy. In addition, the programs originally set up to give relief to depressed rural areas ended up producing materials useful for defense purposes. The only problem was that the plan as a whole required peace, but war with China interrupted progress.

Foreign Incursions: China

Japan would be involved with China militarily until its surrender at the end of the Second World War. China's appeal was of course its natural resource potential, and Japan took advantage of China's weakness to acquire territory there. One threat to Japan's ambitions was the potential response from the Soviet Union, which also had ambitions in China, partly to guarantee its warm water port on the Pacific, but also because of China's resources. (It was partly to offset the threat from the Soviet Union that Japan later in the 1930s entered into an alliance with Germany.)

Japan's interests in China dated from 1895, when it acquired Taiwan-Formosa. Later, it took advantage of the 1911 revolution in China to influence the ruler of Manchuria in order to gain natural resource concessions as well as access to the Manchurian rail line. This was only partly successful, as the Manchurian warlord's allegiances shifted. In the late 1920s, the Chinese political situation became even more uncertain, with the Kuomintang rising, and when the Kuomintang leader Chiang Kai-shek entered Peking (modern Beijing), Japan responded by sending a military expedition to China. There followed a period during which control over Manchuria was contested, but China's forces were too divided to hold on to it and resist Japanese advances at the same time.

Kuomintang

Chinese nationalist political party

Simultaneously, domestic problems within Japan itself were growing, so the increase in military activity in Manchuria promised to divert attention from these problems as well as solve the resource problem. Manchuria was forcibly taken over in 1932 and renamed Manchukuo. Access to Manchurian resources would dramatically assist Japan's industrialization effort, but Japan also eyed the resource wealth of northern China. To get control of these required removing the Kuomintang and creating a pseudo-independent (although nominally Chinese) state under Japanese influence. The problem was that the Kuomintang opposed these incursions, and used the threat of Japanese aggression to call for Chinese unity.[2] From 1935 on, frictions with China increased. For so long as Japan could get access to resources to permit continuation of industrialization, outright warfare was checked. However, also at this time the appeal of an alliance with Germany grew—German strength against the Soviet Union would give Japan freedom of action in Manchuria and northern China and could also give freedom to expand southward to the resource rich European colonies such as Dutch Indonesia, which possessed oil. Japan planned to continue building up its own industrial capability in order to prepare it for war with the Soviet Union by 1941. But to do this implied meeting two requirements, neither of which were met. First, avoid any lengthy military engagement in China. Second, ensure continuing imports from and good relations with the United States Japan did not want to make an enemy of the United States, knowing it did not have the capability to defend itself against American forces. For a considerable period of time, this strategy nearly worked, partly because the United States did not think that Japan's attempt to gain self-sufficiency would be successful, so that she would be forced back to the discipline of the international marketplace.

Industrialization Slowed

The China crisis escalated and turned into outright conflict in 1937, when Japan took northern China. However, what was supposed to be a short, decisive engagement turned into a long, draining action. Because the conflict dragged on, Japan became more dependent on imports of oil, steel, machine tools, and other necessities, and continuing austerity for the civilian population and reallocation of resources away from civilian industries did little to help maintain productive capability, much less build it up.

The United States became much more influential as a supplier. By 1938, three quarters of all the scrap iron used to produce steel came from the United States, 80 percent of all fuel needs were met from United States sources (even the lagging synthetic oil industry depended on United States equipment), and 60 percent of all machine tools came from the United States, which also sold Japan copper, steel alloys and cotton.

Economic conditions worsened in 1939. A drought reduced the size of the rice crop and also lowered water levels, reducing the production of electricity from hydroelectric plants, forcing increases in coal imports. Externally, the signing of the Nazi-Soviet non-aggression pact was devastating, as Japan could no longer rely on Germany to distract Soviet attention from Japanese actions in China. In 1940, however, Japan formally joined forces with the Axis alliance of Germany and Italy.

Southeast Asia Expansion and War

Although Japan industrially was not really prepared for war, a southward advance looked as though it might solve some problems and help supply needed materials. Indonesia was particularly appealing because of its oil reserves, and rubber and nickel were also found there. French Indochina began to take on an increasing importance too, and in 1941 the Vichy government of occupied France effectively permitted a Japanese takeover there, which gave Japan access to Indochina and Thailand.

Because of the importance of control of the oil fields of the Pacific, the Philippines were threatened, which brought the United States into the potential conflict. By this time, Japan's economic situation was so weak that ironically, hostilities to gain access to oil so as to be able to continue fighting for any length of time became the only feasible option. A southward advance also forced conflict with Britain once British colonies in Malaya (rubber and tin) and Burma (rice) were threatened.

The Pacific war has been called a conflict over two different versions of East Asia. One was

Figure 16.2 Begining in the 1970s, imports of Japanese cars took a larger share of the U.S. automobile market. This shows an aerial view of automobiles and containers off-loaded at the Port Newark/Elizabeth Marine Terminal in New Jersey. (Courtesy of the Port Authority of New York and New Jersey)

Japan's vision of a self-sufficient Japanese empire that needed to build up its economic strength. Japan entered the war remarkably unprepared—it was short of shipping, steel and oil, hardly the most propitious start to what did turn out to be a lengthy conflict. On the other side was the American idea of international cooperation in which nations were linked peacefully through trade and finance. Ultimately, neither vision was achieved.

Summary

Japan's defeat in the Second World War left it devastated, and not only because it has the unwelcome distinction of being the only country in the world to have suffered the effects of nuclear warfare. It was subject to American occupation; half its 1930s land area was lost as Taiwan, Korea, and southern Sakhalin were removed from Japanese control; it lost the colonies of its coprosperity sphere, and thus access to the resources it wished to own, not trade for. Losses during the war included 90 percent of its merchant marine, one quarter of its housing and one fifth of its industrial capacity—a total loss estimated at about one quarter of its national wealth. In addition to the loss of physical productive plant, five million military and civilian personnel repatriated to Japan after the war put extra strains on a by-then fragile society.

Special Characteristics?

Seemingly against all odds, Japan recovered (its postwar recovery will be treated more fully in Chapter 22). The question that is always raised is whether anything can explain both this recovery and also the very rapid industrialization that occurred after 1868. There are certain characteristics that were features of pre-1868 society that have survived and were adapted to a modern context. Many of these are reminiscent of qualities associated with European feudalism, and it seems

strange that what had to be removed from Europe to produce the characteristics needed for modernization are now associated with the modernization of Japan. In Europe, the qualities of individualism, risk taking, frugality, rationality, and so on were associated with the adoption of capitalist ways. These are either less significant in Japan or else have been reinterpreted in a Japanese context.

Some of the special social features that have been identified as contributing to the Japanese "miracle" include the following. A greater willingness to accept authority and discipline has supposedly reduced social conflict that accompanies industrialization, although it did not prevent sporadic uprisings, especially in the earlier years, or student protests more recently. These are qualities associated with loyalty, rewards according to birth or seniority, and the individual's willingness to be subjected to the authority of the group. At the present time, this is used to explain the system of paternalist industrial relations and lifetime employment. An individual is loyal to the employer rather than to a peer group (like a union). However, this system applies only to the male work force in the large-scale, modern industrial sector; it does not apply to women nor to the work force in the subcontractor or traditional sector. (In any event, this system is not quite so pervasive now as it used to be.) These qualities perhaps explain the lack of original innovative activity in Japan, as they do not encourage innovation, but at the same time can help account for the success of borrowed ideas and technology.

These features are associated with the power the *zaibatsu* gained over the economy. They first began to appear in banking and finance, and in the 1920s, took control of small-scale commerce and manufacturing. Partly due to their association with the military and the government, they grew into large groupings of heterogeneous enterprises dominating the modern sector. Because all involved saw their interests served, and because no restraints on the growth of monopoly power existed, they dominated the modern sector of Japan and help account for the rapid capital accumulation and modernization of the economy. At the same time, they are characterized by the old traditions of hierarchy and authoritarian control—a tradition that fits in well with paternalism but is at odds with modern ideas of political and social democracy.

However, national stereotyping is a dangerous pastime. What is necessary to know is that Japan, like Germany, emerged very rapidly from a feudal-like past to industrialize quickly. Both have matched an industrialization effort with military goals, and both failed to reach those goals. In the postwar world, both have played significant roles in the world economy and have not rebuilt a military establishment, preferring instead to add their voices to the call for world peace.

Notes

1. These are estimates made by Yuzo Yamada and quoted in W.W. Lockwood, *op. cit.*, p. 135. The footnotes to table 16.1 describe the various statistical problems surrounding these figures. In spite of this, it is clear that structural change was underway.

2. Until 1949, the nationalist Kuomintang and the Chinese Communist Party were united in resisting Japanese and other foreign efforts to control China. Then in 1949 the two split, and the leaders of the Kuomintang were forced to flee to Taiwan, where they established the Republic of China and remained in opposition to the People's Republic of China on the mainland.

Key Concepts

Daimyo
Import Substitution
Industrial policy
Isolationism

Kuomintang (China)
Subsidy
Zaibatsu

Questions for Discussion or Essay Writing

1. What were the problems that Japan had to overcome in order to initiate an industrialization process?

2. To what extent are early industrialization policies in Japan similar to those adopted in Europe under the influence of mercantilist ideas?

3. Are there any advantages in being a late comer to industrialization?

4. Describe Japan's resource endowment. To what extent did it influence subsequent economic development?

5. How important are military and political aspirations in explaining Japan's approach to industrialization?

6. Socio-cultural influences are often said to be the important "hidden" factor in explaining Japan's economic growth. Discuss and evaluate.

7. Japan has often been described as the economy that brought copying others' experience to a high degree. Is this true?

8. Do wars help or hinder economic development? Discuss, using Japan as an example.

For Further Reading

Abramowitz, A. "Catching Up." *Journal of Economic History*, 46 (June 1986): 385-404.

Allen, George C. *A Short Economic History of Modern Japan, 1867-1937*. new ed. London: Allen & Unwin, 1972.

Barnhart, Michael A. *Japan Prepares for Total War: The Search for Economic Security, 1919- 1941*. Ithaca: Cornell University Press, 1987.

Denison, Edward F. and William K. Chung. *How Japan's Economy Grew So Fast: The Sources of Postwar Expansion*. Washington, D.C.: The Brookings Institution, 1976.

Goldsmith, R.W. *The Financial Development of Japan, 1868-1977*, New Haven: Yale University Press, 1983.

Iriya, A. *Japan's Drive to Great-Power Status* in M. Jansen, ed. *The Cambridge History of Japan, vol. 5*. Cambridge: Cambridge University Press, 1989.

Kelley, A.C. and J.G. Williamson. *Lessons from Japanese Development: An Analytical Economic History*. Chicago: Chicago University Press, 1974.

Klein, L. and K. Ohkawa. *Economic Growth: The Japanese Experience Since the Meiji Era*. Homewood, Ill: Richard D. Irwin, 1968.

Lockwood, W.W. *The Economic Development of Japan: Growth and Structural Change, 1868- 1938*. Oxford: Oxford University Press, 1955.

Macpherson, W.J. *The Economic Development of Japan, 1868-1941*. London: Macmillan, 1987

Morishima, M. *Why has Japan 'Succeeded'? Western Technology and the Japanese Ethos*, Cambridge: Cambridge University Press, 1982.

Ohkawa, K. and H. Rosovsky. *Capital Formation in Japan, Cambridge Economic History of Europe*, vol. VII, Part 2, Ch. III, Cambridge: Cambridge University Press, 1978.

Oshima, H. *Meiji Fiscal Policy and Economic Progress*, in W.W. Lockwood, ed., *The State and Economic Enterprise in Japan*, Princeton: Princeton University Press, 1965.

Saxonhouse, Gary. "A Tale of Technological Diffusion in the Meiji Period." *Journal of Economic History*, XXXIV (1974).

Smith, Thomas C. "Peasant Time and Factory Time in Japan." *Past & Present*, vol. 111 (May 1986): 165-197.

Yamamura, K. "Success Ill Gotten? The Role of Meiji Militarism in Japan's Technological Progress." *Journal of Economic History*, XXXVII (1977).

Part IV

The Maturing of Industrial Capitalism

(Nineteenth and Twentieth Centuries)

Chapter 17

Late 19th Century Industrialization

AS WE HAVE SEEN, 19TH CENTURY DEVELOP-MENT was characterized by structural economic change. Manufacturing accounted for a larger share of national output, a change paralleled by the corresponding development of the service sector, especially financial services. Output grew absolutely, due partly to an increase in available resources but also because of increasing productivity due to technological change. The occupational structure shifted away from agricultural work, and proportionately more people were employed in industry and services. The composition of output changed away from heavy industry and toward consumer goods, especially toward the production of previously unknown commodities. All this took place in an increasingly urban atmosphere.

Although one of the costs of capitalist industrialization—poor living and working conditions for the new proletarianized working classes—had long existed, a new cost appeared. This was the relatively new phenomenon of the business cycle, which involved periodic cycles of depression and prosperity, alternating around a general upward trend. Although bad times had existed before, due

Business cycle

Periodic fluctuations in the level of economic activity

to harvest failures or wars, for example, the new element was the periodicity of the capitalist business cycle.

This chapter provides a link between previous and succeeding chapters. It begins with a general summary of the century's common developments, then moves on to examine the internationalization of capitalist development, focusing especially on the financial implications. The chapter closes with a brief description of the opposition to capitalist industrialization and the forms that this opposition took.

Industry and the Factory System

Centralization of Production

Factory production was one of the earliest features of the Industrial Revolution, centralizing production to replace the decentralized putting out system. The factory also changed the location of production by separating workplace from home. There were two motives for centralization. Profit-seeking capitalists had an incentive to bring workers together in one place because they were then able to control the work process and thus the costs of production better. Second, adding power to machines increased labor productivity and gave more control over the labor force because management could change the speed of machines. Power-driven machinery also implied an increase in the scale of operations, and technological developments continually enlarged the minimum size of the most efficient plant, in turn implying that fewer producers would be needed, even in an expanding market. This undermined the competitive conditions of early capitalist industrialization and led to sticky policy questions later.

Search for New Technology

A more systematic search for innovations to expand profit-making ability also occurred. In the first phase of the Industrial Revolution, inventions were typically small and simple, like the flying shuttle, for example. After the transportation breakthrough provided by the railways, deliberate application of scientific technology became more common and innovations became more complex; think of the different types of electrically powered urban mass transit, for example.

There were many further linkages. The expansion of the economy made possible by applying steam power to locomotion not only created larger markets for the output of larger firms, it also widened the area from which resources (old and new) could be supplied. It made possible the exploitation of new resources, such as rubber and

Table 17-1
Growth of Transportation Links: Railroad Mileage, Shipping Tonnage

| Year | Railroads | | Shipping | | | |
| | | | Sailing Ships | | Steamships | |
	Miles	Percent Growth	Gross Tons	Percent Growth	Gross Tons	Percent Growth
1850	24,000	—	9,100,000	—	280,000	—
1860	67,000	179	13,000,000	43	780,000	179
1870	130,000	94	13,500,000	4	2,050,000	163
1880	230,000	77	13,870,000	3	4,400,000	115
1900	490,000	29	7,245,000	−31	22,370,000	170
1910	640,000	31	4,625,000	−35	37,290,000	67
1930	775,000	21	1,585,000	−66	68,025,000	82
1950	770,000	−0.6	720,000	−56	84,580,000	24

Note: These figures are underestimates, as they give no indication of improvements in speed made possible by improved technology. In addition, extension of transportation links requires consideration of roads, inland waterways, and, in the latest period, the growth of air transportation.

Source: Calculation based on C.M. Cipolla, *The Economic History of World Population*, 6th ed, Harmondsworth: Penguin. 1974; p. 79.

petroleum (which required scientific knowledge for their exploitation) and also led to totally new industries such as bicycles, motor vehicles, and chemicals.

Mass Production and Standardized Goods

A third implication of late century development was that standardized goods for a mass market could be produced by the new mass production industries, especially in new branches of manufacture such as the consumer durables industries producing new goods such as the sewing machine or electric lamps. However, not all industrial processes were suitable for large-scale mechanization or mass production, and economic dualism resulted. On the one hand were the core industries such as the capital goods industries which had an effect on just about every other industry, and the consumer durables industries. They were increasingly characterized by large-scale enterprise and dominance by a few producers. On the other hand, many small producers existed where large-scale mechanization was inappropriate or simply not sufficiently developed. They operated either in small factories or workshops, or used sweated labor and outwork. Examples include garment manufacturing, some leatherworking, and millinery.

Finance Capital

As many enterprises grew in size, a fourth implication appeared. Growth required ever larger amounts of finance capital, not only for the initial installation or expansion of large amounts of pro-

Figure 17.1   The S.S. Great Britain was the first steam-powered iron ship, and made its first voyage across the Atlantic in 1845. Many early steamships also had rigging for sails. She was a merchant ship; the gunports are only painted on.

ductive capital but also to finance working capital requirements. Typically, although mass production produces larger amounts of output per worker once in operation, it takes longer to start producing output. The tooling required for installation takes time, the production of parts for final assembly takes time, and suppliers as well as workers have to be paid even before final output is produced and sold. These expanding needs for credit required the refinement of techniques for raising initial capital and for financing working capital, met by selling shares in stock markets or bonds to creditors.

Specialization

As mass production spread, the nature of the work performed changed. Machines can do only simple tasks, so the job was broken down into its specific components to make it possible to develop a machine to duplicate that one specific task. Then an individual did not need to possess a variety of skills; a worker in a mass production industry became only a machine tender, working at one particular fragmented part of the total task. (Work deskilling led to various worker protests and a variety of responses.)

Also, as the labor force in individual enterprises grew, there was a need to organize and control it, which encouraged the development of a managerial hierarchy. So the numbers of white collar office jobs grew, concerned not only with supervising production employees but also with controlling the flow of materials into the production process and distributing the finished products afterwards. Marketing functions became as important as production. Office tasks were also mechanized, permitting fast calculation and reproduction of the necessary information. Early office machines were the typewriter, made more practical by the late 1860s, and the adding machine, introduced in 1888. Growth of white collar employment had a further implication. To begin with, most office personnel were male, but by the end of the century, women became an important source of labor for these jobs, especially at the lower, clerical levels.

Electricity and Other New Industries

All these effects were made possible by improvements in steelmaking and the machine tool industry, and by the deliberate application of scientific technology to industrial uses.[1] Among the new industries were those based on electricity and chemicals. One of the first uses of electricity was in communications, and the electric telegraph, introduced in the 1830s, dramatically speeded up the transmission of information, which continued with the development of the telephone in the 1870s. Electricity was later used for lighting, replacing gas and oil in the 20th century. With the development of the dynamo in 1867, electrically powered motion began to revolutionize urban transport. In 1879, an electric dynamo was used for the first time to power a locomotive in Berlin, and electrically powered streetcars became widely used by 1913, especially in Europe. One of the most significant uses of electricity in urban transport came with its adaptation to the underground railway. Steam was obviously impractical in an underground tunnel—London's first underground railway in 1863 was for the most part set in deep cuttings rather than tunnels for this reason. But the first modern underground line in a tunnel (the Tube) opened in London in 1890 and was powered by electricity from the start. Other large cities such as Paris and New York also developed underground mass transit systems powered by electricity.

After 1890, electricity began to be used for industrial power; its advantages were that it could be used only where and as needed. It also affected domestic life by making possible electrically powered domestic appliances such as refrigerators, irons, washing machines, and vacuum cleaners. Improvements in the generation and transmission of electricity also helped expand markets. Most early generating plants were coal fired, but hydro-electric power (for example, power from Niagara Falls was tapped in 1897-1898) and oil-fired plants began to account for small shares of generating capacity. Transmission of electricity was improved with the invention of the transformer, and high voltage alternating current replaced the previous system of direct current transmission. Although generating plants themselves were scattered (it is difficult to transport electricity over long distances), the production of electrical equipment for the generation and use of electrical power was typically concentrated in a few firms.

The chemical industry also expanded as new technological developments in other industries required its inputs. For example, the electrolytic process for making soda, the most widely used industrial alkali, and improvements in making sulfuric acid, the most widely used acid, affected agriculture and the paper, explosives, and rubber industries, to name only a few. Chemical advances also made possible the development of leisure time activities through innovations in photography and motion pictures, which soon became popular forms of entertainment for a mass market.

Development of the oil industry was encouraged by the discovery of new uses for oil. These included the gasoline-powered internal combustion engine, which was invented in Germany and first powered a car in 1885. Gasoline engines were later used in new motor buses in large cities. Other new uses for oil included power generation and the production of synthetics. The automobile itself had further stimulative effects on the construction industry (road building), the steel, glass, and rubber industries, among others. The bicycle, however, was a much more common method of individual transportation that also put pressure on improving roads, as unpaved roads or cobblestones are not suitable for bicycles. The bicycle had existed since the early 19th century but really became popular with the introduction of the "safety" bicycle in the 1880s. This replaced the penny-farthing, so called because the front wheel, which the cyclist sat over, was large in relation to the small back wheel, just like the relative size of two British coins, the penny and the farthing. The safety bicycle had two wheels of equal size and was much easier to get on and off than the penny-farthing. It was also easier to ride once the pedals did not turn the wheels directly but were connected to them by means of gear wheels. The bicycle was not as popular in the United States as in Europe, where it remained one of the commonest forms of transportation well into the 20th century.[2]

Development of Money and Capital Markets

As enterprises grew in size, their needs for finance capital grew, with three important implications. First, ownership ceased to be in the hands of one person, because one individual's resources were too small to meet the increasing needs for finance. So there was a tendency toward multiple ownership, first through partnerships and later the joint stock company, which was most appropriate for large enterprises.

Corporations and Stock Markets

In England after 1720, establishment of an incorporated joint stock company required specific authorization. Throughout the 18th century most were successful operations, removing the fear of abuse that had occurred during earlier speculative manias. The Bubble Act was repealed in 1825, and in 1844 simply registering the company resulted in incorporation. The joint stock form became even more appealing when limited liability was added in 1855, limiting financial risk to the initial sum used to buy shares. Other countries also relaxed prohibitions on this form of enterprise. By 1860 all of the United States permitted the incorporation of companies;

France relaxed restrictions in 1867; and all restrictions were abolished in Germany in 1870.

One feature of a joint stock company is that its shares are transferable, and markets to make this effective, stock markets, emerged. At first, stockbrokers in London had worked out of coffeehouses and specialized in transferring ownership of government securities (because there were very few corporate securities). But by 1802 their activities were relocated to the Stock Exchange building, and first railway and public utility shares, then corporate shares were also traded. Similarly, the Bourse in Paris was initially established in 1724 to handle government securities but was reorganized in 1816, at which time sixty brokers (compared with five hundred in London) handled seven issues. Stockbrokers first organized in New York in 1792, and the New York Stock Exchange was established in 1817. Other exchanges were developed at the same time in the major commercial centers of Amsterdam, Berlin, Rome, and Vienna.

The development of multiple ownership of companies and a market for the transfer of ownership solved one problem of raising initial capital, but also created a new problem, abuse. This was especially acute in the United States, perhaps because few of the requirements for acceptable business behavior that had slowly developed in Europe were present there. The opportunity for abuse came as ownership of companies by shareholding spread to many people, very few of whom were either interested or actually involved in the everyday operations of their companies. Separation of ownership from control permitted those who knew the true value of the companies to manipulate buying and selling so as to enrich themselves, and the resulting periodic waves of speculation led to occasional stock market crashes that undermined confidence.

The second implication of larger enterprises resulted from their need for larger amounts of working capital to finance operations in advance of receipt of sales revenues. The financial structure became more complex and banks and banking functions grew more specialized. By the end of the 19th century, three specific types of banks existed: central, commercial, and investment banks. (Further consideration of the banking system, especially commercial and investment banking, will be left until the following chapter.)

Money Supply

Finally, the third implication of the growth in enterprises accompanying the growth of output was the need for more money with which to consummate the growing volume of transactions. Not only were more goods being produced and sold, but more resources, including the labor resource, were being used and paid for, and a larger number of purely financial transactions were occurring, a fairly recent development that saw its birth in the late 19th century. Thus, the actual volume of coins in circulation was increasing and in addition, other types of negotiable instruments acceptable for payments were being developed.

This had both a domestic and an international aspect. Domestically, the money question involved the structure of the monetary system and how it was controlled. Internationally, industrial countries were part of a world market where they competed with each other and were also linked to primary producing countries. This required the development of an international financial system facilitating flows of money, goods, and resources across national borders.

From fairly early times, national rulers had recognized the importance of a single government-controlled currency system. However, even in the late 19th century, some countries still had several different currencies in circulation. Switzerland did not replace its twelve different currencies until 1875, Italy unified its currency in 1860, and there were nine different currencies in Germany until 1875. At this time the practice of letting foreign coins circulate also ended. For so long as the only acceptable medium of exchange agreeable to buyers and sellers was a metal, monetary policy consisted of issuing the right quantity of metal coins and preventing debasement.

Two developments disturbed this simplicity. One was the use of paper (bank notes especially) as a convenient supplement to coins in commercial transactions. Another was that institutions besides the mint emerged with the ability to issue this paper, complicating the role of monetary policy. Therefore it became necessary to wield control over banks, paper money and credit in order to maintain confidence in a money-using market system. This led to the development of the central bank, which acts not as a private profit making entity but whose main function is the regulation of money and banks to prevent instability. In addition, the use of paper money in larger amounts made it necessary to adopt a monetary standard that defined the quantity of metal a piece of paper would be redeemed for.

Confronting the issue of the choice of a monetary standard, Great Britain was the first to adopt

Figure 17.2 This 1909 Auburn Touring Car shows the affinity early automobiles had with older horse-drawn carriages. Note the non-pneumatic tires; also note that the road is unpaved. (Courtesy of the Auburn-Cord-Duesenberg Museum, Auburn, Indiana)

a gold standard, which defined the pound sterling in terms of a specific weight of gold. This was formalized in 1821, when paper notes of the Bank of England were convertible into gold. Most other countries adopted a bimetallic standard with a fixed value between the two metals and between them and paper. However, after the 1870's, there was a trend to a single gold standard, either on a de facto basis or on an official basis. This simplified international trade by eliminating doubt about the relative exchange values of different currencies and by having free convertibility into gold.

Gold standard

Monetary system in which a nation's currency unit is defined in terms of gold and exchangeable into gold

Bimetallism in the United States

Bimetallism worked well in spite of some inherent problems relating to changes in the supply of the two metals, except in the United States which experienced crisis after crisis. Its problem was not so much fluctuating supplies of metals (which could be overcome by altering the weights of coins) as lack of effective control over money and banking. In 1791, the United States adopted a bimetallic standard when it replaced the British pound with the American dollar. The dollar was defined as containing 371.25 grains of silver, and the ratio of silver to gold was 15:1. This meant that the mint would exchange one ounce of minted gold for every 15 ounces of silver, and similarly, paper money could be converted into metal in these proportions. A major problem arose when gold was discovered in California and Australia in 1848-1849. From a world annual average of $15.7 million in the period 1801-

Bimetallism

The use of two metals with a fixed relationship to each other as a nation's monetary standard

1850, gold output rose dramatically to $121.2 million in the period 1851-1855. This increase in the supply of gold relative to silver lowered the free market value of gold, but although the mint ratio had been changed to 16:1 in 1834, it was not changed at this time. So silver coins dropped out of circulation, illustrating Gresham's Law.

Gresham's Law states that "bad money drives out the good." Technically, this means that the metal coin that is overvalued at the mint will circulate while the undervalued coin will not, because of the imbalance between market ratios and the price the mint pays for the metals used for coins. Practically, what it means is this: A coin's purchasing power is determined by its face value, so a dollar coin made out of gold and a dollar coin made out of silver will both buy a dollar's worth of goods. Now if the relative supplies of metals change so that one becomes plentiful, then its price falls in the metals market and the relative price of the other rises. No one mining the scarce metal (or holding coins made out of it) will sell it to the mint because its intrinsic value as metal is greater than the purchasing power the mint says it has, making it worth more as metal.

Gresham's Law

When two kinds of money with the same face value but different intrinsic values exist, the one with the greater intrinsic value is hoarded while the other circulates

Hence these coins drop out of circulation (possibly to be melted down or sold as metal), while coins made out of the abundant metal will circulate and miners of this metal will continue to sell it to the mint. However, the United States neither altered the mint ratio nor lowered the amount of silver in its coins, as the other bimetallic countries did at this time.

The problem of imbalance arose again in the 1870s with the opening of Nevada's silver mines, but now gold went out of circulation, as it was relatively scarce in relation to silver. Most countries had simply adopted the gold standard by this time, but in the United States, the money situation had been further complicated by the issue of unconvertible paper money (greenbacks) during the Civil War and an expansion of bank notes afterwards. Silver miners exerted strong pressure for continuation of a bimetallic standard because they wanted the mint to continue to buy their silver.

Greenbacks were partly retired in 1873 by making them convertible to gold, which was a move toward a gold-only standard and a partial setback for the silver lobby. Despite that, it did achieve two successes. One was the Bland-Allison Act, which required continued minting of silver coins, resulting in $378 million worth of silver coins or silver certificates being issued. The second was the Sherman Silver Purchase, authorizing the Treasury to buy 4.5 million ounces of silver each month, paying for them with Treasury Notes, which were legal tender. As a result, the Treasury acquired silver worth $156 million. Further problems occurred in the depression of 1896, when perceptions of an overissue of silver led to an increase in demand for gold, with the result that the Treasury's gold reserves fell. The final phase came in 1900, when the gold standard was finally adopted. What made monetary problems worse in the United States was the absence of a central bank for most of the 19th century, so there was little control over the supply of money and credit.

Central Banking

The modern functions of a central bank involve acting in the interests of the nation as a whole and not as a profit-making enterprise for its shareholders. While many central banks began life as private or partly private banks, most became state-owned in the 20th century. A central bank is the government's banker, holding its income from taxes and paying the government's debts; it has the monopoly of note issue; holds reserves of foreign ex-

Central bank

A bank acting in the interests of the nation as a whole

change; is the "lender of last resort," standing ready to provide credit to private banks, and is responsible for making sure that the amount of money in circulation is adequate for the needs of commercial transactions. In short, it controls the money supply and is responsible for ensuring the stability of the financial structure, and through that, the economy as a whole. Central banks did not acquire all these functions at once. Some developed originally by extending their early banking functions of receiving and safeguarding deposits from customers and making loans. Gradually, the only "customer" they dealt with was the government (Treasury) itself, and the only loans made were to private banks, which gave the ability to operate as a control mechanism.

The central bank gradually acquired the monopoly of note issue, which was necessary if the monetary system required convertibility of paper into metal. There were two competing views on how best to issue paper money. One was the Currency School, which saw paper bank notes simply as a convenient proxy for metal. Accordingly, as international settlements were made in gold, any time the Bank experienced a loss of its gold reserves due to an adverse trade balance, the money supply should be contracted and credit tightened, and vice versa.[3] This ties the domestic money supply tightly to the international economy and leaves the monetary authority with little to do except make sure that paper money outstanding fluctuates in accordance with the level of reserves. It also causes business conditions to prosper or decline as the trade balance is favorable or unfavorable. (To modern economists, this would cause and accentuate depressions and worsen inflation.)

In contrast, the Banking School believed in more flexibility. If, for example, gold reserves fell for a temporary reason, the resulting restriction

Solving Problems in Economic History

Is a central bank necessary?

Central banks in the 20th century perform a variety of functions that in one way or another relate to the need to maintain stability in the economic system. A central bank really only has one client, the government, but because it fulfills various functions affecting the performance of private banks, its decisions and actions affect every single economic agent, directly or indirectly. The central bank acts as agent for the government, but by being able to influence the reserves held by private banks — and ultimately standing ready to be lender of last resort should a liquidity crisis threaten — can influence the volume of credit as well as the terms on which it can be obtained. This gives the central bank tremendous influence in a modern money-using economy.

But central banks, especially with all their modern duties and policy tools, developed relatively recently. We can date the first ones back to the 17th century, but the full complement of functions emerged slowly. The traditional explanation for the emergence of central banking is expressed in evolutionary terms: that as problems developed, so these institutions emerged to deal with them. In particular, the first banks held the government's gold reserves and had a reputation for soundness, so were ideally suited to extend credit to other banks experiencing temporary liquidity crises, thus preventing their insolvency and a collapse of confidence in the financial system.

A second approach disagrees, maintaining that some sort of private insurance scheme could handle any temporary liquidity crisis. According to this view, central banks did not evolve in response to practical problems but were established as favors to the government of the day, which saw these banks as a convenient way to increase their access to revenue sources.

Michael D. Bordo and Angela Redish in "Why did the Bank of Canada Emerge in 1935?" (*Journal of Economic History*, XLVII:2, June 1987 pp. 405–417) investigate these competing explanations in relation to the establishment of the Bank of Canada in 1935. They are testing three possible explanations for its emergence, two of which fit into the evolutionist approach, while the third explains the Bank's establishment as a response to political, not economic, pressures. They use evidence from various published sources, and estimate a time series econometric model to conclude that the Bank of Canada was founded in response to political factors.

The Bank's establishment in 1935 is relatively late, so one would expect that in the preceding period, alternative institutions had developed to perform some of the functions associated with a central bank, which was the case. The issue of bank notes was fairly elastic: The existence of a nationwide branch banking system avoided the seasonal liquidity crisis that plagued the United States; the Bank of Montreal acted as the government's bank; most of the banks kept reserves on call in the New York money market so that they were easily accessible to meet increased demands for liquidity; and after 1914, the banks had a liberal rediscounting facility.

Because these duties of a central bank *were* being performed, the debate over the need for such a bank centered on its role in a gold-standard world. Central banks maintained convertibility into gold, and thus directly controlled the size of the money supply. Before 1914 (when Canada abandoned the gold standard) this con-

Problem continues on next page

Problem continued from previous page

trol was exercised indirectly by the banking system's operations as a whole. Canada returned to the gold standard in 1926, suspended it *de facto* in 1928, and placed a formal embargo on gold exports in 1931. At this time, because Canada was expected to restore the gold standard, a central bank was not needed as an alternative.

Bordo and Redish suggest that an empirical examination of the performance of key macroeconomic variables such as the price level, exchange rates and interest rates may provide indirect evidence of the reasons for its emergence. The hypothesis that the bank was a necessary substitute for the gold standard in controlling the money supply implies that the behavior of the price level would differ from that prevailing under a private banking system after the bank's establishment.

Because data to estimate a structural model of the economy was not available, they constructed a time-series model. If the introduction of the Bank of Canada did make a difference, it would be expected that the evolution of the price series would change in 1935 because the monetary regime changed. In fact, no such structural break was found in the performance of major macroeconomic variables. Hence they conclude that the emergence of the Bank of Canada was due neither to evolutionary necessity nor to provide an alternative control mechanism for the monetary system in a post-gold standard world. Moving away from quantitative data to qualitative evidence supports their reasoning that political motives were important. In particular, there was a perceived need for a Canadian central bank to facilitate cooperation with central banks in other countries and to assert Canadian sovereignty over financial and economic matters. Thus they conclude that political factors rather than economic necessity account for the Bank's establishment.

---

of money and credit under the Currency School's policy would do more harm than good, giving the economy an inherent tendency to instability. The Banking School favored a looser link between reserves and note issue and wanted the bank to be able to influence the stability of the financial structure and the economy as a whole so that available money and credit would change with the needs of the domestic economy.

As central banks developed in the 19th century they veered toward one or the other of these poles. In England, the Currency School won, and after 1844 the Bank of England (whose notes became legal tender in 1797) was the only bank able to issue new bank notes. Private banks' notes continued to circulate but were withdrawn gradually. The Bank was divided into two departments: the Banking Department (which undertook general banking activities) and the Issue Department (which issued paper currency). The motivating

principle, as stressed by the Currency School, was security, so new note issue was subject to more rigorous limitation than elsewhere. It could issue up to £14 million worth of bank notes, backed by government securities, but further issues had to be backed by an equal increase in the amount of gold held in reserves.

The result was a very inelastic money supply, precisely when continued rapid expansion of the economy as a whole required more money. It also meant that in the crises of 1847, 1857 and 1866, the Bank was powerless to provide liquidity to other banks and businesses when this would have helped them to weather the crisis without too much damage. (Although it did issue, illegally, an extra £2 million in bank notes in 1857.)

Whenever development in one area is restricted as it was here, ways around the obstacle will be developed, and this was what happened in England. A growing proportion of the larger volume of transactions was financed by checks— transfers drawn on checking accounts, to which the principle of fractional reserve banking applied. That is, private banks knew that not all of their depositors wished to withdraw all their cash at the same time. Once they knew how much cash to keep on hand to meet demands for cash by depositors, the remainder could be used as a basis for profitable loan making. This permitted the money supply to expand beyond the bank notes in circulation. That is, so long as creditors were willing to accept checks credited to their own bank accounts as payment for debts, there was no need for an exact matching of "money" with gold.

This development expanded the role and importance of the Banking Department, whose most important function was to hold reserves for its clearing house function[4] and to extend or limit credit to the private banks as necessary, enabling it to influence business activity and thus the need for money. For example, if banks wanted to borrow from the Banking Department in order to increase their own reserves and make loans to business customers, the Department could accommodate these demands on favorable terms if it wished to encourage expansion. If it wished to slow business activity, it could limit loans made to banks by raising the discount (interest) rate it charged, and the higher rates would be passed on to business borrowers, limiting their demands. Besides being able to influence business activity by raising or lowering the discount rate, the Department could also stabilize the banking system as a whole during a liquidity crisis by making credit easily available, lessening the chance of a worsening crisis. (Changes in interest rates also influenced movements of gold into and out of the country, and thus the size of reserves and the amount of bank notes issued.)

Discount rate

Interest rate charged by the central bank on loans to commercial banks

---

A central bank operating on a completely different banking principle was the Bank of France, founded in 1800. The Bank gained a monopoly of the bank note issue in 1848, and while it kept metallic reserves of between 50-80 percent, the limit on the amount of bank notes that could be issued was often raised if economic conditions indicated. French note issue was much more flexible and adequate to demands than the English, so checks as a method of payment did not develop to the same extent.

Unlike the Bank of England, the Bank of France also became the ultimate discounter of commercial paper. That is, traders who received bills of exchange maturing in, for example, three months time, could exchange them for cash at a private bank for the face amount less the discount. This bank then passed them to the Bank of France, which is why it needed fairly high metallic reserves to be able to redeem bills for cash. When the bill matured, the issuer would make good the debt to the Bank. The volume of bills of exchange presented to the Bank gave it a good indication of the state of business activity, so it knew the correct amount of bank notes to issue.

In Germany, central banking started when the Bank of Prussia became the Reichsbank (the German central bank) in 1875. This Bank compromised between the two extremes of the Banking and the Currency schools. It gradually achieved a complete monopoly of bank note issue, and while an upper ceiling on the total amount of notes it could issue was fixed, it was a flexible ceiling. Unlike other central banks, which tended not to operate branch banks and deal with individuals, the Reichsbank had 100 branches and 4,000 sub-branches. This network permitted the Bank to fulfill its obligation to provide cash on demand by making transfers between accounts at different branches easy, an effective substitute for the private check.

Banking in the United States

The United States did not develop an effective central banking system until the 20th century, largely because of political disagreement over the whole idea of central banking. Although soon after independence, in 1791, the First Bank of the United States had been established to operate as a central bank, its charter was not renewed in 1811 because private, state-chartered banks were opposed to what they saw as its undue interference in their profit-making activities. They hoped that in the absence of a central bank, government deposits would be left with them, providing the basis for loan-making activity.

Between 1811 and 1816, there was a period of unrestrained banking activity, and the number of state-chartered banks rose from 86 to 246, all of them issuing their own bank notes. While nominally backed by gold and silver, the bank note issue was heavily overextended. To attempt to restore order, the Second Bank of the United States was chartered in 1816 with some of the functions of a central bank. However, it was mismanaged and also became a political football. On the one side were eastern interests, mainly merchants and bankers, who favored tight control over the money supply to keep the value of the dollar stable. On the other side, supported by President Jackson, were western and southern interests who favored expansionary money policies. Politically, they feared centralized (i.e., monopoly) financial control of the country by eastern urban financiers and disliked central government, favoring decentralization and greater powers for the largely agrarian states. They won this battle, and the Second Bank's charter was not renewed.

What followed in the absence of any controls was a period of loose banking. Many new banks were established in the West. (So many that they were referred to as "wildcat" banks, wildcats appearing to be the only customers many of them could hope for.) State supervision was poor, and there was no institution with the ability to extend credit as a last resort. For safety, not trusting private banks, the federal government kept its revenues in vaults at customs houses, so they were not available to be used as reserves by the banking system.

Partial order to the resulting chaos came with the 1863 National Banking Act, at which time some 12,000 different bank notes were in circulation. Many of these were worthless, having been issued by banks that had failed. New nationally chartered banks were established, and any other bank accepting federal regulation could deposit government bonds they owned at the Treasury, to serve as a reserve against which they could issue their own bank notes. In 1875, country banks were required to hold 15 percent of their assets as a nonearning reserve, while banks in reserve cities (mainly New York banks) were required to hold liquid assets of 25 percent. In addition, after 1865, taxes on bank notes issued by unregulated state banks plus the deposit of government funds in the national banks helped curb the unrestricted expansion of private banks. While this put controls on the issue of bank notes, there were still flaws.

The most obvious problem was the reserves held by banks. There was no lender of last resort, which gave an inflexibility to the money supply that the private banks could do nothing about. The money supply thus tended to fluctuate, in accordance not with the needs of business but with the amount of government bonds held by national banks as reserves, which was not very closely related to overall economic needs. New York banks acted as *de facto* reserve banks for country banks but did not have all the powers to make this effective. Country banks left deposits with New York banks, which were required to keep large liquid assets. To get around the liquidity problem and to earn something on these assets, the New York banks lent them to Stock Exchange dealers on call (i.e., they could be called back to the bank at any time). This resulted in a potentially unstable situation, which spilled over to stock market operations whenever there was a drain on bank deposits and a need to restore reserves to the legal amounts.

Federal Reserve System

There were major financial crises in 1873, 1893, 1903, and 1907, and finally, in 1913, the Federal Reserve System was established as the nation's central bank. As a compromise to states' rights advocates, not just one but twelve Federal Reserve Banks were established, each controlling private banks in its own semi-autonomous district, with overall control exercised by the Federal Reserve Board.

The money issue was gradually monopolized by the Federal Reserve, being essentially complete by the 1930s. Gold reserves were held by the Reserve Banks (which were responsible for foreign exchange transactions), each could issue Federal Reserve Bank Notes, and the system as a whole issued Federal Reserve Notes that became much more important as the older national bank notes were eliminated. In this way, the new central bank controlled the size of the money supply. It controlled credit conditions and acted as lender of last resort, which also affected the size of the money supply by influencing the size of reserves held by private banks and the volume of deposit accounts on which checks could be written. Its open market operations—the buying and selling of government securities to banks and the public—influenced the size of private banks' reserves, while the terms on which credit was available was also influenced by the interest rate charged on loans to borrowing banks.

International Finance

Internationally, the existence of central banks in the major trading nations plus the convertibility of paper money under the rules of the gold standard simplified trade between nations by simplifying international settlements. However, having an international gold standard did not mean that international settlements were exclusively made by shipping gold between central banks. Throughout the 19th century they were conducted through a specialized financial institution, the London bill market, a more sophisticated version of the centuries-old trade in bills of exchange.

Discount houses (bill brokers) in London were willing to buy bills of exchange from sellers/exporters, regardless of whether they were British or not. The advantage for the sellers was that they received money now, less the discount retained by the broker, while the broker assumed the risk that the importer, who had issued the bill in payment for goods, would not be able to pay when the bill was due for payment. On their accumulated knowledge of the creditworthiness of the world's importers and exporters, bill brokers established credit ratings. This easy liquidity of international bills of exchange encouraged the trend to the financing of most of the world's foreign trade in London, an internationally oriented financial center.

This international money market collapsed during World War I. It worked for so long as major trading nations followed the rules of the gold standard, with free currency convertibility and liberal trade policies—that is, for so long as all economies believed that they could benefit more from such policies. After the war, the gold standard was effectively abandoned, and the movement toward protection, already apparent in the 1880s, spread to affect not only trade but also currency movements, as controls were put on capital movements across national boundaries. Between the two world wars, London and New York shared dominance in international finance, but after the World War II, New York, in the only country left relatively unscathed by the war and as the financial capital of the world's strongest economy, emerged as the dominant financial center.

Business Cycles

Output rose absolutely in the 19th century, but not always steadily. There were periods of fluctuation, of longer and shorter duration, around the long-term trend of expansion. These were business cycles, which with the spread of capitalist industrialization became a systematic feature of economic development. Great Britain, the first industrialized country, was the first to experience more or less periodic fluctuations of business activity. As industrial activity spread, the effects of depressed or prosperous conditions spread from one country to another. It was increasingly difficult for any one country to isolate itself from international events, especially as more liberal trade policies linked countries together more tightly. The first true international depression hit in the years 1873 to about 1895, a period called the Great Depression until the term was taken over by the events of the 1930s.

Three major types of cycles have been identified. The shortest, from four to eight years in length, are based on adjustments made by producers to an imbalance between output and sales. If sales' growth falls short of output growth, unsold output piles up in inventories and current production plans are scaled downward until sales and output are more nearly in balance. Cycles of intermediate length, eighteen to twenty-five years, have been explained as a result of fluctuations in building activity corresponding to population changes as well as business activity. Longer cycles of between forty and sixty years, geared to fluctuations in major innovative activity, have also been suggested. Thus the early years of the 19th century just after the Napoleonic wars saw a peak of prosperity corresponding to the surge of investment in textiles and heavy industry, with depressed conditions marking the 1840s. The next peak corresponded to worldwide railroad investment, with a decline associated with the years following 1873. The third peak corresponded to the automobile and construction boom of the

1920, with a long depression following in the 1930s. A fourth peak in the 1960s corresponded to the postwar reconstruction period, the air travel revolution, and the beginnings of factory automation. When all three cycles coincide, then depressions are longer and more intense, with prosperity also lasting longer.

All cycles, however long, are rooted in fluctuations in investment activity, which, in a capitalist economy, depends on expected profitability of the proposed investment expenditure. As new innovations appear, they stimulate increased investment expenditures, which pay off in rising profits. As this continues, equally profitable new investment opportunities become scarcer and risk increases. There may also be speculation or over-investment in some areas, which results in falling profits and reduces confidence in continuing prosperity, hence investment expenditures begin to decline. Added to this is another possible squeeze on profits from the cost side. Resources in general may become scarcer as demand for them rises. This is especially true of labor, and the relative scarcity of labor at times when business expansion is occurring may result in rising wages.

Process of a Cycle

The late 1860s were generally prosperous years in all the industrial countries. In midcentury, expansion was largely due to the initial industrialization of countries other than Britain, and with the growth of a worldwide system of transportation based on steamships and the railroads, this expansion also included primary producing countries. The end of the American Civil War saw a resumption of cotton sales and the European textile industry climbed out of its depression; further expansion of the capital goods industries was aided by the use of new techniques in the steel industry (which lowered costs) and the continuation of rail building (which expanded demand); the Suez Canal was built, which lowered shipping costs, and ocean shipping in general expanded with the growth of world trade; Germany was experiencing a building boom; and rising real wages stimulated the expansion of production of consumer goods.

The crisis broke first in the United States. As a result of speculative overbuilding of railroads, and speculation in general, the finance house of Jay Cooke collapsed because it was unable to meet its immediate obligations. This led to a collapse of the New York stock market, which affected European investors in American rail companies, and many European banks shut temporarily. The mid 1870s saw a temporary drying up of new profitable investment opportunities, and this plus the crisis in the United States resulted in depressed conditions in Europe (although Great Britain was hit less severely than Germany, where, for example, sales of iron and coal dropped to half their previous levels). The problems experienced by European investors in the United States were exacerbated by failures elsewhere. For example, loans to the Spanish government turned sour, and Turkey ceased to pay interest on its loans.

From 1873 to the mid 1890s, prices in general fell, but most of this decline was due to cost reductions caused by new technical improvements especially in the heavy industries, which lowered production costs elsewhere in the economy. Agricultural prices fell most of all, but as money wages remained either constant or fell by less than the fall in prices, real wages rose. The fall in prices and profits during this period saw the beginning of the end of competitive capitalism, especially in the United States and Germany, where price fixing agreements between groups of cooperating industrialists were common.

There was a slight recovery from 1879–1882, followed by another downturn in 1882–1886, another recovery and a third slump 1890–1896. This one was triggered by the Panama Canal Company scandal and the near failure of Baring Brothers, a British finance house. Inevitably, more or less depressed conditions led to a reduc-

tion in world trade, which did not regain the peak levels of 1872–1873 until the late 1890s.

There were several implications. First, in Europe (and especially in Great Britain) at the end of the century, population was increasing at a slower rate than before while capital accumulation was faster. The combination implied that foreign investment opportunities looked better than the low profit rates that seemed to be associated with domestic investment. So from the 1880s on, Britain, France, and Germany showed more interest in colonial activity, motivated less by the colonies' trading potential (as in earlier centuries) and more by their resource potential. All three turned their attention to Africa, where five million square miles were taken; France became involved in Indochina, and Britain annexed Burma and controlled Malaya. The United States also engaged in quasi-colonial activities, especially in Central America and the Caribbean.

A second implication was that various types of cooperative agreements between producers were encouraged by falling prices and profits. To the extent that falling profits were the result of cutthroat price competition rather than a decline in demand, this type of agreement was most effective. Demand as measured by sales did fall temporarily but was overall not on a downward trend.

Finally, to a very limited extent but for the first time, governments tried to modify the downswings. The most common method was to raise the central bank's discount rate charged on funds borrowed by private banks to decrease speculation by tightening credit availability, but this was not very effective. France, with the Freycinet Plan of 1879, was the first to try to solve the unemployment problem associated with depression by introducing a public works program. However, such attempts would not be used on any meaningful scale until the 20th century, when governments in general moved from laissez faire policy to more active management of their economies.

Urbanization and Living Conditions

With industrialization in the 19th century, cities grew both in extent and in density. By the end of the century, at least half the population of the industrial countries was living in an urban area, five million alone living in the world's largest city, London, in 1881. City growth had both centralizing and decentralizing effects. On the one hand, the shift of a previously rural population into industrial employment in cities accounted for their absolute growth and increased city density. New York was a prime example of geographical constraints forcing an increase of density through the development of tenement housing for the working classes, but in all industrial cities, working class areas were marked by houses tightly packed together. On the other hand, the growing numbers and wealth of the middle classes—those in white collar and professional occupations—also encouraged an escape from deteriorating conditions. This escape led to the growth of suburban areas that never became as densely built up as the inner city and were made possible through the development of urban transportation.

The first example of urban mass transit was the horse-drawn omnibus, which permitted people to live away from their work. However, the development of urban and suburban rail lines, especially electrified ones, made it possible to live further away yet still be accessible to the industrial cities. By the mid 1890s, the electric trolley or tram and electrified underground and suburban rail lines were becoming more common in the largest cities, and by 1914, the urban motor bus was also in use. For the individual, the bicycle also made it possible to live a greater distance away from the workplace.

Costs and Benefits of Urbanization

City growth had costs and benefits. Granted that the new urban workers had few alternatives, life in the city did provide more employment opportunities than were available in the country and opened up new horizons. For example, cities provided new forms of entertainment, new shopping experiences, and the potential to acquire education. There were also costs. At the individual level, although urban wages were higher than those in the country, so were expenses. Entertainment had been free in the country, but in the city was part of a market system. Rents were high, which led to the common practice of renting space in tenements or houses to boarders, usually single men or women but often an entire family. Furthermore, life in the city precluded the cultivation of a garden. (Although as late as the 1860s, pigs freely roamed through the streets of Washington and New York.)

More important were the social costs. The new industrial cities were examples of pure laissez faire in action. Building was subject to no or minimal control, and its unplanned nature implied a deteriorating urban environment. This deterioration showed physically in increased traffic congestion, dirty streets, crumbling, overcrowded housing, air and water pollution, lack of public amenities, and noise, and was manifested in serious epidem-

---

Social costs

Costs—negative effects—imposed on society as a whole as a result of private action

---

ics that periodically swept through the cities. Industrialization produced deterioration but also produced the means to deal with it, although nothing could be done unless there was a social willingness to do something, which took a long time to appear. The first attempts to correct the most serious problems did not begin until mid-century in Europe, and until the 20th century in the United States

Among the problems were those concerned with sanitation, providing for disposal of sewage, street cleaning, and pure water supplies. In Europe, this came about after the creation of local government units or when the national government itself became involved. It took longer in the United States, where corruption and inefficiency in government plus the private profitability of slums reduced the willingness to attack urban evils. In addition, the continued massive flow of immigrants into the cities from Europe and from rural areas made the problem quantitatively larger.

Most improvements came in related areas. For example, rising real wages and the fact that most urban families were smaller than rural ones raised family income levels. Starting in Germany in the 1880s, spreading to other European countries around the turn of the century and to the United States by the 1930s, the provision of social welfare services, including sickness and accident insurance, and the introduction of retirement pensions further improved material living standards. Social reforms, especially those affecting children (the easiest to bring about) improved life qualitatively. The extension of universal, compulsory education, medical attention provided to children in school, and often the provision of school meals made children's lives better and healthier.

By the 1880s most cities had gaslights, streets were paved and cleaned of refuse, and some provision for police and fire services made them safer and more pleasant to live in. While no one could admit that life for the working classes in cities was a paradise, at least a start had been made to mitigate the worst effects of urban industrialization.

Internationalization of Capitalism

Britain had been the only industrial country at the beginning of the 19th century but was only one among many in the second half, and no longer the unchallenged industrial leader by the end. Further, although throughout the 19th century, Britain was at the center of world trade and financial arrangements, even this dominance was beginning to be challenged and would disappear in the 20th century. In midcentury, Britain produced most of the world's coal, half its iron and cotton textiles, and over half its steel, although only accounting for one third of total manufacturing capacity in 1840. Even as late as 1870, 38 percent of all manufactured goods in world trade came from Britain, but the percentage share fell after that, even though their absolute volume increased. Britain continued to dominate world trade and investment, but in an industrializing world it was inevitable that its share of world output would fall.

Britain's Relative Decline

This decline began in the 1870s, for reasons that were either beyond the control of Britain's industrialists and financiers, or due to causes specific to Britain itself. Among the inevitable causes was the rise of larger industrial competitors, chiefly the United States and Germany. Both had a larger population and a higher rate of population growth, which implied a larger labor force and potential market. This was important as the production of consumer goods for a mass market became characteristic of economic growth. Britain's population of 31.8 million in 1871 increased by 42 percent to reach 45.3 million in 1911, but Germany's population of 41 million grew 58 percent to reach 65 million in 1910, and the United States showed the fastest rate of growth of all—a 138 percent increase from 38.5 million to 91.7 million. Consequently Britain had less incentive to adopt standardization and mass production techniques that would pay off only in a large mass market. Both Germany and the United States had larger land areas and larger resources of coal and iron ore, the basic ingredients of 19th century industrialization. In particular, the United States also possessed oil resources, and oil was an important input for many of the new industries that became the growth industries of the 20th century.

Britain, in fact, made industrialization of its potential competitors possible because of adherence to free trade ideology. Skills, equipment, and finance capital were exported from Britain in large quantities after the 1840s, and while stimulating production and exports in the short run, it helped to build up competitors' domestic industries that later reduced demand for manufactured goods from Britain. It also meant that countries developing later avoided making the mistakes of the pioneer.

This illustrates one irony of capitalist competition. While the individuals involved in producing and exporting these goods profited in the short run, unless other markets elsewhere opened up, it worked against their interests in the long run. This was further intensified by most countries' retreat to protectionism after the 1870s, which closed many overseas markets. To a certain extent, Britain compensated by developing closer ties with still industrially underdeveloped, primary-producing countries, especially those within the British empire. But in the 20th century, the fastest growth occurred with trade in manufactured goods between industrial countries, and here, Britain, once the most dynamic trader, became one of the most sluggish.

Lack of dynamism also showed in industry. For example, although one of the first major uses of electricity was street lighting, British cities already had gas street lighting. There was little impetus to switch, which in turn reduced the market for lighting equipment that appeared elsewhere. In general, only when old equipment had to be scrapped and replaced were new technologies adopted. A possible explanation for this lack of dynamism late in the century was the fact that Britain was the first country to industrialize. In the early phase of industrialization, dynamic risk-taking behavior was a necessity; once the structure was in place, it was both expensive and difficult to change.

For example, although Britain pioneered many of the early developments in chemicals, dyes, electrical manufacturing, and metalworking, new methods were slow to spread and were adopted much more rapidly elsewhere. In already existing industries, it could make sense for an individual firm not to adopt a new technology if the old equipment was still workable, but if all do this, increases in capacity and productivity for the economy as a whole will be below those of other countries, especially if new enterprises adopt the latest, largest, and most efficient productive equipment. Lethargy was not general in Britain. For example, the Midlands area centered around Birmingham did switch from being the center of hardware manufacture to become important in the production of bicycles, engineering, and later, car production.

There was no shortage of talent or lack of interest in technological progress either, but there was a general lack of support. In Britain scientific curiosity remained a somewhat amateur tradition—brilliant, but not widespread. Both Germany and the United States in contrast systematically encouraged the development of scientific and technical skills that could be applied to industrial uses. In 1913, there were 60,000 students in German universities, but only 9,000 in British ones. Most of the new universities established in Britain in the 19th century did put an emphasis on science and technology, but there were too few of them with too few graduates. In addition, the earlier adoption of universal compulsory education in Germany and the United States improved general literacy. A national system of education in Britain was in place by 1870, but education was not compulsory (for ages up to ten) until 1876, and not free until 1891. By 1890, most of the northern states in the United States had a system of compulsory elementary education, and in Germany, education had been made compulsory in Prussia during the reign of Frederick the Great. In both countries, state-provided higher education was also free, which was not true in Britain until the 1940s. This meant that Britain lagged in having the educational support necessary for the application of scientific technology.

Output continued to expand, but an increasing volume of investment funds continued to flow out of Britain in search of higher returns, especially in the new colonial areas. Annual investments made abroad exceeded net capital formation within Britain itself in the 1870s, and not until the 20th century would the home market reassert its appeal.

Britain's response to this relative decline was part complacency—it is difficult to recognize when a leadership role has been lost—and partly a retreat into the safer, noncompetitive world of a new colonial empire. (The topic of this new imperialism will be covered later, as it marks a more mature phase of international capitalism.) In the mid to late 19th century, competition between countries was between industrial and newly industrializing countries. When all have become industrial, there are subtle and not so subtle ways of competing for market shares and leadership that are very different from those appropriate to the earlier phase.

Opposition to Industrialization

The Industrial Revolution had two major effects on the mass of the working population. These effects were felt first by only a few, but as industrialization spread, and as agriculture also demonstrated a tendency to become capitalist in organization, most had experienced a total transformation of their life and work by the end of the century. The first impact involved changing social relationships. One of capitalism's characteristics is a proletarianized wage labor force, a labor force economically dependent on wage income earned by working for a capitalist employer. By the late 19th century, although there were differences of degree among different countries, very few independent artisan-producers or farmers responsible for their own productive activity were left. Instead, most had a propertyless status, in which they no longer owned or had access to the means of production, but rather "sold" their labor power to the capitalist industrialist or farmer.

For this to happen, the old feudal or peasant ties had to be broken, so accompanying the development of a greater economic dependency was the political and legal emergence of the "free" man, one free to enter into a contract, voluntarily, with an employer. This also implied a freedom to enter into other agreements or associations in order to strengthen the individual's position. This type of association took much longer to develop into an effective counterbalance to an employer's economic power.

Along with this change in status also came a change in the nature of personal relationships. For so long as industrial enterprises were small, personal relationships between owner and worker were common. The owner was usually involved in every aspect of the business, and while of a different class than his employees, was of necessity intimately connected with practical operations. Once the scale of enterprise expanded, it was difficult to maintain this type of personal contact. The first obvious example was railroad construction, which involved huge gangs of manual laborers working under gang bosses. Elsewhere, a type of subcontracting was common, where only the prime worker was actually hired by the employer. This practice became much more structured and formalized, especially in the mass production industries. By the 1880s, a management and supervisory hierarchy was emerging to oversee the work of the actual producers. In this situation, impersonalization replaced the previous personal nature of relationships.

Change in the Nature of Work

The second effect resulted from the technological changes of the Industrial Revolution that involved mechanization and increased specialization. This affected workers in three ways. First, with power-driven machinery, the worker worked at the pace of the machine, in contrast to earlier times when the machine was controlled by the producer. Now the pace of work could be deliberately speeded up by the employer, as the employee no longer controlled the power source.

Second, the character of work changed. In older handicraft manufacture, the producer was typically responsible for the variety of tasks needed to produce a finished item. With the introduction of machinery, the task was broken down into its component stages, and each worker was responsible for only one stage, making work monotonous and repetitive.

Third, the effect of the deskilling of work performed under harsh conditions in the factory coupled with the lack of contacts implied the likelihood of potential conflicts between capitalists and the workers. Workers' labor was necessary for profit making, but their control over the actual production process had diminished.

Although mechanization tended to encourage labor homogenization, it was by no means complete. A minority of approximately 15 percent of the labor force were a highly skilled labor aristocracy. Such workers were found especially in the engineering industries or in specialized areas of other industries that were not yet subject to mechanization. In the mass production industries, especially those adopting assembly line techniques, there were proportionately more semi- and un-skilled workers whose skills had been absorbed by the increasing complexity of the machine they were operating.

Whether or not workers were skilled or unskilled, the loss of status associated with being a wage laborer was keenly felt, especially by first generation workers for whom such a status was new. Added to this was the concern about new conditions of work. Wages were low, but this was not of itself cause for protest, as low wages, except for specific groups at specific times and places, were general. However, periodic attempts by employers to cut wages were always resisted, although rarely successfully.

There were two particular problem areas. First, work in a factory meant that the individual no longer controlled either the work environment or the work itself. Factory discipline was harsh and rigorous. Workers had to be in the factory at starting time or lose pay, and stay until the closing bell. The machine set the pace of work and industrial accidents were frequent. There were rules against singing or talking in many factories, even were it possible to be heard over the noise of the machines. Factories themselves were poorly ventilated, a particular concern to workers in textile factories, and machines had no guards. Child labor was common in the first half of the century. Added to the problem of low wages was the common practice of using truck stores, which were company stores in which the workers' pay had to be redeemed for poor quality and overpriced goods.

Second, the worker's insecurity increased. In pre-factory production systems the worker was rarely dependent solely on a wage. In the putting out system, for example, owning a small holding meant that even during depressions, the family was not entirely destitute. Now in the new industrial cities, periods of unemployment were feared because there was no fallback mechanism available. In England after 1834, Poor Law relief was an extreme resort; in the United States, the problem was particularly acute for new immigrants, who not only were in unfamiliar cities but also usually had no extended family or kin nearby to turn to.

Most work followed a seasonal pattern, and few workers could expect year-round employment year after year; business depressions caused widespread hardship. There was no compensa-

---

Truck

A system of paying wages in goods, not money

---

tion for wages lost due to an industrial accident or sickness, and no retirement pension scheme for older workers. With low wages, it was hard, even for the labor aristocracy, to fulfill the self-help ethic prevalent in the 19th century and save enough to support them through periods of crisis. This complete dependency on a money wage marks an interlude between earlier periods, when there was community provision for those in need, and the later period, starting in Germany in the 1880s, of state-provided social services for the economically disadvantaged.

Given both loss of status and poor living and working conditions (the working masses did not really begin to share in the increased material wealth they produced until the second half of the 19th century), it is not surprising that there was opposition to industrialization in general and capitalist industrialization in particular. Although not all workers were factory workers, and thus subject to mechanization and factory discipline, loss of status and poor work conditions did affect all of the new working classes. Especially in sweated labor workshops, wages were low and conditions appalling. Even in the 20th century, when the proportion of workers in manufacturing began to decline as the service sector and white collar employment opportunities expanded, the same trends toward routinization and deskilling of work appeared. Probably the only wage workers who did not become part of a mass movement attempting to reform or improve conditions were domestic servants, who accounted for the majority of female workers and who were the lowest paid of all. However, in the 20th century, domestic service as an employment opportunity declined both relatively and absolutely.

Protest Options

Most attention is usually focused on the conditions and reactions of manufacturing workers because their situation was new and without precedent, and many were involved in protest movements. The decline in the economic status of the working classes contrasted with increasing gains in the political sphere, especially in the United States, where the Constitution had granted equal rights to all, but also in the European countries where political rights were being gradually extended. Political equality was felt to be meaningless unless accompanied by economic rights and justice. For those dissatisfied with their situation, there were three major options.

The first option was to change the system entirely and replace it. This option was based on the belief that the institution of private property caused the problem; that control over the means of production by a few profit-oriented capitalists not only doomed the majority to poor economic conditions but was also socially and humanely unjust. This was the socialist option. The second option involved accepting that a capitalist economic system is not a transitory phenomenon; therefore it is necessary to reform it or adapt it wherever possible to improve conditions. This option led to various cooperative schemes, which attempted to improve particular aspects of life, and to the labor union movement, which focused especially on improving the bargaining power of workers in their contacts with employers. The third option was to opt out of participation in the system entirely, either by becoming a self-employed farmer or by joining a cooperative commune. This option was available to only a few. Changes in farming tended to reduce the small farmer's chance of success, while the communes (except for the religious ones) were generally short-lived. The rest of this chapter will explore these three options as they appeared in the different countries covered.

Early Protest Movements

What form a working class movement will take depends on various factors, and it took a different shape in different countries at different times. When conditions were depressed, protest movements surged, because these were precisely the times at which material hardships were most acute, and the lack of support mechanisms most keenly felt. Conversely, when times were prosperous and there was less immediate pressure from material hardship, opposition to the system was muted. The introduction of new technology was another influence. When new machines or processes first displaced workers, those immediately affected suffered and opposition to a system permitting the destruction of the livelihood of so many without any immediate compensation increased. New machinery embodying new technology was always a target simply because it was very visible. Ultimately, increased productivity made possible by increased mechanization did improve living standards, which reduced workers' opposition. This was not, of course, apparent to displaced workers who were many years, if not many generations, away from benefiting from it.

A third influence on the shape of a protest movement was the legal status of worker organizations, and they were typically illegal in all countries at the beginning of an industrialization process. Under Anglo-American common law, organizations of workers were treated as criminal conspiracies interfering with the freedom to trade. In addition, and this applied also to European countries, worker organizations *per se* were seen as revolutionary and antiestablishment, and were therefore banned. In such a repressive climate, any association of necessity took the form of a secret society or of an association overtly formed for some permitted purpose but covertly concerned with organizing worker protest. The introduction of harsh repressive legislation did not stop them, because for so long as the underlying conditions were unchanged, legislation was no deterrent. Gradually, repeal of old laws, introduction of new ones and judicial interpretations made it possible for new organizations to be formed legally to represent worker interests. For example, the repeal of the English Combination Acts in 1824 permitted trade unions to engage in

collective bargaining with employers for the first time, although complete acceptance of unions took many more years.

Finally, the political status of workers was another influencing factor. If voluntary associations of workers could not achieve the desired ends, then state action was an option if the working classes had political representation. This was not the case in most countries until fairly late in the 19th century. Even where working men had the vote, as in the United States, this did not mean that policies would be adopted to serve their interests. Throughout the 19th century, the formation and activities of more economics-oriented worker organizations paralleled political activity, first to achieve more political representation for the working classes, and second to influence policymaking in their favor.

Initially, and this was common in the first half of the century although it would be less true later, workers' grievances were simply ignored. The transformation of society implied that old organizations such as the guilds had either disappeared or were no longer relevant, while new organizations were illegal and therefore suppressed. Political action also was not possible. Policymakers ignored the working classes' interests. In Britain, this was partly due to the trend toward a laissez faire ideology and the prevalent middle class ethic of self help. It was also colored by an ignorance of working class life and values—factory workers, after all, were simply "hands." In Britain, as elsewhere in Europe, there was also a perception that the working classes were all revolutionaries, eager to gain at the expense of the middle classes, and therefore revolutionary tendencies must be suppressed at all costs. In the United States, where manufacturing was minimal until the Civil War and therefore the problem was of less magnitude, the prevailing attitude was one of indifference. However, later on, political activity, especially at the state level, was more apparent, although trade union formation was slower than in Europe.

Machine Breaking: Luddism

Where there were no formal mechanisms for expressing discontent, the only outlet was either revolution (which happened in some European countries) or mass violence, often accompanied by machine breaking. The occasional revolutions in European countries in the 19th century always contained an element of economic protest by the poor. Machines, as the outward sign of the changes taking place, were a common target. Occasional machine breaking had taken place in 18th century England, usually by artisans trying to bring pressure on employers in the absence of more effective means. However, in the early years of the 19th century, such outbreaks reached a new peak, especially in the Luddite phase of 1811–

Luddism

Outbreaks of machine breaking in England

1816.[5] The timing of this outbreak occurred when the underlying grievances—the powerlessness of the working classes combined with the lack of political representation, no possibility of collective bargaining, low wages, and generally poor living conditions—were felt most acutely in the depressed years of 1811 and 1812. In those years, a commercial crisis and bad harvests resulted in unemployment and high food prices, and also sparked food riots that often degenerated into industrial sabotage.

Luddism was never an organized, coherent movement. All the workers involved in machine-breaking outbreaks, which tended to be concentrated in the textile areas of Nottinghamshire, Yorkshire, and South Lancashire, had their own particular grievances, although ultimately they were based on resistance to new capitalist industrialization. The common thread was the inability to resolve their grievances. Thus, whenever a final catalyst was present, the situation was ready for riot with machines simply a convenient target;

they were visible; the "system" that had led to the workers' new situation was not.

These early outbreaks ended when economic conditions improved after the Napoleonic Wars and when new mechanisms for expressing worker interests appeared, although scattered machine breaking continued to occur in all countries into the 20th century. While the machine breakers gained nothing from their activities—new machines and technologies continued to be introduced—they did not lose, either. They represented for the first time in the new industrial age a political challenge to authority, even if it was incoherently expressed. They gained no immediate results but showed that a large section of the population could no longer be ignored. While it would be incorrect to say that lessons were learned from the Luddite experience, during the rest of the century most working class movements did become better organized, more focused, and more effective.

Option 1: Socialist Movements

Capitalism as an economic system founded on private property resulted in a new class division where a small group of property owners achieved economic wealth and power as a result of their ability to control the labor of the propertyless. Its emergence produced a socialist reaction and competing philosophy. Socialism, both in theory and in the practices of various socialist movements, changed in character over time, although always retaining its emphasis on the evils of private property.

Ideologically, the rejection of capitalism was based on the belief that private property had resulted in a dehumanizing society. By emphasizing the private accumulation of wealth made

---

Socialism

A political theory and economic system centering around the social ownership of productive resources

---

possible by property ownership to the exclusion of other social concerns, those without property were denied the ability to realize their true human potential. Practically, the concentration of wealth in the hands of a few resulted in a polarization of wealth and poverty.

The many propertyless suffered from material deprivation as a result of their exploitation by the wealthy. To change this situation, reform was insufficient, as it merely tampered with the results of the system rather than attacking the root cause of the problem, private property. This recognition gave justification to the practical action, political or otherwise, that frequently accompanied belief in socialist theory.

Early Socialism

Early socialist thinkers suffered from an inability to produce a consistent theory that would also lead to consistent action. In France in the 1790s, the Jacobins simply expressed the hatred of the poor for the rich by revolutionary violence. Also in France, Saint-Simon, who died in 1825, attempted a more constructive course of action, but it turned out to be too vague. He saw history as a process of alternating epochs of destruction and construction, with the French Revolution of 1789 marking the last epoch of destruction. This produced an opportunity to rebuild the social order so as to produce a better life for the masses. Direction for this social order would be given by a vaguely theistic new religion, with social industry replacing private industry so that producers would now be able to control their economic affairs.

Another early French socialist was Louis Blanc, whose "stage" theory of history saw authority in politics and religion alternating between individualism (as in the Protestant Reformation) and a stage of association and fraternity (the ideals of the French Revolutionaries). In economic life, effective socialism required financing cooperative workshops so that workers them-

Hegelian philosophy
Describes how an idea (thesis) is transformed into its opposite (antithesis), with the result (synthesis) emerging as a higher form of truth

selves owned and controlled production. This idea influenced the establishment of National Workshops after the 1848 Revolution, but they failed because there was too little productive work for them to do and too many people to do it.

Both Saint-Simon and Blanc represented the utopian socialist variety of socialist thought, marked by the belief that a new environment would produce a good society and thus permit the flowering of people's innate goodness. The problem with their ideas, which is understandable given the stage of economic development reached by the French economy, was that they failed to appreciate the extent of linkages existing between all sectors of society and the important implications of private ownership of economic resources.

Marxist Socialism

It was the Germans Karl Marx and Friedrich Engels who reconciled the existing socialist views with Hegelian philosophy and gave socialist thought and practice an economic base. In so doing, they not only provided a powerful method for the analysis and critique of capitalist society, but also a much firmer justification for practical action to achieve a classless society in which private property was eliminated. Very simply, applying the Hegelian dialectic method to the study of history showed that internal contradictions in any economic system will produce conflicts that will eventually produce a new system. Capitalism is marked by private property, and private ownership of the material means of production and wealth inevitably produces its opposite in the

Dialectics
A logical practice of examining ideas to determine their validity

form of proletarian socialism. The proletariat, denied the fruits of their labor because they do not own the means of production, become increasingly impoverished. But the intense individualism and competition among capitalists in order to further their own capital accumulation also leads to a greater need for social links between them, which is at odds with the atomistic nature of capitalist production. The proletariat gains a very important role, as they can undermine the increasing fragility of the capitalist structure through combined action.

Also, production tends to increase faster than consumption, resulting in periodic and increasingly acute periods of overproduction, unemployment and falling profits. This occurs because profits are the key to continued capital accumulation, and, other things being equal, can be increased by adding new machinery to increase worker productivity and by holding wages to subsistence level. But the larger the volume of capital, the more difficult it is to prevent the rate of profit from falling. So output can be expanded but sales will not because of the deficiency of purchasing power, and crises occur because of the increasing difficulty of realizing profits. As unemployment grows worse in each succeeding crisis, eventually workers revolt to produce a classless society replacing a capitalist one.

This strand of Marxist socialism contains an element of inevitability in history: Capitalism contains the seeds of its own destruction. Practically speaking, if conditions for the propertyless are to be improved, it is not enough simply to wait around for this to happen. Although economic developments will eventually produce the classless society, it is proper to hurry it along through other means. The justification for revolutionary action comes from Marx's theory of value. Every school of economic thought has a theory of what gives things their value. The French Physiocrats thought land was the source of value because only agriculture could produce harvests larger than the quantity of seeds. After the Industrial Revolution, value theory became based on labor, which is the only input capable of producing more than is needed to replace it. Machines (capital) produce only a transformed version of their original value, but labor adds value greater than is needed to replace the labor used up. Because capitalists controlled production, they could extract the surplus value over and above the subsistence wage paid to labor as the basis of profit.

This analysis, sketched only very briefly here, leads to a view of economic justice that is the opposite of that embodied in capitalism. In capitalism, the income an economic resource receives for participating in market activity is, by definition, a fair value. But Marx showed that as only labor produces real value, only labor deserves an income. Income to property owners in the form of profits, rent, and interest simply represents the results of exploitation by property owners who control the means of production, an income resulting from ownership, not from a productive activity.

Range of Practical Socialism

In the classless socialist (and eventually communist) society that will follow the revolution all means of production are owned in common, and therefore exploitation cannot occur. Until then, the analysis provides a range of possible alternatives for producing economic justice. At one extreme, various specifically revolutionary movements called for the elimination of private property. The only successful one was the Bolsheviks' revolution in Russia in 1917, one of the least likely locations for a true socialist revolution. There were many socialist secret societies in Europe, and socialist ideas helped influence the 1848 revolutions in many countries. However, the collapse of these revolutions led to the disappearance, and in some countries continued repression, of socialist societies.

Politically, as was most apparent in those countries without a developing labor union movement, socialist groups did gain strength. By the end of the century, the German Social Democratic Party was easily the most successful one, although the first example of a true, if short-lived, specifically working class government occurred during the Paris Commune of 1871. The exceptions were in Britain and the United States In Britain, where unions by this time represented workers' interests and worked within the system, no specifically socialist party emerged. (The Independent Labor Party, established in 1893, represented workers' political interests and was only moderately socialist.) The United States never developed anything other than small socialist parties, possibly because the impact of immigration plus generally higher living standards reduced the revolutionary spirit of the working classes. In general, by the end of the century, socialist political parties had become less revolutionary and more reformist.

Moving along the spectrum of socialist alternatives, other socialist-inspired organizations were economic groups, such as labor unions. Again, there was a range of viewpoints, with one extreme calling for the abolition of private property and others attempting to improve the conditions of their members within the system. While to some degree all worker movements could be called socialist because they represent less than complete satisfaction with the capitalist system, it is important to distinguish between totally revolutionary and simply reformist movements. By the end of the century, totally revolutionary movements, calling for the complete abolition of private property and the immediate introduction of a socialist society, were very few and very small. However, reformist movements influenced by socialist ideals were more pragmatic and willing to work within the capitalist system. To the extent that overtly revolutionary goals were modified, these movements became more accepted, if not respectable.

Option 2: Adapting the System

A second option open to those who opposed capitalist industrialization and its effect on the lives of the workers was to work within the system to attempt to improve conditions. This was much more effective in terms of numbers involved and impact. It abandoned the view that capitalism was temporary, and would be replaced with a socialist system. Even if that happened, the event was so far off that it was of no practical concern to today's workers suffering in today's conditions. Therefore, the most practical thing to do was to improve conditions where improvements could be made. This could be done through direct action, collective bargaining or the establishment of new institutions specifically designed to meet particular needs of the working classes.

Three major groups of economic institutions were developed in the 19th century to do this. Some were more successful than others, such as the trade unions that bargained collectively with employers to improve conditions, and the consumer cooperatives, which bought goods in bulk for their members and so directly lowered living expenses. The producers' cooperatives were employee-owned work shops and were less successful in terms of longevity. However, in the 20th century an adapted version of these, agricultural cooperatives, which buy and sell on their members' behalf, are a significant element in many countries.

Consumer cooperative
a retail organization owned collectively by its members who share in its benefits

---

Chartism in England

Before examining these, we shall briefly look at a political attempt at reform within the system, Chartism. It failed as an organization, but is an early example of a working class reformist movement with specified goals and an organization to achieve them, unlike Luddism. The Chartist movement in England was an example of an attempt to increase political representation for the working classes, to work through politics to achieve improvements.

The first 19th century political reform bill, passed in 1832, did nothing to represent the interests of the new workers, and Parliament in the 1830s did nothing positive for the poor. Although the 1833 Factory Act was the first to regulate working conditions in factories, only a few were affected. Many more, however, were affected by the 1834 New Poor Law, which substituted harsh indoor relief for the old system, and so was a perpetual reminder to the working classes of the instability of their position. An early attempt to organize all workers for their mutual economic interest, Robert Owen's Grand National Consolidated Trades Union had failed.

So in 1836, a group of politically minded workingmen in London formed the London Working Men's Association, with the specific purpose of encouraging the reform of Parliament in order to achieve improvements for the working classes. By 1838, they listed six aims in their People's Charter. They were: annual parliaments, voting by secret ballot to replace a show of hands, universal manhood suffrage to extend the vote to the working classes, equal electoral districts to make the principle of equal representation effective, abolition of the property qualification for Members of Parliament so that workers would be able to stand for election, and payment of MPs so that those without independent means would not suffer financially by entering politics.

Support for these proposals spread from London and was particularly concentrated in industrial areas. The movement was predominantly

Chartism

Working class political movement in England, 1840s, advocating democratic social and political reforms

working class, although some of the leaders were middle class. It also attracted support from those with specialized local grievances, such as the hand loom weavers who had been displaced by power looms, skilled craftsmen who were also in the process of being displaced by machinery, and miners, whose working conditions were harsh. In addition, depressed conditions saw an increase in support, especially in the years 1838-1839, 1842, and 1847-1848. As the People's Charter received such a positive response, it was proposed that it be presented as a national petition to be adopted by Parliament. To this end, it was presented in 1839, only to be defeated by middle class interests in Parliament. With visions of revolution always present, the government announced that any protests or risings in support of the Charter would be immediately crushed.

At this point, the Chartist movement began to disintegrate, with most of the middle class sympathizers leaving, fearing potential violence. The split and defections worsened after the second petition to Parliament was rejected in 1842, followed by an outbreak of strikes and riots, which were immediately crushed. Leadership of the movement was then taken over by Fergus O'Connor, an Irish journalist who was an effective orator and publicizer of the Chartist movement but an ineffective organizer and leader. Under his leadership, a third petition was presented to Parliament in 1848. It was supposed to contain five million signatures in support of the Charter, but only contained two million, many of them forged (including that of Queen Victoria). This unseemly action completely discredited the Chartist movement and it collapsed. In addition, once prosperity returned after the mid 1840s, the economic pressures that encouraged its support lessened. Also other issues such as cooperative societies, the Ten Hour movement, and the anti-Corn Law League, which seemed to have a more direct impact on working class life as well as greater chances of being realized, attracted its supporters to their cause.

In spite of its failure, Chartism is significant because it was the first example of a working class political organization. It was ahead of its time. The middle classes' success in gaining control of Parliament, crowned by the 1832 Reform Bill, was too recent to permit the extension of political power to the workers, although the correctness of the Chartists' reform proposals was recognized. Eventually all but one of its demands, annual parliaments, were adopted: Property qualifications for MPs were dropped in 1858; the secret ballot was adopted in 1872; in 1918, MPs began to receive pay and the vote was extended to all men; while after 1885 attempts were made to equalize electoral districts.

Consumer Cooperatives

The problem with attempting a political movement to achieve desired goals is that entrenched political interests have the ability to delay change. This is also true for economic organizations established by the disadvantaged to improve conditions—the slow development of labor unions in the 19th century is an example. In both cases, the problem emerges from the fact that for so long as the disadvantaged want a share in what the advantaged have control of, which implies a smaller share for the advantaged, the advantaged have every interest in preventing this diminution.

However, an organization's chances of success are much greater if it does not present such a direct threat to vested interests. Good examples are the consumer cooperatives, which, unlike Chartism and the unions, achieved immediate success, although producers' cooperatives, which did present a threat to capitalist industrialists, were not so successful. The cooperative movement attempted to make improvements in only one area of life, the purchase of goods. It was one of the few examples of working class attempts at self-help and was also an indirect way of overcoming the failure of the movement, so far, to increase wages. Improving the terms on which goods were

bought, with money wages constant, resulted in higher real wages.

At first, cooperatives bought goods at wholesale prices and resold them to members at below-market retail prices. Very few of the early ones were successful, although many were established. In the United States, for example, about four hundred cooperatives were set up, most of them in New England, but they began to decline in the 1850s. Even when they were successful, success led to the idea of expansion, and an abandonment of the original ideas on which they were based in favor of outright capitalist ideas.

The modern cooperative movement in England took a different track, survived and expanded without losing sight of original principles. In 1844, a group of twenty-eight weavers in Rochdale (the Rochdale Pioneers) each invested £1 to set up a cooperative retail store. Where they differed from earlier attempts was by selling at retail prices competitive with private stores, but returning part of the surplus as a cash dividend to the purchasers, the size of the dividend depending on the amount of purchases made. With the initial capital, later purchases of shares by new members, and by encouraging members to leave their dividends to accumulate as shares plus the non-distributed part of the surplus, their capital grew sufficiently to establish new stores. It was also a convenient way for low-income workers to save, as the dividend or accumulated shares could be redeemed for cash. The appeal of these stores lay not only in this unique feature of their organization but also because they sold pure food—in contrast to the adulteration common elsewhere—at reasonable prices, in contrast to company-run truck stores. The movement spread, especially in northern industrial areas. By 1881, there were over half a million members, and by 1913, three million. (Anyone could shop in a coop, but only members got the advantage of receiving a dividend.)

In 1863, the North of England Cooperative Wholesale Society was set up to buy goods from manufacturers for the different retail societies that operated the retail stores. (It was renamed the Cooperative Wholesale Society in 1873.) Further expansion took place backward into manufacturing and also into services, and it owned such facilities as flour mills, ironworks, footwear factories, and the CWS Bank, one of the first specifically geared to working class depositors. It was also an early pioneer of adult education. While not originally intended to be a political organization, the Cooperative Party was established in 1917. It was officially separate from the Labour Party but worked closely with it, and its funds helped support the election of representatives who supported labor interests.

Producers' Cooperatives

Consumer cooperatives were not seen as a threat because they presented no serious challenge to established retailers when mass purchasing power was expanding. The same was not true of producers' cooperatives, whose aim was not only to cut the production costs of goods but also to undermine capitalist control of the means of production by setting up competing employee-owned workshops.

Producer cooperative

A workplace owned and operated by its workers

They were universally failures. They found it difficult to get credit from banks that were wary, understandably, of financing enterprises aimed at replacing the capitalist system. Suppliers, wholesalers, and shippers refused to do business with them, and larger, better financed capitalist competitors simply undersold them. This was a particular problem during depressions, when the larger resources of competitors enabled them to survive a price cutting war that the cooperatives could not survive. In the 20th century, European cooperative retail societies still exist, but the only examples of producer cooperatives are found in American and European agricultural cooperatives.

Labor Unions

The final example of worker organizations attempting to adapt and improve the capitalist system in the interests of the working classes is the labor union movement. Unions are a product of capitalism itself, because only in capitalism is there a permanent class of wage earners. They date from the Industrial Revolution, after the necessary preconditions for their establishment were met.

Labor union

Association of workers designed to improve their material condition

---

There are earlier examples of producer associations, but they differ from modern labor unions. For example, the medieval guilds were concerned with the wellbeing of their members, but they were associations of all producers, employers and employees. A labor union, by definition, is an association of employees only. From the 16th century on, there had been occasional organizations of journeymen (employees), but these were not successful and were only short-lived.

Two necessary preconditions, a permanent, propertyless status and freedom to form associations, are necessary for a union to exist. In addition, a third factor, technological change, also helps determine the timing of their appearance. Propertyless status for the majority of the population is a characteristic of capitalism. Unions do not appear until this is a permanent condition, which did not happen for most workers until industrialization was well under way. Because the conditions of work under capitalism involve exploitation (the property owner is motivated to increase profits by every means possible) and because of low wages and poor working conditions, workers have incentives to improve their situation. Unlike journeymen, for whom wage labor is only a temporary stage to be passed through before attaining the status of master, the permanence of a wage-earning status and the lack of alternatives make improvement crucial, because it is a lifetime status.

This alone will not result in labor union formation. What is also needed is free status, which means that workers can organize and overcome individual powerlessness by acting as a collective unit. Thus, although working conditions can be bad under any number of alternative economic systems, protest without free status results only in rebellion—as with slave rebellions in the United States, or peasant protests in Europe. Both represent sporadic protest against conditions rather than a basic, organized challenge to their status as such.

Two aspects of freedom are relevant here. First, the emergence of capitalism implies a freedom from feudal ties, that is, a freedom to become a wage worker. But although this implied a freedom from the limitations imposed by feudalism, under capitalist work conditions it did not also imply a freedom to determine one's own life; there were no alternatives to wage-labor status. In addition, given the contradiction between the wealth that the producers were producing and the little that they actually received, an attempt to divert more of this wealth to the producers was also encouraged. Second, although unions can be organized once the necessary preconditions are met, they can grow and flourish only if they have legal freedom to do so, otherwise any contract made between an employer and a union is not legally enforceable. Unions initially did not have this legal freedom and were treated as criminal conspiracies under common law. But gradually, throughout the 19th century, the growth of unions became possible.

Unions and the Labor Market

Mechanization of industry also stimulated union organizing, for two reasons. One was the initial immediate effect of job loss on those displaced by machines and the longer range effect of work deskilling and further loss of status. The initial effect was usually temporary, and a general expansion of demand and production solved the employment problem, but the second effect was permanent. Second, the transition to capitalism and mechanization was connected with greater reliance on the market mechanism. This replaced both the independent status of medieval craftsmen and the paternalism of early employers with an impersonal market mechanism regulating relationships between people. What is more, this mechanism not only treated labor (people) as just another commodity to be bought and sold in a market—which was dehumanizing and degrading—it was also unjust. It was unjust because for so long as employers have economic power, they can control not only the actual work process but also the rewards that come from participating in it. For so long as workers enter into a contract with an employer individually, the balance of power inevitably results in low rewards for them.

Thus labor unions can be seen as organizations with both moral and economic aims: to improve the status of their members and the economic rewards attached to their work. They necessarily involve modifying the free market by reducing or eliminating competition in the labor market to redress the uneven balance of power. In this sense, the growth of unions paralleled the movement to cooperation among business enterprises themselves. Both were a response to what was seen as the unpredictable working of the market mechanism.[6]

Unions' concern with the working of the labor market also helps explain the range of approaches to their goals. At one end are the purely socialist unions, whose goal is the complete elimination of labor market competition that can occur only when capitalism is replaced by socialism. At the other end are the "bread and butter" unions, whose concern is to improve material conditions for their members and do not necessarily have any overly political aims. The socialist end would be represented by French syndicalism, which aims for worker control of industry; the other extreme by American labor organizations. In between are various mixes; while socialism may be desirable as a long-run goal, the unions' immediate concern is to improve conditions now.

Political Implications

Although unions are not necessarily politically oriented, there are political implications in their goals that can lead to actual political action. As union membership grows, the existence of a large number of voters in them is an appealing target for politicians; hence directly or indirectly, unions can have political influence. In addition, many of the improvements unions seek may be better achieved through government action on the national level. Thus, while collective bargaining with an employer is the most appropriate method to influence wage rates, job opportunities, apprenticeships, working conditions, introduction of new machinery, and so on, in the 20th century government action has become recognized as best suited for issues concerned with social security such as retirement pensions and accident and sickness insurance. There is also an impetus to move directly into the political arena if, for one reason or another, collective bargaining fails or is thwarted by restrictions, preventing the attainment of desired goals.

Types of Union Organization

This is a fairly recent development and is based on a sophistication and knowledge of how the capitalist system works that early labor unions did not have. The process of the development of labor organizations in fact mirrored the changes taking place in the economy. To begin with, early organizations were formed at a time when the permanence of neither capitalism nor wage labor was recognized. So in the first half of the 19th century, organizations tended to be broad, all-encompassing ones, including employers, industrial workers, farmers—anyone who did not seem to be benefiting from the capitalist system. They often included schemes to improve these peoples' access to property resources, such as land reform, demands for cheap credit, and producers' cooperatives, for example, which would permit an escape from wage labor status. Examples of these are the Grand National Consolidated Trades Union, formed by Robert Owen in 1834 in England, and the Knights of Labor in the United States, formed in 1869 at a correspondingly early phase of American economic development.

They were short-lived, mainly because by looking back to the past they failed to deal with present realities. Once the permanence of capitalism was recognized, then new organizations accepted the situation, recognized that the interests of employers and employees did not coincide, and attempted to use the collective strength of members to improve their situation. Most of the unions at this stage were craft unions, organized by skilled workers, often cutting across industry lines. Their motivations for organizing were not only to improve their economic position but also to protect their status. Such unions recognized that while mechanization did involve a tendency toward the deskilling of work and the homogenization of labor, craft workers were not the same as semi-skilled machine operators or unskilled manual labor in general.

However, as mass production spread, it became less possible to distinguish between workers in the mass production industries, where most tended to perform the same type of work. Here, the motivation to organize was to improve conditions and strengthen bargaining power, because unlike skilled workers, they could be easily replaced. (Semiskilled workers did not have to go through an apprenticeship period.) The existing craft unions were unwilling to give up their more privileged status by admitting mass production workers, so organizations at this later stage involved industrial unionization, or unions of all workers in one particular industry.

In the 20th century, a third type of union emerged, the general union encompassing workers from different industries, partly due to the general weakening of unionism in the 20th century. This in turn was due to the increased prosperity that had filtered down to the working classes and to the shift in industrial composition away from manufacturing and toward the service sector. Manufacturing had always been the prime area for union activity. With the spread of service and white collar occupations, and regardless of actual conditions of work, union organizing became more difficult with the growth of middle class, anti-union sensibilities. The general union is thus an attempt to prevent the collapse of a union in one area by extending its coverage and increasing its potential strength. (A more complete discussion of union development in different countries will be found in chapter 19.)

Employers' Reactions to Unions

Not unexpectedly, employers opposed unionization and used every method available to prevent them forming. They fired union organizers and members and then blacklisted them, making it difficult to find employment elsewhere. Employers pressed for legislation banning or at least limiting union activity, sued unions in court for damages suffered as a result of a strike, and some even formed company unions (under the control of management) to try to prevent losing control. Frequently employers were temporarily successful, but in the long run, unions survived and grew, often being accepted by management. Although there is controversy about how much of the improvement in wages and conditions was due to actual union activity, there is no doubt that im-

provements did take place. Whether this was voluntary, inspired by the fear of union organizing, or legislated for is irrelevant; at the very least, the goals of unions were being realized.

Possibly more important was the recognition by employers, especially in the United States where unions rarely had socialist tendencies, that a stable, contented work force was important. That is, the unions' most effective weapon was the strike, the collective withdrawal of labor power. If a plant was not operating because of a strike, then no output was produced and therefore no profits made. This was even more critical in times of labor shortage when strikebreakers could not be hired. Hence there was an incentive to introduce various welfare measures and engage in collective bargaining in order to prevent the threat of a strike in the first place by avoiding conditions making it inevitable. In addition, a contented work force was a more productive work force, so although employers may have resented the extra costs incurred, this more than paid off in terms of increased productivity.

Option 3: Opting Out

The third option open to those dissatisfied with a capitalist society was simply to opt out. This was part of the utopian socialist or commune movement. The motivation for taking this option stemmed from the degradation and dehumanizing effects of capitalist industrialization. The utopians shared with the 18th century enlightenment philosophy the belief that God would not transform the world, therefore only by creating a new society now would it be possible to realize the essential goodness in people that was being destroyed by capitalism. Most were not Marxists, because they believed that desirable conditions could be created now, rather than some time after

---

Commune

A group of people living communally who share work and its rewards

the socialist revolution. All were socialist in the sense that in all of the communes that were established, there was no private property: All property was owned in common (hence the name *commune*).

American Communes

Although the earliest idea for such a utopian community can be found in Plato's *Republic*, which outlined the ideal constitution for the development of human potential, Thomas More's *Utopia*, published in 1516, provided the start of modern utopian literature and practice. Actual formation of such communities in any significant number dates from the late 18th century, peaking in the 19th, precisely when actual material conditions under capitalism were most oppressive. Most of them were based on a self-sufficient agricultural community; therefore very few were set up in Europe for the simple reason that not enough land was available for this purpose. Thus the 19th century communes were largely an American phenomenon where empty land was available, even if many of them were set up by groups of European immigrants. They were also mainly, but not exclusively, middle class, although the reason for the formation of a commune was to provide an alternative to wage labor and the conditions that made wage labor necessary.

It is difficult to tell precisely how many communes were established, but approximately one hundred were formed after 1780, most in the 19th century. Only about eleven or twelve were successful in that they lasted more than twenty-five years (a sociological generation), and even fewer lasted into the 20th century. (The shortest-lived one was Fruitlands, a commune established on fruitarian principles, which only lasted eight months—it ran into problems during the winter.) The commune movement was, of necessity, restricted as a viable option to capitalism, because they were established in a capitalist environment

hostile to their continuation. The few communes that applied their principles to industrial work found this hostility too great. Either it was difficult for them to get the necessary supplies or credit from capitalist institutions, or they were unable to sell their products in a capitalist-controlled world. If they were successful, they faced the problem that with material success came a resurgence of interest in private property, which undermined the communistic nature of the original principles. Two successful communes, Amana and Oneida, stopped being communes and became purely capitalist industrial enterprises.

But communes do have a significance because they did represent in an extreme form an alternative to a capitalist way of life. In addition, withdrawal from the world had previously been restricted to purely religious orders. The 19th century communes broadened that idea to include ordinary people. True, they were more or less withdrawn from the world, but did not follow such a specifically religious way of life as the monasteries did.

Religious Communes

Communes can be classified into two groups, religious and socialist. The best and longest-lived example of a religious community was the Shakers. The Shakers emerged in England as millennial "shaking" Quakers (hence the name) and emigrated to the United States in 1774. The parent society, Mount Lebanon, was established in 1792, and at its peak in the 1870s the Shakers had eighteen colonies with nearly five thousand members, mostly American by this time. Membership declined after that, but in 1924, there was one commune left with two hundred members. A Shaker commune was based on absolute communism. Property was held in common, and work was done to meet the needs of the community. Members were celibate, and their simple way of life was very strictly regulated (members were even told which foot to put out of bed first in the morning).

The Amana commune in Iowa was another religious commune, founded by German immigrants in 1842. It had 1,450 members in 1875. Although based on strict communist principles, it did use hired labor from outside the community, like the Oneida community founded in 1848. Oneida was heavily criticized. It was founded as a Perfectionist community and was unusual at that time for the freedom, including sexual freedom, it permitted its female members, which did not endear it to its Puritan neighbors. Oneida began as a purely agricultural society but, like Amana, later branched into manufacturing and, also like Amana, was financially successful. Both stopped being purely communist societies late in the century. Oneida transformed its industrial enterprise into a joint stock corporation, with the shares allotted to its remaining members in 1880.

Socialist Communes

Less successful than the religious-inspired communes were the socialist ones, especially those based on the ideas of Charles Fourier. Both Robert Owen and Fourier believed that the prevailing environment made people wicked and selfish, therefore establishing a new society to change that environment would bring out the good in people. This could be done on a small scale at first, but, it was hoped, the success of these communes would inspire others to follow so that eventually the entire society would be transformed.

Robert Owen established a commune in 1814 (buying Harmony, Indiana, from its owners, a Rappist commune that subsequently moved to a new area in Pennsylvania where it lasted until the late 1870s). However, Owen's New Harmony failed in 1831, mainly because it never developed a true sense of community enabling it to survive without Owen's leadership.

Fourier-inspired communes added a new element of conservatism. They were attempts not only to avoid the dangers of new capitalist industrialization but also to prevent working class revolt that would destroy civilization. Fourier believed this could be prevented by making industrial work more meaningful to the workers by enlisting the assistance of progressive capitalists. Unfortunately, such creatures, with very few exceptions, did not exist.

However, as reinterpreted in the American context, this idea was appealing to the middle class Associationists, who believed in a return to pre-capitalist, pre-Industrial Revolution days. The main aspect of their communes, about forty of them in the 1840s, was the emphasis on economic equality achieved by reforming industry in the phalanx (a reorganized community). These communes went beyond Fourier, who was mainly concerned with the workers' role in actual production to be done in a communist setting. They required that capital, labor, and talent would be entitled to equal shares in the fruits of industry. They were not true communist societies because they applied communist principles only to production. Most of them failed within a relatively short time, not only because they were too artificial but also because the fear of revolution, which was common in Europe, did not exist in the United States.

In general, utopian communities were an example of the attempt to provide an alternative way of life by creating a setting in which members are permitted to perfect themselves. Except for the religious-inspired ones, most were only short-lived, and the impetus to form new ones waned after the 1880s as the actual material conditions of life began to improve. This lessened the need, and desire, to escape from degrading conditions, which in any case was not an option open to many of the working class.

Summary

As more countries became industrialized by the late 19th century, so more people were drawn into the market system and felt the effects of capitalist industrialization. This became characterized by a tendency for enterprises to become larger in size as they adopted new, more sophisticated technologies, which also had an effect on business behavior and competition in general. The periodicity of business fluctuations also became a feature of this period, with one of the first international depressions occurring in the 1870s. Real economic fluctuations also had links to the monetary sphere, and developments in money markets included the adaptation of new forms of financial transfers that supplemented exchanges of actual currency. Currency systems themselves were increasingly based on the gold standard, which simplified international transactions.

Life in a city became a reality for much of the population by this time. Attempts to remedy some of the worst urban conditions brought about by the unplanned construction in cities also began. As increasingly large numbers of people became part of a permanent working class, so there were also attempts to deal with this situation. The most important and longest lasting was the formation of labor unions that tried to improve working conditions for their members. Other working class associations attempted to improve other aspects of life. The most significant here were the cooperative retail societies that increased their members' purchasing power. Both unions and cooperatives accepted capitalism as permanent, in contrast to the socialist reaction, which had as its goal the end of capitalism, and the utopian commune, which attempted to opt out of the system entirely.

Notes

1. One of the first enterprises to have as its sole aim the discovery of new technical innovations was Thomas Edison's laboratory in Menlo Park, set up in 1876.

2. The bicycle also had an influence on women's clothing. Heavy petticoats and long skirts made bicycling difficult; gradually heavy petticoats disappeared and hemlines became shorter.

3. The mechanism is as follows. An importer must buy gold from the central bank (which has the monopoly of holding monetary gold and foreign exchange) in order to pay the foreign exporter. The bank receives domestic paper money from the importer equal to the value of gold that is owed the exporter, and so long as it does not issue new notes, the result is a smaller domestic money supply. In reverse, any domestic exporter receiving gold from a foreign buyer will exchange it at the bank for the equivalent amount of paper money, which represents an addition to the money supply. Netting out all these exchanges results in a gold outflow/domestic money supply fall when the trade balance is adverse, and a gold inflow/domestic money supply increase when the trade balance is favorable.

4. Development of an official clearinghouse is another indication of growing sophistication in the financial system because it permits smoother linkages between independent banks and their customers. A clearinghouse makes it possible for an individual with an account at one bank to write a check to an individual with an account at a different bank. It does this by debiting or crediting the different banks' accounts with the central bank as customers' checks are presented for payment.

5. Machine breaking has been called Luddism, after Ned Ludd, one of the alleged leaders of a machine-breaking group.

6. Interestingly enough, unions in the United States were regarded as monopolies and therefore illegal under the provisions of the 1890 Sherman Antitrust Act. However, Congress had not intended to limit unions in this way, so in 1914, unions were exempted from antitrust prosecution. The argument used was that the antitrust laws were attempts to prevent

monopolization of commodity markets, and that
labor was not a commodity.

Key Concepts

Assembly line

Bimetallism

Business cycle

Central banking

Centralization of production

Chartist movement

Commune

Consumer cooperative

Craft union

Discount house

Economic dualism

Efficiency

Factory system

Fractional reserve banking

Gold Standard

Gresham's Law

Industrial union

Labor union

Liquidity

Luddism

Marxism

Mass market

Money creation

Open market operations

Paper money

Producer cooperative

Proletarian

Public utility

Reserves

Socialism

Standardization

Stock broker

Stock market

Sweated labor

Truck

Urban transit

Questions for Discussion or Essay Writing

1. Late 19th century industrialization has been described as becoming increasingly complex. How would we demonstrate that complexity?

2. How important were the "new" industries that were beginning to emerge in the late 19th century"

3. To what extent were changes in the financial sector a cause of or a result of changes in the productive sector?

4. What role did the gold standard play in the international economy?

5. What are the advantages and disadvantages of a bimetallic standard?

6. Why did central banks emerge? Were there differences in the operations of different central banks?

7. What monetary and financial problems did the United States experience in the 19th century?

8. Why has the appearance of business cycles been associated with the spread of industrial capitalism?

9. What were the urban problems emerging in the late 19th century? How were they solved?

10. What accounts for the changing shares of world output and trade in the late 19th century?

11. What is the relation between invention, innovation and economic growth?

12. What are the major differences between a peasant or artisan in a precapitalist economy and a proletarian industrial worker?

13. What trends in the nature of work can be identified in the 19th century?

14. What prerequisites must exist if employees are to form effective organizations in support of their interests?

15. Why did socialism as an alternative ideology first appear in the 19th century?

16. There were several examples of socialism in practice. What were they, and what impact did they have?

17. What impact did 19th century labor unions have on the labor market?

18. Different types of communes were set up in the United States in the 19th century. What was their impact?

For Further Reading

Dobb, Maurice. *Studies in the Development of Capitalism*. N.Y.: International Publishers, 1964.

Beecher, Jonathan. *Charles Fourier: The Visionary and his World*. Berkeley: University of California Press, 1987.

Bordo, Michael D. and Angela Redish. "Why did the Bank of Canada Emerge in 1935?" *Journal of Economic History*, XLVII:2 (June 1987): 405-417.

Cameron, Rondo, ed. *Banking and Economic Development*. N.Y.: Oxford University Press, 1972.

Cottrell, P.L. *Industrial Finance 1830–1914*. N.Y.: Methuen, 1980.

David, Paul. *Technological Choice, Innovation and Economic Growth: Essays on American and British Experience in the 19th Century*. London: Cambridge University Press, 1975.

Dykes, Sayre L. "The Establishment and Evolution of the Federal Reserve Board, 1913-23." *Federal Reserve Bulletin*, 75:4 (April 1989): 227-243.

Friedman, Milton and Anna Schwartz. *Monetary Trends in the United States and the United Kingdom 1867–1975*. National Bureau of Economic Research, 1982.

Gide, Charles. *Communist and Cooperative Colonies*. N.Y.: Thomas Crowell, 1930.

Hill, C.P. *British Economic and Social History 1700–1975*. 4th ed. Edward Arnold, 1977.

Hobsbawm, Eric J. *The Age of Capital 1848–1875*. London: Wiedenfeld & Nicholson, 1975.

James, John A. *Money and Capital Markets in Postbellum America*. Princeton: Princeton University Press, 1978.

Locke, Robert. *The End of the Practical Man: Entrepreneurship and Higher Education in Germany, France and Great Britain, 1880–1940*. Greenwich, Conn: JAI Press, 1984.

Marshall, Alfred. *Industry and Trade: A Study of Industrial Techniques and Business Organization*, New York: A.M. Kelley, 1970.

Mitchell, Wesley C. *Business Cycles: The Problem and its Setting*. N.Y.: National Bureau of Economic Research, 1930.

Morgenstern, Oskar. "Developments in the Federal Reserve System." *Harvard Business Review*, 66:4 (July 1988).

Ng, Kenneth. "Free Banking Laws and Barriers to Entry in Banking, 1838–1860." *Journal of Economic History*, XLVIII:4 (December 1988): 877-889.

Nordhoff, Charles. *The Communistic Societies of the United States*. N.Y.: Hillary House Publishers, (1875) 1961.

Ostrom, Elinor. *Governing the Commons: The Evolution of Institutions for Collective Action*. Cambridge: Cambridge University Press, 1990.

Rosenberg, Nathan. *Perspectives on Technology*. Armonk, N.Y: M.E. Sharpe, 1985.

Sabel, Charles and Jonathan Zeitlin. "Historical Alternatives to Mass Production: Politics, Markets and Technology in Nineteenth Century Industrialization." *Past & Present*, vol. 108 (August 1985): 133–176.

Thomis, Malcolm I. *The Luddites: Machine-Breaking in Regency England*. N.Y.: Schocken Books, 1970.

Ware, Norman. *The Industrial Worker 1840–1860*. Boston: Houghton Mifflin, 1924.

Chapter 18

Structural Changes I: Rise of the Modern Corporation and the Trend to Concentration

IN THE PRECEDING CHAPTER, SOME GENERAL FEATURES of capitalist economic development were discussed. The next two chapters will consider two more related features of late 19th and 20th century development. The first is the rise of the modern large corporation, which became the dominant organization controlling economic activity, not only in manufacturing but also in other areas of the economy such as finance and transportation. Competition also declined as more cooperative arrangements between firms were made. The growth of a supportive financial structure also took place.

The second development is the emergence of the labor union to act as a collective bargaining agent for its members vis à vis employers. Unionization can be seen as a reaction to industrialization, as described in the last chapter, and it can also be seen as an example of the decline of competition in the labor market mirroring the decline of competition in the production and sale of goods and services. Unions can take many forms. They can be idealistic, attempting to opt out of a wage earner status; aggressively militant, seeking to overthrow the conditions that force a wage labor status on them; or pragmatic, accept-

ing these conditions but attempting to improve the well-being of their members. The history of workers' associations gives examples of all these approaches, but by today, most have adopted the last approach. This topic will be covered in the next chapter.

Increases in the Scale of Operations

The size of the average enterprise increased between 1870 and 1900, and a larger proportion of the economy's output became concentrated in the hands of a smaller number of larger firms, a tendency that became more pronounced in the 20th century. There are two explanations for this, one technological, and one connected with the development of capitalist enterprise. Although the ideology of competitive capitalism is persuasive, forces encouraging concentration are much stronger than those leading to competition. The result is a policy issue: How to gain the greater efficiency and lower costs that may come with an increase in the size of firms without at the same time encouraging monopoly elements. The danger is that if this tendency goes unchecked, monopoly trends may undermine economic democracy and free markets. There is no easy solution to this question, and different countries have approached it in different ways.

Monopoly
A very large firm dominating its market

Technological and Profit Explanations

The technological explanation lies in the very nature of advances made in the 19th century. First, technological advances in general increase the scale of operations. For example, if a machine is improved so that it works faster or produces less waste, then a larger amount of output is generated in the same amount of time with the same labor force. Second, the introduction of new industries or new processes—chemicals and steel are good examples—were done on a large scale for sales in a large market. Both contributed to the rise of mass production industries, new and old, by the late 19th century, and both continued to be effective in the 20th century.

The second explanation lies in the nature of the search for profits, and is closely connected with capitalists' choice of technology. The size of the market determines the size of output it is profitable to produce. Theoretically, the limits of the market occur where the gains from sales are equal to the cost of making those sales. As technology increases the scale of operations, and as transportation improvements lower costs of movement, the effective size of markets becomes first regional, then national, and then international. At each stage, the producer has an incentive to adopt new technologies to take advantage of wider market areas, because this improves the profit potential.

Another incentive to adopt new technologies can also be derived from pure economic theory. Pure theory deals with the case of new methods of production lowering costs. In a perfectly com-

petitive situation where no one producer has any control over selling price, being the first to adopt a cost-reducing technique is advantageous, because the spread between cost and selling price widens, increasing profits, even if only temporarily.

A further trend that also increased the size of the individual firm became observable in the 19th century. This was diversification, where a firm in one industry expands by taking over firms in other industries, which may or may not be related. It

Table 18-1 New Products and Processes by date of introduction	
Transportation	
Wooden rails	mid 17th C
Iron rails	1767
Practical steam locomotive	1814
Dynamo	1867
Underground railway (steam)	1863
Underground deep level (electric)	1890
Electric locomotive	1879
Gasoline engine (auto)	1885
Pneumatic tire	1888
Safety bicycle	1880s
Communications	
Practical typewriter	1868
Adding machine	1888
Monotype (printing)	1885
Rotary press	1880s
Telephone	1876
Telegraph	1837, 1850
Radio	1896
Steel	
Bessemer converter	1856
Siemens-Martin open hearth process	1865
Thomas-Gilchrist basic process	1878
Micellaneous	
Dynamite	1863
Cigarette	1880s
Aspirin	1897

maintains profits if firms with offsetting prosperity cycles or those that provide inputs or markets are acquired. An example of vertical integration is United States Steel. The company expanded backward from steel making by acquiring pig iron furnaces, iron ore mines, coking companies, and coal mines, and forward into a shipping company and railway cars. It was assured a flow of raw materials and other inputs, and it controlled production costs by removing the uncertainties involved with dealing with outside suppliers. Similarly, control of retail outlets, forward integration, was important for oil companies in the 20th century that established company-owned gas stations to serve the growing numbers of motor vehicles.

Rising Fixed Costs and Monopolization Trends

Three important implications result from this trend. First, acquiring new technology usually increased the fixed costs of the firm. Fixed costs include interest expense on money borrowed to finance the new machinery or buildings which must be paid regardless of how much output the company sells. For example, railroad fixed costs, connected with acquiring land for track, laying lines, building stations, installing signals, and buying the rolling stock, amounted to two thirds of the total annual costs in the late 19th century. Such high capital costs are an entry barrier deterring potential competitors: It becomes more and more expensive for a newcomer to try to compete. However, economic concentration and growth in the size of individual enterprises is not *per se* undesirable. It may encourage lower per unit costs of production and lower prices, a larger output for more buyers as well as more choice and, in addition, may lower costs simply by ra-

Fixed costs

Costs that do not change as the output level changes

tionalizing inefficient techniques and methods. Whether it produces desirable or undesirable results depends on the behavior of companies.

The second implication is that the large firm's behavior may eliminate competition. Economies of scale (so called because as output increases, per unit costs of production fall because fixed costs are spread out over a large volume of output) permit a firm to undercut and literally wipe out its competitors. Furthermore, when demand is slack, the large firm also has an incentive to cut prices simply to keep its machines running, even if a loss results. If it does steal sales from its rivals, it can probably emerge from depressed conditions in a stronger position than before. The third implication is inevitable: Smaller competitors are

Economies of scale

Increases in a firm's scale of production that permit lower average costs

forced out of business, either through destructive price cutting or simply because a market of a given size needs fewer large producing units to satisfy its demands. This increases the tendency toward concentration and monopoly in the economy.

The problem then is that mass production involving high fixed costs can ultimately damage competition (in the economic sense). If there are fewer companies in any one area, the chance of monopoly price setting is greater. Only when enterprises are small and many is private profit making compatible with social well-being. In addition, although there is disagreement among economists on this point, the spirit of enterprise flourishes better in a more competitive environment; monopoly can make companies self-satisfied and lazy.

Furthermore, when these tendencies began to appear after 1870, first in railways, then in many of the other new industries, individual companies tried to protect themselves against the loss of profits resulting from price wars. They formed monopolistic combinations attempting to hold prices at profitable levels. These groups involved only a transfer of decision-making authority from the individual firm to the group, unlike mergers, which avoid competition by acquiring competing companies.

Advantages of the Corporate Form

Whatever the *results* of this behavior, fewer firms remained in individual or family hands. The corporation was a more effective method of organizing a large enterprise, as the railroads had shown earlier in the 19th century. For the large firm, given the expenses required to establish it, corporate status was the only practicable way of raising the equity capital required. With the development of financial institutions such as the stock market and investment banks, new sources of financial resources could be tapped more easily. Incorporation limited the individual's financial risk, especially when limited liability became common. The existence of stock markets also increased liquidity. However, owners were no longer involved in the running of companies as specialized managers took over instead.

The corporation does not itself reduce competition and is simply a legal form of organizing a company in which ownership is spread over a number of owners. What makes it different from earlier types of organization is that the corporation itself is legally separate from its owners. This is an advantage in conducting business. It is an advantage because the owners cannot be sued for what the corporation does (or does not do), and its debts cannot be paid by liquidating the property of the owners if their liability is limited: The shareholder-owner is protected from the failure of the company. This contrasts with individual or family proprietorship, where the owners and the company are one and the same, and where the owners' property can be used to pay off the company's debts. The corporate form also improves survival: Unlike the proprietorship, it does

not cease to exist when the owner dies, as ownership claims can be transferred to another owner.

However, the corporate form makes use of anticompetitive agreements easier. The shareholders are not involved personally in cases where legality is questionable. The separation of ownership from control also encourages management to take action without necessarily having the consent of all shareholders. Given the right external conditions, combinations between companies may be used to limit competition and protect prices and profits. These combinations can take many shapes. Historically, the first ones tended to be weaker and most easily suppressed or attacked, so there was a trend to the use of stronger, more effective combinations.

Pools and Cartels

The first method used was the pool, an informal agreement among a group of companies to maintain prices to stop destructive price cutting and establish market shares. Although membership in a pool is not illegal *per se* under the common law of Great Britain and the United States, it can be attacked legally if it is successful, and its members charged with combining in order to restrain trade. In addition, its legal status is weak. For example, if one member of the group believes that individual action, such as shaving price below the pool level to try to attract more sales, would be beneficial to it alone, there is nothing the other members can do to try to control the transgressor. They are unable to prosecute it for stepping out of line because that would be an admission of an attempt to restrain trade, which is illegal.

Pool
An informal anticompetitive agreement

Cartel
A formal anticompetitive agreement

Another weak form of combination is the trade association, formed by groups of companies within a particular industry. It has no power to force agreement between members, but may indirectly reduce competition. It has this effect because it provides a conduit for the dissemination of information of interest to its members (which is why they have an incentive to join), which may encourage further action. For example, if the association publicizes some firms' pricing policies others may tacitly follow along. Uniform prices result, but it is difficult to prove illegality because there is no formal agreement. Trade associations, however, have many other functions that may or may not have anti-competitive results and are perfectly legal unless they provide the basis for a more formal combination.

The cartel is a stronger version of a pool, a formal agreement establishing prices and production quotas for its members. It involves a contract between participants, so it can be upheld in a court of law if one member does not abide by the agreement if the country's legal system permits. Neither the United Kingdom nor the United States recognize the validity of the cartel; it is a combination in restraint of trade, although membership in an international cartel is excepted. Cartels are legal in Germany and have been legal in France since 1884.

Trusts and Holding Companies

Because there was opposition to monopolizing trends in the United States, a variety of other devices to extend control and limit competition were used. One was the trust, in which the participating companies retain individual ownership, but control of their operations passes into the hands of a new body, the trust. This is accomplished when the shareholders of member com-

Trust

A combination of firms designed to control production and prices

Holding company

A corporation holding the shares of other companies

panies transfer their share certificates to the trustees. The trustee controls the companies and makes sure that each acts in accordance with some agreed-on common aim. In exchange, shareholders continue to get a share of the earnings generated.

The trust form of combination ran into problems in the United States after 1880, stimulating a search for a more effective form. The result was the holding company, a new corporation created to hold the securities of the operating companies. Here, holders of shares in the "owned" companies exchanged them for a pro rata amount of shares in the holding company. Economically, there is no difference between the holding company and the trust: The operating companies still make decisions in concert with each other to avoid destructive competition. But legally there is a difference that put the holding company on uncertain ground. Common law prohibits one company from holding stock in another because of the potential for anti-competitive action, so the holding company is illegal unless legislation specifically permits it. This is why some states in the United States were pressured to pass legislation permitting corporations chartered within their borders to hold securities of others. The first to do so was New Jersey (1889, 1893), and other states soon followed. Many trusts then re-formed as holding companies. Holding companies were still not immune from attack on anti-competitive grounds, so the final stage of the search for protection against destructive competition resulted in the merger or amalgamation of rival companies.

Both the trust and the holding company are based on ownership of securities or claims to property, and both increase the nominal number of firms by one. The merger involves ownership of assets and reduces the number of firms to one as one firm acquires the property of the others, which then lose their identity as independently owned enterprises. This is the most complete form of combination. Unlike the pool or cartel, which cannot influence the internal structure and management of member companies (and may be composed of both efficient and inefficient firms), the merged company can make changes. Because one large company is created out of the component parts, only one management remains in control of decision making. Competition is reduced: Only one large company now exists where previously there had been many smaller ones. The company resulting from a merger has an incentive to close down some plants to eliminate excess capacity and use the remaining capacity more effectively to tap economies of scale. In the absence of monopolistic behavior, production is rationalized, and lower cost units permitted, but the reduction in competition often prevents translation into lower prices.

Concentration in Britain

Although they pioneered, British enterprises were slow to use the corporate form. Even in 1914, most manufacturing firms were still relatively small family firms. Only in new areas requiring large initial financing such as public utilities, iron and steel, heavy engineering, and shipbuilding, or in the "traditional" corporate areas of railway transportation and banking was the use of the corporation widespread. A few major monopolies did exist in sewing cotton, cement, wallpaper, and flat glass, but they had little impact on the economy because they were typically not in key industries. This contrasted with the United States experience, where significant core industries were monopolized.

Concentration increased after 1914, boosted by the demands and disruptions of the First World War and depressions in the early 1920s and early 1930s. Government policy also supported it, although economic ideology favored competitive capitalism. By the mid 1930s (statistics are poor for the period before 1930), this trend was well under way. While there were many workplaces in Britain, most of them employed fewer than twenty-five workers, but a tiny handful of firms (one third of one percent by number) accounted for one fifth of total employment. The disparity between the growth of a few large firms surrounded by many small ones increased: In the "average" industry, about one quarter of the work force was employed in the three largest firms, but in the most highly concentrated new industries of chemicals, engineering, vehicle manufacture, and iron and steel, the percentage rose to 40 percent or more.

In output, too, the trend to concentration was becoming clear. In 1935, 170 products were produced in industries dominated by three or fewer large firms. The 130 rail companies of 1914 had become 4 large noncompeting monopolies by 1921. In banking (which had already experienced many mergers during the 19th century), the 38 joint stock banks of 1914 had merged into 12 by 1924, although the "big five" dominated.

Most of these large undertakings resulted from mergers, and some had an international influence. For example, the domestic monopoly of J & P Coats in sewing thread also dominated foreign markets; and Lever Brothers (later called Unilever in the United States) which first began using vegetable oils in the manufacture of soap in the 1880s, owned copra mills in Australia, cotton seed mills in the United States, and soap factories in Germany and Switzerland. An international combination that later resulted in a merger occurred in the new oil industry where Shell Transportation transported oil from the Dutch West Indies, the United States, and Russia. It merged with the Netherlands Royal Dutch Company 1902–1907, and became involved in oil production in order to compete with American oil companies better.

Mergers tended to occur in waves, and the resulting companies, directly or indirectly, benefitted from government policies. Overall, four elements contributed to concentration. First, depressed conditions in the interwar years encouraged a defensive reaction to merge in an attempt to maintain profits by eliminating competition. This contrasted with experience in the United States, where merger waves tended to occur during periods of prosperity. Second, although British industry had been oriented to the international market in the 19th century, the rise of stronger industrial competitors plus the intensification of protectionism and the resulting decline of world trade in the 1930s led to a focus on the domestic market. Government policy was no longer influenced by free trade ideology at this time, and began to protect the home market from foreign competition, encouraging the growth of protected mass production industries geared to satisfying domestic demand. This was particularly important in the new auto industry, where auto makers were unable to reach the same economies of scale as United States producers. Closely related was the third element, the expansion of technologically new industries, organized on a mass production basis and relying on government support. Important here were the development of aircraft manufacture, which depended on government orders for military planes, and the growth of electrical manufacturing industries, which supplied the public monopoly of electrical power generation and distribution.

Public Sector Involvement

Finally, in both "problem" and emerging industries, public sector involvement was much greater than in the United States, and often resulted in a virtual monopoly. It was justified by the need to meet international competition, national security reasons, the desire to avoid wasteful competition in cases of "natural" monopoly, or the desire to maintain quality standards by means of the public monopoly. Hence, even as early as 1914, the British government was a part owner of the Suez Canal Company (important to national defense as well as trade by improving transportation links to the East); the Anglo-Persian Oil Company (later renamed British Petroleum, one of the few major non-United States oil producing companies, which was important not only for national prestige, but also to ensure a supply of oil controlled by British owners); the Cunard Steamship Company; and the Marconi Radio Telegraph Company (an emerging technology). The natural monopoly argument was used to justify the Post Office's acquisition of the major telephone company and also the creation of national and regional monopolies in electricity production and distribution. In the new entertainment and information industry of radio broadcasting, the four-year-old British Broadcasting Company was made into a public monopoly when it became the British Broadcasting Corporation in 1926.

Natural monopoly

A company that is large relative to the size of its market

Making private industry more efficient was another argument for greater government involvement. This meant that in many cases, amalgamations or cooperative agreements were encouraged in order to rationalize production, lower costs, and produce a stronger industry. This influenced the railway amalgamations in 1921, the iron and steel pricing agreement in 1932, and the national coal agreement in 1936, as well as various state-sponsored marketing schemes in agriculture (which covered one third of total agricultural output, including pigs, milk, potatoes, and hops).

By the end of the 1930s, the British economy, which had begun the century as one of the least concentrated economies, was one of the most concentrated. Economic disruption during the Second World War and the coming to power of a Labour Government in 1945 further encouraged concentration through nationalization of key areas of the economy, such as coal, iron and steel, road transport, and railways. Concentration was also apparent in areas of the economy not subject to direct government involvement. In the 1960s, a merger wave reduced the number of firms listed on the Stock Exchange from over 1,300 in 1961 to slightly over 900 in 1968, with over half of this activity occurring in the food, beverage, metal manufacturing, paper, and printing industries.

Concentration in Germany

Germany industrialized later than Britain, so many of its new companies were large from the start. In addition, the lack of a tradition of laissez faire and competition and government assistance implied that cooperative agreements were acceptable. Thus monopolies and cartel agreements were much more common in Germany. In 1879, there were 16 cartel agreements; by 1900, there were 300 cartels; by 1911, the number had risen to 600, to 1,000 in 1922, to 1,500 in 1925 and to 2,100 in 1930.

Use of Cartels

The basic justification for permitting cartels was the desire to preserve freedom of trade and thus the freedom of the consumer. If destructive price cutting forced firms out of operation, the resulting reduction in numbers was not beneficial and reduced the choice available to the public. Hence it was ultimately beneficial to use cartels to prevent price competition. In addition, it was also argued that if an agreement resulted in prices that covered costs, a cartel would help keep more firms in operation during periods of slack demand by preventing failure due to excessive losses. This would help prevent depressions by avoiding unemployment, and thus falling incomes and purchasing power.

Consequently, cartel agreements as a method of rationalizing competition were common, espe-

cially in important economic sectors. One of the first was made by the largest Ruhr coal producers in 1893. It ended price competition among its members, resulting in more profitable prices, and regulated production by establishing output quotas. (These aims are complementary. In general, given a certain level of demand, limiting output will produce higher prices.)

The coal cartel also dealt with competition from nonmembers in various ways. Members could charge lower prices if faced with competition from outsiders, and they bought new but unworked coal mining areas in order to eliminate the threat of future competition. A trend towards greater concentration of production in the hands of a few—which is not automatically an aim of a cartel—was also observable. Larger companies bought out smaller ones and took over their production quotas, thus the number of members was reduced.

The cartel also tried to minimize output fluctuations, remembering the declining sales of the 1870s. This was more difficult to achieve, as coal producers alone could not control demand conditions. However, cooperation with the German Steelwork Union, a combination of existing cartels formed in 1904, helped. This cartel wanted to price high enough to cover the costs associated with the large capital investment required to construct a modern steelmaking facility. If they also acquired their own coal mines to avoid purchasing from the coal cartel, they would have more control over costs. But at the same time, some coal cartel members also had an incentive to become involved in steel production to ensure a market for their coal. The result was closer ties between the two cartels, which effectively produced a mixed cartel cutting across industry lines, operating to the benefit of members of both groups.

Another raw material cartel was formed by German potash producers, who had a world monopoly in commercial potash production (potash is used mainly in fertilizers) until 1914. It was formed in the 1870s, when unregulated competition drove down prices and profits. This monopoly was broken after the First World War when the province of Alsace, where many producers were located, was ceded to France. However, an international agreement between French and German producers effectively restored a cartel agreement.

Other cartels appeared in the new chemical and electrical industries, spurred not so much by destructive price competition as by the need to recoup the high costs of starting up new enterprises in a new area and to try to control markets. By the 20th century, cooperation in the electrical industry was assured by the dominance of AEG (Allgemeine Elektrizitäts-Gessellschaft) which specialized in lighting, and Siemens-Halkse, which specialized in motors. They agreed on pricing, markets, and product specialization. Similarly, chemical companies had early combined to eliminate destructive competition, when I.G. Farbenindustrei was formed in 1926, a combination of existing combinations. This unit was also a partner in an international market sharing agreement with British and American chemical companies.

A cartel is easier to establish in an industry where there are only a few large producers, but there are other examples of cartels in industries with many producers. Their purpose was to regulate competition to encourage the survival of the members. The question of survival was also important to German banks. They were closely associated with the new companies which they had helped establish by providing investment capital, and had every interest in schemes that would protect this investment and avoid destructive competition. To this end, banks' representatives sat on corporate boards of directors, and the links between banks and industry also helped the development of cooperative agreements between companies.

Concentration in France

France did not experience as many cooperative agreements as other countries, even after cartel agreements were legalized when the law preventing companies from making price agreements was repealed in 1884. This is because mass production was less highly developed, and most companies in most industries remained relatively small and family owned. Membership in trade associations gave a greater potential for cooperative agreements. While usually intended to improve efficiency through information gathering and dissemination, they could also be used for policy making purposes.

However, there were some exceptions. The steel industry reduced competition through agreement between firms. In addition, the trend to a more concentrated economy via state intervention or ownership was also present, especially after the Second World War. Broadcasting and tobacco became state monopolies, and state ownership in steel, public utilities, railways, air transportation, postal communications, auto manufacture, banking, chemicals, oil, and computers is either complete or a significant force in the industry.

Concentration in the United States

As in Britain, use of the corporate form of organization was very slow to be adopted, but it became more common as the United States industrialized, and also paralleled the tendency to increased concentration of economic power in the economy. Even as late as 1878, only 520 manufacturing enterprises out of a total of 11,000 were corporations. They were significant because while representing barely 5 percent of the total number of manufacturing firms, this five per cent included large firms producing one third of total manufacturing output. By 1909, corporations composed 26 percent of all industrial enterprises, employed

76 percent of all wage earners, and produced 79 percent of the country's total output.

Rail Pools

Forces encouraging cooperation rather than competition emerged during periods of destructive cutthroat price competition in the search for ways to end price wars and maintain profits. Government policies and activities also offered indirect encouragement. Cooperative agreements tended to come in waves. The first was in the 1870s, a period of price warfare that affected the emerging mass production industries most, but the rail transportation industry developed the first response. Lower rates resulting from price wars obviously benefitted shippers, but they eliminated profits. So the rail companies formed pools that fixed rates and shared traffic. One of the first was a pool of three rail companies operating for fourteen years after 1870 between Chicago (an important rail terminus) and the agricultural center of Omaha. In 1877, another pool of the four main lines connecting the Ohio Valley to the East Coast was formed. These agreements raised prices and increased profits, and attracted attention. Farmers and shippers in general were strongly opposed, and a pattern in which each wave of combinations was paralleled or preceded by legal and legislative activity emerged. Among the pools formed in the late 19th century were agreements in cast iron pipes, meat packing, tobacco, and wallpaper, while a patent-sharing pool existed between General Electric and Westinghouse in the electrical equipment industry.

Trusts and Antitrust Action

Pools were a weak form of cooperation because an agreement could not be enforced on a wayward member. In addition, public opposition, state legislation, and the possibility of effective federal action against them stimulated a search for a better form of cooperation. This was the trust, emerging in the 1880s. There were trusts in the

new oil industry, sugar refining, and tobacco, for example. They could control the activities of the companies involved better, so increasing profitability. The most notorious of all trusts was the Standard Oil Company (SO), created in 1882, at which time it controlled over 90 percent of refined petroleum production.

Antitrust

Legislation concerned with the regulation of monopolies such as trusts

---

Partly because of its activities (including industrial espionage, illegal rate rebates from rail companies, and physical violence to noncooperating refiners), SO ran into opposition and legal problems at both the state and the federal level. The decade ended with the first federal legislation designed to prevent the monopolizing tendencies that were appearing in many industries, the Sherman Antitrust Act, so called because a trust was identified with a monopoly and monopolizing behavior.

While this law became the cornerstone of American legislative activity, it did not prevent increased concentration in the economy effectively. In any event, corporations began to use the holding company to avoid antitrust prosecution, which became possible once the states, led by New Jersey, permitted it. For example, the sugar trust was reorganized as a holding company in 1891, and Standard Oil dissolved itself as a trust and reorganized in 1892, with the Standard Oil Company of New Jersey created as the holding company of Standard Oil companies.

Mergers

While the holding company seemed to have solved the problems encountered by the trust, it was still open to legal attack, and some holding companies were subsequently prosecuted under the Sherman Act. Formation of new ones was discouraged, and the preferred form of combination became the merger, a combination owning property rather than securities.

The merger wave that followed at the turn of the century resulted in many large companies, including International Harvester, du Pont, United Shoe Machinery, Bethlehem Steel, Republic Iron and Steel, Allis-Chalmers, and Eastman Kodak. It also resulted in a very high degree of concentration in the affected industries. They were key industries, including the metals, machinery, chemicals, and agricultural equipment industries.

Merger

Formation of a single large company through the amalgamation of several companies

---

The timing of this merger wave depended not only on reactions to earlier forms of combination but also on financial developments, especially the presence of a stock market. A stock market helps the development of the corporate form of business organization because the corporation's shares are transferrable, and the transfer is effected through the stock market. In addition, because a company attempting to acquire the assets of another frequently issues new stock to raise the necessary financing, a rising stock market is also helpful. First, the rise reflects the willingness of purchasers to acquire new shares. Second, rising share prices mean that an acquiring company can raise the required funds without diluting its stock too much—that is, for any given amount it wishes to raise, it need issue fewer new shares if prices are rising. These conditions were present by 1897.

Between 1898 and 1902, there were 2,653 reported mergers of companies, involving a total capitalization of $6.3 billion. (As a point of reference, there were over 207,000 manufacturing firms in 1899 whose assets were valued at over $11 billion.) The result was the existence of 200 firms each with a capitalization of over $1 million,

controlling 40 percent of the production facilities of all manufacturing industry.

U.S. Steel alone, which the banking interests of J.P. Morgan acquired from Andrew Carnegie in 1901, controlled two thirds of all steel ingot capacity and 60 percent of the total steel industry. (However, it lost market share later and was never the lowest cost steel producer, probably because it grew larger than the size needed to tap economies of scale most efficiently.) Another company formed at this time was the Aluminum Company of America, which had an absolute monopoly of aluminum ingot production. Other large monopolizing companies included the American Sugar Refining Company (formerly the sugar trust) which controlled 90 percent of its market; International Harvester, which produced between 80 and 90 percent of all farm machinery; and United Shoe Machinery, which produced almost all the shoemaking equipment.

This merger wave was effectively over by 1903. Mergers had taken place in most of the areas where mass production techniques and the potential for economies of scale were present, which were highly concentrated. In addition, extensive new stock issues to finance the acquisitions had led to speculative overexpansion in the stock market. (For example, the new U.S. Steel Company was capitalized at $1.4 billion, while the actual value of its physical assets was only $700 million.) This led to an adverse reaction, the prices of shares traded on the stock market fell sharply, and a recession followed.

The 1920s, another decade of prosperity in industrial America, also saw a wave of mergers coinciding with a rising stock market. Between 1925 and 1931, over 5,000 mergers were recorded, particularly affecting second-tier companies. By 1931, the 100 largest industrial enterprises had increased their share of total manufacturing assets from 36 percent to 44 percent.

Another merger wave in the late 1960s created many conglomerate companies. The turn of the century merger wave resulted in horizontal mergers of companies at the same stage of production in the same industry. This was considered anti-competitive, because it directly reduced the number of competitors, so vertical mergers—either forwards or backwards in the same industry—

Horizontal merger

Merger of companies at the same stage of production

---

were preferred later. A conglomerate company is formed by merging companies in different industries. One of the best examples resulting from the 1960s merger wave was International Telephone and Telegraph. This company at one point owned not only its original operations in the foreign telephone equipment and service market, but also a hotel chain, an insurance company, a rental car company, a bakery company, a fiber and fabrics company, a manufacturer of alarm systems, and a

---

Vertical merger

Merger of companies in the same industry but at different stages of production

---

housing developer, becoming in the process the eighth largest industrial firm in the United States.

Effects of Larger Firms

While the merger and acquisitions route is a fast way for the individual company to grow, a larger firm is not automatically guaranteed continued profitability, although larger firms have historically done better than small ones. Economic opinion is generally opposed to most of them, both on grounds of economic equity and because they do not, *per se*, encourage economic growth, an important aim of modern economies. If mergers lead to greater market power, then markets become less competitive. Mergers do not increase employment. In fact, if duplicative facilities or excess capacity is scrapped, employment is reduced. Also, while the individual firm may believe it has made an investment by acquiring others, this is not the economic meaning of investment that expands overall productive capacity which does lead to economic growth. But the economic issue is clouded by the fact that while economic goals include growth and fairness, they also include efficiency. This produces a problem when evaluating the trend to larger scale, because if larger size produces economies of scale and the potential for lower cost production (i.e., more efficiency), it conflicts with the desire for fairness and competition. It is this problem of balancing conflicting goals that has led to differences in reaction to the growth of concentration in different countries.

Reactions to the Growth of Monopoly Elements

All countries want their economies to work well, ideally by harmonizing the private decisions of industry to produce the greatest possible social well-being. However, this is not automatic, and the mechanisms used to achieve this aim differed. Thus, while the goals of growth, stability, and economic equity are common to all, actual policies vary. Attempts to prevent monopolization and concentration have not been successful. Present day economies are significantly more concentrated than they were at the beginning of the 20th century.

One philosophy influencing government policy on monopoly derived from 19th century Classical economic theory, and was prevalent for the longest time in Great Britain. This was the belief that laissez faire and small companies operating in a free market would produce the best results. It influenced all countries, but in no case has policy actually succeeded in reversing the impetus towards greater concentration.

Great Britain

Great Britain had the longest capitalist tradition and the most clearly expressed ideology of the free market. In addition, political conflicts during Stuart times led to opposition to the monopolies granted by the Stuart kings. Both elements produced public hostility to combinations and legal and legislative action to prevent them. Under common law, and reinforced by statute law, any agreement resulting in a limitation of trade was illegal; the contract leading to such an agreement was legally unenforceable; and anyone injured by such an agreement could sue for damages. (This anti-combination bias of common law was also adopted by the United States.) In addition, adherence to free trade policies in the 19th century limited the effectiveness of any domestic attempt to monopolize, so long as foreign- made products could enter the country. This potential competition was not effective until the end of the 19th century, when the rise of foreign competition helped weaken Britain's industrial leadership. But competitive conditions did not lessen substantially because internal pressures encouraging increases in size were weak.

This changed in the 20th century. Both Germany and the United States had industrialized at a time when large scale techniques were state-of-the-art technologies, producing at low cost. In addition, tariff protection closed many former export markets to British producers. The resulting weakening of Britain's position led to a curious contradiction, although there was also a pragmatic realization that change was necessary. The result was that opposition to concentration was weaker in practice than in theory, and both industry and government encouraged agreements and amalgamations that would, it was hoped, restore Britain's industrial strength by creating internationally-competitive large companies. So most amalgamations came later in Britain than in the United States but resulted in a similar degree of concentration.

Germany

Germany did not have the same historical traditions as Britain, and combinations were accepted as both desirable and necessary. However, there was no *carte blanche* for monopolizing producers, and the two principles of social responsibility and freedom of trade remained important. The idea of social responsibility derived from the medieval guilds where both producer and consumer were protected by regulations made in their mutual interest. In order to make sure that this continued in the late 19th and 20th centuries, government supervised monopolies and combinations to encourage continuing freedom of trade. While this freedom included the ability to make a legally enforceable contract, actual court decisions did not uphold all business contracts. Only those not interfering with the public interest were permitted and thus cartels were to some extent controlled. (Because of this emphasis, cartels were common in Germany, while the common law bias against it in the United States and the United Kingdom encouraged mergers.)

In addition, large-scale enterprise under public ownership existed in Germany as in most other European countries. Most of the electricity generation and supply system, the national airline, the rail system, post office, waterways, ports, and many banks are publicly owned, while broadcasting is composed of a federally owned system and a set of provincial systems. As elsewhere, the rationale for widespread public ownership derives both from economic theory and the desire to produce more economic equity. Most publicly owned enterprises are natural monopolies, where the scale of operations necessary to produce low-cost production is so large that competition would be wasteful, duplicative, and therefore expensive. Also, because many provide essential services, it is felt that social ownership captures the gains that accrue only to a privileged few should they be in private hands.

United States

Opposition to combination and monopolizing tendencies was most pronounced in the United States. Built on a base rooted in common law, a succession of antitrust laws after 1890 and some judicial decisions were intended both to encourage the maintenance and development of competitive conditions and to prevent monopolizing trends. This was the outcome of several influences. They included the belief that competition produced beneficial results (although at the same time, belief in laissez faire encouraged the development of large enterprises and behavior that undermined the working of free markets); the strong anti-monopoly legacy of Thomas Jefferson and Andrew Jackson; and political pressures exerted by farmers, shippers, and the general public against the abuses associated with the rise of monopolistic combinations.

The first surge of protest came during the 1870s, directed against the railroad pools which were charging different rates to different groups of rail users. Rates were higher where there was no alternative form of transportation (such as water), and for farmers and shippers of agricultural products in general. Pressure from these groups, especially in agricultural areas (in the industrial East, there was generally competition between companies along most routes), led to some state laws designed to eliminate rate discrimination, but they had limited effectiveness because the states had no authority over interstate lines; only the Federal government could regulate commerce between the states.

Interstate Commerce Act

The first federal law to involve itself in the anti-monopoly movement was the Interstate Commerce Act of 1887. It required that rates charged by the railroads (the dominant form of transportation at this time) be "just and reasonable," prohibited discriminatory rates (for individuals or shipments or between places), and required that rates be published and not changed without prior notice. In order to enforce the law, the Interstate Commerce Commission (ICC) was established, but it had only limited powers that were trimmed even further by Supreme Court decisions. The ICC was supposed to oversee rates charged by the rail companies, but it was not until the first decade of the 20th century that it got the power to acquire the information it needed and set price ceilings. Ironically, by this time the railroads were beginning to face competition from road transportation, which put downward pressure on prices. Thus, by the time that the ICC was in a position to regulate the railroads effectively and prevent their abuse of monopoly power, it was no longer needed.

Meanwhile, the rise of trusts in manufacturing was also beginning to arouse opposition. Farmers opposed high rail rates, high interest rates and high prices for agricultural equipment and manufactured items in general, because their own incomes were falling as a result of declining agricultural prices. Raw materials producers found themselves selling at artificially low prices to monopolized manufacturers who could choose between suppliers and determine what price to pay. Independent manufacturers who refused to join in combinations found the trusts threatened their ability to survive.

Sherman Antitrust Act

State antitrust laws were not effective, because the operations of the trusts were rarely confined within the boundaries of any one state. Pressure for effective action at the federal level was almost overshadowed by campaigns to raise the tariff to give greater protection to domestic businesses, and to raise farm prices by increasing the coinage of silver by helping create inflationary conditions. In spite of this, and almost as an afterthought, the first federal anti-monopoly law, the Sherman Antitrust Act was passed in 1890. It had two major sections. The first made any contract or combination to restrain trade illegal; the second made attempts to monopolize illegal. Anticompetitive actions thus became federal offenses.

While seemingly all-inclusive and absolute, and providing the base on which all subsequent antitrust laws have been grounded, Sherman was not effective and legal interpretations further weakened it. Some exemptions were made deliberately. Agricultural organizations (such as cooperative marketing groups), regulated industries (which became subject to direct government supervision), some professional sports, and export cartels were exempted. Other exemptions exist as a matter of usage. They include local trades, the professions, urban services, health, education, government services and enterprises, national defense suppliers, and patent-intensive industries.

Probably application of the "rule of reason" in 1911 was the most significant modification of the Sherman Act. In that year, both the Standard Oil Company of New Jersey and the American Tobacco Company were found guilty of monopolizing *unreasonably*. In other words, a successful prosecution had to demonstrate not merely the existence of a monopoly, but prove that it had bad effects. If a monopoly could show that it was a "good" trust and did not have adverse effects on the economy, it was home free and clear. This was the ruling in the case brought against U.S. Steel in 1920. Another requirement was added later. If the monopoly were broken up into its component parts, it must be shown that no loss of economies of scale would occur. These additions weakened the application of the antitrust laws as antimonopoly tools. Between 1905 and 1920 (Theodore

Roosevelt's "trustbusting" years) almost every company with a large market share was prosecuted under the Sherman Act. However, only three were actually found guilty of being bad monopolies and broken up into smaller units: American Tobacco, Standard Oil, and du Pont. (Although du Pont was found guilty of monopolizing the gunpowder market, it was rescued when the outbreak of the First World War required its output.) In the other eight major cases, they were either acquitted outright (because they were good trusts) or required to undergo such trivial restructuring that no serious readjustment was required. Even the dissolution of the Standard Oil holding company into separate Standard Oil companies did not end the community of interests among the parts: the Rockefeller family and groups allied to it remained dominant. In addition, the importance of oil increased as the auto industry expanded.

Clayton Antitrust Act

Although the outbreak of World War I and the practical effects of the rule of reason ended any further attempts at enforcing the Sherman Act, the pre-war cases did have an impact. While legally most of the companies were cleared of being bad trusts, the evidence presented in court showed that their behavior lessened competition. The Clayton Act was therefore passed in 1914, the result of an effort to define anti-competitive acts clearly enough to be used in legal cases. It made four major points. First, it became illegal to acquire the stock or assets of competing companies, although stock purchases were still permitted for investment purposes, as in these cases the acquirer was assumed to be unable to exert control over operations.

Second, it became illegal to enter into exclusive or tying contracts. Now a manufacturer could not require a retailer to handle only his products, excluding a competitor's, or require a purchaser to buy a second product if they only wished to

Tying contract

Requirement that the purchase of one item is conditional on the purchase of a second

acquire one product. Third, it was illegal to charge different prices to different consumers for the same item unless the difference reflected genuine cost differences. This was intended to prevent the abuse of market power and prevent one company forcing another out of business by deliberately undercutting its prices. Fourth, it was illegal for one person to serve as a director on the boards of two or more large companies. This was intended to prevent nominally independent companies from acting in concert through the influence of overlapping directorates. The Clayton Act also specifically exempted labor unions from antitrust coverage, on the grounds that labor was not a commodity and that monopolization of commodity markets was the proper subject of the antitrust laws.

The Federal Trade Commission Act was also passed in 1914. It included a general clause against unfair competition, and established the Federal Trade Commission (FTC), as an independent administrative agency that overlaps slightly with the Antitrust Division of the Department of Justice, the main antitrust enforcement agency. The FTC has very limited powers and resources, and can only issue "cease and desist" orders to a company engaging in illegal practices, in effect simply telling it not to do it (whatever "it" is) again.

However, these new tools were barely used during the 1920s, and mergers and concentration both increased. Pressure for more effective action against big companies and their activities appeared during the 1930s from a new source, food retailing, which was revolutionized by the emergence of the supermarket and large food chains. Small grocers suffered from this competition, because the large food chain stores' buying power gave them an ability to negotiate bulk discounts from food processors, permitting them to under-

cut prices charged by their small competitors. The result was the passage of the Robinson-Patman Act in 1936 which effectively amended certain sections of the Clayton Act by tightening up the clauses on price discrimination. It also attempted to equalize the bargaining power of small as against large concerns.

In the same way that merger activity in the United States tended to come in waves, so enforcement of the antitrust laws also came in waves, a period of active enforcement being followed by no action. However, until recently (with the required breakup of AT&T in 1984) antitrust action has not required restructuring of large, dominant firms. This reluctance comes from the belief that efficiency gains will be small or nonexistent if size and economies of scale are correlated, that the costs of restructuring are not justified by possible benefits, that it may hinder innovation, that shareholders will see a loss of the value of their shares, and that market power is declining anyway.

In any event, the existence of antitrust laws and their enforcement has not stopped the growing dominance of big business, even where there are new technologies that do not automatically need large production facilities or large markets. Part of the explanation is that development of new technologies is a very capital-intensive undertaking. Large companies with financial resources to exploit them have an advantage. Because of the enormous outlays involved, entry barriers are effectively raised against potential new competitors. The record is on the whole mixed, but cooperation and abusive practices do seem to have been reduced.

Scientific Management

The corporation proved to be capable of dealing with the external environment, and it also encouraged the development of new ways of organizing the work process internally. By the end of the 19th century, mass production technology was used in

Scientific management

Method of organizing the work process by subdividing tasks into their component parts

some industries, becoming more widespread and more refined in the 20th. Many implications result that are also closely tied to other developments occurring at this time.

First, mass production techniques became increasingly mechanized, tending to reduce the skill requirements needed to accomplish any given task. Historically, the division of labor and mechanization dramatically increased productivity for several reasons, as Adam Smith first noted in *The Wealth of Nations*. First, if each worker learns only one task, it shortens learning time, enabling more time to be spent actually producing something saleable. Second, another time saving occurs because the worker does not have to switch between tasks. Third, there is a saving on materials. Learning to do anything involves some necessary waste and spoilage of materials, but if only one task is learned, spoilage can be minimized. Fourth, if frequent repetition is involved, the worker can accomplish the task faster as dexterity increases. Fifth, specialization can lead to innovation in tools and equipment. Because the worker's entire attention is devoted to one particular task, it encourages the development of ideas about how to improve the way work is done.

Once the task has been broken down into its component parts, each involving a simple mechanical movement, it is then easier to mechanize; machines do simple repetitive movements faster and more accurately than humans. Then people with a wide variety of specialized skills are no longer needed; at the extreme, all that is required is a machine tender. In any event, skill requirements became fewer, and in any one industry, fewer grades of labor were needed, in contrast to artisan techniques of production. In the 20th century, office functions have undergone a similar routinization. Paperwork tasks have become in-

creasingly mechanized and power driven: a good example of office machinery that has become highly sophisticated is the typewriter. Office work has also become fragmented. The typical office worker today rarely has to accomplish the range of tasks that an early 20th century office worker did.

The employer can then hire semi- or un-skilled workers who need go through only a short training period and who are paid lower wages, which increases profits. Many workers feel they have lost status by becoming a wage worker, and because work has become monotonous and dehumanized, it no longer uses all the individual's creative potential. Hence the development of organizations attempting to re-exert control by workers over the work process. The problem of dehumanized work remains important in the 20th century, and a variety of approaches have been suggested to overcome it. How can organizations and work systems that provide for society's needs (the output and productivity issue) as well as for the individual's needs (how to tap and satisfy people's innate creativity) be developed?.

The second development involves the expansion of plant size associated with the increase in the scale of operations; in contrast to early factories, thousands of employees may be located in any one plant. It can be rational and efficient to bring large numbers of workers together in one place from the engineering point of view. But there are also costs involved that do not appear on the company's balance sheet, costs borne by individuals or society. These include the cost of travel time to a workplace that is increasingly distant from the home as the number of employees increases, and the costs of building roads or transport facilities, which tend to be paid by society as a whole.

Development of a Management Hierarchy

Third, and becoming especially apparent by the end of the 19th century, management hierarchies develop. Integrated corporations need coordination of all the different components involved with running the company and producing its output(s). Raw materials and semifinished goods must be in the right places at the right times, flows of goods-in-process to the different parts of the plant have to be organized, new machines acquired, and goods transported to selling places or the customer. These are just a few of the functions that need to be accomplished.

Management increasingly takes over the intellectual part of the producer's task, as well as fulfilling the new ones involved with the increasing scale and complexity of larger production units. This is the final stage of the development of the work process. To recap, in medieval times, the producer was responsible for all aspects of the job: its conception, accomplishment, and sale. The merchant-capitalist was the first to separate the production of something from its marketing. The organization of the factory reduced the production part from a complex whole to a fragment. The final stage involves the separation of the

Figure 18.1   When office jobs first began to expand, they were predominantly filled by men. (Courtesy of the Museum of the City of New York)

conception of, and therefore control over, the task from the worker, who becomes simply a human adjunct to the machine.

Frederick Taylor's Standardization

That this is possible owes much to the scientific management movement associated with Frederick Taylor and Frank Gilbreth. While few plants actually adopted this system in its entirety, it was both practically and ideologically influential. Practically, scientific management made it possible for management to control the "brainpower" part of the worker's task. Ideologically, it helped justify the development of a managerial hierarchy.

Taylor realized that mechanization and the division of labor did not necessarily produce maximum output at the lowest cost. He studied all the different operations involved in production, selected the fastest way of accomplishing any given function (which involved eliminating inefficient movements) and then recombined the operations into an efficient series. This series became the "standard" method of performing a particular task, that would then be taught to the workers. Management took on a new role: To acquire the traditional knowledge of workers, classify it and reduce it to a set of rules and laws that then became the standard method. In other words, management did the brainwork and was responsible for transmitting it and supervising the workers, intensifying work deskilling in the process. Management engineers absorbed part of the functions of the skilled craftsman who could then be replaced by lower skilled workers. Responsibility of supervision, coordination, and motivation rested with management, leaving the worker with less control over the job.

There is a further implication. The logic of Taylor's system was that work could be measured, therefore establishing the time needed to accomplish it. Then the pay for any particular job could be computed according to how much work was done and how long it took to do, to provide an unambiguous method of establishing wage rates independent of collective bargaining between employer and employees. It could be used to break unions by establishing a technological determinism to wages. It was precisely this aspect that met opposition from employees and their unions by removing a role for collective associations and collective bargaining over a wide range of work-related issues.

Taylor's method did not in fact produce the labor harmony he thought it would. It was seen as yet another way to accomplish work speedups and reduce wages, and threatened a breakdown of collective bargaining. This ties in with the ideological aspect, which was that management now had a justification for existence: controlling the labor force and the work process. When companies were owned and managed by their founders, their right to management functions was acceptable. But with the corporation, and the separation of the management from ownership, this justification disappeared because the managers were not the owners of the "capital" factor of production. However, the idea of organization based on management superiority in conceptualizing, coordinating, and supervising work justified the development of a management hierarchy, and was a very persuasive idea also supported by Social Darwinists.

Growth of Women's Clerical Employment

The development of management hierarchies also had an impact on women's employment, including middle class women. Lower class women had always been much more likely to work than middle class women. (In fact, the "traditional"—but never absolutely accurate—ideal of the proper place for women being in the home applied only to middle class and leisured upper class women.) In the United States, black women had always worked, before as well as after emancipation, just like black men. Most women who worked in the

19th century in all countries were domestic servants or agricultural laborers, the latter often being unpaid and therefore not appearing in official counts of the labor force. (It is difficult to visualize the expansion of new settlements and family farming in the American West occurring without the labor of women.)

As manufacturing expanded, a significant proportion of its labor force was female, for three major reasons. First, given the generally patriarchal structure of society, women were paid less than men, which was important to factory owners who also saw women as a more docile labor force than men. Second, and closely associated with this, factory work was often non-craftsman work which had not previously involved women to any significant degree. The expansion of factories utilized first the skills women already possessed such as spinning, or required fewer skills than existing technologies, without immediately threatening the jobs men were doing. So women were highly in demand as a new supply of labor. Third, practical necessity made it imperative for most lower class women to work: A single wage was insufficient to maintain an entire family. This became more relevant as traditionally male jobs disappeared, were deskilled or accompanied by wage cuts.

With 19th century economic development, there was an increasing demand for more services in general and socially provided services in particular. This opened up new areas of employment, some of which even provided new opportunities for middle class women. For example, the provision of public education increased the demand for teachers, many of whom were women; greater attention to health care led to an increased demand for nurses; expansion of retail shops expanded the opportunities for women to work as shop assistants.

But the most dramatic expansion of women's employment, both absolutely and as a percentage of the labor force, came in clerical employment, and is closely associated with the development of a managerial hierarchy. Managers were men, and they made decisions that required an increasingly large army of clerical subordinates to manipulate the expansion of paper work that paralleled the production of goods and services. To begin with, these office functions were performed by men, but—as became obvious in the 20th century—women took them over. Today, typing, stenography, and other secretarial functions are almost exclusively "women's work," and account for the largest single occupational category for working women.

Development of a Financial Structure

Growth of corporate firms in the late 19th century was assisted by the parallel growth and increasing sophistication of financial institutions and markets. Money and its movement had not played too important a role in precapitalist economies simply because in nonmarket economies, money and monetary values did not dominate people's lives. In these economies, there were relatively few questions relating to money and financial institutions. One of the most important was how much coinage to produce; another related to money lending.

Types of Banks

The supply of money and the provision of credit became much more important once market relationships connected with the spread of capitalism became more common. As we have already seen, central banks appeared to issue the nation's money supply and exercise general control over monetary conditions. They are not primarily profit-oriented. Profit-making banks tended to specialize, and two broad categories of banks, commercial and investment, or industrial, banks, can be distinguished. Commercial banks undertook the traditional banking functions of providing safe places for customers' deposits, making loans, and, in the 19th century, of providing check-clearing facilities. They were distinguished from investment banks by making short-term, self-liquidating loans to business as well as mortgage loans. Investment banks, on the other hand, made long-term financing available to business, and often owned the stocks or bonds of companies.

In England, most commercial banks became joint stock banks after 1825 and showed a tendency to merge before industrial companies did. This meant that a few large banks, operating many branches across the country, dominated commercial banking. Although a trend to concentration was obvious in the United States in industry, it was not so apparent in banking because most banks were chartered to operate in only one state, and limits on the number of branches they could own further encouraged a proliferation of banks. Because banks can extend credit, within the limits established by the central bank, they have a powerful influence in a money-using economy.

Investment banks do not deal with retail customers but instead provide long-term financing to new or expanding enterprises, acting either as an intermediary between borrower and suppliers of funds, or on their own account. For example, they can arrange to underwrite (agree to provide a market for) new equity shares of a company, or find lenders willing to provide credit by buying company bonds (debt). Alternatively, the bank itself can provide financing, thus ending up as part-owner or creditor of the company. Such banks originated in the family-owned banks of Western Europe, and were important in providing loans for governments. Their role expanded with the rise of large new industries with large capital requirements, such as railways. This was particularly relevant for late industrializing countries that could not tap an already-accumulated pool of financial resources, and investment banks were more important in these countries than in Britain. In the 20th century, there has often been

a merging of commercial and investment functions with the rise of mixed- or full-service banks. Overlap is particularly clear with business operations: A full service bank can provide short term working capital (like a commercial bank) as well as long-term capital.

Development of Stock Markets

As larger companies became more common, most were or became joint stock corporations, which was possible only if corporate securities could be bought and sold in specialized stock markets. Such markets helped mobilize the capital needed for the growth of large companies. Stock markets made it possible to issue new shares to provide financing for companies, and increased the liquidity of individual shareholdings. That is, one feature of the joint stock company is the ability to transfer ownership shares from one to another, and the existence of an organized market makes it easier for an individual to exchange shares for cash or acquire new shares.

While many of the activities connected with stock markets were beneficial, there was also the potential for abuse. Unlike family-owned firms or partnerships whose owners were closely involved with the actual management of their companies, investors in corporate securities were rarely interested in management. They provided funds (and the fact that they could is an indication of rising income levels and the existence of large sums of money not needed for everyday needs in the hands of some of the population), but company management frequently acted in its own interests, at the expense of shareholders. This could be done by speculating in stocks, watering stock, issuing phony certificates for nonexistent companies, and so on. Often, such abusive practices undermined confidence in the stability (and ethics) of a system built on the widespread dominance of money. Consequently, stock market panics resulted as shareholders tried to unload their shares before prices fell, which automatically produced the very fall they were trying to avoid.

In spite of that, financial markets did develop into a major mechanism controlling modern economies. Because they provide credit and financing, funding both new ventures and expansion, they are involved in the existence and performance of nonfinancial companies. They can thus determine which enterprises start, succeed, or fail by providing or withholding finances; they can influence the way management operates because of this power. On the individual level, they can also influence who gains or loses personal wealth as a result of their decisions. Because of the profit motive and the desire to lessen risk, the development of a sophisticated financial structure was closely connected with the increase in concentration in the economy. That is, to put it in the simplest terms, loans to large companies that are already established and have some market power are less risky than loans to smaller, newer companies. Larger companies have easier access to the financial resources that can help them grow larger, and in turn, only the largest finance houses can provide funding on the increasingly large scale needed. So while all firms have close ties to their major sources of finance—banks, investment houses, underwriters, and so on—links between larger banks and larger firms tend to be more pervasive. Because this tends to reduce support to smaller firms, it is anticompetitive and provides another explanation for the increasing concentration of the economy.

Summary

This chapter has focused on the emergence of the modern corporation and the development of a more concentrated structure that characterizes modern economies. Socialist economies are concentrated too, but while the technological incentive is common to both capitalist and socialist economies, the profit motive is missing from the latter.

Increasing scale and complexity of operations had two important implications, one external and one internal. Externally, because a capitalist business is profit-oriented, there was a strong incentive for companies to grow larger in order to exert market power that could accomplish the profit goal more easily, and/or come to an agreement with rivals that made it easier for all of them to attain this goal. This may involve various types of behavior such as price fixing or market sharing, and various mechanisms could be used. Internally, growth of companies implies a need to organize production in order to control costs. This was complicated by the fact that any one company includes many different production processes, using a variety of raw or semi-finished inputs, and employing a labor force possessing different degrees of skill. A simple example of a one-product firm using a simple one-step production method is totally inadequate to explain the internal organization of the company and its output. Efforts to deal with this increasing complexity involved the expansion of the management function, and the increasing specialization of managers occurred as the work force was increasingly homogenized. The idea of "rationalizing" work also showed the influence of market relationships. Here, the idea was that if the work task can be precisely defined and measured, its value could be unambiguously measured. Then rewards for work would no longer be dependent on tradition, market power, or any non-economic factor.

None of this growth could have taken place without a parallel growth of the financial structure. Modern economies produce goods and services for sale in a market, thus as markets become widespread, the financial and monetary aspects must also develop to permit and encourage it.

Key Concepts

Antitrust

Cartel

Conglomerate

Corporation

Economies of Scale

Fixed costs

Holding company

Horizontal integration

Management structure

Merger

Natural monopoly

Pool

Price competition

Scientific Management

Trust

Vertical integration

Questions for Discussion and Essay Writing

1. Why does technological progress tend to increase the scale of operations of firms?

2. How did companies react to the changes in the economic environment of the late 19th century?

3. Discuss the advantages and disadvantages of different types of anticompetitive agreement emerging in the late 19th century.

4. In what ways was the emergence of a more concentrated economy encouraged in Britain in the 20th century? What were the results?

5. Why were cartels more widely used in Germany than elsewhere? What was their economic impact?

6. Why was the formation of rail pools opposed?

7. In what ways did different countries deal with the trend to monopolization and concentration?

8. Was antitrust policy effective in the United States?

9. Why were corporate managers so interested in Scientific Management?

For Further Reading

Berle, Adolf A. Jr. and Gardiner C. Means, *The Modern Corporation and Private Property*, N.Y.: Macmillan 1932.

Alfred D. Chandler, Jr. *The Visible Hand: The Managerial Revolution in American Business*, Cambridge, Mass: Harvard University Press, 1977.

Davis, Lance. "The Capital Markets and Industrial Concentration in the United States and the United Kingdom: A Comparative Study." *Economic History Review* (1966): 255–272.

Davis, Louis E. and James C. Taylor, eds. *Design of Jobs,* Harmondsworth: Penguin, 1972.

Goldin, Claudia. *Understanding the Gender Gap: An Economic History of American Women*, New York: Oxford University Press, 1981.

Haber, Stephen H. "Industrial Concentration and the Capital Markets: A Comparative Study of Brazil, Mexico and the United States, 1830–1930." *Journal of Economic History*, 51:3 (September, 1991): 559–580.

Hoxie, Robert F. *Scientific Management and Labor*, N.Y.: Augustus Kelley (1915) 1966.

Lamoreaux, Naomi. *The Great Merger Movement in American Business, 1895–1904.* Cambridge: Cambridge University Press, 1985.

Nadworny, Milton J. *Scientific Management and the Unions 1900–1932: A Historical Analysis*, Cambridge: Cambridge University Press, 1955.

Nelson, Ralph. *Merger Movements in American Industry, 1895–1956.* Princeton: Princeton University Press, 1959.

O'Brien, Anthony Patrick. "Factory Size, Economies of Scale and the Great Merger Wave of 1898–1902." *Journal of Economic History*, XLVIII:3 (September ,1988),: 639–649.

Parker, William N. *Europe, America and the Wider World: Essays on the Economic History of Western Capitalism.* Cambridge: Cambridge University Press, 1984–1991.

Payne, P.L. "The Emergence of the Large-Scale Company in Great Britain, 1870–1914." *Economic History Review* (1967): 517–542.

Reid, Samuel Richardson. *The New Industrial Order*, N.Y.: McGraw Hill 1976.

Rosovsky, Henry, ed. *Industrialization in Two Systems.* New York: Wiley, 1966.

Rotella, Elyce J. *From Home to Office: United States Women at Work, 1870–1930.* AnnArbor: University of Michigan Research Press 1981.

Tilly, Richard. "Mergers, External Growth and Finance in the Development of Large Scale Enterprise in Germany, 1880–1913." *Journal of Economic History* (September 1982): 629–655.

Chapter 19

Structural Changes II: Creation of a Permanent Wage Labor Force

Labor Unions and the Labor Force

If labor unions are to appear and survive, two essential preconditions must be met. First, the labor force must be composed of permanent wage workers. If it is not, workers have little incentive to organize in order to improve their condition because they know their status is temporary. Second, such organizations must be legal. Both these preconditions were met in the 19th century, although the exact timing varied in different countries. However, while industrial capitalism gave birth to labor organizations, the first true unions were not formed by industrial factory workers. The first were protective associations formed by craftsmen-artisans trying to protect their status and livelihood from the competition of factory-produced output and machine technology. They were not successful, but the idea of collective action persisted. Then instead of trying to turn the tide back and prevent change, labor organizations accepted the permanence of a capitalist economic system. So the purpose of collective action became to work within the system and improve wages and working conditions—important aims once employee status was lifelong. [1]

Formation of labor groups represents action by large numbers of ordinary people trying to overcome their individual powerlessness in a large, impersonal economic system. They express both hopes and fears: Hope of improving their situation, fears of the changes that affect their lives but over which they have little control. Labor organizations did not make steady progress. They faced hostility from most employers who were often supported by the government, and could not count on fair treatment from the legal system. In addition, the working class was not a homogeneous mass (as was recognized in the 19th century when it was referred to in the plural as "the working classes"), and both regional and industrial differences delayed the development of a common working class consciousness. Even when these were overcome by transportation developments and the spread of machine technology, which reduced skill differences, national differences between immigrant groups and racial differences between whites and blacks continued to slow down a unionization movement in the United States.

Collective bargaining was one of the major mechanisms used to reach union aims. Presenting a united front could overcome the individual worker's powerlessness, who otherwise was more easily subject to the employer's demands. The major weapon was the strike, the collective withdrawal of labor power, then seen as the only weapon for exerting pressure on employers who needed the workers to run factories and workplaces. Especially in the early stages of capitalism, few other options were open to workers for expressing their interests, and only much later did more become available. However, the strike was used relatively rarely, and then only as a last resort.

Common Elements of Unions

While each labor movement had different characteristics in different countries, there are some common elements. The very first stage of development (covered more fully in Chapter 17) was the recognition of changes that upset the traditional order. At first, it was thought to be temporary; it was difficult for displaced workers to see capitalism as a permanent phenomenon. Labor organizations at this time were idealistic: They either looked backward to a return to simple agrarian or artisan ways of life, or sideways, with schemes to help people avoid a permanent wage-labor status.

Then true unions, in the form of craft unions, emerged. They were associations of the craftsmen who were most threatened by new technology and who were therefore trying to protect themselves. Usually formed on a local basis, they were unlike the previous all-inclusive organizations, and were restricted to practitioners of one craft. As transportation improvements broke down local and regional barriers and encouraged the formation of a national market, links between these locals grew. So forming national unions, which united workers in one particular craft or trade, was the next step. Nationals were either created by amalgamating existing local unions or started

from scratch with local branches representing the interests of local workers.

The linkages between changes in industrial capitalism and labor movements became clearer in the next stage of industrial unionism. The development of machine technology and the increasing size of plants both reduced the different types of work being done and increased the number of employees working at any one location. At the same time, the distance between workers and employer widened, and the greater economic power of a smaller number of capitalist employers tipped the balance of power even further toward employers. Craft unions did not organize the growing numbers of semiskilled workers who did not fit into a traditional craft category, which encouraged the creation of industrial unions including all workers in a particular industry regardless of type of work done.

A final stage appeared early in the 20th century. As corporations grew larger by merging, they often also diversified and merged with other companies in completely different industries. Similarly, a trend toward a general union was noted—a union with a membership not restricted to one particular craft or industry. To some extent, this was a reaction to two developments. On the one hand, union membership, after peaking in the 1950s, has declined since then, and a union had an incentive to expand organizing outside its original area to maintain membership. On the other, continuing industrial changes have altered the structure of industry. This means that some industries and occupations, especially in manufacturing, are no longer major employers, while new industries and occupations have appeared that do not fit into the traditional pattern of unionization. However, on the whole, unions have been slow to meet the challenges posed by continuing economic changes.

Craft union

Association of workers sharing a specific skill

General union

Association of workers from different industries and crafts

A final common characteristic is that, to a greater or lesser extent, labor organizations have both an industrial and political aspect. That is, although a labor union is primarily concerned with improving material conditions for its members by collective bargaining with employers, some goals can also be attained through state action. Given the large numbers of potential voters in unions, they could exercise political leverage to influence policy making. This can be important in the area of social reform or legislation that has a direct impact on the conditions of life of the mass of the population.

Collective bargaining

Negotiations between an employer and an employee organization acting on behalf of its members

Politics and Unions

This linkage had different results in different countries. American labor unions have shown the least inclination to become politically involved, while European unions have been much more closely associated with a political party representing labor's interests. Although some early

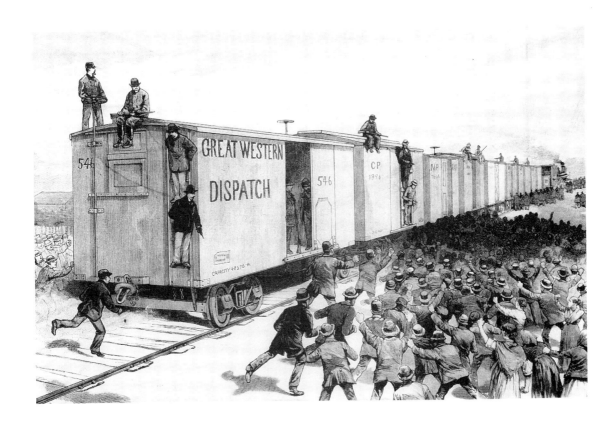

Figure 19.1 Disruption of transportation by a strike was greatly feared by rail companies. Shown here are armed guards on a train surrounded by striking workers in East St. Louis. (First appeared in *Leslie's Illustrated*, April 1886. Courtesy of the Tamiment Institute Library, New York University)

American organizations did have specifically political aims, the permanent unions developed in the United States after the 1880s disavowed such links and became what have been called "business unions." This means that they are concerned with purely economic concerns: wages, working conditions, fringe benefits, job security, and so on, using collective bargaining. In Europe, links between parties and unions are closer, although there are important distinctions between different countries. In Britain, the political party representing labor's interest, the Labour Party, emerged from the union movement itself. Its inclination is mildly socialist, and even when the

---

Business union

A union concerned only with the material welfare of its members

---

Labour Party was in power, no attempts were made to eliminate capitalism. British unions never became identified with the State, preferring to retain their freedom of action in economic affairs. This follows two important strands of thinking. On the one hand, socialism in Britain has been of the gradualist type, working within a long-established Parliamentary tradition rather than adopting a revolutionary or direct action approach. On the other hand, unions have guarded their status as voluntary associations bargaining collectively on their members' behalf as an effective safeguard against centralizing tendencies. Strangely enough, while British unions do have much stronger links with a political party than their American equivalents, they are much freer from state intervention than in the more laissez-faire, anti-union United States. As will become clear later, the American labor movement has been subject to much more legislation limiting their activity.

It was very different in Germany. In contrast to the British experience, and influenced both by the later start of industrialization and the limits imposed by repressive policies in the 19th century, the union movement was the creation of the Socialist movement itself. Germany has also been dramatically affected by wars and preparation for wars. Modern unionism in Germany is a development of the post-World War II era and does not show an unbroken tradition dating back to the 19th century. The French labor movement is also very different. In France, the traditions of syndicalism—the attempt to introduce socialist economic relations by direct action rather than through Parliamentary means—remained strong, and the labor movement, while socialist in inclination, has in consequence a very different appearance. Both France and Germany have a dual labor movement: Some unions are openly socialist, and they coexist with unions formed on a competing religious basis.

England: Unions Before 1851

In medieval times, guilds regulated wages, prices, quality of work and other aspects of life. Guilds were not unions because they included both masters and journeymen. In the 16th century, Parliament also became involved in regulating wages when it passed the Statute of Artificers in 1563, which gave local justices of the peace a role in setting wages. However, this type of paternalism broke down late in the 17th century with the spread of production not regulated by guilds. Guilds declined because of the introduction of new technology and capitalist types of business organization. Now, becoming a master craftsman-producer took a larger amount of capital. When selling was separated from production, as in the putting-out system and also in some handicraft industries, the old pattern of life was disturbed.

Consequently, it was increasingly difficult for the former journeymen-artisans to become independent master-craftsmen, and they became instead employees working for a "small master" whose output was sold by a merchant. The employee had lost status while the master's functions were reduced. The master-employers were also caught in a profit squeeze that intensified later with the spread of competition from factory production. The squeeze occurred because they were no longer responsible for selling, so they could not set sales prices, forcing them to increase pressure on journeymen, frequently by cutting wages.

Early Organizations

In the 17th and 18th centuries journeymen-workers in some occupations set up trade clubs. They were mainly social organizations, often with benefit features (such as sickness or burial benefits) that filled part of the gap left by the decline of the guilds. They could also be used to try to protect those rights and privileges previously granted either by the guilds or by Parliament, which made them begin to look like unions. Attempts to regulate work often took the form of restricting the number of apprentices in order to keep the number of workers scarce and wages high, and wage cuts were opposed directly by withholding labor. These organizations were conservative and traditional; they wanted to maintain the status and standard of living of the more skilled artisans during a time of economic change.

Although in their more unionlike form they were illegal under common law (by acting collectively and withholding labor, the workers were a "combination in restraint of trade"), many did exist and were difficult to suppress. Small employers needed their workers' cooperation, and as they too were under pressure, there was often a community of interests facing the merchant capitalists. Not all employers were sympathetic, and it was probably the fact that some associations *were* successful that opposition to them increased at the end of the 18th century. In addition, this period saw revolution in France, and fears of revolution and the upset of established interests in England also helped contribute to hostility to them.

Opposition to Early Organizations

In any event, such associations were attacked by the Combination Acts. The first, passed in 1799, forbade formation of any group (combination) of workers trying to reduce hours or increase wages. The second, passed in 1800, provided penalties and speeded up court procedures. To a large extent, these Acts were symbolic rather than effective, and it could easily be argued that their existence made the situation worse, for several reasons. First, the existence of legislation did nothing to deal with the underlying economic conditions that led to group formations, so they continued to be formed. However, because they were illegal, many were formed as secret societies and, because they were unable to express their grievances openly, violence was undoubtedly encouraged. This was particularly true in those areas where large numbers of people were most dependent on employers—the lower skilled workers or those whose manual work could be done by machines—and the following years saw an increase in sporadic acts of violence. Second, while combinations of employers were also banned, none was ever prosecuted. This clearly showed the class nature of the legislation, designed to protect employers' interests by imposing repressive measures on employees. Third, penalties were mild, which reduced the number of prosecutions under the Combination Acts in favor of other, harsher, measures available. For example, the 1797 Mutiny Act against unlawful oaths had heavy penalties. It was used against secret societies and to crush union formation; one example was the case of the Tolpuddle Martyrs (see below). Fourth, the Acts were not applicable to Scotland, which was also experiencing many of the same industrial changes as England.

This period of repression of worker associations and outbursts of violence climaxed after the

Combination Acts
English laws used to prevent the formation of unions

depression following the end of the Napoleonic Wars. It seemed that there was no way in which ordinary people could be heard. Worker associations were banned, and political pressure was useless, as the majority of the population could not vote, which led to a movement for parliamentary reform. Even peaceful protests were suspected of being preliminaries to revolution and therefore were put down. One that had tragic consequences, the Peterloo Massacre, occurred in Manchester in 1819, when eleven participants in a peaceful political demonstration were killed by troops. It also presented a problem that was never satisfactorily resolved. On the one hand, political authorities must maintain law and order. But on the other, if the conditions that lead to the necessity to use force are not dealt with, this legitimate exercise of power is meaningless and can only be interpreted as repression. The problem for British governments in this period sprang from the acceptance of laissez faire and the desire to protect propertied interests. The combination meant that little was done either to improve economic conditions for the bulk of the population or to provide an acceptable mechanism for the expression of popular opinion.

The realization that the Combination Acts only encouraged violence and ill feeling resulted in repeal in 1824. The immediate consequence was an outburst of strikes: Times were prosperous, so workers believed they could put pressure on employers and win their demands. In turn, this resulted in the 1825 Act, which made employee combinations legal but limited them. Employees could bargain (peacefully) with employers over hours and wages, but could not "molest" or "intimidate." Therefore it was difficult to strike and withhold labor, which could easily be interpreted as intimidation of employers and therefore illegal.

Robert Owen's Grand National Consolidated Union

Some craft unions were formed in this period, but they were short-lived. Most of the workers' atten-

tion was turned to parliamentary reform, which was logical given uncertainties surrounding their ability to use industrial action (see chapter 17). However, while the 1832 Reform Bill was a success from the middle class point of view, it did nothing to improve the political rights of the working classes, which were simply nonexistent. Given the effective closing of two outlets of expression, there was a reaction against capitalism itself, which surfaced in Robert Owen's formation of the Grand National Consolidated Trades Union (GNCU).

Owen himself was an anomaly. Although he became a capitalist manufacturer, he criticized the industrial system and introduced conditions at his New Lanark cotton mills that were very uncharacteristic of 19th century capitalism and industrial towns. He paid high wages and did not employ children under ten. Believing that a good environment produced good people, he built houses for his employees (with sanitation), provided schools for their children, and also established stores selling good products at reasonable prices. To the amazement of his competitors, Owen's mills were profitable. Because he believed that cooperation would be a better basis for society than competition, he also influenced the cooperative movement and tried (unsuccessfully) to establish a utopian commune in the United States. Back in England, and influenced both by the lack of progress for parliamentary reform and by the classical theory of value, he organized this new union.

The Grand National, open to all employees irrespective of trade or industry, had as its ultimate goal the replacement of capitalist industry by a cooperative system of worker control. It also tried to get improvements in wages and give financial and moral assistance to strikers. It was initially supported by workers and resisted by employers. Workers were locked out, and/or had to sign an agreement not to join the union as a condition of employment (called a yellow-dog contract in the United States). The union collapsed in 1834, as workers had no resources to fall

Yellow-dog contract

Agreement made by a worker not to join a union as a condition of employment

back on. It also suffered from the aftereffects of the Tolpuddle Martyrs case, which symbolized a peak of repression against the working classes. The Martyrs were six farm laborers in Dorset who formed themselves into a union in 1833 in order to resist a cut of one shilling in their weekly wage of nine shillings. This in itself was not illegal, but the authorities were anxious to make a stand against worker organizations and accused them under the 1797 Mutiny Act of using an illegal oath when planning to join the Grand National. They were sentenced to seven years in a convict settlement in Australia (but were subsequently pardoned in 1836).

Between the collapse of the GNCTU in 1834 and 1851, working class activity was muted. Some craft unions were formed by those artisans either unaffected by industrial changes or actually gaining from them, such as engineers and boiler-makers. Most were short-lived and rarely touched the growing numbers of factory workers. Much more attention was given to political reform—the 1840s was the decade of the Chartist movement (refer back to Chapter 17)—but little was achieved.

England: Unions After 1851

New Model Unions

Idealistic and/or anticapitalist unions thus were unable to provide an effective mechanism for working class expression, which was also denied an outlet in politics. After 1851, however, the labor movement entered a new phase and more permanent unions with limited aims were formed. Because they were based on very different principles than their predecessors, they were called the "new model" unions. The pioneer was

the Amalgamated Society of Engineers (ASE), formed in 1851. It was an exclusive national organization for engineers, whose skills were crucial to the success of new industrial technology. As these men were relatively highly paid, the union charged high dues, but it also provided benefits as well, payable during times of sickness or unemployment. It and similar unions formed by the boilermakers, carpenters, and bricklayers also broke new ground by being much more conservative than previous unions. The ASE admitted that the interests of employers and employees did not coincide, but it was nonrevolutionary and tried to avoid the direct confrontation of the strike. In other words, the new model accepted capitalism and limited its goals to the immediate issues of improved economic conditions for members.

Even though these unions affected only the most skilled minority of the labor force, their sheer survival was an achievement. Their legal status was still uncertain, they had no recourse if their funds were embezzled (which was serious given that union benefits were all their members could rely on in times of distress), and they still met opposition from the middle class, although a few employers were sympathetic. Opposition to them was based not only on fear of *any* combination by workers but also on the widely accepted wages fund theory. This held that if the total amount of wages paid to all employees was fixed, a gain made by one organized group of workers must come at the expense of another. Ironically, economic theory also helped end resistance to unions. Believers in pure laissez faire opposed unions as combinations preventing the free working of the laws of supply and demand in a free market. However, if these laws were as fixed and immutable as the theory held, then unions were bound to collapse anyway because they interfered

Wage fund theory

Economic theory holding that the total amount of wages paid to all employees was a fixed amount

with the maximization of society's well-being. That unions survived and grew not only surprised the theorists but also indicated that life was not governed by economic laws alone.

National Unions

Further economic changes—the widening of the market, continued introduction of new technologies, and faster economic growth—encouraged the development of national unions. These were nationwide mergers of the already-existing local craft unions, and their growth was also helped by legislation. The Friendly Societies' Act, 1855, gave legal protection to unions with benefit functions, which solidified their legal status. Two further strands of development became apparent in the 1860s. First, the importance of increasing political representation for workers was reasserted. In this respect, American workers had an advantage because they could vote, while British workers still suffered from the denial of political rights. However, political demands were brushed to one side for a few more years, although by the mid 1860s, popular demonstrations of workers' concerns had become significant, and urban male workers did gain the right to vote in 1867.

Industrial union

Association of workers in a particular industry

The second strand centered around the importance of strengthening the union movement itself. This involved three aspects. First was the continuing formation of new unions in new areas and the growth of membership. Initially, new unions were formed in the important textile and mining industries, but after the generally depressed 1870s, some industrial unions appeared among gas workers, transportation workers, building workers, and railwaymen in the more prosperous 1880s. These unions differed from the older craft unions. Their membership was generally composed of the lower-skilled and lower-paid work-

ers, not the highly skilled craftsmen, and instead of focusing on the provision of benefits, they made much more use of the strike as a way of achieving their aims. Such unions were typically all-inclusive because there were fewer levels of skill differentiation in new industries.

The Trades Union Congress: A National Forum

Second, the 1860s also saw the beginning of a national leadership for the union movement. The London Trades Council was formed in 1860 as a grouping of national unions headquartered in London. It developed a common policy on various issues of interest to unionists, and, reflecting its composition of older craft unions, was basically conservative. However, continuing changes led to the establishment of the Trades Union Congress (TUC) in 1868, at first on an informal basis then as a permanent national forum for unions. Like its later equivalent in the United States, the American Federation of Labor (AFL), the TUC (to which unions were affiliated) was dominated by conservative craft unions. But unlike the AFL, it also provided the link between unions and political action. So while it provided assistance in organizing unions and presented "labor's" view on important issues (but was never directly involved in collective bargaining with employers, which remained the prerogative of the individual union) it also encouraged Parliamentary representation of workers' interests, which eventually led to the formation of the Labour Party.

Improving Climate for Unions

Both these developments, the formation of new unions and the creation of a central official voice of labor unions, were assisted by the third aspect, favorable legislation and a change in public attitudes toward unions. Continuing opposition to unions remained strong and was increased from time to time by excessive violence by unionists. One of the most notorious at this time was known as the Sheffield Outrages, 1866-1867, when rival unions of cutlers (Sheffield was an important center for the production of cutlery) went literally for each others' throats. The murders and violence horrified respectable opinion and often reconfirmed the prevailing middle class attitudes about the lower classes.

A Royal Commission was created to examine the union movement, and it reported in 1867 that the typical union was more like the Amalgamated Society of Engineers than the Sheffield unions. It found that much of the work done by unions was beneficial and proposed that they receive legal protection. This finding led to the passage of the Trade Union Act in 1871, which legally recognized unions as legitimate organizations so that their funds would now be fully protected. However, peaceful picketing during strikes was still banned.

Thanks partly to the votes of the newly enfranchised urban workers, opposition to this part of the Act led to the defeat of the Liberal government in 1874, and the new Conservative government in 1875 repealed the offending section. It was replaced by the Protection of Property Act, which legalized peaceful picketing in a dispute with an employer, with penalties being applied only if an act would have been a criminal offense if done anywhere else. In addition, the Employers' and Workmens' Act modified the penalties applicable to any worker who broke a contract. Now, they would be liable only for damages and not a prison sentence as before.

Late Century Unionization

The last two decades of the 19th century saw further changes in the union movement as an increasingly large proportion of the labor force became unionized. Industrial unions open to lower-skilled and lower-paid workers became more common and more permanent. However,

there was a curious contradiction at this time. On the one hand, some workers' efforts did gain middle class support, even if involving a strike. For example, in 1888 the matchgirls of London won their strike for increased wages. Public sympathy was easily come by in this case: The matchgirls were very badly paid and their work—dipping matches in phosphorous—admittedly dangerous. Then there was a strike of dockworkers a year later in support of their claim for a minimum wage of sixpence an hour, which was hardly excessive at that time, and again, support for them was widespread.

On the other hand, while continuing developments encouraged the growth of industrial unions as the increased scale of operations and reduction of skill differentiation increased the numbers of semiskilled workers, there was also a widening of the distance between the middle and the lower classes. The growth of scale of industry meant that the old paternalist form of company ownership was increasingly replaced by the more impersonal joint stock form, and "management" saw itself as distinct from production line workers, encouraging class divisiveness. This was mirrored by changing residential patterns in the industrial towns. Rising incomes and improved transportation facilities meant that those able to afford it could move to new residential, middle class, suburbs. So work distance was reinforced by the separation of residential areas, intensifying the lack of contacts. Separation was even apparent in the educational system. By 1891, when state-provided education became free, the children of manual workers were assured an education, but their education took place in schools in working class areas, and children from different social backgrounds rarely went to the same schools.

The experience of this period showed that while individual groups could gain widespread public sympathy for their struggles with employers, there was also a general antipathy to working class movements. This was apparent in the 1890s when some employers' associations designed to counterattack the unions were formed. In the earliest factories, the balance of power had been tilted toward employers, assisted by laissez faire attitudes and the powerlessness of individual employees. With the rise in living standards after midcentury came both a desire of employees to share in the prosperity they were creating and a growing social consciousness that a wealthy country did have a social responsibility to attack the worst abuses accompanying industrialization. Both the willingness and the ability to form unions expressed a desire of working people for a larger voice in society. When this seemed to threaten employers' power, they too grouped together to try to prevent this erosion.

The union movement also encouraged political representation for the working classes. In general, acceptance of unions as legitimate bodies, plus the responsibility of unions during the upheavals of the 20th century, led to fewer attacks on them than in other countries. However, many problems remained unresolved. Because the labor movement had been dominated by craft unions and the TUC had a generally conservative attitude, there has been a relative lack of adjustment to continuing structural changes in industry. Not only is there a multiplicity of craft unions in many areas, leading to jurisdictional disputes between different unions, but there are also "new" areas where unionism is weak, especially the service and white collar occupations. This is also an issue in other countries.

Political Implications

With the exception of the United States, the new industrial working classes accompanied efforts to unionize and make economic gains with political demands. Most modern industrial economies that are capitalist are also political democracies, but political representation of all sections of society has been fairly recent. Progress toward greater political democracy through the extension of the franchise often involved worker associations ex-

erting pressure. Nowhere is this clearer than in Great Britain, where, to a greater or lesser extent, workers' groups were always involved in Parliamentary reform movements, and where the creation of a political party to represent labor's interests owed much to union involvement. Consequently, much of its 20th century industrial history overlaps with political history.

Birth of the Labour Party

The origin of the Labour Party dates from 1900 when the TUC formed its Labour Representation Committee to encourage the election of working class Members of Parliament. However, the possibility for its success goes back to 1867, when the electorate was doubled by extending the vote to all urban male householders and most rural ones. (The remaining males became enfranchised in 1884.) In addition, the adoption of pay for MPs in 1911 removed the disadvantage that working class candidates had when running against propertied candidates with greater financial resources.

Although the extension of the franchise was a necessary precondition for the development of a working class party, it was not sufficient. Two more elements were required. First, the spread of socialist ideas, while more influential in Europe than in Britain, helped to increase awareness of political opportunities and thus the legitimacy of a separate working class party. As reinterpreted in Britain, the gradualist views of the Fabian Society (founded in 1884), which rejected revolutionary socialism in favor of parliamentary methods, were more influential in developing the ideology of the 20th century Labour Party than the more radical but smaller socialist groups. This produced a platform emphasizing the gradual improvement of the condition of the people through legislative action and enlightened administration. It sup-

Fabian Society
An organization of English socialists who favored gradual reform rather than revolution

Solving Problems in Economic History

Were immigrants to the U. S. "pushed" or "pulled"?

One influential explanation of immigration to the New World is that immigrants were fleeing economic distress—they were being pushed to leave by the lack of economic opportunity at home. An alternative explanation maintains that immigrants were pulled by the potential opportunites of a new land—the desire to achieve a better life. If the first explanation is correct, we would expect that in any given period, the immigrant population into the United States contained a disproportionately large percentage of those from occupations under stress compared with the proportion in the population in the country of origin. So, during the enclosures or the early stages of the Industrial Revolution in England, we would expect to find a larger proportion of dispossessed small farmers, agricultural laborers, or pre-industrial workers among English immigrants when compared to the population remaining in England. Alternatively, if the second explanation is correct, then the immigrant population should resemble the remaining population more closely—it would include those from industries not experiencing rapid technological change, suggesting that immigrants were motivated by a desire for economic improvement.

This is difficult to test, mainly because statistics on immigration are neither complete (especially the further back we go) nor particularly comparable with other demographic data. Also "motivation" is difficult to demonstrate. Several researchers have made the attempt, including Raymond L. Cohn in "The Occupations of English Immigrants to the United States, 18361–1853." *Journal of Economic History*, 52:2, June 1992, pp. 377–387. This article also provides a good example of how statistical analysis can help throw light on historical questions. After 1819, information on immigrants' occupations was included on passenger lists filed by ship captains on arrival in the United States. Cohn used information on 2,409 males arriving on 55 ships between 1836 and 1853, and compared them with other studies.

If the traditional view is correct, Cohn expected that the passenger lists during this period would contain higher proportions of poorer farmers, agricultural laborers, and industrial workers—who were probably travelling alone because their economic status did not permit them to buy tickets for their entire family. If the newer view is correct, then better-off farmers and other occupational groups would be represented in proportion with their representation in the general population.

In fact, the evidence does not support either view strongly; both "push" and "pull" factors can be identified for different groups. Farmers were well represented in the immigrant population, but they were not poor—they could afford to travel with their families, suggesting that the pull factor was more important than the push factor. The relatively largest group was the laborers, most likely agricultural laborers, who were young and apparently poor as they travelled alone which suggests that economic distress was an important cause of immigration for them.

In summary, it seems that at this time different migrant groups immigrated to the United States for different reasons, which appears to reflect the complexity of reality more appropriately than a simple "either-or" solution.

ported the policies of nationalizing some industries, in whole or in part, and the introduction of the welfare state. (These policies were, by and large, also accepted by the rival Conservative Party, which made only minor efforts before 1979 to limit the expansion of the welfare state. However, in the 1980s, most of the nationalized industries including telecommunications, utilities, and the national airline, have been returned to private ownership.) This emphasis distinguished democratic socialism from other forms of socialism.

Second, some adverse judicial decisions plus the rise of employer anti-union efforts also stimulated attempts to influence more favorable legislation by increasing the influence of the votes of workers. In the 1895 general election, all the candidates put up by the Independent Labor Party were defeated, and only two were elected in 1900. So, many union leaders became more concerned about the security and permanence of their legal rights. One legal ruling in particular helped reconfirm the need for a greater voice for workers in Parliament. This was the Taff Vale decision of 1901. In this case, the owners of the Taff Vale Railway brought a civil suit against a railway union to recover damages resulting from a loss of business it experienced during a strike. The judge ruled in the company's favor and ordered the union to pay £123,000. This was a landmark decision of great concern to unions: The right to use the strike weapon was ruled out if it was possible to file a civil suit. Previously, claims to compensate for actual physical damage done during a strike could only be made in a criminal suit. Now, even when a strike was called after collective bargaining failed, was peaceful, and did not result in any physical damage, strikers faced being liable for what could have happened to the employer's business. In addition, it threatened the security of union funds held for other purposes, a security unions had long fought for.

This led to the formation of the Labour Representation Committee, which worked together with the Independent Labour Party and other groups to increase voters' support. (The LRC officially became the Labour Party in 1906.) This was successful. In the general election of 1906, forty-four Labour representatives were elected plus twelve Lib-Labs (representatives who stood for the Liberal Party but who favored Labour's interest). It was not a majority, but was sufficient to influence the new Liberal Government to include new legislation that did meet some of the new Party's demands. The first of these was the 1906 Labour Disputes Act, which removed union funds from liability for civil damages, thus closing the loophole opened up by the Taff Vale judgement. More and wider social legislation followed after 1908, some of it initially opposed by unions, but eventually this opposition was overcome.

Pro-Union Moves

Legislation established labor exchanges to facilitate a match between job seekers and jobs available, which improved the mobility of the labor force by increasing available information. At first, unions were opposed to the reform because they thought the exchanges would be agencies to supply blacklegs (strike breakers) to help companies break unions. Another important reform was the establishment of health and unemployment insurance on a national basis. The craft unions were initially opposed to this reform because they thought that this scheme (which became universal in 1946) would conflict with their own arrangements for benefits. But opposition was overcome by making friendly societies agents for the scheme's operation, which incidentally led to a large increase in union membership.

On the economic front, some remaining problems in collective bargaining were attacked. Unions had jealously guarded their status as collective bargaining agents, but bargaining was not possible in poorly organized or unorganized

Blackleg
Strikebreaker

areas where wages were low. In addition, the multiplicity of unions in other areas frequently led to disputes that disrupted entire industries, even if only one union was directly involved. Trying to deal with this situation involved two mechanisms. First, in some low-wage areas, agencies were established to fix wages—the first came in the garment industry in 1909. Second, conciliation boards (Whitley Councils) were set up in other industries to try to mediate disputes that had not been settled through collective bargaining. This was opposed by most unions, which remained wedded to the 19th century view of industrial relations, even though the structure of the economy was changing and would undergo further changes. Whitley Councils, composed of employers and union leaders, were not very effective. None were established in the major industries of cotton, engineering, and mining.

Economic Uncertainty

The next few years were unsettled. In the years leading up to the First World War, economic uncertainty resulting from Britain's loss of economic leadership contributed to economic unrest, which was made worse by political problems. The Liberal Government struggled to end the undemocratic block on some legislation made by the House of Lords (at that time, a hereditary upper chamber of Parliament). The suffragette movement campaigned for the enfranchisement of British women. (The first step toward this goal was taken during the First World War.) There were renewed attempts to gain home rule in Ireland. Another problem was inflation.

The First World War added to international problems and was followed first by a short boom, then an intense depression in 1920. This depression increased the bitterness of industrial relations in some industries, most notably mining and rail transportation, but as depression spread, active industrial unrest lessened. However, poor industrial relations were the result of many causes, not

only union duplication and militancy. The decline of former leading industries, especially textiles, reflected on conditions and wages, while the spirit of cooperation between labor and management during the war was embittered later as companies tried to eliminate concessions made to workers. Politically, the Liberal Party, the bulwark of 19th century politics, proved unable to meet the challenges of the 20th century and nearly disappeared in 1922. However, this presented a no-choice situation: On the one hand stood the Conservative Party, dominated by employers' interests, and on the other, the new, politically inexperienced Labour Party, which in 1924 briefly found itself in power as a minority government (until November 1924). Even though it owed its origins and support to organized labor, in no way did this imply significant legislative assistance for the labor movement.

1926 General Strike

Worsening conditions climaxed in 1926 in a General Strike, when about two and one half million workers—miners, transportation workers, printers, and workers in metals, chemicals, and utilities—stopped work. This idea of joint industrial action was influenced by syndicalism (especially the views of the Frenchman Georges Sorel, who proposed a general strike so that workers could take control of the State), but more important was the existing potential for industrial conflict. The strike ended after nine days but represented a loss of prestige for the labor movement. One lesson learned was that a general strike would not be an effective weapon for labor to use to reach its goals.

Other setbacks in industrial action during the 1920s saw unions become more politically involved. In particular, they opposed the anti-union Trades Disputes Act in 1927. This legislation made sympathetic strikes illegal (although this clause was never actually used); prevented civil servants from joining a union affiliated with the

TUC; made intimidation of strikebreakers illegal; and enforced the contracting-in system [2] for payment of the political levy to the Labour Party that was included in union dues. The Labour Party's income from union subsidies was reduced by one third, but there were closer union ties to the party as a result.

Conditions improved after 1926. Regardless of which party was in power, the government recognized the need for union cooperation in government policy and legislation. This was further encouraged by the desire to prevent a further loss of economic position, which in some cases involved active assistance to particular industries. Linkages between employers and unions improved and were further strengthened by the requirements of the Second World War.

Unions in the 1930s

The depressed 1930s saw some gains but many losses for organized labor. An earlier tendency for unions to amalgamate had increased their average size, but there were still demarcation problems only partly solved by jurisdictional agreements. Industrial change had further effects. Declines in employment in mining and the cotton textile industry saw membership losses, but more important was the failure of unionization in new areas. Domestic service and agriculture (both declining areas), clerical employment and distribution (which were expanding), and unskilled labor in general remained least unionized. However, the Amalgamated Engineering Union grew both by amalgamation and by opening its ranks to the lesser skilled, while the Transport and General Workers Union by 1937 was the largest union in the world with 654,000 members. As in the United States, British unions also faced a problem with a few Communist activists. The TUC advised unions to exclude Communists from leadership positions, with expulsion from the organization as an extreme resort. This was mirrored by political rejection of the Communist position.

World War II and After

However, British unions gained in prestige and membership during the 1930s and the Second World War. (Total membership reached 7.8 million in 1945, with 6.7 million affiliated to the TUC, and climbed further to 9.5 million in 1951.) In addition, during this time the labor movement did not suffer the divisiveness of American unionism or the repression of European unions. Union responsibility increased both during and after the war, when the Labour Party finally achieved a majority government.

In keeping with its campaign platform, some key industries were taken into public ownership. The Bank of England became a public corporation in 1946; the coal industry was nationalized in 1947; the railways, canals, and road haulage came under the control of the British Transport Commission in 1947; the electrical industry was nationalized in 1948, followed by the gas industry in 1949, and the iron and steel industry in 1951. One concession to union demands was the repeal of the 1927 Trade Disputes Act.

However, the problems of rebuilding a war-shattered economy remained, and attempts were made to restrain wages in order to keep industrial costs down. This was not successful because boom conditions in the export industries and the boost given by spending for the Korean War generated inflation. Although unions had voluntarily given up their bargaining rights during wartime, they refused to abandon them during peacetime.

The emphasis on the role of unions as voluntary associations remained important in keeping organized labor in Britain at some distance from governmental policy. This preserves some important aspects of democracy, but at a cost—the legacy of a somewhat irrational union structure that has not adapted sufficiently fast to changing economic conditions.

Unionization in Germany

Industrialization started later in Germany than in Great Britain, and so did the development of a labor movement. But the union movement grew fast, and by the start of the First World War, both labor movements were roughly equivalent in size. There is, however, one very important difference between the two countries. In Britain, unions developed first, followed by the creation of a political party specifically representing working class interests. This party was only mildly socialist, as the long tradition of parliamentary government in Britain encouraged the adoption of gradualist methods for the attainment of socialist goals. In Germany, the birth of a union movement was the outcome of a political movement. To some extent, this can be explained by the very different political, social, and economic background in Germany. As previously noted, the introduction of capitalist industry in Germany owed less to the autonomous development of a liberal-minded middle class than to the desire of the State to improve economic and thus military strength. Liberal views were ignored during the unification process, and there was little development of an independent urban middle class as in Britain. Political repression limited liberal sentiments but did not succeed in preventing the development of socialist thinking or socialist parties. In 1863, Ferdinand Lasalle established the first political party specifically oriented to workers' representation. It merged with a Marxist party in 1875 to form a new party then called the German Social Democratic Party. The SDP remained the largest political party in Germany until Adolf Hitler succeeded in crushing it in the 1930s.

The Social Democratic Party and Unions

The SDP encouraged the formation of socialist trade unions, even though Chancellor Bismarck banned both socialist political parties and socialist labor unions. Unions tended to be industrial un-

ions because the early adoption of mass production techniques in Germany limited the development of craft unions along British lines. Most of them tended to be socialist, but there was a parallel growth of nonsocialist, usually Catholic, unions, too. When the ban on socialist organizations was lifted in 1890, both political parties and unions were formed. A central union organization, the General Commission of German Trade Unions, similar to Britain's Trades Union Congress, developed in the 1890s, and the trade unions associated with the SDP were affiliated to it. The unions' socialist tendencies became muted as they grew. They focused more on working within the capitalist system to improve working and living conditions rather than on overthrowing it, an experience similar to that in Britain and the United States. Many craft and independent unions remained in Britain, while German unions tended to merge with each other. This meant that by the end of the century two thirds of a total of about 2.5 million unionists were in the five largest unions, with 20 percent in the metalworkers' union alone. (In 1913, there were four million unionists in Britain, with almost three quarters of them affiliated with the TUC.)

This modification of socialist goals worked to the SDP's advantage during the First World War. The orthodox socialist position opposed workers' participation in the war on the grounds that it was instigated by capitalist interests. If workers of one country fought and killed those of another, the common struggle of the working masses against their capitalist exploiters, regardless of nationality, was denied. Consequently, in many countries socialist unions encouraged their members not to enlist as pawns in a capitalist struggle for dominance of world markets. But patriotism proved stronger than socialist class feelings, and German workers supported their country's war efforts. In fact, the SDP emerged as the only political party not discredited by the war, in which Germany was defeated. In the 1920s it was the largest political party and helped establish the Weimar Republic to replace the German Empire, which had led Germany into the war. This boost to the moderate socialist movement was also reflected in increases in union membership, which reached nine million in 1921. Then events of the 1920s and 1930s resulted in a loss of power for both unions and the socialist movement.

Setbacks in the 1920s and 1930s

The first setback was the hyperinflation of 1922-1923. One important cause of the massive rise in

Hyperinflation
Extremely high rate of inflation

the price level was the demand for reparations for war damages to be paid by Germany to the victorious allies. Against the best advice of some leading economists, Germany's bill for reparations in 1921 was 132 billion gold marks. There was no way that even a fully employed economy, recovered from war devastation, could pay this amount; it was far greater than Germany could raise in taxes, so the Weimar Government, already

Figure 19.2 A Labor Day Parade taking place in New York City in 1884. (First appearing in *Leslie's Illustrated*, September 17, 1884. Courtesy of the Tamiment Institute, New York University)

facing a budget deficit, simply printed more money to pay its bills. The combined effect of the drain of funds and exports abroad plus the increase in the nominal money supply had a disastrous effect. In 1922, the price level rose 5,470 percent—and in 1923, rose 1,300,000,000,000 percent!

In the late 1920s and early 1930s, both unions and the SDP came under further attack. Big business launched an antiunion drive, while the SDP faced opposition from the Communist far left and the Nazi right. Final destruction of the left, the labor movement, and any democratic traditions in Germany was due to the growth of the National Socialists (Nazis) under Adolf Hitler, a movement that was socialist only in name. Many explanations have been offered, including Germany's defeat in the war, humiliation after it, the weakness of the Weimar Government and a liberal middle class, and the discrediting of the SDP for its association with the hyperinflation and following deflation. Once Hitler gained power in 1933, the labor movement was destroyed, all left-wing political parties abolished, and the leaders of both either imprisoned or executed. (The events of this period are covered more fully in Chapter 21.)

Postwar Labor Organizations

Not until 1945, after Germany suffered another defeat in the Second World War, were trade unions permitted again. This time, Germany was divided into two, with East Germany (the German Democratic Republic) coming under the influence of the Soviet Union and West Germany (the Federal Republic of Germany) occupied by the allied forces of the United Kingdom, United States, and France. Unionization was rapid in West Germany, with 40 percent of the labor force unionized by 1949. Unions were politically neutral and were affiliated to a new central organization, the German Federation of Labor. What was unique in this period was the operation of the

principle of codetermination, achieved in the important coal and steel industries. Codetermination means that labor has an input into industrial policy-making decisions, and union representatives sit with stockholders on the boards of directors of companies. Although meeting one of the traditional socialist demands for effective democracy on the economic as well as the political front, codetermination was not introduced in order to achieve an idealistic principle. Rather, it was forced on the union movement by the occupation authorities as a pragmatic response to the existing situation. This situation was one of serious devastation of Germany's industrial plant. Given the need to rebuild and restore the eco-

---

Codetermination

Union representatives in Germany are included on company boards of directors in some industries

---

nomic structure, it was vital that labor cooperate fully in the rebuilding effort. The right to strike and disrupt the recovery was taken away, and this denial of liberty was compensated for by the introduction of codetermination in the leading areas of the economy. Such cooperation effectively helped restore the German economy to the strength it had at the end of the 19th century.

Unionization in France

Both Britain and Germany developed a labor union movement closely allied to a political party, recognizing a moderate socialist tradition of working for improvements within an existing capitalist system rather than its overthrow. It also recognized that no one body could accomplish goals on both the economic and the political front. Thus, unions were organized to represent workers in their bargaining with employers to improve wages and conditions, while workers' parties were seen as necessary to express labor's views in politics and government.

Syndicalism

No similar development occurred in France, where there was no linkage between unions and politics, and where a strand of syndicalism was influential. Syndicalism favors direct action (such as the use of strikes and other industrial weapons) to achieve worker control of the means of production. It is anticapitalist insofar as it maintains that economic issues should be influenced by the participants. As wage earner status is so prevalent in a market exchange economy, there must be wage earner input into economic decisions. This goes much further than the gradualist, compromising approach of unions in Britain and the United States, which have not tried to preempt owners' or managers' roles in running industry. These unions prefer a more or less adversarial role in facing management on their members' behalf to being involved in actual managerial decision making.

Syndicalism

Theory advocating direct action to achieve workers' control over industry

---

French union development reflects the revolutionary tradition of 1789. Successive periods of repression demonstrated the futility of political action and compromise with the government, encouraging direct action by syndicalists instead. At the same time, socialist parties were struggling for survival but rarely cooperated with the unions as elsewhere. The 1789 Revolution showed the working classes that one group could seize power from another—the middle class had succeeded. The 1848 Revolution also gained the support of workers, but again hopes that their interests would be attended to were dashed. The closest they came to producing a government occurred with the establishment of the Paris Commune in 1871, but this was short-lived and was brutally put down—20,000 members of the Commune died. Such repression therefore forced attention

to the control of industry by workers, to an overthrow of capitalism where it was most rapidly growing.

Before 1884, unions did not have a legitimate legal status. They were merely tolerated, and were too weak to threaten industrial interests in any serious way. However, many local and national unions were formed after 1884, and for a time it seemed as though unionization might follow the experience elsewhere. In 1895, most unions became affiliated to a new central organization, the Confederation Générale du Travail. The CGT was somewhat like Britain's TUC or the American AFL, a national forum for the expression of labor interests. But unlike these two organizations, it was neither conservative nor gradualist nor interested in politics. It was dominated by syndicalists, so union activity became much more aggressive. It rejected cooperation with French socialists, who, although representing a wide variety of viewpoints, thought that social transformation by political means was possible. (The various socialist parties in fact merged in 1905 to form a unified socialist party.)

With the outbreak of war in 1914, the same dilemma confronted syndicalist unionists as occurred elsewhere: Whether or not to fight in support of capitalist interests. And as elsewhere, patriotism was stronger than class interests. French workers' participation in the military was a signal of the decline in sympathy for the syndicalist viewpoint.

The following period until the end of the Second World War in 1945 saw many reforms at the national level. A comprehensive social security law roughly along the lines of Germany's was introduced in 1928, and family allowances (state subsidies to families, depending on the number of children) were introduced in 1933. These helped improve the living conditions of workers and further reduced support for more aggressive tactics to achieve the overthrow of capitalism. Partly because of the seeming co-option of some workers into the system, some of the more extreme left-wing unions disaffiliated from the CGT to ally with the Communist party in the early 1920s, but they returned to affiliate status in the mid 1930s.

The prestige of the unions and their members increased during the Second World War. Early in the war, Germany had defeated and then occupied France, setting up a puppet government centered in Vichy. This was supported by leading financial and industrial interests, anti-socialist right wing politicians, the Church and the military, and collaboration with the Nazis was widespread. Resistance to occupation was led by labor groups, always at intense risk. The resistance movement's role in providing links with the Allies and information as well as escape routes was seen as the true patriotic and nationalist spirit of France. Hence after the war, labor groups were highly regarded.

Unions as such had not been officially permitted during the war, and they began a new period of fluctuating fortunes after it. The disrepute in which the Vichy government was held, added to the long tradition of worker distrust of government in France combined to force a distance between unions and government. At this time, the leadership of the CGT became dominated by Communists, and as in Germany, unions tended to be either left wing or Catholic, even within the same industry. Thus there is a dualism in the French union structure, with one part aiming for the overthrow of capitalism and the other more in favor of a gradualist approach focusing on the improvement of conditions.

Unionization in the United States

Union development in the United States followed the British pattern of development, rather than the German or French, with a lag of about thirty to forty years accounting for the later start of industrialization. Thus the earliest unions were started by skilled craftsmen attempting to protect their status, and other early unions were idealist,

rather like Robert Owen's Grand National Consolidated Trades Union. Craft unions proper, affiliated with a central organization, developed later. When mass production industries appeared, so did industrial unions.

However, important differences distinguish the American labor movement. First, unionization has never affected as large a proportion of the labor force as in Europe. (For example, even in 1924, only 15 percent of the United States labor force was unionized, compared to 75 percent of the German labor force and 65 percent of the British.) Second, although attempts to combine labor unions with political activism were made in the early 19th century, they were unsuccessful, and the mainstream of American unionism did not become associated with a labor party as in Britain. Third, union development in the United States has been associated with a much higher level of violence than in Britain. Finally, opposition to union organizing was more successful in the United States, and union activities were subject to more anti-union legislation and adverse legal action than was the case in Britain. So unionization in the United States was slowed down. In general, however, the similarities are that unions in both countries tend to accept capitalism and work for improvements in their members' material conditions, while overtly socialist aims are disavowed. While socialist, even syndicalist, philosophy has influenced the development of labor unions, the effects were only sporadic and short-lived.

Early Protective Associations

Some early worker associations can be traced back to the 17th century, but the first true unions did not appear until the 19th century, when the conditions that encourage them first appeared. The very first association was formed by Boston shoemakers in 1648. It was more like a guild than a union; it aimed to control the quality of footwear by suppressing shoes made by itinerant shoemakers as well as by regulating the work done by its members.

The first true unions appeared in shoemaking in the 1790s, when a more capitalist form of organization was introduced. These unions are instructive; they show the pressures on workers trying to protect themselves from changes in the structure of production. In Philadelphia, the Federal Society of Journeymen Cordwainers was formed in 1794, lasting for twelve years. It was formed in response to the split of shoemaking, when sales were made by the merchant-master employer, while the journeymen, who worked at home, produced the shoes. The journeymen's loss of control plus declining material well-being intensified in the first decade of the 19th century. Some employers expanded into wholesaling functions that generally involved lower quality output competing with the custom output of small master producers. By the 1830s, a new stage was reached with the entry of the merchant-capitalist, who manufactured on a large scale (although still using traditional hand production methods). Journeymen were left with two options: Either

---

Cordwainer

A leatherworker, especially a shoemaker

---

work for the merchant-capitalist or work for the small masters who were subcontractors for the wholesale manufacturer. In either case wages were lower; by this time, weekly wages had fallen to $4-6 per week, compared with $9-10 at the beginning of the century. The relative wage differential between these skilled workers and unskilled workers in general also declined. For example, the demand for labor in canal building had almost eliminated any pay differential by raising wages of the lower-skilled. At first the small masters, who were formerly independent producer-retailers, sympathized with the journeymen, as both were pressured by the new capitalists, but now they were in the position of being employers without capital. Their income de-

pended on the spread between what they received from the merchant-capitalist and what they paid out as wages to the journeymen. In this situation, they had every incentive to force down wages in response to pressure from merchant-capitalists.

Given this, the journeymen associations attempted a defensive strategy: Protection against both low wages and the inferior quality of output directly controlled by the new capitalists. As the sales function had been separated from production, there was little they could do to control quality, so they focused on wages. However, these early unions were not successful. Unions were treated as criminal conspiracies (only in 1842 was the right of workers to organize for their mutual benefit granted), so any attempt to strike to further their aims resulted in the employers getting court protection against them. The ability of employers to coopt the courts in their struggle against workers' associations also resulted in most unions of this period being formed as secret societies.

Political Action

Lack of success encouraged political action to improve conditions. In the most economically advanced states of Pennsylvania, New York, and Massachusetts, unions urged their members to nominate candidates for public office to replace what they saw as a government favoring moneyed interests. They wanted to reduce monopoly (especially the banking monopoly), make public education free, abolish imprisonment for debt, have directly elected public officials, and separate church from state. Once the property qualification for voters was removed, many of the wage-earning class could vote, and their votes in 1828 helped elect Andrew Jackson, who favored many of the antimonopoly issues supported by wage earners. But this brief flurry of labor's involvement in political issues ended by the mid 1830s. Their parties had won political recognition and were especially important in local elections, but they were weakened as a political force by internal divisiveness, and they lost their support because the major parties had taken over some of the most important issues.

By this time, the feeling that political activity was fruitless was general, and unions retreated to focus on economic issues. With a few minor, and short-lived, exceptions, the American labor movement never became politically active and never established a national party to represent the interests of the working classes. This was partly due to the fact that American workers could already vote; one of the major forces leading to European workers' political activism was the demand for enfranchisement.

Unions in the 1830s

Prosperous conditions in the 1830s encouraged a spread of union activity beyond the traditional groups of craftsmen such as shoemakers and printers, to textile workers. Prosperity increased workers' bargaining power and throughout the 19th century union activity always rose in prosperous periods, only to decline during depressions. Efforts to increase ties between unions were also made, first through associations of unions in one city (by 1836, there were thirteen such central trades councils in the major manufacturing cities) and later by combining local unions in one industry into a national union. These unions collapsed in the depression of 1837-1839. The decade of the 1840s saw workers' efforts change. New labor organizations began to be more aggressive in their efforts to improve material conditions as industrial workers continued to experience real-wage declines. This contrasted with the defensive approach of earlier unions and partly reflected the changes caused by mechanization.

Knights of Saint Crispin

Unions remaining defensive were not successful. For example, shoemakers had always resisted the growing capitalist nature of their work, in part because of its inferior quality and lower pay compared with custom work. After 1850, first with the introduction of machinery and later with the addition of steampower, however, factory-produced shoes were no longer inferior. A new shoemakers' union, the Knights of Saint Crispin, was founded in 1867. With a peak membership of about 50,000 in the early 1870s, it was the largest American labor organization at the time. It did not oppose machinery as such but objected to the substitution of unskilled machine operatives for trained journeymen, because it lowered wages. While its strikes were at first successful, its defensive position was unsustainable in the long run. Factory output was not inferior, and the availability of nonjourneyman labor reduced the need for employers to use higher-paid journeymen. So the Knights collapsed in the depression of 1873.

The more aggressive nature of unions formed at this time was easier to sustain in new areas, especially in industries organized along factory lines from the start, which therefore had no previous tradition of craft organization and no threatened status to protect. For example, the textile industry in New England at first had not been particularly encouraging to union organizing efforts because the workers did not see themselves as permanent wage earners. Then during the 1840s, speedups, wage cuts, and long hours stimulated protests and the formation of unions to press for better conditions. These too were short-lived. Union organizers were fired and blacklisted. Employers replaced union workers with more docile immigrant workers, who were too afraid to join a union for fear of losing a desperately needed job.

National Labor Union

Permanent unions did not appear until after the Civil War, coinciding with the real start of industrialization in the United States. As had been the case in Britain at a similar stage, unions went through an idealistic phase when workers attempted to attach broader reform aims to the more narrowly economic aims of later unions. One example was the National Labor Union, which existed from 1866 to 1872. It was an all-inclusive association of trades' councils, local and national unions, and reform associations with political aims. Among its demands were an eight-hour day, the establishment of cooperatives, easier credit, the abolition of the use of convict labor, the restriction of immigration, and easier availability of public lands for homesteaders. This list included issues directly affecting workers (shorter hours), defensive aspects (elimination of competition from convict or immigrant labor), and mechanisms to assist those who wished to opt out of the capitalist system, an important refrain. Those who opposed demands made by eastern industrial workers for better wages and conditions always pointed to the availability of land in the West: The idea of the frontier as an escape valve for the industrializing East. However, this ignored the fact that low wages did not allow for land purchases, the establishment of a farm, or the support of a family in a new area, and city dwellers rarely knew much about farming.

Knights of Labor

Another example of an idealist, all-inclusive union was the Knights of Labor, founded in 1869, which dominated the labor movement in the 1880s before collapsing in the early 1890s. The Knights were also reformist and anticapitalist, but rather than adopting socialist goals, looked backward to a simpler, precapitalist idealism. It was one big union, open to all with the exception of bankers, stockbrokers, lawyers, gamblers, and liquor interests, but mainly attracting lower-skilled workers. Membership peaked at over 700,000 in 1886. As in Britain, unions were being formed by skilled workers who were not interested in organizing the unskilled. These craft unions had more success precisely because their skills gave them

Knights of Labor
An idealistic union, late 19th century

more bargaining power with employers than the unskilled had, and they did not want to lose this advantage.

The Knights' aims were similar to those of the National Labor Union, but as well as having broad political and reform goals, they also became involved in strike actions. While some of the strikes protesting wage cuts were successful—especially against the rail companies, where a disruption seriously threatened the transportation so necessary to the large national market—these successes were short lived. Later strikes were crushed, employers refused to make concessions and the Knights became weaker as disillusioned members withdrew.

Craft Unions and the AFL

Craft unions formed after 1870, affecting only a minority of the labor force, were much more successful at organizing, especially after 1880. They were patterned after the new-model unions in Britain, and were restricted to the most highly skilled (and relatively highly paid) workers. They charged high dues, but also provided benefits, and were basically conservative, resorting to a strike threat only as a last resort when collective bargaining failed. One of the first was the International Cigar Makers' Union, which was reorganized by three European immigrants, Adolph Strasser, Ferdinand Laurrell, and Samuel Gompers.

The idea of strengthening the union movement by having an alliance along the lines of the TUC was first raised in the 1880s. Many existing unions were affiliated with the Knights of Labor, but the skilled workers felt that a pure union alliance, focusing on economic interests and not sidetracked by political concerns, would be more to their benefit. So the American Federation of Labor (AFL) was formed in 1886. It was a loose confederation of craft unions whose primary concern was the economic betterment of their members. It intended to end rivalry and conflict between unions by guaranteeing each member union its own jurisdiction (by craft, cutting across industry lines) to prevent union raiding. It also helped produce labor unity through education and persuasion, and supported affiliated unions in their drive to be recognized as legitimate collective bargaining bodies by employers. The AFL deliberately chose not to become politically active, even opposing legislation on issues affecting workers such as schemes for social security, minimum wages, and working hours. Opposition was based on the fear that legislation would encroach on the gains craft unions' members were achieving in their bargaining with employers. These gains were impressive. In the 1920s, wages of skilled workers were six or seven times higher

---

American Federation of Labor
Alliance of craft unions, founded 1886

---

than those of unskilled, unorganized workers, compared with a differential of only two or three times in Europe, while in steel, unionized workers had a work week of thirty-five hours as opposed to the seventy-two worked by unorganized steel workers. (In Britain, craft unions had also opposed legislation on social issues, but changed their position when unions and friendly societies became agents handling benefit claims.) AFL membership grew slowly, but survived the depression of the 1890s, continued attacks from employers, adverse court decisions, and antiunion legislation. By 1920 membership in affiliated unions (rail unions were not affiliated) peaked at four million, but only 10 percent of the labor force was organized. However, membership fell during the prosperous 1920s.

Industrial Unrest

Both workers and industrialists faced problems caused by depressed conditions during the 1890s.

Industrialists tried to cope with falling profits resulting from earlier competitive price cutting with renewed efforts to hold labor costs down and develop new methods of cooperation with rivals to avoid further price wars. Workers, including the unorganized ones, resisted wage cuts. There was an upsurge of industrial violence and strikes, paralleling the unrest occurring in western agricultural areas. Strikes were a response to worsening conditions for many workers plus stepped up antiunion activity. For example, in 1892 there was a strike at the Homestead plant of the Carnegie Steel Company, where an AFL-affiliated local had 800 members. Management demanded a pay cut of 18 percent in a new contract. It was rejected, and the plant manager locked out the workers, announced replacements for the strikers, and called in the Pinkerton Detective Agency. Pinkerton detectives fired at the pickets, and seven detectives and nine workers were killed in the resulting melee. The state militia was later called in to restore order. The union collapsed and was not re-established until the 1930s. Only eight hundred out of four thousand strikers were re-hired, and the new workers were not unionized. Management's demands were more than met: A twelve-hour workday was imposed, with no overtime pay on Sundays, and wages were cut to half their former level.

Another important strike, also lost, took place in 1894 at the Pullman plant in Chicago, where railroad cars were made. What made this strike unusual was that Pullman was both employer and landlord—Pullman workers lived in a company town where rents were higher than in nearby areas. The company laid off 3,000 of its 5,900 workers and cut wages for the rest, but did not simultaneously reduce rents so those still working ended up with less than $6 a week. A further inequity was that the company still paid dividends to stockholders. The plant was organized in locals of the American Railway Union, which called a strike to protest the wage cuts. As at Homestead, the response was a lockout. The ARU then an-

Lockout

Industrial action when an employer closes down a plant in order to influence collective bargaining

nounced a boycott of all railroads using Pullman cars, threatening chaos in the transportation system. This time, the company hired Canadian strikebreakers to replace striking workers and used armed guards on the railways, which led to clashes between them and picketing strikers. Federal troops were sent to restore order. What ended the strike and crushed the union was a federal injunction to prevent anyone interfering with mail carried on trains, and union leaders were prosecuted and subsequently jailed. This action was based on a broad interpretation of the Sherman Antitrust Act: The union was held to be a conspiracy in restraint of interstate commerce, even though its original action was intended to restore laid off workers and prevent pay cuts.

This is one example of the use of the court injunction by companies to fight unions. Companies found it very easy to get judicial support, regardless of the justice of their case. The injunction reflects the importance of property ownership. The courts were always ready to rule against unions to restore the status quo because strikes were seen as depriving the employer of his property without due process of law. The injunction was only one of many weapons used to prevent the development of unions, and only ceased to be used in 1932. Other anti-union measures included the yellow dog contract (not declared illegal until 1932), blacklists to prevent union workers from getting jobs after being fired by one employer, and anti-union campaigns waged by a newly formed employers' association, the National Association of Manufacturers. There was a particularly gruesome episode in 1913, when eleven children and two women were burned to death after the militia attacked a colony of strikers in Colorado. They had struck a mining company to force it to recognize their union, the United Mine Workers. Even though public opinion was outraged, the company, controlled by Rockefeller interests, refused to recognize the union.

The Wobblies

Although the Progressive Era (1901-1917) produced some reforms and improvement in public attitudes to organized labor, effective counterattack slowed union growth. Many large industries such as steel, autos, agricultural machinery, electrical machinery, public utilities, tobacco, and meat packing remained unorganized. The AFL was not interested in organizing the semi-skilled, and remained an organization of craft unions. Some new areas did organize. For example, aided by government pressure, the United Mine Workers succeeded in organizing the anthracite mines of Pennsylvania; and the garment industry, long considered a poor area for unionization because it was mainly composed of women and/or immigrant workers working in small shops, was organized by the International Ladies Garment Workers' Union.

This period also saw the last episode of radical socialism in United States labor history as the unskilled, upset not only by their lagging economic gains but also by the lack of interest shown them by the AFL, moved away from mainstream unionization. The result was the Industrial Workers of the World (popularly called the Wobblies), in 1905.

It was formed by miners, lumberworkers, and immigrant farm workers in the West who joined with unorganized eastern industrial workers. The IWW was an anticapitalist, syndicalist movement attempting to promote the spread of industrial unionism. It was first based on the principle that employers and workers were mutually incompatible, but later split and most of the western groups withdrew. While it was openly revolutionary and faced much opposition, it achieved a notable, and

Industrial Workers of the World

A radical industrial union, founded 1905

orderly, victory in a 1912 strike of the Lawrence, Massachusetts, textile workers. The strike protested a wage cut, which would have reduced the average full time wage of $9 a week. Public sympathy for the strikers ran high when, even in spite of the company's attempts to discredit the IWW and the police attack on a group of children being evacuated from the area, the strikers refused to resort to violence. Eventually the company did meet the union's demands.

Membership in the IWW peaked at 60,000, but, as with syndicalist unions in Europe, it lost support during World War I. It opposed United States entry into the war and tried to prevent workers enlisting. Popular feeling turned against it; many states passed laws outlawing it; many of its members were jailed or subject to private vigilante action; and it consequently lost members.

Actions in the 1920s

The Communist Party then took over the radical socialist opposition to capitalism, and after 1919 it remained as a small splinter group challenging the mainstream of the American labor movement. This opposition remained an issue for the next several decades. The AFL gained prestige during the war by supporting the war effort but remained committed to craft unionism. Then it found itself in an awkward position. After the war, many companies wanted to negate their agreements with organized labor made during the war. For example, the National War Labor Board had been established to settle industrial disputes, and in return for a no-strike agreement, gave unions support in organizing, collective bargaining, and equal pay for equal work. The NWLB was abolished with peace, and many strikes followed companies' attempts to return to the pre-war situation. Government no longer supported organized labor, and the continued use of the court injunction crushed strikes. Anti-union campaigning was revived during the 1920s, gaining from

the exposure of corruption and racketeering in some unions.

Union organizing was also weakened by a new tactic used by some companies. Instead of trying to break unions, they introduced "welfare capitalism" as a way of preventing organization in the first place. By 1926, some four hundred company unions were formed, while other companies provided profit sharing schemes, group insurance policies, pension plans and so on. While helping improve working conditions for the relatively small number of workers involved, they limited labor mobility as workers became tied to a particular employer. Average wages rose, and by 1928 real wages in these companies and were 20 percent higher on average than a decade earlier. But there was no real employee representation, and welfare capitalism did not solve the basic problems that initiated formation of worker associations. For example, rewards were frequently accompanied by work speedups and renewed anti-union drives, and workers often felt that company unions did not truly represent their interests, a conflict with the democratic values absorbed through education. In addition, welfare capitalism applied only during prosperity. It disappeared after the 1929 crash, and wages were cut as unemployment rose to seven million by 1930 and to fifteen million by 1932.

Industrial Unions and the Mass Production Industries

The depression years of the 1930s saw gains for labor on two fronts. First, after the election of Franklin Roosevelt in 1932, New Deal policies recognized for the first time that working conditions were too important to be left to the whims of the individual employer. They were of wider social concern, as capitalism in a democratic society should protect the political freedom and economic security of workers. Several laws were passed to redress the balance of power by increasing workers' ability to organize. Second, the more favorable climate for labor organizations gave a boost to the formation of industrial unions, much later than in Europe, although at the cost of the relative weakening of the AFL. The fight for industrial unionism occurred within the AFL itself when some union leaders, led by John L. Lewis of the UMW, tried to form industrial unions within the AFL via a newly formed group, the Committee for Industrial Organization. There were still conflicts, which came to a head in 1937 when the AFL expelled CIO members, charging them with violating AFL principles. The Committee then renamed itself the Congress of Industrial Organizations, and rivalled the AFL for the next 20 years.

It was most concerned with the mass production industries, and made gains even when facing intense opposition. It was conservative, like the AFL. The CIO made a major breakthrough when U.S. Steel and General Motors finally recognized CIO unions as legitimate bargaining bodies in 1937. U.S. Steel's recognition was crucial, as conditions were poor. For example, average annual wages were as low as $560, while estimates of annual income required for a minimum standard of living were $1,500. After U.S. Steel's recognition, wages were increased 10 percent and a 40-hour workweek instituted. In return, workers agreed to a no-strike pledge. However, smaller steel companies resisted recognizing the steelworkers' union, and sporadic violence continued until 1941, when the National Labor Relations Board (a newly established government agency) ordered them to recognize the United Steelworkers Union and reinstate employees they had fired. By this time, the steel union had 600,000 members.

Congress of Industrial Organization
Alliance of industrial unions

The struggle to organize the auto industry took nearly as long to resolve. While hourly wage rates were high, the practice of closing plants to prepare for new models each year involved massive seasonal layoffs, and consequently annual wages averaged below $1,000. The AFL had established an industrial union, the United Automobile Workers, to organize the industry, but strikes in 1934, in support of union recognition, had failed. The UAW broke away from the AFL in 1936 and demanded recognition under CIO auspices instead. General Motors refused to bargain, and in 1937 an unusual form of industrial action took place. The workers took over the plant in a sitdown strike to preempt a management lockout. The action was peaceful and well organized. The company, obviously, opposed it and requested the assistance of the state militia to remove the strikers, but the governor refused to send them. After forty-four days, the company finally agreed to negotiate, and the UAW was recognized as the bargaining unit for the auto workers at GM. (Ford refused to recognize the union until 1941.)

Sitdown strike
Industrial action taken when employees occupy a plant to preempt an employer's lockout

These successes were followed by recognition of other unions in other key mass production industries such as rubber, aluminum, and electrical products. Because such large numbers were involved, total union membership rose from six million in 1936 to twelve million in 1943 and seventeen million by the mid 1950s, when two thirds of the nonagricultural labor force were covered by collective bargaining. Of this number half were in AFL affiliated unions, 20 percent in CIO unions and the remainder in unaffiliated railroad brotherhoods and independent unions. Industrial unions' success in organizing in new areas stimulated the AFL to expand its own organizing efforts. To a certain extent, this involved recognizing that the original jurisdictional lines were blurring with the extension and increasing sophistication of machine technology. The next few decades were not easy. Union organizing continued to face industry opposition; public sympathy was weakened by charges and revelations of internal disputes, racketeering, and Communist infiltration; and some favorable labor legislation during the 1930s was followed by a conservative reaction.

Postwar Unionism

The Second World War brought both gains and losses for labor. Strikes threatened the defense effort in 1941, but cooperation followed. A no-strike/no-lockout agreement was agreed on, and the National War Labor Board was established to deal with issues that were not resolvable by peaceful means. One union aim was not conceded—the closed shop, in which a workplace is staffed by union members only—but the board did encourage the maintenance of union membership. A bigger problem was dealing with the inflation that accompanied the war effort. Wage increases were restricted to 15 percent, but prices rose by more, an obvious injustice to employees. To get around this problem, the tactic of granting fringe benefits (in effect, raising the standard of living without raising hourly wage rates) was used.

Collective bargaining was restored in 1945, although unemployment and continuing inflation were present, but it did not settle the unresolved disputes, and there was a new outbreak of strike activity. Widespread anti-union feeling also resurfaced, reflected in the 1947 Taft-Hartley Act. Its purpose was to restore to management the power it was thought to have lost to unions during the New Deal years. Secondary boycotts (in which workers in an industry not party to a strike refused to handle products from a struck employer), jurisdictional strikes, and the closed shop were banned; unions could be sued by employers; unions could not give contributions to political campaigns (although employers still could); unionists were not permitted to join the Communist Party; and a sixty-day notice before a labor contract could be terminated or modified

was required. In addition, states were permitted to pass more restrictive antiunion laws. These were the so-called right-to-work laws that some states, especially in the south, passed to outlaw the provision that employment be conditional on union membership. While the Taft-Hartley Act supported elections among workers to determine union representation, it was not an effective antistrike weapon. For example, it was not invoked in strikes involving coal miners, steelworkers, or New York dockworkers. Some of its provisions were strengthened with the passage of the Landrum-Griffin Act in 1959. The ban on secondary boycotts was broadened, picketing during strikes was further limited, and states were permitted to intervene in industrial disputes that were not sent for resolution to the National Labor Relations Board, a mediation agency. However, the Act, partly in response to developments in the 1950s, strengthened democratic procedures within unions, gave protection to union funds, and imposed penalties for criminal or Communist activity within unions.

Efforts were made by both union central organizations to clean up their acts and end the conflicts between them. The first problem centered around Communist infiltration and corruption. Here, the CIO was most active, as it had been prepared to accept support from any group during its initial years. Many unions had communist activists in their hierarchy since the decline of the IWW. The union involved was expelled if it would not, or could not, deal with this problem itself. The CIO expelled eleven unions, with 20 percent of its total membership, in 1950. Both the AFL and the CIO became much more active in dealing with corruption and Communist infiltration after this time. The second issue of conflict between the rival organizations was resolved in 1955, when the AFL and CIO agreed to merge. This made sense, as the cause of the original split—conflict over craft versus industrial unionism—was disappearing with the continuing elimination of skill differentials. In addition, both groups had new leaders who were committed to unity and who shared similar views on the role and activities of organized labor. Thus the labor movement supported various social welfare measures and civil rights activism during the 1960s. (Individual unions have not been too active in the antidiscrimination fight, preferring instead to focus on job security for their remaining members by institutionalizing the seniority system, which does little to help the employment history of newly hired minority groups.) Since then, unionization in the United States has weakened, and membership has fallen. This is partly due to the expansion of employment in areas where unionizing activity has always been weak, such as white collar and service occupations. In addition, continuing technological change has reduced total employment in the manufacturing areas where unions have traditionally been strongest, and has also encouraged a return to a focus on job security.

Why is the United States Least Unionized?

While unionism has weakened in all industrial countries since midcentury, the United States remained one of the least unionized. Explanations rely on differences in industrialization between different countries. Slower and less extensive unionization in the United States has been explained as the result of several influences not experienced elsewhere. First, the generally higher standard of living and absence of class consciousness have worked against the labor movement. In general, prosperity encourages conservatism, and when gains from material growth are shared, action to improve the well-being of specific groups is less likely. The persistence of a middle class ethic implies to many that an employee-wage earner status is not permanent. This belief can persist even when the structure of the economy does not encourage a self-employed status for the majority, and when there are real differences of status between middle and working class. Thus, a major

force encouraging the development of a working class consciousness in Europe was the recognition of economic inequality plus a desire to gain political equality through the extension of the vote. That real inequality existed in the United States seems to have been offset by other factors militating against the development of a strong labor movement.

Second, European working classes can trace a common, national heritage, which was not true in the United States. Immigration was important to United States industrialization, and it left several effects on unions. First, immigrants were desperate for work and could be more easily intimidated by employers, so they were less likely to join a union and risk loss of a much needed job. In addition, few of them could rely on accumulated savings or family support, so possession of a job was vital to survival. Second, immigrants were themselves separated by language, national origin, and religion, and were less likely to develop a consciousness of themselves as members of a common working class. Third, these differences were exploited by employers in their anti-union drives; they could play off fears of different groups against each other. Fourth, differences were also exploited by the early craft unions, which were anxious to protect their more privileged status against the encroachments of mass production and the new immigrants. (The conflict between skilled and unskilled workers was overcome at a much earlier stage of labor development in Europe, hence industrial unions there appeared much earlier than in the United States.) Fifth, while many immigrants brought socialist ideals with them—which were important in the European labor movement—the desire to become Americans often prevented these values from being passed on to new generations because prevailing opinion opposed socialism.

The third explanation is that the absence of any continued link with a political party removed both a unifying element and potential support for organizing efforts. Both were present in Europe, where the working class was important in political and economic movements. Finally, anti-union tactics proved effective for much longer in preventing permanent union organization. Employers could count not only on their own power in resisting unionization, but also on the support of the courts and the government. But this frequently led to much more violence in industrial disputes, which furthermore increased general hostility to unions and their members, aided by the feeling that unions were not part of a middle class way of life.

The very success of collective bargaining between established unions and employers continued to widen the gulf between unionized and unorganized workers and was even encouraged by many employers. If the price of labor peace was recognition of a union, it was a price that was willingly paid, as disruption of production by a small group of skilled workers could be damaging. Thus, the conditions of work and job stability improved in unionized areas but often remained poor in the unorganized ones.

Summary

The development of unions can be looked at from many different angles. On a very general level, unions can be seen as an attempt by workers to protect themselves against the workings of a competitive labor market, which guaranteed neither economic security nor adequate rewards. In this sense, unionization mirrors the attempts of companies that were also trying to protect themselves against the effects of competition. While economic theory uses the example of unions to demonstrate the introduction of monopoly elements into a competitive market, historical reality has never provided an example of a perfectly competitive market. Employers could always use their market power to take advantage of the mass of powerless individual workers. While it can be argued that this power was necessary to assist profit-making ability and the capital accumula-

tion process, it also produced economic inequality. Hence unions were formed both to try to offset the economic power of employers and to produce greater shares for workers in the wealth they were producing through collective action.

Also, on a very general level, and this was particularly true in Europe, unions as part of a broader labor movement were also concerned with attaining political equality as well as economic democracy. While capitalism is an economic phenomenon and is not synonymous with political democracy, most capitalist countries are also political democracies, but it took a long time for workers, who made up the majority of the population, to achieve political equality. It has been suggested that the earlier enfranchisement of workers in the United States weakened its labor movement by removing the unifying element found in European movements.

On a more specific level, unions have slowly eliminated the more idealistic of their original aims, to become instead more conservative, economic institutions. The major institution of collective bargaining dominates their efforts to improve the situation of their members within the capitalist system. This is not to deny that some more anti-capitalist elements may be found in different union movements, but they do not characterize the mainstream tradition. Economists remain divided over the question of the extent to which unionization has contributed to the higher material standards enjoyed by workers as a whole. Some argue that rising incomes made possible through the expansion of output would in any event have increased workers' incomes; others give greater credit to unionization or even to fears of unionization, which stimulated employers to make concessions so as to avoid outright unionization. In some respects, however, this debate is immaterial. Workers are both absolutely and relatively better off now than in the 19th century, and an individual worker today is unlikely to quarrel over the cause—the result is what matters.

Notes

1. Ironically, at the present time the wheel has turned full circle. Once more, new changes, especially technological changes associated with automation and robotics, are threatening the status of workers in many industries who fear loss of their jobs. This has led to an increasing emphasis on job security provisions in union contracts, often at the expense of wage gains, which is very similar to the aims of the earliest labor associations.

2. Contracting-in concerned the mechanism by which union dues were paid. Unions preferred a contracting-out system, whereby dues were automatically deducted from wages unless the worker specifically requested that this not be done. Anti-union forces preferred a contracting-in system in which the worker had to specifically request that union dues be deducted from wages. Given the reality of inertia, the former raised union income, the latter lowered it.

Key Concepts

Blackleg
Blacklist
Closed shop
Collective bargaining
Company union
Craft union
General strike
General union
Industrial union

Labor union
Lockout
New Model union
Open shop
Scab
Sitdown strike
Strike
Syndicalism
Yellow dog contract

Questions for Discussion or Essay Writing

1. Why were labor unions not formed until the 19th century?

2. In England, 1851 was a significant date for the development of labor unions. Why?

3. What legal and other remedies did employers have to oppose union formation in England?

4. What was the reason for the formation of the Labour Party in England?

5. What impact did various judicial and legislative decisions have on the development of the union movement in England at the turn of the century?

6. Why was there a General Strike in England in 1926? What were its results?

7. What were the major differences between unionization in the different countries covered in this chapter?

8. What were the problems, issues, and events that led to the elimination of the labor movement in Germany in the 1930s?

9. Why did French unions develop the syndicalist tradition rather than the reformist tradition?

10. Are there any hypotheses concerning the slower growth of unions in the United States?

11. Is prosperity or depression more likely to encourage unionization? Explain.

For Further Reading

Beard, Mary R. *A Short History of the American Labor Movement,* N.Y: Macmillan, 1927.

Briggs, Asa and John Savile, eds. *Essays in Labor History, 1886–1923.* Hamden, Conn: Archon Books, 1975.

Clegg, Hugh, *A History of British Trade Unions Since 1889.* Oxford: Clarendon Press, 1964.

Cole, G.D.H. and Raymond Postgate. *The British People 1746–1946.* London: Methuen, 1961.

Dubovsky, Melvyn. *Industrialism and the American Worker, 1865–1920,* N.Y: Thomas Crowell, 1975,

Dulles, Foster Rhea. *Labor in America: A History,* 3rd ed. Arlington Heights, Harlan Davidson (1949) 1966.

Ely, Richard T. *The Labor Movement in America,* N.Y: Thomas Crowell 1886.

Foster, John. *Class Struggle and the Industrial Revolution.* London: Weidenfeld & Nicolson, 1974.

Galenson, Walter, ed. *Comparative Labor Movements,* N.Y.: Russell & Russell, 1968.

Grob, Gerald. "Labor and the Negro, 1865–1900." *Labor History,* vol. 1.

Gutman, Herbert. "Work, Culture and Society in Industrializing America, 1815–1919." *American History Review* (June 1973): 531–588.

Hay, Douglas. *Property, Authority and Criminal Law* in Douglas Hay, *et. al.* eds, *Albion's Fatal Tree.* New York" Pantheon Books, 1975.

Hill, C.P. *British Economic and Social History, 1700–1975.* 4th ed. London: Edward Arnold, 1977.

Katznelson, Ira and Aristide Zolberg, eds. *Working Class Formation.* Princeton: Princeton University Press, 1986.

Kiernan, Victor. *Working Classes and Nation in 19th Century Britain,* in Maurice Cornforth, ed. *Rebels and their Causes*

Montgomery, David. *The Fall of the House of Labor: The Workplace, the State and American Labor Activism, 1865–1925,* N.Y.: Cambridge University Press, 1987.

Moore, Barrington. *Injustice: The Social Bases of Obedience and Revolt.* White Plains: M.E. Sharpe, 1978.

Painter, Nell Irvin. *Standing at Armageddon, The United States 1877–1919,* N.Y: W.W. Norton 1987.

Pelling, Henry. *A History of British Trade Unionism,* Harmondsworth: Penguin Books, 1963.

Stearns, Peter N, ed. *The Impact of the Industrial Revolution: Protest and Alienation.* Englewood Cliffs: Prentice Hall, 1972.

Thompson, E.P. *The Making of the English Working Class,* London: Victor Gollancz, 1963.

Ware, Norman. *The Industrial Worker 1840–1860,* Boston: Houghton Mifflin 1924.

_____ *The Labor Movement in the United States, 1860–1895,* New York: Appleton- Century- Crofts, 1929.

Webb, Sidney and Beatrice. *The History of Trade Unionism,* N.Y: Longmans, 1935.

Part V

The Internationalization of Mature Capitalism

Chapter 20

Imperialism and the Collapse of the International Order: I

I Trade and International Relations

THE LAST DECADES OF THE 19TH CENTURY WERE CONTRADICTORY. While the industrialized nations cooperated by adopting a common gold standard for regulating monetary relationships, and there was greater conformity and interdependence among financial institutions and methods, other developments increasingly undermined this seeming stability.

After 1870, and before the First World War, a world economy very different from the one existing at the beginning of the 19th century emerged. Several distinctive features have already been covered in earlier chapters; this one will focus on features that, while appearing to increase economic interdependency, had the contradictory effect of producing a breakdown of the international economic system. This was most apparent in the violence of the First World War, a destructive struggle between the leading industrial nations on a much larger scale than any previous war.

Attempts to return to the pre-1914 international situation after the end of the war were unsuccessful. Between the two world wars, a series of improvisations failed to restore cohesive-

ness to the international scene. This period included years of prosperity as well as the longest, widest, and deepest depression ever experienced by modern capitalism and was essentially one in which nations retreated inside their own borders in an attempt to solve their problems, not even paying lip service to the facts of international economic life that were tying them more closely together. Only after the Second World War was an international system that had stabilizing effects finally put into place. By this time, economic conditions were so different that the new system had very few pre-1914 characteristics.

Several characteristics of mature capitalism were already apparent in the late 19th century. Those already discussed include the spread of industrialization, the development of a second generation of new industrial techniques and industries, the increasing use of the corporate form of business organization, a tendency to concentration in industry that was helped by the rise of finance capitalism, and the development of workers' associations. Another very significant phenomenon with its roots in these changes affected international relationships between countries. There was increasing competition between capitalists in different countries, at first, simply an extension of the competition for markets in produced goods that had always existed. But then the growth of large integrated firms and the development of larger, more sophisticated financial institutions encouraged attempts to control raw material sources, partly in response to the perceived needs of advanced industrial capitalism. This often seemed to be easier if there was political control over the country where these sources were located, encouraging a new wave of colonization. It was called the "new imperialism" because of features distinguishing it from earlier colonizing activities, and it will be a major topic in this chapter.

Strangely enough, although these developments pushed countries further apart by increasing conflicts of interest among them, the late 19th century was also a time when almost all the industrialized countries were linked by adherence to a single system for regulating international economic relations. This was the gold standard, which supposedly adjusted international payments flows automatically and linked domestic economies to the outside world. It is ironic that although the "rules of the game" were widely agreed on, as will be seen below, the results of and adjustments to them were ultimately destabilizing. The "golden age" of competitive capitalism, already under strain because of the growth of monopoly elements in the late 19th century, was further strained by the inherent contradictions of the gold standard, attempts of countries to protect themselves from the automatic workings of self regulating markets, and the conflicts encouraged by the new imperialism.

Industrializing Economies

Before investigating these issues, let us recap briefly. The spread of industrialization from Great Britain involved an expansion of the wage relationship, both absolutely and relatively. By the end of the 19th century, 80 percent of the economically active population in Great Britain were wage earners, and between 1881 and 1911, the

number of industrial workers increased from 5.7 million to 8.6, with an additional 1.5 million workers employed in the transportation industry. Similarly, in Germany by 1907, 8.6 million workers were industrial workers, at which time about two thirds of the economically active population were wage earners. Although France had a large population, comparative figures are slightly lower because of the persistence of small shops, trades, and peasant farms, but the number of those people classified as "working class" increased from three million at the end of the 19th century to five million in 1913, when about three fifths of the economically active population were wage earners. Similar reasoning applied to the United States, where a proportionately larger part of the labor force were independent farmers. Even so, the growth of factory employment was very rapid. In 1870, only two million wage earners worked in factories; this number more than doubled to 4.5 million by 1899, and then almost doubled again to 8.4 million by 1919.

Changing Composition of Trade

Industrial output rose following productivity increases associated with innovation, and the volume of international trade expanded in spite of increased protectionism. Exports from all countries grew. Between 1875 and 1913, Germany and the United States, the two new capitalist powers, increased exports by four and five times respectively, while even the old capitalist economies of France and Great Britain saw exports increase by a factor of 1.8 and 2.2 respectively. What was significant was not only the absolute size but also the composition of trade, which shows the development of new industries—oil, chemicals, transportation, mass consumer goods—the second significant feature of late 19th century development. Trade between industrialized nations reflected a changing industrial structure as well as an expanding trade in the needed primary products. This involved closer links be-

Primary products
Unprocessed raw materials

tween industrial and underdeveloped economies, as the former tried to acquire the raw materials required for new industries such as tin, rubber, oil, and nickel as well as food items. In the thirty years before 1900, most of the previously underdeveloped agricultural areas of the world were opened up: the American West, Canada, Australia, Asiatic Russia, Latin America, for example, and many of the new mineral-yielding areas were discovered.

The total value of trade (i.e., including both exports and imports) was estimated at £800 million in 1850, and grew to £8 billion by 1913; almost half was trade between the industrialized nations. Although all countries experienced an absolute increase in trade, relative trade shares changed, mainly at the expense of France and Britain. Britain's share of world trade, 19 percent in the 1881-85 period, declined to 14 percent in the 1911-13 period although it still represented the largest foreign trade position of any country. The decline was chiefly due to the increase of German exports to America and to the industrialization of the United States itself, which reduced imports of manufactured goods.

Demand and Price Changes

The characteristics of goods traded had implications for the economies of producing countries. In general, the supply of primary products, whether agricultural or extractive, is fairly inelastic, so production levels do not change very quickly in response to price changes resulting from changes in demand. For example, once trees or bushes have been planted to produce tree crops such as fruit, coffee, or rubber, potential output depends on the number of mature trees that remain productive for many years. This implies that any given change in demand will produce much greater price variations than are observed

with manufactured goods, so producers' incomes tend to fluctuate more.

The pattern of relative price movements of manufactured and primary products depended on the extent of investment in productive facilities and the amount and pattern of demand. After 1850, the increase in industrialization and growth in urban labor forces favored primary producers, and the terms of trade moved in their favor as demand for their food exports increased. By the mid 1880s, the situation reversed. The new imperialism expanded the areas producing primary commodities, and investment in the necessary productive facilities—mines, plantations, transportation links, for example—resulted in falling prices relative to industrial goods as output increased. In addition, more bulky commodities and food were shipped across the world at much lower prices than before because of improvements in transportation. Thus, the timing of the growth of this type of trade reflects many factors: increased demand for food by urban industrial labor forces, especially in Europe, increased demand for new materials involved in new industries and processes, and the creation of a simplified mechanism for making international payments, as well as lower transportation costs. Primary producers' terms of trade reversed slightly around 1900 as the industrial countries recovered from the effects of the preceding depression. The demand for primary products grew, and renewed investment in manufacturing implied that industrial prices fell relative to those of primary products; the terms of trade again favored primary producers.

Terms of trade
Relative prices of imports and exports

The major implication for economic development emerging from this brief analysis concerns the emergence of a dual market structure. Given the characteristics of the supply of both types of goods and the tendency to increased concentration in the production of manufactured goods, primary goods' producers face a more competitive market situation. They are more subject to market fluctuations that affect their prices and incomes than are industrial producers, who can take advantage of their greater market power and insulate themselves somewhat from changing demand conditions. They adjust mainly with quantity changes rather than price changes, which are more usual in markets for primary products.

Focus is usually put on the trade in goods between countries, but there was also an impressive movement of productive resources (both labor and capital) across national borders in the late 19th century. The migration of labor both helped an industrialization process—especially in the United States—and also made the exploitation of agricultural areas possible. Between 1820 and 1930 the gross number of international migrants was 62 million, most moving from Europe and Asia to the Americas. Of these people, 61 percent emigrated to the United States, 12 percent to Canada, 10 percent to Argentina, 7 percent to Brazil, and the remainder to the white dominion areas of the British Empire: Australia, New Zealand, and South Africa. Internal migration was also significant in many countries. Agriculture in the American West became commercialized, and the steppes of Russia were opened up, and without contract laborers, much of the new plantation agriculture or mining operations in Asia would not have been undertaken.

Development of the Gold Standard

The international movement of money also took on new significance in this period. Increased trade would not have been possible without the growth of international banking institutions and the creation of a world payments system. International money flows included short-term capital flows associated with financing trade and long-term flows associated with foreign investment in pro-

ductive facilities. Exports of finance capital became more important and were associated with the new imperialism. Briefly, money flows across national borders in exchange for goods and services. However, unless trade is on barter terms and goods exchange directly for goods, differences in national currencies limit flows of goods unless buyers and sellers in different countries have some way to agree on their relative value in money terms. Also, if capital is exported from one country to another, for whatever reason, it is easier if there is a network of banks and financial institutions operating in a *world* market.

The two types of financial flows, short-term and long-term, are linked. Trade financing arises as one country acquires imports from another and its payments provide the means whereby the exporting country can acquire imports in turn. The advantage of a world market using a common payments standard is that trade does not have to be exactly balanced between any two countries. That is, the revenues each earns by exporting to each other do not have to be spent on the trading partner's goods. Instead, credits arising from exports can be used to acquire imports from anywhere. At the same time, because all payments in total have to balance, this also gives rise to the export of capital; if one country imports more than it exports, the difference is made good by exporting capital. This money flow is itself equivalent to an export but has results very different from an export of goods or services.

Capital Exports

The first capital exporter was Great Britain, joined by the other industrial countries by the end of the century. Britain had an adverse trade balance on its merchandise trade throughout most of the 19th century, offset by an increase in its invisible trade—earnings from shipping, banking, and

Merchandise trade
Trade in goods between countries

Invisible trade
Trade in services

other services—as well as by the export of capital. There are long-run implications. If capital is used to develop productive resources in foreign countries successfully, then profits in the form of interest or dividends flow back to the capital exporting country. So important were these in Britain's case that by 1870 the return flow of dividends and interest was large enough to produce a surplus on the entire balance of international payments, amounting to 20 percent of all income earned abroad by 1914.

Capital exports from the major industrial countries expanded at a faster rate than merchandise trade. The annual flow of foreign investment from Great Britain doubled from 1880-1884 to 1890-1894, then quadrupled from this level by the 1910-1913 period; France's foreign investment over the same period of time tripled; while foreign investment flows from Germany doubled in the decade 1883-1893 and doubled again in 1893-1913. By 1914, of all foreign capital invested abroad, 43 percent came from Great Britain, 20 percent from France, 13 percent from Germany, 12 percent from Belgium, Switzerland and the Netherlands, 7 percent from the United States and 5 percent from other sources. What could be seen initially as a short-term stop-gap measure—financing a merchandise trade deficit—resulted in a long-term issue with important economic and political implications.

Reasons for Adopting a Single Payments System

Two other pressures encouraged the development of a single, integrated payments mechanism, one pragmatic and the other related to the ideology of the automatically self-regulated market and the desire to maintain currency stability. Pragmati-cally, international trade was encouraged and payment for it simplified if there was certainty about the relative worth of one currency in terms of another. Even if a country's currency (coins) was defined in terms of a specific weight of gold or silver, exchange rates can still vary widely. Variation was caused by the slow speed at which coins or gold were shipped from one country to another, and by the lag of information about economic conditions in other countries. However, in the 19th century, both transportation and international communications improved, especially after the introduction of the electric telegraph and cable. Uncertainty about relative exchange values was reduced, and they were also stabilized as national monetary authorities controlled currency values more effectively.

The way was cleared to the adoption of an international gold standard once monetary units were defined in terms of gold, and gold became the common denominator in international payments. All the major trading countries adopted the gold standard by 1897. It defined the value of their currency unit and assisted the expansion of international trade once easy convertibility of currency into gold was required. In practice, most international trade was actually financed in sterling, mainly due to the large international trade position of Britain and the development of an internationally oriented banking and money center in London. Initially, financing of foreign trade was short-term (the time depending on the speed of making foreign contracts and shipping goods), and tended to turn over quickly. It was also advantageous that trade financing was centered in only a few places, so that foreign exchange "released" when the debt was paid could be used for another transaction. The earliest development of trade financing was undertaken by merchant bankers who, because British trade was so extensive, played an important role as foreign exchange intermediaries by discounting foreign bills of exchange.

London Money Market

The development of the London money market as the major international banking center took a new direction after 1871 and also gained when the Paris money center weakened after the debacle of the Franco-Prussian War. Change occurred when bill brokers, who were chiefly responsible for discounting internal bills of exchange, expanded their operations and borrowed from domestic banks. The domestic banking system was growing extremely rapidly at this time, implying that more funds were available, and the existence of a large pool of sterling funds enabled the bill brokers to start discount operations internationally. Because they were themselves borrowing in sterling, it was easier for importers—wherever in the world they were located—to issue sterling promises-to-pay to their creditors, who in turn were willing to accept them because of the discounting services available and their faith in the stability of sterling's value. But mere availability of sterling was not sufficient for the development of a world market for money, so why were the years 1870 to 1914 the only period of an almost complete, functioning gold standard? An explanation of the prevalent theory of the self-regulating economy is needed, which shows the importance of maintaining exchange stability. All nations were trying to maintain stability, and as sterling accounted for so large a proportion of international finance, its widespread acceptability helped reduce uncertainty to a greater degree than if all countries were trying to coordinate trade using their own currencies.

Gold Standard and Self-Regulating Markets

The 19th century laissez faire economists treated money as only a medium of exchange, and the development of a market for money represented the spread of a market system to regulate economic activity. They thought that no interference from a noneconomic body was necessary. If a currency was tied to gold, the domestic economy could be left to adjust itself automatically to international trade and money flows. Automatic adjustment depended on free convertibility of gold to or from any domestic currency and the widespread existence of markets for goods as well as productive resources. That is, an integrated money mechanism worked to produce self-regulation because all economic activity was regulated by money.

This simplified view of the operation of economic mechanisms ignored many factors that help explain why the international system disintegrated later. Four important omissions are worth mentioning. First, it forgot the role of currency in the national state. One of the first functions of a ruler in the new nation states of earlier centuries was to control the nation's money supply; it was a visible symbol that a single nation did in fact exist. To expect nations to forgo control over a domestic money supply in the interests of a self-regulating international system belittles the importance of national sovereignty. Second, this view ignored the interdependencies existing between the economy and the society; they are not two separate entities. Automatically adjusting economies would impose impossible strains on the social fabric and make perfect economic freedom incompatible with the maintenance of social stability. Thus it is not surprising that the adoption of the gold standard, seemingly a move toward greater nonintervention, was in fact paralleled by increasing protection, both domestically and internationally. The third oversight lay in assuming money's neutrality.

Money is more than simply a medium of exchange and it does influence economic decision making. If domestic enterprises depended on bank credit, then they would be affected by changes in the money supply, and thus the auto-

---

Bill broker

Specialized financier who buys bills of exchange (at a discount) from holders

matic regulating mechanism works—but it could also adversely affect company survival and thus output and employment. In addition, the flexibility of, and speed with which, markets and prices adjusted to an external stimulus also determined the degree of success of the adjustment mechanism. Many governments in the late 19th century were at least beginning to consider the implications of economic breakdown, and industrialists, farmers, and workers were also trying to protect themselves from the uncertain fluctuations of the market. Finally, on the international level, not all countries were equal players, and some had greater political and economic power than others. This makes it difficult to imagine one country doing nothing if another's currency fell in value and it became unable to repay its debts. What was more likely to happen—and did happen in a few cases—was that a prospective default would be met with an application of gunboat diplomacy or the extension of political control over the debtor country. It should therefore be remembered that the gold standard system worked, not because it was left to itself, but because governments did actively intervene to keep money markets functioning in an orderly way.

How the Gold Standard Worked

Adoption of the gold standard represented the high point of the spread of the market system in the 19th century. First goods, then labor and land, and now money, and money on an international scale, became subject to market forces. The theoretical advantage of linking money and thus the domestic economy to an international market was to remove any possibility of domestic governmental interference, thereby achieving the purest form of laissez faire by removing currency questions from politics. In the purest and simplest version, if a country imported more than it exported, the deficit on its balance of merchandise trade was made good by an outflow of gold. This reduced the money supply, and therefore domes-

tic prices were supposed to fall. Simultaneously, another country would be experiencing an inflow of gold caused by its surplus balance; therefore its money supply and domestic prices would rise. The market reaction is that exports from the deficit country rose as its prices became relatively cheaper, while those from the surplus country fell as its prices became relatively more expensive. In this way, continual trade and price adjustments worked to restore balance of payments equilibrium.

In exactly the same way, governments were preempted from adopting any policy designed to overcome a domestic problem. For example, a public works program to alleviate unemployment could not be adopted if it produced a government budget deficit financed by an expansion of money. The central bank could not ease credit to industry to stimulate business and ease unemployment. The result in either case would be rising prices, therefore lower exports and therefore a deficit in the balance of payments that would result in an outflow of gold, which was to be avoided. This was the mechanism that was supposed to produce an automatic adjustment and preserve the value of the currency.

Public works program
Government-financed projects to help remedy unemployment, usually involving infrastructure projects

---

Unstable Conditions

However, while the actual international payments system did make trade and money flows easier, exchange stability and economic stability was not always automatic. For example, a gold outflow did not automatically restrict the money supply and thus produce deflation—this would occur only if businesses were heavily dependent on bank credit and/or if money were exclusively specie (commodity) money. Deflation was also limited by the decrease in competition resulting from increased concentration and protectionism. One of the reasons farmers in all countries wanted tariff protection was to escape from the uncertainties caused by price fluctuations in world markets for their output, markets which were much more competitive than those of manufacturing industries. In addition, the worldwide network of commercial and financial transactions characterizing this period had the effect of increasing interdependency. After midcentury, economic influences originating in any one country spread to others, making it difficult for any one to remain isolated from international events. For example, while financial panics (usually declines in stock prices and bank failures) were often transmitted from one to another early in the 19th century, fluctuations in levels of output, employment, and income were not. A depression in Great Britain remained a British phenomenon and would not necessarily be experienced elsewhere. But later, the linkages coming with increased trade and money flows tended to export depressed or prosperous conditions in one country to others. So, of seventeen large countries, ten experienced a recession in 1890-1891, fifteen were in recession in 1900-1901 and again in 1907-1908, and twelve were in recession in 1912-1913. The same pattern was observed with price trends.

The reason lies with the increase in trade. If one country experienced a balance of payments deficit, and lowered its imports as a result, it reduced demand for exports from its trading partners. With limited price flexibility, the industries producing export goods adjusted by cutting back production and thus employment. Lower employment levels in these industries in turn affected industries producing for the domestic market; less purchasing power translated into less demand for their output, so output and employment cutbacks spread into other industries. Lower national income as a whole led to a lower demand for imports, which affected other countries. This was exaggerated if bank credit were not eased to offset short term liquidity problems, but playing by the strict rules of the gold standard prevented such domestic measures. So the problem spread more easily from one country to another, whatever the original cause. Similarly, an improvement in one country easily stimulates demand and thus production levels in another country. This transmission mechanism increased the stress on international relationships. The increase in world production associated with initial industrialization could not be repeated. However, the potential for increased political and social tension grew because continued growth, and therefore prosperity, depended on growing markets and adequate supplies of inputs. This was particularly acute for European powers, which depended much more on foreign trade than the United States with its huge internal market and resources.

Rising Tensions

Internationally, there was no major war in the period 1871-1914 but there were minor conflicts and many "incidents." For example, Britain fought the Boers in South Africa in 1899-1902, disagreed with Germany over possession of some Pacific Ocean islands, and argued with Russia over spheres of influence in Persia and Afghanistan; France faced problems in Egypt (with Britain), and in dealing with anticolonial uprisings in North Africa; in 1911, Italy gained control of Libya from Turkey; Japan, the emerging Asian capitalist power, wrested Formosa from China in 1894 and fought a war with Russia in 1904, successfully taking control of Manchuria; and the United States fought Spain in 1898, ending up with control over the former Spanish colonies in the Caribbean and Pacific.

The increase in international trade, adoption of the gold standard, and increasing protectionism occurred simultaneously. Domestically, for so long as markets for productive resources were not universal, it was possible to accept the idea of self-regulation of markets, because there was always a safety valve in the nonmonetized, nonmarket sectors that cushioned the shocks coming from the monetized market sector. This was no longer true by the last third of the century, even in the United States. This meant that truly automatically adjusting markets would have threatened the survival of society, if, for example, falling wages in a nonclearing labor market pushed wages below what was needed for survival. To avoid this, social legislation and unionization protected labor against the impersonal workings of the economic system, and farmers also demanded protection, via tariffs, against what they saw as unjust results of market forces. Tariffs were difficult to remove once they were in place, and they also stimulated demands from industry for protection against foreign competition. These demands are linked: Tariffs on agricultural products increased living costs, encouraging wage demands from labor, and both helped justify tariffs on industrial goods to give industry the same advantages as agriculture and justify higher prices. Industrialists were also developing mechanisms to isolate themselves from the working of the market mechanism. Various forms of cooperative agreement to eliminate rivalry helped them to control their environment better, rather than being controlled by it.

In addition, depressed conditions after 1873 encouraged protective reactions. The length of the depression—it lasted until 1896—made it difficult to retain faith in a speedy automatic market adjustment and showed the hardships resulting from unemployment and a shifting industrial structure. Thus, the extension of automaticity (although never as complete as in the textbook example) implied by the adoption of the gold standard had to be accompanied by devices intended to protect societies by providing security and stabilizing incomes. So the consequences of the unfettered workings of free markets were modified by turning competitive markets into monopolized ones, even though it resulted in new problems. This reasoning eliminates the seeming paradox of the spread of free

trade in free markets combined with increasing protection and restraints on the working of these markets. However, there was yet another protective device that could be used: Acquire new colonies to which the pressures could be diverted.

II Imperialism: Justification for the New Colonialism

European powers in the 16th and 17th centuries had acquired many colonies in non-European areas, motivated partly by economics (colonies were essential parts of mercantilist empires) and partly by strategic reasons. In the 18th and 19th centuries enthusiasm for colonization waned, and a few former colonies became independent. This anticolonial bias was also helped by the prevailing liberal view that saw colonies as expensive luxuries. The costs of administering them and protecting them against outside attack or internal unrest was a drain on national treasuries, and also their

---

Imperialism
Colonization, especially in the late 19th century

---

value as exclusive sources for some primary products decreased as improved transportation opened up new, lower-cost, sources. Also, domestic industrialization provided a more profitable outlet for surplus capital funds than overseas ventures. In addition, laissez faire attitudes encouraged the separation of politics from economics, and colonies did not fit in well with a noninterventionist view.

But after 1870, a mad scramble for the remaining politically unprotected areas of the world resulted in two thirds of the world's population having some form of dependency on the advanced capitalist nations by 1914. The "old" European colonizing powers, with the exception of Spain and Portugal, and with the addition of the new colonizing powers of Germany and the United

Table 20-1
Decolonization: Dismantling the old Colonial Empires
Country,* date of independence, and colonizer**

Country	Date	Colonizer
Haiti	1804	France
Chile, Columbia, Mexico	1810	Spain
Paraguay, Venezuela	1810	Spain
Argentina	1816	Spain
Costa Rica, El Salvador, Guatemala		
Honduras, Nicaragua,		
Panama, Peru	1821	Spain
Brazil	1822	Portugal
Ecuador	1822	Spain
Bolivia	1825	Spain
Greece	1827	Turkey (Ottoman Empire)
Uruguay	1828	Brazil
Canada	1867	UK
Cuba	1898	Spain
	1902	US
Australia	1901	UK
Bulgaria	1908	Turkey (Ottoman Empire)
South Africa	1910	UK
Albania	1912	Turkey (Ottoman Empire)
Czechoslovakia	1918	Austria
Yemen, Yugoslavia		Turkey
Afghanistan	1919	UK
Egypt	1922	UK
Vietnam	1945	France
Indonesia (Dutch East Indies)	1945	Netherlands
Philippines	1946	US
India, Pakistan	1947	UK
Myanmar (Burma),		
Sri Lanka (Ceylon)	1948	UK
Laos	1949	France
Libya	1951	Italy
Cambodia	1953	France
Morocco, Tunisia	1956	France
Sudan	1956	UK
Ghana (Gold Coast), Malaysia	1957	UK
Guinea (French Guinea)	1958	France
Cyprus	1960	UK

Table 20-1 (continued)

Country	Date	Colonizer
Benin (Dahomey), Burkina Faso (Upper Volta), Cameroon, Central African Republic, Chad, Congo (Congo-Brazzaville), Gabon, Ivory Coast, Madagascar (Malagasy Republic), Mali (French Sudan), Niger, Senegal, Togo	1960	France
Algeria	1962	France
Jamaica, Trinidad & Tobago, Uganda	1962	UK
Kenya	1963	UK
Malta	1964	UK
Gambia, Maldives	1965	UK
Barbados, Botswana (Bechuanaland), Guyana (British Guiana), Lesotho (Basutoland)	1966	UK
Equatorial Guinea (Spanish Guinea)	1968	Spain
Mauritius, Swaziland	1968	UK
Fiji, Tonga	1970	UK
Bahrain, Qatar	1971	UK
Bahamas	1973	UK
Guinea-Bissau (Portugese Guinea)	1973	Portugal
Grenada	1974	UK
Surinam (Dutch Guiana)	1975	Netherlands
Angola, Cape Verde, Mozambique, Sao Tome	1975	Portugal
Comoros	1975	France
Seychelles	1976	UK
Djibouti	1977	France
Dominica, Soloman Islands, Tuvalu	1978	UK
Kiribati (Gilbert Islands), St. Lucia St. Vincent & Grenadines	1979	UK
Antigua & Barbuda, Belize (British Honduras)	1981	UK
St. Kitts & Nevis	1983	UK
Brunei	1984	UK

* Colonial name in parentheses   ** UN Trusteeships (mainly for German colonies) are not given.

States extended the territories under their control. Britain (including Ireland), with a population of only 41 million people added 4.75 million square miles and 88 million more people to its empire by 1914; France added four million square miles and 56 million (the population of France was only 36 million); Germany gained colonies of one million square miles in extent; tiny Belgium's possessions amounted to .9 million square miles; Italy's were 185,000 square miles, and even the United States, after an internal colonization process against the American Indians, acquired effective control of 125,000 square miles outside its borders.

Why did this renewed surge of colonizing activity occur, and occur when it did? The motivation for and timing of this new imperialism are related to the progress of industrial capitalism. However, much of the justification for colonial expansion was not valid. The new imperialism did not enrich the colonizing countries, although many individuals did gain enormous fortunes as a result. It did not improve conditions in the colonized countries to any great extent, although one justification was to expand productive facilities and "civilize" the native populations.

Colonies as New Markets

To consider timing first, colonization appears an almost inevitable stage of development. Industrial expansion in more countries than before had reached the stage of mass production, with several results. Higher incomes increased domestic demand for goods, but because there was significant inequality in the distribution of incomes, demand increased by less than the increase in output. So there was a search for overseas markets to absorb the surplus to avoid a problem with overproduction. At the same time, many formerly open export markets were being at least partly closed by the late 19th century surge of protectionism. The reluctance of industrial countries to expand trade with each other encouraged a movement into new protected market areas. As it turned out, they were not very important as markets because they were low income areas—but the important point is that the motive emerged from the logic of the industrialization process at that time. The long depression of 1873-1896 also encouraged the desire of many industrial groups to obtain protected markets where risks might be lower than in existing ones. That they successfully enlisted their government's support further demonstrates the weakness of laissez faire ideology to provide a guide to practical action.

Mass production also generated higher savings, a result of the higher level of national income. For so long as outlets for investment existed at home—and initial industrialization, development of transportation networks, and the emergence of new, capital intensive second generation industries and technologies were important outlets for most of the century—there was no problem finding profitable uses for these funds. But toward the end of the century, rates of return on domestic loans fell, and domestic investment increasingly tended to flow into foreign outlets. It occurred in many ways: loans to governments, acquisition of foreign bonds or securities, direct investment in social overhead capital projects (such as railways), mining or plantation enterprises. Here again, political and military weakness in host countries could be taken advantage of by promoters, who knew that their interests would be protected by their own governments. Any doubt that expected returns would not be generated was resolved by the application of military power, meshing economic and political interests. Investors were anxious to stake out claims in colonized areas as part of the competitive struggle against capitalists from other countries. Governments, even when anti-imperialist elements were influential, were willing to support these efforts for fear that new areas would fall under the domination of other powers.

Colonies and Mature Industrialization

All this was encouraged by the concentration of production and finance capital, another feature of the late 19th century. The transformation of competitive markets into more monopolized ones, while seeming to provide greater certainty for the participants, weakened the ability of the economy to correct itself. Concentration, and the resulting behavior of corporations, made prices and costs stickier so that adjustment to economic shocks did not come through price adjustments, as expected by economic theory. So recessionary conditions lengthened, unprofitable assets had to be liquidated, the industrial structure became less flexible, and social tensions increased, producing an incentive to look outside the domestic economy for ways to relieve these tensions. One mechanism was the formation of international cartels that effectively shared the world market among members. Another led to a territorial division of the world in which each country had exclusive influence over markets or raw material sources. This could be done and capital exported to these areas because the growing world financial networks made it possible. Larger and more powerful financial institutions in turn had every incentive to support industrialists because the profitability of their loans and financial backing depended on continued industrial expansion.

All these factors were important in explaining the participation of the United States in imperialist rivalries, a participation that began in the 1890s. While the United States, unlike the European powers, had no heritage of colonial expansion, it faced similar strong economic pressures. By 1890, the basic elements of a mature capitalist economy were in place: An industrial structure that was increasingly concentrated in core areas, a transportation network that made a huge continental market a reality, and a large agricultural sector. But the depression of 1893 had brought with it a sense that economic opportunities were now fewer; the western frontier was effectively closed, and it seemed as though few new productive investment opportunities existed. Increasingly large amounts of surplus capital were all too often diverted into purely speculative ventures. At the same time, it was important to merge the huge numbers of immigrants into the mainstream of American life.

There were large enterprises with the ability, need, and finances to move overseas and also a belief that continued prosperity depended on colonial expansion that would produce a true sense of nationalism in all countries. This merged patriotic and materialistic motives. Finally, industrial growth provided a motive for imperial expansion, and also provided the means to make it effective. Nonindustrialized peoples, even in long-established civilizations such as in China, were economically and militarily powerless to prevent Western encroachment on their sovereignty.

In summary, the timing of the new wave of imperialist activity is related to increasing strains in three areas. First, structural changes in the domestic economy threatened declines of production, employment, and earnings unless pressure could be reduced by international expansion. Second, social and political tensions could be partly offset by domestic intervention measures such as social legislation, but external involvement also provided a safety valve. Third, an increase in tariff protection and the resulting potential loss of markets for manufacturers increased international strains.

Noneconomic Justification

Justifying imperialist ventures had both economic and noneconomic elements. The noneconomic reasons are related to the cultural arrogance of Western nations when facing peoples of different cultures, races, and colors. For a long time, Christian missionaries had been active in many non-Western areas, and frequently their persecution gave an excuse for military invasion. The idea of "the white man's burden"—the idea that the natives of other countries must be "saved" or civilized—was widespread. It implied that non Western races and cultures were inferior, and that imperialists had a duty to bring them into the civilized modern (Western) world. (This arrogance when faced with an alien culture probably resulted in worse treatment of colonized peoples than was acceptable in the treatment of the working classes or minority groups in the home country.) For example, the United States fought Spain in 1898, ostensibly to free the Spanish colonies of Cuba and the Philippines. The advantages of retaining control then required an excuse for staying. President McKinley justified staying in the Philippines by stating that the Filipinos were unfit for self-government, so the United States should stay there to educate and convert them to Christianity in order to improve their capability for independence.

Although the origin of American expansionism could be traced back to 1823, no action took place until later. In 1823, President Monroe presented what later became known as the Monroe Doctrine. It contained two messages to influence foreign policy decisions. First, the United States would not sit idly by if any European power attempted to colonize in the Western Hemisphere because it would be seen as a threat to United States national safety. Second, the United States would not become involved in European affairs. It was restated in 1895, and became much more activist in its insistence that the United States was dominant in the Western Hemisphere. That is, it reaffirmed United States resistance to European "intervention" in Latin America, and justified United States intervention in Latin American countries in the interests of preserving civilization, punishing wrongdoing or "correcting" a

---

Monroe Doctrine

Influence on United States foreign policy; the Western hemisphere is within the United States' sphere of influence

---

weak government. United States intervention in weak countries was rationalized as protecting civilization and independence against the encroachments of the European powers.

In addition, it is possible that this national prestige argument, wherever it was used, helped relieve social tensions at home. Even the lower classes, most of whom were only just beginning to share in the benefits of industrialization, could be pacified by a belief in their innate superiority to colored and non Western peoples, as well as by the feeling of national pride gained through foreign conquests.

Economic Justification

Much more important as a justification for imperialism was the idea that it was economically necessary. This argument, in brief, stated that imperialist expansion was necessary. This necessity emerged from the need to secure foreign markets and sources of supply for the industrialization process and to provide new outlets for investment funds—three related arguments based on the belief that imperialism would be profitable. That it proved not to be was immaterial. Past colonial expansion had often been profitable, at least for the individual investors and companies engaged in it, and there was a fairly general support for overseas expansionism for other reasons. If colonial expansion was to provide new and protected markets, both domestic supply and demand conditions were relevant. Improvements in production technologies had created the potential for an expansion of output greater than the expansion of purchasing power and effective demand. Therefore, selling excess output abroad maintained sales at levels high enough to keep up producers' profits.

Expanding exports to generate high sales ran into the tariff barriers being erected by many industrial nations. Therefore, these former export markets were unreliable as permanent and growing markets, so the only solution was to acquire colonies to provide the necessary markets for the surplus output of the metropolitan country. As further discussed by John Hobson, the gap between potential output and aggregate demand was caused by an unequal income distribution, which, if left unaltered produced business cycles of expansion followed by contraction. This inequality resulted in low incomes for the working classes, so they had insufficient buying power, while at the other end of the income scale, capitalists and rentiers (whose incomes came from financial investments) had so much income they could not possibly consume all the output the economy was capable of producing. Again, the existence of foreign markets was necessary.

Not all industries required this extra outlet, but it was important for those whose production depended on large capital investments to establish production facilities. This was because only growing sales, and as a corollary, no unsold inventories, would justify making that investment in the first place. In addition, there are links between foreign sales and foreign investment. For example, if capital is exported to build a rail network, it stimulates demand for related items such as electrical systems, rolling stock, and so on, providing markets for many other industries. Rail construction in other countries was an important outlet for European industries once the United States no longer needed it. British companies built railways in India, German companies built them in the Middle East, and the Russian rail network was partly financed with French investors' money.

Colonies as Sources of Raw Materials

The second argument, that colonial expansion was necessary to secure supplies of raw materials, reflects the changing nature of industrialization, especially the emergence of new industries. Many new industries required materials either not found in Europe or not available in sufficient quantities, so it seemed vital for companies requiring them to exploit foreign sources overseas. Furthermore,

exclusive control denied access to foreign rivals, giving a new growing company an advantage over its international competition. Also, vertically integrated companies tried to reduce risks by controlling their input sources. Even when exclusive control was not obtained (which it rarely was), this practice still provided more security and helped keep nonintegrated competitors in line by limiting their options, thus limiting competition. This argument was less relevant for the United States, which as a continent-sized country had access to a much wider variety of new resources within its own borders, including the vitally important new resource, oil. But it was appealing to the European countries, and the case of Britain is instructive. The British Isles are in general resource poor, and while existing coal and iron ore deposits had been important for the first Industrial Revolution, lack of materials such as minerals, oil, and timber stimulated efforts to acquire exclusive sources to avoid total reliance on the unpredictable free market for obtaining supplies.

So cotton growing in Egypt was encouraged, Malaya became the location of cultivated rubber plantations and an important source of tin, Australia and New Zealand increased in importance for both agricultural and mineral resources (especially copper and zinc), while Africa presented new opportunities for exploitation of raw material resources. Other European countries too developed colonies for precisely the same reason, while even the United States justified its right to intervene in Cuba to protect American sugar growing interests there.

Foreign Investment in Colonies

Finally, the third argument for imperial expansion focused on the role of capital exports from the industrialized country to the colony. Foreign investment was seen as necessary to develop the foreign market and exploit foreign resources. Much more important, the existence of foreign outlets for surplus capital had implications for the domestic economy itself, especially for the continued profits so necessary for continued capitalist expansion. There are several complementary elements. One is that the process of capital accumulation depends on continued investment expanding profit-making ability. Continued investment is not automatic; even if funds exist, there may be no incentive to further investment. This became particularly relevant in the late 19th century. Initial industrialization had provided incentives earlier; second generation industry development and the absorption of funds involved in the concentration of industry had done so later. Now the problem of equating aggregate demand to potential output became crucial. With new or improved technologies, potential output expanded faster than demand, but if the gap was not filled up somehow, unsold output and unused financial surpluses would accumulate, resulting in depression, a rise in unemployment, and an increase in social tensions. Expansion of other forms of expenditure, especially government expenditure, would achieve balance, but this was not seriously considered in the 19th century because it upset the laissez faire distinction between the political and economic spheres. As previously noted, inequality in income distribution plus a slow rise of the lower classes' incomes prevented consumption expenditures from rising sufficiently to justify expanded investment in new industries at home.

Furthermore, widespread acceptance of the idea of diminishing returns encouraged the export of capital. That is, if there were no new opportunities, continued investment produced smaller and smaller additions to profits. If further investment at home could not produce a sufficient increase in aggregate demand necessary to maintain profits at an acceptable level, capital should be exported to maintain high rates of profit at home. Underdeveloped countries, by definition, were capital short, therefore investment there should produce higher returns than were available at home. This investment both increased demand

for the output of industry and absorbed funds that would otherwise be unused or used for speculative paper ventures. Even the possibility that poor countries might be poor risks because of weak government or the potential for internal upheaval was not a problem. Bringing them under the political control of a colonial administration, backed if necessary by superior military strength, minimized political risks and guaranteed the interests of investors by providing a greater certainty of returns.

Whether or not these justifications were valid, the fact remained that the new colonies were not significant as outlets for either investment or exports. In 1914, total British capital invested abroad—and Britain had by far the largest foreign investment position—amounted to £3.763 billion. Some 20 percent was invested in the not-very-risky United States, a further 20 percent in Latin American countries, chiefly Argentina, 5 percent in Europe, and about 8 percent in other countries. The remaining 47 percent was invested within the empire with 80 percent of this placed in the temperate zone, white dominion countries of Australia, Canada and South Africa, leaving only a relatively small amount for the large colony of India and all the new acquisitions. The same was true of both France and Germany. Only 8 percent of France's private foreign investment was in her colonies, while most was invested in Europe, and only 12 percent of Germany's foreign investment was in her colonies. The pattern of trade followed the same lines—in spite of all the barriers, most trade was between already industrialized countries, although there was a perceptible shift in Britain's trade. In 1914, 37 percent of all exports went to the empire, and 25 percent of all imports came from the empire, but half of all this trade was with the older dominion countries.

Also, while much foreign investment was attracted by the promise of higher rates of return than were available at home, actual returns were usually lower, demonstrating that poorer countries were poorer credit risks. Unforeseen events could result in a default, as in Russia after 1917, when the new Soviet government refused to honor the debts of the old Czarist regime. It is hardly surprising that, as such eventualities could not be foreseen, most foreign investment continued to go to areas that seemed more stable.

Overseas investment did make a contribution to the continuing problem of deficient demand at home, the result of enlarged expenditures made by the state for the administration and control of the new colonial areas. Thus, ironically, an increase in public expenditures was necessary—but it represented a drain on government revenues that did little to improve national wealth. It was supported by businesses with foreign interests because it helped give an extra guarantee for their investments. In addition, such spending helped keep employment high without the drawbacks businesses associated with other forms of public expenditure, such as social programs. The danger with imperialist policies, which climaxed early in the 20th century, was that they intensified competition and led to the potential for actual conflict. Because investors and companies operating overseas knew they could count on government support in the event of any problem, this implied that what started as a commercial rivalry could escalate to open warfare.

Process of Colonization

Up to 1800, the New World and parts of Asia were the main areas for European colonization. Sometimes the acquisition of a colony was incidental. This might occur if a group of missionaries or traders clashed with local authorities, initiating a military takeover by the colonizing country. Or colonization was the outcome of either military adventurism or a deliberate attempt to produce commercial settlements—both were frequent in the New World. Many of the older colonies changed hands frequently. For example, Sri Lanka (the island of Ceylon) was first taken by the Portuguese, passed into Dutch hands from 1660 to 1796, and then became a British possession until independence in 1947. Similarly, the area of Vietnam was a tributary state of China, but after a struggle for independence (which was only a brief interlude) it became drawn into the French overseas empire. European interest in Asia was long-standing. The Dutch and Spanish were the first to set up trading and military posts (the Dutch were the only European traders permitted to trade with Japan after 1641), followed by the Portuguese in the 16th century (Goa and Macao), the British in the 17th century (Madras, Bombay, Calcutta) and the French. China remained untouched, even though Britain and France in the 18th century extended their influence over Asian countries formerly considered to be part of the Chinese sphere of influence.

At the beginning of the 19th century, many of these possessions had changed hands or been lost entirely. Britain lost its American colonies, and France, which formerly had a large colonial empire in India, Canada, and the West Indies in addition to slave-trading stations in Senegal (West Africa), retained only a few islands in the West Indies and off the coast of Newfoundland, Cayenne in South America, and trading posts in Africa and India. Similarly, Spain and Portugal saw the disappearance of much of their colonial empires. Later in the 19th century, when interest in colonization was renewed, the major phase of imperialist land grabbing occurred after 1870, and Africa, the only continent not greatly affected by previous colonization, was divided up by the Great Powers.

Special Case of China

China, center of an ancient civilization, was a major prize. For as long as long distance trade had existed, China was an important source of many items desired by Europeans, but did not become a colony of any power, although many attempts were made. Many of its client states were colonized, however, and China itself ended the 19th century a powerless, humiliated country that had been forced to concede parts of its territories to the "barbarian invaders" and grant them lucrative concessions for railway building and mineral extraction. The process of humiliation began in 1840, with the Opium Wars between China and Britain. What was at issue here was the desire of British traders to sell something to China in exchange for the valuable goods—silks, porcelain, tea, for example—that China exported, but the Chinese aristocracy did not care for Western goods. The traders found that opium, grown in India, could be profitably sold in China, although its sale was illegal. Inevitably, the Chinese authorities tried to prevent the sale of so damaging a substance, but were defeated in the war. The treaty following in 1842 forced China to open five ports to British merchants.

China was thus forced to open up to Westerners. Extraterritorial rights were granted to all the major trading nations, and China's southern borders became dominated by the French, British, and Germans, and its northern borders by Russia and Japan. In addition, Britain extended its influence in Malaya and Burma, France extended its influence in Vietnam (Cochin China in 1862, Tonkin in the 1870s, and Annam in 1884) and Cambodia, while the Russians took Port Arthur in 1898. China became divided into "spheres of influence"; actual physical partition of the country was discouraged by two factors. One was fear of war—not war with China, but rather fear of war among European powers themselves resulting from conflict over the spoils. The other was the rise of Japan. Japan, which had been opened to trade by the Dutch, escaped actual colonial status and showed an ability to learn Western ways when necessary. Thus, Japan quickly industrialized late in the 19th century to avoid the threat of Western domination, but still left much of its social structure intact.

Japan's success also alerted it to the advantages of imperialism. First, it seized Formosa in 1894 and then fought a war with Russia in 1905. To everyone's surprise (and presenting a blow to the idea of Western superiority to oriental races), this Asian upstart defeated Russia, for the first time producing a successful challenge to Western expansionism. Victory was followed in 1910 by annexation of Korea. Meanwhile, China tried to fight back but was unsuccessful. The Boxer Rebellion of 1900 was an attempt to remove all foreign influences from China, but Western troops crushed the rebellion and occupied Peking, forcing China to pay indemnities.

India

Britain's major colony was India. For a long time, the British East India Company dominated India, but its policies, while producing personal fortunes for company officials, had few redeeming features. Indian cotton manufacture was discouraged in order to promote English cotton manufacture, and the destruction of artisan production led to the creation of a semifeudal state where the majority of the peasants were in perpetual bondage to large landowners and moneylenders. (By 1901, 90 percent of the population were small farmers, with average holdings of under five acres.) The Company's administration of the areas it controlled became a national scandal in England, and caused numerous uprisings in India itself. After the Indian Mutiny of 1857, an imperial government replaced government by the East India Company, officially adding India to the extensive holdings of the British Empire.

A period of extensive railway building began that effectively opened up the interior of India. It improved the profitability of cotton growing for the Lancashire cotton mills. The opening of the Suez Canal speeded up transportation from India by eliminating the need for a long journey around Africa. Railway building in India also demonstrated one aspect of this new type of economic imperialism in guaranteed returns to investors, which were not available in earlier foreign investment ventures. For example, many British investors bought shares in American railway companies; some gained huge returns, but others did not. In India, on the other hand, investors were guaranteed a minimum 5 percent return. If the railway was itself unable to produce such returns, then the Indian population would be taxed to make up the difference, in effect a unilateral transfer of wealth to investors.

Colonial Activity in Africa

The most spectacular example of economic imperialism at work took place in Africa. In 1800, little was known of this vast continent, except for its coastal areas and the fact that it provided slaves for commercial plantations in the Americas. Ignorance was partly due to its sheer size, and to the disastrous effect tropical diseases had on northern Europeans. All this changed by 1900, when not only had much of the interior been explored, but 90 percent of the continent was owned by the major European powers. France obtained 40 percent of Africa's territory, mostly in north and west Africa. Britain ended up with 30 percent, a vaguely north-south slice running from Egypt in the north to South Africa, with holdings also on both east and west coasts. Other countries also joined in. Italy, which had no previous colonial possessions, acquired part of Somalia in 1885 and 1889, and wrested Libya from Turkey in 1911-1912, but was unsuccessful in its designs on Ethiopia in 1896. Another latecomer to colonialism was Germany, which wanted to acquire colonies to demonstrate German strength. Germany acquired East Africa (later Tanganyika, later still Tanzania) in the 1880s, Cameroon in West Africa in 1884-1885, and Southwest Africa (now Namibia). Portugal, an old colonial power, extended its trading-post activity into Angola on the west Coast and Mozambique on the east, while Spain, which had long had an interest in the northwest part of Africa, did little to extend its influence and ended up splitting Morocco with France.

Most activity took place after the Berlin Conference of 1884-1885, which effectively divided up Africa between European powers. One of the most unusual, and notorious, outcomes of this Conference was that the entire huge central area of the Congo was given to Leopold II of Belgium as a personal possession. The subsequent exploitation of this area became a world scandal. The most valuable resources were ivory and rubber (from wild, not cultivated, rubber trees). Exploitation of resources required the use of forced labor because no European could, or would, do manual work there, and the Congolese had no conception at all of the meaning of a free labor force. Therefore each village was "taxed," with the taxes to be paid in specific quantities of rubber and ivory, an idea foreign to the Congolese way of life, and incredibly brutal methods were used by the white overseers to enforce it. Men refusing to work or not producing the right quantities had hands or fingers cut off, while village women were often held hostage until the quotas were filled. In addition, all land not directly cultivated by the villagers was confiscated. This created such an uproar that the Belgian government eventually assumed administrative responsibility, but not until after Leopold had gained a huge personal fortune. After that, the rubber industry declined because it could not meet the competition from cultivated rubber plantations of Malaya and Indonesia (then a colony of the Netherlands). Later on, however, discovery of copper led to the exploitation of copper mines, which reinforced the importance of the area to the industrial world.

French Colonies in Africa

France and Britain got the major shares of Africa. France, which had seen its old colonial empire partly demolished by Britain after the war of 1763, started rebuilding a new one after 1830. At first, attention was focused on North Africa, and

Algeria was conquered in 1830-1848. Algeria proved to be an unwilling colony and continued to present problems, manifested in a series of anticolonial uprisings which were expensive to control. Settlement by French emigres was an important part of French colonial policy, and by 1911 there were 800,000 French settlers there. In 1881, France moved into Tunisia to protect French foreign investments, imposing taxes to meet the necessary interest payments, causing local antiFrench hostility. (It was necessary to control Tunisia because it was an important source of the phosphates used to make fertilizers and other mineral ores.) But France met Italian opposition, as Italy also eyed Tunisia's potential wealth, and French rejection of Italian claims contributed to Italy later allying with Germany and Austria.

France also met German opposition when attempting to exert influence in Morocco. Morocco was officially independent in 1880, but the Sultan was in debt to foreigners, giving an opening for the exercise of French power. An international agreement gave Morocco to France, Egypt to Britain, and Libya to Italy, but excluded Germany, which then tried to force Morocco open to German trade and investment. Germany even dispatched a gunboat to Agadir in southern Morocco in 1911, a crisis that ended only when France ceded part of its holdings in French Equatorial Africa to Germany. (Germany held this area until 1914, and it was returned to France after Germany's defeat.)

After 1880, France also gained colonies in French West Africa (including Dakar, Senegal, Ivory Coast) and Equatorial Africa (French Congo), but failed in its scheme to control most of Africa. France had less success here than in North Africa. The climate and communications were both difficult, and development of a rail system after 1882 was expensive, although necessary for exploitation of ground nuts and rubber. However, little was done to build all the necessary infrastructure, and the policy of giving monopoly concessions to privileged companies in the 1890s did not result in any meaningful development. Of all French colonial holdings, those in Indochina proved to be the most important, accounting for half of all French colonial trade.

British Holdings in Africa

Britain had very few holdings in Africa at the beginning of the 19th century but ended up as the second largest colonial power there by the end, and as the largest colonial power in the world as a whole. Extension of holdings came about through a mixture of government diplomatic dealings, private adventurism, and military power. Egypt provides an example of diplomatic maneuvering. Egypt was nominally part of the Turkish Ottoman Empire but in practice fell within the French sphere of influence. The French built the Suez Canal in the 1860s, dramatically shortening transportation times from India and the East to Europe; and therefore Egypt took on a new importance to Britain. The opportunity to do something to gain a foothold resulted from the indebtedness of the Viceroy of Egypt to European financiers. He could not repay his debts, so in 1875, Prime Minister Disraeli of Britain bought the Viceroy's controlling interest in the Canal. This did not solve the repayment problem, so both French and British governments were urged to take steps to protect their respective bondholders' interests. The result was a system of dual control over Egyptian affairs by France and Britain until 1882. Egypt protested this situation, and so British troops were sent there in 1882— and for the next 70 years, Britain alone remained in control. Egypt was made into a protectorate during World War I to avoid its entry into the war in support of Turkey, then an ally of Germany, and became an internally self-governing colony in 1922.

At the southern tip of the continent, Britain had seized Cape Colony from the Dutch in 1806. The Dutch farmers (Boers) then moved north to form two independent Dutch republics, Orange Free State and Transvaal. However, toward the end of the century, South Africa once again became the focus of British attention, this time through the activities of Cecil Rhodes. Rhodes gained control of gold and diamond exploitation through his interest in the British South Africa Company, chartered in 1889 to exercise both economic and political power in the area. (Using the holding company mechanism, Rhodes controlled De Beers Diamond Mining Company, which monopolized the world sale of diamonds, and Consolidated Gold Fields, which controlled gold mining in South Africa.) This power resulted from agreements made with nominally sovereign African tribes, who granted mining concessions to the Company. Because Western-style contracts were alien to the tribes, some excuse could be manufactured to violate the treaty, then the Company asked for British military support to take control of the area. In this way, Zululand and Bechuanaland were added to Britain's South African holdings in the 1880s.

Rhodes found the Boers an obstacle to the further extension of his, and Britain's, interests in South Africa. Worsening relations between the British and the Boers pushed Rhodes out of Cape Colony, forcing him to move north where he founded a new colony in Rhodesia, another important source of mineral ores. The climax came in the Boer War, 1899-1902, after which the Boer Republics were absorbed into the Union of South Africa, which included all the other British holdings in South Africa. Ironically, the Boers were given political equality with British white settlers, and successfully gained control of the government, which they held until 1993. As an incidental, but important, note, the doctrine of racial inferiority and Manifest Destiny that influenced the imperialist surge retained a strong hold in South Africa. Up to 1990, the official policy of apartheid separated whites from black Africans, who were considered politically, economically,

and socially second-class citizens, although they made up the majority of the population.

In the middle section of Africa, Britain gained possession of Nigeria in 1900, adding to holdings in West Africa that already included Sierra Leone and Ghana. Sierra Leone was created in 1787 as a state for freed British slaves, and it provided a model for the later creation of Liberia, the only United States foothold in Africa.

United States Imperialism

The United States by the end of the 19th century was becoming a world economic power, but as yet was still somewhat unwilling to become a world political power. At first, much expansionist activity occurred internally in the Indian wars. The result was a decimated Indian population and the commercial exploitation of their lands by mining and timber companies and commercial farmers. After the 1870s, pressured by some expansionist industry groups, and motivated by the Monroe Doctrine's premise of the Western Hemisphere being an American sphere of influence, the United States moved into the Pacific and Caribbean. Samoa was acquired in 1878, and later agreements divided the Samoan Islands between the United States and Germany. All the other powers also acquired islands in the Pacific, with the result that by 1900, 99 percent of all the Polynesian islands were colonies or dependencies of the major powers. In 1887 the United States set up a naval station at Pearl Harbor in the island kingdom of Hawaii and followed this by successive encroachments on Hawaiian sovereignty. American sugar interests gradually achieved control over most of the sugar grown in Hawaii, and on various occasions, United States marines landed there, ostensibly to preserve the peace and protect the safety of American business interests. The islands were formally annexed in 1898.

However, the war fought with Spain in 1898 was the most important event turning the United States into an imperialist power. At issue were sugar interests of Americans in Cuba, then a colony of Spain. A long-standing accusation of Spain's "interference" with American trade and interests in Cuba gave rise to the potential for conflict with Spain. In addition, United States protest over the existence of European colonies in the Western Hemisphere came to a head when the United States battleship *Maine* was sunk. This gave the excuse to declare war on Spain, and as a result of its victory the United States gained possession of Cuba, Puerto Rico, Guam, and the Philippines. Cuba became nominally independent, but the United States reserved the right to intervene to protect American interests—a right exercised militarily in 1906, 1911, and 1917. This war turned the United States into a power with interests in the Caribbean and Pacific, increasing the importance of developing naval power to protect them. Awareness of Japan's growing strength as an Asian power with emerg-

Figure 20.1 The Hawaiian Islands were the focus of attention from American sugar growers. Shown here are workers harvesting sugar cane. (Courtesy of Kauai Museum Photographic Collection)

ing expansionist aims also reinforced the necessity of greater military strength. But there was one problem: The length of time required to sail from the Atlantic to the Pacific around the southern tip of South America. This renewed interest in the construction of a canal in the Central American isthmus connecting the two oceans to dramatically shorten lines of communication. The idea of such a canal had existed for some time, but French attempts to construct one had collapsed in scandal in the early 1890s.

The major problem was the acquisition of land needed for the canal. Colombia, then an independent country containing the land most suitable for a canal, opposed the idea and in 1901 refused to sell the necessary strip of land. To get around this problem, an insurrection was organized in the area that later became the country of Panama. Invoking the Monroe Doctrine, United States warships prevented Colombian troops from moving in to reexert control, which effectively gave the United States control. By 1903 the United States had gained exclusive possession of the Canal Zone on much more favorable terms than were originally offered to Colombia. In order to reinforce United States strength in the area once the Canal was built, it was proposed that United States enterprises should locate in nearby areas to provide a justification for intervention in the case of outside (or inside) aggression. However, such enterprises were slow to locate there and required guarantees of adequate returns.

Types of Colonial Control

As a country that had once been a colonial possession, the United States denounced outright colonization but then found itself in an awkward position: How to expand overseas, exerting political control needed to assure the economic returns required, without becoming a formal colonizing power. To this end, the areas in which the United States had an interest were not colonies *per se*. They often retained their nominal

independence, with the United States reserving the right to intervene in order to protect American business interests. In consequence, in 1906 and 1912, marines invaded Nicaragua; they invaded Haiti in 1915, and in 1916, troops set up a military government under American control in the Dominican Republic (another former Spanish colony). Hawaii and Puerto Rico both had a status short of formal colonization. In these ways, effective control could be exercised at the same time that adherence to the principle of national sovereignty was maintained.

In fact, political and economic mechanisms for exerting control were numerous. At one extreme were colonies proper where internal administration was the direct concern of the colonial authority. Halfway to independent status was the dominion, which was characterized by internal self-government, with external defense remaining in the hands of the metropolitan country. But even if the country was fully sovereign, as with most of the Latin American countries, for example, dependency status was still a reality because of the importance of foreign investments. Thus, Argentina was effectively a commercial dependency of Great Britain because it depended on imported capital. In this way, financial dependency solved the problem connected with infringement of political sovereignty through direct colonization, and was frequently observed in practice. The issues connected with dependency status will be looked at later.

Contribution to International Conflict

Although colonial expansion at the end of the 19th century was intended to provide greater certainty for foreign investment in protected areas, it was not risk free. Colonies were costly to administer and little of the wealth they generated seeped back into national treasuries. Internal unrest and anticolonial uprisings were also costly and were consequences both of the actual treatment of subject populations and of the discrepancy between the principle of national self-determination and the reality of dependency. Although the First World War ended further colonial expansion, not until the end of the Second World War was the process of decolonization begun in earnest. Even then, economic dependency often remained, especially in countries where foreign companies operated. These operations were only a small part of the total activity of the company itself, but they represented a very large proportion of market economic activity in the host country, thus having a very large impact on the economy of the country in question.

Uncertainty increased when continued colonial expansion raised the problem of national rivalry. The end of the 19th and the beginning of the 20th centuries were marked by frequent minor clashes as the ambitions of one country collided with those of another. The obvious danger of "losing" one's claims in such a conflict was represented by the loss of the overseas investment, and once started, imperial expansion took on a momentum of its own. That is, the existence of military or political bases and economic enterprises made continued military aggression much more likely. The aim was to protect the possessions already held, which implied the likelihood of acquiring more territory to act as a buffer or to present too large a challenge to a rival. This is why colonial rivalries are cited as a contributing cause of the First World War. Industrial progress could present greater chances for peace because of the development of greater economic linkages among countries but it also increased the possibility of destruction. Not only did industrial progress strengthen nations militarily (giving the means for destruction), it also increased tensions because of imperial rivalries (giving the motive).

The First World War can be considered to have its origin in 1912, when the Balkan peoples began a movement in support of their claims for national independence from Turkey, at a time when Turkey was otherwise engaged in fighting Italy. Once again Europe became a battleground.

Colonialism and Dependent Development

One question plaguing development economists in the 20th century is why so many countries failed to experience significant economic development. Why does the world remain divided into a small group of highly developed industrial nations and a much larger group of lesser developed ones where per capita output is only a fraction of the level in the advanced countries? Further examination of this issue shows that most of today's lesser developed countries were the victims of the late 19th century imperialist surge. As it is usually

---

Dependent development

economic development dependent on forces outside the control of the economy concerned

---

presented, this question can be subdivided into two related components. First, why was the spread of the market economy into these new areas limited, given that imperialism forced an extension of contacts with developed market economies? Second, why did not capitalist institutions spread, even though imperialist expansion was an expansion of capitalism? Subdividing the question in this way avoids the issue of economic development within a noncapitalist framework, which is outside the scope of this book. However, it should not be forgotten that economic development can take many forms (as the early chapters demonstrated), that advanced industrial status can be achieved in a noncapitalist society, and that markets are features of all economies. But given that capitalism is a dominant form of economic organization, it is appropriate to narrow the issue.

In order to explain this lack of development, it is useful to summarize the process of the emergence of capitalism in Europe. Four elements are noteworthy. First, precapitalist societies went through a process of disintegration of their existing social and political structures. This was accompanied by the second element, a slow but noticeable rise in agricultural output that was also associated with the development of a "surplus" population, one not needed for agricultural production at the then-existing level. Third, this also accompanied the beginnings of industry and urbanization, the early stages of a broad division of labor into urban-industrial and rural-agricultural classifications. Fourth, a class of merchants also emerged to begin the process of capital accumulation in which wealth permitted the creation of more wealth that was deliberately used, not for conspicuous consumption or wastefully, but for productive investment. Capital accumulation fed on itself in an intricate cause-effect relationship, so that changes in one area stimulated changes in others until almost all aspects of life became dominated by money and market relationships.

Receptivity to Capitalist Institutions

As capitalist contacts spread from Europe, whether or not capitalist institutions took hold in enough areas to produce a growing capitalist economy depended very much on the nature of the receiving society. In general, in new "empty" countries or those where a small existing population could be easily overwhelmed, it was easier to develop along capitalist lines. Examples are countries such as Canada, the United States, and Australia, which emerged from a colonial status with rapidly developing capitalist institutions. Where Europeans faced already-established societies, capitalist contacts destroyed some aspects of these societies, but the existence of others implied that the growth-producing elements of capitalism would be absent or thwarted. In addition, new areas were not seen as areas where development was to be encouraged; rather their existence and activities were to support development in the colonizing country.

Many colonizing activities were necessary as preconditions for development. For example,

building transportation and communications networks had economic as well as administrative implications, while the introduction of western style legal and political institutions introduced relationships characteristic of advanced capitalism (although often ahead of the need). But many others were not so helpful. The result was that the existing structure disintegrated, and development turned these countries into economic dependencies without much ability to achieve internally self-generated economic development as in Europe. So the resulting social structure did not have all the necessary elements to encourage capitalist development. Several characteristics of today's developing countries are rooted in imperialist expansion. First, they are producers of raw materials and primary products. If production is agricultural, the shift to the production of crops for export destroyed the agricultural self-sufficiency of the old society. If production is extractive in nature (minerals) it is controlled by foreign capitalists, as the capital investment required was not generated internally, and the existing society was not at a level that either recognized or valued the necessity of such activity. If the initial contact was exploitative, then this mineral or agricultural wealth was unilaterally transferred to Europe or the United States, thus removing a potential economic surplus that could have been used internally.

As a result, these countries are dependent on events in other countries, such as fluctuations of market demand that lead to altering demands for their output and thus to fluctuations in income over which they have no control. This is intensified if production is specialized, such as coffee, cocoa, copper, bananas, or bauxite, which are examples of exports from monoculture economies. Specialist producers are even more vulnerable to instability in buying countries. Much specialized production, because of its nature, requires large amounts of long-term investment, so vulnerability persists even after political independence.

Difficulty of Industrializing

Often a development program based on industrialization to achieve economic diversification is seen as the answer, but this too is difficult. During the period of imperialism, if not before, much of the local artisan production of colonies was destroyed by competition from industrial imports, so modern industrialization had no base of skills on which to build. Although this destruction created a large surplus labor force (which then tended either to migrate into towns as a permanent class of unemployed paupers or back to the countryside where it was surplus to the requirements of agriculture), it proved difficult to use in an industrialization process. Early 19th century industrialization did require large amounts of labor, but the problem now is that the evolution of industrial techniques results in lower labor requirements. In addition, because no capital goods industries exist, capital equipment must be imported, but is limited by revenues earned from exporting primary products, which are subject to their own difficulties. Borrowing abroad does not help either, as unless exports rise to increase earned foreign exchange, developing countries become permanently indebted to their creditors. Furthermore, the old problem of how to survive the first stages of industrialization when faced with competition from already established, efficient producers remains. To attempt to deal with this behind tariff barriers invites retaliation from trading partners on whom export revenues depend.

In addition, as the inhabitants were seen as sources of unskilled labor, education and skill levels were not developed. Even when an education system was set up, it was restricted to urban areas or oriented to Western-style education and did not meet local needs adequately. This lack of investment in people further retards development. Even if education is widespread, because there are too few local opportunities to exercise skills, the result is either a drain of the highly skilled abroad or a situation of unsatisfied aspirations, which leads to social unrest.

Dual Economy

Many development economists today are concerned with the problems faced by developing countries with a dual economy. This is composed of a small modern sector using Western technologies and oriented to serving export markets, surrounded by a much larger, backward agricultural sector. This could be attributed to a dependency status. That development has not occurred or does not spread from the modern sector is the result of many influences. At the most basic level is the lack or misuse of any economic surplus generated. If much enterprise is foreign-owned, profits are repatriated and are not available for further investment locally, as was the case in Europe or the United States. If the surplus does remain in the country, it is too often absorbed by the luxury consumption of the small upper class, used for the maintenance of a political bureaucracy or military establishment (especially if internal unrest exists), or drained abroad in private hoards; not enough is used in productive ways. In other words, there is a lack of both motive and facilities to establish new enterprises that will support, reinforce, and stimulate others. This is a vicious circle. Modern developed economies are self-sustaining because so many linkages (technically called external economies) exist to increase the likelihood of success of new enterprises. In their absence, it is difficult to start one and hope that others will quickly be established to make the investment worthwhile. A short-term analysis of the existing situation simply indicates its unprofitability because of the lack of a supportive environment.

The new form of economic colonialism, the establishment of modern manufacturing facilities by foreign companies, also does little to help. The problems of capital ownership and retention remain; the company is attracted precisely by the low labor costs of a low-skilled labor force, so it has no incentive to provide training; and usually these enterprises are export ones, with few linkages to the rest of the economy. Assembly operations are typical here, but even service operations, such as vacation resorts, have similar characteristics. They use few if any material inputs from the rest of the economy and usually do not sell to the local population.

Japan, as we saw in Chapter 16, did escape this pattern. What is instructive about Japan is that capitalism did develop, but old social relationships did not disintegrate, being instead absorbed into the new ones, providing an element of continuity missing elsewhere. The result was that Japan successfully developed both economic and military strength without losing its own identity. This further indicates that if development is to be successful elsewhere it is necessary to reconstruct the economy. If the existing economic and social structure does not permit internally self-generated development in which the economic surplus can be productively used, then it must be restructured so as to permit it.

Summary

In summary, late 19th century imperialism completely changed the pattern of capitalist development. It resulted in most of the then-nondeveloped world being brought, either formally or informally, within the orbit of the advanced industrial nations. However, ties between nations did not become closer, as the inherent tensions endemic to imperialist rivalry exploded in the violence of the First World War. Imperialist expansion was thought to be not only economically necessary by providing markets, sources, or outlets for surplus capital, but also morally justified. Economically, imperialism can

be thought of as an inevitable extension of the stage of capitalist industrialization. But the high hopes for profits were rarely realized and subsequent analysis and behavior shows that political control is not necessary for continued economic expansion. Also it is possible that by thwarting the development of colonized countries, imperialism helped slow down the overall economic progress of the world as a whole.

World trade expanded dramatically at this time, due to the spread of industrialization, as trade between industrial nations is greater than that between agricultural ones. Strangely, this was happening even as companies and industries were trying to protect themselves from the uncertainties of competitive markets. As we saw in Chapter 18, at the end of the 19th century, various types of cooperative agreements between companies were being used, adding elements of oligopoly. At the same time, companies were also pressuring their governments to raise tariffs to protect them from foreign competition.

As trade expanded, the development of an international monetary system also became more effective. At this time, most of the major countries adopted a gold standard; the theory implied that trade imbalances would be corrected automatically, but domestic policies increasingly modified the effects of complete adherence to the gold standard "rules of the game."

Much of the rising pressure associated with the spread of advanced industrialization forced a new wave of colonization, especially in Africa. However, in spite of various arguments raised in support of this imperialist activity, it is questionable whether it did anything positive to help continued economic growth in either the advanced or the colonized areas—although some individuals and companies did become wealthy.

Key Concepts

Capital export
Colonization
Dependent development
Dual economy

Gold standard
Imperialism
Monroe Doctrine
Protectionism

Questions for Discussion or Essay Writing

1. To what extent is it true to say that the end of the 19th century was marked by contradictions?

2. To what extent do trade statistics give information about economic development?

3. Why was it more likely that countries would experience business cycles at the same time later in the 19th century rather than earlier?

4. Why did the industrialized nations engage in a new wave of colonization in the late 19th century?

5. How did colonization affect the development of colonized countries?

6. What are some of the development issues arising from the colonization experience?

For Further Reading

Bakeless, John E. *The Economic Causes of Modern War: A Study of the Period 1878–1918.* N.Y.: Garland, 1972.

Bordo, Michael and Anna Schwartz. *A Retrospective on the Classical Gold Standard, 1821–1913.* Chicago: University of Chicago Press, 1984.

Buiter, W.H. "A Viable Gold Standard Requires Flexible Monetary and Fiscal Policy." *Review of Economic Studies,* 56 (January 1989): 101–117.

Cairncross, A.K. *Home and Foreign Investment, 1870–1914: Studies in Capital Accumulation.* Cambridge: Cambridge University Press, 1953.

deCecco, Marcello. *Money and Empire: The International Gold Standard, 1890–1914.* Totowa, N.J: Rowman and Littlefield, 1975.

Edelstein, Michael. *Overseas Investment in the Age of High Imperialism: The United Kingdom, 1850–1914.* New York: Columbia University Press, 1980.

Feis, Herbert. *Europe: The World's Banker 1870–1914,* N.Y.: Norton, 1965.

Fieldhouse, David. *Economics and Empire, 1830–1914,* Ithaca: Cornell University Press, 1973.

Hoffman, Ross J.S. *Great Britain and the German Trade Rivalry, 1875–1914.* Philadelphia: University of Pennsylvania Press, 1933.

Kindleberger, Charles P. "Foreign Trade and Economic Growth: Lessons from Britain and France, 1850–1913." *Economic History Review* (1961).

Frankel, S. Herbert. *Capital Investment in Africa: Its Course and Effects.* New York: H. Fertig, 1969.

Hobson, John. *Imperialism,* Ann Arbor: Michigan University Press, 1965.

Hymer, Steven. *The Multinational Corporation and the Law of Uneven Development,* in Jagdish Bhagwati, ed. *Economics and World Order from the 1970s to the 1990s.* New York: Macmillan, 1972.

LaFeber, Walter. *The New Empire: American Expansion, 1860–1898*, Ithaca: Cornell University Press, 1963.

Landes, David. *Bankers and Pashas: International Finance and Economic Imperialism in Egypt*, Cambridge, Mass: Harvard University Press, 1979.

Lebergott, Stanley. "The Returns to United States' Imperialism, 1890–1929." *Journal of Economic History* (1980): 229–252.

Lenin, V.I. *Imperialism: The Highest Stage of Capitalism*, Moscow: International Publishers, (1916) 1939.

Priestley, Herbert I. *France Overseas: A Study of Modern Imperialism*. New York: Appleton Century Co., 1938.

Pollard, Sidney. "Capital Exports, 1870–1914: Harmful or Beneficial?" *Economic History Review* (1985).

Saul, S.B. *Studies in Britain's Overseas Trade 1870–1914*. Liverpool: University of Liverpool Press, 1960.

Scammell, W.M. *The London Discount Market*. New York: St. Martin's Press, 1968.

Taylor, A.J.P. *Germany's First Bid for Colonies, 1884–1885*. Hamden, Conn: Archon Books, 1967.

Townsend, M.E. *Origins of Modern German Colonialism, 1871–1885*. New York: Columbia University Press, 1921.

Wilkins, Mira. *The Emergence of Multinational Enterprise: American Business Abroad from the Colonial Era to 1914*, Cambridge, Mass: Harvard University Press, 1970.

Woodruff, William. *Impact of Western Man: A Study of Europe's Role in the World Economy 1750–1960*, Washington, D.C.: University Press of America, (1967) 1982.

Zevin, Robert. "An Interpretation of American Imperialism." *Journal of Economic History* (1972): 316–360.

Chapter 21

World War I and the Collapse of the International Order: II

IF THE PERIOD PRECEDING THE FIRST WORLD WAR was marked by an intensification of strains on the international order, the period after it saw the effective collapse of any pretense to a "world" international order. Military conflict was the visible sign of that collapse, but even the return to peacetime conditions did not restore stability or order, either internationally or internally. Attempts to manage problems raised by the war only led to new crises, partly because the balance of military and economic power had been dramatically altered by the events leading up to the war and by the war itself. There was a failure to recognize the nature of these changes, and attempted remedies were both unrealistic and based on poor economic theory. Short-term solutions were unable to solve long-term problems and they contributed to the total collapse of the international system.

The interwar period marked the end of Britain's role as world economic leader and saw the rise of the United States as the strongest economic power. But unlike Britain in the 19th century, the United States was unwilling to assume the international responsibilities that went with economic strength. Consequently, following the failure of postwar actions to restore the prewar status quo (an impossible task), there was no generally accepted international system to regulate international relationships or to resolve longstanding contradictions. The retreat of nations inside their own borders proved to be no solution either to their domestic or to their international problems. The gold standard finally collapsed for good, trade shrank, and in spite of a veneer of prosperity in the late 1920s, domestic retreat did not insulate economies from the depressed conditions of the 1930s.

World War I and its Immediate Aftermath

Two important economic causes of the First World War were related to industrialization. The first was apparent in the international rivalries accompanying the expansion of imperialist ambitions. As noted previously, many of these rivalries led to actual conflict, but until 1914 the conflict was usually limited. The second related to the shift in the balance of power in Europe due to the rapid industrialization of Germany after unification in 1870.

Historically, and at the risk of gross oversimplification, political and diplomatic rivalry in Europe very loosely followed religious differences between states. From the point of view of north European, Protestant Britain, first Mediterranean Catholic Spain and then Catholic France was seen

Rationing

Allocation of scarce goods during emergencies, usually using coupons authorizing a specified quantity per person

as the major threat. Traditional enmity between France and Britain was longstanding, but since the Napoleonic Wars at the beginning of the 19th century, and given the economic and military supremacy of Britain throughout most of the rest of the century, rivalry had been muted. For so long as Germany had been a collection of fairly weak independent states, the balance of political and military power in Europe rested with Britain and France. After German unification, and as a result of its rapid industrialization, this old reality no longer provided a guide to diplomatic stability, and the balance of power shifted. Bismarck had been acutely aware of the potential of economic strength for military strength and to define Germany's sense of nationhood, and he used war as a mechanism to achieve unification. By the end of the century, Germany was not only economically strong but also able to demonstrate that strength internationally by encroaching on what other countries saw as their exclusive preserves.

The problem was that even a realignment of France and Britain against Germany did not produce a new "balance" of power, as it was always possible that the exercise of German power could crush both countries, adding a new threat to an already smoldering international environment. International tensions were increasing because of the rivalries connected with imperialist expansion, the deliberate application of economic policies intended to gain advantages for one country while denying them to another, and an intensification of nationalist feelings in general. In this situation, it was all too easy for what could otherwise have been a minor diplomatic incident to explode into outright war—because of the generally accepted view that there was no alternative to war to safeguard a nation's honor.

The War and New Technologies

The war itself broke new ground. It was definitely a modern war in both economic and military terms. Economically, the enormous industrial strength of both sides meant that what some thought would be a short, decisive conflict dragged on for four years. Only when the United States entered the war in 1917 did the balance of economic strength tilt firmly in favor of the allies. In addition, it was a modern economic war because it involved the output of new industries. Thus, poison gas, a product of the expanding chemicals industry, effectively supplemented traditional armaments as a fighting weapon, and airplanes and submarines, both using totally new technologies, were used for the first time. Militarily, the war was far removed from the older idea of set battles between two armies on a defined battlefield. Now civilians and civilian targets were drawn into the conflict, and destruction of property was far more extensive than ever before. Even so, the actual strategy of much land fighting still seemed medieval, helping prolong it. This was especially apparent with the use of trench warfare to defend territory and/or gain more territory.

As in the Napoleonic Wars, controlling the seas and blockading enemy ports was an important economic weapon, designed to weaken the enemy by denying access to vital food and raw materials. The Allies blockaded German and Austrian shipping, closed many land routes, and prohibited the export of goods to neutral countries for fear that they might eventually find their way to Germany. Consequently, German imports by 1915 had fallen to two thirds their 1913 level, food shortages were chronic, and supplies of such imported goods as rubber and oil were scarce. Inevitably, this invited retaliation, and starting in 1915, Germany used the new submarine (U-boat) to sink both enemy and neutral ships going to or from Britain. This was extremely effective. By 1917 the Allies had lost about 11 million tons of shipping out of a total 25 million tons existing in 1915, and their shipyards could not work fast enough to make good the loss. There was, however, one unintended consequence—these attacks also affected American shipping and influenced the entry of the United States into direct combat, marking the turning point in the Allies' favor.

Internal Wartime Measures

Internally, wartime pressures forced governments to act decisively, often in directions previously considered unthinkable. The prevalence of laissez faire attitudes, which only applied in peacetime conditions, had left most unprepared to cope with the new role of managing a war economy. In general, the government had to become involved in domestic economic matters to assure that military needs were met and to deal with the problems of the civilian economy. Intervention took place in three major areas: food supplies, industry in general, and financing. Food shortages, occurring as a result of both the blockading of imports and the reduction of domestic agricultural production, were particularly crucial in Europe. Only Russia and the United States were normally self-sufficient in food production; all the other belligerents relied on imported food to a greater or lesser extent. Dealing with shortages led to similar responses. To ensure an equitable distribution of available food, rationing was introduced. This meant that each family was allocated a right to purchase a specific amount of those items in short supply, so that purchases required both money and a coupon specifying the allotment.

On the whole, food supplies remained adequate in Britain, and only late in 1917, following the intensification of the German submarine campaign, was rationing introduced. This was first applied to sugar then later imposed on meat, fats, and some other basic items. Quality of food was another issue, and nutrition deficiencies did result from the use of poor quality substitutes. To prevent food producers from reaping windfall profits as a result of shortages, prices of most basic items were controlled. It was considered to be against the national interest that certain favored groups should make excessive fortunes while the rest of the population suffered. In spite of these measures, food prices increased significantly in all European countries. In addition, all countries tried to assure an adequate supply of imported food. Governments soon realized that if each acted individually when dealing with foreign suppliers, prices were forced up; but the rise could be limited if they all negotiated in concert. In addition, shortages of specific products led to a renewed interest in developing substitutes, a search that also applied to nonfood items.

Industrial intervention involved the broad question of resource allocation in order to shift industry onto a wartime basis. Those industries whose output was vital to the war effort, such as armaments, were guaranteed inputs. Industries normally producing civilian goods were reoriented to producing goods needed for the war, such as armored cars or trucks instead of passenger cars, and nonessential civilian goods came last on the list of industrial priorities. Control also extended to the labor force, as labor was directed first to priority industries. Because of the enormous manpower needs of the military services (a total of sixty-five million men in all countries were mobilized between 1914 and 1918), the resulting labor shortage was made good by encouraging women and retirees to work. In this way, women in significant numbers made their first step into what had previously been all-male occupations. France and Britain also recruited workers from their colonial possessions in order to keep their economies working at full capacity. Manpower policy not only aimed at making good the loss of men into the armed services, it was also concerned with the skill distribution of the labor force, as the new recruits could not be expected to learn new skills immediately. Therefore workers with specific skills needed in the most vital industries (armaments, shipbuilding, and steel among others) were exempted from military duty.

How to Pay for the War

The third area of involvement was financial—how to pay for the war. The basic problem was that even though the economy was working at full capacity, because so much output was diverted to military uses, it was both unsalable (and therefore nontaxable) and inflationary. That is, incomes were earned, but there was less output for civilian purchase, and the resulting excess purchasing power could push up prices. Thus, any wartime policy requires several elements, one of which is a tax structure to reduce inflationary pressure in general, reinforce the restructuring of output to meet wartime needs, and also generate revenues to pay for the war. It is also advisable that it impose an equitable burden on the population. Although patriotic fervor is high during wartimes, patriotism should not be relied on to ignore obvious injustices in the tax burden. Income taxes were either introduced (as in France and Russia) or increased, both to reduce consumers' purchasing power and to provide government revenues. In addition, specific taxes were used to achieve other desirable ends. For example, the question of how to share the war's burdens equitably was partly answered by imposing an excess profits tax to reduce the gains from war profiteering, while taxes on luxury goods were intended to discourage their production, encourage the production of nontaxed essential goods, and reinforce the shift in the composition of output toward military and essential goods. (The combination of new or higher tax rates in an economy working at high levels of capacity utilization resulted in tax revenues doubling in France and tripling in Britain.)

Internal taxing and borrowing measures met 85 percent of the Allies' war efforts, but were insufficient, thus requiring recourse to external funds. The difference was met by loans between the Allies, and the question of repayment of these loans had enormous implications after the end of the war. The major lenders were the United States and the United Kingdom, each of whom lent $7 billion to other countries, while a further $2.2 billion was lent by France. The war effectively ended the operation of the gold standard because internal financing had independently increased the supply of both paper currency and bank credit, so free convertibility of currency into gold became impossible. In addition, European governments banned private exports of gold in order to prevent a flight of gold out of their countries. However, interallied loans did help maintain the exchange ratios of currencies, which otherwise would have suffered from the loss of export markets (which could not have been serviced anyway, given the diversion of industry) and the need to maintain imports.

Losses Due to the War

Return to peacetime conditions in 1918 was not easy after a war that was long and destructive and had involved immense dislocations. The immediate impact, although serious, was manageable, and it was expected that within a few years everything would be more or less back to normal. The war did not discriminate between victors and the defeated, and both faced similar immediate problems. The first of these was the extent of carnage, which would of course have an effect on the future operation of the economy, as well as leaving an unquantifiable psychological scar. Deaths alone amounted to over 8 million: 2.7 million in Germany, 1.7 million in France and Russia each, 1.5 million in Austria-Hungary, 930,000 in Great Britain and 150,000 in the United States In addition, a further 5 million people were declared missing, presumably dead, 7 million were permanently disabled, and 15 million more were seriously wounded. Loss of manpower was greatest in France and Germany, where 10 percent of all men of active age were killed; the figure was 5

Inflation

Generalized rise in the price level

---

percent in Great Britain. This was a permanent loss, so some of the labor force changes intended as temporary stopgap measures during the war became permanent.

In terms of physical destruction, much of the capital equipment in Europe was either destroyed or worn out, because all savings generated during the war had been channelled to military uses and had not been used to maintain or replace the capital stock. Furthermore, the difficult task of shifting industry back to meeting civilian needs had to be faced and was made more complicated by several additional factors. First, the demobilization of the armed forces immediately increased unemployment. It also increased tension between the "new" workers and those wanting to return to the jobs they held before military service. Second, the pent-up demand for civilian goods, if unleashed, threatened to put new inflationary strains on the economy. Both of these could not be held in check by calls to patriotic duty—now that the war was over, patriotism was less fervent. There was an outbreak of strikes in France, Britain, and the United States, demands for land reform in Central and Eastern Europe, and political upheavals in many other countries. In October 1917, the Czarist regime in Russia was overthrown and replaced by a socialist, then a communist government, while in the losing countries of Germany, Austria, Bulgaria, and Turkey, the discredited governments were replaced.

International economic as well as political relations had been shattered, but, as will be seen in more detail later, they proved difficult to restore. One basic need was to return production to its prewar levels; this required not only the rebuilding of domestic economies but also the restoration of old export markets. Many had been lost entirely, either for political reasons (the new Soviet Union) or because previous customers had been able to build up their own productive structures, or because new suppliers had emerged. Japan in particular had been able to expand its manufacturing capability and consequently ex-

panded its exports. In addition, the war resulted in the creation of many newly-independent states, and the proliferation of tariff barriers in these and elsewhere prevented a return to the old patterns of trade. For example, Britain's exports in 1921 were only half what they had been in 1913, and a greater proportion of trade than before was within the Empire (to be renamed the British Commonwealth of Nations in 1932). Some capital that had been tied up in international trade and foreign investment was completely lost. For example, the new Soviet government simply refused to pay debts contracted by the old Czarist regime. The distribution of the remaining assets had changed. By 1921, 40 percent of all gold reserves were now in the United States which saw its gold holdings quadruple to $2.5 billion. This increase occurred because the United States sold necessary equipment and supplies to its European allies for gold, transferring gold ownership from Europe to the United States. This itself was one of the symbols of the shift in economic power that had taken place: the United States, not Great Britain, was now the world's major creditor.

In summary, the total cost of the war, including estimates of economic losses plus direct war expenditures, was estimated at $603.5 billion; as a point of reference, the total National Income of the United States in 1918 was about $50 billion. Expressed as percentages of national wealth, the cost of the war was 32 percent for Britain, 30 percent for France, 22 percent for Germany and 9 percent for the United States. Excluding money borrowed from other countries, total public debt increased from $26 billion before the war to $225 billion by 1920. Including foreign debts, the direct costs plus the indirect costs associated with restructuring economies were enormous.

Difficulty of Recovery

In spite of many efforts made to contain inflationary pressures, they did not go away, further complicating recovery efforts. Inflation reduced the value of monetary savings, which made funding private investment activities harder, further delaying reconstruction and often putting a premium on speculative activities which promised greater returns. Inflation also produced discrepancies between internal price levels and exchange values. This hit France, Italy, and Central and Eastern Europe hardest and added to recovery problems. Recovery required increased imports, especially of raw materials and capital equipment, but how could exports be increased to generate needed foreign exchange if production levels had not yet recovered? Thus, further loans were needed after the war. Economic analysis provided no solution or policy recommendations. The fact that even though exchange values were lower, exports could not rise and the balance of payments could not return to equilibrium provided another example of the failure of orthodox economic theory to indicate the correct adjustment mechanism. The reasoning behind the gold standard policy was that if inflation reduced the external value of a currency, exports would be stimulated, but this worked only when an ability to produce existed. In other words, what was needed was a quantity adjustment or an incentive to expand production itself, rather than an incentive to divert existing production from the domestic to the international market in response to the alteration of relative prices.

While Western Europe was not as devastated as Central Europe (although the postwar depression of 1920-1921 hit hard), it was not until the mid 1920s that production levels regained 1913 levels. Much more disruptive, both to individual economies and to the international order, were the issues concerned with war debts.

International Problems

In general, the long-term impact of the First World War was a shift of economic and financial power from Western Europe to the United States. One indication of this was that United States foreign investments rose from $3.5 billion in 1913 to $6.4 billion in 1919 and to $15.1 billion by 1930. This new international distribution of wealth, with former creditor nations such as France and Britain becoming debtors while former debtor nations such as the United States became creditors, was either not recognized, or if recognized, resisted. Recovery efforts of both winners and losers therefore became much more difficult. Economic organization had broken down both internally and internationally, and the international economy lurched from one crisis to another until 1945. The first crisis period was the war itself, which was followed by attempts to return to the prewar situation. Efforts were made to restore the exchange values of different currencies to their prewar relationships and to return to the gold standard with full convertibility. After 1925 it seemed as though these efforts might work, as reconstruction improved the domestic economies of the European countries. But appearances belied reality, and increasing strains after 1929 led to another crisis, followed by more improvised repairs after 1931, followed by a final collapse of any pretense to an organized international system after 1933.

German Reparations

The major problems preventing a return to normality were those related to German reparations and the repayment of international debts. Proposed solutions made neither economic nor practical sense. The European victors wanted Germany to make good war damages and costs, but the payments at first had little relationship to Germany's ability to pay, and no account was taken of their impact on receiving countries. Normally, international payments are payments for something, but reparations are unilateral financial

Reparations
Payments made by a defeated country to compensate for losses in the victorious countries

flows with no corresponding movement of goods or services. They would impoverish Germany, but the countries receiving reparations would not necessarily become economically wealthier. Whether or not this happened depended on their own ability to absorb the inflow of money and resources, which in turn depended on their productive capability. If this was lacking, then the "repair" aspect of reparations would not be forthcoming. In fact, there was a strong element of punishment for punishment's sake in the demand for reparations. Combined with efforts to return to exchange-rate parity and gold-standard convertibility, and given internal problems in many

countries that resulted in strains on their international position, the international system became very vulnerable to stress, and this intensified local problems.

Looking first at the reparations issue and its effect on Germany, it was decided at the Versailles Conference in 1919, where the peace treaty ending the war was signed, that the precise amount of reparations would be determined by a commission due to report in 1921. Until then, Germany was subjected to very onerous requirements. Allied armies occupied Germany, which was required to pay $5 billion in commodities, securities, and gold; give up part of its merchant

Map 21.1   European Borders Before and After the First World War
The most significant result of the Peace Treaty following the First World War was the creation of new states, especially Czechoslovakia and Yugoslavia. New borders are shown by heavy lines.

fleet to the Allies as well as build 200,000 tons of shipping each year to make good the losses suffered by Allied shipping; grant trade preferences to the Allies for five years; and deliver livestock, railway equipment, and coal to them. The immediate effect was that Germany exhausted its supplies of gold and industrial securities (most of which ended up in American hands); that German shipyards were busy while others in Europe were forced to close down or operate at very low levels; and that Britain lost important export markets for coal, previously a large source of foreign exchange earnings. In addition, Germany was forced to give up certain territories. The provinces of Lorraine (location of much German industry), the Saar, and Upper Silesia (location of one third of German coal resources) were lost, and this loss plus the requirements for coal reparations meant serious energy shortages for German industry. But delay in restoring industry made it more difficult to pay reparations by imposing taxes on an expanding economy and/or by producing enough exports to earn foreign exchange. German markets were freely opened to exports from other countries, which closed their markets to German exports in an attempt to build up their own production and export capability, intensifying the German problem of payment.

Full repayment of all that Germany owed would have required an export surplus derived from reconstruction of the economy. But the strength of German industry before 1914 was one factor that the Allies believed had led to war, and they were not really interested in rebuilding German economic strength. This is indicated by the territorial changes and other impositions on Germany made in the Peace Treaty. Yet repayment required a massive expansion of exports. Before the war, Germany ran a deficit on the merchandise balance of trade, and it was only other earnings—interest on foreign investments, sale of ships, shipping services—that produced a balance of payments surplus. Now these other earnings no longer existed; the merchant marine was taken

over and no income from shipping could be expected, while Germany's foreign assets were either confiscated or frozen. This put the burden onto expanding actual exports, but there were no markets for them. Furthermore, there was as yet no effective mechanism for transferring to the government the private claims on foreign exchange resulting from trading activity.

Raising money by taxation was troubling and would have involved a massive tax burden on the population for many years. How such taxes were structured, and thus their impact on different groups, stirred political and social conflicts. In short, and this became apparent when the reparations commission reported, the Allies were demanding payments from Germany but at the same time limiting its ability to make them.

In 1921 the commission determined that Germany should make reparations of 132 billion gold marks ($33 billion). This was to be paid over a period of 30 years, by issuing three sets of bonds (for 12, 38, and 82 billion gold marks respectively), paying one billion in 1921, and then an annual sum of three billion plus the revenues from a 26 percent tax on exports. If these payments were not made, France and Belgium were authorized to occupy the Ruhr, a major industrial center. Part of the 1921 payment was made by selling new paper marks to foreigners, but the effects on Germany were disastrous—continuing balance of payments problems, the start of a hyperinflation, near collapse of the economy and a corresponding increase in labor unrest and social tensions.

Complexity of Repaying War Debts and Loans

Some economists, notably J.M. Keynes, recognized that the burden of reparations was too great. But it was difficult for governments to agree to make them more realistic because they were connected with war debts, and probably also because of sheer thirst for revenge. The European allies needed reparation payments from Germany

Hyperinflation

An extremely large, rapid rate of inflation

in order to honor their own debts—especially to the United States The debt network was complex, involving loans both to and from some countries. Only the United States owed no war debts, and by 1922 was a net creditor for $10 billion. Great Britain was a net creditor for $4.5 billion and France a net creditor for $3.5 billion of war debts.

Unfortunately, the United States did not recognize the connection between war debts and reparations. It insisted that all war debts be repaid in full. President Coolidge's position ("They hired the money, didn't they?"), though legally correct, raised the ethical question of whether war loans should be regarded as a business investment. What was at stake here was the type of war assistance given by the United States. Most was in the form of military equipment, which was "paid" for by the European ally obtaining a financial loan from the United States, that thus had to be repaid. But if the composition of the assistance had been different so that more American soldiers had been fighting with American guns, this issue of repayment would not have arisen. Europe's manpower losses were much greater, but there

Figure 21.1 Office work was becoming increasingly feminized, as this photograph of a late 19th century insurance office shows. (Courtesy of Met Life Archives)

was no mechanism to take them into account. France and Britain attempted to distinguish between war debt proper and the post-1919 debts incurred in order to reconstruct European economies. They wanted war debts to be forgiven because they were part of a common war effort, and did in fact grant concessions to countries in debt to them. The United States did not make this distinction and insisted on complete repayment, giving France and Britain a reason to insist in turn on reparations payments from Germany.

Wealth Shifts to the United States

Even after rescheduling and readjustments of debts (which were never completely repaid), the result was a massive shift of ownership of financial wealth to the United States. By 1931, the United States received $2.7 billion in repayments. Britain, which had made concessions to its debtors, received a total of $881 million from its principal debtors while repaying $1.122 billion to the United States. It lent twice what it had borrowed, so its lower repayments adversely affected its international position. France, which received $1.426 billion in reparations from Germany, repaid $418 million to the United States and Britain, so ended up with a net monetary gain. Repayments from all debtor countries, including Germany, were possible only because of the continuing extension of international loans, which added to the increasing fragility of the international situation. All countries had unfavorable trade and payments positions with the United States, the result of contradictory elements. On the one hand, to earn foreign exchange dollars required that European exports to the United States increase, but this became almost impossible after United States tariff barriers were raised in 1922 and 1923. But on the other hand, if dollars were used to repay war debts to the United States, then they could not be used to acquire United States goods, which would have an adverse impact on the United States economy by lowering

its exports. This was essentially a no-win situation. Even if these blocks had not existed, a very large expansion of production and trade was required to permit the building up of international balances necessary to repay all the international debts. This would have been difficult even in the most ideal environment, and the situation in the 1920s was far from ideal.

Return to the Gold Standard

Britain returned to the gold standard in 1925 at the prewar parity of sterling to gold, but this worsened international problems, already acute because of the reparations issue. The 1921 depression lowered exports to half their 1913 level, and they fell in value until 1926. This was partly due to the fact that Britain's return to gold convertibility was at the wrong rate; sterling was overvalued in relation to other currencies, so British export prices in sterling were relatively high in terms of other currencies. Not until 1929 did British exports reach the levels of 1924. With the return to gold, many other countries became tied to sterling, which meant that a gold exchange standard coexisted with a gold standard for some countries. The prewar system had been characterized by some relevant relationship existing between productive capacity, relative costs, exchange rates, and international reserves. All these old relationships no longer held good, but the 1920s situation did not reflect this. Now international flows of gold and finance had little

Financial panic
Collapse of the financial system resulting from falling financial asset prices

Depression
Downturn in the business cycle characterized by falling output, high unemployment, low profits, and extensive business pessimism

connection with domestic economic strength or the volume of internal credit.

Britain's former position as the major international lender and financial center was based not only on expertise but also on its position as a major trading nation with large gold reserves gained from its exports, earnings from shipping, and returns on foreign holdings. In the new situation, few of the former sources of income were available, making the resumption of sterling as a major international currency very shaky. Exports were lower and many former earnings from invisibles had disappeared, which left Britain earning only a small current surplus. Also gold and foreign exchange reserves were much lower than before because of the drain to the United States in debt repayments. This meant that any strain on Britain would also be transferred to those gold exchange countries holding their international reserves in the form of British currency, bank deposits in British banks, and British securities. Since their currency units were defined in terms of pounds sterling, their currency's exchange value also fell irrespective of their own economic strength if the exchange value of sterling against currencies outside the sterling bloc fell because of strains on Britain.

Clearly, the trading world needed one strong financial center able to provide loans to allow countries to maintain liquidity in a world economic crisis, but such a center did not exist. London banks had fulfilled this function in the prewar period, but now they did not have the power. American banks, in spite of the transfer of wealth to the United States, did not have the ability—their emergence on the international scene was too recent. In addition, the United States was not willing to accept international responsibilities. Its emergence as a world power was confirmed by United States participation in the First World War, and in the Versailles negotiations President Wilson approved the establishment of the League of Nations, an international body to promote stability and peace.

But Congress refused to ratify the Versailles Peace Treaty, and the United States never became a member of the League of Nations. The isolationist attitude of the United States was further expressed in tariffs and controls on trade and immigration in the early 1920s.

Inflation in Germany

Against the background of the international events of the 1920s, Germany's problems were paramount. Soon after the reparations commission reported, it became obvious that Germany could not meet its terms. Both Germany and Austria were suffering from balance of payments problems, government deficits and acute inflation. The exchange rate had been four marks to the dollar in 1914, rose to 270 in November 1921, and by November 1923 it reached a meaningless peak of 4,200 billion marks to the dollar. In Austria, the exchange rate in August 1922 was 83,600 crowns to the dollar, as against five in 1914.

Many elements contributed to this disastrous collapse in Central Europe. The war left much devastation, a large government deficit, and a balance of payments deficit, accentuated by the demand for reparations. Thus, after all available gold and securities had been used to meet the first reparations payments, some of the next were paid in 1921 by selling paper marks to foreign speculators, who had bet that because Germany's basic industrial capability was good, the mark's value would be maintained. German businessmen were speculating against the mark. Exporters receiving foreign currency could take advantage of the fact that the internal price level was rising more slowly than the mark was depreciating externally. Holding foreign currency for a while before converting it to marks resulted in a gain in domestic purchasing power, which was then used to buy land and other real assets. In addition, the government was also printing money in order to cover its increasing debts, and public debt rose twenty-fold as taxation proceeds were not enough to cover enormous outlays. With the diversion of so much of Germany's industrial output, the money supply increased, rising from 50 billion marks in 1919 to 496,585,345,900 billion in 1923, and resulting in a spiralling of prices almost hourly in late 1923. The economy collapsed; monetary values had lost all meaning.

Even before hyperinflation had reached such disastrous levels, Germany announced that it could not continue the coal deliveries and other reparations payments in kind and in money. French troops immediately occupied the Ruhr, to be met by a refusal of the Ruhr miners to dig coal. The government supported the strike and undertook to pay the miners' wages, further increasing the budget deficit and pushing the hyperinflation into its final stages. Normally, a government makes every effort to avoid or end work stoppages in key industries but the political situation did not permit such strong action. The sense of humiliation and resentment in Germany after defeat in the war was keen. Only the combination of economic, political, and psychological effects of the war can explain the subsequent events.

Restructuring the Currency

Obviously, something had to be done. Internally, the currency was reformed, effectively restoring stability. A new monetary unit, the Rentenmark, replaced the mark at a rate of one trillion old marks to one new Rentenmark. This was "backed" by agricultural land but was not convertible into anything, and strict limits on the issue of Rentenmarks were enforced. Also, the government's budget was balanced. These measures were the prelude first for the Rentenmark's replacement by the Reichsmark on a one-to-one basis in 1924, and for Germany's subsequent return to the gold standard. At the same time, the Dawes Plan of 1923 drawn up by an interallied commission attacked the question of reparations. While the total was left unchanged, repayment

schedules were rearranged so that repayments would rise gradually as the economy strengthened, and they were tied to specific revenues. Thus 50 percent of the payments were to come from federal tax revenues, 12 percent from a tax on the gross revenues of railways, 12 percent from an issue of bonds secured by a first mortgage on the capital equipment of industry, and 26 percent from an issue of bonds secured by a first mortgage on railway assets. (Simultaneous attempts by the Allies to renegotiate their war debt repayments with the United States were unsuccessful.)

Meanwhile, the first exercise of international authority by the new League of Nations was a success. The scene was Austria, also facing economic collapse and hyperinflation. The League sponsored a loan to Austria and provided international supervision of debt repayment. This resulted in Austrian stability by 1926; prices stopped rising and the currency was reformed. The return to stable conditions in Austria and Germany seemed to have resolved international problems, but it was an illusion. International stability depends on real and financial flows having a reasonable relationship to underlying economic strengths and needs, but this did not occur, as reparations and war debt repayments added an arbitrary element. In particular, the recovery of foreign lending, although seemingly a sign of normality, only underscored international fragility. By 1927, international lending by Britain had surpassed its prewar level, but the United States replaced Britain as the single largest international creditor. United States gross foreign investment, excluding war debts, amounted to over $15 billion by 1930, with most going to Canada and Latin America.

United States Becomes a Financial Power

The development of the United States as a major lender and of New York as a world financial center (which became effective after World War II) was not due only to lack of war destruction. There were several contributory elements. First, war-related sales (especially of steel, ships, munitions, and food) until 1919, and sales of manufactures for reconstruction needs in Europe in the 1920s resulted in an export surplus. This in turn permitted the repurchase of United States securities held by foreigners (representing prewar foreign investment in the United States) which effectively reduced the drain of foreign exchange involved in making interest and dividend payments to foreigners. In addition to war debt repayments after the war, there was capital flight from Europe to the United States resulting in a transfer of funds to the United States and a surplus on its balance of international payments. These factors led to large amounts becoming available for overseas investments or loans and in turn increased the obligations of foreigners to the United States by requiring contractual flows of funds back to the United States later.

Three problems emerged as a result, one related to the United States position in particular, the others to the nature of international loans in general. First, unlike Britain in the prewar period, lending from the United States was a smaller proportion of its current balance of payments surplus, which meant that until 1924 there was a net inflow of gold and foreign exchange into the United States. United States claims on the assets of other countries were increasing, and this tied events in other countries much more closely to developments within the United States. This proved especially dangerous after 1929.

Second, unlike the loans of the prewar period, few were made for directly or even indirectly productive uses, so they did not stimulate increased production levels immediately. Loans went to Europe as loans to governments; some were used to improve public works or for relief payments, while others went to increase the production of commodities that were not in short supply. This fed back to the first problem. These loans committed the borrowers to repayment, but

were not increasing productive capability, thus making repayment much more difficult.

Third, while long-term lending increased absolutely, short-term loans increased as a proportion of the total. There were two problems with this. One was that the need in the 1920s was for meaningful reconstruction, especially long-term projects, so reliance on short-term borrowing was inappropriate as the repayment potential of the project would not become effective until after the loan matured. This increased the dangers of default. The second problem was that short-term lending developed a momentum of its own, as new loans had to be taken out in order to repay maturing loans. In effect, capital was being used to pay interest, which is economically unjustified. For example, between 1924 and 1931, Germany borrowed £465 million worth of long-term loans but £586 million worth on short-term (and until its final default in 1929, borrowed three times more than it was required to make in repayments).

Development of the Late 1920s Crisis

By 1927, problems with international financial flows, revolving around reparations and war debts, were clearly leading to a crisis, to which underlying economic problems were also contributing. Britain never fully recovered during the 1920s, and its weakness was not fully confronted by policymakers. Unemployment levels, too, were much higher than were usually associated with economic expansion. The lowest annual unemployment rate achieved in Britain was 9.7 percent in 1927, a level usually associated with depression, not recovery. There was some industrial expansion, especially in mass consumption goods, which masked weakness, as did the fact that food prices were falling, which meant that real wages were rising. Falling food prices resulted partly from increased supplies of many basic commodities, particularly wheat, sugar, and coffee, many of which came from developing countries, but this added yet another element to the emerging crisis. Many primary producing areas were producing at high levels, but rapid population growth (which was faster than in industrial countries) plus only slowly growing or falling income levels in these countries meant that their rate of economic growth was insufficient to absorb the surplus output of the manufacturing countries. This basic imbalance, however, was hidden by the appearance of prosperity elsewhere, especially in the United States, which now had the role of economic powerhouse.

Initially, speculation in the United States resulted in a financial crash, but the weakness apparent elsewhere, both underlying economic weaknesses and international crises, resulted in a widespread depression in the 1930s. Financial speculation had always been a feature of United States economic life but had not seriously affected the basic growth of the economy. This growth was impressive. In the 1920s, the United States accounted for half the world's output of steel and two thirds of its output of oil, its electricity production was equal to that of Europe as a whole, and in coal, machinery, automobiles, and other consumer durables it had a commanding position. Between 1921 and 1929, American industrial output increased by 90 percent, largely through increases in labor productivity, itself the result of mechanization and work rationalization. All this growth was based on exploitation of internal resources and purchasing power; while American trading had increased, foreign trade was never so important, or so large a proportion of total economic activity as it had been in Britain. Postwar reconstruction needs in Europe had provided an important stimulus to the United States manufacturing industry through the 1920s.

But even in 1928, cracks were beginning to appear. Wholesale prices were declining (the result of overproduction of some commodities), agriculture was not sharing in the general prosperity, and new construction was falling. Profits were still rising (although auto company profits fell in 1929), credit was easily available, and much financial wealth was being channelled into stock and bond market speculation rather than into productive investment. As stock prices seemed to be moving in only one direction, upward, this speculation seemed to be an easy way to make money; in 1929, the index of security prices rose to the range 200-210.

The Crash of 1929

The Federal Reserve Bank of New York raised interest rates to try to control stock market speculation, but it only attracted more foreign funds into the country and did not check speculation. Other countries were also affected. The inflow of foreign funds into the United States was the counterpart of an outflow of funds, especially from Europe, which put pressure on the gold reserves and foreign exchange held by central banks, most of which were back on the gold standard by 1929, because domestic currency had to be exchanged for gold or dollars before moving to the United States for speculation or investment. Central banks responded to this outflow by tightening credit availability, and the resulting rise in interest rates accelerated or initiated weakness in domestic economic activity. One reaction led to another. The New York stock market crashed in October 1929 (by 1932, the index of security prices had fallen to the range 3-40), wiping out tens of thousands of paper fortunes. American foreign lending dropped, reducing the volume of international trade; by 1932, its value was only one-third the 1929 level. This contraction in trade led to a reduction of British foreign lending, and growing balance of payments problems appeared in all countries except France and the United States

Export of Problems

In an effort to solve these foreign exchange problems, all countries began restricting trade and this filtered back to depress domestic economies further. By 1932 industrial production fell by one-third to one-half, depending on the country, and commodity prices fell by 30 percent to 40 percent. Primary producing countries, the unwilling victims of industrial problems, were then affected, and their subsequent reduction of imports further lowered world trade levels by removing markets for manufactures. The initial problems resulting from financial overspeculation had thus led to a decline in economic activity caused by credit restrictions, declining trade, trade imbalances, falling prices, and renewed problems of debt repayment, made worse by generally falling incomes. By 1931, it seemed briefly as though the worst was over, but instead, a new shock wave overwhelmed the world economy.

New Crises in Germany

This deeper crisis again revolved around the interrelated problems of reparations, war debts, and international lending. For years, Germany had been borrowing abroad, especially from the United States, in order to make its reparations payments. Those countries expecting reparations relied on them to repay their loans from the United States, which in turn lent money abroad. Germany was thus central to this financial cycle. Although Germany seemed to be recovering after 1924, its financial position was still shaky, and in 1929, when new long-term loans were no longer available from the United States, there was another prospect of default in reparations payments. To try to deal with this, the Dawes Plan was replaced by the Young Plan in 1929, which both reduced the total due and reorganized the repayment schedule. But this came too late. A worldwide depression was visited on the world economy. In Germany, the National Socialist Party, one of whose aims was to end Germany's humiliation by the Great Powers by eliminating reparations payments, was making electoral gains. About £50 million in short-term assets held

in Germany were withdrawn by their foreign owners. On top of this, a banking crisis hit in Austria in May 1931, when her largest commercial bank was declared insolvent. This occurred partly because its assets had depreciated and partly because foreigners withdrew the securities held in it for fear of further loss of value. A rescue operation was mounted by the Austrian government, and the bank continued operations with loans from the Bank for International Settlements[1] and some national central banks, but confidence was destroyed.

Attention then shifted to Germany, where, after Austrian banking assets had been frozen, foreign withdrawal of assets held in Germany had accelerated. An announcement that Germany's financial position was weakening further worsened the crisis, which was intensified by the likelihood that the next installment of reparations, due on July 1 under the Young Plan, would not be paid. The United States proposed that this installment be delayed for a year, and this, plus some short-term loans made to Germany by other central banks slowed down the rate of capital withdrawal.

Crisis in Britain

The center of the crisis then moved on to Britain, which throughout July 1931 was experiencing massive withdrawals of foreign-owned assets. This was occurring precisely because the complex financial flows of the 1920s required the meshing of all parts. If one link in the chain was broken, the whole collapsed, and this was what was happening in 1931. Thus, Germany ceasing to pay reparations led to other European countries experiencing difficulties in meeting their obligations, which was further intensified by depreciation of foreign assets, restrictions on their withdrawal, desire to rebuild depleted national reserves, and a lessening of confidence in sterling. Sterling was one of the major currencies used in international trade and finance, but the relative weakness of the

Solving Problems in Economic History

Why did Britain's productivity levels decline in the interwar period?

Britain was the world's industrial powerhouse throughout most of the 19th century, but declined relatively speaking in the 20th century. Especially in the interwar period, productivity growth was lower than in the United States, increasing the gap between the two countries. Why? Various explanations have been suggested. Most emphasis has been placed on the failure of British companies to adopt the efficient structures of their American counterparts—merging with other companies to develop multi-unit, vertically integrated firms which captured economies of scale, for example—or inefficient managerial decisions—managers were rarely professionally trained, for example.

This article, "Britain's Productivity Gap in the 1930s: Some Neglected Factors," by S.N. Broadberry and N.F.R. Crafts, (*Journal of Economic History*, 52:3, September 1992, pp. 531-558), holds that these traditional explanations account for only part of the gap. When attempts were made to quantify the effects of these failures, the gap appears less significant. Also, later structural reorganizations and mergers after World War II did not raise productivity by much, if at all, which seems to reduce the importance of the structural explanation.

When the authors looked at the dramatic productivity increases of the 1980s, they linked them to changes in behavior, rather than structure. With this in mind, they hypothesized that the poor productivity performance of the interwar period was mainly due to behavioral rather than structural problems. These were made worse by official policy which reduced competi-

tive pressures. Policy measures at that time included raising tariff barriers, encouraging cartelization, and devaluing the pound, for example, which were actions that raised entry barriers, made it more difficult for inefficient firms to exit, and encouraged the persistence of restrictive practices, especially accomodative bargaining in labor markets. They also noted that poor training may have contributed to a low level of labor force skills.

The explanatory value of these ideas were examined in two stages. First, a regression equation was set up to explain cross-sectional productivity growth, with labor productivity growth as the dependent variable. Results were consistent with the hypothesis that conditions in labor and product markets encouraged a "low effort" equilibrium. That is, while high unemployment in the early 1930s improved productivity, it was offset by increasing market power of protected firms. Official policy had the effect of encouraging inefficient firms to remain for fear of the resulting increase in unemployment if they went out of business.

The second step was to explain the productivity gap between American and British industries in the 1930s. It used an equation based on a Cobb-Douglas production function to explain the impact of factor endowments on output growth, and included the effects of scale of operations and various structural distortions (the extent of unionization, concentration, and tariffs). Interestingly enough, the effects of tariffs and union strength were insignificant; more significant were the human capital variable and the concentration ratio (the extent to which a

Problem continues on next page

Problem continued from previous page

product market is dominated by a small number of firms with market power). In summary, it seems as though the most important explanation of the productivity gap was the lower level of human capital in British industries. Lower productivity was also affected by less competitive, more cartelized conditions which made it possible for inefficient firms to remain in operation. In other words, factors of production were used inefficiently, and an attempt to restructure (encourage mergers) would therefore be the wrong response to this problem; what would be needed would be behavioral changes.

British economy in the 1920s and the decline in foreign trade after 1929 put severe strains on Britain's continued ability to act as an international banker. This position was further weakened because Britain still clung to the gold standard, which meant easy convertibility of foreign claims into gold, but Britain's own assets held abroad were not readily liquid, because international commitments had grown faster than the ability to replenish reserves through exports and other international earnings. Britain's reserves, even after borrowing £50 million from the Federal Reserve and the Bank of France, continued to run dangerously low as foreign creditors withdrew funds in

---

Depreciation

Decline in the value of one currency relative to another

---

ously low as foreign creditors withdrew funds in order to restore their own reserves to adequate levels. Finally, in September, Britain abandoned the gold standard, allowing the exchange rate of sterling to fall. This had further consequences because so many other countries were tied to sterling, and they also came under increasing pressure, which was reduced by allowing their currencies to depreciate in terms of gold and of the United States dollar too. By April 1932, a total of 24 countries had ended their ties to gold, and the gold standard was effectively ended in 17 others. The only major country still on the gold standard was the United States.

By this time, the worst of the international crisis was over, but oddly enough, more stable conditions were due not to international agreements but to governments acting independently. A further deterioration was prevented, but economic activity was at its lowest level since the war. These decisions could not have been made without abandoning of the gold standard because they involved actions at odds with gold standard rules. Thus, governments applied strict exchange controls to prevent capital flight and increased tariffs in an attempt to stimulate domestic production by keeping foreign competition out. The most dramatic change was the imposition by the United Kingdom of a general 10 percent tariff on imports and a 33 percent tariff on some manufactured items, reversing a century of adherence to free trade. Inevitably, the immediate result was a fall in the volume of international trade, but partial recovery of European national production levels did begin.

Germany Defaults

Still remaining was the perennial problem of reparations and debts, which could not be handled unilaterally—common action was needed. In 1932 the link between reparations and war debt repayments was finally publicized, but still the United States refused to make concessions, even though the European powers wanted an end to reparations to force the United States into a settlement on their debts to it. Later that year, the Lausanne Conference attempted a final settlement. It proposed that Germany make one final payment by issuing 5 percent bonds starting in

1935, with the Bank for International Settlements acting as issuing agent, and with any unsold bonds to be cancelled in 1950. This loan was based on the fundamental strength of the German economy, and on the presumption that Germany would be able to pay interest and principal within fifteen years. However, the arrangement was never put into effect. While Britain agreed to forgo repayments due it, the United States continued to insist on full repayment, but the scheme collapsed on the coming to power of the National Socialist Party under Adolf Hitler in Germany.

The resulting complete default on reparations payments did eliminate one element of uncertainty but resulted in very little else. International rivalries, political fears, and an unwillingness to take concerted action implied that financial weakness and a lack of economic growth would persist. The final illustration of the complete disintegration of an international system came in 1933. The League of Nations planned a world economic conference to attempt to deal with the problems, but just before it was due to meet, the United States finally went off the gold standard; conversion of paper money into gold was prohibited. This was not the result of international strain, as it had been for Britain, because the United States did have a strong foreign exchange position. Rather it was due to poor economic theorizing and diplomacy, and the hope that it would lead to a unilateral strengthening of the United States. The depression following the 1929 crash had hit the United States hard, and the beginnings of recovery had been too weak. Then in 1933 a wave of bank failures exacerbated the existing depression. So it was thought that if the dollar was not tied to gold, it would depreciate and the internal price level would rise, stimulating domestic production, while falling prices of goods sold on the world market would give a boost to exports. By the middle of the year, the value of the dollar in relation to other currencies had fallen 30 percent, but the volume of trade did not increase and real recovery with full employment and full use of

industrial capacity did not return to the United States until the Second World War. At that time, renewed demands for military goods increased aggregate demand and stimulated production levels.

Internal Impact

The First World War and the international events of the 1920s obviously affected the domestic economies of both Europe and the United States, and in turn, internal developments had an impact on the international scene. In brief, this period saw a shift of the international distribution of wealth, as the United States gained and Europe, especially France and the United Kingdom, lost ground, relatively speaking. Britain experienced slower recovery during the 1920s, partly because of a dependence on declining industries and too few new growth industries. (Ironically, this relative weakness also implied that the 1930s depression would be moderated; a decline from a low level is less burdensome than a decline from a high one.) Germany's internal development was complicated by the peculiar position it was forced into after the war, which encouraged political extremism.

The postwar period did not return the Western world to "normal" peacetime conditions, although attempts were made to restore the pre-1914 situation, chiefly through an emphasis on the return to the gold standard. But the war had changed the economic environment, so these attempts were incompatible with others that were specific results of the war (including reparations and war debts). The result was confusion, and there was a breakdown of concerted action to come face to face with the new international reality. The United States did not admit the connection between reparations and war debts, and had not yet come to terms with its new role as economic leader and major financial lender. Britain was unwilling to recognize that the war had signalled the end of its role as world economic leader and tried, unsuccessfully, to reestablish dominance. Germany was paralyzed by the economic burdens put on it, and its attempts to recover from psychological humiliation led to an extremist political reaction. This was the most glaring example of the wave of right-wing fascism that emerged at this time in some European countries such as Italy. In many ways, this confusion, improvisation, and lack of real progress contributed to the length and severity of the depression of the 1930s, the most severe in the history of capitalism. The changes and responses to those changes also contributed to the events leading up to another worldwide conflict. Unfortunately, the "war to end all wars," as the First World War was called, proved to be a misnomer. The remaining section of this chapter will cover some of the internal developments of different countries that were closely tied to international events.

Germany

Germany ended the war not only as a defeated country but as a smaller one with a reduced industrial base. Its redrawn boundaries did not make economic sense. For example, although increased demands were made on the coal industry to ship coal as reparations in kind, one-third of Germany's coal resources were lost, and although the iron resources of Lorraine were also lost, Lorraine ore continued to be shipped to the industrial Ruhr for processing. When industrial output did begin to recover, much was diverted abroad, especially coal and shipping, although a stepped-up export drive was needed in order to earn foreign exchange for reparations. The situation was irrational, and the combination of diverted output, reparations demands, a government deficit, international borrowing, and currency speculation all contributed to the disastrous hyperinflation of 1921-1923, one of the worst in history, as discussed above.

Effects of Inflation

Although currency stability was restored in 1923, the combination of defeat in war and redistribution of wealth after the inflation had adverse economic, political and social effects. Any inflation redistributes wealth from savers to debtors and to those with the ability to speculate against the currency. In Germany's case, the inflation was so long and so extreme that it also destroyed any pretense at liberal democratic values, which had always faced a struggle for influence in Germany. Those who gained were landowners and large businesses. Landowners, especially large ones who held mortgages (which were expressed in money terms), gained as the value of the currency fell because their debt was literally wiped out. Small landowners gained only to the extent that the fall in the real value of what they owed was greater than the rise in the monetary value of their incomes; in fact, most small farmers suffered. Many sophisticated businessmen gained. Those who understood the process of inflation borrowed and then repaid with depreciated currency, and those whose production was sold at prices higher than costs gained, especially if the monetary gains were quickly used to buy real property. Similarly, speculators or those receiving foreign currency could also make paper gains by holding that currency for some time before conversion into a larger amount of marks. The key to capitalizing on inflation lies not merely in making a paper profit (which will soon become worthless itself) but in turning those paper profits into something that will retain value. Wage earners suffered some loss of real incomes, as money wages did not rise in pace with prices.

The major losers in Germany were the middle classes. Salaried workers found that their incomes lost ground compared with the cost of living; those on fixed incomes, especially retirees, lost as their incomes did not increase as fast as the prices of food and other basics. Those receiving interest income, particularly those who had bought war bonds to help finance the war effort, found their holdings and interest payments were now worthless. These effects eliminated any incentive to save, because inflation wiped out the value of saving. Inflation also reduced the faith of the middle class in the virtues of the capitalist system. They had long been its supporters, especially against the perceived threats from socialist workers, but now they suffered as it careened out of control. Even if control and stability were restored, it would be too late to restore their savings.

Rise of the National Socialists

This adverse impact provided fertile ground for the growth of the National Socialists. Until the hyperinflation, it had been seen simply as a crackpot party, but the economic and psychological damage suffered since 1919 resulted in the middle classes becoming its most solid supporters. To them, the idea of restoring German dominance to atone for their suffering was most appealing. Up to this time, the most strident opposition to both the Democratic coalition government of the Weimar Republic and socialism came from the conservative National Party. Its leadership came from the large landowners, especially in Prussia, with a long tradition of support for the monarchy and the army, and of opposition to Socialism, Catholicism, and Judaism, so it was favorable to the idea that Germany had been betrayed by the Versailles Treaty. These ideas overlapped with those of the National Socialists, and an alliance between them meant the end of democratic Germany and the coming to power of a fascist dictatorship.

Potential middle class and landowner support was insufficient to produce the electoral gains and visible economic advantages needed by this opposition to seize the government. To do this required an alliance with big business, and here the common ground was opposition to socialism and the working classes. However, between 1924 and 1929 economic conditions were improving, as exports grew and public works, financed by borrowing, helped restore the infrastructure needed for rebuilding the economy. In this period, extremist parties did not do well. Then the crash of 1929 and the ending of American loans to Germany set off a severe depression in Germany providing the last straw for continued middle class support for democracy and the Weimar Republic. Unemployment rose to over three million in 1930 and to 5.6 million in 1932.

In that year, the possibility of effective power for the National Socialists became a reality. The elderly war hero, Field Marshall von Hindenburg, the candidate supported by the Nationalists, won the election for President of the Republic, outpolling Adolf Hitler of the National Socialists by 20 million votes to 13.4 million. Persuaded by leading Nationalists who favored a collaboration with Hitler's Nazis, Hindenburg appointed Hitler Chancellor in January 1933. Then in April, the Reichstag, which was barely dominated by Nazis following elections, voted to delegate its powers to the Hitler government, effectively beginning the Third Reich. (The Holy Roman Empire counted as the first, and Bismarck's empire as the second.) On Hindenburg's death in 1934, Hitler also became President.

The economic recovery that took place under a system of tight central control reinforced Hitler's position. Unemployment was reduced to two million by 1935 and to only one million by 1937; Germany was the only major industrial country to "solve" its unemployment problems in the 1930s. National output doubled by 1939, when it was 26 percent higher than in 1929. These goals were accomplished by a program of public works projects, stimulation given to various industries (chemicals, metals, textiles, and food especially) and a process of rearmament. This was forbidden under the Versailles Treaty but began secretly in 1933 and openly in 1935 with the construction of fortifications and armaments facilities and the development of a military aircraft industry. State control was closely allied to large industrial groups without whose support the economy could not have begun to strengthen to permit military development. Then it became clear that the restoration of German glory depended on war, especially to annihilate France. To this end, military service was reestablished in 1935, the Rhineland reoccupied in 1936, Austria absorbed in 1938, Czechoslovakia occupied in 1939. The year 1939 also saw an alliance with Italy (under the right wing fascist dictatorship of Benito Mussolini), the signing of a nonaggression pact with the Soviet Union, the appeasement of Britain, and the invasion of Poland. Thus began the Second World War, which was much more destructive than the first: Its death toll was fifty million, six times the death toll of the First World War.

France

France, which was occupied twice by Germany in the 20th century, suffered in the interwar period from political weakness, fluctuations between left and right wing governments, inflation, and colonial problems. Inflation was linked with the general problem of German reparations. Much of the rebuilding of the economy was predicated on assuming that reparations would pay for it, but when they did not materialize in the amount expected, the difference was made up by printing money and borrowing. While nowhere near as disastrous as inflation in Germany or Austria, it had much the same impact on redistributing wealth, contributing to political difficulties. In addition, inflation encouraged a flight of capital from France.

The development of the French overseas empire was encouraged during the 1920s, but had less impact than expected. In 1928 a system of imperial preference favoring trade within the empire was established, and, as was the case with Britain, a larger proportion of French trade was diverted to its colonies. In 1928, 12 percent of French imports came from within the empire and

19 percent of its exports went to the colonies, proportions that rose to 27 percent and 30 percent respectively by 1938. To strengthen colonial ties, French banks were established in Africa and the Middle East. Development in the colonies was slight. Only about 10 percent of all French capital invested abroad was in the colonies, and most of this financed commerce rather than manufacturing or extractive industries. In addition, the colonies were not easy to hold. Anticolonial revolts required France's intervention in 1920-1921 and again in 1937-1938 in Tunisia, while Morocco was in upheaval in 1925-1926 and in 1937-1938, and peasant revolts took place in Indochina in 1930-1931, all of which represented a drain on French resources.

Internally, the 1920s saw a catch-up effort in industry. The index of industrial production, 100 in 1913, fell to a disastrous war-induced level of 57 in 1919, but recovered to 109 in 1924 and to 127 in 1928. Much of this was due to the adoption of techniques common elsewhere. The use of power increased, there was more mechanization and modernization in general, and this increased worker productivity, which also helped compensate for the loss of manpower during the war. In addition, there was more rationalization and the growth of large companies. The auto industry, for example, became dominated by three companies (Citroen, Peugeot, and Renault). The sector gaining most was the capital goods industries, where France had long been weak in relation to her industrialized rivals. In spite of this, large companies were still the exception; only 20 percent of all French workers worked in firms employing five hundred or more, while 40 percent worked in firms employing fewer than ten. Some incentive to industry was given by the falling exchange rate of the franc, and exports in particular gained from the fact that internal inflation was slower than the fall in the franc's external value. Only 7 percent of manufacturing output had been exported before the First World War; this proportion rose to 10 percent in the 1920-1924 period but fell dramatically in the 1930s.

Britain

Britain's economy, like France's, had been particularly hard hit by the war, and although a victory had been achieved over its major industrial rival, it was a pyrrhic one. Not only was the actual cost of the war in money and men very high, but also some of the provisions of the Peace Treaty did not seem like the spoils of war due the victor. Underlying this was the decline of three basic industries on which British prosperity and leadership during the 19th century had depended, a decline accentuated for two of them by the Treaty. This implied that even after the economy returned to peacetime working, unemployment ran at levels higher than previously. It averaged 12 percent, never fell below one million and reached a maximum of three million in 1932, and was always higher in the old industrial areas, especially in one-industry, nondiversified areas.

Declines in Coal, Shipbuilding, and Textiles

The requirement that Germany make reparations in coal adversely affected coal mining in Britain, which was further depressed during the 1930s. From a level of 287 million tons in 1913, coal output fell to 227 million by 1938. Coal was typically produced in areas relying almost exclusively on that one industry, so some areas were severely affected. For example, in the 1913-1914 period, only 3 percent of workers in Wales, a coal mining area, were unemployed, but by 1934, 36 percent were, and in some mining valleys up to 70 percent were out of work.

Similarly, British shipyards had built one million tons of ships for British shipowners alone in 1913, but saw their order books empty as German shipyards built ships to make good the destruction of Allied shipping. Recovery did not start until 1927, but then was overtaken by the Great Depression when the fall in foreign trade left existing ships idle and many yards closed.

The third basic industry was textiles, which was adversely affected by events in Asia in the postwar period. By 1933, Japan was exporting more cotton textiles than Britain, while India, previously the largest single importer of British cottons, had been able to increase its own production during the war. In 1913, exports of cottons accounted for one-quarter of all Britain's exports; by 1938, output of cotton was only half its previous level and exports of cotton about one quarter. Fortunately, Lancashire (center of cotton manufacture) was a more diversified industrial region, and growth in other textile areas (carpets, hosiery, synthetics) also mitigated the worst impact of the decline.

In general, production after the war was one fifth lower than before, and although recovery proceeded during the 1920s, the crash of 1929 reduced production by one third. Manufacturing output had grown faster during the 1924-1935 period than in the 1907-1924 period, and industrial output per capita rose by one third 1924-1937. This was mainly due to the growth of new industries, especially consumer goods industries. The problems with trade during this time encouraged a shift toward supplying the domestic market, which had not been considered a prime growth area during the 19th century, so there were some new opportunities. This shift toward greater reliance on the home market plus the fact that Britain's traditional industries were already depressed modified the impact of the 1929-1932 depression. The index of industrial production stood at 100 in 1913, then fell from 109.9 in 1929 to 90 in 1932, compared with a fall from 112.7 to 58.4 for the United States and a fall from 108 to 64.6 for Germany.

Policy Creates Problems

Some of Britain's problems during the 1920s can be traced to the effects of the war, but others were due to either specific policy decisions or general international changes. The major policy decision causing problems was to return to the gold standard in 1925 at the prewar parity of the pound. The problem was that although it was an effort to regain prestige and a former international position, the pound was overvalued. This made exports relatively expensive and, because Britain now faced industrial competition, exports were reduced and did not recover their 1924 value until 1929. In turn, this led to efforts to cut wages in order to reduce production costs (one of the factors influencing the General Strike of 1926), which in turn led to many "hunger marches" by unemployed workers to dramatize their plight. On the bright side, for those holding jobs real wages did rise, as although money wages fell, wholesale prices fell more.

Figure 21.2 Unemployment was high in Europe throughout the 1920s and 1930s and scenes such as this soup kitchen in Germany were common. Unfortunately, such persistently depressed conditions often contribute to the rise of the extremist right-wing political movement. (From "Sieg Heil! An Illustrated History of Germany from Bismarck to Hitler," by Stefan Lorant, published by W.W. Norton, New York, 1974, p. 180. Courtesy of Stefan Lorant)

Even without the return to the gold standard, Britain's former position would have been difficult to regain because world trade was also declining. To some extent, trade within the empire held up better than trade with other countries. This situation plus the ever-present problems of war debts also affected Britain's overseas investments. While overseas investment and earnings and invisibles had recovered to their former levels by the mid 1920s, the shocks of the 1929-1932 period resulted in a second period of decline. Between 1929 and 1932, dividends earned on investments abroad had fallen from £250 million to £150 million, while invisibles earned only £86 million, down from £233 million.

But some changes that were made resulted in Britain looking more like a modern economy by 1939. There was more emphasis on science and technology, with notable achievements being made in the totally new forms of entertainment, radio, and later television. While pure science discoveries opened up the fields of nuclear physics, computers, and biochemistry, Britain failed to build on these achievements. Only with radar and

jet propulsion did original British discoveries reach practical application, and then only because of State sponsorship. More consumer goods were also produced, although the level of production of durables such as refrigerators and cars was lower per capita than in the United States.

United States

The decline of Europe throughout this period was matched by an increase in the economic and financial power of the United States, a power increasingly wielded on an international scale. The war had given a stimulus to industrial production and National Income as a whole almost doubled to $61 billion by 1918. Participation of the United States in the war and peace negotiations was visible evidence of its role as a world power, but isolationism triumphed in the 1920s and the 1930s, first with the raising of barriers against goods and people in 1922-1924 and again more dramatically in 1930. So although the United States was the largest international creditor during this period, growth in the 1920s was largely based on internal markets and industry.

Table 21-1
Effects of the Great Depression, United States

I Index of Industrial Production (1923–25 = 100)	
May 1929	May 1932
126	61

II Unemployment (millions)			
1930	1931	1932	1933
3	6	10	13 (25% of the labor force)

This basic strength overcame fears that financial overspeculation and international fragility could lead to problems threatening the real economy, but when the crash occurred, the results were dramatic. Paralleling declines in industrial production, unemployment rose to three million in 1930, doubled to six million in 1931, and reached a peak of thirteen million in 1933, when one quarter of the labor force was out of work. Wholesale prices fell by one third between 1929 and 1932. In a vain attempt to stimulate domestic industry, new tariffs were introduced in 1930. These had the effect of reducing imports, which had been $4.4 million in 1929, to $1.3 million in 1932. Although foreign trade was not too important for the American economy, this reduction served to remove vital markets for other countries, for whom trade was significant. Without export earnings, they in turn reduced their demand for United States goods, and United States exports consequently fell from $5.2 million in 1929 to $1.6 million in 1932, an example of the export of depression among interrelated economies. Then the United States abandonment of the gold standard and the devaluation of the dollar in 1933 further affected export industries.

The length and severity of this depression forced a new approach to economic problems. Although Germany had solved its internal economic problems, that particular approach, with all its implications, was looked on with distaste by democratic societies elsewhere.

Deflation
Generally falling price level

Summary

Although economic recovery and reconstruction did take place in Europe in the 1920s, it was influenced strongly by the dual problems of German reparations and Allied war debts. These problems were made worse by the United States refusal to treat war debts as anything other than business investments. Given that the United States was achieving a position of dominance as a major world lender and financial power, this implied that international financial flows were increasingly unstable. When repeated difficulties with German payments forced rescheduling of debts, the problem was not solved. The world economy went from crisis to crisis, and a problem in one country became transmitted to another because of the linkages between reparations, war debts, and trade.

There was no concerted effort to deal with internationally caused problems. The League of Nations, the new international body, did not have the authority to handle such problems, and the United States declined to be a member. Instead, countries adopted unilateral actions to solve problems. This may have seemed to be the only feasible option, but it delayed practical, workable solutions. The United States, especially after 1929, retreated inside its own borders. Both Britain and France tried to use their colonial empires to make good losses suffered elsewhere, but neither managed to restore their previous strengths, although the foundations for modernity were laid. Of the advanced industrial nations, only Germany succeeded in emerging early from the depression. But the cost of this would haunt the world for generations: Loss of democratic values, annihilation of opponents of a vicious right-wing regime, and another, even more disastrous world war that led to the possibility of the destruction of the entire planet.

Notes

1. The Bank for International Settlements was established in 1929. Originally, it was hoped that it would develop into a true international central bank facilitating settlements between national central banks and providing liquidity in emergency situations like the Austrian one, but this did not happen.

Key Concepts

Deflation

Depression

Financial Panic

Gold Standard

Great Depression

Hyperinflation

Inflation

Rationing

Reparations

Tax Structure

Unemployment

Questions for Discussion or Essay Writing

1. Why did the balance of economic power shift after the First World War?

2. Explain the difference between unilateral capital transfers and trade-related capital flows in the context of the 1920s.

3. Why were reparations the key to the effective functioning of the international monetary system?

4. What were "the economic consequences of the peace" following World War I?

5. What were the pros and cons of returning to the gold standard in the 1920s?

6. Explain the causes of the German inflation of 1923. What were its effects?

7. To what extent is it true to say that political extremism finds fertile ground in economic misery?

8. What economic factors slowed down Britain's recovery after the First World War?

9. How can policy retard or encourage economic activity? Illustrate, using examples from the interwar period.

For Further Reading

Arndt, H.W. *The Economic Lessons of the 1930s*. London: Frank Cass, 1963.

Ashworth, William. *A Short History of the International Economy Since 1850*. 3rd. ed. London: Longman Group, 1975.

Bordo, Michael D. and Barry Eichengreen, eds. *A Retrospective on the Bretton Woods System: Lessons for International Monetary Reform*. Chicago: University of Chicago Press, 1993.

Bradford de Long, J. and Andrei Shleifer. "The Stock Market Bubble of 1929: Evidence from Closed-End Mutual Funds." *Journal of Economic History*, 51:3 (September 1991): 675-700.

Broadberry, S.N. and N.F.R. Crafts. "Britain's Productivity Gap in the 1930s: Some Neglected Factors." *Journal of Economic History*, 52:3 (September 1992): 531-558.

Galbraith, J.K. *The Great Crash*. Boston: Houghton Mifflin, 1961.

Eichengreen, Barry. *Elusive Stability: Essays in the History of International Finance, 1919-1939*. Cambridge: Cambridge University Press, 1990.

_____ "The Origins and Nature of the Great Slump Revisited." *Economic History Review*, XLV:2 (May 1992),: 213-239.

Garraty, J.A. *The Great Depression: An Inquiry into the Causes, Course and Consequences of the Depression of the 1930s*. San Diego: Harcourt, Brace Jovanovich, 1986.

Hacker, Louis M. *The Course of American Economic Growth and Development*. N,Y: Wiley, 1970.

James, Harold. "The Causes of the German Banking Crisis of 1931." *Economic History Review*, XXXVII:1 (1983): 68-87.

Hayes, Peter. "Carl Bosch and Carl Krauch: Chemistry and the Political Economy of Germany, 1925-1945." *Journal of Economic History*, XLVII:2 (June 1987): 353-363.

Kindleberger, Charles P. *The World in Depression, 1929-1939*. Berkeley: University of California Press. 1975.

OECD, *Industrial Statistics, 1900-1955*. Paris: OECD, 1955.

Potter, Jim. *The American Economy Between the World Wars*. 1974.

Rees, Goronwy. *The Great Slump: Capitalism in Crisis, 1929-33*. London: Wiedenfeld & Nicholson, 1970.

Romasco, Albert U. *The Politics of Recovery: Roosevelt's New Deal*. N.Y.: Oxford University Press, 1983.

Schlesinger, Arthur M, Jr. *The Coming of the New Deal*. Boston: Houghton Mifflin, 1959.

Sundstrom, William A. "Last Hired, First Fired? Unemployment and Urban Black Workers During the Great Depression." *Journal of Economic History*, 52:2 (June 1992): 415-430.

Temin, Peter. "Soviet and Nazi Economic Planning in the 1930s." *European Economic History Review*, XLIV:4 (1991): 573-593.

Chapter 22

Post World War II Reconstruction and Cooperation

Objectives

IN THIS CHAPTER WE WILL SEE HOW WESTERN EUROPE, once the center of the economic world, struggled out of the devastation of World War II. Following that struggle, the small nations of Europe began to cooperate, recognizing the advantages accruing to large continent-sized countries in the 20th century. European integration is continuing in the 1990s. The moves toward economic integration by the European Community reverse the experience of centuries of development of the region as a set of competing nation states. Integration has contributed to the recovery of European economies and to their rapid growth since then. We will analyze the reasons for integration, political as well as economic, a complex process.

A second theme of this chapter is macroeconomic policy making in an environment of modern large-scale industrial organizations and mass production techniques. Government has become more involved in economic affairs and there is a greater concern for social welfare everywhere. However, exactly what shape this involvement took differed from country to country. We will

look at six examples: the United States, West Germany, France, the United Kingdom, Italy, and Japan.

Finally, although much late 19th and 20th century economic development involved mass production and a trend to increasing size of enterprise, there are also other developments. In some new late 20th century industries—for example, electronics, software development, specialized production—smaller companies seem to have an advantage. Although they are highly specialized, they are also highly flexible. Is this significant or is it just an interesting oddity? A second trend, more compatible with the move to increasing size, is the incentive to cross-national cooperation. The huge research and development expenses associated with new technologies such as those in space research or superconductivity encourage it. It should be distinguished from multinational corporations, which are single-ownership entities operating across borders. Cross-national enterprises in contrast involve government support for cooperation between several different national enterprises.

Need for Economic Recovery

The Second World War marked a new high in death and destruction. Although destruction of

---

Economic integration

Countries join together to gain some of the advantages of a single country

---

518

physical property was enormous, oddly enough the Western European economies were still left with greater productive capacity in 1945 than they had at the end of the First World War. Instead of collapsing into chaos and depression, the international economy began a period of impressive growth after 1947, thanks to a deliberate effort to encourage international cooperation to solve problems. Some lessons had been learned.

No attempt was made—as had been in the 1920s—to return to the prewar situation. The element of revenge, imposing an impossible burden on Germany, was minimal, meaning that interallied loan repayments and reparations did not lead to international collapse. The financial problems of waging this war had been handled very differently. Instead of the financial loans of World War I, a lend-lease "exchange" of goods and services was used, and European war loan obligations to the United States were simply cancelled at the end of the war. Except for small deliveries of equipment, neither Germany nor Japan, the major belligerents, was required to pay reparations. The United States did not retreat into isolationism; the 1950s was a decade of its unchallenged economic dominance in the world economy.

Beginning at the Yalta Conference in February 1945, a new threat in the form of Soviet expansionism stimulated a response from the Western powers. After 1945, another shift in the balance of power became obvious. Europe was dwarfed in comparison to the rise of two continent-sized superpowers, the United States dominant in the West, and the Soviet Union, which was dominant in Eastern Europe. No peace conference was held after the war because there was no recognized government in Germany after its surrender. It was partitioned into zones of influence, and the occu-

Lend-Lease

Material aid (arms, equipment, food) provided by the U.S. to its Allies during the Second World War

Multinational corporation

A company with production facilities in many different countries

pying forces took on the responsibilities of government. The Russian zone became the German Democratic Republic, or East Germany, in 1949, while the American, British, and French zones formed the basis for what would become the Federal Republic of Germany, commonly referred to as West Germany. Also, while there had been extensive redrawing of boundaries and the creation of new states including Czechoslovakia, Yugoslavia, and a redrawn Poland after the First World War, very little territory changed hands as a result of World War II. With the exception of Germany's partition, the borders of 1938 or 1939 were largely restored, although the Baltic states were reorganized as Soviet Republics within the Soviet Union.

Extent of World War II Damage

World War II was without precedent in world history in the extent of damage inflicted and the number of countries and populations involved. Many countries in Europe and the Pacific area were occupied by invading armies; others—in Europe, North Africa, the Middle East, Indochina, and the Pacific—had been fought over. Still others like Britain were not the scene of land battles but were subject to air bombardment, a weapon that was also turned against the major cities of Germany.

The war was also unprecedented in the use of new military technologies. The submarines and aircraft of the First World War had evolved by this time into highly sophisticated fighting instruments. Aircraft had become differentiated; there were fighter planes, high-flying surveillance craft, bombers, and also cargo-carrying planes that provided a new method of supplying land-based forces. New pilotless flying weapons, the V-1 jet-propelled flying bomb and the V-2 rocket bomb, were developed in Germany—a technology later put to peaceful uses in revolutionizing commercial aircraft. Naval warfare using a variety of extremely sophisticated weapons and devices such as radar was responsible for turning this into a truly worldwide conflict. But the beginning of a new stage of modern warfare came when two atomic bombs were dropped on Japan in August 1945, one on Hiroshima and a second on Nagasaki. Scientists were not quite sure how destructive they would be. Afterward, and after decades of further refinement and testing, it became clear that the use of nuclear warfare in a subsequent major war dooms life on the entire planet to destruction.

Relative economic strength determined the war's outcome. With the enormous economic power of the United States and Russia to count on, the Allied forces were able to outlast the Axis forces. Estimates of the actual costs of the war are difficult and probably underestimated, especially in respect to civilian deaths. Overall, close to forty million people died (equivalent to the entire population of Portugal, Greece, the Netherlands, and Denmark), a further thirty-four million were wounded, and thirty million displaced. The country suffering the largest death toll was Russia, where it is estimated that about twenty million people were left dead and twenty-five million homeless.

Actual outlays for war materials and expenses have been estimated at $1,154 billion, seven times those of the First World War. Its estimated cost, including an allowance for property destruction, was $3,000 billion. To put it into perspective, the United States, with one third of the world's production of manufactured goods, had a national income of just over $66 billion on the eve of the war.

The United States, Canada, and Australia were fortunate enough to be spared actual combat on their territory, but sent fighting personnel and equipment to Europe. Capital equipment deteriorated during the war years, but these countries' economies remained strong, and they ended the war with usable productive capacity that was called on to help meet Europe's postwar reconstruction effort.

Germany

Germany suffered heavy war damage, as bombing had hit civilian as well as military targets. Damage to the transportation system was particularly serious—it was a priority target for Allied bombing because wartime military strategy depended on effective transportation. However, damage was not total. Although industry in the American zone in 1945 could produce only 10 percent of its 1936 level of output, this was due more to materials shortages, the uncertain financial system, and lack of transportation than to actual destruction of equipment. While buildings had been destroyed, much of the industrial equipment could be salvaged, which helped Germany's rapid growth after 1948. In particular, the machine tools industry survived enough to reproduce equipment.

Great Britain

Losses in Britain were due not so much to physical destruction of industrial capacity as to obsolescence and financial problems. Industry had been geared to producing for military needs, so very little new investment had taken place; hence by 1945 industrial capacity desperately needed replacing and modernization. Financial problems turned Britain into the world's largest debtor in 1945, a complete reversal in the course of the 20th century. Public expenditure had risen from £1,147 million in 1938 to £6,190 million by 1945; high taxation covered 25 percent of war expenditures, which meant that the rest had to be financed somehow.

The interwar years had not been kind to Britain. In the 1920s, her recovering industries were unable to recapture markets lost during the War. In addition, the industrial leaders were not innovative and lagged in developing new goods for which demand was rising. Returning to the gold standard in 1925 hurt, because the pound in terms of gold was overvalued. Exports were less competitive in world markets, and deficits in the balance of payments characterized the 1930s even after the 1931 devaluation. The most significant earnings on invisibles were those from shipping and interest and dividends from overseas investment, but were nowhere near enough to cover trade deficits. Britain's international debt increased from £476 million to £3,335 million by 1945—but by this time, there were few earnings from shipping, as a large part of the merchant marine had been sunk during the war. About 25 percent of overseas investments had been sold to help finance the war effort, and these overseas holdings could not contribute much to paying off this debt. Much of the country's postwar experience revolved around the problem of external balance.

Europe's External Problems

In fact, Britain's experience was only the most extreme example of a more general Western European problem. Before the war, earnings on European overseas holdings were roughly equivalent to one third the value of their exports. During the war, these holdings were liquidated, and in 1950–1951, their earnings represented only 9 percent of the value of export earnings. The more general problem was that the European economies desperately needed to expand exports to start earning foreign exchange in order to pay off debts accumulated during the war. But to do this, they needed foreign exchange to acquire the raw materials and capital equipment needed to restart production—where was this foreign exchange to come from? Even if it was available, the problem of finding export markets remained; many old markets had disappeared because some previous importers had industrialized; the division of Europe into East and West meant that East Euro-

pean markets were lost; and yet other markets had been lost to American exporters.

Japan

Japan's war damage was also considerable. There were 1.5 million military deaths and countless civilian deaths, including 100,000 killed as a result of the atomic bombs. Physical destruction was estimated as equivalent to about one-quarter of national wealth. It included the loss of 90 percent of the merchant shipping fleet, one quarter of the housing and one-fifth the industrial capacity. In addition, after the war, Japan no longer had control over Taiwan, Korea, and southern Sakhalin—losses effectively reducing the nation's land area to one half that claimed as Japanese in 1930.

Japan had entered the war on an economic shoestring, so her immediate postwar position was gloomy. The most immediate need was for food (which was imported from the United States), and industrial recovery was very slow. This was partly due to the loss of access to the raw material resources of the former empire, and like Europe, Japan also needed to export to earn foreign exchange. As in Europe, this was difficult, both because of low production levels—industrial output in 1946 was only one fifth of the 1939–1944 average—and because of the difficulty of earning foreign exchange with which to import needed materials.

Internal Issues

In addition to these problems, all countries involved in the war had imposed various restrictions on domestic activity as part of restructuring the economy to military production or dealing with war-related issues. If the international economy was to move to peacetime conditions, these restrictions would have to be removed to permit a freer, more liberalized movement of goods. As will become clearer, one of the lessons of the interwar period was that "beggar-my-neighbor" policies beggared everyone. That is, each country's attempts to improve its own position by imposing tariffs on imports simply reduced the total volume of world trade and reduced internal economic activity, because there were too few buyers of exports. Removing trade restrictions was a very important part of international negotiations after 1945.

Beggar-my-neighbor policy
One country's attempt to improve its international balance by limiting imports reduces world trade and spreads recession to its trading partners

---

In addition, various exchange controls had been imposed on international flows of money and capital. The European countries felt controls were necessary in order to conserve scarce foreign exchange needed to acquire war-related goods. (Exchange or currency controls limited the ability of domestic nationals to acquire foreign exchange, and only the government in each country had the power to authorize access to limited foreign exchange reserves.) Controls were gradually relaxed after 1945 as economies converted back to peacetime operations.

During the war, both the armed forces and industry needed personnel. Industry relied on older men, women (many of whom entered the paid labor force for the first time), and, in some cases, immigrants from colonial possessions to keep running at full capacity. Unemployment was at a bare minimum. However, because so much of industry's output was intended for military uses, less was available for sale, but total earned incomes were high. Most countries had raised taxation rates during the war, and high tax rates served to reduce inflationary pressures by siphoning off purchasing power from consumers. High tax rates were also a financing device for large government expenditures, and special taxes were imposed to prevent war profiteering and to dis-

courage the production of items not important to the war effort. Price controls were also imposed to hold inflation in check.

Wartime measures also included rationing, various schemes by which scarce goods could be allocated without using the price mechanism. Rationing had the most effect on the civilian population in the allocation of foodstuffs, especially imported ones, and also gasoline and fabrics.[1] Countries relying on imports for a substantial proportion of their total food supplies rationed them to get a fair allocation. In Britain, sugar, fats, and meat were rationed, and certain groups in the population such as children and pregnant women were given preferential treatment. Once production levels began to return to normal after the war, rationing was eliminated. By the early 1950s, most of these internal controls and restrictions had been lifted.

Planning for Postwar Relief

A focus on Western Europe in the immediate postwar period showed that although problems were immense, they were not insurmountable. This was partly due to the recognition—begun as early as 1941 while the war was still in progress—that a concerted cooperative approach was needed. The problems of economic development, military security, and political democracy subsequently became intertwined.

This became increasingly clear once it was obvious that the European nations could no longer claim economic dominance, especially given the economic realities of the 20th century in which size gives advantages. Although there is a range of physical differences (climatic and topographic), the western European countries are small in land area. The twelve EEC countries have a total land area of 2,349,000 square kilometers, which is small compared with the 9,363,000 square kilometers of the United States or the 22,402,000 square kilometers of the former Soviet Union.

The nation-state and capitalist industrialization on the whole took hold early. European countries are, however, culturally and linguistically distinct. Their economic superiority began to diminish in the late 19th century, when forces encouraging divisiveness rather than cooperation increased. Britain responded to her relative industrial decline by looking away from Europe toward her empire; Germany unified and became increasingly powerful and militarily aggressive; France grew slowly though steadily, but did not show the evidence of development that her resources promised; while southern Italy and the Mediterranean countries remained peasant agricultural economies.

Europe's fragmentation and weakening continued in the 20th century. The advantages of relatively small land areas disappeared once efficient transportation and communications networks developed, permitting the exploitation of the huge natural resource wealth of the United States. Size also gave an advantage in modern industrialization, because access to a large market permitted successful exploitation of economies of scale. Loss of markets as former importers industrialized hurt European economies highly dependent on trade. Devastation following the world wars and the beginning of the decolonization process effectively reduced the size of European colonial powers.

Developments in the rest of Europe underscored Western Europe's problems. The old Austro-Hungarian and Ottoman (Turkish) empires were broken up into small independent nation-states after the First World War. After the Second World War, Europe split into East and West, divided by an "iron curtain," an expression first coined by Britain's wartime Prime Minister, Winston Churchill. This division represented an ideological barrier between the socialist planned economies in the East and the mixed capitalist market economies in the West.

Continuing problems of fragmentation and the threat to security posed by the rise of totalitarian states as well as military aggression led to three main concerns that became the principles underlying postwar development. First, there was a need for a mechanism to guarantee collective security, initially against a resurgent Germany and potentially against an expansion-minded Soviet Union. Second, there was a desire to encourage democratic processes in all countries. Third, there was a desire to relax trade restrictions as a way of revitalizing European economies.

The first formal indication of what would be needed came in 1941 when Churchill and Franklin Roosevelt, then United States President, jointly issued the Atlantic Charter. It made a start in identifying problems that would emerge when hostilities ended, and enunciated several desirable principles. They included a rejection of aggression; a statement that no territorial changes should be made without the consent of the people involved; general statements affirming the rights to free choice of government and freedom to travel; and a statement about future international financial arrangements. The pro-peace ideal and the need for a peace-keeping mechanism led to attempts starting in 1943 to establish the United Nations Organization (effective in 1945). Although the United Nations has not been able to prevent all wars since then, it has played a significant role. The League of Nations failed because individual nations were unwilling to subordinate their own interests to the peace of the world. The United Nations had a better chance because by this time, international cooperation was recognized as essential if world peace were to be assured.

The Atlantic Charter also led the way to the establishment of other international financial and economic institutions, such as the International Monetary Fund, the International Bank for Re-

Iron Curtain

Term used to describe the barrier isolating the Soviet Union and its allies from the rest of the world

construction and Development (the World Bank), and the General Agreement on Tariffs and Trade, an institution that would be instrumental in helping reach agreements to lower tariffs and other trade restrictions. What is significant about the charter is not that its ideals were accomplished—they were not—but that it represented an *international* approach. It was followed by a series of international conferences that addressed the practical issues of how to reach these ideals. These conferences largely established the framework for the international economy that we are familiar with today.

Immediate Postwar Relief and UNRRA

Idealism is all very well, but in the last years of the war, practical relief was needed. In many areas, low agricultural production and the cutoff of trade created widespread food shortages, and a few places were near starvation. During 1944, as Allied armies began their final sweep to victory, most immediate food needs were provided by the distribution of emergency rations by the armies. After the war ended (May 1945 in Europe and August 1945 in the Pacific) this sort of relief was still needed, as farmers began to return to a normal routine. In some cases, however, even this was not possible, because farmland had to be cleared of land mines and other military detritus before it was safe to work.

Postwar relief was accomplished by the United Nations Relief and Rehabilitation Administration (UNRRA), which spent $1 billion distributing food, clothing, blankets, and medical supplies where needed between 1945 and 1947. Major funding came from the United States, which as an economy emerging stronger than ever before had to take a leading role in Europe's recovery. The United States also provided the raw materials and capital equipment needed for industrial revival. After 1947, UNRRA'S work was continued by the International Refugee Organization

and the World Health Organization (one of the branches of the new United Nations).

Marshall Aid and International Cooperation

However, by 1947 it was also becoming clear that economic recovery was not occurring as quickly as expected. The main reason was that the European economies were simply too short of dollars to continue importing from the United States, so the time they took to return to "normal" peacetime production levels was increasing. To earn the foreign exchange needed to buy imports from the United States required expanding exports, but exports would not grow unless productive capacity was replaced and modernized, which would not happen unless imports from the United States were acquired. In other words, everyone wanted dollars but no one was in a position to earn enough dollars. The United States also had an incentive to act, because unless Europe was buying American products, its exports would be lower. Although it experienced a postwar expansion due to the unleashing of pent-up wartime domestic demand, the risk of recession if trade was adversely affected was real.

The solution came in 1947 when the European Economic Recovery Plan (Marshall Plan) was set up. It was essentially a straight capital transfer from the United States to Europe, distributing about $13 billion in loans and grants between 1948 and 1952, when it ended. All participants benefitted. Available dollars meant that European enterprises could acquire the resources needed for renewing their industrial capacity, which then gave them the ability to expand exports and start earning foreign exchange. American producers benefitted, because now there were buyers for their products. The increase in economic activity

Marshall Plan

European recovery plan financed by loans and grants from the United States

set off by this transfusion of purchasing power paid for itself many times over.

The principles underlying the ERP illustrate the three related economic, military and political issues that motivated the Atlantic Charter and gave an incentive for an international approach. The United States intended to give aid to Europe as a whole, but there was no Europe-wide mechanism for doing it and for allocating aid within Europe. Hence, the first requirement was to create such a mechanism to organize the aid distribution, the first step on the long road toward European integration. This mechanism, the Committee on European Economic Cooperation (CEEC)—later renamed the Organization for European Economic Cooperation (OEEC)—was responsible for distributing aid with a more ambitious goal of rebuilding Europe's economy by removing barriers to trade.

The Soviet Union was originally going to receive Marshall aid, but it balked at the requirement that a single European agency distribute funds. It wanted bilateral aid instead, but when it became apparent that this was not forthcoming, the Soviet Union refused to be part of the CEEC and took a much more aggressive stand toward the Western nations.

Freer trade was another objective of the United States, connected with rebuilding an effective, and nonrestrictive, international financial system. The United States wanted the European countries to stop relying on bilateral trading arrangements, which they were using to overcome the postwar problems of foreign exchange scarcity. Such arrangements always balanced trade, therefore avoiding problems associated with unbalanced balance of payments or shortages of foreign exchange or inconvertible currencies. However, they also artificially held trade to levels below what it could otherwise have been. In other words, while each nation was solving its own problems, the result was less desirable than if there had been more flexibility permitting an overall expansion of trade, even if resulting in temporary balance of payments problems.

European Payments Union

The creation of the European Payments Union (EPU), a system for the multilateral settling of trading accounts, solved the problem. Each month, each country's imports and exports within the region were tallied, and any balance of payments deficit was financed with automatic credits granted by other countries.

Together, Marshall aid and the EPU provided the necessary catalyst to recovery; by 1951 all the OEEC countries had achieved levels of industrial production well above their 1938 levels, and recovery was essentially complete by the mid-1950s. The international approach to solving mutual problems certainly seemed to work. While the postwar period in the early 1920s and the entire decade of the 1930s were depressed, a similar major postwar depression did not occur after the Second World War. The OEEC, even after Marshall aid ended, continued to work for freer trade within the region. By the late 1950s, western European trade was almost entirely free from restrictions. Over the decade 1950–1960, the average increase in the volume of trade was 47 percent, although some individual countries did better. In 1958, the EPU was replaced by the European Monetary Agreement and enlarged to include the sterling area (composed of those countries belonging to the British Commonwealth of Nations that used sterling in international trade and held their international reserves in sterling) and the French franc area (all the French colonial possessions that gave a similar role to the franc). At this time, most European currencies that had previously been convertible only within the EPU became freely convertible with the United States dollar.

NATO and Collective Security

The need for collective security was the third principle expressed by Churchill and Roosevelt in the Atlantic Charter. At first, it was felt that the establishment of the United Nations would accomplish this, but developments later in the 1940s demonstrated the need for some more formal arrangement.

It had always been assumed that Germany would be included in any arrangement for Europe. The partitioning of Germany made this difficult, but West Germany did receive Marshall aid money. However, strict limits on rearmament were imposed. (Similar restrictions were also imposed on Japan, and the consequent effect of limited defense spending in both countries has been offered as a partial explanation of their rapid economic growth in the postwar period.)

When relationships between East and West deteriorated in 1948, coming to a head with the Berlin Blockade,[2] the Western nations agreed to form the North Atlantic Treaty Organization (NATO) in 1949, a military alliance assuring mutual military support to any member. (A similar organization, the Council for Mutual Economic Assistance, was formed at the same time by the Soviet Union and its allies, partly to counter the implications of and respond to the Marshall Plan.) NATO was composed of the United States, Canada, Belgium, the Netherlands, Luxembourg, France,[3] the United Kingdom, Denmark, Iceland, Italy, Norway, and Portugal. In 1952, Greece and Turkey joined; then West Germany in 1955; and Spain in 1981. In keeping with yet another principle of the Atlantic Charter—and also influencing the expansion of the EEC—some of the newer members were permitted to join later only when democratic governments had replaced dictatorships.

To summarize, the Western European economies had fully recovered and started an impressive expansion by the late 1950s, stimulated by aid and internal policies such as direct loans and low tax rates to encourage an expansion of investment. Laissez faire may have been an ideal, but in practice, governments everywhere recognized the need for some form of economic planning. This may have been as general as simply expressing certain socially desirable goals, such as full employment. But in Europe, there was an increasing recognition that prosperity and security did not just happen, that they had to be carefully nurtured, preferably within a larger grouping than the borders of the individual nation state.

Moves Toward European Integration

Much European political history is the history of conflicts, alliances, rivalries, and wars between the various European states. But after the ravages of two European-centered world wars, the postwar period has witnessed a remarkably successful process of European integration. It falls considerably short of full political union—which is unlikely to occur—but still represents a unique endeavor.

Types of Integration

Economic integration includes different degrees of integration, all of which are or will be represented in Europe. In the larger free market of a regional grouping, each country's producers can expand production and achieve economies of scale that are not possible in the domestic market alone. There are other advantages that depend on how the group is structured.

The least comprehensive scheme is a free trade area. This is composed of a group of countries that eliminate tariffs and quotas on trade among themselves. Each retains its own commercial policy regulating trade with nonmembers. An exam-

Free trade area

Members eliminate tariffs on trade between themselves

Table 22-1
Postwar European Recovery, 1948-54
Industrial Output and Employment Indexes (1950=100)

Year	West Germany		Italy		France		United Kingdom	
	Output	Employ-ment	Output	Employ-ment	Output	Employ-ment	Output	Employ-ment
1948	55	—	79	—	90	—	87	—
1949	79	—	87	—	94	—	93	—
1950	100	100	100	100	100	100	100	—
1951	119	108	113	101	109	102	105	102
1952	128	112	116	101	108	101	101	102
1953	139	116	127	101	109	99	106	103
1954	154	125	137	106	110	100	105	106

Source: United Nations, *Economic Survey of Europe*, 1953, 1954

ple of a free trade area is the European Free Trade Association. A more limited version is also possible in which free trade applies to products of only one sector, such as an industrial free trade area. An example of this is the European Coal and Steel Community (ECSC), which affected only production and trade in coal, iron, and steel.

A more comprehensive integration scheme is the customs union. It adds a common tariff policy to internal free trade so that all members have the same policy with respect to trade with nonmembers. The advantage is that it adds a measure of protection against foreign competition by closing up a loophole of the free trade area. This loophole is that producers in nonmember countries can evade high tariffs in some member countries by exporting only to the member with the lowest tariffs. Once inside the area, the goods are treated as intra-area trade and can move freely to other

members of the area, effectively escaping their own high tariffs on imports. Examples of customs unions are the Prussian-led Zollverein in the mid 19th century and the European Economic Community in the 1960s and 1970s.

Economic community
Free trade in goods and resources between members of the community

Although a customs union frees trade, it still falls short of the advantages available to a *large* nation-state. The difference is that only traded goods move freely within a customs union, while within a nation-state, productive factors also have freedom of movement. The next stage of integration then is to add this freedom of movement by creating a common market, in which labor and capital are freely transferrable across national frontiers. This means that people can take a job anywhere so long as they meet the requirements, while companies can establish operations anywhere within the region. In principle, this is the

Customs union
Like a free trade area with the addition of a common tariff on imports from outside countries

current situation within the European Economic Community. The final stage, which takes the integrating countries one step short of statehood, is the economic union. This is the stage where each country's economic policies are harmonized with the others, a single set of economic institutions is developed, including a common monetary system, a single central bank, and a unified tax and benefits system, and there is complete freedom of movement for financial flows. This is a much more difficult step to achieve, because while the earlier stages involve the *removal* of restrictions, this one requires the *creation* of something new. It is also difficult because it requires agreement from all countries involved to give up their economic sovereignty to a new supranational entity[4] and national sovereignty is very hard to give up. However, steps have been taken to approach economic union in Europe after 1992, with the creation of the so-called single market. The grouping is now called the European Union; it has been enlarged by the inclusion of west European countries such as Austria; and some of the post-Communist, formerly centrally planned east European countries, such as Poland and Hungary, have applied for affiliate status as a prelude to full membership.

The advantages of economic union go beyond the provision of a larger market and the opportunity to gain economies of scale. Specialization may increase, and production of some items may be concentrated in the hands of the most efficient producers. Costs may be lower, and, depending on the pro-competition, antimonopoly policy in existence, may be passed on to buyers. All these normally have the effect of creating trade and increasing the overall level of economic activity within the union—the effect of the whole being greater than the sum of its parts.

There are also dynamic effects that are particularly important for smaller countries. Investment usually increases—perhaps as a result of the benefits from the larger market or the pressure to improve efficiency when facing competition from

other producers within the scheme. Technological advance is more likely, especially if there are information and research-sharing provisions. Also, external economies may appear when advances made in one industry permit lower costs in another, through either subcontracting or increased specialization.

External Economy

Improvement in one industry lowers costs in another

Initial Stages of European Integration

The original incentive toward closer ties within Western Europe came as a result of the Marshall Plan. As we saw above, the distribution of American aid was made by the OEEC, made up of sixteen nations, which jointly determined the allocation of aid. Plans for defense and cultural unity fell through (although NATO was established later, it was a different type of military alliance). However, the idea of closer economic and security links was considered important in guaranteeing future European integrity and peace. Once aid had been distributed and economic recovery assured, the OEEC evolved into the Organization for Economic Cooperation and Development in 1961, composed of the original OEEC countries plus the United States, Canada, Japan, Australia, and Finland. Its main purpose is to encourage growth through trade with a secondary purpose of encouraging the industrialization of less-developed countries by drawing them into the international trade environment. While it was successful in the 1960s by creating a "club" for wealthy industrialized nations, it has been less successful in encouraging the development of the nonindustrialized economies.

European Coal and Steel Community (ECSC)

What was to be done to link the European economies together for their mutual benefit and that would also assist their mutual security? The ECSC was formed next, as a limited free trade area. In 1950, during the Korean War (the first time the peace-keeping mandate of the new United Nations was tested), there was a world-wide shortage of steel for military purposes coexisting with excess steelmaking capacity within Europe, and it seemed sensible to take advantage of this situation. The ECSC was initiated by France and Germany, which already had some experience in international industry organization: Lorraine iron ores were French, but were mostly shipped to Germany for processing. They proposed to formalize this arrangement and jointly manage coal, iron, and steel production to guarantee supplies to many other industries. Belgium,

the Netherlands, and Luxembourg joined because the scheme represented an extension of their own "Benelux" grouping. Italy also joined, although at that time it did not have a steel industry worth mentioning, but it was desperate for international recognition and also needed a stimulus for economic expansion. These six countries were to be the original six founders of the EEC. The United Kingdom did not join, because it had recently nationalized its steel industry, and feared that the adjustment to ECSC requirements would be too great.

The ECSC began functioning in 1952 and was an interesting organization because it tried to do more than just eliminate tariffs and other restrictions. The whole point was to make the industry

Figure 22.1 Transportation was revolutionized after the middle of the 20th century with the development of jet-powered airplanes. Shown here are jet planes at J F Kennedy International Airport, one of the world's busiest. (Courtesy of the Port Authority of New York and New Jersey)

more efficient and more competitive, so its administration had extensive powers over modernization, subsidies, closures, and mergers in different countries, which was unique. It was successful in rationalizing and modernizing production units, but was not an unqualified success because of other factors. The market for coal was shrinking in the late 1950s as oil became a preferred energy source. In 1951 coal provided two thirds of the energy needed by its six members; this had shrunk to less than one quarter by the late 1970s. It is frequently the case that when the overall economy is expanding, international cooperation is easy because gains are easy to come by, but when contraction begins, international cooperation is more difficult.

Treaty of Rome: EEC

In spite of this drawback, the feasibility of an economic union remained, and the six nations explored ways of developing a more complete form of integration. In 1957 these efforts were crowned with the signing of two Treaties of Rome, one establishing the European Economic Community (EEC) and the second establishing the European Atomic Energy Commission (Euratom). As the two largest powers in the grouping, France and Germany dominated the EEC. France wanted to ensure that its farmers could get free access to Germany's large industrial cities, and also wanted to be able to influence the progress of German industrial development. Germany wanted freer access to France's market for industrial goods. Italy wanted to end its relative isolation, and the Benelux countries, the smallest in the group, favored international cooperation in principle as well as wanting access to larger markets for their industrial producers. All of them hoped that creating a larger market (160 million at that time) would expand trade and production, encourage greater efficiency, raise living standards, and encourage greater harmony between them.

The Treaty of Rome covered various issues that would have to be dealt with in order to achieve the final aim of an economic community. It proposed establishing a customs union, policies for agriculture and transport (with the details left for later), methods for harmonizing social security and tax programs, and coordination of different national legal systems.

Setting up the customs union was the first project. Tariffs and quotas on industrial products were abolished on intra-EEC trade—easily coordinated with the more general moves to liberalize trade that the General Agreement on Tariffs and Trade[5] was coordinating. There was a timetable of twelve to fourteen years (although all tariffs were effectively abolished ahead of schedule by 1968). In 1968, the EEC, ECSC, and Euratom merged into a single structure. Policies dealing with agriculture provided many more problems, and will be dealt with more fully later.

European Free Trade Area

At the same time that the EEC was being established, a rival organization, the European Free Trade Association (EFTA), was formed, coming into effect in 1960. Britain was the leading force here, because she feared losing some European markets as a result of the creation of the EEC, which she had not wanted to join because of the extensive system of preferences covering trade between Britain and the Commonwealth nations. Instead, Britain favored an association dealing only with industrial commodities, allowing each member to retain its own agricultural policies. The EEC's emerging agricultural policy was one that protected farmers and kept prices high, which was very different from the British situation where low-cost imports from the Commonwealth and direct payments to British farmers kept prices to consumers low. So EFTA was designed to free trade in industrial goods while still permitting each country to protect other sectors of the economy in any way they chose.

Furthermore, because it was a free trade area, each member retained its own external tariff. The seven members of EFTA were the United Kingdom, Sweden, Switzerland, Austria, Norway, Denmark, and Portugal.

Comparing both groupings shows the trade-creating effects of integration. Trade increased, with trade between members increasing even faster, a more pronounced effect in the EEC than in the EFTA. However, the EEC countries, with the possible exception of Italy in the early years, were similar in terms of level of industrial development. There was more diversity in size and level of economic development within EFTA, which included highly industrial and wealthy countries like Britain and Switzerland as well as poor agricultural Portugal.

Although Europe was at sixes and sevens for some time, Britain applied for membership in the EEC when her economic ties with the Commonwealth countries began to weaken. All the EFTA countries (except Portugal) applied for inclusion in 1961, but de Gaulle of France vetoed Britain's application, fearing loss of French influence should both Britain and West Germany be in the EEC. Britain's application was again vetoed by France in 1967, but in 1973 the EEC was expanded with the entry of the United Kingdom, Denmark, and Eire, leaving EFTA much smaller. (The remaining EFTA members do, however, have a Special Relations Agreement with the EEC.) The EEC was expanded again in 1981, when Greece became a member. Spain and Portugal were admitted in 1986.

This expansion may create problems. The smaller EEC was made up of relatively similar economies. With the expansion of the 1980s, the EEC has to face the problem of integrating poor agricultural nations into the grouping without disruption. However, because encouraging democratic governments in all countries was one of the initial motives for integration, the latest expansion was done mainly to help preserve these relatively new democracies.

Common Agricultural Policy

One of the most controversial aspects of the European Community has been its agricultural policy, especially after enlargement from six to nine and then to twelve members with very different resources and needs. The EEC is one of the most productive agricultural areas in the world, capable of producing a wide variety of items because the area includes many different climatic conditions, ranging from the cool northwest latitudes to the hot Mediterranean region. No single country is totally self-sufficient in food production, but the EEC as a whole is. For example, the United Kingdom and Eire have advantages in dairying; France and West Germany's main crops are cereals; viniculture is found mainly in France, Italy, Spain, and to a lesser extent, in Germany; the Mediterranean countries produce olive oil, rice, and citrus fruits. This diversity is a key to understanding the Common Agricultural Policy (CAP).

Common Agricultural Policy
European Community policy protecting agriculture

Another element influencing the CAP's construction is an inherited feature: Large numbers of people left in agriculture in some countries even as industrialization progressed. In 1949–1950, the average percentage of the labor force in agriculture was 21 percent in West Germany, 27 percent in France, 37 percent in Italy, compared with 12 percent in the Netherlands, 9 percent in Belgium and 5 percent in the United Kingdom. (Comparable percentages were 40 percent in Eire, 48 percent in Greece and Portugal and 46 percent in Spain; and only 10 percent in the United States.)

Extensive shortages and low industrial production in the postwar period was paired with excessive underemployment in agriculture. However, farming was encouraged through a variety of

Underemployment

Situation where employed people have too little work to do, resulting in low labor productivity

traditional protective measures (such as tariffs) and price supports, because of these shortages and lack of foreign exchange. In most cases, the result was high-cost production that was often not suitable for the country's economic resources. Although lower-cost food was obtainable through trade, lack of foreign exchange, the desire to use scarce foreign exchange for industrial restructuring, and the historic preference for self-sufficiency in food meant that agricultural problems remained. But trying to develop a *common* policy was difficult, as land tenure patterns and productivity levels differed widely.

The CAP's aims were desirable but somewhat contradictory. Productivity should rise by encouraging technical progress. Farmers should have higher incomes so their standard of living becomes comparable to nonagricultural workers. Consumers should pay reasonable prices. All these aims were to be accomplished with market stabilization. Social goals were also apparent—especially the goal of easing labor out of agriculture without the labor displacement and social misery that accompanied the "classic" agricultural revolution in Britain. This does seem to have been accomplished. In the original six members, the percentage of the population engaged in agriculture dropped considerably: In 1980, the largest percentage was in Italy at 13 percent (representing 2.9 million people, the largest absolute number).

Agricultural Policy in Operation

The CAP began in 1962 by creating a single market for agricultural goods protected from outside competition by variable import duties that remove the price advantages of a lower cost producer. It is unlike a customs union for industrial goods, however, because of its pricing arrangements. In theory, industrial producers set their own prices and compete with other enterprises. But competition among farmers produces uniform prices. So instead, target and support prices and subsidies are established by the CAP. Target prices are at a level that would generate an adequate income for producers; if support prices are not met subsidies make up the difference. There are separate policies to encourage restructuring in agriculture, such as schemes for retraining or modernization and a system of annuities to older farmers who give up farming.

In the end, CAP is both highly political and highly controversial and may not even have reached one of its goals—to help the smaller farmer. This is because the system benefits larger, more commercialized farmers who can take advantage of the various incentives. In effect, this has resulted in the subsidization of overproduction and the consequent creation of the "butter mountains" and "wine lakes" that make good newspaper headlines.

Such a system, of course, is expensive to maintain—about two thirds of the EC budget is taken up by these subsidies, although this proportion has been declining. Moreover, by reflecting various interest groups, notably French farmers with large surpluses to dispose of, the agricultural policy involves a transfer of income to agriculture away from food importing to food exporting countries, especially those with excessive numbers of farmers. Most of the EC's income comes from levies on imports, so food importers with an efficient agricultural sector gain nothing from the CAP. The United Kingdom and other net food importers such as West Germany fall into this category. On the other hand, France, Italy, and Eire gain the most. They are food exporters with large structural problems, and they gain both from access to a larger market and from the system of guaranteed prices, subsidies and grants. While British farmers have also benefitted because they are among the most efficient in the Community, thus gaining from their low costs and the

Community-set high selling prices, there are very few of them (532,000). The country as a whole became a net loser on entry to the EEC, when low-cost food imports from the Commonwealth were replaced by high-cost food imports from Europe, an example of trade diversion. This controversial issue was raised in the United Kingdom's application to join the EC and has remained unsettled ever since.

A third problem relates to the persistence of many structural problems even though numbers of farmers are declining. There are still many small farms, especially in areas highly dependent on agriculture. Changes have left older farmers in place in many areas, while younger ones have departed. Such rural depopulation makes traditional village life impossible to maintain; the complaints first voiced decrying the enclosures in England in the 16th and later centuries are heard again.

Trade Diversion

When imports are diverted from a low cost supplier to a high cost supplier

---

European Industry

As previously noted, Europe's industry completed its recovery by the mid-1950s, and continued expanding after that. The role of the EEC in providing a larger market helps to explain continued expansion in the 1960s—roughly half the members' trade is within the EEC, and most is trade in industrial goods. The experience of the United Kingdom is instructive in showing the impact of the customs union on trading patterns. In 1960, when it was not a member, 38 percent of its exports went to the sterling area and 16 percent to the six EEC countries. But by the late 1980s, roughly half its trade was with the EEC countries.

The EEC countries, individually and as a group, rely much more on trade than the United States. They account for about one third of world

---

ECU

A unit of account used in the European Community

---

trade and for 70 percent of trade of the industrial countries of the EEC, North America, and Japan. The pattern of imports and exports also reflects their industrial maturity: Manufactured goods account for 65 percent of imports and 80 percent of exports.

In 1980–1981, the EEC's population was 271 million compared with 227 million in the United States. It produced more steel than the United States but consumed less; and it produced more cars—9.6 million compared with 6.4 million. It exported more than the United States: Its total value of exports was 478.8 million ECUs compared with 159.5 million ECUs. (An ECU is an artificial currency unit devised by the EC's central bankers. It is the sum of specified amounts of member countries' currencies; rates of each currency against the ECU are defined for the purpose of keeping the exchange value of the currency within an agreed range.) In steel production, the rise of Italy as a major producer has been significant. Italy is now second only to West Germany within the EC, although unlike West Germany it relies on imported ore. The steel industry in Europe has been extensively modernized. Most EEC steel is now made using basic oxygen converters, which are faster and bigger and can also be adapted to use steel scrap as an input, and most of the open hearth and Bessemer converters have closed.

New Industrial Characteristics

Industrial development in the postwar period has several characteristics, so that most modern industrial economies look remarkably similar and produce more or less the same things. The first characteristic is the role of multinational companies. At first, they were responsible for direct foreign investment from the United States; previously, capital transfer had been government-to-government loans or bond purchases. Most went to the United Kingdom, but significant United States operations were built up in West Germany, Belgium, and the Netherlands, with most in oil refining, automobiles (all three major United States producers have subsidiaries in Europe), chemicals, electronics and consumer products. By the mid-1970s, foreign-controlled firms accounted for between 20 and 30 percent of industrial production in the leading European economies. The EEC is attractive for direct foreign investment by the United States not only for its high level of development, but also because of the desire to establish United States-owned production facilities *inside* tariff walls; the same reasoning also applies to Japanese direct foreign investment in the late 1980s and after. By the 1970s, also, European multinationals were becoming more significant, not only in other European countries but reversing the trend and establishing operations in the United States. Within the EEC, as we would expect, this is easier as many restrictions on the movement of productive resources and capital within the Community have been removed.

A second element involves a very different migration pattern compared with that of the 19th century. Due to agrarian overpopulation, about fifty-five million people emigrated from Europe in the years between 1820 and 1914, with thirty-eight million going to the United States. This was mostly for economic reasons, and most of the emigrants intended to establish permanent residence in their adopted country. In Europe in the 20th century, some of the movement across borders was politically inspired—the result of redrawn borders or of political repression. As noted earlier, immediately after World War II ethnic Germans moved into West Germany, enabling industrial expansion by providing an extra pool of labor to draw on. However, this was a one-time movement. Later, the practice of using "guest workers" from countries on the fringe of the EEC

(such as Yugoslavia or Turkey) was adopted to avoid any labor shortage. What is different here is that the motive is economic, not political, and the movement is essentially temporary in nature rather than for permanent settlement. This is underscored by the policy of the host country: Once the need for the migrants' work is over, they are expected to return home. In the late 1980s, foreign workers (who are not usually seasonal workers so much as workers hired for a short period of time in industrial and service operations) numbered eight million. This is the ultimate version of free labor, an advantage for the host country, as they can be attracted into the country when the demand for labor is rising, but sent home when the demand for labor falls; there is no further commitment involved. The employment rate for native workers stays high—any fluctuations in business conditions are borne by the guest workers—and because they are not citizens or permanent residents, they have limited claims to social security benefits.

Guest Worker

Usually a temporary immigrant worker who does not take up permanent residence

The extent of part-time farming in some countries is associated with this, and it also adds some flexibility to economic activity, although it is a different type than in previous centuries. In the late 1980s, on average in seven countries of the EEC, agriculture employs 7 percent of the working population, but 31 percent of those with second jobs. Part-time farming is particularly important in West Germany, Eire, and Italy, countries with many small farms that are uneconomical for full-time work. Part-time farming is defined as taking place when one or more members of a farm family is employed in a nonfarm job. This can be one of two types. First is the entrepreneurial type, as when a farm is combined with tourism, such as operating a guest house on the farm. The second type occurs when work is undertaken away from the farm area, usually in an industrial or commercial setting.

Future Developments: Monetary Union

In the late 1980s, the EEC began final steps toward more complete integration. Political integration is highly unlikely. Although policy harmonization took place, it occurred because decisions were made by each national government. There is a European bureaucracy (the European Commission operating out of Brussels) and a European Parliament (sitting in Strasbourg) but neither has powers equivalent to those of a national government or executive.

The final stages of economic union, however, are hard, and strongly resisted by the United Kingdom, which does not want to lose either its sovereignty in this area or its place with New York and Tokyo as one of the three important centers of international finance. Some EC sovereignty over monetary issues came in 1979 with the creation of the European Monetary System (EMS), which was intended to create a stable exchange rate system. The Exchange Rate Mechanism (ERM) is at the center of the System. EC members agreed to limit fluctuations in their currency to within a narrow band, although reserving the right to adjust its value through de- or revaluation if necessary. Linkage with the ERM did prove to be advantageous in terms of relative monetary and balance of payments stability.

Full membership in the EMS is seen as a first step toward a single currency and central bank for Europe as a whole. Together, they remove any possibility of independent monetary policy, and also limit fiscal policy if the country's central bank is involved in the financing aspects of fiscal policy. This in turn could affect political party platforms and national election processes, which contain policy implications: Are nations willing to give up these rights to a supranational authority? The cost of a commitment to European unity rises as a

Fiscal policy
Use of government's taxation and expenditure policies to accomplish macroeconomic goals

result, and a decision to meet this higher cost has not yet been made.

Final Steps to Integration

In fact, it became clear in the 1980s that the provisions of the Treaty of Rome were insufficient to produce a truly integrated Europe. The Treaty has had three major accomplishments: The elimination of tariff barriers between EC countries, freedom for nationals of member countries to work anywhere in Europe, and the right of companies to establish themselves anywhere in the Community (under rules established by the host country).

Barriers preventing a perfectly free market such as exists within the United States still exist, so it is more costly to move goods within Europe, for example, than within the United States. Some of the more obvious barriers are those associated with the fact that EC members *are* sovereign nations. Examples are border stops at a country's borders, capital controls (permitted under certain circumstances), different systems and rates of taxation, and restrictions on some cross-border selling, affecting mainly financial services. Other less obvious ones include discrimination in buying for public enterprises (domestic suppliers are favored), differences in safety and technical standards, and road transport restrictions, especially weight and size limits on trucks. The net result is that the European market is still much more fragmented than the United States market.

The single European Act was passed in 1987, to overcome some of these barriers with the intent of creating a single European market by 1992. It identified thirty legal changes that will be required to eliminate remaining restrictions on freedom of movement to make unification effective. Agreement is difficult because different countries have different interests, and they also vary in their perception of the best way to achieve a single market.

Mass Production and Macroeconomic Policy

Industrialization, as we have recognized by now, does tend to make the industrial structure in different countries similar. Techniques tend to be similar, especially when multinational corporations are involved. Most companies have become organized on the joint stock principle, which has advantages for financing and legal issues. They have also tended to develop highly sophisticated and large managerial structures, made necessary both by the increasing size of the enterprise and by increasing specialization within the enterprise.

If one looked only at the trends, it might be expected that the advanced industrial countries would come to resemble each other. But in spite of all the pressures, this has not happened. Strong traditional forces still distinguish one country from another, and policy differences imply that although industrial techniques may be the same, each country's social and economic reality has its own distinctive features. A brief picture of each of six countries in the postwar age follows, showing the different approaches to macroeconomic policy taken by each.

United States and "Traditional" Policy

After the Second World War and for the next twenty years or so, the United States was at the height of its economic powers. The economy expanded until the late 1960s, with the exception of a couple of mild recessions. The government reversed its previous protectionist stance, and like Britain a century earlier, took advantage of its economic dominance to be the standard bearer of free trade and laissez faire ideas. Interestingly enough, calls for protectionism were heard once

international competition began to strengthen in the 1970s once again.

What differentiated the United States from other countries at this time is that this expansion was not consciously planned or regulated or controlled. The main economic involvement of the Federal Government was in what has now become called traditional economic policymaking, especially fiscal policy. Changes in taxes rather than changes in government spending were the most important mechanisms used to influence the direction of the economy.

Immediately after the end of the war, Congress passed the Employment Act in 1946, to express a commitment to the three related goals of high employment, price stability, and economic growth. No mechanism for attaining these goals was suggested, however. With the disastrous memory of the 1930s, a commitment to preventing economic collapse was politically advisable. Although postwar demobilization sent ex-servicemen flooding into the labor market, the expected postwar recession did not occur, for two main reasons.

One was that pent-up domestic demand for consumer goods—which had been held in check during the war—was unleashed, providing a high level of demand for the consumer goods industries. The second was that demand from other countries, especially for the capital goods needed to rebuild war-damaged economies, was also strong. Together, sufficient demand was generated to offset the decline in production of military goods. That this demand could be met owes much to the fact that the United States escaped war damage and had the capacity to meet the demands placed on it. Ironically, the problem was not so much recession as excess demand pushing up inflation—prices rose 25 percent by 1947.

There was a mild recession in 1948–1950 that ended when spending for the Korean War increased demand. There were three other very mild recessions before 1960, but they did not seriously interrupt the overall expansion of the economy.

Several contributory factors have been offered as explanations. First, although the government expressed its opposition to socialism, it adopted several social welfare programs, which helped maintain a high level of demand and thus business profitability. In the 1960s, the Great Society program was introduced to eliminate poverty. It increased spending on education, health programs, and job training, for example. Expansion of the Social Security program meant that more retired workers received government retirement pensions; the introduction of medical assistance for the indigent and the elderly also gave a boost to the health care industries and their suppliers. Second, a high level of military spending boosted the defense industries, and it remained high throughout the postwar years. (Even in 1980, expenditures on defense were 13.4 percent of GNP, compared with only 2.5 percent in Japan.) This was due not only to involvement in wars such as the Korean and Vietnam Wars, or military "engagements" in places such as Iran, Central America, or the Lebanon, but also to the Cold War. Although this was not a shooting (or "hot") war, it involved a high level of military preparedness in case it erupted into a hot war. In addition, during these decades the United States either had armed forces in other countries (in Germany and Japan) or was the major military presence in various defense alliances.

A third way that the government helped stimulate economic activity was by using monetary and fiscal policies. Before 1960, the government was committed to the orthodox policy of a balanced budget, a preoccupation that led to periodic federal spending cuts, which have been used to explain the onset of mild recessions in the 1950s. After 1960, deliberate stimulative policy was applied: Taxes were cut in 1964, and the economy expanded. However, when spending for the Vietnam War began increasing in 1967, the problem was not so much how to stimulate the economy as how to damp down inflationary pressures. Restrictive policies were not fully imposed,

and inflation became the central issue in the 1970s, made more difficult to handle because the economy's growth was slowing and external factors were pushing up input costs.

A final factor relates to the position of dominance of the United States in the world economy. Although trade has never been so important for the United States as for other countries, it is a significant player in world trade. Even a tiny change in United States imports or exports—although having little effect on the domestic economy—can have a large effect on its trading partners. This dominance had several effects. First, the size of United States buying power kept the prices of many raw materials and other inputs low, which helped hold down production costs. Second, its role in keeping world peace plus the process of removing restrictions to world trade produced a stable international situation. United States producers were able to move production to wherever profits might be higher—and use the threat of moving plants overseas to extract wage and tax concessions at home to help keep costs down. Many subsidiaries were established abroad at this time as the flow of direct foreign investment from the United States increased. Finally, particularly in the earlier postwar period, American producers faced little competition from foreign producers, so exports were high. All these factors generated a favorable climate for business and economic expansion.

Loss of Competitiveness

This favorable climate began to reverse in the early 1970s, and by the 1980s, United States dominance in world markets had been seriously eroded. It was particularly obvious in areas where the United States had been a leader, in cars and consumer durables, for example, but also in newer industries such as electronics. Cars are instructive. In 1955, imports of autos into the United States were insignificant and were mainly prestigious luxury cars. But by 1970, imports had risen to 15 percent, and by the early 1980s, accounted for a third of all sales. Much of the increase came about because foreign producers were more flexible in adopting new technologies and new designs more in keeping with changes in the car buying market.

Several reasons have been given to explain this loss of a competitive position. One is very similar to the explanation for Britain's loss of markets at the very end of the 19th century. Put into the context of the 1970s, once the European and Japanese economies had been rebuilt, American producers no longer had a monopoly position in the world marketplace. Now they faced international competition. A related reason is that these producers were no longer quite so competitive. Many were less interested in maintaining an international position once they faced competition as they were able to depend on a large internal market. Also, American investment in productive facilities was less than in other countries, which affected productivity and competitiveness. A dynamic, growing economy has a high rate of investment, so productivity growth is high (and is probably also technologically innovative), and industry is competitive. Once the cycle is broken, as it appeared to be in the 1970s, it became harder for the United States to regain its former position. Internationally, the dominant role of the dollar in international trade and finance complicated matters—a topic that will be dealt with in the next chapter.

In summary, the United States moved from a position of unchallenged international dominance to one where it faced considerable competition in the postwar period. It is still the world's largest economy, but it is less dynamic than others, and there has been no serious attempt to manage this change in position. As Britain found, a laissez faire approach is feasible if the monopoly position is strong; when it is not, then some action is needed. This lesson has been learned by other countries in the postwar period. But in the 1980s, no clear policy direction oriented to regaining competitiveness emerged.

Germany's "Economic Miracle"

West Germany in the postwar period started as a defeated nation to become one of the three most important Western economic powers in the 1970s. This "miracle" began in 1948 and was based on a combination of private enterprise and public investment—the social market economy.

As previously noted, at the end of the war Germany was partitioned and demilitarized, but not significantly weakened economically. Reparations were not imposed, with the exception of some German factories that were relocated to the Soviet Union (which lost 60 percent of its mining and metallurgical capacity during the war). Although the financial system needed rebuilding and there was a housing shortage, the existence of excess productive capacity plus a large pool of skilled labor permitted growth. (The labor pool increased as ethnic Germans immigrated into West Germany after the war and because the agricultural sector released labor.)

Social market economy

A private enterprise economy with a social conscience

Immediately after the war, controversies among the Allied Powers led to delays in economic recovery. France (which regained the provinces of Alsace and Lorraine) wanted to make sure that German economic strength would never again threaten her. When it became apparent that the economy was becoming revitalized, France supported European integration as one way of controlling it. The Soviet Union was not in favor of a strong, united Germany, either, and its insistence on control over East Germany was a significant factor in the start of the Cold War (and see also note 2). Currency reform was not accomplished until 1948 because of disagreements between the United States and the United Kingdom. The United States wanted a decentralized banking system similar to the Federal Reserve System; the United Kingdom favored a centralized system. So there was uncertainty in the years before 1948, which kept goods from being offered for sale—producers hoarded them because they were unwilling to be left holding currency that might turn out to be worthless, exacerbating the postwar goods shortage.

In the 1948 reform, the old Reichsmark was replaced by the Deutschemark. Many commercial banks' assets were now worthless, and the central bank in each state made good their asset shortage in relation to liabilities. This set off inflation. Commercial banks gained Deutschemark credits from the central banks, generating excess reserves. Excess reserves were the basis for making loans to businesses whose existing bank accounts had been blocked. It was inflationary because the blocked accounts were being slowly released at the same time that the expansion of loans also increased liquidity. At the same time, the goods that had been held off the market reappeared. The inflation was short, but since then, remembering the 1920s experience, Germany has tended to favor restrictive anti-inflation policies, achieved mainly through the operation of monetary policy.

After 1948, the occupation forces took less responsibility for West Germany's internal affairs. Progress began to formalize a constitution, and a German-directed policy emerged to govern the economy.

Social Market Economy

The social market economy policy was announced by Economics Minister Ludwig Erhard in 1948, coinciding with the formal constitution of the Federal Republic of Germany. It was a policy based on private property and free enterprise in competitive markets (although the Germans applied a different meaning to the word *competition*). It was neither pure laissez faire nor a planned economy, but was oriented to achieve various social goals. Government policy was limited to maintaining price stability, and if market failures appeared, then government intervention would deal with them through the tax and social benefits system. Government was active in other ways too. Although not adopting an official policy of nationalization, the government ended up owning a significant part of the economic structure anyway.

The Central Bank (responsible for monetary policy as well as monopolizing the note issue) was 100 percent owned; 60 percent of all credit institutions were owned; 72 percent of the aluminum industry, 62 percent of the electrical industry and 40 percent of the domestic coal and iron mining industries were publicly owned in the 1960s. In fact, government control extended further than these percentages imply. Public ownership was accomplished by government participation in holding companies and by asset and share ownership, which effectively widened its influence. Government ownership of credit granting institutions is very important in allocating finance and thus in influencing what does and what does not get produced. In addition, active investment spending by government, both for infrastructure and in strategic industries, kept the investment rate high and provided the capacity for continued productive expansion.

This policy set off a period of rapid industrial growth, as shown by the index of industrial production (1936=100): in 1948, reflecting war damage, the index was 63, in 1949 it was 90, in 1950 it was 114, and in 1951, it was 136. Much of the newly-produced output was exported, although heavy requirements for raw material imports resulted in a trade deficit in the early postwar years. However, investment was directed largely to expanding the capacity of the capital goods industries, which formed an important part of West Germany's exports. By 1951, West Germany had repaid all the $120 million credit it received from the European Payments Union, and it subsequently ran a surplus on its balance of trade.

Further expansion took place in the 1950s, when West Germany was Europe's fastest growing economy. Using a new index of industrial production in which 1950=100, net industrial production had nearly tripled to 284 by 1963. Germany was at that time second only to the United States in the production of autos and was the world's third largest producer of iron, steel, and ships.

The only sector that did not share in this expansion was agriculture. After the war, one quarter of the labor force was in agriculture, and, as in France, holdings were small and fragmented in many parts of the country. The proportion subsequently dropped to 14 percent in 1960 and to 6 percent in 1980, at which time the absolute number of agricultural workers was 1,528,000. Productivity improvements were held back by the persistence of small holdings. In 1968, 84 percent of all farms (covering 57 percent of the entire cultivated area) were between five and fifty acres in size. This had the effect of encouraging part-time farming, which also occurred in other countries for the same reasons.

Explanations for Germany's Expansion

Many contributory factors have been suggested as explanations for growth. Some are directly related to the war; others are policy related. One of the war-related reasons focuses on the economic benefits of losing the war. Requiring German demilitarization removed the necessity for public spending to maintain a military establishment. Although Germany contributed to the costs of occupation, this was offset by the spending of the occupying forces within Germany. And even though some factories were removed to the Soviet Union, they were replaced with the most up-to-date equipment. Modernization was helped by the receipt of Marshall aid, which made it possible for Germany to finance necessary imports for industrial restructuring from the United States.

(Total United States aid to West Germany amounted to about $3.5 billion.)

Another war-related contribution was demographic. In the 19th century the German area experienced rapid population growth, and emigration was high before industry expanded to absorb surplus labor. In 1921 the population of the German Republic was 61 million; in 1941 it was 69.8 million. After partition, the population of West Germany alone was much less, but was subsequently swollen by the immigration of about ten million ethnic Germans from Central and Eastern Europe. By 1970, the population of West Germany was 60.7 million, making it the most populous country in Western Europe.

What was significant is that many of these immigrants were skilled and, as is very often characteristic of immigrants, they were willing to work hard for low wages. In fact, throughout the 1950s the rate of growth of wages was below the rate of growth of output, which increased the profit share of national income and encouraged the maintenance of a high rate of investment. Pressure on wages was further weakened as a result of the shift out of agriculture during the entire postwar period. This was also an advantage shared by Italy, and both countries grew significantly faster than the United Kingdom, which had no similar pool of labor to draw on—in 1949, only 4.9 percent of the British labor force remained in agriculture, compared with 21 percent in West Germany and 37 percent in Italy.

Deliberate policy actions were consistent (in contrast to the United Kingdom) and also specifically oriented to rebuilding the economy. Throughout the 1950s and 1960s total domestic fixed investment averaged 22 percent of GNP (16.6 percent in the United Kingdom). There was public investment, and fiscal policy was coordinated with overall aims. Government tax revenues were used to provide investment funds in both public and private sectors, including agriculture, coal, housing, and shipbuilding. Differential tax rates were also used to influence investment in particular areas.

Industrial policy as a whole was clearly oriented to strengthening the German economy. Although Erhard's social market policy was based on the presence of competitive markets, it was not the Anglo-American idea of competition, which sees competition based on active price competition in atomistic markets, with no domination by large companies. The German vision of competition is based on the 19th century idea of company survival in a possibly hostile environment, hence state intervention is justified. That is, if vicious price competition reduces the number of market participants through bankruptcy, for example, the result is anticompetitive because fewer firms survive, and consumers have less choice.

Some large companies were split into smaller units in an antimonopoly effort, but this was short-lived, and was reversed in the 1960s. The reason was that if the world as a whole was the appropriate boundary for competition, a large German company might be a monopoly domestically but not internationally, where large size was needed to meet global competition. It was important to have a German presence in the global marketplace, which encouraged industrial concentration; by 1972 the four largest steel producers accounted for 90 percent of industry sales, and the four largest chemical firms controlled 70 percent of their market. Encouraging size implied that pricing was not market pricing as presented in the economics textbooks.

The final element in Germany's success story has been more harmonious labor-management relations than elsewhere, which has limited the number of work stoppages. This is due to the policy of co-determination, where union representatives sit on company boards of directors to get a labor input into corporate decision making.

Co-determination

representatives of workers are included in corporate decision making

This was imposed on Germany after 1951 and is most prevalent in the vital areas of mining and steel. The idea was that because strikes would disrupt essential economic reconstruction, co-determination should replace the right to collective bargaining in these areas. In fact, the original idea dates back to 1925, when it was first proposed as a way of improving working conditions, and recognizing the reality that businesses should serve the society in which they exist. The idea of encouraging enterprise social consciousness fits in nicely with the principle of the social market economy, even though co-determination as practiced now still leaves most decision-making in the hands of management.

France and Indicative Planning

France was another success of the postwar period, although it had lost its status as a Great Power, and many holdovers from the past remained to slow down development. The economy is a modern industrial one, and France has taken the lead in some areas, such as the use of nuclear power for the generation of electricity. However, in spite of many changes, much agriculture remains small scale and traditionally oriented. France's success has been credited to membership in the EEC,

Indicative planning

Government sets goals and targets and private companies use them to guide their own decision making

which gave a necessary competitive push, plus the use of indicative planning, which is based on cooperation between government and industry. Another push came from a demographic factor. After stagnating in the 19th century and into the early postwar period, France's population began to expand. This was the result of a falling death rate and a rising birthrate that resulted in the average age of the population falling. This "increase in youthfulness" may also have given a boost to the modernization process. (France's population was 39.4 million in 1880, 39.3 million in 1921, 39.8 million in 1940 and then it rose to 50.8 million in 1970.) However, while some of the other European countries (West Germany and Italy especially) found that population growth and a rural to urban shift provided a growing supply of labor that kept wages and inflation down, this did not happen in France, which suffered from recurring inflation.

Immediately after the war, when German occupation forces had been removed from the northern part of the country, France faced the common European problem of goods shortages and excess liquidity. Industrial capacity—much of which had been commandeered to meet German wartime needs—had on the whole been spared war destruction. However, it was in need of modernization and rationalization, as much French manufacturing was dominated by small, family firms protected from competition.

Modernization and growth were both desirable goals—the experience of three defeats by Germany since 1870 was too humiliating to ignore. A three-pronged approach was used. First, promoting regional integration (covered above); second, selective nationalization in key areas of the economy; and third, indicative planning to encourage private enterprise. Roughly one fifth of the industrial sector became publicly owned. This included some credit and deposit banks, the Bank of France, electricity generation, coal mines, the national airline Air France, the railroad system SNCF, and Renault, a major motor vehicle producer.

Indicative planning was introduced in a series of plans, starting with the Monnet Plan, 1947–1952. In this type of planning, government suggests the goals to be achieved, "modernization committees" spell out the details, and actual implementation is up to private enterprise. No coercion or detailed quotas or allocation of inputs—as associated with central planning—are involved. In other words, by presenting a vision of what the future could look like, government hopes that private decision makers will take it into account and make the vision a reality. Plans were drawn up by sector (e.g., coal, heavy industry, textiles), by activity (e.g., health, education), and also covered multisectoral issues such as finance.

Government provided various inducements to encourage the cooperation of private enterprise. Immediately after the war, a major inducement was the provision of funds, made necessary because the private capital market had suffered greatly as a result of the war. Later, government loans at low interest rates, various tax preferences, and government contracts were used to encourage greater production. The first plan was successful: By 1950 France had regained its 1929 standard of living chiefly due to the increase in productivity that caused a 4.5 percent growth in national output, a faster rate of growth than the United Kingdom but slower than Germany or Italy.

Special Factors: Colonial Wars

However, some special factors hindered French growth in this period. First were France's problems with decolonization, affecting colonial possessions in Indochina, North Africa and Africa. Only the French colonies in Africa became independent by agreement rather than bloodshed[6]. In North Africa, France ruled Tunisia and Morocco (although they were officially only French protectorates) and Algeria. The first two became independent in 1956; Algeria, which was regarded as part of metropolitan France, involved France in a bloody and costly nationalist war for seven years after 1954. The Algerian crisis divided France, and in 1958, to try to heal the divisions, Free French war hero General Charles de Gaulle returned to politics. As a result, a cease-fire and ultimate independence was negotiated.

In Indochina (including Vietnam—formerly called Annam—Laos, and Cambodia) France was again involved in a costly colonial conflict. She resumed control of her possessions in 1946 after the Japanese defeat. Soon after, a nationalist movement led by Ho Chi Minh surfaced in Vietnam, and his Vietnamese forces engaged French forces in a hopeless guerrilla war. French forces were defeated in 1954, and Vietnam split into two, North Vietnam under Ho Chi Minh, and South Vietnam. France in effect ceded influence over South Vietnam to the United States, which later found itself embroiled in a long, costly, and exhausting war in the late 1960s—a war that it too could not hope to win.

Inflation and Balance of Payments Problems

A second special factor was recurrent inflation after wartime price controls were abandoned. The wholesale price index measured 100 in 1938; by December 1945 it was 469; in 1947 it rose to 1,217; by 1948 to 1,974; and in 1950 it measured 2,409. In the later 1950–1966 period, France's implicit GNP price deflator had increased 143 percent compared with a rise of 69 percent for West Germany and 80 percent for the United Kingdom. The causes were related to both supply and demand. For example, wages were frozen until 1950, but because prices had risen so much, prewar wage levels were not restored until 1955. The trade union movement was divided into two opposing factions, the larger Communist-dominated Confédération du Travail and the smaller Catholic Confédération Française des Travailleurs Chrétien. Strikes were a common method of French worker expression in the absence of collective bargaining before 1950. Because there was no official anti-inflation policy, inflation spilled over to affect France's external relations, a third special factor.

During the war, like other European countries France had imposed trade and exchange controls, and the government requisitioned private foreign investment holdings, which obviously distorted international movements of trade and capital. After the war, necessary imports were financed with emergency loans from the United States and the United Kingdom. But the movement toward more "normal" conditions was made difficult by the absence of anti-inflation policies, which distorted the structure of French domestic prices in relation to world prices. This was hidden by a series of bilateral trade agreements and devaluations that took the place of market-oriented adjustment. That is, bilateral agreements glossed over the possible lack of price competitiveness, while occasional devaluation, by making the franc cheaper in terms of foreign currency, brought French prices more in line with world prices without the need for domestic restructuring to improve productivity. The franc was devalued in 1948, 1949, 1957, and 1969. The balance of payments was in deficit until 1954, even though imports were restricted. However, involvement in the EEC forced planners to correct this problem. While French farmers continued to be protected by the operations of the Common Agricultural Policy, manufacturers were facing more competition in the European market and could no longer rely on traditional restrictive policies to shield them.

Low Investment

Lack of investment and persisting traditionalism, both features of 19th century France, were a fourth factor influencing French postwar development. In 1949, 27 percent of the labor force was engaged in farming and although this percentage fell to 8 percent by 1982 (1,870,000 people), the effect was muted.

French agriculture suffered from low productivity per laborer, mainly due to the inherited problem of small-sized farms held in fragmented rather than compact holdings. This slowed modernization because it is much more costly to improve small, fragmented farms. In a cause and effect relationship, most of the reduction in numbers of the French agricultural labor force came as younger farmers left—intensifying the pressure for conservatism in rural areas. Some attempts were made to consolidate holdings, but most were resisted, the older farmers favoring higher support prices instead. While there has been a faster growth of agricultural productivity in the most recent period, the farm sector still remains relatively inefficient compared with others in the EEC, such as Denmark.

Lack of investment also characterized industry, for a variety of reasons, some of which date back to the 19th century. The persistence of small firms oriented mainly to meeting local needs and protected by favorable tax treatment does not encourage investment. In addition, slow population growth does not encourage rapid technological progress, which benefits from the incentive of expanding markets. While many French firms are as modern as those found anywhere else, they simply underscore the duality present in the economy. In the early 1960s, only 17 percent of all French firms employed over a thousand employees, compared with 28 percent of German firms.

Another problem with investment is that even if the incentive is present, mobilization of finance is not as easy as in other European countries. Until 1954, new issues of shares and large issues of bonds had to be authorized by the Ministry of Finance because the government wanted priority access to the pool of private savings for its own borrowings. Bank credit is available but is expensive, and banks tend to favor their larger customers. Self-financing is limited by the small profits made by firms.

Entry into the EEC has to a certain extent helped offset some of these negative elements. For example, membership in the European Coal and Steel Community in the 1950s forced modernization of the coal and steel industries. Exposure to a larger, freer market also encouraged the development of larger firms, often through merger, which are able to tap economies of scale. Within the Community, the need for modern-

---

European Coal and Steel Community
Free trade area in coal and steel sectors in Europe

---

ization intensified, and French industry has shown a much more progressive nature as a result.

U.K: "Stop-Go" Policies and External Problems

Much of the mixed experience of the British economy in the postwar period can be traced to the problems of a former world power adjusting to a changed environment. Unlike some of the other European countries, structural change had already reduced the pool of surplus labor in agriculture, and inflexibility in the industrial labor force made responsiveness to changing conditions more difficult because there was less slack in the economy. The goals set were ambitious and conflicting: To maintain a high level of employment,

---

"Stop-go" policies
Policies that shift abruptly from stimulation to contraction

---

price stability, and external balance with some nationalization in key areas, but most emphasis was on retaining the viability of private enterprise. Unfortunately, this was hard to do, as an emphasis on external balance led to deliberately induced recessions to hold down imports whenever a balance of payments deficit occurred. This did not encourage investment spending, and the alternation of first stimulative and then restrictive policies was dubbed "stop-go" because it alternately stimulated and then reduced growth. The *net* effect slowed growth below the levels of other European countries. During the 1950s and 1960s, investment remained below that of Britain's industrial competitors, with the result that both the growth rate and the economy lagged.

In the immediate postwar period, as noted above, Britain faced a large external debt, an obsolescent industrial capacity, a loss of overseas income due to the selloff of many foreign assets, and serious problems with returning the economy to peacetime production. The prospect of demobilization led policy makers to fear a recession and deflation, although the huge buildup of liquid assets (due to high levels of saving during wartime) threatened inflation.

Public Ownership

Given this, nationalization of the economy's basic sectors was begun to help restructure the economy, develop efficient economic planning, and encourage an adequate level of investment in order to maximize industrial activity. The coal industry was nationalized in 1946 and faced a critical need for modernization; steel firms were initially subject to "directed" reconstruction, then in 1947, 107 major steel producers were taken into public ownership; the railway system and the canals were nationalized in 1946; followed by electricity generation and distribution in 1947; and the Bank of England and the commercial airlines also became publicly owned. By 1951 about 20 percent of industry was publicly owned.

There were several reasons for nationalization. First, by providing guaranteed supplies of essential inputs (such as coal, electricity, steel, transportation) at reasonable prices, it was hoped to assist private industry's modernization. Second, in cases where economies of scale existed, production would be rationalized by closing small, inefficient plants and concentrating production in larger, more modern units. This would be easier if there was a single owner rather than several struggling for survival. Third, if economies of scale existed and rationalization occurred, a privately owned company would be in a strong monopoly position, able to dictate prices and terms of sale. So perhaps a public company could capture these potential monopoly gains for the social benefit.

Many wartime controls still existed, some remaining until the early 1950s. They included rationing of some consumer goods, restrictions on imports, and mechanisms to allocate fuels and raw materials for industry. Their retention held down excess demand and gave some flexibility to expansionary policy. In the late 1940s, the government wanted to expand the economy to avoid the problem of unemployment. Interest rates were lowered hoping that easier financing would boost investment spending, income taxes were reduced, and the excess profits tax (a wartime measure) was abolished. Remaining price controls reduced inflationary pressures and a potential unfavorable impact on the balance of payments due to economic expansion was avoided because dollars were available—the result of a loan from the United States—and also because various import restrictions and exchange controls were in place.

Exchange controls
Limits on availability of foreign currency

Policy Alternation

However, that loan would itself create problems and lead to the first of the "stop" periods. Although the interest payments were not due until 1951, the United States granted the loan on condition that the pound sterling became fully convertible in 1947 and that discriminatory trade policies be eliminated. This proved difficult. The winter of 1946–1947 was very cold, and too little coal was being produced to meet all needs. Then energy cutbacks lowered industrial output and exports and Britain's terms of trade deteriorated. When the pound became freely convertible later in the year, there was still a scarcity of dollars in the sterling area, but sterling holders converted pounds into dollars, reducing Britain's international reserves. So exchange controls were reapplied, the terms of the dollar loan suspended, and imports restricted. Inflation and unemployment both rose, and wage demands increased.

The situation began to stabilize in 1948. In that year the unions agreed to limit wage increases, and Marshall aid helped the foreign exchange situation. A production and export boom began but was cut short as a United States recession reduced exports from Britain later in the year. Further pressure occurred after the American government publicly recommended sterling's devaluation, causing a flight from sterling and another deterioration in Britain's international reserves. The pound was devalued by 30 percent in 1949, and although other European countries also devalued at the same time, exports rose. The balance of payments improved and was in surplus every year except three until 1957. (These surpluses were used to lower international debt rather than to increase Britain's international reserves.) Devaluation, however, also raised import prices, and prices rose because Britain imported many of its raw materials and much of its food. To counter this inflation, public expenditures were cut in 1950. The preceding period had seen industrial gains: industrial production was one third higher in 1950 than in 1949, exports were up 60 percent, and in 1950 the United Kingdom ceased receiving outside aid.

Unfortunately, the start of the Korean War in 1950 began another set of external problems. Fears of war often lead to stockpiling of raw materials in case war cuts off supplies, and 1950 was no exception, so import prices increased. Problems also occurred with oil supplies. Britain at this time depended entirely on imported oil, and when Iran seized British-owned refineries there in 1951, oil supplies fell and prices rose in Britain. Defense expenditures grew because of Britain's involvement in the Korean War (as part of the UN military force). Rising import prices lowered dollar reserves held by Britain, and there was another balance of payments crisis in 1951. Restrictive policy and controls on imports turned the crisis around—but at the cost of slower

growth. This pattern repeated again in 1955: Whenever expanding domestic demand threatened external balance, the brakes were slammed on.

Hence, overall growth was slow. Industrial output grew only by 1.8 percent annually between 1946 and 1955; the entire period between 1950 and 1962 saw Britain's GNP growing by only 2.6 percent annually on average, similar to Belgium's 2.8 percent (Belgium is another resource-poor, heavily industrialized economy that also industrialized early), but well below the average for other European countries. The main reason was inadequate investment spending—again, slow growth does not encourage productivity growth, which reinforces low investment spending. Low investment spending was the result of the relative lack of modernization in industry at this time, although there are many important exceptions to this rule, such as the chemicals industry. In addition, a labor shortage and a tight labor market until the 1980s added a degree of rigidity to the employment structure.

However, discovery of natural gas in the North Sea (off the Netherlands' coast in 1959) and later the discovery of oil in areas within the territorial waters of Norway and the United Kingdom at least partially reversed the resource situation. Although extraction conditions in the North Sea are difficult and oil is high in cost compared with Middle East oil, oil exports eased the perennial balance of payments problems in the 1970s and later.

Britain's growth in the later period was still slow, but some restructuring occurred, especially after entry into the EEC, where the international orientation of some British enterprises gave them an advantage. The most significant change was built on one of Britain's 19th century strengths, London's role in the international financial market. The problem with periodic investment shortages still hovers, as do fears that investment is not in the best areas that promise the most growth in the future, and investment in infrastructure, especially in education, remains low.

Italy's Postwar Industrialization

Italy is another economic success story of the postwar period, changing from a heavy dependence on agriculture to become a modern industrial state. Like Germany, Italy did not become politically unified until late in the 19th century (1861–1870). An unfavorable land-labor ratio (too little of the former, too much of the latter) made the escape valve of emigration important in the last years of the 19th century and the first years of the 20th.

Problems with developing industry stem from Italy's resource poverty; she has no iron ore deposits, delaying an industrialization process based on steam power. Agriculture also suffered from many of the same problems experienced elsewhere in other European countries, with small, fragmented, not very productive holdings. In the middle of the 1930s, nearly half the working population was in farming; the percentage was still 37 percent in 1949. However, the postwar period saw a massive rural to urban shift, and after falling to 33 percent in 1960 and to 20 percent in 1970, the percentage of the labor force in farming in 1980 was 13 percent. Within the expanded EEC, Italy's farm population of 2,925,000 is the Community's largest.

Postwar Italy also had to deal with the legacy of prewar fascism. Many of the same forces that encouraged the rise of fascism in Germany also contributed to the rise of Benito Mussolini in Italy in the 1920s. Mussolini used public works projects and colonial expansion to deal with economic problems, especially the problem of unemployment. A project to resettle "surplus" Italian farmers in Libya (then an Italian colony) nearly succeeded—the farms were just beginning to become productive when the Second World War broke out, ending the experiment.

Public Investment and Regional Development

The economic situation in Italy was mixed in the immediate postwar period. There was massive unemployment due to several factors, including the elimination of the prewar public works program that had employed a large number of otherwise unemployed people; the loss of Italian colonies and consequent repatriation of the colonists; demobilization and continuing rapid population growth. Population was 43.8 million in 1940, 54.5 million in 1970, and 57.3 million by 1988—this growth occurred without the traditional safety valve of emigration until after 1947. Although the large labor pool—swelled by a shift out of agriculture during the three postwar decades—permitted low-cost industrial growth, Italy was almost unique in the 1950s by experiencing a high rate of unemployment, averaging 10 percent annually. This occurred mainly because the industrial expansion taking place in the North (the most highly industrialized region) was highly capital intensive, and output increased faster than labor input. Between 1948 and 1961, real gross national product increased 120 percent while industrial output increased by 215 percent.

Two features characterized postwar expansion: A high rate of public investment and public involvement in the economy, mainly using the holding company approach. Indicative planning along French lines was not used because it was considered to be tainted with Mussolini's fascism. Instead, much of the industrial restructuring was done by the IRI agency, a government-owned holding company that could stimulate activities in crucial areas by either making outright loans for financing or financing them by buying shares in the company. It also funnelled some Marshall aid into these areas to help modernize industry. In 1953 a similar public holding company, ENI, also controlled both public and semipublic enterprises including AGIP, which developed the natural gas resources discovered in the Po valley. State

Figure 22.2 White collar office work became a predominantly female occupation in the middle of the 20th century. (Courtesy of Met Life Archives)

involvement helps explain the expansion of gross investment—by 222 percent between 1948 and 1961. By 1955 national income after adjusting for inflation was 54 percent larger than in 1938.

One area not modernizing significantly was agriculture, and even in 1950 agricultural output only just returned to its 1938 level. In that year, encouraging mechanization, use of more fertiliz-

ers, and consolidation of highly fragmented farms was started to modernize agriculture and improve productivity. (One reason labor productivity was so low was that so much time was lost moving from one patch of land to another.) However, these attempts were abandoned as peasant hostility was too great; resistance was based on an unwillingness to part with one's ancestor's land.

Another problem in the agricultural sector was excessive rural unemployment and underemployment. Some large estates were subdivided and given to peasants, but did not solve the unemployment problem and only added to the existing problem of too many small, inefficient farms.

Another attempt to improve agriculture was made by the *Casse per il Mezzogiorno*, another feature of Italian postwar development, but unfortunately one with mixed success. In 1950, the Plan for the Mezzogiorno was introduced to deal with the extreme disparity between northern and southern income levels. It was designed to stimu-

---

Casse per il Mezzogiorno
Regional development plan for southern Italy

---

late both agriculture and industry in the south and in Sicily, which were much less industrialized and more traditional, had lower income levels and higher illiteracy rates, and access to fewer energy sources. While some industrial activity has taken place, the regional disparity still exists. This in fact is one aspect of policy that remains to be adequately dealt with within the European Community because it is not an exclusively Italian problem. That is, the problem is how to establish a regional development policy to deal with lagging regions—lagging either because they have never industrialized or because they are locations for declining industries and have not been able to attract the new or expanding ones.

In summary, Italy's growth to become one of the most advanced industrial nations in the EC is a postwar achievement. In the late 1980s, its GNP per capita was close to that of the United Kingdom and the Netherlands, while its absolute GNP level was the third largest after West Germany and France. Growth can be attributed to the ability to tap a large pool of labor that permitted a movement out of low productivity areas into high productivity ones, a large public sector that maintained a high level of investment, and an expansion of exports of those products for which

international demand was increasing. Italy became the EC's second largest steel producer; it has a significant car industry (Fiat in fact was the first Western car producer to establish production facilities in the Soviet Union and the first to establish an assembly line entirely operated by robots). It also remains the European country attracting the most tourists, which gives rise to a large tourist industry getting its appeal precisely from the inheritance of Italy's past nonindustrial glories.

Japan: Business and Government Cooperation

Japan's postwar experience shows a very different pattern of government involvement, one which was remarkably successful in stimulating both economic recovery and an extremely fast growth rate. We must, however, bear in mind that the cultural background and system of values is different in Japan, so principles that may seem appropriate or objectionable to a Western mind may be viewed in a very different light in Japan. This implies that direct comparability is misleading. We should also remember that the early postwar events in Japan were largely shaped by the demands of the occupation authorities. Some observers divide this period into pre- and post-1960, depending on the influence of government involvement, which, in combination with the dynamism of private business, helps explain the growth of the economy.

Immediately after the war, the Japanese economy was one of the most damaged. Agriculture did not recover its mid-1930s level of output until 1950, and until then, food imports were needed. Industry recovered more slowly. In 1946 industry was producing a level of output barely one fifth of what had been produced during the war. Several attempts to improve this situation were made, including easy credit, but several years of severe inflation resulted. Prices rose 364 percent in 1946, 196 percent in 1947, and 166 percent in

1948. Inflation lessened after that as more practical measures were adopted and as output expanded.

In 1948, the occupation authorities introduced economic measures designed to stabilize the economy. Restrictive policies intended to produce a surplus in the government budget and restrictions on credit availability and bank lending were applied. At the same time, the prewar *zaibatsu*—powerful family-controlled groups which had dominated finance and industry—were dismantled. The resulting gap was filled by a greater degree of bureaucratic involvement. At first state trading companies were formed, lasting until the mid 1960s, when the private general trading companies, or *sogo shosha*, inheritors of the *zaibatsu* tradition, took over. Also in the early period, many other companies were publicly owned, such as the rail and telephone systems. However, while this was a deliberate policy move in Europe, nationalization was not intended to be permanent in Japan.

Zaibatsu

A powerful family-controlled commercial combine

Directly encouraging policies introduced at this time included extensive subsidies to rebuild and reequip industrial capacity; they were replaced by low interest loans in the 1950s. The aim of policy was to improve efficiency as well as rebuild the economy. Policies included import restrictions to protect the domestic market; subsidies, especially for research; tax breaks; favorable access to financing; and assistance in finding and exploiting overseas markets. They were successful in encouraging industrial rebuilding, so much so that when the Korean War started in 1950, Japanese industry benefitted from the boost in demand accompanying it. Japan was not involved in the fighting, but became a major workshop supplying the forces that were sent to Korea from other countries.

The rebuilding process plus the special factors associated with the Korean War resulted in full recovery by the early 1950s, accompanied by a resumption of price stability. A long boom period of high growth based on large investment expenditures by Japanese business followed, helped by continued encouraging government policies. Initially, government support was given to the capital goods industries, important in providing a strong industrial base, and to other industries with extensive linkages throughout the economy. For example, shipbuilding was protected throughout the 20th century, and in the mid 1930s, Japan became the world's third largest shipbuilder. In the postwar period, the closing of the Suez Canal in 1956 increased the demand for large, oil-carrying supertankers. (The Suez Canal in Egypt had shortened transportation times between the large Middle East oil producers and the important European oil importing market. After its closure, there was a boom in the supertanker market because they carried large quantities of oil at lower cost on the longer journeys made necessary by the Suez crisis.) This extra boost turned Japan into the world's largest shipbuilder in the mid 1950s, when half the world's tonnage was built in Japanese shipyards.

Similarly with autos, the policy of support in the 1950s led to the dramatic growth of Japanese auto production. The Japanese market itself was protected from competition, but the small geographic size of the country implied a limited domestic market anyway. Between 1955 and 1970, Japanese production of passenger cars expanded 155-fold, and production of trucks expanded 46-fold. By the late 1960s, Japan had replaced West Germany as the second largest producer of cars after the United States. In 1972, four million cars were produced, with much of this production geared for export markets in the United States and Europe where Japanese cars had a cost advantage. This occurred because, as production had started from scratch in the 1950s, the equipment was the most up-to-date possible, incorporating the latest technology, whereas other countries with older established industries had both older equipment and work practices.

Export growth was encouraged by the activities of the Ministry of International Trade and Industry, one of the special features of Japanese development. MITI actively promoted the development of new industries by sponsoring research and the development of new technology by providing financing and information on new markets. Not only autos but also computers, electronics in general, and consumer durables have gained from this support and expanded into foreign markets. MITI's role is short of French indicative planning, although it does establish a set of desirable goals on the macrolevel, setting out priorities for different sectors. Given the cooperation between government and business and the respect accorded to the bureaucracy, these goals and priorities will be accepted. Business, it is said, respects the competence of government and the desirability of consensus is maintained.

Another special and unique feature is the role of the general trading companies, *sogo shosha*, which although they began as merchant trading companies, have extended also into manufacturing and finance. They have an important role in helping make it possible for the many small companies in Japan to coexist with large enterprises. They have preferential access to bank credit, give assistance in international selling, provide information, and in some cases take a direct equity position. As in Germany, there is a strong commitment to the survival of the firm, and the support of the trading company is crucial to the smaller firm whose survival helps the profitability of larger firms by acting as a cushion for economic fluctuations.

Many observers have also remarked on Japan's so-called lifetime employment characteristic. This helps generate intense employee loyalty to the company and thus commitment to the company's goals, which increases the consensus noted in Japan. From the company's point of view, a stable environment is necessary, which is why government intervention to generate stability is welcomed. But it must be remembered that this lifetime employment applies only to male employees in the "core" industrial firms. It does not apply to women or part-time employees or to employees of small firms or subcontractors. It is these latter groups' role in buffering economic fluctuations that makes a privileged position for a minority of employees possible. Whether this employment practice will continue is uncertain. Already in the 1980s, there were signs that even the largest Japanese companies were beginning to adopt American employment practices in which even senior executives can be fired.

In summary, Japan's success in becoming the world's third largest economy is not due to its resource endowment, because it has few natural resources. Observers usually credit the success to the cultural factor (which produced results similar to the Calvinist work ethic), and the close communications between business and government and the general trading companies. This environment produced a high rate of investment that is important for maintaining dynamism and a growing economy.

Implications of New Technology

The text stressed earlier the importance of expanding markets paralleling industrial changes that expanded productivity. In Britain's case, for so long as overseas markets were opening up, industrial expansion could continue without too much attention being given either to the domestic market or to deliberate policy designed to expand markets. Later in the 19th century, and in the 20th, and ignoring wartime upheavals, most market expansion occurred internally, tied to rising real income levels. However, for the group of industrial countries as a whole, productive capacity has tended to expand faster than effective demand. If this is the case, how will it be possible to maintain the impetus for growth?

There are not too many possibilities. Perhaps new markets in the as-yet nonindustrial world will open up, which may have limited applicability if industrialization does come to these areas. Or perhaps government can be persuaded to adopt policies that guarantee continued expansion. This helps explain the postwar experience we have just examined. That is, as mass production techniques expand, it becomes increasingly important not only to find new markets or expand old ones but also to avoid economic fluctuations. This is necessary because if recessions occur and sales are not made, all the calculations justifying large investment expenditures in mass production facilities become meaningless when the expected profit does not appear. Hence the simultaneous appearance in industrial countries of demand management policies. As we saw, they can range from countercyclical policies through social welfare policies to regional development policies—the aim is the same. A problem, however, began to appear in the 1970s.

Mass production is large-scale production, and being large also tends to be relatively inflexible. Its advantage lies in being able to produce at low cost if production runs are large enough, but it is not capable either of a fast turnaround to changing demand conditions or of specialized production to satisfy particular submarkets (which is why mass production techniques may dominate an economy but do not entirely take it over—large companies coexist quite happily with small ones). Mass production is most apparent in sectors such as oil, steel, transportation equipment, and consumer durables.

In the 1970s, after government demand management policies had successfully prevented major business downturns, general economic

---

Mass production

The production of large quantities of standardized goods

---

conditions became less supportive. There were several supply side shocks that raised production costs. In 1974, when the Organization of Petroleum Exporting Countries raised oil prices and limited production, it hurt the oil consuming countries, because oil had replaced coal as the basic energy source. This was repeated in 1979 after the Iranian revolution and the start of the Iran-Iraq war. Both countries are major oil producers, so the effect in cutting off oil supplies was severe. There were also agricultural problems throughout the 1970s that raised agricultural commodity prices. The problem for policymakers was that inflation had traditionally been countered with demand reducing policies, which had no effect on inflation originating from the supply side, as in the 1970s. So the decade saw the unusual combination of inflation and stagnating economies, reducing the credibility of the demand management approach.

However, what was also happening was that the direction of technological change was not unilaterally toward larger and larger size. Increasingly, and this was especially true with knowledge-based activities, technological change began to favor smaller firms. They had always existed; now they were gaining a new lease on life as a result of computerization, for example. Their advantage lies in their flexibility—being small, they can easily adapt to demand changes—and in their ability to specialize, thus meeting atypical needs. Like the knowledge-based industries, specialized metalworking areas such as the machine tool makers, fashion industries and segments of the consumer goods areas are characterized by what is called small-batch production (as opposed to large-batch or continuous process production). Small-scale, flexible production firms have different policy needs. They need a supportive environment, good infrastructure and transportation, training and retraining facilities, for example.

This development will by no means reverse other trends, especially the trend to increasing size, and further adaptations are appearing. As already noted, the multinationals are one example of enterprises operating across national borders, but another example is the logical extension of the trend to increasing size. This is especially apparent in the research-based industries, where research financing needs are so large that it is difficult for one country to justify that type of expenditure in a competitive environment. There has been cross-country cooperation in Europe in the development and production of commercial aircraft and computers, where a joint venture is commercially feasible and has a better chance of countering the marketing power of large United States companies. A further extension of this type of cooperation exists in Europe's space program (Ariane) and also the possibility of worldwide cooperation in space research, which is no longer automatically ruled out by ideological differences.

Summary

This chapter has been wide-ranging, covering the reconstruction of the European economies in the postwar period and continuing with the creation and development of the European Economic Community. Much of what has happened has been both a continuation of past trends—the development of larger industrial processes—and also a reversal of them—the movement to create a unified Europe. The progress of the European Community, a regional integration scheme, has been a major feature. It has encouraged the economic development of its members, although the most recent expansion (in the late 1980s) has not been as easy as expected. Future problems may occur when some of the Eastern and Central European nations, the formerly centrally planned economies, apply for membership, because there are political and security considerations to account for as well as economic ones. However, European integration has stimulated other countries to consider similar schemes, notably in North America, Central America, and the Pacific Rim.

A final consideration in this chapter has been the direction of technological change. It seems that new technology has produced alternative possibilities for growth. If small-scale, flexible production does become more significant, it will require a change in government policymaking to produce the supportive environment that historically has been so important in encouraging economic development. This discussion has been done within the context of the further development of the international economy, and the evolution of international financial arrangements will be the focus of the next chapter.

Notes

1. Clothing and fabric for civilian clothing was also rationed, because uniforms and other military uses of textiles (such as parachutes and medical supplies) took priority. This required an alteration in fashion-consciousness, and was especially noticeable in women's clothing where new fashions economized on fabric. Hemlines became shorter, skirts skimpier and bodices more fitted. After the war when fabrics became more available, fashion reversed itself. This was clearly demonstrated in 1947 when Christian Dior, a leading Paris couturier, introduced his A-line, which featured longer and much fuller skirts.

2. The Berlin Blockade began in June 1948 and lasted for a year. The problem was the result of the indecision of the Powers about Germany's future at the Potsdam Conference (1945). All that was decided was that Germany be occupied by military forces. Later, it was agreed that the Prussian state would no longer exist, and that Germany would be divided into states, five in the Russian zone and twelve in the Western zones. Berlin, the former capital, was geographically in the Russian zone and was not included in this arrangement, being put instead under the joint control of all occupying nations. When West Germany's currency was reformed in 1948, legally this represented a violation of the Potsdam

Agreement because the Soviet Union had not been consulted. In protest, it blocked all road and rail access to West Berlin (the Western forces' zone) from West Germany, effectively ending the period of cooperative occupation, and beginning the Cold War. For the next year, American and British airforces mounted a relief airlift, bringing the necessary food, fuel, and raw materials into West Berlin. A year later, having realized that the original blockade had served no useful purpose, all roads to West Berlin were once more reopened.

3. France withdrew from practical participation in NATO in 1966, but remains a member.

4. The United Nations is an international, not a supranational, organization, so the same problems did not occur before its establishment. That is, the UN exists because its members wish to have some international mechanism to achieve various goals; it is based on voluntary cooperation between sovereign states. A supranational organization, in contrast, takes away states' sovereignty, uniting them under one sovereign authority.

5. The establishment of the General Agreement on Tariffs and Trade was agreed on at a postwar international conference in Geneva in 1947. At this conference, twenty-three nations agreed to pursue multilateral tariff reductions. In the following twenty years, five sets of reductions took place, covering about 80 percent of world trade engaged in by thirty-seven nations. GATT also established other principles to influence trade: nondiscrimination, no quantitative restrictions, and disagreements to be resolved through negotiation.

6. In 1960, these colonies became independent. Some chose to remain within the French Community, keeping certain ties with France; two, Guinea and Togo, did not. Because name changes frequently occur after independence, the country's new name appears in parentheses in the following list of former French African colonies: Sudanese Republic (Mali), Dahomey (Benin), Niger, Mauritania, Upper Volta (Burkina Faso), Ivory Coast, Congo, Malagasy (Madagascar). Cameroon and Togo had been German colonies administered by France after 1919.

Key Concepts

Common Agricultural Policy

Common market

Customs union

Economic community

Economic recovery

ECU

European Coal and Steel Community

European Economic Community

European Free Trade Area

European Payments Union

Free Trade area

Guest worker

Indicative planning

Integration

Macroeconomic policy

Marshall Aid

Productivity

Public ownership

Regional policy

Social market economy

Value Added Tax

Questions for Discussion and Essay Writing

1. What were the major differences between the way the two world wars were financed?

2. What were the major differences between the recovery efforts after the First and after the Second World Wars? What were the major problems that the different countries engaged in World War II had to face at the end of the war?

3. "Modern wars are less struggles between rival armies, and more struggles between economies." Discuss.

4. Marshall aid was criticized in the United States because it was seen as a "drain" of money out of the country that would not benefit the economy. Was this criticism justified?

5. To what extent may economic integration schemes help or hinder economic development? What different types of schemes exist?

6. International cooperation characterized the post World War II period. What were its characteristics and why was it significant?

7. Describe the evolution of the European Community since its inception.

8. The EC was originally created not only to encourage economic integration but also to encourage political stability in the region as well. How did it do this?

9. The Common Agricultural Policy is both an economic and a social policy. Evaluate.

10. To what extent does the macroeconomic policy making adopted by a government depend on its economic strength? What other factors may also influence policy?

11. How did the United States adjust its macroeconomic policy making in the postwar period?

12. Germany experienced what has been called an economic miracle in the postwar period. What was it? Why did it happen?

13. "France's indicative planning combines the benefits of a plan with the voluntarism of capitalism." Discuss.

14. Britain's problems in the postwar period have been due to the frequent reversal of policy. How true is this?

15. Italy achieved a remarkable structural shift in the postwar period. Describe and evaluate.

16. Japan's postwar success has been explained in terms of a high degree of cooperation between industry and government. Describe and evaluate.

17. Technological change has tended to increase the scale of production. Discuss.

For Further Reading

Alford, B.W.E. *British Economic Performance 1945–1975*. London: Macmillan, 1988.

Clout, Hugh, Mark Blacksell, Russell King and David Pinder. *Western Europe: Geographical Perspectives*. London: Longman, 1985.

Colchester, Nicholas and David Buchan. *Europower*. London: Economist Books, 1990.

Eatwell, John. *Whatever Happened to Britain? The Economics of Decline.* Oxford: Oxford University Press, 1982.

Fennell, Rosemary. *The Common Agricultural Policy of the European Community* London: Granada, 1979.

Gardner, Richard. *Sterling-Dollar Diplomacy.* Oxford: Clarendon Press, 1956.

Harrison. Mark. "Resource Mobilization for World War II: The USA, UK, USSR and Germany." *Economic History Review*, XLI:2 (1987): 171–192.

Harrod, R.F. *The Life of John Maynard Keynes.* New York: Harcourt, Brace, 1951.

James, Harold, Hakan Lindgren and Alice Teichova. "The Role of Banks in the Interwar Economy." *Journal of Economic Issues*, 26:4 (December 1992): 1303–1305.

Kerr, A.J.C. *The Common Market and How it Works.* Oxford: Pergamon, 1977.

Kossoudji, Sherrie A. and Laura J. Dresser. "Working Class Rosies: Women Industrial Workers During World War II." *Journal of Economic History*, 52:2 (June 1992),: 431-446.

Liberman, Sima. *The Growth of European Mixed Economies, 1945–1970,* Cambridge, Mass: Schenkman Publishing, 1977.

Minshull, G.N. *The New Europe: An Economic Geography of the EEC.* New York: Holmes & Meicr Publishers, 1985.

Organization for Economic Cooperation and Development (OECD), *Progress and Problems of the European Economy.* Paris: OECD, 1954.

Postan, M.M. *An Economic History of Western Europe, 1945–1964.* London: Methuen, 1967.

Stein, Herbert. *The Fiscal Revolution in America.* Chicago: University of Chicago Press, 1965.

United Nations, *A Survey of the Economic Situation and Prospects of Europe.* New York: United Nations Annual Survey, 1948.

Vatter, Harold G. *The United States Economy in World War II.* New York: Columbia University Press, 1985.

Note: The following Statistical Sources will also be useful:

European Economic Community: *Basic Statistics of the Community*

OECD Economic Surveys, *Annual*

United Nations, *Statistical Yearbook of the United Nations*, annual

United States, *Survey of Current Business* (Commerce Department)

Chapter 23

Development of the International Economy

One of the themes developed in this book is the successive widening of horizons. In the feudal period, the focus of economic life turned inward, and the village/manor was the relevant universe for economic activity. With the development of the nation-state and associated mercantilist policies, economic boundaries were pushed out to the borders of the state and, from the policymakers' point of view, included the entire mercantilist empire. (This was not very meaningful for most of the population, whose life styles were barely affected by the great decisions made by their rulers.) Similarly, following industrialization and the extension of production for a market, the earliest firms were small, often producing for a local market. As firms grew in size, so too the size of their relevant market expanded, first to national borders, later extending to the international market. With the spread of industrialization and the development of modern communications, more and more people were brought into contact with a modern market economy, and those people and communities living very much as their ancestors had done became fewer and fewer. Although today there are many exceptions to globalization where local markets still remain appropriate—haircuts and restaurant meals, for example, will never be traded internationally—and although many producers have no interest in making inter-national sales or acquiring foreign inputs, the internationalization of the world economy is a definite reality in the modern world. There are very few people in the world today who have never come across an imported item—American wheat or movies, Arabian oil, or Japanese electronics are among some of the most well-known, and there are few manufactured items produced with absolutely no imported components in them.

Much of this internationalization is relatively recent, even for the Western nations that have long looked beyond their national borders. As we saw in the last chapter, the pace of globalization speeded up after the Second World War. At this time, partly to help accelerate the European economies' reconstruction effort, a deliberate attempt was made to prevent a return to exclusively nationalist preoccupations. Thus, Marshall aid from the United States became available through a conscious international effort. The barriers and restrictions that were necessary to organize economic activity and international relationships during the extraordinary conditions of wartime were slowly dismantled. Commercial and trade relationships between nations became liberalized. Trade expanded as the European and Japanese economies recovered. With general economic growth occurring worldwide, and with the industrialization of new economies—particularly the Pacific Rim countries—trade and financial relationships between countries grew.

Another feature of the postwar age that combined both recognition of national aspirations and the disappearance of the old-style colonial empires was the granting of independence to former colonies. Especially during and after the 1960s (although important examples such as India and Pakistan occurred earlier), a process of decolonization speeded up (refer back to Table 20-1). Independent self-government was stimulated by the surge of nationalist feeling in many colonies after the Second World War and was further accelerated by pressure from the United Nations, which officially expressed approval for the granting of independence in 1960. (Over eighty states became independent after 1945.)

Decolonization
Process of granting independence to colonies

Need for an International Monetary System

What is needed to facilitate and encourage this—a need recognized during the Second World War—is an effective international monetary system. This need arises because trade and other international economic relationships take place between sovereign independent nations. Each has its own currency system (the earlier development of national monetary systems was covered in Chapters 6 and 17), and there is no "international money" acceptable as currency in all countries, although at different times suggestions for creating it have been made.

Trade between countries involves not only an exchange of goods but also an exchange of national currencies, which raises another issue. How

International monetary system
Links between trading nations facilitating money flows between them

do traders know they are getting the right amount of foreign currency when selling abroad? For a long time, the question of relative value was solved by expressing each country's monetary unit in terms of a weight of gold. In the late 19th century, the expansion of world trade occurred with the major trading nations accepting the gold standard as the control over their international exchanges. This acceptance implied also a commitment to domestic policies that were consistent with the gold standard, chiefly the obligation to contract or expand the domestic economy as the trade balance went into deficit or surplus respectively.

As we saw in Chapter 21, the collapse of the international economic order in the late 1920s and 1930s generated a recognition that the gold standard was not adaptable to the needs of a modern world. Although not an issue at that time (but it would be later), there was also a problem using a commodity like gold as an international money. The problem is that for international trade to expand smoothly, the supply of gold must keep pace. But gold is mined in only a few countries, and if its supply does not grow as fast as trade does, or if its costs of production rise, then it becomes less suitable as an international exchange medium. This has frequently happened—the supply of new gold grew more slowly than the growth of world trade, putting pressure on the international monetary system.

Another problem with gold production was political in nature. The world's two largest gold producers were the Soviet Union and South Africa, and reliance on these two countries for gold supplies was politically embarrassing, since the first was ideologically opposed to the capitalist system (until its disintegration in 1989), while the second (until the late 1980s) operated a repressive system of apartheid abhorrent to the Western democracies. The possibility that, because of the size of each country's output relative to total world demand, either could hold the world trading community to ransom by raising the price of

Table 23-1
Comparative Economic Statistics:
US and EC Countries, 1982
(1949-59 share of agriculture in employment in parentheses)

Country	Population (000)	Urban Percentage	Distribution of Labor Force (Percentage of Total)			Exports as % of GDP
			Agriculture	Industrial	Services	
U.S.	227,658	75	4 (5)	30	66	5
W. Germany	61,566	79	6 (21	44	50	26
Italy	57,070	52	13 (37)	37	49	22
U.K.	56,010	77	3 (5)	36	61	21
France	53,714	72	9 (27)	35	56	18
Spain	37,400	na	19 (46)	36	45	na
Netherlands	14,150	77	5 (12)	30	65	49
Portugal	9,900	na	27 (48)	37	37	na
Belgium	9,859	87	3 (9*)	33	64	58*
Greece	9,599	53	30 (48)	30	40	12
Denmark	5,123	80	9 (24)	27	64	28
Ireland	3,401	52	19 (40)	32	48	47
Luxembourg	365	69	6	37	49	

* includes Luxembourg

Source: G.N. Minshull, *The New Europe: An Economic Geography of the EEC,* New York: Holmes and Meier Publishers, 1985; *Economic Report of the President*, Washington, DC: U.S. Government Printing Office, various years

gold extremely high was one factor encouraging the demonetization of gold. Although gold was kept as part of many countries' international reserves, it became less and less important in this role after the 1970s. The development of an effectively "cashless" or bookkeeping method of keeping track of international transactions further encouraged this trend. It was also assisted by improvements in international telephonic communications and by the spread of computerized record-keeping mechanisms in the world's largest banks.

Functions of an International Monetary System

Even before the war, economic analysis had developed sufficiently to identify three requirements of an international monetary system (IMS). The first requirement was that it must provide sufficient liquidity to meet demands. In practical

Liquidity
The ease by which an asset can be converted into money, the most liquid of all assets

Table 23-2
Rates of Growth of Population,
National Product and Per Capita National Product at constant prices

Country	Period	Percent Average Annual Change		
		Population	National Product	NP per capita
United Kingdom	1860/69–1949/53	0.8	2.2	1.3
France	1841/50–1949/53	0.1	1.5	1.4
Germany	1860/69–1950/54	1.0	2.7	1.5
Italy	1862/68–1950/54	0.7	1.8	1.0
United States	1869/78–1950/54	1.7	4.1	2.0
Japan	1878/87–1950/54	1.3	4.2	2.6

Source: S. Kuznets, *Six Lectures on Economic Growth*, Glencoe, Ill: Free Press 1959, p. 20-21, quoted in C.M. Cipolla, *The Economic History of World Population*, Cambridge, Mass: Belknap Press of Harvard University Press 1978, p. 77.

terms, what this means is that if total international exchanges are expanding by, say, 3 percent annually, then the medium used as an international currency must also expand at the same rate, or, in a modern world with a sophisticated financial structure, access to supplementary liquidity must be present. If sufficient liquidity exists, there will be no adverse spillover effect on a trading country's domestic economy due to a shortage of the international exchange medium.

Stability can also refer to the characteristics of stable foreign exchange rates between different currencies. This was not too important in the nineteenth century, when governments believed that maintaining a nondebased currency convertible into metal was enough. A commitment to convertibility was considered sound monetary policy. However, especially in the post-World War II period, exchange stability became much more important to some governments, possibly reflecting the increased importance of international trade links to their economies. Up until the early 1970s, the exchange rates of the major

trading nations were remarkably stable, and only very infrequent adjustments were made. After 1973, however, the situation changed, and the question of stability once more became important to economists and policymakers.

Second, an international monetary system must make adjustment to changing conditions possible. What this means is that if any one country's currency value falls out of line with the others, a simple, fast, and effective adjustment mechanism should be able to restore parities between currencies. If it is not available, then persisting imbalances in exchange rates can worsen already existing domestic conditions that caused the problem, producing instability. Alternatively, if the imbalance was caused by an unrelated factor such as speculation against the currency based on unfounded rumors, then it could lead to a domestic problem where none existed before. Problems with the gold standard's adjustment mechanism were many and frequent in the interwar period and helped its final collapse in the 1930s.

Finally, the third requirement is that the IMS encourage confidence in the system—that is, confidence that unexpected developments can be managed in a stabilizing way. How this is done depends on the technical characteristics of the specific system. For example, in a gold standard system, confidence is maintained for so long as currency or gold holders know the central bank will convert these holdings into gold or currency on demand. In fact, in the 19th century, because confidence in the British central bank's ability to do this was so high, few such conversions actually took place. Instead, traders were as willing to hold sterling as to hold gold because it was more useful. Not only did it serve as an international currency but it could also be used for purchases within Britain and for buying British securities that paid interest.

The Bretton Woods System

Very early in the course of the Second World War, ideas for reconstructing a new, cooperative international order in the postwar period began to be discussed. We have already looked at the discussions between political leaders that led to the Atlantic Charter, which was instrumental in helping rebuild the European economies once the war was over. Now we will turn to the proposals that led to a new international monetary system—the Bretton Woods adjustable peg system.

Bretton Woods system

International monetary system based on fixed but adjustable exchange rates

---

Economists' and Bureaucrats' Contribution

The Bretton Woods system emerged as the result of Anglo-American joint discussions, which had begun as early as 1941. The system marked United States acceptance of its responsibility to the international economy for the first time. It was the world's largest market economy which had not been affected by war damage, so its acceptance was a practical necessity. While the resulting system contained a heavy dose of United States paternalism, it was preferable to the situation that had prevailed after the First World War, when the United States retreat into isolationism was one of the elements contributing to international collapse in the interwar period.

On the British side of the Atlantic, the great economist John Maynard Keynes was the principal thinker and negotiator. As early as 1941 he recognized how fragile Britain's position would be after the war once the various emergency restrictions were removed. These problems were related to several factors. First, the size of British citizens' foreign investment holdings abroad fell as they were sold to pay for the costs of the war or as a result of having been seized by enemy forces. This meant that after the war, fewer foreign earnings would be available because there were fewer income-producing foreign assets left. Second, the remaining foreign assets were not very liquid. Third, the postwar requirement was that foreign exchange should be immediately accessible in order to start the process of rebuilding the economy, but the assets that existed were primarily long-term in nature, so the result was an imbalance in the maturities of assets (long) and liabilities (short) which was not very helpful.

Keynes favored international cooperation, because many other countries were also going to face similar problems, and the attempt to solve problems individually had created the crisis of the late 1920s. Although recognizing that international problems had to be solved on an international level was the result of logical thinking, there was also a practical aspect. As became clear later in the war and in the immediate postwar period, the American position was that any favorable treatment for Britain must be conditional upon Britain's acceptance of trade liberalization. But this would be disastrous for the British economy without restructuring assistance. Before the beginning of the cold war, the United States Congress was also somewhat hostile towards approving what could be seen as a charitable handout to Britain. Hence, the need to gain congressional approval meant that the final scheme was international in scope, limited the financial liability of the United States, and gave it a large role in running the system.

On the American side of the Atlantic, Harry White at the United States Treasury was most responsible for preparing American thoughts on the future international monetary system. Both White's and Keynes' first ideas on the subject were dismissed as too utopian; subsequent negotiations produced a compromise more closely reflecting American views. (Following the collapse of the Bretton Woods system, it is interesting that proposals for a new international monetary system were favorably inclined toward Keynes' original ideas.) All this was done assuming that restrictions on world trade would be removed.

Keynes' Clearing Union

Although never completely adopted, some of Keynes' original ideas are interesting because they not only represented a complete reversal of previous thinking on international payments mechanisms but are also undergoing a revival of interest at the present time. The requirements for stability, adjustment, and confidence are all met in one way or another. The creation of a clearing union was central to the proposal, which was essentially an international central bank. It would be instrumental in facilitating international trade by operating as a bank, using its own medium of exchange that could expand as international trade expanded. Keynes suggested also that the adjustment mechanism should be structured to put pressure on any country whose balance of payments was in dise-

---

Clearing union

International central bank responsible for coordinating financial flows between countries

---

quilibrium in *either* direction. This made sense—a country generating a *persistent* surplus put as much strain on the overall international economy as one running a trade deficit, because it was accumulating payment claims against its trading partners. Unless it "recirculated" these claims, or adjusted its domestic economy to expand imports and/or reduce exports, the possibility of the overall level of trade and economic activity shrinking remained high. Thus, one country's actions could have an adverse effect on others because of these international linkages. This proposal was strongly opposed by the United States, which would be the only surplus country in the immediate postwar period. It objected to the possibility that penalties would be imposed on countries running a surplus. The final version penalized only deficit countries, even though for international stability, persistent surpluses also cause international economic problems.

Keynes also suggested that after the war, each country have a stock of reserves sufficient to see it through the difficult period of transition toward more open trade. This proposal was intended to increase confidence and encourage governments to begin the process of relaxing restrictions without having to face the resulting problem of temporarily adverse financial constraints. Unfortunately, the United States saw these suggested credits as handouts, and they were subsequently scaled down dramatically. It also did not like the idea that the central institution had an automatic expansion capability. Instead, it preferred the principle of a fund, where the borrowing ability of deficit countries would be limited to the size of the initial assets establishing the fund. Therefore the final plan's ability to accommodate the expansion of world trade that did in fact take place was limited in a way that a true international bank would not have been. Both Keynes and White addressed the short-run problems to be faced, but only Keynes' scheme was adaptable for the long run. (Partly because of its lack of flexibility, the final scheme adopted was incapable of surviving the pressures imposed on it, and it collapsed in 1971 when the United States refused to honor any more requests for currency exchange into gold from foreign central banks.)

The Bretton Woods Conference

By 1943, discussions and negotiations were taking place in Washington on the two plans that eventually resulted in a final compromise. The United Kingdom agreed to eliminate the expansion proposal and to establish the new international institution with gold and foreign currencies rather than a new international medium of exchange. It also gave in on the structure of the institution, accepting the fund rather than the bank principle. These negotiations, and their outcome, were one more indication of the change in the balance of world economic power.

In July 1944, the final draft was presented for negotiation at the Bretton Woods Conference. This conference was organized to discuss what was needed for the effective establishment of a new international order. It was a major international achievement, representing a commitment from the forty-four countries attending, including China and the Soviet Union, to agree on international cooperation to face the enormous international problems of the postwar period.

The conference was a breakthrough. It was unlike peace conferences of earlier years, which were small groupings of the major powers who took on themselves the "responsibility" of rearranging the world. Although most of the proposals had been worked out beforehand, there was still a tremendous amount of work achieved at Bretton Woods. Unlike previous mechanisms—before World War I markets were supposed to reach some solution, while before World War II what cooperation existed was achieved by informal contacts between national central banks—the conference genuinely tried to reach effective solutions for a difficult environment.

To repeat, the international order was a shambles. Only the American dollar and Swiss franc were fully convertible; although there was convertibility within the sterling area centered on London, payments made outside the area were restricted. Each nation had its own goals, controls, and restrictions, and bilateral trading arrangements were common. There was a shortage of goods, but an excess of purchasing power domestically, a lack of productive capacity, and a shortage of dollars (the European countries had large trade deficits with the United States). Many controls and restrictions had been used and fixed exchange rates retained to try to manage in this environment. It was the success of the conference and the system it put in place that helped in reestablishing order and the moves toward a liberalized international system.

Operation of the New International System

In the short run, and in coordination with other developments such as the control of inflation and increase of production levels and trade, the new system moved toward a multilateral system of trade and payments, although the socialist planned economies finally declined to participate. Recovery after the war plus economic aid from the United States resulted in the OEEC countries generating surpluses on the current account in 1952-1955, surpluses mirrored by the appearance of deficits in the United States. These surpluses increased their reserves[1] of gold and foreign exchange. By the mid-1950s most countries had returned to easy currency convertibility.

Restoration of exchange rate stability was a longer term aim, the point being to prevent the competitive rounds of devaluations associated with the depressed conditions of the 1930s. This was done by setting a par value for each country's currency in terms of either gold or the dollar. Effectively speaking, most countries pegged their currency value to the dollar, and the dollar was defined in terms of gold. (Because of this characteristic, the Bretton Woods system was also called a gold exchange standard.) Up until 1971, most countries held most of their international reserves in United States dollars because they had confidence that the dollar would retain its value in terms of other currencies and that it would remain convertible into gold. This feature was a holdover from the past; traditionally gold was the most acceptable form of international money. The gold exchange system differed from a pure gold standard, which specified a value for the currency in terms of gold and also provided for full convertibility of currency into gold. In the gold exchange standard, by contrast, gold convertibility applied only to transactions between nations, with the United States exchanging gold with foreign central banks at the rate of $35 per ounce after 1968. (Before then, private parties could buy gold from central banks, but gold was not used as domestic currency.)

At one time, gold was the only form in which international reserves were held, but this was no longer true in the 20th century. By 1970 gold composed about 40 percent of the reserves of the major trading nations and it continued to play a role in the international payments system until 1971. Later, partly due to increasing weaknesses, it was phased out of this role by agreement.

International Monetary Fund and Rate Adjustment

Associated with the aim of exchange rate stability was the introduction of a new adjustment mechanism. Essentially, the Bretton Woods system established fixed rates that could be adjusted periodically in cases of serious disequilibrium. Central to the adjustment process was the International Monetary Fund (IMF), a new international institution created by the Bretton Woods Conference and reflecting the United States insistence on the fund principle for organizing the international payments system.

International Monetary Fund
International organization lending reserves to countries with temporary balance of payments deficits

The IMF, which began operations in 1946, was intended to lend reserves to countries experiencing temporary balance of payments deficits, encourage the trend toward a more liberalized system of international payments, and supervise the "orderly adjustment" of exchange rates. Its ability to make loans so that reserves could be rebuilt came from contributions from member countries. These contributions were made in gold and member countries' currency, and they totaled $9 billion by 1957. The initial amount of IMF assets was only slightly more than a third of the amount Keynes had suggested—it was felt that the smaller amount would limit the responsibility of the United States to bail out countries with problems. In the event, their limited size was a constraint on the IMF's ability to act, and they have been periodically increased by new contributions from members since then.

Any member could vary its exchange rate by up to 1 percent each side of its par value, but any larger adjustment had to be approved by the IMF. Each member was assigned a quota, which was based on its national income, extent of available international reserves, level of imports, variability of exports, and the ratio of exports to national income. This quota then determined the member's initial contribution to the fund and defined the amount that could be borrowed. A member could borrow up to 25 percent of its quota for up to five years.

The combination of minor economic fluctuations and the ability to borrow reserves to protect a currency's value successfully avoided frequent and large devaluations. In the years before 1973, changes of exchange rates were rare. West Germany and the Netherlands altered rates in 1961; Denmark and the United Kingdom devalued in 1967; France and West Germany devalued in

1969; and Austria changed its rates in 1971. But in 1973, after the turbulence caused by the United States ending gold convertibility in 1971, commitment to the orderly adjustable peg mechanism was broken as nations ended their attempts to maintain it.

Collapse of Bretton Woods

Although the new system of international cooperation worked well during the 1950s, it came under increasing strains in the 1960s, some of which were related to the limitations imposed on the IMF and some to the problems associated with the use of the United States dollar as a reserve currency. In the early postwar years, the United States was a surplus country (i.e., in simple terms, it sold more to other countries than they sold to it), but these surpluses were "returned" to the international economy in the form of economic and military aid. In the mid 1950s, the European economies had been rebuilt, economic aid was no longer needed, and instead of being the preeminent economic power, signs

Figure 23.1 Water transportation developed the capability of carrying huge amounts of cargo following the development of the container ship. (Cargo is packed into containers simplifying loading and off-loading.) (Courtesy of Hapag-Lloyd AG)

were beginning to appear that the United States was coming under increasing pressure from international competition. This did not become a major issue until the late 1960s, but, possibly lulled into a false sense of security, nothing much was done earlier.

The growth of both Japan and West Germany posed the most serious challenge to United States dominance. This challenge was reflected in the dollar's overvaluation in the late 1960s, but because of its central role as reserve currency in the system, a downward adjustment was out of the question; all other currencies would simply follow suit. What was needed was a *relative* decline in the value of the dollar, but this was impossible for a reserve currency whose monetary unit was used as the standard to which other monetary units were pegged. In addition, the United States trade deficit, which had been modest earlier, grew. By 1972 it exceeded $10 billion and was dominated by a declining trade balance due largely to a faster growth rate of imports than of exports. In terms of shares of world exports, the United States share fell from 21 percent in 1953 to 14 percent in 1971, and the United Kingdom's share fell from 10 percent to 7 percent. These relative declines were almost exactly matched by a rise in Germany's share from 6 percent to 12 percent and a rise in Japan's share from under 2 percent to 8 percent.

Special Drawing Rights

Such a rapid expansion of world trade had not been foreseen by the creators of the Bretton Woods system, and the amount of international credit lagged behind demands made on it during the 1960s. The problem could be traced to two major issues. First, foreign countries became less willing to hold their international reserves in dollars. They were willing only for so long as they were confident that the United States would remain able to convert these holdings into gold, but this confidence disappeared. Confidence weak-

---

Special Drawing Rights
Artificial expansion of international liquidity

---

ened because United States deficits appeared, and because throughout the 1960s, dollar holdings were growing but the stock of monetary gold was not.

Second, the supply of newly mined gold did not expand, limiting the growth of the stock of gold held for monetary purposes. This was partly due to purely financial considerations: the official price of gold was fixed, but costs of producing it rose, reducing the incentive for mine owners to produce more. A new phenomenon also appeared: Hoarders who bought gold as a purely speculative asset, anticipating that a crisis would send up the price of gold.

The central banks created a two-tier market in 1968 in an effort to stabilize the situation. They agreed to stop selling gold to private parties, which effectively turned gold into a freely traded commodity sold in a private, international gold market. Since that time, the price of gold has fluctuated wildly. However, having made this decision, the question of how to expand official reserve assets remained and was answered by the creation of Special Drawing Rights (SDRs) in the IMF in 1969. Trading countries' shares of SDRs depended on the size of their IMF quotas. SDRs are a purely artificial construction: They are not an international currency and could be used only by a deficit country to buy foreign currency from countries with payments surpluses or from the IMF. However, they did represent an expansion of international liquidity and could have taken on a much more important role than they actually achieved. Presumably, if the dollar did stop being used as an international reserve currency, SDRs could be used to replace it, but they never accounted for more than a tiny share of international reserves. In 1977, total reserves amounted to nearly $500 billion in the United States dollars, of which SDRs accounted for only $10 billion.

Growth of the Eurodollar Market

Only indirectly related to the growing pressure on the United States and the emerging weaknesses of the gold exchange standard, but directly related to the adaptability of financial institutions was the development of the Eurodollar market. A Eurodollar initially referred to a dollar deposit held in a bank outside the United States, but for convenience it can refer to any foreign currency held outside its home country. Although it began as a protective device, the Eurodollar market has dramatically expanded and it has also taken on an independent existence. That is, although a dollar held outside the United States is potentially a claim against that country, Eurodollars have become almost like a pure currency because they have a value independent of their use within the United States.

Eurodollar

A dollar deposit held in a non-United States bank

The emergence of Eurodollars is related to the start of the cold war, when the early postwar spirit of cooperation between the United States and the Soviet Union was replaced by the arms race and increasing competition and hostility. Because there was some trade between the United States and the Eastern European countries, these countries were accumulating dollar holdings. But fearing that a crisis between East and West could lead to the United States freezing their dollar assets if they were held in American banks, Eastern European-owned dollars were deposited, as dollars, in Western European banks instead, thus avoiding a complicated, three-way currency transaction with possible political overtones.

The European banks could not mingle these dollar deposits with their own local currency deposits, and they maintained two sets of records to distinguish them. The deposits grew for two reasons. First, any foreign entity acquiring dollars can deposit them into what then became known as a Eurobank rather than converting them into local currency via the central bank, if there are no restrictions or currency controls. The second reason is more important. Because Eurobanks are profit oriented, they began to loan dollars based on their holdings of Eurodollars to both local and foreign borrowers who preferred dollars rather than local currency. Thanks to the magic of fractional reserve banking—which means that because not all holders of dollar accounts will want to withdraw them simultaneously, only a fraction of all deposits need be held in cash reserves for withdrawal purposes—the total volume of loans and hence Eurodollars outstanding ballooned. In addition, because they are denominated in dollars, they are outside the control of European monetary authorities, and because they are held mainly in Europe, they are outside the control of the Federal Reserve System in the United States. There were thus no restrictions on the expansion of this market such as exist on the supply of liquidity within each country.

Growth was also assisted by developments in the United States and in Europe. In the United States, the imposition of Regulation Q in the 1930s established maximum interest rates that commercial banks could pay on time deposits. It was extended to thrift institutions in 1966, during a period when there was competition for deposits because the economy was generally expanding, and banks found it profitable to extend loans. (That is, it was hoped that by imposing maximum rates that banks could pay on deposits, rates charged on loans would not become outrageously high.) But starting in the 1950s, and accelerated by the extension of Regulation Q in the 1960s, large depositors searched for more attractive rates elsewhere. This "elsewhere" turned out to be Europe, where interest rates were higher than in the United States, and where some remaining exchange controls made short-term capital movements through the foreign exchanges difficult. So both United States residents (including United States banks) and Europeans were attracted to the

Figure 23.2 New technologies continue to be developed. This photo shows an artist's conception of the Terminal Doppler Weather Radar System, designed to detect hazardous weather conditions at airports. (Courtesy of Raytheon Company)

Eurodollar markets. United States residents could get higher returns on dollar deposits, while European borrowers could get loans in dollars without the red tape and restrictions they met if trying to get dollars through official channels.

Another boost came in 1957, when balance of payments problems for the United Kingdom led to restrictions on the use of sterling to finance trade outside the sterling area. London banks active in such trade financing avoided a potential loss of business by using Eurodollars instead, and the entire Eurodollar market rapidly expanded. In 1960, it totaled $1 billion; by 1972, it had grown to $91 billion, of which three quarters were held in dollars.

The growth of this unofficial international currency market helped undermine confidence in the Bretton Woods system by creating an unrestricted, uncontrolled parallel source of international liquidity. It could be, but has not yet become, a potential threat to the stability of the United States monetary system. Theoretically, if all holders of Eurodollars, for whatever reason, decided to transfer them to American banks, which, also theoretically, they could do because these holdings are dollars, the United States money supply would dramatically expand. Another possible result could be a shift in the ownership of real United States assets (depending on what Eurodollar holders wanted to do with their funds). That this has not yet happened indicates that commercial interests are best served by the flexibility and increased international liquidity offered by the Eurodollar market. It also demonstrates the importance of the confidence factor. Although it is extremely unlikely, should confidence in the strength of the United States economy, and thus in the ability of the United States to recognize claims on it, ever waiver, the entire international financial structure would become subject to unacceptable stress.

Changing Role of the IMF

Whether the Bretton Woods system ended in 1971 or in 1973 depends on which aspect one is considering. Attempts to stabilize the gold market and create sufficient extra liquidity by expanding the IMF's facilities were insufficient. These extra facilities dated from the early 1960s, and included standby credits (a country could arrange ahead of time to borrow from the IMF if need be); special arrangements whereby the leading economies agreed to make extra funds available if needed by any of the others; and special compensatory financing to meet requirements of developing countries whose export earnings fluctuate in value. Later, after 1973 when the fixed rate regime of the Bretton Woods system was abandoned, the IMF added longer-term loans to deal with structural readjustments, and in 1974, after oil prices rose, it made loans available to help developing countries finance higher oil import costs.

These developments indicate a changing role for the IMF beyond those originally associated with easing short-run balance of payments adjustments. They have given the IMF a much greater role in influencing the growth of developing countries, and a reduced role in the developed ones that evolved more "non official" adjustments especially using links between private international institutions such as banks and stockbrokerages. (Interestingly enough, they also vindicate Keynes' original proposal for a true international central bank.) The IMF also became much more active in demanding *domestic* economic changes in countries suffering from persistent balance of payments problems. It therefore has been strongly criticized as representing the views of the United States rather than in attempting to understand what might be the most appropriate course of economic development given the existing situation.

Pressure on the United States

Returning to the international situation at the beginning of the 1970s, it was becoming apparent that the postwar payments system was not adaptable to change. Attempts to stabilize the gold market by creating a two-tier system did not end pressure on the dollar, and the expansion of IMF lending functions to create extra liquidity was insufficient. Foreign central banks were enrolled to help ease the pressure against the dollar by buying dollars. But again this was not enough, and in August 1971 the United States decided to suspend its willingness to sell gold to foreign central banks, effectively ending the gold exchange standard. In 1973, the fixed exchange rate regime was abandoned in favor of a managed floating rate system. In this, theoretically "the market" decides what the value of each currency will be relative to the others, with the possibility of central banks intervening to limit the amount of float.

There was a new problem, however, that was not present earlier—even with management, there has been extreme exchange rate volatility, both on a day-to-day level and over the longer term. For example, from 1980-1985, the dollar appreciated by roughly 70 percent in real terms, then depreciated by 70 percent from 1985–1988. According to economic theory, the exchange rate is supposed to reflect real values, but it is difficult to imagine that real values change so rapidly by such large amounts.

Unfortunately, given the realities of the present international environment, it is difficult to anticipate a return to fixed rates. This is because a system of fixed but adjustable rates producing stability on the international level requires some similarity of and coordination in domestic macroeconomic policy objectives and mechanisms of the major players, which is unlikely (and a topic lying outside the scope of this book). This does not absolve monetary authorities from action. As this book is being written, there is serious concern about the state of the international monetary system and many proposals to deal with it—but so far, no answers, and no action equiva-lent to the negotiations leading to the establishment of the Bretton Woods system.

Note

1. International reserves can be used to defend the nation's currency internationally and consist of foreign exchange or assets that can be easily converted into foreign exchange. Reserves plus a country's ability to borrow compose its international liquidity position. Typically, the central bank holds these reserves. They increase when domestic exporters receive payments in foreign currencies that need to be converted into domestic currency, and the central bank has the monopoly on this activity. They fall when domestic importers need to buy foreign exchange in order to purchase from other countries. The ability to control these exchanges, and determine the terms on which they are made, is a powerful policy tool.

Key Concepts

Bretton Woods system
Clearing union
Convertibility
Devaluation
Eurodollar

Foreign exchange rate
International Monetary Fund
International monetary system
Special Drawing Rights

Questions for Discussion or Essay Writing

1. What are the functions of an international monetary system?

2. What problems became apparent in the international economy before and after the Second World War?

3. Describe the issues and events leading up to the introduction of the Bretton Woods system.

4. The International Monetary Fund was a new development on the international scene. Why was it established and what did it do?

5. An international monetary system must provide liquidity, stability and an adjustment mechanism. Discuss.

For Further Reading

Agnew, John. *The United States in the World Economy*. Cambridge: Cambridge University Press, 1987.

"A Brief History of Funny Money." 314:7636 *Economist* (January 6, 1990): 21-24.

"When Money Makes News and News Makes Money." *Economist* 305:7530 (December 26, 1987): 89-91.

Ellsworth, P.T. and J. Clark Leith, *The International Economy*. London: Macmillan, 1975.

Hamouda, Omar, *et al.*, eds. *The Future of the International Monetary System*. Armonk, NY: M.E. Sharpe, 1989.

Kennedy, William P. *Industrial Structure, Capital Markets and the Origins of British Economic Decline*. Cambridge: Cambridge University Press, 1987.

Kindleberger, Charles P. and Andrew Schonfield, eds. *North American and Western European Economic Policies*. NY: Macmillan, 1971.

Porter, Richard and Alexander K. Swoboda, *Threat to International Financial Stability*. Cambridge: Cambridge University Press, 1987.

Postscript

It is difficult to know where to begin any history; it is similarly difficult to know where to end. No attempt has been made to bring this text up to date. By the late 1980s it was becoming apparent that enormous economic changes are taking place, changes whose consequences, though they cannot be predicted, are bound to be important, especially the dramatic changes taking place in Eastern Europe and the former Soviet Union.

In spite of the need to be cautious, some insights can be derived, and possibly some predictions. The first point to be made is that change is inevitable in human society. This is not a new insight, but it is relevant, especially for the beneficiaries of Western development, who sometimes argue as though history has come to an end. If this book has shown anything, it is that nothing lasts forever—no economic system, no ethic, no tradition. While it might take many generations to change—or almost no time at all— we do know that today's rulers are not guaranteed security of tenure for tomorrow.

- We have seen economic systems themselves change; feudalism disappeared, capitalism emerged. Capitalism itself has undergone change, not only to meet specific needs of different countries, but also because the very logic of the system necessitates change and adaptation. For example, in the 20th century, we have seen the growth of white collar and service occupations, and an increasing role is being played by the providers of finance capital. Work itself has also changed, chiefly due to the impact of computerization, which affects both job content and job numbers.

The lesson of this insight, for those who are congratulating themselves on the fall of Communism in the East, is that what may be the right answer for today may not work tomorrow. As we have seen throughout this book, while improving the human condition for all has become an increasing possibility, the reality of doing this depends on various non economic factors. They include the balance of power, both within and between nations and peoples, the precise policies that are adopted, and the commitment to their enforcement. It remains as true today as it was in the Middle Ages that the interests of the ruler rarely permit any *voluntary* dilution of power or reduction of economic interests. The connection between economics and politics is complex, and continues to attract the attention of scholars.

Closely associated with this is another problematic concept. A central theme of the book has been the importance of industrialization. In simple economic-theoretical terms, industrialization has meant the application of non-human energy sources and a dramatic increase in productivity. The result has been an enormous increase in output and consequently in the standard of living of those in the industrialized countries. However, this has had several consequences. First, the few developed countries now lay claim to a disproportionate share of the Earth's resources in order to maintain their high standards of living. Unless industrial requirements are significantly reduced downward, it will be impossible for all the currently underdeveloped and developing countries to reach the same levels of industrialization and living standards. The Earth's resources—as we currently measure them—are simply incapable of meeting all demands on them at current levels of use.

- Industrialization, the application of nonhuman power sources to the production of material things, has been the most significant development of modern history. When paired with the development of market mechanisms and the profit motive, the potential for economic growth is enormous, but problems also arise.

  The implication here is that unless the trend to increased international cooperation noted in the last two chapters is maintained and extended, the likelihood of international conflict over access to resources increases. And unfortunately, the internationalization of communications means that the world's poor have a better knowledge of how the world's rich live than vice versa—which is likely only to make things worse. The revolution of rising expectations has risen faster than the ability to realize them. Furthermore, it is easier to disseminate knowledge than understanding, and easier to pass on knowledge of "how to start" than "how to stop." Combine this with knowledge of military expertise, which unfortunately has been one of the few things developed countries have willingly traded with the less developed, and the stage is set for a vicious potential conflict between the have-nots who want, and the haves who are not about to give anything up.

- International cooperation is not out of the question. Beginning in the 1950s, the Euro-

pean nations began to link their economies more closely together. Similar regional integration schemes have been suggested or applied in other parts of the world, in Asia, Africa, and North America. Not all have succeeded, but a willingness to start thinking about cooperation is a first step. If cooperation for the purpose of furthering economic growth is possible, then it is also possible to cooperate to deal with other problems of human existence that need to be faced.

Human understanding can potentially solve this problem, because social institutions and arrangements, being made by humans, are amenable to adjustment. The problem of international inequity is difficult to solve and requires more innovative action. For example, the market system's approach to externalities is to ignore them unless forced to do otherwise. One of the most damaging externalities, with the saddest of consequences for the natural environment, is pollution resulting from industrial waste. Unfortunately, although the spread of industrialization and urbanization has had many positive social results—lengthened life expectancy, lowered infant mortality, improved quality of life for many—it has come at the expense of encroachment on the others who share the planet. In the relatively short experience of industrialization, many species have become extinct, and the survival of others is precarious. It seems as though our "improvements" are gained at enormous, perhaps even insupportable, expense if we consider the entire living planet rather than just the human part of it. Some economists take the technologically determinist approach that there is always a solution to everything, but so far, humans have yet to find a solution to death. Just because 19th century concerns about over-population and famine were solved by agricultural improvement does not automatically imply that acceptable solutions will always turn up for every problem.

- A third lesson has perhaps a more favorable outcome. One theme of this book has been the progressive broadening of horizons: from local to national to international. But as economic potential has broadened and been paralleled by an increase in political horizons, there has been an interesting countertrend, especially in the late 20th century. That is, while an increase in scale seems to characterize many (but not all) industrial and economic operations, and has encouraged a trend to international cooperation between nation states, increasing education has reaffirmed the importance of ethnic and cultural roots. In many cases, this can be compatible with democratic nationalism: A stable state can incorporate many ethnic and regional loyalties within its borders so long as there is a built-in tolerance for difference. Unfortunately, the process of drawing boundary lines in the 19th and 20th centuries was often arbitrary or designed for some purpose other than keeping ethnic groups together. So a "state" was often created without the corresponding "nation" to give it popular legitimacy. The result has been many political states containing many separate, occasionally even conflicting, ethnic peoples within them. This in itself need not create problems, but when separate ethnic groups do start to demand their own political state, the potential for upheaval surfaces. One possible solution is to encourage a certain amount of fractionalization so that these groups are better represented in a political democracy, while the advantages of increased size for economic affairs is gained through regional integration scheme such as the European Community. Then those functions that are best provided at the local level will be retained at that level, while those where economies of scale are important become the responsibility of the regional grouping. Such a division of responsibilities makes sense, as the different sizes of existing nation states are essentially accidents of history, so there is no reason why there should not be different groupings formed for different purposes.

- The implication here is that political democracy can extend economic rights and accomplish many desirable functions.

On a final note, these problems are potentially solvable and one hopes they will be solved. One more, however, needs to be mentioned at this point, because it is the most important. We could get all the answers to the economic problems right, but this will be useless unless we manage to guarantee world peace. It is vitally necessary to solve the problem of militarism and achieve peace. Modern military technology has accomplished what has never been possible before: The ability to totally destroy all life several times over. If this ever happens, then having succeeded in achieving economic plenty and justice for all will become totally meaningless. As has also been stressed throughout the book, values are integral to an economic system. To be able to accomplish the goals that we think are desirable, and that we now have the means to accomplish, should not be too difficult if those values are already incorporated into existing systems. History never ends, so it remains important for us to remember that decisions made today influence tomorrow's reality.

Glossary

Abolition of feudal tenure The ending of customary rights to use land, usually contemporaneous with the introduction of private property in land

Ad Valorem Duty A duty or tariff imposed as a percentage of the commodity's price

Agrarian Democracy (U.S.) The principle that a strong nation is one built on a base of independent farmers who do not owe their livelihood to the whim of an employer

Agricultural Processing The stage of production transforming crude agricultural products into more usable ones, such as flour milling

Agricultural Revolution 1. enclosures, which changed land owning practices; 2. the application of scientific knowledge to increase productivity in agriculture

Alienation of the Demesne The process by which lords of the manor ceased to accept their feudal rights and obligations regarding cultivation of demesne land by feudal serfs. Instead, they leased it out to tenant farmers for a money rent payment

Anarchism Political theory advocating the replacement of governments with voluntary associations of cooperative groups

Anti-Industrial Bias Opposition to industrialization

Antitrust (U.S.) Laws that prohibit monopolies, the attempt to monopolize or monopolistic behavior

Apartheid Official policy of separation of the races practiced in South Africa

Apprentice A person who works for a specified length of time for a master craftsman in return for learning the skills of the craft or trade

Arable Farming The growing of crops as distinguished from raising livestock

Artificial Barrier Any manmade impediment to free trade or free movement of resources, such as tariffs or legal restrictions

Artisan A self-employed skilled worker

Assembly Line A production arrangement in which each specialized worker performs a particular task on the product which moves past on a moving track or belt

Balance of Trade The balance sheet of a nation's merchandise trade with other countries; a favorable balance of trade occurs when the value of exports exceeds the value of imports

Bank Note Originally a receipt issued by a private bank in return for a customer's deposit of coined money; later, they circulated and were accepted as money

Benefice An area of land granted to a feudal tenant in return for services provided to the grantor; later, it referred exclusively to Church livings, while a fief referred to the estate of a lay noble

Bill of Exchange A debt instrument, originally a promissory note written by a buyer promising to pay the seller a specified amount of money at a specified future time and place

Bimetallism The use of two metals with fixed values in relation to each other as a nation's monetary standard

Blackleg A strikebreaker

Blacklist An employer-circulated list of people who are to be denied employment

Bondholder A bond is a debt instrument issued by a borrower who promises to repay the principal amount borrowed plus interest at a specified future date; the bondholder may be the original lender or someone who later bought the debt from the original lender

Bourgeois Originally a freeman living in a medieval town; applied to one engaged in a non-traditional, non-feudal occupation handling money; later extended to apply to the middle class between the landed aristocracy and the peasant or working class

Bourse An exchange where goods could be bought and sold; specifically for financial transactions

Bretton Woods System International monetary system established after the Second World War, featuring fixed but adjustable exchange rates

Bubble   A period of speculative fever in which unlimited optimism drives up the price of shares of an affected company beyond any "reasonable" level. When adverse news or a rumor hit, the bubble bursts and the shares may become worthless

Bullionism   Bullion refers to gold and silver, and bullionism refers to the earliest stage of mercantilist philosophy advocating the acquisition of large amounts of bullion

Burg, Burgh, Burh   A fortified town; originally any building with a palisade or fortification around it

Business Cycle   The alternation of periods of prosperity and of depression characteristic of modern economies

Canal   An artificial waterway

Canon Law   The body of law of the Church

Capital Accumulation   In general, the increase of wealth by individuals or society; in capitalism, capital accumulation occurs when profits are plowed back into the enterprise to expand productive capacity

Capital Deepening   Occurs when relatively more capital equipment is used with labor; specifically, the capital-labor ratio increases

Capital Export   Usually exports of finance capital, but may also refer to exports of capital goods

Capital Good   Productive assets such as tools, equipment, machines, and buildings used to produce output

Capital Intensity   The proportion in which productive capital is put to use relative to other inputs

Capital Mobilization   The process of getting finance capital from where it is available to where it will be used to acquire productive capital

Capital Scarcity   A situation in which productive capital is scarce relative to the demand for it

Capital Widening   Occurs when the stock of productive capital expands at the same rate as the growth of the labor force

Capitalism   An economic system in which economic resources are privately owned and operated for profit

Capitalist Ethic   The system of values characteristic of and justifying capitalism, specifically the justification of the profit motive

Capitation   A head or poll tax

Cartel   An association of producers establishing a joint monopoly by fixing prices, determining production quotas, and so on.

Central Bank   An agency, usually government-established, with the functions of controlling the nation's money supply and credit conditions, and supervising private commercial banks

Centralization of Production   Focusing production activities in a limited number of places, as in the factory system, as distinguished from a domestic system of production

Ceteris Paribus   (Lat.) All other things remaining the same

Chartist Movement, Chartism   (Eng.) A movement in England in the 1840's advocating democratic social and political reform

Check   A third party draft authorizing a bank to pay a certain amount of money from the payer's account to the payee

Chonin   (Japan) Merchants

Clearing Union   A multilateral arrangement for settling international trading accounts

Cliometrics   The study of history using advanced methods of mathematical analysis in order to quantify historical experience

Closed Shop   A workplace in which union membership is a condition of employment

Co-determination   (Germany) Participation by representatives of labor unions in policymaking for the business enterprises in which they work

Collective Bargaining   A process of negotiation between an employer and organized workers to reach an agreement on wages, working conditions, and hours

Colonization   Process in which one country (the colonizer) brings others (colonies) under its political control

Command Economy   An economic system in which the decisions regarding what to produce, how much to produce, and who to produce for are made by a noneconomic authority such as a government

Commercial Policy   Government policy affecting commerce and trade

Common Agricultural Policy   (Eur.) The agricultural policy of the European Economic Community

Common Law   The law of a country based on custom and usage, distinguished from canon law, mercantile law, and statute law

Common Market   A closer form of regional integration than a customs union, in which not only is trade in finished goods free from tariffs but also free movement of resources across borders is permitted

Commons, Common Land In feudalism, the area of land open to all to use for pasture, and so on; land not owned by an individual

Commune A group of people who live together and share in work and the rewards from work

Commutation The process by which a feudal serf ceased to be a feudal serf, usually by substituting a money payment for feudal obligations

Company Union An association of workers at a particular company, unaffiliated with any other labor organization, and usually controlled by the company

Conglomerate A large corporation usually formed by a merger of companies operating in unrelated industries

Consumer Cooperative A retail organization owned collectively by its members who share in its benefits (especially those resulting from buying in bulk)

Continental System A system of blockade initiated by Napoleon in 1806, aimed at excluding Great Britain from commerce with those parts of Europe under French-control. British ships were excluded from French-controlled ports, and British property and subjects could be seized. After 1807, any ship going to or from a British port or colony was considered to be a lawful prize

Convertibility The ease (or otherwise) with which one currency can be exchanged for another

Copyholder A landholder who was not a freeholder but whose right to hold land was proved by a written record in the rolls of a manorial court

Corn Laws (Eng.) Protectionist laws imposing tariffs on grain imported into Britain; repealed 1846

Corporation A form of business organization in which the firm is owned by individuals; it has a legal identity separate from its owners (see also Joint Stock Company)

Corvée A special "tax" requiring able-bodied men to work on the upkeep and repair of roads in France

Craft Union An association of workers in the same trade or occupation, cutting across industry lines

Crop Rotation The practice of successively growing different crops with different nutritional requirements on the same piece of land in order to prevent soil depletion

Customary Tenant One whose right to hold/use land depended on the goodwill of the lord of the manor; one whose presence on the land was established through inherited custom

Customs Union A form of regional integration between nations that agree to eliminate tariffs on trade between themselves and impose a common tariff on trade with all other nations

Daimyo (Japan) Feudal lords

Danelaw The north and east part of England occupied by the Danes in the 9th and 10th centuries and subject to the code of laws established by the Danish invaders

Debasement Process by which the intrinsic value of coins is lowered

Decentralized Production See Domestic Industry, sense 1

Deflation A fall in the general level of prices

Demesne In feudalism, the area of the manor reserved for the use of the lord

Dependent Development A situation in which the economic development of one country is not self-generated or sustaining, but dependent on events in another, as with the provision of a market, financing, or entrepreneurial activity

Depopulation Reduction in population

Depression A period of unemployment, low investment, low/falling output, and business pessimism

Devaluation A reduction in the price (the foreign exchange rate) of one currency in terms of another

Dialectics A method of examining ideas logically in order to determine their validity

Discount House A financial institution that specializes in buying debt instruments (bills of exchange) at a discount

Discounting The practice by which a lender or an institution such as a discount house deducts interest in advance. The discount rate is the rate of interest charged for discounting

Dissenter (Eng.) A Protestant who does not accept the doctrines of the Anglican Church

Division of Labor A method of organizing production in which different workers each specialize in one particular task rather than having all the skills necessary to complete the entire product

Domestic Industry 1. Work for an employer undertaken at the worker's home, as distinguished from factory industry; 2. All industry within one country as distinguished from industry in foreign countries. See also Putting Out System

Dual Economy See Economic Dualism

Economic Community A regional integration scheme that goes beyond the requirements of a common market to encourage the harmonization of fiscal, monetary, and socioeconomic policies

Economic Dualism A situation in which part of a nation's economy is characterized by modern organization and technology and high productivity, while another part is characterized by the persistence of traditional methods

Economic Efficiency Same as Efficiency; may also be the situation in which some desired outcome is obtained

Economic Recovery A period of recovery from a disaster or depression, characterized by expanding output and employment

Economic System The organization of society that influences economic activity, and thus determines how society's economic needs are met

Economics The study of how the material conditions of life are arranged

Economies of Scale Increases in output per input (increases in productivity) that result from an increase in the size of the operating unit

ECU (European Currency Unit) An artificial monetary unit of account created by central bankers in the European Community; it is equal to the sum of defined amounts of the national currencies of EC members.

Effective Demand Demand that is made effective by the exercise of purchasing power in a market

Efficiency A situation in which, given technology, maximum output is obtained with the existing level of usable inputs

Elastic Demand Demand is said to be elastic if there is a proportionately greater change in purchases in response to a given change in price

Elizabethan Poor Law (Eng.) To deal with the problems of poverty accompanying enclosure, each parish was responsible for the poor within its own boundaries

Enclosure Narrowly, the erection of fencing, and so forth, around a property; more generally, enclosure in 16th century England and later referred to the process by which land became privately owned

Equilibrium Technically, a state of rest. In economics, it may also imply attainment of an optimizing position

Eurodollar Reserves, deposits or loans denominated in dollars but held in banks outside the United States

European Coal and Steel Community The sectoral integration scheme rationalizing production of coal and steel in member European nations

European Economic Community The regional integration scheme first formed in 1958 as a customs union by six European nations

European Free Trade Area A free trade area formed in 1958 by seven European nations

European Payments Union Agreement between European nations after World War II intended to encourage the normalization of international settlements and currency convertibility

Excise Tax A tax imposed on a specifically identified commodity

Export of Industrialization Export of capital goods that will be used to build up the industrial capability of the importing country

Extent of the Market Maximum size of the market

External Economy Situation where an improvement lowering costs in one industry results in lower costs in another

Factory Act (Eng.) 19th century laws attempting to regulate work and workers in factories, e.g., by restricting the use of child labor or limiting working hours

Factory System A system of centralized production separated from the workers' homes

Fair In medieval times, a gathering of international merchants held infrequently for a few days or weeks at a time, distinguished from local retail markets

Fallow Land left uncultivated

Favorable Balance of Trade See Balance of Trade

Feudal Tenure In feudalism, the system of land holding in which the land holder owed certain duties to the overlord. The right to hold land (for both nobles and serfs) was heritable although dependent on the lord's will

Feudalism An economic, political, and social system, chiefly in medieval Europe. The system revolved around the landholding relationship of the fief, which incorporated a particular type of relationship between lord and vassal

Fief See Benefice

Financial Panic A period of successive defaults on loans causing bank closings that may also affect other financial institutions such as the stock market

Financing The process of acquiring money resources in order to acquire or build real assets

Fixed Costs of Production Those costs that do not increase or decrease as output increases or decreases, such as machinery and equipment costs or interest payments

Fodder Crop   Food grown to feed cattle and other livestock, such as hay

Forced Labor   Unfree labor required to do their master's bidding, as distinguished from free labor

Foreign Exchange Rate   The price of a country's currency in terms of a foreign currency

Fractional Reserve Banking   A banking system in which banks are required to keep some fraction of customers' deposits in the form of cash or non-interest bearing deposits with the central bank

Free Labor   Workers who are not tied to the land and who are therefore legally free to enter into a contract with an employer and work for wages

Free Trade   A situation in which trade is not subject to regulation, tariffs, or quotas imposed by government

Free Trade Area   The weakest form of regional integration scheme in which tariffs on trade between member nations are eliminated

Freeholder   One who holds or owns land for life or with the right to pass it on through inheritance, as distinguished from leaseholder

Friendly Society   (Eng.) A mutual aid society formed by industrial workers. In return for payment of dues, it could provide life insurance, sickness allowances, payment of funeral expenses, and provision for old age, for example

General Strike   A strike by all the workers in an industry or throughout an entire country; specifically the 1926 General Strike in England

General Union   A labor union open to workers that cuts across craft and industry lines

Gold Standard   A monetary system in which a nation's currency is defined in terms of a specified weight of gold and is convertible into gold

Grange   (U.S.) Name given to the Patrons of Husbandry, an association of farmers organized in 1867 to promote their mutual interests

Great Depression   An extended period of declining output, high unemployment, low investment, corporate bankruptcies and bank failures; specifically, the 1930's

Greenback   (United States) Any legal tender, non-interest bearing notes first issued by the United States in 1862, printed on the back in green ink

Gresham's Law   "Bad money drives out the good;" in a bimetallic monetary system, the coin whose metallic value exceeds its purchasing power (face value) drops out of circulation

Guest Worker   Immigrant worker in a country who has no permanent right to residence there

Guild, Gild   In medieval times, an association of producers in the same craft or trade, designed to maintain standards and protect the common interests of members

Hanseatic League   In medieval times, an association of towns (originally Bremen, Lübeck and Hamburg) designed to promote and protect the economic interests of their members by offering mutual assistance to merchants from affiliated towns

Heavy Industry   Those industries considered to be the core of an industrialized economy, especially metal working, transportation, and power generation

Hectare   An area roughly 2.47 acres in size

Holding Company   A corporation organized to hold the bonds or stocks of operating companies

Holy Roman Empire   An empire in west central Europe created by Charlemagne in 800 A.D.; in later centuries it was a nominal empire only, and it ceased to exist in 1806

Horizontal Integration   Merger or other close links between enterprises at the same stage of production

Hyperinflation   Extremely severe and rapid inflation

Immigrant   A man or woman who leaves their country of birth to move to a new country, usually to settle there

Imperialism   The practice of establishing a colonial empire in order to control sources of raw materials and markets, especially the colonization associated with the late 19th entury

Import Substitution   A policy of industrialization that encourages the domestic manufacture of previously imported items, especially to improve the trade balance

Income Distribution (functional)   The division of National Income into wage, rent, and profit shares associated with the land, labor, and capital factors of production

Increasing Returns to Scale   Returns to scale give the rate at which output grows when input use expands. If they are increasing, then output expands by proportionately more than inputs

Indentured Servitude   A type of unfree labor in which a person enters a contract binding the servant to work for an employer for a specified period of time

Indicative Planning   A system of planning in which certain economic goals or guidelines are established, and private enterprises are encouraged to reach them

Indulgence   In the Roman Catholic Church, the issuing of a remission of temporal or purgatorial punishment due for a sin after the sinner has confessed guilt, repented and been forgiven in the sacrament of penance

Industrial Concentration The degree to which a market or industry is marked by competition or monopolizing trends. The higher the degree, the more an industry is dominated by a few large firms

Industrial Linkage The connections between different industries or parts of industries via input or market requirements

Industrial Policy Any type of government policy that affects industrial activity

Industrial Union A labor organization whose members are employed in the same industry cutting across skill and craft lines

Infant Industry Tariff A tariff imposed on competing imports in order to protect a newly established domestic industry from foreign competition

Inflation An increase in the general price level

Infrastructure The basic facilities necessary for the effective functioning and growth of society and private industry, such as roads, bridges, schools, communications systems, and so forth (also called social overhead capital)

Innovation The use of a new production technique

Integration Process of bringing together different enterprises, institutions, or economies

Intensive Agriculture A system of farming aimed at maximizing crop yield per unit of land

International Monetary Fund Created as part of the Bretton Woods system to encourage and coordinate easy currency convertibility and stability, and to promote international liquidity

International Monetary System The system governing monetary exchanges and financial flows between nations

Invention The creation of a new idea

Investment The acquisition of new productive capital assets

Investment Bank A bank that makes long-term loans available to business for capital-investment purposes

Invisible Export Non merchandise exports such as tourism, banking services, insurance, shipping, and so forth

Isolationism A policy or belief that opposes a country's participation in any type of international activity or arrangement

Joint Stock Company A business enterprise owned by stockholders who have the right to sell or transfer their shares independently

Journeyman In medieval times, a worker who had completed an apprenticeship and was working for wages prior to becoming a mastercraftsman

Just Price In medieval times when production was done by artisans selling mainly in local markets, this was the selling price that would maintain the seller in his customary position in society

Kuomintang (China) Nationalist political party of China, organized in 1911 by Sun Yat-sen, and later controlled and led by Chiang Kai-shek

Labor Shortage A situation where free labor is scarce relative to the demand for it

Labor Union An association of employees designed to promote the economic position of its members, usually through collective bargaining with employers

Laissez Faire The view that government should not interfere in economic activity

Land Grant Policy in the United States in the 19th century in which federal and state governments gave public land to states, railroad companies, or other enterprises or institutions

Landed Gentry Originally large landowners who were not nobles but who had made money in commerce or trade which was then used to buy land. Later, it referred to nonaristocratic landowners who ran their estates along business rather than feudal lines by renting the land out to tenant farmers

Leaseholder One who has entered a contract with the owner of land and thereby gains the right to use the land for a specified period of time and for a fixed payment (rent)

Legal Tender Money that, by law, must be accepted for payment of debts

Lend-Lease After 1941, program designed to assist the war effort during World War II; material aid such as arms, tools and food was provided by the United States to countries whose defense was determined to be vital to United States interests

Limited Liability Characteristic of a modern corporation in that shareholders are at risk of loss only up to the value of their finance capital invested

Liquidity Characteristic of money or of assets that can be easily converted into money

Lockout An industrial action in which an employer refuses to let his employees work until they agree to his demands

Luddism Machine breaking, specifically the machine-breaking movement in early 19th century England

Machine Tool Tools or equipment used to make machines or machine parts

Macroeconomic Policy Government policy that aims to influence the operation of the entire economy

Management Structure The hierarchical organization of the managers of an enterprise

Manor In feudalism, the area of land under the control of a noble; it was the fief granted the lord by his military or political superior to whom he owed allegiance

Manorial System The economic organization of feudalism centering around the manor and the rights and obligations of the two classes living on the manorial estate

Margin Loan A loan used as a partial downpayment for the purchase of stocks.

Market Economy An economic system in which the decisions regarding who does the work and who to produce for is determined through markets, usually in response to a monetary motive

Marshall Plan Program of United States' economic assistance to help rebuild European economies after the Second World War

Marxism Version of socialist thought developed by Karl Marx

Mass Market A very large market, usually for standardized products

Mass Production Production of goods in large quantities, using machines and division of labor

Mechanization The process of using machines rather than hand labor to accomplish an industrial task

Mercantile Law Commercial law developed by merchants to regulate trade and commerce in late medieval times. It was administered in "pie-powder" courts

Mercantilism The doctrine expressing the view that the economic interests of a nation are best encouraged through active government policies to protect private industry and to generate a favorable balance of trade through monopoly grants and tariffs

Mercantilist Empire The entire unit of a colonizing European power and its underdeveloped colonies seen as a mutually complementary whole

Merger The acquisition of one corporation by another

Metal Working The process of making things out of metal

Money Creation Process by which banks in a fractional reserve banking system can expand money by making loans to borrowers

Money Wage The payment to free laborers

Monopoly Control of a market or industry by one seller or producer; a monopoly grant gives this exclusive privilege to an enterprise

Monroe Doctrine (U.S.) The doctrine dating from 1823 and influencing United States foreign policy, stating that the United States would regard any attempt by a European nation to interfere in any country in the Americas as an unfriendly act

Most Favored Nation Refers to a clause in international treaties by which a nation commits itself to grant to another nation the same terms as are currently or will be granted to any other nation. Effectively, it grants favorable tariff status

National Bank (U.S.) In the 19th century, a bank chartered by the Federal Government issuing its own bank notes secured by government bonds

Nationalization The process of transferring ownership or control of facilities to the national government

Natural Monopoly An enterprise in which the scale of operations is so large relative to the size of the market that one firm could supply the required output more efficiently than several competitive firms

Naval Stores Products used for building and maintaining ships, such as timber, pitch, tar, turpentine, hemp, flax

New Model Union (Eng.) Labor unions created after 1851 focusing strictly on the attainment of economic goals such as wages, fringe benefits, working conditions

Nonconformist See Dissenter

Open Field System The technical aspect of rural life in medieval (and later) times, referring to the organization of agriculture. The tenants' fields were held and cultivated in common, with the land divided into strips "owned" by individual families

Open Market Operations Process by which a central bank can increase/decrease the size of the money supply by buying/selling government bonds from/to the public in the open market

Open Shop A workplace in which union membership is not a condition of employment

Outdoor Relief   A system of relief for the poor who live in their own houses and are not required to become institutionalized as a condition for receipt of aid

Paper Money   Noninterest bearing notes issued by a government or its central bank that circulate as legal tender

Peasant Farming   Small-scale farming by independent peasant farmers who may or may not produce for a market

Physiocracy   18th century French theory holding that land and what can be produced on the land are the only true sources of wealth, because of the belief that only nature can produce a surplus. Its policy implication was for the removal of restrictions on agriculture

Piecework   System of payment for work; pay depends on the amount of work done and not the time taken

Plantation   A commercial estate cultivated by workers living on it

Political Fragmentation   A situation where a nation is not unified

Pool   A combination of business firms attempting to monopolize a particular area

Positivism   From the system of philosophy that bases knowledge on observable, scientific facts and the relationship between these facts, rejecting normative value judgement

Predestination   The Calvinist doctrine that God has predetermined which souls will be saved and which damned

Price Competition   In economic theory, this occurs when business enterprises compete with each other solely on the basis of price

Primary Product; Primary Producer   A primary product is one extracted from the earth (mineral deposits) or grown (trees, field crops) and which has not undergone further processing. A primary producer usually refers to the country with an economy dominated by the production of these commodities, i.e., a nonindustrial economy

Primogeniture   Legally, the exclusive right of the eldest son to inherit property

Producer Cooperative   A productive enterprise owned and operated by its workers

Productivity   The ratio of output to inputs. Productivity increases when more output is produced by the same amount of inputs

Profit   The financial or monetary gain derived from the use of capital, often expressed as a percentage of the capital invested (the profit rate) or as the amount left from business income after all costs have been deducted

Proletarian   A member of the working class, especially an industrial worker

Protectionism   A policy affecting international trade adopted by a government to protect domestic industries from foreign competition

Provost   The steward, bailiff, or overseer of a manor

Public Ownership   See Nationalization

Public Utility   An enterprise producing and selling water, power, transportation, and so forth to the public; usually government-owned

Putting Out System   A domestic system of industry in which work was "put out" on commission by the capitalist employer to the employee, who owned the fixed capital (buildings, equipment). It economized on scarce capital

Rack Renting   The practice of charging excessively high rent; at the limit, the annual rent is close to the value of the land

Rail Network   The creation of a transportation network by the connection of different private/public rail lines

Rationing   The system of allocating scarce goods during times of emergency

Real Wage   The purchasing power of the money wage

Reeve   An administrative official of a manor; the reeve's powers and duties varied with the source of his appointment and the jurisdiction he was placed over

Regional Policy   Policy oriented specifically to assist one particular region of a country

Rentier   A person providing financing for projects who receives interest or dividends in return, but is not involved in management

Reparations   Payments to be made by a defeated country to make good economic losses in other countries caused by the war

Reserves   (Banking) The part of customers' deposits that banks hold as cash or as a non-interest bearing deposit at a central bank

Resource Endowment   The relative quantities of economic resources (land, labor, capital) within a country

Returns to Scale   The rate at which output increases when all inputs are increased

Robber Baron   (U.S.) The term given to some late 19th century American capitalists who gained their wealth by exploitative and/or ruthless means

Rotten Borough   (Eng.) A borough (electoral district) with only a few voters but with the right to elect a representative to Parliament (abolished in the Reform Act of 1832)

Salic Law   Code of laws originating among the Germanic tribe of Salian Franks; the name given to the law excluding women from succeeding to the monarchy in France and Spain

Scab   A worker who refuses to strike or who takes the place of a striking worker

Scientific Management   A system of work management originated by Frederick Taylor in 1903, also called efficiency engineering. It focuses on identifying the elementary operations of any task through time and motion studies

Scrivener   A professional or public writer; a notary whose occupation is to draw up contracts or prepare documents

Serf   A person belonging to any of the various grades of the non-noble class in feudalism who was bound to the soil and more or less subject to the will of the lord of the manor

Servile Status   The status of a feudal serf who had rights and obligations by virtue of living on a medieval manor

Sharecropping   The practice in which a tenant farmer works the land and "pays" the landlord with a share of the harvest

Sitdown Strike   A strike in which the workers stay at the workplace until a settlement is reached

Slavery   The practice or institution of owning people as slaves

Sleeping Partner (Silent Partner)   A part-owner of an enterprise who helps finance the enterprise but who plays no role in managing it

Social Darwinism   The philosophy developed by Herbert Spencer who adapted Darwin's idea of biological evolution to society, in which wealth was the measure of success of the economically fittest

Social Ethic   The code or standards regulating behavior in a society

Social Market Economy   (F.R.G.) An economy that is predominantly a private enterprise economy but in which a strong socialist commitment is also present

Social Welfare   The well-being of society

Socialism   1. an economic system based on communal ownership of the means of production; 2. a political theory and movement advocating the establishment of such a system

Société en Commandité   (Fr.) A form of partnership in which there are one or more silent partners who provide financing but who are liable only up to the value of their capital invested. A forerunner of the *société anonyme*, French term for a corporation with limited liability

Special Drawing Rights   IMF-created international reserve assets on which member nations could draw to meet needs for international liquidity

Specialization   Process of narrowing down job skills; concentrating on only one part of an activity

Specie Money   Coins, as distinguished from paper money

Specific Duty   A fixed tax or duty imposed on an item, as distinguished from an ad valorem duty

Speculative Bubble   See Bubble

Speenhamland System   (Eng.) A system of outdoor relief of poverty in which unemployed or low-wage families received relief based on the price of bread and the size of family (1794-1834)

Standardization   A process of reducing irregularities; making uniform

Steam Power   Power used to operate machinery, for example, generated by steam

Stock Exchange; Stock Market   A specialized market where stocks are bought and sold

Stockbroker   A specialist who is the intermediary between buyers and sellers of stocks and bonds in a stock market

Strike   An industrial action in which workers refuse to work until certain demands have been met

Strip Farming   See Open Field System

Subsidy   A grant of money by a government to an enterprise producing a product or performing a service, usually designed to encourage greater production

Sweated Labor   Workers who work in a work place for low wages under poor conditions (sweatshop)

Syndicalism   A theory, plan, or movement of trade union action, originating in France, advocating direct ownership of industry by unions, and favoring its attainment through direct action and general strikes

Syndicat   (Fr.) A labor union advocating the control of workers over the production and distribution processes

Synthetics   Artificial equivalents of natural things

Taille   (Fr.) A tax levied by the king or lords on their subjects or on land held of or under them; it became an exclusively royal tax in the 15th century, although nobles and clergy were exempt

Tallage   A toll or fee paid by a feudal tenant to a lord, originally in commutation for previously-performed services or for a tax-in-kind

Tariff   A tax imposed on an imported good

Tax Farming   A system of tax collection where certain individuals contract with the government to collect taxes and can keep any amount in excess of the contracted-for amount

Tax Structure   The organization of a country's taxes, specifically the importance of different types of taxes to taxpayers and to the government's tax revenues

Technical Efficiency   The state of getting maximum physical output from the given inputs

Technology   The proportion in which inputs are used to produce output. Technological change occurs when these proportions alter

Tenant-at-Will   A customary tenant whose continued occupation of land depends not on possession of a copyhold or some other formal record of occupation, but only on the goodwill of the lord of the manor

Tenant Farming   Situation where land is cultivated by leaseholders as opposed to freeholders cultivating their own land, or feudal tenants cultivating land as of right

Terms of Trade   The relative prices of imports and exports; specifically the ratio of an index of export prices to an index of import prices

Toll   A tax or fee imposed for the use of something, especially of a road or bridge

Trade   Specifically the buying and selling of goods and services across national boundaries; generally, any exchange activity

Trade Regulation   The practice of limiting or constraining the operation of private enterprises, usually to attain some socially defined purpose, as distinguished from laissez faire

Trade Union   See Labor Union

Traditional Economy   An economic system in which the organization of production and distribution of output is based on custom or habit

Truck   A system of paying wages in goods produced rather than in money; usually an employee's "pay" could be redeemed for goods only in the company-run store

Trust   A combination of enterprises in which control of the member corporations is vested in the trust, thus eliminating competition between them

Turnpike Road   A toll road for the use of which a fee is charged

Underemployment   1. an employed person has too little work, so labor productivity is low; 2. a person is employed in a low-skilled job that does not utilize skills or training adequately

Unemployment   The state of having no work

Urban Regulation   In medieval times, the process by which towns put limits on the activities of merchants and craftsworkers in order to protect the interests of the town

Urban Transit   A transportation system within an urban area designed to move large number of people

Urbanization   The process of urban expansion; the change from a rural to an urban way of life ife

Usury   Lending money and charging interest on the loan

Value Added Tax   A type of indirect sales tax in which tax is imposed and paid at each stage of production, depending on the value added to the product at that stage

Variable Costs of Production   Those costs, chiefly of labor, energy and raw materials, that vary directly with the amount of output produced

Vassal; Vassalage   In feudalism, the vassal held a fief and thus owed loyalty to a superior, vassalage was the state of being a vassal

Vertical Integration   A merger or other close links between enterprises in the same industry so that different stages of production come under the same control

Vingtiéme   (Fr.) A direct tax imposed on peasants

Wage Labor   Labor done in return for a money wage; an employee's status

Waltham-Lowell System   (U.S.) The first capitalist manufacturing system in the United States in Massachusetts, which provided chaperoned boarding houses for its female workers in textile mills

Work Discipline   The rules and procedures governing conduct in the work place

Working Conditions   The conditions under which people work, including such factors as wages, fringe benefits, working hours and days, physical conditions of the workplace, degree of discipline, and so forth

Yellow Dog Contract   A contract between worker and employer in which the worker agrees not to join a labor union while employed

Zaibatsu   (Jap.) A powerful, family-controlled commercial combine

Zollverein   (Ger.) A German customs union

Index

A